General Editor
David Roberts

rock
chronicles
every **legend**. every **line-up**.
every **look**.

Foreword by
Alice Cooper

FIREFLY BOOKS

A FIREFLY BOOK

Published by Firefly Books Ltd. 2012

Second printing, 2013

Publisher Cataloging-in-Publication Data (U.S.)

Roberts, Dave, 1954–
    Rock chronicles : every legend, every line-up, every look /
Dave Roberts, general editor ; forward by Alice Cooper.
[576] p. : photos. ; cm.
Includes index.
ISBN-13: 978-1-77085-117-7 (pbk.)
1. Rock groups – History. 2. Rock music – History and criticism.
I. Cooper, Alice. II. Title.
781.6609 dc23   ML3534.R6347 2012

Library and Archives Canada Cataloguing in Publication

Roberts, David, 1954–
    Rock chronicles : every legend, every line-up, every look
/ Dave Roberts. — 1st ed.
Includes index.
ISBN 978-1-77085-117-7
    1. Rock groups—History. 2. Rock music—History and
criticism. I. Title.
ML3534.R552 2012   781.6609   C2012-901050-2

Published in the United States by
Firefly Books (U.S.) Inc.
P.O. Box 1338, Ellicott Station
Buffalo, New York 14205

Published in Canada by
Firefly Books Ltd.
50 Staples Avenue Unit 1
Richmond Hill, Ontario L4B 0A7

Colour separartion by KHL Chromagraphics, Singapore
Printed in China by Midas Printing International Ltd.

This book was designed
and produced by
Quintessence Editions Ltd.
230 City Road
London EC1V 2TT

Project Editor: Simon Ward
Editors: Bruno MacDonald, Olivia
McLearon, Frank Ritter
Editorial Assistants: Sara Di-Girolamo,
Olivia Young
Designers: Alison Hau, Tom Howey
Design Assistant: Isabel Eeles
Production Manager: Anna Pauletti
Editorial Director: Jane Laing
Publisher: Mark Fletcher

contents

foreword by alice cooper

Rock 'n' roll is over a half a century old. The British Invasion is forty years old. If you're around seventy right now, you were probably a Beatles or Rolling Stones fan. Why does this music keep going on? Most of the bands from the fifties and sixties are still touring and making records. Is there something magical about this music, or is it just a refusal to grow old? I'm starting to think it's a psychochemical reaction. Rock 'n' roll is all about attitude and image. It's mostly blues-based, and it's akin to an ongoing rebellion against the safe, conservative, acceptable music that our parents and grandparents wanted us to appreciate.

Since most of these artists refuse to die or simply fade away, here's a book about what they did then, what they're doing now, and what they might do later. And even though I have a ladies' name, the old adage "it ain't over till the fat lady sings" will never ever apply to me. Since I'll never be fat, and I'll never quit singing. Long live rock 'n' roll—rock 'n' roll is NOT DEAD. You might want to take your own pulse. If it's too loud, maybe you're dead.

Alice Cooper

introduction by david roberts

Rock Chronicles is a new way of telling the story of this powerful and enduring genre. More than 250 of rock's finest, spanning seven decades, get an in-depth examination, presented in a unique and revealing display that starts and ends with archetypal purveyors of classic rock: AC/DC and ZZ Top. Along the way, you'll be introduced to the personnel who created subgenres, from glam to grunge and psychedelia to punk.

A new kind of rock encyclopedia for the twenty-first century, the book features elements that give a visual overview of each act's long and winding career. A team of experts has compiled the essential biographies found at the core of each act's entry—together with the birth and, sadly, ever increasing death dates of the cast of many hundreds of rock stars.

So far, so traditional. But this is where the similarity to other rock encyclopedias ends. *Rock Chronicles* boasts at-a-glance graphic timelines of the comings and goings of group members set against the albums they made and the labels that signed them. These cleverly designed infographics will help you to pinpoint the key moments in rock history: when line-ups changed, breakthrough albums were released, record deals were brokered and singers departed. Want to know who played drums on Pearl Jam's debut album? Find out how many copies *OK Computer* has sold worldwide? Remind yourself what The Kinks' bassist looked like or when Frank Zappa was inducted into the Rock and Roll Hall of Fame? You'll find all the answers to these and an unimaginable stack of other questions in the fact-packed pages of a very different kind of book.

Delving into *Rock Chronicles,* you will undoubtedly, like me, learn all sorts of trivia. Not facts that you would necessarily look up, but good-to-know, intriguing stuff like the simple story behind how Canadian stars Nickelback got their name and the bizarre fact that French progressive rockers Magma have invented their own lyrical language.

Away from these intriguing diversions, let's answer the big questions most of you will consider when using a rock encyclopedia. First, just how did we make the selection as to which acts are included? Not without a huge amount of thought, debate and argument is the unsurprising answer. The issue of what constitutes a rock act at all, as opposed to a pop outfit, is enough for starters, before determining who fits the bill.

At the heart of most decision-making was the symbol which very firmly dominates the front cover of this book: the electric guitar. Synths made a half-hearted attempt to usurp the guitar in the seventies and eighties, but the definition of a classic rock band is built around the six-strings of Chuck Berry through to present day Kings of Leon.

So, having established a very basic definition, who of the thousands of potential bands to choose and who to lose? Your list and mine will, I'm sure, have been different but there's no exact science in deciding who makes the final cut. Highest record sales and best chart statistics just won't do. That way leads to the omission of so much music that is commercially lacking but creatively inspirational. So, fear not, Captain Beefheart and His Magic Band, the Buzzcocks and Pavement all have their place. That said, all the British, Irish and North American rock heavyweights you'd expect to see are included, plus significant acts from across Europe, China, Japan, South America and Australasia.

To get the most out of the book, start by checking out the visual guide to *Rock Chronicles* overpage. Here you can get acquainted with the timelines that run throughout the book and the symbols and graphic devices used to reveal the vast amount of information at your fingertips.

Each timeline covers the period each act has been active, punctuated by core members (and, in the case of solo acts like Bowie, Elvis, and Neil Young, significant others), together with a full chronological rundown of studio albums. All compilations and soundtracks, and most live albums, have been excluded to keep discographies to manageable proportions, but exceptions have been made where the entries would be simply incomplete without them. Fear not, fans of the MC5, Dave Matthews, and Jane's Addiction: those live debut albums are in here. And in a few selected cases—notably Tangerine Dream and Frank Zappa—we have cherry-picked highlights of their huge back catalogs, including live albums (which fans of those acts regard as equally canonical).

All types of album—studio, live, and compilation—qualify for the big four sellers at the top of each double-page spread. A great deal of research has gone into establishing the most accurate estimate for each release. Record sales are often prone to much exaggeration but our figures are based on a combination of expert advice and record industry certifications for platinum, gold and silver sales or shipments. These certifications are given per disc, not per album release—so in the case of George Harrison's terrific triple album, *All Things Must Pass,* the often reported sales total of more than ten million is in fact 3.5 million.

The all-important rock stars highlighted in the biographies and on the timelines are pictured on each page for easy identification. For a selection of the more visually exciting and most enduring bands, there are picture features that show the visual changes undergone throughout the decades of fashion changing, hard rocking, touring and general debauchery associated with the "hope I die before I get old" brigade. These are color-coded to key albums, also pictured on those spreads.

Every decade since the seventies has seen predictions of the death of rock. However, although the twenty-first century has seen a slow-down in the production line and a lessening of the grip the recorded product has on us, rock is still a massive draw for the world's buoyant live performance sector. It's also pop music's most fascinating genre to read about—so immerse yourself in the astonishing wealth of fact that is *Rock Chronicles.*

how to use this book

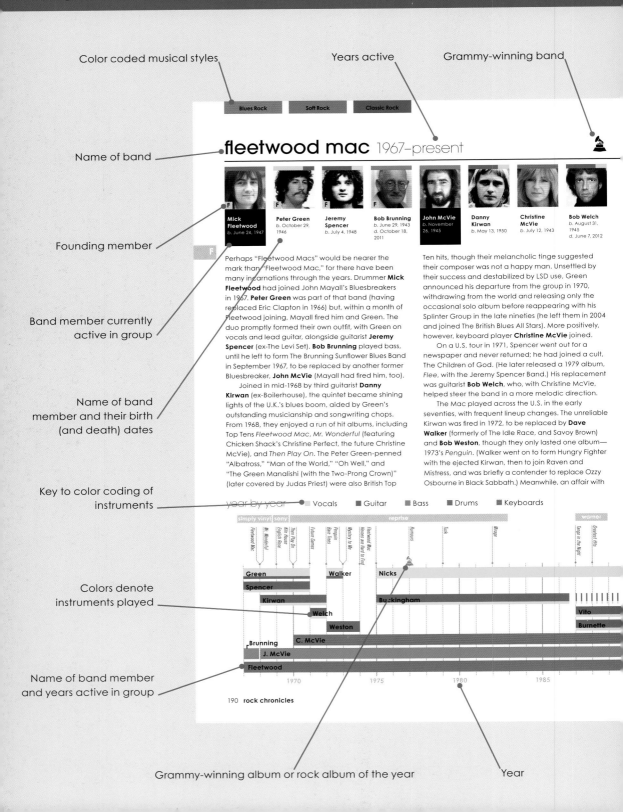

Color coded musical styles

Years active

Grammy-winning band

Name of band

Founding member

Band member currently active in group

Name of band member and their birth (and death) dates

Key to color coding of instruments

Colors denote instruments played

Name of band member and years active in group

Grammy-winning album or rock album of the year

Year

Blues Rock   Soft Rock   Classic Rock

fleetwood mac 1967–present

Mick Fleetwood	Peter Green	Jeremy Spencer	Bob Brunning	John McVie	Danny Kirwan	Christine McVie	Bob Welch
b. June 24, 1947	b. October 29, 1946	b. July 4, 1948	b. June 29, 1943 d. October 18, 2011	b. November 26, 1945	b. May 13, 1950	b. July 12, 1943	b. August 31, 1945 d. June 7, 2012

Perhaps "Fleetwood Macs" would be nearer the mark than "Fleetwood Mac," for there have been many incarnations through the years. Drummer **Mick Fleetwood** had joined John Mayall's Bluesbreakers in 1967. **Peter Green** was part of that band (having replaced Eric Clapton in 1966) but, within a month of Fleetwood joining, Mayall fired him and Green. The duo promptly formed their own outfit, with Green on vocals and lead guitar, alongside guitarist **Jeremy Spencer** (ex-The Levi Set). **Bob Brunning** played bass, until he left to form The Brunning Sunflower Blues Band in September 1967, to be replaced by another former Bluesbreaker, **John McVie** (Mayall had fired him, too).
Joined in mid-1968 by third guitarist **Danny Kirwan** (ex-Boilerhouse), the quintet became shining lights of the U.K.'s blues boom, aided by Green's outstanding musicianship and songwriting chops. From 1968, they enjoyed a run of hit albums, including Top Tens *Fleetwood Mac*, *Mr. Wonderful* (featuring Chicken Shack's Christine Perfect, the future Christine McVie), and *Then Play On*. The Peter Green-penned "Albatross," "Man of the World," "Oh Well," and "The Green Manalishi (with the Two-Prong Crown)" (later covered by Judas Priest) were also British Top

Ten hits, though their melancholic tinge suggested their composer was not a happy man. Unsettled by their success and destabilized by LSD use, Green announced his departure from the group in 1970, withdrawing from the world and releasing only the occasional solo album before reappearing with his Splinter Group in the late nineties (he left them in 2004 and joined The British Blues All Stars). More positively, however, keyboard player **Christine McVie** joined.
On a U.S. tour in 1971, Spencer went out for a newspaper and never returned; he had joined a cult, The Children of God. (He later released a 1979 album, *Flee*, with the Jeremy Spencer Band.) His replacement was guitarist **Bob Welch**, who, with Christine McVie, helped steer the band in a more melodic direction.
The Mac played across the U.S. in the early seventies, with frequent lineup changes. The unreliable Kirwan was fired in 1972, to be replaced by **Dave Walker** (formerly of The Idle Race, and Savoy Brown) and **Bob Weston**, though they only lasted one album—1973's *Penguin*. (Walker went on to form Hungry Fighter with the ejected Kirwan, then to join Raven and Mistress, and was briefly a contender to replace Ozzy Osbourne in Black Sabbath.) Meanwhile, an affair with

year by year   ■ Vocals   ■ Guitar   ■ Bass   ■ Drums   ■ Keyboards

simply vinyl | sony   reprise   warner

Green
Spencer
Kirwan
Welch
Weston
Brunning   C. McVie
J. McVie
Fleetwood

Walker   Nicks
Buckingham
Vito
Burnette

1970   1975   1980   1985

190 rock chronicles

Global sales of top-selling albums

35.2M
Rumours
(1977)

8.9M
Fleetwood Mac
(1978)

11.3M
Tango in the Night
(1987)

16.1M
Greatest Hits
(1988)

Colors denote instruments played

Dave Walker
b. January 25, 1945

Bob Weston
b. Nov 1, 1947
d. January 3, 2012

Lindsey Buckingham
b. October 3, 1949

Stevie Nicks
b. May 26, 1948

Rick Vito
b. October 13, 1949

Billy Burnette
b. May 8, 1953

Bekka Bramlett
b. April 19, 1968

Dave Mason
b. May 10, 1946

Alphabetical index

Fleetwood's wife Jenny saw Weston fired in September 1973. Then, toward the end of 1974, Welch departed to form Paris and embark on a successful solo career.

With Fleetwood and the McVies now settled in California, the drummer's interest was piqued by a tape of an album by **Lindsey Buckingham** and **Stevie Nicks**. The duo were invited to join the band, creating the band's tenth and most successful incarnation.

After a slow climb, the West Coast-flavored *Fleetwood Mac* made No. 1 in the U.S. in 1976. By the next year, the relationships between Fleetwood and his wife, the McVies, and Nicks and Buckingham were collapsing. "A complete disaster zone…" Fleetwood told writer Craig Rosen. "Emotional hell laced with musical pleasure." Despite (and even inspired by) their friction and cocaine habits, 1977's melodic *Rumours* became one of rock's all-time best-sellers.

Eager to avoid making *Rumours Pt II*, Buckingham pushed for an experimental approach for *Tusk* (1979). The title track and "Sara" were both hits, but the band returned to less controversial waters for *Mirage* (1982).

With Nicks having launched a platinum-selling solo career with 1981's *Bella Donna*, the Mac went their separate ways for three years. They re-formed in late 1985 to create *Tango in the Night* (1987), which proved another huge hit. However, plans for a tour broke down and Buckingham quit, to be replaced by guitarist **Rick Vito** and vocalist **Billy Burnette** (who had played with Fleetwood in the latter's band The Zoo).

The six-strong lineup cut 1990's *Behind the Mask*, but Nicks and McVie quit at the end of the year. The full return of the Mac came in 1993, at the request of President Bill Clinton: Buckingham, Nicks, Fleetwood, and the McVies performed *Rumours*' "Don't Stop" at his inauguration party. However, it proved a one-off—instead, Fleetwood and the McVies recruited vocalist **Bekka Bramlett** and former Traffic guitarist **Dave Mason** for 1995's disappointing *Time*.

The famous five re-grouped again for 1997's live *The Dance* (1997). Coupling originals with old hits, it returned them to the multi-platinum status of old, and preceded a spectacularly successful reunion tour.

Christine McVie departed again in 2003, but the remaining four produced that year's *Say You Will* (despite renewed tension between Buckingham and Nicks) and mounted a hits tour in 2009. "I don't believe Fleetwood Mac will ever tour again," Fleetwood told *Playboy* in 2012, "but I really hope we do." **RD**

Bold type for first mention of each band member

Contributor's initials

Record label

reprise

warner

reprise

Behind the Mask

Time

Say You Will

Name of studio album

Bramlett

Mason

Featured band and page number

1990   1995   2000   2005   2010

Broken lines indicate time away from group

ac/dc 1973–present

Angus Young
b. March 31, 1955

Malcolm Young
b. January 6, 1953

Dave Evans
b. July 20, 1953

Larry Van Kriedt
b. 1954

Colin Burgess
b. November 16, 1946

Bon Scott
b. July 9, 1946
d. February 19, 1980

"When everybody else was getting into cleverness and synthesizing…" Keith Richards reminisced of late 1970s AC/DC, "these cats [were] laying it out." It's a fitting compliment for a band who, along with the Stones, did much to bring Chuck Berry's formula of addictive riffs and witty wordplay to the masses.

Malcolm and **Angus Young** had been inspired by the success of their elder brother George, who, as part of The Easybeats, had been the first Australian beat group to have a U.K. Top Ten hit. The early days of AC/DC saw a shifting lineup hone their chops on the pub circuit, Angus Young turning heads both with his nimble lead guitar skills and his characteristic school uniform stage attire, which he still wears today.

A key moment in their progress came with the replacement of original singer **Dave Evans** by Ronald "**Bon**" Scott, a friend of brother George. At the end of 1974, the new lineup recorded *High Voltage*. Success at home came quickly, with AC/DC establishing a reputation for noisy good-time rock 'n' roll with laddish lyrics ("She's Got Balls"). The following year, *T.N.T.* featured the band's first popular anthem, "It's A Long Way to the Top (If You Wanna Rock 'n' Roll)"—which would become a signature tune for Bon Scott. As 1975 drew to a close, they were Australia's top rock act.

The first throes of world domination came in 1976, when the band signed an international deal with the Atlantic label. Spending much of the year touring Europe, they gained valuable experience supporting the likes of Black Sabbath, Kiss, Blue Öyster Cult, and Aerosmith. To coincide with the tour, an "international" version of *High Voltage* was released, compiling tracks from the first two Australian albums.

AC/DC hit their stride with 1976's *Dirty Deeds Done Dirt Cheap*. Like *High Voltage,* this would be issued as an international edition (which hit No. 3 in the U.S. in 1981), although both versions include its three classics: the anthemic title track, the kinetic "Problem Child," and the atypically reflective "Ride On." (Scott later sang "Ride On," just days before he died, with French rockers Trust, who also covered "Problem Child.")

For the remainder of the 1970s, AC/DC continued their upward global trajectory, moving toward rock's top table with *Let There Be Rock* (1977) and Keith Richards's favorite, *Powerage* (1978). Then, in 1979, the group's sound was overhauled by producer Mutt Lange: the harsh edge of earlier recordings was refined, while retaining the all-important energy of their live sound. The resulting *Highway to Hell* (1979) saw AC/DC in the U.S. Top Twenty for the first time.

year-by-year   ▨ Vocals   ▪ Guitar   ▪ Bass   ▪ Drums

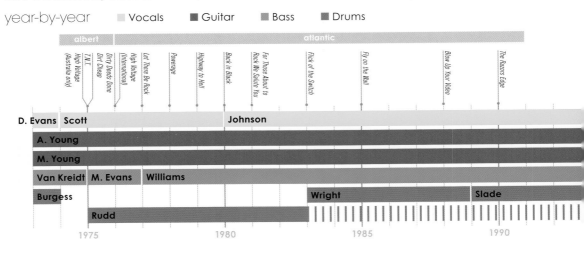

10M	15M	36M	8M
Dirty Deeds Done Dirt Cheap (1976)	*Highway to Hell* (1979)	*Back in Black* (1980)	*For Those About to Rock We Salute You* (1981)

A

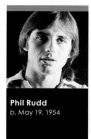

Phil Rudd
b. May 19, 1954

Cliff Williams
b. May 12, 1959

Brian Johnson
b. October 5, 1947

Simon Wright
b. June 19, 1963

Chris Slade
b. October 30, 1946

Mark Evans
b. March 2, 1956

A new decade kicked off with AC/DC poised to conquer the globe. But on February 19, 1980, after a night of heavy drinking at a London club, Bon Scott was found dead in an associate's car, his passing officially listed as "acute alcohol poisoning." Rejecting their initial instinct to break up, Angus Young recalled that Scott himself had talked about the singer from Geordie, an English band who'd enjoyed a brief flurry of success the previous decade. **Brian Johnson** was invited to audition: within days he was in the studio working on the material they had begun with Scott.

These were inauspicious beginnings for an album expected to turn AC/DC into superstars. But *Back in Black* (1980) proved they were anything but a band in crisis. Fears that fans might reject a new front-man proved spectacularly unfounded, as they unleashed a benchmark classic in heavy rock (oddly, producer Lange was unconvinced by "Back in Black" itself, arguably the album's finest cut). Topping the U.K. and, later, Australian charts, *Back in Black* was certified platinum within three months of release and went on to spend 131 weeks on the *Billboard* chart. Over the next three decades it would sell more than twenty-two million copies in the U.S. alone, helping to make it one of the top ten best-selling albums of all time.

With the demise of Led Zeppelin, AC/DC had become the world's most successful hard rock act (subsequently, only Metallica would challenge their supremacy). *For Those About to Rock We Salute You* (1981) gave them their first U.S. No. 1, *Who Made Who* (1986) mixed songs old and new, *Blow Up Your Video* (1988) reunited the band with original producers Vanda and Young, and *The Razors Edge* (1990) bore a new classic, "Thunderstruck." Even lesser regarded albums like 1983's *Flick of the Switch* and 1985's *Fly on the Wall* maintained AC/DC's unbroken run of U.S. platinum-sellers. (Along the way, drum duties passed from **Phil Rudd** to **Simon Wright** and **Chris Slade**.)

In latter years, the gaps between albums have widened: 2008's *Black Ice* (by which time Rudd had rejoined) was the group's first new studio album in eight years. The band's return was greeted with open arms and wallets: the album debuted at No. 1 in twenty-nine different countries. The hugely successful stadium tour that followed confirmed that AC/DC were back in business. They capitalized on a new generation's exposure to their brand of pile-driving rock with a soundtrack for the blockbuster movie *Iron Man 2* (a "greatest hits" in all but name) confirming their standing at the top of the classic rock genre. **TB**

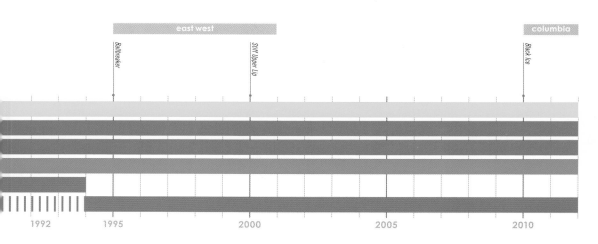

east west

columbia

Ballbreaker

Stiff Upper Lip

Black Ice

1992   1995   2000   2005   2010

High Voltage
(1975)

T.N.T. (1975)

Dirty Deeds Done Dirt Cheap (1976)

Let There Be Rock (1977)

Powerage (1978)

Highway to Hell (1979)

Back in Black (1980)

Blow Up Your Video (1988)

The Razors Edge (1990)

Black Ice (2008)

Very early AC/DC—the school uniform would stay longer than the platform boots.

Bon Scott (left) and Angus Young (right) in Hollywood in 1977.

Young and Scott explode onstage in the mid-seventies.

Young meets the fans at the Oakland Coliseum in California, 1978.

The band get mean 'n' moody at Shepperton Studios, London, in 1976.

Studio shot of AC/DC in 1979: **Malcolm Young**, **Scott**, **Cliff Williams**, **Angus Young** and **Phil Rudd**.

Simon Wright in Australia in 1988, on his last tour with the band.

Bon Scott, **Malcolm Young**, **Angus Young**, **Phil Rudd**, and **Cliff Williams** in a good mood at Shepperton in 1976.

Malcolm Young in Sydney, Australia, on the *Razors Edge* tour.

Brian Johnson giving it his all in 1980.

Johnson (left) and **Angus Young** rock Washington, D.C., on the 2008 *Black Ice* tour.

A

bryan adams 1977–present

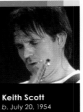

Bryan Adams
b. November 5, 1959

Jim Vallance
b. May 31, 1952

Mickey Curry
b. June 10, 1956

Tommy Mandel
b. June 2, 1949

Keith Scott
b. July 20, 1954

Dave Taylor
b. February 20, 1953

Bryan Adams has conquered the world, re-written record books, and transcended musical genres during a solo career that has spanned more than a quarter of a century. But this superstar is also blessed with a "guy-next-door" image that would endear him to your drinking mates *and* your rock-shy grandmother.

The Canadian vocalist, songwriter, guitarist, photographer, and philanthropist was born to British parents in Kingston, Ontario in 1959. His CV is bulging with records, awards, nominations, and accolades, including seventeen Juno (Canadian music) awards, a Grammy for a movie hit, two Ivor Novello awards, a star on the Hollywood Walk of Fame, and much-deserved recognition for his contributions to music and charity. He has been awarded the Order of British Columbia and been made a Companion of the Order of Canada—the country's highest honor for lifetime achievement. So far, so good, for the artist who has sold more than 65 million records worldwide.

Adams bought his first guitar with money made from scrubbing dishes. Rehearsals in his mother's Vancouver basement led to an audition with glam rockers Sweeney Todd, for whom he provided

vocals on *If Wishes Were Horses* (1977). However, the album's closing track, "Say Hello, Say Goodbye," was indicative of the temporary appointment. By 1978, an eighteen-year-old Adams had forged an alliance with songwriter and drummer **Jim Vallance** that survives to this day. Together, the pair knocked out numerous demos and the track that would become Adams' first single, "Let Me Take You Dancing." However, despite placing tracks on Kiss's *Creatures of the Night* (1982), commercial success would initially prove elusive.

Fast forward to 1984. Following his first venture into the Canadian and U.S. Top Tens with *Cuts Like a Knife* (1983), Adams made his bow on the world stage with *Reckless*, an album that would go on to sell more than five million copies in the U.S. and spend 115 weeks on the U.K. chart. *Reckless* featured six hits, including arm-waving classics like "Run to You," "Heaven," and "Summer of '69," the latter described by Adams as a song about "making love in the summertime."

In the early nineties, with arena rock on the wane and grunge in full, angsty swing, Adams took aim at the mass market with mid-tempo ballads, hitting the bullseye with a cut co-penned by Pink Floyd/

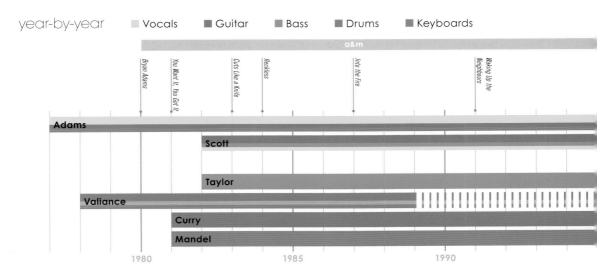

year-by-year   ■ Vocals   ■ Guitar   ■ Bass   ■ Drums   ■ Keyboards

a&m

Bryan Adams · You Want It, You Got It · Cuts Like a Knife · Reckless · Into the Fire · Waking Up the Neighbours

Adams

Scott

Taylor

Valiance

Curry

Mandel

1980   1985   1990

11.3M	10.8M	15.4M	4.7M
Reckless (1984)	*Waking Up the Neighbours* (1991)	*So Far So Good* (1993)	*18 Till I Die* (1996)

Phil Thornalley
b. January 5, 1960

Gary Breit
b. October, 1960

Norm Fisher
b. October 22, 1963

David Bowie orchestrator Michael Kamen and super-producer Mutt Lange (who made Adams's *Waking Up the Neighbours* and Def Leppard's *Adrenalize* sound like the work of the same act). Clocking in at 6 minutes 34 seconds, "(Everything I Do) I Do it for You," from the soundtrack to the movie blockbuster *Robin Hood: Prince of Thieves*, amassed seven weeks at No. 1 in the U.S. and an unprecedented sixteen consecutive weeks at the top in the U.K., wiping Slim Whitman's thirty-six-year-old "Rose Marie" from the record books.

Chart longevity aside, the track's enduring legacy was to force a change to regulations that had restricted airplay in Adams' homeland for songs lacking sufficient Canadian content. "Everything…" flouted the rules for its recording location (the U.K.) and producer (Zambian-born Lange). Wading into the political debate, Adams declared: "Who wants to have an international record and then be called un-Canadian? It's a disgrace." The resultant publicity prompted a rethink and the rules were amended to allow collaborations with non-Canadians.

With "Everything…" threatening to eclipse his entire eighties output, and no doubt invigorated by his run-in with the Canadian government, Adams returned to the studio and successfully removed the metaphorical millstone from around his neck with moments of heart-wrenching beauty ("Please Forgive Me") and barefaced cheek ("The Only Thing that Looks Good on Me is You"). He also courted more box-office blockbusters: "All for Love" from *The Three Musketeers*, featuring Rod Stewart and Sting, and "Here I Am" from *Spirit—Stallion of the Cimarron*.

In more recent times, Adams has proved an astute judge of musical trends, cashing in on the success of the Spice Girls by hooking up with "Sporty Spice" Melanie C for "When You're Gone" and joining British dance maestro Chicane (aka Nick Bracegirdle) for the U.K. chart-topper "Don't Give Up."

Away from the recording studio, the Bryan Adams Foundation—an educational charity working with young people worldwide—heads a long list of worthy causes supported by the singer. He is an award-winning photographer, his face has graced Canadian postage stamps, and, in 2011, he became a father when his Personal Assistant, Alicia Grimaldi, gave birth to the splendidly named Mirabella Bunny. **MW**

■ Other percussion

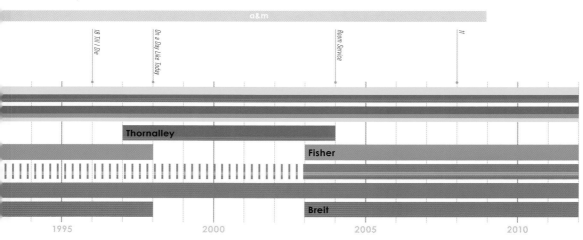

aerosmith 1970–present

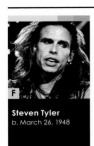

Steven Tyler
b. March 26, 1948

Joe Perry
b. September 10, 1950

Ray Tabano
b. December 23, 1946

Tom Hamilton
b. December 31, 1951

Joey Kramer
b. June 21, 1950

Brad Whitford
b. February 23, 1952

"Oh gawd, Aerosmith," moaned Mick Jagger in 1977. "They're just rubbish." A generation disagreed. "There was," recalled Guns N' Roses guitarist Slash, "nothing cooler than Aerosmith coming out of America."

Boston's bad boys convened in 1970. Frustrated at being stuck behind drums in previous groups, **Steven Tyler** insisted on fronting a union with guitarist **Joe Perry**, bassist **Tom Hamilton**, and drummer David "Pudge" Scott. The latter was usurped by **Joey Kramer**, who named the band "Aerosmith," a word he dreamt up at school. **Ray Tabano** came on board as second guitarist, but was replaced in 1971 by **Brad Whitford**.

Aerosmith was released in 1973 to, as Perry noted, "no fanfare." Nonetheless, it heralded their rock-R&B fusion, featuring sax player David Woodford, whose resume would stretch from The Shirelles to P. Diddy. (Woodford toured with Aerosmith and featured on vintage cuts added to 1978's explosive *Live! Bootleg*.)

Get Your Wings (1974) maintained the brass, courtesy of jazz stars Michael and Randy Brecker (who also graced Bruce Springsteen's *Born to Run*) and Elephant's Memory alumnus Stan Bronstein. Keyboards were by producer Ray Colcord, the A&R

man who persuaded Columbia to sign the group. Colcord subsequently joined Lou Reed's band, while Jack Douglas took over Aerosmith's production.

Relentless touring fueled the success of *Toys in the Attic* (1975), featuring pianist Scott Cushnie, late of The Hawks (the group that became The Band). In 1976, *Rocks*—featuring banjo by Paul Prestopino—and a reissue of 1973's "Dream On" were U.S. Top Ten hits.

Momentum carried *Draw the Line* (1977) but—having cut five tracks for a follow-up—Perry quit the fatigued band. *Night in the Ruts* (1979) was completed with guitarists Richie Supa and **Jimmy Crespo**.

Crippled by drugs and debt, Aerosmith entered limbo. Columbia plugged the gap with the eventually multi-million-selling *Greatest Hits* (1980). Whitford quit and was replaced by **Rick Dufay**, but 1982's *Rock in a Hard Place*—featuring Paul Harris (formerly of Stephen Stills' Manassas) and John Turi (of Cyndi Lauper's pre-fame band Blue Angel)—halted neither their commercial decline nor their narcotic dysfunction.

A reunion of the vintage lineup was inevitable. However, 1985's *Done with Mirrors* fared even worse than *Rock in a Hard Place*. Producer Rick Rubin threw

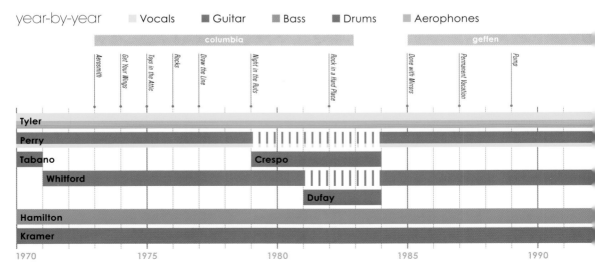

year-by-year   ■ Vocals   ■ Guitar   ■ Bass   ■ Drums   ■ Aerophones

11M
Toys in the Attic
(1975)

13.9M
Aerosmith's
Greatest Hits
(1980)

11.1M
Pump
(1989)

13.5M
Get a Grip
(1993)

A

Jimmy Crespo
b. July 5, 1954

Rick Dufay
b. February 19, 1952

them a lifeline, recruiting Tyler and Perry to guest on Run-DMC's 1986 cover of Aerosmith's hit "Walk This Way." Although its video featured members of metal group Smashed Gladys deputizing for Whitford, Hamilton, and Kramer, the front-men's appearance catapulted Aerosmith back into the limelight.

Purged of their addictions, the band rose from the flames with the smashes *Permanent Vacation* (1987) and *Pump* (1989), featuring a brass section led by new producer Bruce Fairbairn. Thom Gimbel, later to join Foreigner, handled sax and keyboards on tour.

Now even bigger than in their seventies heyday, they scored their first U.S. No.1 hits with *Get a Grip* (1993) and *Nine Lives* (1997). The former featured Don Henley and Lenny Kravitz; the latter arrangements by David Campbell (father of Beck, and a conductor who worked with Kiss and Metallica, and on Bono and The Edge's *Spider-Man* musical). In between, *Big Ones* (1994) became their second multi-million-selling hits set and Russ Irwin—late of Curt Smith's post-Tears for Fears group, Mayfield—joined as tour keyboardist.

The resurrection was crowned by their first No. 1 single, "I Don't Want to Miss a Thing," from the 1998 movie *Armageddon* (starring Tyler's daughter Liv). However, 2001's *Just Push Play* boasted hi-tech production at odds with their sleazy sound, despite the presence of soul horn legends Tower of Power, and was outsold by *O, Yeah! Ultimate Aerosmith Hits* (2002).

Aerosmith returned to their R&B roots with the covers album *Honkin' on Bobo* (2004). Produced by the returning Jack Douglas, it featured vocalist Tracy Bonham, Chuck Berry's pianist Johnnie Johnson, and soul label Stax's brass section The Memphis Horns.

Ongoing touring yielded the live *Rockin' the Joint* (2005), but a health problem-plagued 2009 outing to promote the *Guitar Hero: Aerosmith* game saw them grind to a halt. With Tyler relapsed into painkiller addiction, Perry announced Aerosmith were seeking a new singer (an invitation Lenny Kravitz declined).

After protracted wrangling—during which Jimmy Page tried to recruit Tyler for a revived Led Zeppelin—the band hit the road once more in 2010. Attempts to complete another album were interrupted by Tyler becoming an *American Idol* judge, but, as Kramer remarked in 2011, "The only thing that's going to stop us is if someone out-and-out dies." **BM**

■ Other percussion

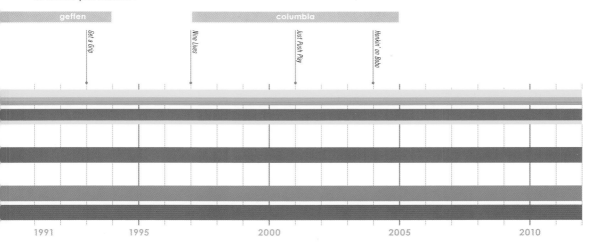

aerosmith 23

Aerosmith (1973)

Get Your Wings (1974)

Toys in the Attic (1975)

Rocks (1976)

Draw the Line (1977)

Rock in a Hard Place (1982)

Permanent Vacation (1987)

Get a Grip (1993)

Nine Lives (1997)

Just Push Play (2001)

Tom Hamilton (left) and **Steven Tyler** (right) backstage in 1973.

An exuberant **Tyler** performing onstage in 1975.

Studio shot of Aerosmith circa 1974: **Joe Perry, Brad Whitford, Tyler** (front), **Hamilton** (back) and **Joey Kramer.**

Tyler cools down after performing at Washington RFK stadium, on May 30, 1976.

Kramer (drums) and **Tyler** (front) performing live in 1984.

Tyler and Perry—a.k.a. "The Toxic Twins"—live in Germany in August 1977.

Whitford and Hamilton in Minnesota in 1987.

Tyler and Hamilton rehearsing at the 1993 MTV Music Awards.

Tyler rocking out onstage in August 1997.

One of rock's greatest pairings, Perry (left) and Tyler (right) on the *Just Push Play* tour in 2001.

a-ha 1982–2010

Morten Harket
b. September 14, 1959

Magne Furuholmen
b. November 1, 1962

Pål Waaktaar
b. September 6, 1961

Formed in 1982 by singer **Morten Harket**, guitarist and principal songwriter **Pål Waaktaar**, and keyboard player **Magne Furuholmen**, Norwegian pop outfit a-ha became a major success of the eighties. Their timing was good: as they tasted initial success in 1985, teen-appeal rivals Duran Duran were fading and Wham! were anticipating George Michael's departure. The stage was set for a band with good looks and indelible hooks to swoop in and clean up.

The first song they worked on was the future smash "Take on Me," originally called "The Juicy Fruit Song" and later "Lesson One." It didn't come easy: a version recorded with producer Tony Mansfield had little impact but a-ha persevered through re-recordings until an Alan Tarney-helmed take hit paydirt.

The clincher was a groundbreaking video mixing live action with animated sketches. This captured MTV viewers' imagination and propelled the catchy "Take on Me"—with Harket's trademark falsetto and Furuholmen's deathless synth riff—to No. 2 in the U.K. and No. 1 in the U.S. *Hunting High and Low* (1985) consolidated the breakthrough, making No. 2 in the U.K. and No. 15 in the *Billboard* 200.

In the U.K., even greater singles success was to follow with "The Sun Always Shines on T.V." It grabbed the No. 1 slot, which had eluded "Take on Me," at the start of 1986. The trio were quick to follow up with *Scoundrel Days* (1986), a muscular record that was even more accomplished than their debut and

again racked up multi-million worldwide sales. Their stock remained high as Waaktaar penned the theme for the 1987 James Bond movie *The Living Daylights* with stalwart composer John Barry. The track was the third of an eventual eight No. 1 singles in their native Norway, and a hit around the world (bar the U.S., where their profile slumped after 1986's "Cry Wolf").

The downbeat side to a-ha, always present in their more glacial tracks, was drawn out fully on *Stay on These Roads* (1988). This attitude would be equally prominent on *East of the Sun, West of the Moon* (1990) and its lead single, a cover of The Everly Brothers' "Crying in the Rain"—another opportunity for Harket to stretch his lovelorn croon.

Memorial Beach (1993) was the final album of a-ha's first phase and reputedly difficult to record. An ensuing hiatus—filled by Harket's attempt at solo fame and Furuholmen and Waaktaar's dabblings in other groups—was broken by the return to form *Minor Earth Major Sky* (2000). a-ha had slipped nicely into maturity, still unashamedly pop but careworn with it. *Lifelines* (2002) and *Analogue* (2005) continued the thread, the latter featuring Graham Nash of Crosby, Stills & Nash on backing vocals, and springing a surprise U.K. Top Ten hit, "Analogue (All I Want)."

After *Foot of the Mountain* (2009), a-ha chose to call it a day, packing things up neatly with a farewell tour in 2010. Impressive global ticket sales proved how well they had endured. **MaH**

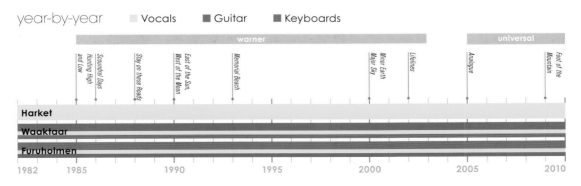

year-by-year ▪ Vocals ▪ Guitar ▪ Keyboards

warner · universal

Hunting High and Low · Scoundrel Days · Stay on these Roads · East of the Sun, West of the Moon · Memorial Beach · Minor Earth Major Sky · Lifelines · Analogue · Foot of the Mountain

Harket
Waaktaar
Furuholmen

1982 1985 1990 1995 2000 2005 2010

alice in chains 1987–present

Jerry Cantrell
b. March 18, 1966

Layne Staley
b. August 22, 1967
d. April 5, 2002

Sean Kinney
b. May 27, 1966

Mike Starr
b. April 4, 1966
d. March 8, 2011

Mike Inez
b. May 14, 1966

William DuVall
b. September 6, 1967

"Pretty music that makes you want to die" was drummer **Sean Kinney**'s verdict on Alice in Chains, whose famous fans range from Metallica to Elton John.

Kinney, singer **Layne Staley**, guitarist **Jerry Cantrell**, and bassist **Mike Starr** convened in 1987. They drew on Black Sabbath-type influences common to Seattle contemporaries Soundgarden and Nirvana, blended with an Eagles-esque flair for melody. Other distinctive elements on their 1990 debut *Facelift* included Cantrell's talkbox on their breakthrough "Man in the Box" and Kinney's piano on "Sea of Sorrow."

A year of touring pushed *Facelift* to gold sales. Then Alice fashioned 1992's acoustic EP *Sap*, featuring Heart's Ann Wilson, Mudhoney's Mark Arm, and Soundgarden's Chris Cornell. With "Man in the Box" a hit, Soundgarden touring with Guns N' Roses, Pearl Jam ascending *Billboard*'s chart and all three acts appearing in Cameron Crowe's *Singles*, "grunge" had arrived. *Dirt* (1992) duly crashed the U.S. chart at No. 6, sharing the Top Ten with the *Singles* soundtrack (featuring Alice's "Would?," a tribute to Andrew Wood of Pearl Jam precursors Mother Love Bone). On the ensuing tour, Starr was fired for drug-fueled apathy and replaced by ex-Ozzy Osbourne bassist **Mike Inez**. *Dirt* itself, featuring Tom Araya of Alice's touring buddies Slayer on the Sabbath pastiche "Iron Gland," sold over four million, while Slash loved it so much that he enlisted Inez for his GN'R sideline Slash's Snakepit.

The bleak *Jar of Flies* (1994) became the first "shortform album" to debut atop *Billboard*'s chart. (Guests included viola player April Acevez, wife of Soundgarden's Matt Cameron.) However, Alice vanished for much of 1994–95, Staley being unwilling—and, given his heroin addiction, unable—to tour. Instead, the singer focused on *Above* (1995) by Mad Season, a short-lived "supergroup" with Barrett Martin (Screaming Trees) and Mike McCready (Pearl Jam).

The defiant *Alice in Chains* (1995) was the band's second U.S. No. 1. However, after *MTV Unplugged* (featuring Heart's Scott Olson) and shows with Kiss in 1996, Alice effectively ceased to be. Staley's fatal overdose in 2002 ended further speculation.

Cantrell, Kinney, and Inez reunited as Alice in Chains in 2005. Early shows featured guests such as Tool's Maynard James Keenan, Ann Wilson, GN'R's Duff McKagan, Pantera's Phil Anselmo, Queensrÿche's Chris DeGarmo, and Puddle of Mudd's Wes Scantlin. However, by the time the group hit the festival circuit, **William DuVall**—latterly of Comes with the Fall and Cantrell's solo live band—was their front-man. With him, *Black Gives Way to Blue* (2009) ranked alongside the best of Alice's back catalog. More remarkably still, its title track featured former Prince associate Lisa Coleman and Elton John. "A dream for me," marveled Cantrell. "To be able to collaborate and make music with the people that inspired *you* to make music." **BM**

year-by-year   ■ Vocals   ■ Guitar   ■ Bass   ■ Drums

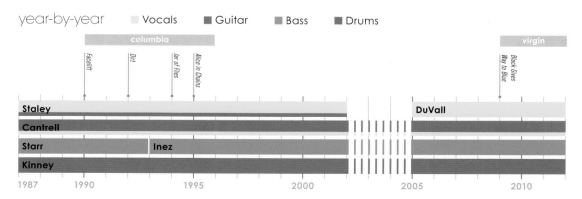

the allman brothers band 1969–present

Duane Allman
b. Nov 20, 1946
d. October 29,
1971

Gregg Allman
b. December
8, 1947

Dickey Betts
b. December
12, 1943

Berry Oakley
b. April 4, 1948
d. November
11, 1972

Butch Trucks
b. May 11, 1947

Jai Johanny "Jaimoe" Johanson
b. July 8, 1944

Chuck Leavell
b. April 28, 1952

Lamar Williams
b. April 14, 1949

With a heady mixture of hard rock, country, jazz, and blues on trademark intertwining guitars, The Allman Brothers Band set the standard for Southern rock.

The group was formed in Jacksonville, Florida, in 1969 by brothers **Duane** and **Gregg Allman** (guitar and keyboards respectively) with **Dickey Betts** (guitar), **Berry Oakley** (bass), and both **Jai Johanny "Jaimoe" Johanson** and **Butch Trucks** on drums. Although they quickly established a great live reputation in the South, their debut album, The Allman Brothers Band, was only a moderate success. Nevertheless, tracks such as "Whipping Post," "Black Hearted Woman," and "Dreams," all written by Gregg, would become classics. Meanwhile, the group relocated to Macon, Georgia, with which they were to be indelibly linked.

Idlewild South followed in 1970—with "Midnight Rider" by Gregg and "In Memory of Elizabeth Reed" by Betts among its highlights—and found a better commercial reception. But, perhaps unsurprisingly for a group who made their name with stupendous performances, it was a recording of two March 1971 concerts, At Fillmore East, that catapulted them to the forefront. In particular, versions of "Whipping Post," "In Memory of Elizabeth Reed," "You Don't Love Me,"

and the comparatively succinct "Statesboro Blues" epitomized what the group could accomplish in the field of sophisticated improvisation. The Allman Brothers Band had truly arrived.

However, double tragedy soon struck. First, Duane was killed in a motorcycle accident in Macon in October 1971. The group had already begun Eat a Peach (1972), on which live numbers (such as the epic "Mountain Jam") would flesh out the studio tracks, several recorded after his death. But it proved impossible to replace his unrivaled tone and gloriously free style. "It's really hard for me to believe that what we accomplished with Duane happened in two years —beginning to end," Trucks told Mojo. (Apart from the group's early recordings, Allman also made a huge contribution to Eric Clapton's Derek and the Dominos hit album, Layla and Other Assorted Love Songs.)

The Allmans had barely recovered from the shock when Oakley died in a bike crash, a year later, barely three streets from the scene of Duane's demise. **Chuck Leavell** (keyboards) had already been added to the roster to free Gregg for more guitar duties; **Lamar Williams** replaced Oakley to finish the recording of Brothers and Sisters (1973). The album topped the

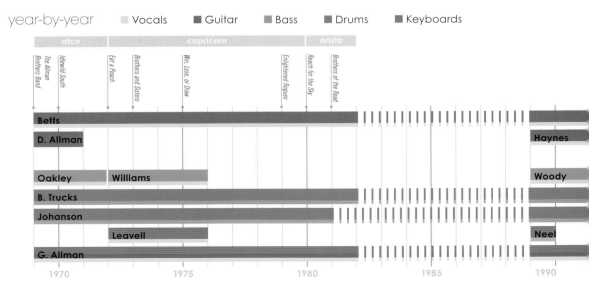

year-by-year · Vocals · Guitar · Bass · Drums · Keyboards

○	○	○	○
3M	**2.5M**	**2M**	**2.8M**
At Fillmore East (1971)	*Eat a Peach* (1972)	*Brothers and Sisters* (1973)	*A Decade of Hits* (1991)

A

Warren Haynes
b. April 6, 1960

Allen Woody
b. October 3, 1955
d. Aug 26, 2000

Johnny Neel
b. June 11, 1954

Marc Quiñones
b. 1963 or 1964

Oteil Burbridge
b. August 24, 1964

Derek Trucks
b. June 8, 1979

Jimmy Herring
b. January 22, 1962

charts while the single "Ramblin' Man" moseyed to No. 2 in the United States. The mellifluous instrumental "Jessica" was also a stand-out (both written by Betts).

While still a huge live draw, the surviving band members were wracked by drink, drugs, and friction. *Win, Lose, or Draw* (1975) was, by their high standards, uneven. Gregg, in a stormy marriage with Cher, was arrested on drugs charges in 1976 and controversially blamed his minder. The other members vowed not to work with him again and the group effectively split, though they reformed in 1978 to record *Enlightened Rogues* (1979). Guitarist Dan Toler and bassist David Goldflies came in, the latter replacing Williams, who had formed Sea Level with Chuck Leavell (Leavell later became a longstanding associate Rolling Stone).

Having replaced Johanson with David "Frankie" Toler, the group recorded *Reach for the Sky* (1980) and, with Mike Lawler on keyboards, its follow-up *Brothers of the Road* (1981)—but, disappointed by the reception to the latter, decided once more to split. By 1982, the Allman Brothers Band seemed to have run its course, apart from a few impromptu jam sessions and benefit shows arranged by promoter Bill Graham. "I went into a big slump for years," Gregg confessed.

So it stayed until 1989 when the surviving founders, with Johanson restored, reunited for a revival, boosted by guitarist **Warren Haynes**, keyboard player **Johnny Neel**, and bassist **Allen Woody**. Three new albums earned critical plaudits, while they were inducted into the Rock and Roll Hall of Fame (1995) and even won a belated Grammy in 1996 for "Jessica."

Apart from the arrival of **Marc Quiñones** in 1991, the departure of Neel and the replacements of Woody by **Oteil Burbridge** and Haynes by Jack Pearson (soon followed by **Derek Trucks**, Butch's nephew), the nineties were relatively serene—but the harmony could not last. After a rift with Gregg, Betts left the group for "personal and professional reasons" and, having been replaced first by **Jimmy Herring**, then by the returning Haynes, took the others to court. Meanwhile, Allen Woody was found dead.

Fortunately, the modern age has proved kinder. With a stable lineup and a 2003 studio album, *Hittin' the Note* ("The best record we ever made," Trucks maintains), they continue to be an exciting live draw. Meanwhile, Gregg Allman's smash solo album *Low Country Blues* (2011) earned a Grammy nomination for Best Blues Album. **MiH**

■ Aerophones   ■ Other percussion

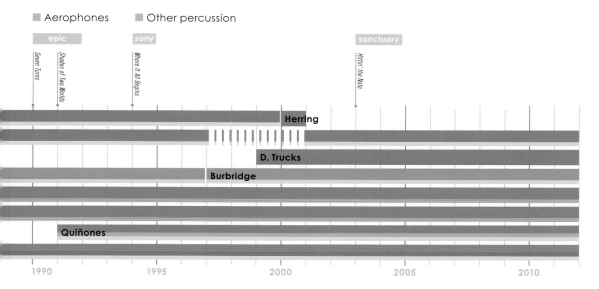

the animals 1962–1969

Eric Burdon
b. May 11, 1941

Hilton Valentine
b. May 21, 1943

Alan Price
b. April 9, 1942

Chas Chandler
b. Dec 18, 1938
d. July 17, 1996

John Steel
b. February 4, 1941

Danny McCulloch
b. July 18, 1945

The grittiest of Britain's "beat boom" bands, The Animals were formed in Newcastle in 1962. Appearing first as the Alan Price Rhythm and Blues Combo, the original lineup consisted of **Alan Price** (keyboards), **Hilton Valentine** (guitar), Bryan **"Chas" Chandler** (bass), and **John Steel** (drums). The group were soon joined by sultry, scowling vocalist **Eric Burdon**, and their uninhibited, energetic performances earned them a local reputation as "animals"—a name they quickly chose to adopt.

Like The Beatles, they were attracted to the money that could be earned performing to lively around-the-clock audiences in Hamburg, Germany. Starting in May 1963, they undertook a two-month fixture at the city's Star Club, where the Fab Four had recorded thirty songs the previous December. They themselves recorded an EP for fans, and this led to offers of work in London.

However, it took a meeting with Yardbirds' manager Georgio Gomelsky to convince The Animals that a move to London was necessary to secure a record deal. Now delivering impressively tight, fiery versions of American blues staples by the likes of Jimmy Reed, John Lee Hooker, and Nina Simone, the group were ready to up their game. Traveling south to the capital, The Animals quickly established themselves as one of the hottest R&B bands on the London scene. Central to The Animals' sound were the growl of gravel-voiced Burdon and the nimble fingers of Price, who was one of the very few skilled organists working in popular music at that time.

Signing to EMI's Columbia label, The Animals enjoyed immediate Top Twenty success with "Baby Let Me Take You Home," a rocking take on a traditional folk song, "Baby Let Me Follow You Down," that had recently been revived by Bob Dylan. With Valentine's unaccompanied, arpeggiated guitar intro and Price's Vox Continental organ dominating the sound, this debut recipe was repeated to sensational effect on the group's follow-up single (and another old folk tune)—"The House of the Rising Sun." With Burdon giving one of the defining, instantly recognizable vocal performances of the period, this brooding pop masterpiece topped the charts on both sides of the Atlantic, despite EMI arguing that its four-and-a-half-minute duration was too long to attract radio play.

Hits continued in much the same manner over a two-year period, with beat classics "Don't Let Me Be Misunderstood" and "We Gotta Get Out of This Place" (both 1965) reaching the Top Twenty in both the U.S. and the U.K. In common with most of their material, those hits were covers, this time of songs by Nina Simone and Sam Cooke respectively. Another 1965 hit was a cover of bluesman John Lee Hooker's

year-by-year

■ Vocals ■ Guitar ■ Bass ■ Drums ■ Keyboards ■ Strings

* Not released in the U.K.
** Eric Burdon and the Animals

columbia

The Animals

Animal Tracks

Burdon				
Valentine				
Price				
Chandler				
Steel				

1962   1963   1964   1965

John Weider
b. April 21, 1947

Barry Jenkins
b. December 22, 1944

"Boom Boom," which rose to No. 43 on the U.S. chart. Yet notwithstanding these triumphs, internal pressures began to emerge. Increasingly at odds with the group's musical direction, and with a fear of flying that threatened to jeopardize their U.S. campaign, Price left the band (he would enjoy enormous success of his own over the two decades that followed). He was replaced by Mick Gallagher (later Hammond organ player with Ian Dury and the Blockheads), then Dave Rowberry (whose audition was reportedly helped by the fact that he looked quite like Price).

At the beginning of 1966, Steel announced his intention to leave the band and go into business in Newcastle. Among names reported in the press for his replacement were The Who's Keith Moon, but the position went to **Barry Jenkins** of English pop group The Nashville Teens. Jenkins played on the 1966 hits "Don't Bring Me Down," a Gerry Goffin/Carole King song that made the Top Twenty in the U.S. and the U.K., and "See See Rider," a Gertrude "Ma" Rainey blues song that, released only in the U.S., reached No. 10 and gave The Animals one of their biggest hits. (It was later a staple of Elvis Presley's performances.)

Despite all this apparent success, the writing was on the wall for The Animals. The group had management problems and their finances were in a desperate state. Another sore point within the

group was Burdon's enthusiasm for LSD and the counterculture, while the others were content to sup their beer. With Burdon having begun his own chart career and Chandler quitting to manage Jimi Hendrix (to be replaced by **Danny McCulloch**), The Animals fell apart in late 1966.

Relocating to California, Burdon created a second version of The Animals. This time around, the driving blues of their classic singles was usurped by the prevailing psychedelic sound of the time. Billed as Eric Burdon and the Animals, the new band enjoyed hits such as the anti-Vietnam War song "San Franciscan Nights," including a bizarre and lengthy spoken-word introduction paying tribute to the "beautiful people of San Francisco." The period's stand-out track, "When I Was Young," showcased the electric violin of guitarist **John Weider** (later to be bassist with Brit group Family).

Following a period of shifting personnel (including guitarist Vic Briggs, keyboardist Zoot Money, and future Police man Andy Summers), Burdon disbanded this edition of the Animals in 1969. The final straw was thought to have been a traumatic Japanese tour that, unknown to the band, was being run by Yakuza—organized crime syndicates. It terminated with The Animals abandoning their equipment and fleeing the country for their lives. Burdon went on to join the funk band War before resuming a modest solo career. **TB**

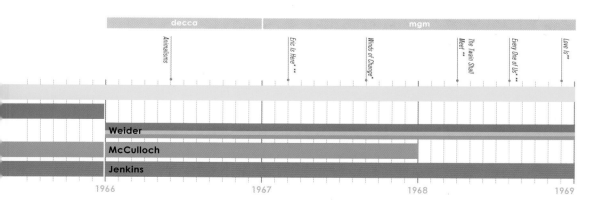

A anthrax 1981–present

Scott Ian
b. December 31, 1963

Dan Lilker
b. October 18, 1964

Greg D'Angelo
b. December 24, 1963

Neil Turbin
b. December 24, 1963

Matt Fallon
b. September 30, 1965

Joey Belladona
b. October 13, 1960

John Bush
b. August 24, 1963

Dan Nelson
b. June 21, 1976

"It'd be great to make a lot of money, appear on *American Bandstand* and *The Johnny Carson Show,* have my picture in *16 Magazine* and all that," Anthrax singer **Joey Belladonna** admitted to *Kerrang!* magazine in 1985. "But I can't see it happening!"

History has proved him right, but Anthrax are firmly established alongside Metallica, Megadeth, and Slayer as one of the "Big Four" bands of thrash: the super-speedy metal variant that energized the genre in the same way as punk did to rock in the seventies. To the *de rigeur* howling vocals and histrionic solos, Anthrax added humor and hip-hop—the first distinguishing them from virtually every major thrash act, and the second predating the nü-metal likes of Korn, Limp Bizkit, Linkin Park, and Slipknot.

Two drummers (Dave Weiss and **Greg D'Angelo**), two bassists (Kenny Kushner and Paul Khan), two guitarists (Greg Walls and Bob Berry), and three singers (John Connelly, Jason Rosenfeld, and Tommy Wise) passed through the ranks after **Scott Ian** and **Danny Lilker** conceived Anthrax in 1981. By the time of their 1984 debut, *Fistful of Metal,* the lineup had settled on guitarist Ian, bassist Lilker, drummer **Charlie Benante**, guitarist **Dan Spitz**, and singer **Neil Turbin**.

Falling short of the standards set by Metallica

and Slayer's debut albums the previous year, *Fistful* marked the swansong of both Turbin and Lilker. The former found himself largely written out of Anthrax's history, despite having written lyrics for classics like "Armed and Dangerous." The latter formed Nuclear Assault with early Anthrax singer John Connelly, and resurfaced alongside Ian and Benante—and front-man Chuck Billy—in their hardcore side-project Stormtroopers of Death (whose classic, albeit highly unpleasant, *Speak English or Die* was issued in 1985).

After a short stay by singer **Matt Fallon** (later to spend an equally forgotten period in Skid Row), 1985's splendid *Spreading the Disease* introduced Anthrax's new singer Joey Belladonna and, on bass, Benante's nephew **Frank Bello**. The album crept into the lower reaches of the U.S. chart while the band toured with W.A.S.P. and Black Sabbath. A triumphant outing with former Megaforce label-mates Metallica included, in September 1986, one of the loudest shows ever held at London's hallowed Hammersmith Odeon. Five months later, Anthrax returned to headline at the same venue, a performance eventually issued on 2007's *Caught in a Mosh: BBC Live in Concert.*

Among the Living (1987) made them the thrash band it was okay to like. Their skate shorts, comic

year-by-year ■ Vocals ■ Guitar ■ Bass ■ Drums

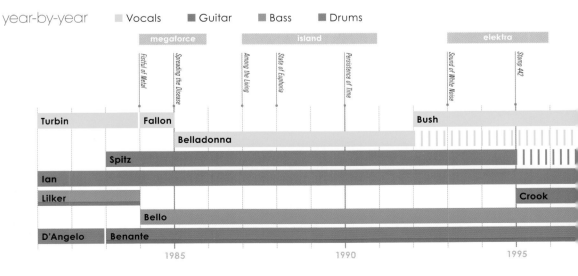

| 1M
*Among the
Living*
(1987) | 1M
*Persistence
of Time*
(1990) | 1M
*Attack of the
Killer B's*
(1991) | 1M
*Sound of White
Noise*
(1993) |

A

Dan Spitz
b. January 28, 1963

Paul Crook
b. February 12, 1966

Rob Caggiano
b. November 7, 1976

Frank Bello
b. July 9, 1965

Charlie Benante
b. November 27, 1962

book references (such as the Judge Dredd-inspired "I Am the Law"), and tongue-in-cheek anthems like "Caught In A Mosh" appealed to folks who didn't buy into metal's *sturm und drang*—and those who did. The former delighted in the mock hip-hop of 1987's *I'm the Man* EP, the latter sent 1988's *State of Euphoria* into the Top Thirty on both sides of the Atlantic.

Persistence of Time (1990) proved another smash, although the lyrics had turned more serious. A cover of new-waver Joe Jackson's "Got the Time" proved their ongoing willingness to defy expectations, though even that was eclipsed by a 1991 hook-up with rap's greatest act, Public Enemy. A reconstructed version of PE's "Bring the Noise"—the original of which included a name check for Anthrax—was the starting gun for a pioneering co-headlining tour by the two groups.

Disenchanted, Belladonna left for a low-key solo career, and was replaced by singer **John Bush**, from metallers Armored Saint. With him, Anthrax scaled new musical and chart peaks with the excellent *Sound of White Noise* (1993), which included orchestration by *Twin Peaks* composer Angelo Badalamenti.

Unfortunately, a debilitating series of personnel upheavals meant they never made good on this second wave of success. Spitz quit, leaving six-string

duties on *Stomp 442* (1995) and *Volume 8: The Threat is Real* (1998) to his guitar tech **Paul Crook**, drummer Charlie Benante, and Pantera's Dimebag Darrell. By 2003, Boiler Room's **Rob Caggiano** had displaced Crook, but not even a return to musical form—plus cameos by Dimebag and The Who's Roger Daltrey—could save *We've Come for You All* from achieving Anthrax's worst chart placings in two decades.

A reunion of the Ian-Benante-Spitz-Belladonna-Bello lineup held up long enough for a 2005 tour, but fans campaigned for Bush's return. They fleetingly got their wish in 2009, before **Dan Nelson** stepped into thrash's least stable shoes. (Nelson resurfaced in 2012 alongside bassist Rudy Sarzo, latterly of Blue Öyster Cult, in a band called Tred.)

After yet another brief Bush revival in early 2010, a Belladonna-fronted lineup, with Ian, Benante, Bello, and Caggiano, embarked on that year's "Big Four" festival tour with their old compadres Metallica, Slayer, and Megadeth. Remarkably, this incarnation of the band stuck together long enough to record *Worship Music* (2011), which garnered enthusiastic reviews and sufficient sales to land it just outside the U.S. Top Ten. They were still at it in 2012, playing the U.S. Mayhem festival alongside Slipknot, Slayer and Motörhead. **BM**

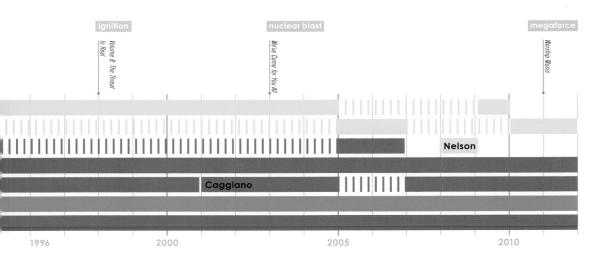

A

arcade fire 2001–present

Win Butler
b. April 14, 1980

Régine Chassagne
b. August 18, 1977

Myles Broscoe
b. December 31, 1969

Brendan Reed
b. March 21, 1978

Richard Reed Parry
b. October 4, 1977

Will Butler
b. October 6, 1982

"They're fantastic," said David Bowie of Arcade Fire in 2005. "I discovered them a year ago. Coldplay's Chris Martin has been saying he's discovered them first, but I did. So there. Na na na na na!" It is not hard to see why this multi-instrumental alternative band with theatrical overtones has won admirers from Bowie and Martin to U2 (who took the band on tour and used "Wake Up" as their intro music), Dave Grohl (who, having listened to "Keep the Car Running" on a daily basis, performed it with his Foo Fighters), Bruce Springsteen (who brought them onstage for rapturously received versions of songs by them and him), and even Kanye West (who tweeted "Arcade fire!!!!!!!!!! I feel like we all won when something like this happens!" when *The Suburbs* became the first "indie" release to win a Grammy for Album of the Year).

In the grand art rock tradition, Arcade Fire has achieved the winning combination of critical acclaim and a devoted fan base, while maintaining an enigmatic air, avoiding being over-exposed, and producing challenging yet rewarding music.

Originally called The Arcade Fire, the group began performing together as the trio of **Win Butler**, Josh Deu, and Tim Kyle (now in Wild Light) in Boston in 2001. On moving to Montreal, Win Butler met **Régine Chassagne**, with whom he began writing songs and, before long, forming a romantic attachment.

Kyle left, but the group expanded, adding **Myles Broscoe** on bass, Dane Mills on drums and guitar, and **Brendan Reed** on drums and vocals. Broscoe left before they had finished recording their self-titled and self-distributed debut EP (2003), and **Richard Reed Perry** joined soon afterwards.

During a show to celebrate the release of that EP, Reed quit live on stage after an argument with Butler. Mills swiftly followed, so **Tim Kingsbury** and **Will Butler** (Win's younger brother) joined to form a new lineup (Deu also left in 2003, but still works with them occasionally). Before the year was out, their impressive live form saw them signed to Merge Records.

Its title coined after several band members lost relatives during the recording, their debut album

year-by-year ■ Vocals ■ Guitar ■ Bass ■ Drums ■ Keyboards

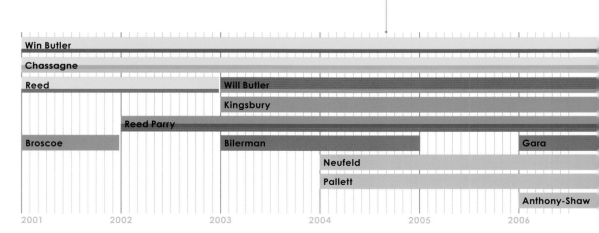

| 1.1M | 1.3M | 1.1M |
| *Funeral* (2004) | *Neon Bible* (2007) | *The Suburbs* (2010) |

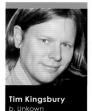

Tim Kingsbury
b. Unkown

Howard Bilerman
b. September 25, 1970

Sarah Neufeld
b. August 27, 1979

Jeremy Gara
b. July 6, 1978

Owen Pallett
b. September 7, 1979

Marika Anthony-Shaw
b. Unknown

Funeral appeared in 2004. New additions to the expanding lineup included **Sarah Neufeld** on violin/strings and **Howard Bilerman** on drums. A success in Canada, the conceptual collection became a slow-burning sensation in the U.K.—where four of its singles hit the Top Forty—and the U.S. In 2005, U2's infatuation began: drummer Larry Mullen Jr. said they were the only band he wished he'd been in, and singer Bono sighed, "I wouldn't want any other group to support us ever again." And when the *Fashion Rocks* TV show requested Bowie's participation, "I told them I'd do it only if they got Arcade Fire to perform." (They duly performed his "Five Years" and their "Wake Up.")

Recording sessions in a deserted church led to the epic *Neon Bible* (2007)—influenced by Dylan, Springsteen, and Elvis, but featuring a pipe organ, military choir, and full orchestra. Another lineup change—**Jeremy Gara** replaced Bilerman on drums—proved no obstacle to Arcade Fire's commercial ascent: buoyed by the hit "Keep the Car Running," *Neon Bible* debuted at No. 1 in Canada and

Ireland, and No. 2 in the U.S. and U.K. Win Butler and Chassagne's guest appearance at a Springsteen show in Canada sealed their extraordinary year.

In the aftermath, Arcade Fire participated in free concerts in support of U.S. presidential candidate Barack Obama. In January 2009, at the new president's request, they joined Jay-Z as the musical guests at the Obama Campaign Staff Ball.

The Suburbs duly topped international charts on its release in 2010. Influenced by the Butler brothers' upbringing in Houston, the album was described by Win as "a mix of Depeche Mode and Neil Young." Its singles ranged from the pounding "Ready to Start," through the Velvet Underground-esque "City with No Children," to a collaboration with David Byrne of Talking Heads, "Speaking in Tongues." The gorgeous "Sprawl II" even introduced an element once lacking in the Arcade Fire experience: a dance routine (albeit an odd and faintly disturbing dance routine).

Now able to command stadium-sized audiences, the group's next move is eagerly anticipated. **OM**

■ Aerophones   ■ Strings   ■ Other percussion

merge

Neon Bible

The Suburbs

2007   2008   2009   2010   2011   2012

A arctic monkeys 2002–present

Alex Turner
b. January 6, 1986

Jamie Cook
b. July 8, 1985

Matt Helders
b. May 7, 1986

Nick O'Malley
b. July 5, 1985

Andy Nicholson
b. Unknown

Glyn Jones
b. Unknown

In 2005, Arctic Monkeys, a young quartet from Sheffield, England, had a spectacular leap to fame when they came from nowhere to score U.K. No. 1 hits with their first two singles, "I Bet You Look Good on the Dancefloor" and "When the Sun Goes Down."

The debut album, *Whatever People Say I Am, That's What I'm Not*, wasn't an obvious blockbuster. It was indie rock released at a time when many were predicting that genre's demise, topped with wry, witty lyrics sung in a distinctively northern English accent. Yet *Whatever People Say…* became the fastest-selling debut album in British history upon its release in January 2006. It also achieved phenomenal international success, topping the Australian and Irish charts, reaching the U.S. *Billboard* Top Twenty and becoming a Top Ten hit all over western Europe.

The story began in 2002, when five friends formed a band. The first Arctic Monkeys lineup consisted of singer **Glyn Jones**, guitarists **Alex Turner** and **Jamie Cook**, drummer **Matt Helders**, and bassist **Andy Nicholson**. Jones soon dropped out, apparently lacking the necessary dedication, and main songwriter Turner took over as frontman. By the following year they were regularly gigging around Sheffield and recording demos.

The Monkeys' masterstroke was to give away CDs of said demos at their live shows. Fans uploaded their songs onto the Internet and news spread not so much by word-of-mouth, as by click-of-mouse—the band's songs went viral. By 2005 a frantic bidding war raged between record companies eager to sign them. Arctic Monkeys rejected offers from major labels and signed to Laurence Bell's indie label Domino.

Their subsequent leap to fame was too much for Nicholson, who took a temporary break "due to exhaustion." He was replaced by **Nick O'Malley** on their first U.S. tour; he would soon become a permanent member after the tour when Nicholson officially left the group. *Favourite Worst Nightmare*, released in April 2007, was another (U.K.) platinum hit, with many declaring it to be even better than their critically lauded debut.

Turner next took a brief break from the group to team up with Miles Kane (then the frontman of The Rascals), to form The Last Shadow Puppets. The duo recorded *The Age of the Understatement* (2008), a collection of dramatic, string-laden sixties-styled songs that gave Turner his third U.K. No. 1 album.

Arctic Monkeys reconvened for *Humbug* (2009)—co-produced by Josh Homme—which featured a denser, darker tone than its predecessors. *Suck It and See* (2011) combined their earlier melodicism with *Humbug*'s heavier sound to great effect and near-universal acclaim. Both albums were huge international hits, *Suck It and See* giving Arctic Monkeys their fourth consecutive U.K. chart-topper. **DJ**

year-by-year   ■ Vocals   ■ Guitar   ■ Bass   ■ Drums

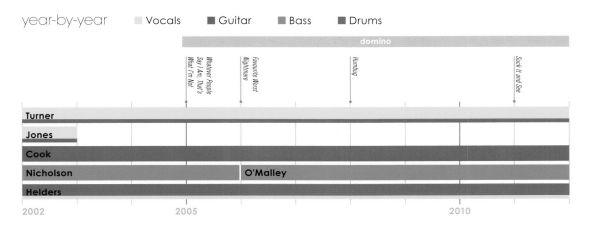

domino

Whatever People Say I Am, That's What I'm Not

Favourite Worst Nightmare

Humbug

Suck It and See

Turner				
Jones				
Cook				
Nicholson	O'Malley			
Helders				

2002   2005   2010

asia 1981–present

John Wetton
b. June 12, 1949

Carl Palmer
b. March 20, 1950

Geoff Downes
b. August 25, 1952

Steve Howe
b. April 8, 1947

Greg Lake
b. November 10, 1947

Scott Gorham
b. March 17, 1951

John Payne
b. 1958

Steve Lukather
b. October 21, 1957

Asia were big, but they could have been much bigger if they had had fewer personnel changes and avoided excessive reliance on founder-member **John Wetton**, who left and rejoined the supergroup several times. The group grew out of a progressive rock background and were formed in 1981 by Wetton (ex-King Crimson), **Carl Palmer** (from Emerson, Lake and Palmer), **Geoff Downes**, and **Steve Howe** (both from Yes). Their self-titled debut album, released in March 1982, got heavy airplay on MTV and sold ten million copies worldwide, with two singles from it—"Only Time Will Tell" and "Heat of the Moment"—making the U.S. Top Forty. The latter became, with another track from this album, "Sole Survivor," one of the anthemic show-stoppers of their live act.

Asia were off to a flying start with their debut topping the *Billboard* album chart for nine weeks but it was on stage that they really made their mark as one of the prototype arena bands. Their second album, *Alpha*, went platinum, but some fans objected to the spotlighting of Wetton's vocals at the expense of the other band members. Then suddenly the *Alpha* tour was suspended in September 1983. By the time the group next played live—at the "Asia in Asia" Tokyo gig in December—Wetton had been replaced by Palmer's friend from ELP, **Greg Lake**.

Asia's material—rock with a hard core but an MOR casing—did not suit Lake. He quit in early 1984

and Wetton rejoined the group. Then Howe left and was replaced by Mandy Meyer from Krokus. These changes undermined their identity; sales of their third album, *Astra*, were so disappointing that Polydor canceled the planned tour.

Shortly after, the group split. In 1987, Wetton and Downes re-formed Asia with guitarist **Scott Gorham** (ex-Thin Lizzy) and drummer Michael Sturgis (ex-a-ha) but despite this they failed to land a recording deal. They had better luck with their 1989 lineup, which featured John Young on keyboards, and first Alan Darby, then Holger Larish on guitar. A successful European tour prompted the release of *Then & Now* (1990), a best-of compilation with four new tracks featuring Toto guitarist **Steve Lukather**.

In 1991, Wetton left again and was succeeded by **John Payne**, who, together with another new recruit, Al Pitrelli, joined Downes, Howe, and Palmer on *Aqua*. Yet the players remained as fluid as the album title and a myriad of lineup changes in the nineties included Palmer leaving for an ELP reunion.

In 2006, Wetton, Palmer, Downes, and Howe got back together as The Four Original Members of Asia. The following year saw the emergence of Asia Featuring John Payne. The former played only Asia material in which Payne had not been involved; the latter performed songs from the entire history of the band as the complex Asia timeline rumbled on. **GL**

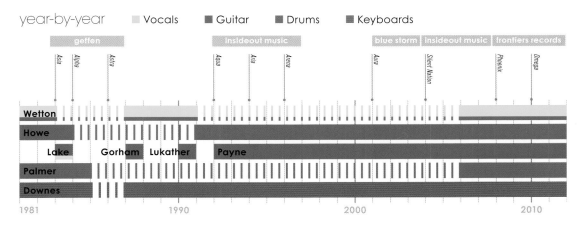

b-2 1988–present

Igor "Lyova" Bortnik
b. 2 September 1972

Aleksandr "Shura" Uman
b. 3 February 1970

Victoria Bilogan
b. Unknown

Grigori Gaberman
b. July 29, 1977

Andrey Zvonkov
b. 1 December 1973

Maxim Andrusschenko
b. 15 October 1978

Boris Lifshitz
b. 9 July 1981

Yanik Nikolenko
b. 25 February 1973

One of Russia's most important rock bands of the past two decades, B-2 have only been releasing albums since the late nineties, although their history stretches back a further one-and-a-half decades.

The story begins in 1985 in Minsk, Belarus, then a republic of the Soviet Union. **Aleksandr "Shura" Uman** and **Igor "Lyova" Bortnik**, two Jewish teenagers with ambitions to be actors, formed the new wave band Bratya Po Oruzhiyu ("Brothers in Arms"). Three years later they adopted the name Bereg Istini ("Shore of Truth"), soon abbreviated to B-2. With it came a new style of music: a kind of eastern-tinged classic rock.

In 1991, Uman and Bortnik moved to Israel. A year later, they won a "battle of the bands," enabling them to make their first professional recordings. Bortnik remained in Israel, serving in the army, while Uman moved on to Australia. In separate continents, the duo collaborated via mail and the Internet, while Uman formed the post-punky Chiron. In 1998, Bortnik joined his colleague's band but, within a year, they opted to concentrate on B-2.

In Australia the duo recorded tracks for what was intended as their debut album, Byespolaya e Grustnaya Lubov ("Sexless and Sad Love"); "Serdze" was a hit on Moscow radio. B-2 moved to Russia in 1999 but, with the country in financial crisis, they were unable to secure a release for the album.

Expanding to a full band, B-2 had a breakthrough a year later thanks to Aleksei Balabanov's film Brat 2. The soundtrack album was a hit, as was B-2's "Polkovnik." On the back of this success they were able to record their award-winning self-titled album in 2000. Meow Kiss Me was an even greater success, as B-2's videos were in heavy rotation on MTV Russia.

Success continued with albums from Inomarki ("Foreign Cars", 2004) to Spirit (2011), all of which achieved gold sales status. Among their more popular songs is "Bowie," which suggestively twins a reference to the Vladimir Nabokov novel Lolita with the simple inquiry, "Do you like David Bowie?"

B-2 often collaborate with other Russian rock acts like Splean, ChayF, Nochniye Snaiperi, and Zemfira. In 2005, with lyricist Mikhail Karasev (Uman's uncle), they produced Nechetny Voin ("Strange Warrior"), a CD featuring many of Russia's top pop and rock artists. A second volume emerged two years later.

B-2 continue to enjoy a following in Eastern Europe: the Spirit stadium tour continued well into 2012. Unfortunately, however, singing in their native tongue has prevented serious success in the West. **TB**

year-by-year ■ Vocals ■ Guitar ■ Bass ■ Drums ■ Keyboards

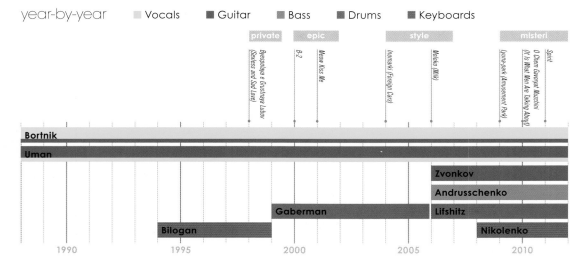

private — Byespolaya e Grustnaya Lubov (Sexless and Sad Love)
epic — B-2 / Meow Kiss Me
style — Inomarki (Foreign Cars) / Moloko (Milk)
misteri — Lyuna-park (Amusement Park) / Spirit / O Chem Govoryat Muzchini (It Is What Men Are Talking About)

Bortnik

Uman

Zvonkov

Andrusschenko

Gaberman

Lifshitz

Bilogan

Nikolenko

1990   1995   2000   2005   2010

the b-52's 1976–present

Cindy Wilson
b. February 28, 1957

Ricky Wilson
b. Mar 19, 1953
d. October 12, 1985

Keith Strickland
b. October 26, 1953

Kate Pierson
b. April 27, 1948

Fred Schneider
b. July 1, 1951

Julee Cruise
b. December 1, 1956

Sterling Campbell
b. May 3, 1964

"The women looked like they were from outer space," enthused Dave Grohl of The B-52's, "and everything was linked in: the sleeves, the sound, the clothes, the iconography, the logo... When you're a kid, that's what you're after—a real unified feel to a band."

Fueled by cocktails, siblings **Cindy** and **Ricky Wilson**, **Keith Strickland**, **Fred Schneider**, and **Kate Pierson** decided to form a band on the way home from a meal in their Athens, Georgia hometown. It was a suitably idiosyncratic start for a group who named themselves after southern lingo for the beehive hairdos adopted by Pierson and Cindy Wilson. The quintet made their live debut in Athens on Valentine's Day, 1977, then headed to New York to seek fame.

A self-financed single, featuring "Rock Lobster," snared deals with Warner and Island, and even inspired John Lennon's return to the studio. "It sounds just like Yoko's music," he told *Rolling Stone*, "so I said to meself, 'It's time to get out the old axe and wake the wife up!'" After two gold sets—*The B-52's* and *Wild Planet*—the band pioneered the remix album with 1981's *Party Mix!*. Then, seeking to expand their sound, they worked with Talking Heads' David Byrne. The sessions collapsed in disagreements, but the abortive results were issued as the mini-album *Mesopotamia*.

After 1983's *Whammy!*, the band's profile dipped, but the most serious blow was the death of Wilson, caused by complications from AIDS, in 1985. With the guitarist having co-written the band's music with Strickland, it seemed unlikely they could continue. Yet they bounced back with the hits "Love Shack" and "Roam" from 1989's *Cosmic Thing,* produced by Nile Rodgers and Don Was. Meanwhile, Pierson guested on R.E.M.'s *Out of Time* and Iggy Pop's "Candy."

Despite Cindy Wilson opting out to start a family, 1992's *Good Stuff* and 1994's "(Meet) The Flintstones" maintained the momentum. Live, Wilson was replaced by Strickland's old schoolmate Kim Basinger for one show, then for a tour by "Falling" singer **Julee Cruise**. In the ensuing hiatus, Schneider issued 1996's *Just Fred,* his second solo album (after 1984's *Fred Schneider and the Shake Society,* featuring Pierson and Ricky Wilson alongside Patti Labelle). But with Cindy back in the fold, the band returned to the road and issued the retrospectives *Time Capsule—Songs for a Future Generation* (1998) and *Nude on the Moon* (2002).

Funplex (2008), their first studio album in sixteen years, hit U.S. No. 11, while *With the Wild Crowd! Live in Athens, GA* (2011) proved The B-52's—now featuring Strickland on guitar and former Duran Duran/Soul Asylum/David Bowie drummer **Sterling Campbell**— to be as vibrant as ever. Of the party band that has championed causes from AIDS research to animal rights, Schneider remarked: "We're out there to entertain people, but it's great to get people thinking and dancing at the same time." **BM**

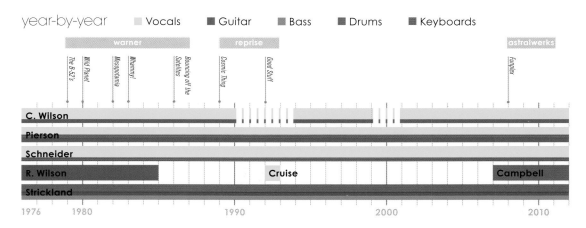

year-by-year   ■ Vocals   ■ Guitar   ■ Bass   ■ Drums   ■ Keyboards

B

bachman-turner overdrive 1973–present

Randy Bachman
b. September 27, 1943

Chad Allan
b. March 29, 1943

Robbie Bachman
b. February 18, 1953

C.F. "Fred" Turner
b. October 16, 1943

Tim Bachman
b. August 1, 1951

Blair Thornton
b. July 23, 1950

This Canadian band did much to keep alive the hard rock tradition during a period when most of the leading groups were soft-centered like Yes or glam like *Ziggy Stardust*-vintage David Bowie. While Bachman-Turner Overdrive's detractors point to their lack of musical ambition, their many fans liken them at their best to mid-period Led Zeppelin.

They were formed by two refugees from The Guess Who—lead guitarist **Randy Bachman** and singer **Chad Allan**—who called in Bachman's kid brother, **Robbie Bachman**, on drums and bassist **C.F. "Fred" Turner** to form Brave Belt, and cut a couple of albums for Reprise. (Turner had been recommended to Randy by compatriot rock star Neil Young.)

Thereafter, they bid farewell to Allan and enlisted another Bachman brother, **Tim Bachman**. Record companies, however, did not flock to their door. "I received about twenty-five or twenty-six refusals," Randy Bachman told *Billboard* book author Craig Rosen. Bachman funded their first album and paid the band's wages with his Guess Who royalties, which ran out just before Mercury finally snapped them up.

BTO's self-titled 1973 debut album was a slow-burner. It took six months to chart in the U.S. (but was eventually certified gold), and the single "Let It Ride"

took a year to reach the U.S. No. 23 spot. But by then *Bachman-Turner Overdrive II* had consolidated their growing reputation. However, Tim Bachman left to become a producer and the band replaced him with guitarist **Blair Thornton**, whose licks and looks helped 1974's *Not Fragile* achieve platinum sales, a *Billboard* No. 1 and the band's only U.K. hit LP (No. 12). Its title was a nod to Yes's breakthrough 1971 album *Fragile*—which, Randy Bachman told Rosen, "was very delicate and symphonic and kind of classical in a way. Ours was the exact opposite. It was just blunt, 'hit them over the head with a guitar and drum beat' kind of thing. But it wasn't a slam against Yes."

This was followed by two hits—"Takin' Care of Business" (U.S. No. 12) and their best-known track, "You Ain't Seen Nothin' Yet" (U.S. No. 1/U.K. No. 2). Although they never repeated this success, *Four Wheel Drive* (1975) went platinum and they had six more U.S. Top Forty singles before the end of 1976.

A year later the band's fortunes took a dip. "My Wheels Won't Turn," was a single from *Freeways*, the band's sixth studio album, which failed to chart. Turner, who took lead vocals on only two of the album's eight tracks, felt that he had been sidelined and refused to appear full-face on the cover.

year-by-year ▫ Vocals ▪ Guitar ▪ Bass ▪ Drums

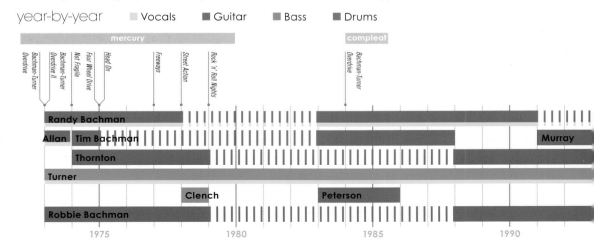

	2M	2.2M	1.5M	3.2M
	Bachman-Turner Overdrive II (1973)	**Not Fragile** (1974)	**Four Wheel Drive** (1975)	**Best of BTO (So Far)** (1990)

B

Jim Clench
b. May 1, 1949

Garry Peterson
b. May 26, 1945

Randy Murray
b. Unknown

In 1978 Randy Bachman left the band, saying that he and his fellow members just "ran out of common interests." Now without its founder, the group was creatively exhausted, but it soldiered on with **Jim Clench** (ex-April Wine) under the name BTO (Randy retained and zealously guarded rights to the full original moniker). The new-look BTO's first album, *Street Action*, was a disappointment; their second, *Rock 'n' Roll Nights*, a disaster (no more than a quarter of a million sales worldwide); after the promotional tour for the latter, the band split.

The members then did their own things until 1983, when Randy Bachman—who had meanwhile performed in Ironhorse and written some songs with Carl Wilson of The Beach Boys—re-formed the group with brother Tim, Fred Turner, and **Garry Peterson** (the drummer from The Guess Who). When they toured to promote their new album—to which, confusingly, they gave the same title as their first—their drum tech, Billy Chapman, joined them on stage playing keyboards.

In 1986 Bachman-Turner Overdrive opened for Van Halen on the *5150* Tour with the same lineup bar Turner, who, it was said, had been unavailable when the organizers tried to contact them. At the end of the run, Randy Bachman split again but Tim kept

the band going in cut-down form until 1988, when the *Not Fragile* lineup (Randy, Fred, Blair, Robbie) reconvened once more. Only one recording from this incarnation of the group survives—a cover of "Wooly Bully" (originally a 1965 hit for Sam the Sham and The Pharaohs) that was used on the soundtrack of the 1989 Sandy Wilson movie *American Boyfriends*. Then Randy again went his own way and was replaced by **Randy Murray**. This was the dawn of BTO's longest period of stability—the members stayed together from 1991 until the end of 2004. Then, it was announced, they would take a break from touring.

What had been planned as an intermission turned into a hiatus and, when their management company was disbanded, it looked like the end of a very long road. Not quite: In January 2009, Tim Bachman played at a Randy Bachman show and, in December of the same year, the latter got back together with Fred Turner in Winnipeg, Manitoba, Canada. This reunion led to a full-blown tour of North America and Europe in 2010, with the pair backed by Randy's band (Marc LaFrance, Mick Dalla-Vee, and Brent Howard). All was not well in the world, however, as Rob Bachman and Blair Thornton threatened legal action over this group's adoption of the name Bachman & Turner. **GL**

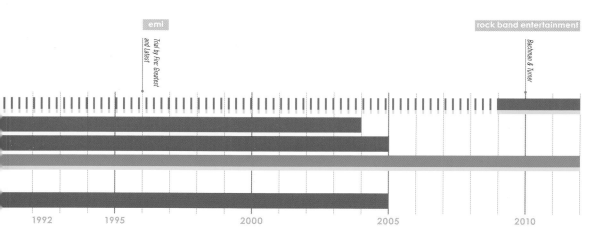

bad company 1973–2010

Paul Rodgers
b. December 17, 1949

Mick Ralphs
b. March 31, 1944

Simon Kirke
b. July 28, 1949

Boz Burrell
b. August 1, 1946
d. September 21, 2006

Brian Howe
b. July 22, 1953

Steve Price
b. Unknown

Larry Oakes
b. Unknown

Gregg Dechert
b. May, 13, 1952

A swaggering supergroup formed in 1973 upon the final demise of Free, Bad Company had instant and meteoric success. The chemistry between Free's **Paul Rodgers** (vocals) and **Simon Kirke** (drums), Mott the Hoople's **Mick Ralphs** (guitar) and King Crimson's **Boz Burrell** (bass) was obviously right, and the group soon established a formidable live reputation.

They also proved they were able to reproduce their live punch on record. *Bad Company*, the first album, came out in 1974 and sold extremely well in both the United States (where it went to No. 1) and the United Kingdom. Studded with terrific riffs like "Ready for Love" (which also featured on Mott the Hoople's *All the Young Dudes*) and "Can't Get Enough" as well as the title track, the group had a fuller sound, with bolder brushstrokes, than Free's relatively lean (yet effective) palette. The follow-up *Straight Shooter* (1975)—blessed with more great songs such as "Feel Like Makin' Love," the elegiac "Shooting Star," and "Good Lovin' Gone Bad"—also quickly went gold.

Paul Kossoff, the guitarist from Free who struggled with heroin addiction, formed Back Street Crawler after that group's demise. Free bandmates Rodgers and Kirke invited him to tour with Bad Company in

1976, but it proved an ill omen. Kossoff died before the tour started and, despite *Run with the Pack,* their third album in three years, going platinum in the United States, some of the group's impetus was lost. *Burnin' Sky* (1977) sold gold but made less chart impact, its songs being arguably somewhat formulaic. *Desolation Angels* (1979), aided by the hit "Rock 'n' Roll Fantasy," was a return to form and commercial favor, but more problems were to beset the group.

Peter Grant, Led Zeppelin's legendary manager, had been guiding Bad Company's fortunes and his business acumen made a vital contribution to their triumphs. But Grant was badly affected by the death of Zeppelin's drummer, John Bonham, in 1980 and rather lost interest in managing anyone. The group released the under-performing *Rough Diamonds* in 1982, but were growing disillusioned (punch-ups were not unknown) and decided to call it a day.

Rodgers, his taste for supergroups unsated, set up The Firm with Jimmy Page, who had escaped the Zeppelin wreckage, future AC/DC drummer Chris Slade, and future Blue Murder bassist Tony Franklin. Ralphs entered into a brief partnership of equivalent stature, touring with David Gilmour of Pink Floyd.

year-by-year ■ Vocals ■ Guitar ■ Bass ■ Drums ■ Keyboards

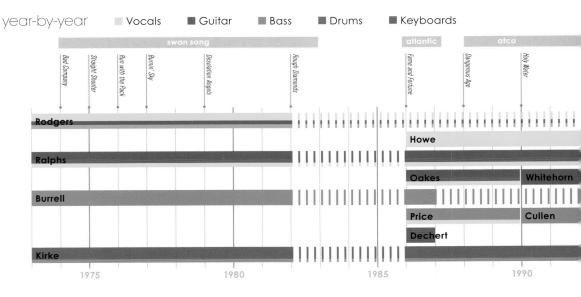

5M	4.2M	3M	3M
Bad Company (1974)	*Run with the Pack* (1976)	*Desolation Angels* (1979)	*10 from 6* (1985)

Paul Cullen
b. Unknown

Geoff Whitehorn
b. August 29, 1951

Dave "Bucket" Colwell
b. Unknown

Rick Wills
b. December 5, 1947

Robert Hart
b. November 1, 1958

Jaz Lochrie
b. Unknown

Lynn Sorensen
b. Unknown

Howard Leese
b. June 13, 1951

That is how it stayed for four years until Ralphs and Kirke reformed the group with **Brian Howe** (who had sung with Ted Nugent), **Steve Price** (bass), and **Greg Dechert** (keyboards). With Foreigner's Mick Jones as executive producer and Burrell fleetingly returning (he quit before the ensuing tour), they issued *Fame and Fortune* (1986) to no commercial interest. But with **Larry Oakes** on guitar, the Howe-dominated *Dangerous Age* (1988) returned them to gold sales.

However, problems were mounting once again. There were tensions in the group between Howe and just about everyone else and the recording of *Holy Water* (1990) was fraught with difficulty, although it turned out to be commercially very successful. Ralphs was unable to join the subsequent tour owing to personal problems and was replaced by **Geoff Whitehorn** from Back Street Crawler, then **Dave "Bucket" Colwell**. Meanwhile **Paul Cullen** came in on bass, to be followed by former Roxy Music/Foreigner man **Rick Wills**. The group's *Here Comes Trouble* (1992), another Stateside success, appeared aptly titled.

Howe quit in 1994 to be succeeded by future Manfred Mann's Earth Band singer **Robert Hart** for *Company of Strangers* (1995) and *Stories Told & Untold*

(1996), the latter a mix of new songs and re-recorded favorites, with guests including Alison Krauss, Bon Jovi's Richie Sambora, and the Eagles' Timothy B. Schmidt. But their commercial fortunes once more declined.

In a dramatic turn of events, the group's founders reunited as Bad Company in 1998. Once again, it could not last: Burrell left again the following year and Ralphs had to give up in 2000. Wills (soon succeeded by **Jaz Lochrie**) and Colwell resumed their places but Bad Company dissolved again in 2002. Rodgers returned to his solo career, which included a high-profile stint with Queen from 2004 to 2009.

Bad Company reformed yet again in 2008. With Burrell having died from a heart attack in 2006, Rodgers' solo touring bandmate **Lynn Sorensen** came in on bass, while Heart's **Howard Leese** joined on guitar and keyboards. In Burrell's memory, Rodgers sang his fine composition "Gone, Gone, Gone" (from *Desolation Angels*). An extensive tour in 2010 showed they had lost none of their old pizzazz.

Bad Company's future is uncertain, but it would be wise not to count them out just yet. The group surfed the 1970's hard rock wave with aplomb and wear a rugged, timeless crown today. **MiH**

■ Aerophones   ■ Other percussion

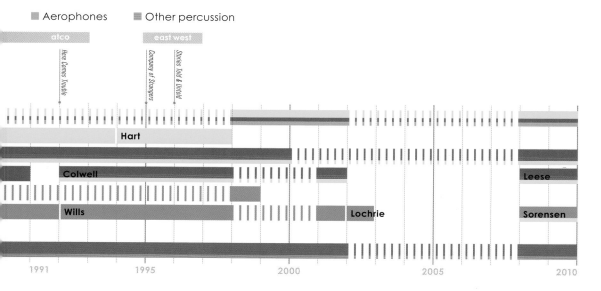

the band 1964–1999

Rick Danko
b. December 29, 1942
d. December 10, 1999

Levon Helm
b. May 26, 1940
d. April 19, 2012

Garth Hudson
b. August 2, 1937

Richard Manuel
b. April 3, 1943
d. March 4, 1986

Robbie Robertson
b. July 5, 1943

Jim Weider
b. 1951

The Band began life in the early sixties as The Hawks, backing Canadian hellraiser Ronnie Hawkins. **Robbie Robertson** (guitar), **Richard Manuel** (piano), **Rick Danko** (bass), **Garth Hudson** (organ), and **Levon Helm** (drums) would enjoy a successful recording and performing career of their own, but their big break came in 1965 when they hooked up with Bob Dylan.

Having "plugged in" at that year's Newport Folk Festival and declared himself a rock 'n' roller, Dylan needed a band for a world tour. The relationship proved beneficial to both parties. Said Robertson, "I learned from Bob that it's okay to break those traditional rules of what songs are supposed to be."

After a motorcycle accident, Dylan moved to Woodstock, New York, in 1967 and put The Band on a retainer as he recuperated. *The Basement Tapes*, a widely circulated bootleg (officially released eight years later) documented the time. They made their own music, too: namely 1968's electric folk masterpiece *Music from Big Pink*. Part of their strength was an ability to switch instruments: Helm doubled on mandolin, Hudson and Manuel on saxophone, while Manuel, Danko, and Helm were all distinctive vocalists.

The album was named after their communal Woodstock house and featured three songs written or co-written by Dylan ("This Wheel's on Fire," "Tears of Rage," and "I Shall Be Released"). Another track, "The Weight," was featured in the cult classic movie *Easy Rider* and remains their best-known song. "After *Sgt. Pepper*, it's the most influential record in the history of rock 'n' roll," declared Pink Floyd's Roger Waters. "It affected Pink Floyd deeply… Sonically, the way the record's constructed, I think *Music from Big Pink* is fundamental to everything that happened after it."

Robertson penned evocative classics like "The Night They Drove Old Dixie Down" for 1969's *The Band,* while 1970's *Stage Fright* contained some of his best writing. He assumed characters like the Confederate Virgil Cane in "…Dixie…" because he felt "embarrassed by the self-indulgence of 'me me me… here's a little song about me.'"

Cahoots (1971) was the first album to be cut at Woodstock's Bearsville Studios and featured horns arranged by Allen Toussaint. Woodstock neighbor Van Morrison also guested on "4% Pantomime." The Band finished 1971 with a residency at New York's

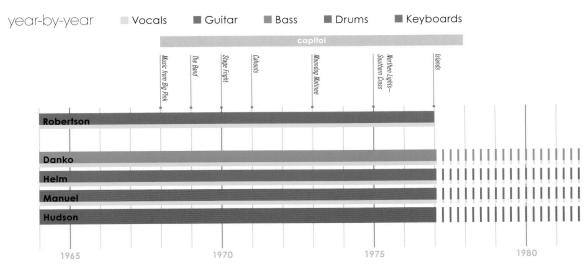

year-by-year ▪ Vocals ▪ Guitar ▪ Bass ▪ Drums ▪ Keyboards

1.4M	2.6M	1.4M	1.3M
Music from Big Pink (1968)	The Band (1969)	Stage Fright (1970)	The Best of the Band (1976)

Blondie Chaplin
b. July 7, 1951

Fred Carter Jr
b. December 31, 1933
d. July 17, 2010

Stan Szelest
b. February 11, 1943
d. January 20, 1991

Randy Ciarlante
b. unknown

Richard Bell
b. March 5, 1946
d. June 15, 2007

Academy of Music, augmented by a horn section: recordings from it were issued as *Rock of Ages* (1972), which became their highest-charting U.S. album.

After *Moondog Matinee* (1973)—a set of oldies whose title was taken from a radio show by rock 'n' roll DJ Alan Freed—The Band backed Bob Dylan on his *Planet Waves* album. Much of 1974 would be taken up touring with Dylan, playing their own set as well as his, and appearing on his live *Before the Flood*.

Yet 1976 would bring not only their penultimate album, *Northern Lights Southern Cross*, but also The Band's retirement from live performance. A historic farewell show at San Francisco's Winterland venue on Thanksgiving Day saw them joined by special guests including Dylan, Eric Clapton, Neil Diamond, Ronnie Hawkins, Dr. John, Joni Mitchell, Ringo Starr, Muddy Waters, and Neil Young. The four hours of performance were immortalized on film courtesy of Robertson's former roommate, filmmaker Martin Scorsese. A triple vinyl album (*The Last Waltz*) of highlights appeared alongside the movie, containing many extra songs. However, Helm believed the film concentrated too much on Robertson, whose

decision had prompted the disbandment. This would be the last time the five graced a stage together—*Islands* appeared in 1977 to fulfill their contract.

The Band re-formed without Robertson in the eighties, but their ranks were tragically depleted when Manuel, whose life had been plagued by addictions, hanged himself after a 1986 show. He was replaced by **Stan Szelest**, then by **Richard Bell**. Other additions included **Fred Carter Jr** and **Blondie Chaplin**, while drummer **Randy Ciarlante** came on board in 1990. (That year, The Band appeared with Roger Waters at a re-staging of *The Wall* in Berlin.) Hard-living Danko died in 1999, while Robertson entered the soundtrack realm. In 1994, the year The Band entered the Rock and Roll Hall of Fame, he returned to his roots with the TV soundtrack *Music for the Native Americans*.

The Band are credited with helping to create the Americana genre that would be successfully mined by Ryan Adams, Gillian Welch, and the like. Their second album was belatedly declared platinum in 1991—suggesting that, while they were never big sellers, many important musicians in America and beyond were among those lending them an ear. **MHe**

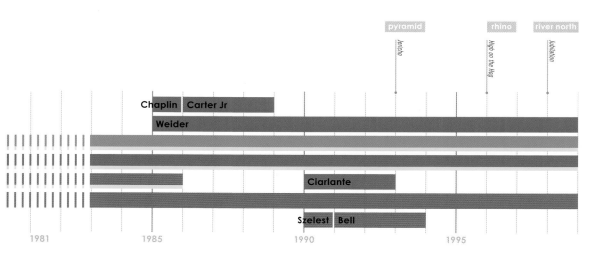

B

bauhaus 1978-2008

Daniel Ash
b. July 31, 1957

David J
b. April 24, 1957

Kevin Haskins
b. July 19, 1960

Peter Murphy
b. July 11, 1957

"British bands sound the way they do because Britain is overcast and gray and there are lots of churches with gargoyles. That's where Bauhaus come from." So said Perry Farrell of Jane's Addiction, just one of many U.S. groups to cite Bauhaus as an influence.

Little did Walter Gropius know when he founded Staatliches Bauhaus—more commonly known as just Bauhaus—in Weimar, Germany in 1919, that the art school's legend would one day be carried forward by theatrical rockers from Northampton, England.

He also probably didn't suspect that the school's name would later be whispered with reverence by generations of disenfranchised young teens as they shopped at malls for dark eyeliner and vampire gear. Or that if you were making "alternative" music in the late eighties/early nineties in the U.S., Bauhaus were probably a big influence. Nirvana, The Smashing Pumpkins, Soundgarden, and the aforementioned Jane's Addiction are just some of the groups who have cited Bauhaus as inspiring their sound. Chalk all three up as unexpected bonuses in the legacy of the man most responsible for creating the influential Bauhaus Movement in art and architecture.

The members were certainly aware of the school's significance—and relished all the implications that came with borrowing such a lofty title. It was, after all, a more striking moniker than The Craze—the name of

an early group that guitarist **Daniel Ash** and the sibling rhythm section of bassist **David J** and drummer **Kevin Haskins** were in prior to uniting with Ash's school chum **Peter Murphy** in 1978 to form Bauhaus 1919.

The new group honored Gropius's school in more than just name: they also, from the start, showed a commitment to creating a signature style that differed greatly from anything else at the time. Bauhaus 1919 came at the perfect moment, with young Brits hungry for an alternative to what was left of the country's punk scene, as well as to the flash of new wave.

Yet nobody could have expected Bauhaus, who dropped "1919" from their name in 1979, to live up to their potential as quickly as they did with "Bela Lugosi's Dead." That debut single from 1979 was about as far from the norm as possible: a darkly appealing nine-minute tribute to the horror movie icon best known for playing Dracula in Universal Pictures' fabled series. The song, unsurprisingly, failed to dent the charts, but provided notice of a new sound emerging from England's post-punk scene. Bauhaus, and their remarkable debut single, would serve as the definition of what is now known as gothic rock, characterized by dark soundscapes, menacing vocals, and bleak lyrics.

"Bela Lugosi's Dead," the genre's anthem, garnered some radio play and was attractive enough to land Bauhaus a deal with 4AD, on which they

year-by-year   ▦ Vocals   ■ Guitar   ■ Bass   ■ Drums

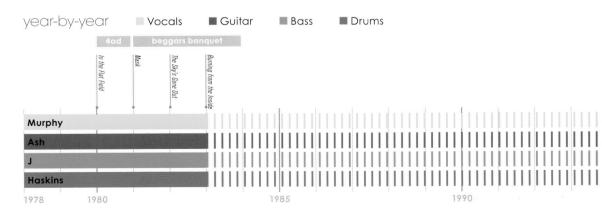

200,000	250,000	200,000	150,000
Mask	The Sky's	Burning from the	1979–1983
(1981)	Gone Out	Inside	(1985)
	(1982)	(1983)	

B

would issue three more commercially unsuccessful singles. The quartet's full-length debut, 1980's *In the Flat Field*, confused critics, who didn't understand what the moaning was all about, but gave Bauhaus their first mini-hit, peaking at No. 72 on the U.K. album chart. More significantly, it stirred a cult-like following, among whom *In the Flat Field* was a badge of honor.

The cult expanded once Bauhaus moved to 4AD's parent label, Beggars Banquet, and released *Mask* (1981). Elevated by its Top Thirty success in the U.K., the group were poised for a commercial breakthrough in 1982. That year brought the quartet their greatest taste of mainstream success, thanks to a hit cover of David Bowie's "Ziggy Stardust" (a non-album track, recorded at a BBC session), a raised middle finger to critics who dismissed them as Bowie clones. The same year also brought them their highest-charting record, *The Sky's Gone Out*, which peaked at No. 4 in the U.K.

Along the way, Bauhaus fans went beyond just listening to a song about Bela Lugosi: they began dressing like him, showing up to gigs in capes and other corpse-chic apparel. Bauhaus's role as posterboys for goth was secured when they featured in the 1983 Tony Scott vampire flick *The Hunger* (starring Bowie), performing, of course, "Bela Lugosi."

The wheels began to fall off around the time they ventured into the studio to record 1983's *Burning from the Inside*—mainly without Murphy, who was too ill with pneumonia to contribute to either writing or recording. Absurd as it now sounds, Bauhaus were attempting to cut an album with hardly any input from their singer. The result, not coincidentally, was less thrilling than the first three albums, but momentum helped carry *Burning...* to No. 13 on the U.K. chart. However, Bauhaus never recovered from those recording sessions, disbanding as the album hit stores.

The Haskins boys and Ash formed Love and Rockets, whose U.S. commercial success—notably 1989's hit "So Alive"—eclipsed their previous band's sales. Meanwhile, Murphy built a low-key solo career, becoming known as the face of a Maxell cassette tape advertisement. In 1984, disbelief greeted his union with Japan's Mick Karn in Dali's Car, often regarded as the most pretentious group of all time.

All the while, however, the group's legacy grew and young goths dreamed of getting the chance to see Bauhaus in concert. The group gave the fans what they wanted with the "Resurrection Tour" in 1988 and a fully fledged reunion in 2005, which lasted three years and included a tour with Bauhaus devotees Nine Inch Nails and an allegedly final album, *Go Away White* (2008). "We come together, burn up, and we leave Bauhaus with fires burning..." said Murphy. "But it's not viable as a band anymore." **JiH**

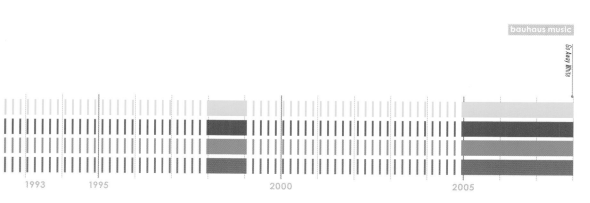

bauhaus music

Go Away White

1993   1995   2000   2005

the beach boys 1961–present

Brian Wilson
b. June 20, 1942

Carl Wilson
b. December 21, 1946
d. February 7, 1998

Dennis Wilson
b. December 4, 1944
d. December 28, 1983

Mike Love
b. March 15, 1941

Al Jardine
b. September 3, 1942

David Marks
b. August 22, 1948

If there was a U.S. equivalent of The Beatles during the sixties, it was The Beach Boys. They notched up sixteen U.S. Top Thirty singles, plus ten hit albums, with their infectious surf-orientated pop, and—unlike their Brit peers—they are still going over half a century later.

Brothers **Brian**, **Carl**, and **Dennis Wilson**, cousin **Mike Love**, and school pal **Al Jardine** formed The Pendletones (named after the surfing shirts they wore on stage) in L.A. in 1961. Within months they were The Beach Boys and had cut "Surfin'" as their first single.

By the close of 1962 they had signed to Capitol Records and released *Surfin' Safari*, which reached No. 32 in the U.S. chart. They lost Jardine for a year (replaced by **David Marks**), but hit the U.S. top spot with "Help Me Rhonda" and "I Get Around."

In the U.K., "I Get Around"—the group's first U.S. million-seller—became their first Top Ten entry and led to a further nineteen chart hits during the decade, including the chart-topping "Good Vibrations" and "Do It Again." However, despite their success, Brian Wilson opted out of live work in 1964 to focus on writing

and producing and was briefly replaced by **Glen Campbell**, then permanently by **Bruce Johnston**.

The result of Brian's studio efforts was *Pet Sounds* (1966), which saw him hailed as "a pop genius" by Eric Clapton and was seen, by producer George Martin, as the inspiration for The Beatles' album *Sgt. Pepper's Lonely Hearts Club Band* (this was fitting, as the Fab Four's *Rubber Soul* had helped to inspire *Pet Sounds*).

With Brian collaborating with creative spark Van Dyke Parks and rarely performing live, a stream of greatest hits albums eclipsed The Beach Boys' studio albums in the seventies. However, releases on their new Brother label showed a change of direction with the rock-orientated *Surf's Up* (1971) and *Holland* (1973), boasting environmental and political themes on tracks such as "Student Demonstration Time."

Sandwiched between these two was *Carl and the Passions/So Tough*, which saw Johnston depart (until 1978). Bassist **Blondie Chaplin** and drummer **Ricky Fataar**—Dennis had put his hand through a window—were recruited to a lineup that still, mostly, lacked

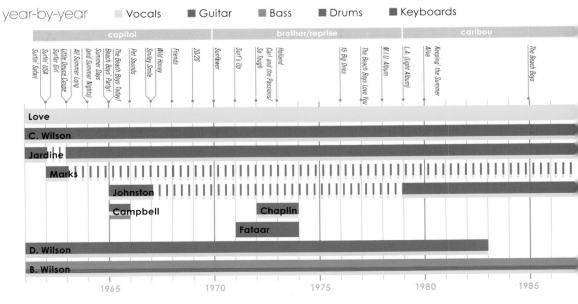

year-by-year   ▨ Vocals   ▪ Guitar   ▪ Bass   ▪ Drums   ▪ Keyboards

| 3M | 1.9M | 1.8M | 1M |
| Best of the Beach Boys (1966) | Pet Sounds (1966) | Endless Summer (1974) | 20 Golden Greats (1976) |

B

Bruce Johnston
b. June 17, 1944

Blondie Chaplin
b. July 7, 1951

Ricky Fataar
b. September 5, 1952

Glen Campbell
b. April 22, 1936

Brian Wilson. Such was their overhaul at the time that Chaplin took lead vocals on *Holland*'s standout, "Sail on Sailor." The surfing look was also over: the bearded Beach Boys looked more like the Grateful Dead or The Band. (In 1979, Bruce Johnston and a trio of session singers provided the Beach Boys sound on Pink Floyd's *The Wall*. The group had been up for it but declined when they learned they had to sing about worms.)

The first signs of a Beach Boys dissolution came in 1981 when Carl Wilson left (albeit for eighteen months) and brother Brian was fired (although he returned in 1989). Then Dennis—the only actual surfer—drowned while swimming off the Californian coast in 1983.

With Brian Wilson busy on his debut solo album, the Beach Boys avoided the singles charts during the bulk of the eighties until they teamed up with rap act The Fat Boys on "Wipe Out." This was followed by "Kokomo," featured in the movie *Cocktail*, which became their first U.S. No. 1 in twenty-two years.

Legal disputes involving song copyrights and former band manager Stephen Love, brother of Mike, ran well into the nineties. The group continued to use Terry Melcher as producer on the unsuccessful 1992 *Summer in Paradise*, an album which also saw Jardine suspended from the group.

Carl remained the only Wilson to perform with the band—alongside Love and Johnston—until he died of cancer in 1998, while Brian and Jardine developed their own new groups. The new millennium saw the release of yet more compilations alongside Brian's 2004 version of the long lost album *Smile* (started and abandoned in 1967). While Carl, Dennis, and Love all issued solo albums with little commercial success, Brian's track record as a solo artist spans over twenty years and includes nine U.S. and U.K. chart albums.

In 2006, on the fortieth anniversary of *Pet Sounds*, the surviving Beach Boys—Brian Wilson, Love, Jardine, Johnston, and Marks—assembled for a celebration at Capitol Records in LA. In 2011, they celebrated their fiftieth anniversary with *The Smile Sessions*, a collection of the original recordings made forty-four years previously, and tour and recording plans. **BS**

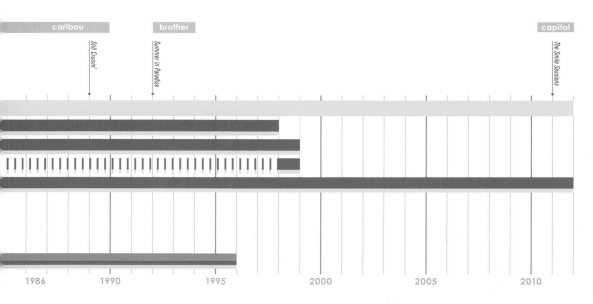

Surfin' Safari (1962)

All Summer Long (1964)

Pet Sounds (1966)

Sunflower (1970)

Surf's Up (1971)

Holland (1973)

Love You (1977)

Keepin' the Summer Alive (1980)

Summer in Paradise (1992)

The Smile Sessions (2011)

Clockwise from top left: **Mike Love**, **Brian Wilson**, **Carl Wilson**, **David Marks**, and **Dennis Wilson**—The Beach Boys circa 1962.

The Beach Boys perform "Wendy" on *The Ed Sullivan Show* in New York in 1964.

Left to right: **Bruce Johnston**, **Al Jardine**, **Dennis Wilson**, **Carl Wilson**, and **Love** during a tour of the U.K. in 1966.

The Beach Boys did a passable imitation of The Band or The Grateful Dead in the seventies: **Ricky Fataar**, **Blondie Chaplin**, **Jardine**, **Love**, and **Carl Wilson**.

Carl Wilson performs onstage in Amsterdam, the Netherlands, in 1971.

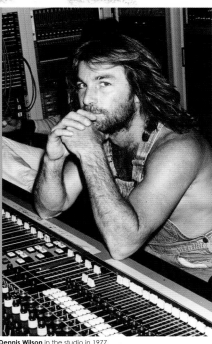

Love, Jardine, Dennis Wilson, and **Carl Wilson** in 1973.

Jardine, Ed Carter, **Love**, and **Carl Wilson** at Wembley Arena, London, in 1980.

Dennis Wilson in the studio in 1977.

Love and **Johnston** appear with John Stamos in the U.S. sitcom *Full House* in May 1992.

Brian Wilson performs *Smile* in 2005, six years before The Beach Boys' version finally saw the light.

the beatles 1960–1970

B

John Lennon
b. October 9, 1940
d. December 8, 1980

Paul McCartney
b. June 18, 1942

George Harrison
b. February 25, 1943
d. November 29, 2001

Ringo Starr
b. July 7, 1940

Pete Best
b. November 24, 1941

Stuart Sutcliffe
b. June 23, 1940
d. April 10, 1962

"When it comes down to pop," mused Nirvana's Dave Grohl in 1991, "there's only one word—the 'B' word. The Beatles." Added bassist Krist Novoselic: "They started it, they did it best, they ended it."

"They" started as teenagers in The Quarry Men Skiffle Group, led by **John Lennon** and named after a line from his Quarry Bank High School song. **Paul McCartney** joined in 1957; McCartney's younger friend **George Harrison** joined in 1958, and by 1960 they were a five-piece rock 'n' roll group called The Silver Beatles, with **Pete Best** on drums and Lennon's best friend **Stuart Sutcliffe** on bass.

Marathon sets in the clubs of Hamburg morphed the quintet—now The Beatles—into no-frills rockers loved by the German art-school crowd. Back in their home town Liverpool (minus Sutcliffe, who died in Hamburg), a residency at The Cavern club attracted record store owner Brian Epstein. He offered to manage them and, in 1962, secured a contract with Parlophone (EMI's comedy subsidiary). Shortly afterwards, Best was out and **Ringo Starr** was in.

Debut single "Love Me Do" made No. 17 in the U.K. and "Please Please Me" made No. 2. The *Please Please Me* album (1963), recorded in one ten-hour session and closing with Lennon's raw reading of "Twist

and Shout," shot to the top. *With The Beatles* (1963) followed it, giving the band fifty-one straight weeks atop the U.K. albums chart. Cue Beatlemania.

The Beatles' career was a series of fresh peaks topped with breathless regularity. "I Want To Hold Your Hand" became their first U.S. No. 1 on February 1, 1964. Eight days later, an unprecedented 73 million viewers watched their Stateside debut on *The Ed Sullivan Show*. By April 4, they held four out of the Top Five on the *Billboard* Hot 100. The same year, their big-screen debut *A Hard Day's Night*—funny, inventive, its soundtrack penned solely by Lennon and McCartney—rewrote the book for pop movies. Follow-up movie *Help!* (1965) boasted the Dylan-esque "You've Got to Hide Your Love Away," the thrilling title tune, and McCartney's much-covered "Yesterday."

Seeking out new horizons, The Beatles discovered marijuana (in 1964, courtesy of Bob Dylan) and LSD, and embraced world music via George Harrison's burgeoning love of Indian music. *Rubber Soul* (1965) and *Revolver* (1966) brimmed over with invention and songcraft; *Revolver* in particular saw them test the studio's capabilities—witness the psychedelic "Tomorrow Never Knows." The astonishing double A-side "Strawberry Fields Forever"/"Penny Lane"

year-by-year   ■ Vocals   ■ Guitar   ■ Bass   ■ Drums   ■ Keyboards

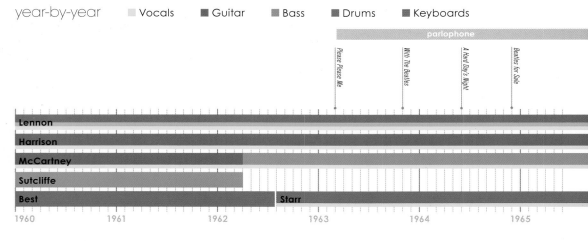

28.5M	32M	13.5M	30.3M
Abbey Road (1969)	Sgt. Pepper's Lonely Hearts Club Band (1967)	Beatles 1967–70 (1973)	1 (2000)

B

followed in 1967 (the songs, later included on the U.S. release of *Magical Mystery Tour,* were kept off the No. 1 spot in the U.K. by Engelbert Humperdinck).

The group's snowballing innovations peaked with *Sgt. Pepper's Lonely Hearts Club Band* (1967), iconic in every way, from its Peter Blake-inspired sleeve to the kaleidoscopic range of music within—notably the dreamlike "Lucy in the Sky with Diamonds" and epic closer "A Day in the Life." Lennon's "All You Need Is Love" captured the zeitgeist of the Summer of Love.

Following Epstein's untimely death in mid-1967, McCartney strove to maintain momentum with the (poorly received) TV movie *Magical Mystery Tour* (1967)—the accompanying double E.P. was much better. Under Harrison's influence, they sought inspiration from Indian guru Maharishi Mahesh Yogi, studying with him in Rishikesh, where they wrote a host of new songs. The resulting double album, *The Beatles* (1968; a.k.a. "The White Album") was sprawling and contained more instant classics ("Back in the U.S.S.R.," "Dear Prudence," "Blackbird," "While My Guitar Gently Weeps"). The same year they released the seven-minute-plus "Hey Jude" ("Revolution" was its rousing B-side). The psychedelic cartoon *Yellow Submarine* (1968) involved precious little new Beatles

music, though Lennon's raucous "Hey Bulldog" and Harrison's acid epic "It's All Too Much" impressed.

A bored Starr had quit during "The White Album." A disillusioned Harrison did the same during the depressing sessions for *Let it Be* (1970)—which nonetheless yielded the rousing rocker "Get Back," Lennon's pretty "Across the Universe," and the reflective title track. Recorded after that album, but released before it, *Abbey Road* (1969) was a superior swansong, boasting Lennon's "Come Together," two of Harrison's best songs ("Here Comes the Sun" and the divine "Something"), and a scintillating side two medley masterminded by McCartney.

With the decade they had encapsulated now behind them, The Beatles broke up in a miasma of bad blood. The legend lives on, though, reinvigorated by projects such as 1995's *Anthology* series—for which the "Threatles" reconvened, adding music to two Lennon demos: "Free as a Bird" (U.K. No. 2/U.S. No. 6) and "Real Love" (U.K. No. 4/U.S. No. 11). The singles compilation *1* (2000) remains the fastest-selling album ever (3.6 million copies sold on its first day). And, within a year of their back catalog appearing on iTunes in November 2010, more than ten million tracks, and around 1.8 million albums, had been downloaded. **RD**

■ Aerophones

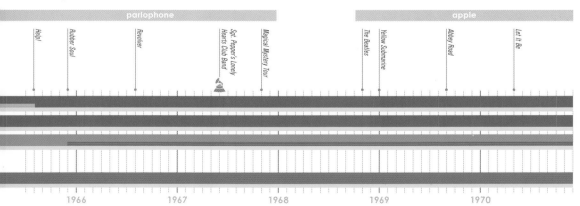

Please Please Me
(1963)

With The Beatles
(1963)

A Hard Day's Night
(1964)

Help! (1965)

Rubber Soul (1965)

Revolver (1966)

**Sgt. Pepper's
Lonely Hearts
Club Band** (1967)

The Beatles (1968)

Abbey Road
(1969)

Let It Be (1970)

Beatlemania is born. **Paul McCartney**, **George Harrison**, **Ringo Starr**, and **John Lennon** performing at the London Palladium in front of 2,000 screaming fans in October 1963.

Performing together in 1963—**George**, **Paul**, **John**, with **Ringo** in the background.

The Beatles outside Buckingham Palace, after receiving their MBEs from the Queen.

Harrison during the filming of 1964's *A Hard Day's Night*.

Starr strikes a Winston Churchill-style pose outside 10 Downing Street, London, in 1965.

Their last live public concert, on the rooftop of Apple, London, 1969.

McCartney, **Harrison**, **Starr**, and **Lennon** at Abbey Road studios in April 1966.

Harrison, **Starr**, **McCartney**, and **Lennon** before the global TV broadcast of *Our World*.

The Beatles and their partners in Rishikesh, 1968. Left to right from **Starr**: Maureen Starkey, Jane Asher, **McCartney**, Maharishi Mahesh Yogi, **Harrison**, Pattie Boyd, Cynthia Lennon, and **Lennon**, who is talking to Mike Love of The Beach Boys.

Lennon toward the end of the band's extraordinary career.

beck 1993–present

Beck
b. July 8, 1970

Carl Stephenson
b. unknown

**Michael Simpson
(E.Z. Mike – Dust
Brothers)**
b. unknown

**John King (King
Gizmo – Dust
Brothers)**
b. unknown

Nigel Godrich
b. February 28, 1971

**Brian Joseph
Burton (Danger
Mouse)**
b. July 29, 1977

Beck Hansen's bohemian upbringing had a significant influence on his music. His mother, Bibbe Hansen, had been a protégée of Andy Warhol and was also active on the Los Angeles art scene. Her father, Al Hansen, was the most celebrated artist of the Fluxus movement, close friends with John Cage and Yoko Ono, and a vital influence on Beck. And Beck's father David Campbell is a composer who has worked on albums by artists as diverse as Kiss and Leona Lewis, as well as on several of his son's releases.

Dropping out of high school in 1986, Beck traveled to Europe and busked around Germany. Returning to the U.S., he launched himself on the New York punk and anti-folk scene, before heading home to L.A.

There, in 1993, he made his first studio album, *Golden Feelings*, full of the humor and eclecticism that would become a feature of his output. That year, he signed to the independent Bong Load Custom label and released "Loser." Recorded with hip-hop producer **Carl Stephenson**, its unusual mix of acoustic slide guitar, ironic lyrics, and dance beats was striking, and quickly attracted the attention of major labels. Beck signed to Geffen primarily because they agreed to allow him to continue making less commercial work available for independent release (hence *One Foot in the Grave* and *Stereopathetic Soulmanure*, issued within months of each other in the first half of 1994).

The first Geffen release was *Mellow Gold*, from which the single "Loser" was reissued. Promoted with a mash-up video made for $300 by Beck and his friend Steve Hanft, the song—with its droll yet catchy chorus "I'm a loser, baby, so why don't you kill me?"—became an instant slacker classic. Supported by a world tour and energetic performances at 1995's Lollapalooza festival, both the single and album unexpectedly hit the U.S. Top Twenty.

Beck cemented his "Generation X" credentials in 1996 with *Odelay*, his second major-label album. Hooking up with celebrated hip-hop producers the **Dust Brothers**, *Odelay* had a substantially more upbeat feel than his previous efforts, playfully mixing a witty array of disparate influences. Breakbeats, a brilliantly baffling selection of samples—Mantronix, Lee Dorsey, Schubert, and Grand Funk Railroad, to name a few—and lo-fi electric guitars were combined with the catchiest of chanted choruses to produce one of the defining albums of that era. *Odelay* won Beck a Grammy, went platinum on both sides of the Atlantic, and found a place in *Rolling Stone*'s 2003 list of the greatest albums of all time.

Beck's love of diversity took a very different line with his follow-up album, *Mutations*. Losing the samples and hip-hop sounds, here was an album of acoustic simplicity that highlighted his appealingly

year-by-year ■ Vocals ■ Guitar ■ Keyboards ■ Programming

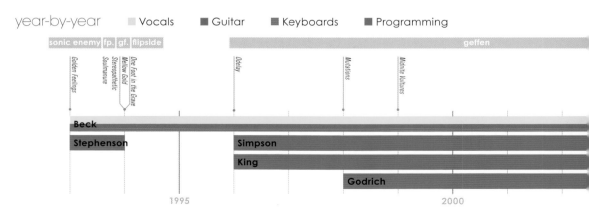

1.9M
Mellow Gold
(1994)

3.2M
Odelay
(1996)

1M
Sea Change
(2002)

1.3M
Guero
(2005)

B

languid vocals and increasingly introspective lyrics. *Mutations* had been intended for an independent release but, having heard the album, Geffen backtracked, causing Beck to launch a lawsuit against his own label. Quietly presented by Geffen as an interim album, rather than a true follow-up to *Odelay*, *Mutations* nonetheless won the star a Grammy and reached the U.S. Top Twenty.

The much-anticipated *Midnite Vultures* (1999) saw Beck's ever-present chameleon tendencies alighting on funk, with the influence of Prince clearly audible throughout. Beck promoted the album by taking his new brass-heavy band on an extensive, critically acclaimed world tour. Although not quite the commercial smash that might have been expected, *Midnite Vultures* sold respectably, spawned the hit "Sexx Laws," and earned Beck a Grammy nomination.

It would be three years before his next album. *Sea Change* saw a deeply introspective man, who had broken up with his long-standing fiancée, grappling with the more personal themes of heartbreak and solitude. This was pared-down Beck, both musically and lyrically. With predominantly acoustic instrumentation, and his lines delivered with a hitherto unheard sincerity, it could not have been more different from its predecessor. Not expecting such a low-key album to perform well, Geffen gave

Sea Change little promotion. Yet its somber tone resonated in post-9/11 America: blessed with a five-star review in *Rolling Stone* (one of only two releases so adjudged that year), it gave Beck his first Top Ten success, peaking at No. 8 on the *Billboard* Top 200.

Confounding expectations once again, in 2004 Beck reunited with the Dust Brothers to produce *Guero*. Boasting a collaboration with Jack White, and dividing critics with a return to the sample-heavy beats of *Odelay*, it nevertheless became Beck's biggest hit to date, entering the *Billboard* album chart at No. 2. A remix version of the album—*Guerolito*—appeared later that year, with its songs reworked by the likes of Diplo, Air, and Beastie Boy Adam Horowitz.

Beck teamed up once again with Radiohead producer **Nigel Godrich**—overseer of his "quiet" albums—to produce 2005's superb *The Information*. Another transatlantic hit, Beck said of it, "My previous work with him was *Mutations* and *Sea Change*… this new one is sort of bringing these two worlds together."

In 2008 he forged a musical alliance with **Danger Mouse**. The result, *Modern Guilt*, was a fine slab of twenty-first-century paranoia. Grammy nominated, it gave Beck his first British Top Ten hit. In July 2011 it was announced that Beck was working on an album with country singer Dwight Yoakam, likely to be as eclectic, ever-changing, and interesting as ever. **TB**

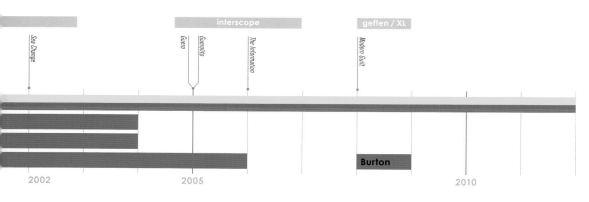

interscope

geffen / XL

Sea Change

Guero

Guerolito

The Information

Modern Guilt

Burton

2002

2005

2010

the bee gees 1960–2011

Barry Gibb
b. September 1, 1946

Robin Gibb
b. December 22, 1949
d. May 20, 2012

Maurice Gibb
b. December 22, 1949
d. January 12, 2003

Colin Petersen
b. March 24, 1946

Vince Melouney
b. August 18, 1945

Some groups reinvent themselves on a regular basis but few have matched the Bee Gees for their enduring ability to switch genres and career paths successfully. This adaptable family effortlessly mastered rock, pop, disco, and songwriting during a forty-year span, a feat made even more remarkable by some significant dips in popularity.

The Bee Gees arrived in the world of pop via the Isle of Man, Manchester, and Australia. **Barry Gibb** and younger twin brothers **Robin** and **Maurice Gibb** were born on the small island off the west coast of Britain, raised in the northern British city, and formed "down under" in Brisbane. After playing at a local speedway track in 1960, the trio took on the name The B.G.'s—after the race organizer and a local radio DJ, both of whom had those initials—and eventually re-located to Sydney. There, they signed to a local record company and finally hit the top spot in Australia with their eleventh single—"Spicks and Specks"—in 1966.

Upon their return to the U.K., the group—now formally known as the Bee Gees—signed with pop entrepreneur Robert Stigwood. They also recruited drummer **Colin Petersen** and guitarist **Vince Melouney** in advance of their debut international hit "New York Mining Disaster" (U.S. No. 14 and U.K. No. 12). Its haunting melody led some listeners to think that it was by The Beatles. Later in 1967, the Bee Gees earned their first U.K. No. 1 with "Massachusetts," while their international debut album *Bee Gees 1st* hit the Top Ten in both the U.S. and the U.K.

Follow-up albums *Horizontal* and *Idea* were both hits, as were the singles "I've Gotta Get a Message to You" (U.K. No. 1), "I Started a Joke," and "First of May." However, Petersen and Melouney left in 1969—as did Robin Gibb. Brothers Barry and Maurice continued as the Bee Gees but achieved little commercial success.

But then, in 1971, the three Gibb brothers were reunited successfully when "How Can You Mend a Broken Heart" became their first U.S. No. 1 single and, a year later, "Run to Me" became their first U.K. Top Ten hit in three years. Another dip in fortunes followed *Odessa* (U.S. No. 20 and U.K. No. 10): the Bee Gees failed to register a Top Thirty entry with their next six albums. But in 1974 the trio linked with American soul producer Arif Mardin and subsequently returned to the charts with the album *Main Course* (1975).

What came next was one of rock and pop's most astonishing career path changes: their newly adopted disco style resulted in the hits "Jive Talkin'" (U.S. No. 1), "Nights on Broadway," and "You Should Be Dancing" (another U.S. No. 1, from 1976's *Children of the World*). These led Barry, Robin, and Maurice to

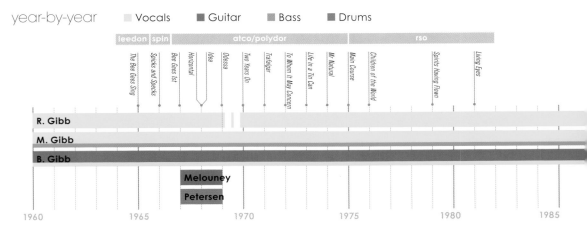

year-by-year   ▢ Vocals   ■ Guitar   ■ Bass   ■ Drums

15.5M	3M	2M	3M
Saturday Night Fever (1977)	Spirits Having Flown (1979)	Bee Gees Greatest (1979)	Still Waters (1997)

B

create the Grammy-winning soundtrack *Saturday Night Fever*. It topped the charts in both America and Britain in 1978 and went on to sell more than fifteen million double LPs worldwide, making it pop's biggest-selling album until *Thriller*. That same year also saw them starring in the movie *Sgt. Pepper's Lonely Hearts Club Band* (alongside Aerosmith, Alice Cooper, Peter Frampton, and Earth Wind & Fire)—a deserved flop.

The brothers' stature as songwriters earned them a record-breaking run of five U.S. No. 1s in 1978 with "How Deep Is Your Love" (U.K. No. 3), "Stayin' Alive" (U.K. No. 4), "Night Fever" (U.K. No. 1), "If I Can't Have You" (written for Yvonne Elliman), and "Shadow Dancing" (written with—and performed by—fourth brother Andy Gibb). After eldest brother Barry's hit theme song for the movie *Grease* (sung by Frankie Valli), the group's album *Spirits Having Flown* (1979) topped both the U.S. and U.K. charts, as did the single "Tragedy." The album boasted two other U.S. No. 1s: "Love You Inside Out" and "Too Much Heaven."

After 1979's U.S. chart-topping *Bee Gees Greatest*, the trio's fortunes plummeted amid a backlash against disco. However, Barry won a Grammy for *Guilty*, a gorgeous hit album with Barbra Streisand, while the brothers' compositions "Heartbreaker," "Islands in the Stream," and "Chain Reaction" were

chart-toppers for Dionne Warwick, Kenny Rogers and Dolly Parton, and Diana Ross respectively.

The Bee Gees' own success was restored in 1987, when "You Win Again" (from the Top Five album *E.S.P.*), made them the only band to top the British singles chart in the sixties, seventies, and eighties. The trio continued to tour America and Europe, and returned to the U.S. Top Five in 1989 with "One"—their first U.S. Top Ten hit for over a decade. *High Civilization* and *Size Isn't Everything* maintained their enduring appeal.

In 2001 the Gibb brothers released what would turn out to be the last Bee Gees album: *This Is Where I Came In*. Maurice died in January 2003, aged fifty-three, from a cardiac arrest. Barry and Robin continued to work on a variety of solo projects in the new millennium, although they reunited for TV guest appearances and for charity concerts.

Honored in 1997 with both a World Music Legend Award and a Brit Award for Outstanding Contribution to British Music, the Bee Gees amassed global record sales of over 100 million, released fifty U.S. and U.K. chart singles—including eleven No. 1 hits—and have had their songs covered by more than 2,500 artists (including relatively young bucks like The Flaming Lips, Billy Corgan, and Feist). These were incredible and outstanding achievements. **BS**

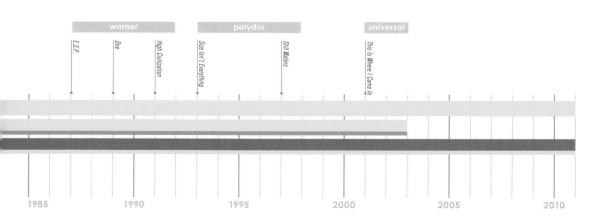

Bee Gees 1st
(1967)

Horizontal
(1968)

Main Course
(1975)

Children of the World (1976)

Saturday Night Fever (1977)

Sgt. Pepper's Lonely Hearts Club Band (1978)

Spirits Having Flown (1979)

Staying Alive (1983)

One (1989)

Still Waters (1997)

Left to right **Barry Gibb, Colin Petersen, Robin Gibb, Maurice Gibb,** and **Vince Melouney:** the less celebrated five-man incarnation of the Bee Gees.

The five-man lineup outside a TV studio in Hamburg, Germany, in 1968.

In New York's Central Park in 1975, just weeks before "Jive Talkin'."

On New York City's Long Island Expressway—and on the road to superstardom.

Barry Gibb in 1977—one of the era's most successful songwriters.

Posing with Peter Frampton (right) in costumes for the ill-conceived and ill-fated 1978 movie version of The Beatles' *Sgt. Pepper's Lonely Hearts Club Band*.

At a UNICEF charity show at the United Nations General Assembly, New York, in 1979.

Robin in 1983, the year of the *Saturday Night Fever* sequel *Staying Alive*.

Maurice, **Robin** and **Barry** relax before a tour in March 1989.

Back on top, collecting International Artist trophies at the American Music Awards in 1997.

chuck berry 1955–present

Chuck Berry
b. October 18, 1926

Johnnie Johnson
b. July 8, 1924
d. April 13, 2005

Willie Dixon
b. July 1, 1915
d. January 29, 1992

Fred Below
b. September 16, 1926
d. August 14, 1988

Lafayette Leake
b. June 1, 1919
d. August 14, 1990

Otis Spann
b. March 21, 1930
d. April 24, 1970

One of the most influential figures from the early days of rock 'n' roll, **Chuck Berry** produced an endless succession of period classics: driving electric rhythm and blues combined with pioneering lyrics that neatly summed up teenage life in fifties America.

Charles Edward Anderson "Chuck" Berry arrived on the music scene relatively late in life. Although he had taught himself a few chords as a high school student, he did not take music seriously until his mid-twenties. Berry's principal influence had been bluesman T-Bone Walker, who was not only a guitarist of rare finesse but also something of a showman.

Moving to Chicago, the hub of the electric blues scene, Berry served his apprenticeship with the **Johnnie Johnson** Trio—their work together continuing until Johnnie's death in 2005. (He also worked with influential blues musician **Willie Dixon**, drummer **Fred Below,** and pianists **Otis Spann** and **Lafayette Leake**.)

A chance meeting with bluesman Muddy Waters put him in contact with Leonard Chess, owner of the famous blues label, Chess Records. Having initially followed a straight blues path, Chess was particularly impressed with Berry's own up-tempo material. A first single at the end of 1955, "Maybellene," was Berry's take on an old country song, "Ida Red." It sold more than a million copies and became the first R&B record to make a big impact with white audiences.

Between 1956 and 1959, Berry enjoyed a succession of million-selling hits, including "Roll Over Beethoven," "Rock and Roll Music," "Sweet Little Sixteen," "Memphis, Tennessee," and "Johnny B. Goode." These tunes would become part of the standard repertoire for the first generation of white beat groups, such as The Beatles and The Rolling Stones: indeed, the latter's Keith Richards would use Berry's guitar playing as a template—an economic style that combined elements of rhythm and lead.

Berry was also vital in the evolution of the pop lyric. His songs were full-blooded mini-soaps at a time when most popular songs of the time skirted around "real" issues. In fact, Berry put the case for the American teenage lifestyle of the fifties better than just about anyone—mildly ironic, given that he was in his thirties when he wrote his classic hits.

By 1959, Berry was one of the most popular figures on the American music scene. However, his career crashed to a halt in December 1959 when he was arrested after an allegation that he had slept with a fourteen-year-old waitress and transported her across state lines. After a series of trials and appeals, in which

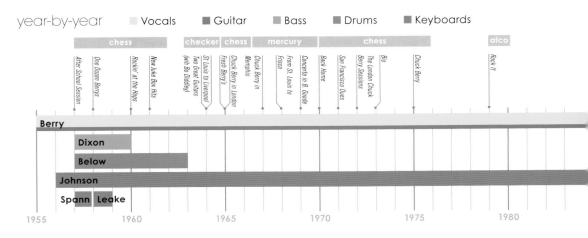

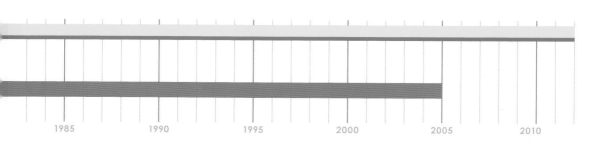

| 1M | 250,000 | 250,000 | 250,000 |
| Chuck Berry on Stage (1963) | Chuck Berry's Greatest Hits (1964) | The London Chuck Berry Sessions (1972) | Bio (1973) |

B

his claims of a racially prejudiced jury were aired and upheld, Berry served eighteen months in prison.

Following his release in October 1963, Berry tried to rebuild his career. His cause was aided by the "British Invasion" bands (both The Beatles and The Rolling Stones covered his songs) and by new young American groups, such as The Beach Boys, who acknowledged him as an important influence.

He continued to have hits with "Nadine," "No Particular Place to Go," and "You Never Can Tell"—the latter finding a new audience in the nineties following its memorable use in Quentin Tarantino's movie *Pulp Fiction*. In spite of Berry's controversial fall from grace, he still fared better during the sixties than most others from rock 'n' roll's first wave.

He remained a major concert draw throughout the decade, the appealing raw edge of his music being captured in 1967's *Live at the Fillmore Auditorium*, where he was backed by an early incarnation of The Steve Miller Band. In this instance, he was fortunate to have such a group at his disposal. Berry, always conscious of the business side of his work, rarely employed musicians of his own, and was often found playing with unrehearsed local pickup bands of varying (and often sub-standard) quality.

Returning to the Chess label in 1972, having spent most of the sixties with Mercury, Berry enjoyed his biggest and most unexpected chart success. The novelty singalong ditty "My Ding-a-ling" was recorded live in Coventry, England (where his backing group were members of the Average White Band) and this became his first single to top the charts—a feat it achieved on both sides of the Atlantic. The song, based on a series of phallic *double entendres* that, even then, anyone over the age of twelve would have found embarrassing, was about as far away from classic Chuck Berry as anyone could imagine.

Berry has produced no new material of any great worth since the sixties, but even now—well past the age of eighty—he continues to perform in concert. In spite of his indisputable importance in the history and development of rock music, Berry himself seems to have been ambivalent toward such accolades, viewing himself more as a working entertainer than one of *the* great "artists" of the post-war era—a case that many would argue in his favor. Primarily a singles artist, Berry rarely produced memorable studio albums; the casual listener is certainly better served by the many chart compilations that cover the first decade of his recording career. **TB**

1985   1990   1995   2000   2005   2010

the black crowes 1989–present

Chris Robinson
b. December 20, 1966

Rich Robinson
b. May 24, 1969

Steve Gorman
b. August 17, 1965

Johnny Colt
b. May 1, 1966

Jeff Cease
b. June 24, 1967

Ed Harsch
b. May 27, 1967

Marc Ford
b. April 13, 1966

Sven Pipien
b. May 30, 1967

Like The Kinks two decades before them, The Black Crowes have thrived despite—or possibly because of—a volatile fraternal relationship at the group's core. Two-and-a-half years separate singer **Chris Robinson** and guitarist **Rich Robinson**, but their close bond and songwriting chemistry have led to a series of good-time sleazy rock records and an enviable knack for bouncing back.

Emerging in Atlanta, Georgia, in 1989 from the remains of earlier band Mr. Crowe's Garden, The Black Crowes wasted little time getting their act together. Their signature style—more or less unchanged over twenty years in the business—was in place from the start, aping a louche blues-rock preserved in aspic in the early seventies. Obvious touchstones were *Exile on Main St*-era Rolling Stones, The Allman Brothers, and The Faces. The Black Crowes dressed to match, as if an entire generation of musical and sartorial fashion changes simply didn't happen. For all the throwbacks, in an age of hair metal and production excess the Crowes' approach to rock was almost radical.

As they shook off their old identity, The Black Crowes were signed to Def American by George Drakoulias. With Drakoulias also in the production

seat, and joined by guitarist **Jeff Cease**, bassist **Johnny Colt**, and drummer **Steve Gorman**, the brothers wrote all of their debut album *Shake Your Money Maker* (1990), save the cover of Otis Redding's "Hard to Handle." The album was a commercial success—making the *Billboard* Top Five and picking up Top Thirty hits with "Hard to Handle" and "She Talks to Angels"—and enjoyed a fair ride from the critics, but they would soon perfect their whisky-soaked swagger.

The Southern Harmony and Musical Companion (1992) would come to be seen as their masterpiece. Cease had been fired, to be replaced by guitarist **Marc Ford**, but the recalibrated Crowes sounded meatier, funkier, and, crucially, equipped with better songs. Drakoulias was again at the controls and the album—brimming with classics like "Remedy," "Hotel Illness," and "Thorn In My Pride"—strode to the top of the *Billboard* chart and to No. 2 in the U.K.

Amorica (1994) endured a more fraught birth: an entire album, provisionally titled *Tall*, was scrapped before the group settled on a harder but more varied sound. Remembered by many for its pubic hair cover, *Amorica* made the U.K. Top Ten and narrowly missed the same back home. Its promotion saw the

year-by-year   ■ Vocals   ■ Guitar   ■ Bass   ■ Drums   ■ Keyboards

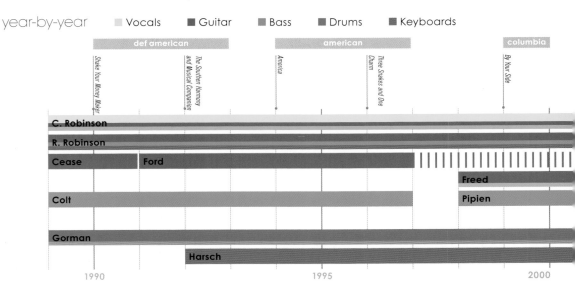

6.9M
*Shake Your
Money Maker*
(1990)

2.8M
*The Southern Harmony
and Musical Companion*
(1992)

1M
Amorica
(1994)

1M
*Live at the
Greek*
(2000)

**Adam
MacDougall**
b. August 1974

**Luther
Dickinson**
*b. January 18,
1973*

Audley Freed
b. Unknown

Greg Rzab
b. 1959

Andy Hess
*b. December
4, 1966*

Bill Dobrow
b. Unknown

Paul Stacey
b. Unknown

Rob Clores
b. Unknown

Crowes supporting the Grateful Dead in the U.S., Chris Robinson's insistence on performing barefoot on a rug fitting in nicely with their hippie-rock elders.

Three Snakes and One Charm (1996) saw the Crowes' rougher surfaces dulled and prefaced upheaval: Ford was fired and long-term bassist Colt left. Another album—*Band*—was shelved before the Crowes got back to bluesy basics with *By Your Side* (1999), an effort received as a return to core rock-soul values but only a vague success in commercial terms.

To the delight of fans, the Crowes mounted a two-night engagement in L.A. with Led Zeppelin's Jimmy Page. The resulting cocktail of Zep and blues classics was issued as 2000's *Live at the Greek*. Meanwhile, Chris Robinson carved an unexpected niche in the celebrity spotlight with his marriage to Hollywood star Kate Hudson. The trappings of fame did not prevent one more album—the adventurous *Lions* (2001)—but the group soon bowed to the inevitable with that most modern of splits, the "hiatus."

As it turned out, they had every intention of coming right back—in 2005—once again with the hardy kernel of the Robinson brothers and drummer Gorman, along with bassist **Sven Pipien** and the

returning Ford. *Warpaint* (2008), now with keyboard player **Adam MacDougall** and versatile guitarist **Luther Dickinson** on board, enjoyed an unusual publicity boost when *Maxim* magazine gave it a sniffy review, apparently without even hearing it. The consequent uproar saw it become the Crowes' first U.S. Top Ten album since *The Southern Harmony*—but credit is also due to the songs, which were as rich as anything the band had released since that chart-topper.

A looser feel permeated the double album *Before the Frost... Until the Freeze* (2009), recorded in front of an audience as the group continued to explore their abilities. They experimented with release tactics, too, pushing *Before the Frost...* into stores and offering its partner *Until the Freeze* as an online download, but forward motion was then put on hold. *Croweology* (2010) was a mainly acoustic root around the back catalog—an opportunity to show how far the Crowes had come from enthusiastic revivalists to established keepers of the loon-panted, blues-rock flame. As they prepared for another break, Chris Robinson told fans: "With a smile so wide you can count my teeth, and with a heart so full of love that it is spilling over the rim, I offer a humble and simple thank you." **MJH**

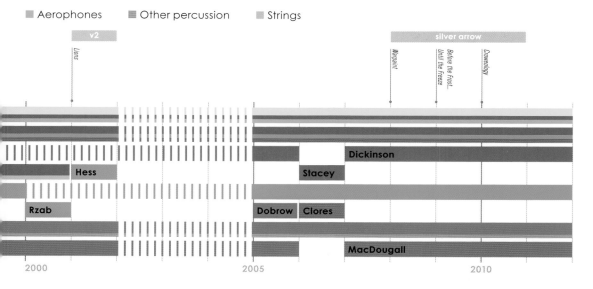

■ Aerophones   ■ Other percussion   ■ Strings

black flag / henry rollins 1976–present

Greg Ginn
b. June 8, 1956

Dez Cadena
b. June 2, 1961

Keith Morris
b. September
18, 1955

Ron Reyes
b. 1960

Henry Rollins
b. February 13,
1961

**Glen "Spot"
Lockett**
b. 1951

**Chuck
Dukowski**
b. February 1,
1956

**Roberto
"ROBO"
Valverde**
b. 1955

Black Flag were pioneers of the original California hardcore scene. Formed in 1976 by guitarist and UCLA graduate **Greg Ginn**, they embraced the DIY ethic of punk, forming their own SST label to release their early recordings. Defining the U.S. hardcore sound, Black Flag took the basic punk template, but added elements of metal, experimental noise, and even jazz.

Heavy U.S. touring built a small but fervent group of followers. At a 1981 New York gig, twenty-one-year-old fan **Henry Rollins** jumped on stage to sing: impressed by his intensity, the band asked him to join. Black Flag's first full-length album, 1981's *Damaged*, was a milestone in post-punk intensity. The murky grind of the music proved ideal backing for Ginn's emotive lyrics, delivered by Rollins with stark aggression.

Signing to Unicorn, an MCA subsidiary, and with punk peaking in popularity in the U.S., Black Flag seemed on the cusp of a commercial breakthrough. Instead, they were almost crushed by the business. MCA refused to release the record, citing its content as dangerous and "anti-parent." Ginn pushed on regardless, releasing *Damaged* on SST to huge critical acclaim. But as soon as it appeared in stores, Unicorn sued for breach of contract. The band continued to tour, but for two years were unable to use their name or distinctive logo on any recordings. The dispute ended in 1983, but only because Unicorn filed for

bankruptcy. Meanwhile, Black Flag lost commercial ground that proved impossible to recoup.

With a huge backlog of material, the band, now without vocalist/guitarist **Dez Cadena** (later to join the Misfits), proceeded to record at a prolific rate. In 1984 alone they produced the highly praised *My War, Slip It In,* and *Family Man* albums—the latter featuring one side of Rollins' spoken-word material.

The following year proved no less fruitful, with two further albums—*Loose Nut* and *In My Head*—plus an instrumental EP and heavy touring. The concerts were increasingly aggressive affairs, with Rollins—by now an avid body-builder—at times forced to fend off physical attack. Furthermore, tensions within the band, who began to resent the relentless touring and near poverty, began to reach a critical point.

Black Flag disbanded in August 1986. Ginn focused on SST, by then a key independent label, releasing early works by the likes of Sonic Youth, the Minutemen, Hüsker Dü (on whose *Zen Arcade* Dez Cadena appeared), Soundgarden, and Dinosaur Jr.

Rollins, meanwhile, became the group's highest-profile success story. His solo career has taken in the popular Rollins Band (who reached their peak with 1994's U.K. and U.S. chart-buster *Weight*), poetry and spoken-word performances, book publishing, acting, and presenting TV shows. **TB**

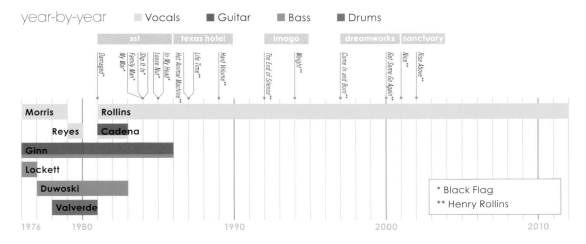

year-by-year   ▨ Vocals   ▪ Guitar   ▪ Bass   ▪ Drums

sst · texas hotel · imago · dreamworks · sanctuary

*Damaged** · *My War** · *Family Man** · *Slip It In** · *Loose Nut** · *In My Head** · *Hot Animal Machine*** · *Life Time*** · *Hard Volume*** · *The End of Silence*** · *Weight*** · *Come In and Burn*** · *Get Some Go Again*** · *Nice*** · *Rise Above***

Morris · Rollins
Reyes · Cadena
Ginn
Lockett
Duwoski
Valverde

* Black Flag
** Henry Rollins

1976   1980   1990   2000   2010

black panther 1987–present

Li Tong
b. November 28, 1964

Guo Chuanlin
b. Unknown

Ding Wu
b. December 30, 1962

Wang Wenjie
b. May 11, 1965

Dou Wei
b. October 14, 1969

Zhao Mingyi
b. October 7, 1967

Qin Yong
b. July 13, 1968

Zhang Kepeng
b. April 19, 1972

The People's Republic Of China: possibly the toughest territory in which alternative music could attempt to evolve for much of the twentieth century. Under Chairman Mao, pop and rock was, to say the least, stifled. In a post-Maoist culture, however, Black Panther (Hei Bao in their native language) helped introduce a new sound to the masses.

Singer-songwriter Cui Jian popularized the electric guitar in the late eighties, but Black Panther were one of the first groups to exploit the rock genre. Guitarists **Li Tong** and **Guo Chuanlin** formed the collective in 1987, Guo's eyes having been opened to the rock scene some years earlier: "In 1982, a Filipino surf band did a show at a park. It was all covers, Beach Boys and stuff. We stood there stunned. We had no idea a guitar could make those sounds."

Guo stepped behind the scenes to become the band's manager. Completing the lineup were singer and guitarist **Ding Wu**, bassist **Wang Wenjie**, and drummer Wang Wenfang. Ding was barely out of the starting blocks when he quit in 1988 to form China's first metal band, Tang Dynasty. **Dou Wei** replaced him on vocals, and Luan Shu joined on keyboards.

Their self-titled debut album was issued in Taiwan and Hong Kong in 1991, reaching mainland China more than a year later. The hits "Don't Break My Heart" and "Ashamed" hooked a nation, helping the album sell more than a million copies in China.

Despite being the best-selling mainland Chinese rock band ever, Black Panther could not hold down a frontman, as Dou left to go solo. Luan took up the reins for a nationwide tour and *Spirit of Light* in 1993.

Luan's tenure as vocalist proved short-lived too. In 1994, the band signed to Japanese label JVC, which reissued *Spirit of Light*, with its title track re-recorded by their fourth singer in seven years, **Qin Yong**.

After third album *No Right No Wrong* was released in 1996, Black Panther made themselves known in Japan, playing live in Tokyo and representing China at the Come Together Event for East-Asian acts in Osaka.

Can't Let Worries Have No Chance for Expression appeared in 1998, but the next few years yielded only the live *Hurricane Fervor*, a cameo on a love songs compilation, and the single "Without You."

Finally, in 2002, *Black Panther V* was released. Eight months later—and after a comparatively eon-like eleven years as singer—Qin departed, with **Zhang Kepang** taking his place.

The rise in illegal downloads has been blamed for poor sales of the band's fifth album, though the rotation of vocalists cannot have cheered their fan base. But Black Panther remain a perennial live draw, with drummer **Zhao Mingyi** conceding there is still one platform guaranteed to beat the heart of any rock fan. "The record industry is dead in China," he said. "The festival is the only way to survive." **RJ**

year-by-year

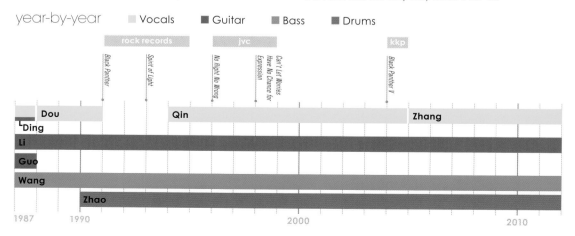

■ Vocals ■ Guitar ■ Bass ■ Drums

black sabbath 1969–present

Tony Iommi
b. February 19, 1948

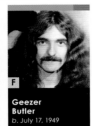

Geezer Butler
b. July 17, 1949

Bill Ward
b. May 5, 1948

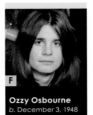

Ozzy Osbourne
b. December 3, 1948

Ronnie James Dio
b. July 10, 1942
d. May 16, 2010

Geoff Nicholls
b. May 31, 1948

Beloved of everyone from Metallica and Slayer to Kurt Cobain and Beck, Black Sabbath's first six albums soundtracked the grisly era of the Vietnam War and *The Exorcist*—and wrote the rulebook for heavy metal.

Hailing from Birmingham, England, singer John **"Ozzy" Osbourne**, drummer **Bill Ward**, guitarist **Tony Iommi**, and bassist Terry **"Geezer" Butler**—first Polka Tulk, then Earth—toured Europe, then re-christened themselves after their song "Black Sabbath." Its doom-laden invocations of Satan built an image the band would never escape, despite their disavowals of devil worship and onstage deployment of crucifixes.

Brutally out of step with progressive rock trends, Sabbath soared in popularity as critics united in vitriol. *Black Sabbath* (1970) smashed into the U.K. Top Ten, then *Paranoid* (1970), *Master of Reality* (1971), *Vol. 4* (1972), and *Sabbath Bloody Sabbath* (1973) went gold in the U.S. (all five would later be certified platinum).

The perception of their music as sludge masked myriad subtleties. Ozzy blew a distinctive harmonica on the debut album's "The Wizard," the U.K. chart-topping *Paranoid* featured the beautiful stoner jam

"Planet Caravan," and Ward and Butler's thunderous rhythms often boasted almost jazzy inventiveness. Keyboards were phased in from 1971, played variously by Iommi, Osbourne, and Butler (and, on *Sabbath Bloody Sabbath*, by Yes man Rick Wakeman).

However, Sabbath were riven with management problems, compounded by drugs and alcohol. After 1975's fine *Sabotage*, the patchy *Technical Ecstasy* (1976) and *Never Say Die* (1978) presaged Ozzy's firing in 1979. (Between the two, he was fleetingly replaced by one-time Fleetwood Mac singer Dave Walker.)

When a disillusioned Butler briefly quit in 1979, Rainbow's Craig Gruber came in. But with the bassist returned, alongside former Rainbow singer **Ronnie James Dio**, Sabbath proved they were still a force to be reckoned with on 1980's *Heaven and Hell*. Ward, grappling with alcoholism, quit on the ensuing tour and was replaced by **Vinnie Appice**, with whom Sabbath made another strong set, 1981's *Mob Rules*.

Simmering tensions erupted during the mixing of 1983's *Live Evil*. Dio and Appice quit to form their own band, Dio, while Butler and Iommi enlisted Bill Ward

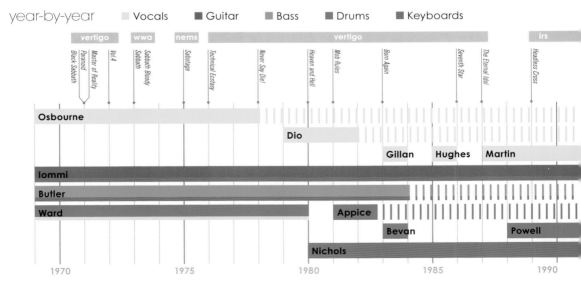

year-by-year   ■ Vocals   ■ Guitar   ■ Bass   ■ Drums   ■ Keyboards

Vinny Appice
b. September 13, 1957

Ian Gillan
b. August 19, 1945

Bev Bevan
b. November 24, 1944

Glenn Hughes
b. August 21, 1951

Tony Martin
b. April 19, 1957

Cozy Powell
b. December 29, 1947
d. April 5, 1998

and former Deep Purple singer **Ian Gillan** for 1983's *Born Again*. But when they hit the road with a Spinal Tap-inspiring "Stonehenge" stage set, Ward was out again, replaced by the Electric Light Orchestra's **Bev Bevan**. By 1985, Sabbath—bar an Osbourne/Iommi/ Butler/Ward reunion at Live Aid—were effectively over.

Conceived as an Iommi solo album, *Seventh Star* (1986)—with Deep Purple's **Glenn Hughes** on vocals— was instead issued under the Sabbath name. Hughes' swift exit was the first of myriad lineup changes over the next four years, including singer Ray Gillen, bassists Dave Spitz, Bob Daisley, Laurence Cottle, and Neil Murray, and drummers Eric Singer (later of Kiss), Terry Chimes (ex-The Clash), and **Cozy Powell** (ex-Rainbow).

With Powell, Nicholls, and new singer **Tony Martin**, Iommi clawed back credibility with *The Eternal Idol* (1987), *Headless Cross* (1989), and *TYR* (1990)—only to destroy it with an ill-fated reunion with Butler, Dio, and Appice for *Dehumanizer* (1992). When the quartet's tour was scheduled to climax with a show supporting Ozzy (whose solo career had outstripped Sabbath), Dio quit, to be replaced by Judas Priest's Rob Halford.

Iommi and Butler recalled Martin and enlisted Rainbow drummer Bobby Rondinelli for 1994's *Cross Purposes*. By the end of the ensuing tour, Rondinelli had quit (to be replaced for a handful of shows by Ward), as had Butler. Iommi, Murray, Powell, and Martin fulfilled contractual obligations with Sabbath's final studio album, 1995's rotten *Forbidden*.

Ozzy, Iommi, and Butler, with Faith No More's Mike Bordin, toured as Black Sabbath in 1997. Ward rejoined in time for a Birmingham homecoming issued as 1998's *Reunion*, and the classic lineup headlined the Ozzfest tours in 2004 and 2005. But with Ozzy sidelined by his TV show *The Osbournes*, Iommi and Butler once again reunited with Dio and Appice as Heaven & Hell. Their *Live from Radio City Music Hall* (2007) and *Bible Black* (2009) were the finest "Sabbath" albums in decades, rendering Dio's death in 2010 even more tragic.

Another reunion of the classic lineup in 2011, for an album to be produced by Rick Rubin, seemed doomed when Ward complained about his contract and Iommi was diagnosed with cancer. But, as their 1978 song declares, Sabbath "never say die." **BM**

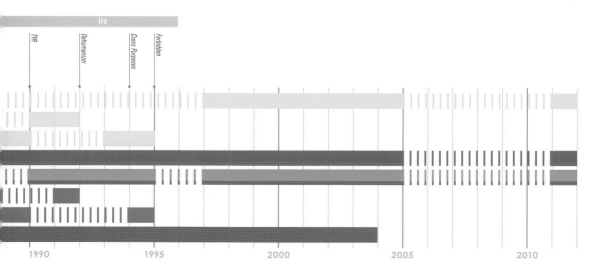

Black Sabbath
(1970)

Paranoid (1970)

Master of Reality
(1971)

**Sabbath Bloody
Sabbath** (1973)

Sabotage (1975)

Heaven and Hell
(1980)

Mob Rules (1981)

Born Again (1983)

Headless Cross
(1989)

Dehumanizer
(1992)

Ozzy Osbourne in 1969, the year Black Sabbath made their debut.

Bill Ward, **Osbourne** (with back to camera), **Geezer Butler**, and **Tony Iommi** conjure an early masterpiece.

Doubtless fueled by "Sweet Leaf," **Butler**, **Iommi**, and **Osbourne** storm Amsterdam in 1971.

Flower power: **Ward** at London's Alexandra Palace in 1973.

Nearing the end of a golden era that shaped an entire genre, **Butler**, **Iommi**, **Osbourne**, and **Ward** rock Copenhagen in October 1975.

Rockin' but sadly far from stylish, **Dio** and **Iommi** at London's Hammersmith Odeon in 1981.

With new singer **Ronnie James Dio** in Paris, where they recorded part of *Heaven and Hell.*

Butler, singer **Ian Gillan**, and **Iommi** with part of 1983's infamous "Stonehenge" stage set.

Mob Rules drummer **Vinnie Appice**, **Dio**, and **Iommi** reunite in '92.

Iommi—the only member to appear on every album—live in 1989.

The *Dehumanizer* lineup that would become Heaven & Hell.

blink-182 1992–present

B

Tom DeLonge
b. December 13, 1975

Mark Hoppus
b. March 15, 1972

Travis Barker
b. November 14, 1975

Scott Raynor
b. May 23, 1978

Blink-182 started out as snotty skate-punks, but grew into highly influential stars. Guitarist **Tom DeLonge** teamed up with bassist **Mark Hoppus** in San Diego in the early nineties. With drummer **Scott Raynor**, they became Duck Tape, then Blink. From the early days, vocals were shared by DeLonge and Hoppus.

Blink built a local following with frequently chaotic live shows. In 1993 they arranged a limited-edition commercial release for *Buddha*, a collection of demos. Several songs from it were re-recorded for the following year's *Cheshire Cat*, which drew threatened litigation from an Irish band named Blink. As a result, the Californian trio picked a random number to append to their name and became Blink-182.

Domestic success came with 1997's teen-angst anthem "Dammit (Growing Up)" and the album *Dude Ranch*, winning them a major label deal with MCA. Raynor left midway through a tour the following year, and **Travis Barker** was hastily drafted in to replace him, formally joining Blink-182 at the end of the tour.

Enema of the State (1999) was dominated by noisy guitar pop songs about youthful relationship problems. This formula provided the first two hits from the album, "All the Small Things" and "What's My Age Again?," but a third—"Adam's Song"—was a brooding ballad dealing with suicidal depression. With Blink-182 having comprehensively outpaced their pop-punk predecessors Green Day, *Enema...* sold five million at home and went platinum in the U.K. and Australia.

The U.S. chart-topping *Take Off Your Pants and Jacket* (2001) contained radio-friendly hits like "The Rock Show," alongside more serious songs such as "Stay Together for the Kids," written by DeLonge about his parents' divorce. The band's serious side took over on a self-titled 2003 album, featuring cameos by The Cure's Robert Smith and actress Joanne Whalley. Arguably their finest and, eventually, most influential album, *Blink-182* was less well received at the time, despite the gold-selling smash "I Miss You." Internal tensions—some resulting from DeLonge and Barker forming the successful side-project Box Car Racer without Hoppus—developed during a U.S. tour, and an indefinite hiatus was announced in February 2005. Hoppus and Barker formed the Blink-esque +44 for the U.S. Top Ten album *When Your Heart Stops Beating* (2006), while DeLonge issued the gold-selling *We Don't Need to Whisper* (2006), the first of four albums with his U2-flavored project Angels & Airwaves.

On September 19, 2008, Barker was badly burned when a plane in which he was a passenger crashed, killing four of the other five people on board. Hoppus and DeLonge visited him in hospital and, in February 2009, Blink-182 announced their reunion at the Grammy Awards. After a rapturously received tour, *Neighborhoods* appeared in 2011. Its experimentation and somber lyrics were a far cry from early Blink-182, but strong sales suggested hardcore fans were happy to accompany them into darker territory. **DJ**

year-by-year   ■ Vocals   ■ Guitar   ■ Bass   ■ Drums

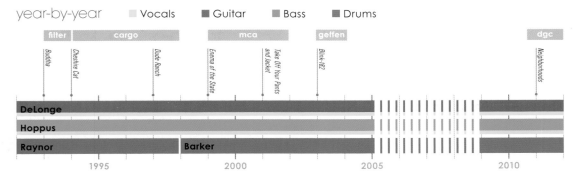

blondie 1975–present

B

Deborah "Debbie" Harry
b. July 1, 1945

Chris Stein
b. January 5, 1950

Clem Burke
b. November 24, 1954

Jimmy Destri
b. April 13, 1945

Gary Valentine
b. April 24, 1951

Frank Infante
b. November 15, 1951

Energetic guitar-led pop, an ear for trends, and the photogenic looks of **Debbie Harry** made Blondie the most successful band to emerge from the U.S. new wave of the seventies. "We were," said the singer, "fighting the idea that the only decent music was the Eagles or Chicago." Formed by Harry, guitarist (and Harry's partner) **Chris Stein**, and future Television bassist Fred Smith, they stabilized with the recruitment of organist **Jimmy Destri**, bassist **Gary Valentine**, and drummer **Clem Burke**. From their 1976 debut album came their first hit: "In the Flesh," a No. 2 in Australia.

Valentine quit before *Plastic Letters* (1978), then "Denis" became a success in Europe. Blondie expanded with bassist Nigel Harrison and guitarist **Frank Infante**, and producer Mike Chapman added a commercial sheen to *Parallel Lines* (1978). The disco-nuanced "Heart of Glass" finally brought them success in the U.S., where it topped the singles chart, while the album became the first of three global million-sellers. "Sunday Girl" followed "Heart of Glass" to the top of the U.K. chart, and they scored the hat-trick with "Atomic" from 1979's *Eat to the Beat* (1979).

With producer Giorgio Moroder, they conjured "Call Me" for the soundtrack of the movie *American Gigolo*. This combination of Harry's soaring, sensual voice and an aggressive groove created Blondie's

second U.S. No. 1. The eclecticism continued on *Autoamerican* (1980), with chart-topping excursions into reggae ("The Tide Is High") and rap ("Rapture").

After Harry's gold-selling solo debut *Koo Koo* (1981) and Blondie's under-rated *The Hunter* (1982), Stein was diagnosed with a skin disease, and the group disbanded at the end of the year. Stein recovered, and contributed to Harry's *Def, Dumb & Blonde* (1989).

No longer a couple but still friends, Harry and Stein re-launched Blondie in 1997 with Burke (who had played with the Ramones and Eurythmics in the interim) and Destri. Valentine initially joined in, but quit before *No Exit* (1999), which included their sixth U.K. No. 1, "Maria." *The Curse of Blondie* followed in 2003, before drug problems forced Destri to depart.

Blondie were inducted into the Rock and Roll Hall of Fame in 2006, but the occasion was marred by an argument between present and former members: Infante pleaded to be allowed to join in Blondie's performance at the ceremony, but he was refused.

In 2008, session bassist Leigh Foxx, keyboardist Matt Katz-Bohen, and guitarist Paul Carbonara became full-time members (the latter was replaced by Tommy Kessler in 2010). *Panic of Girls* (2011) proved the inspirational spirit that had influenced many—notably Madonna—was alive and well. **DJ**

year-by-year   ■ Vocals   ■ Guitar   ■ Bass   ■ Drums   ■ Keyboards

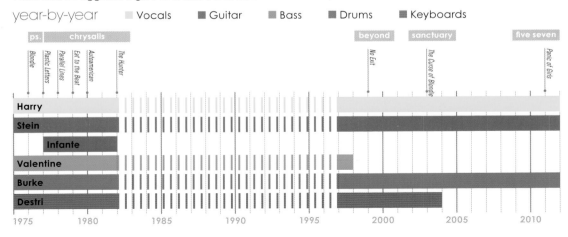

blood, sweat & tears 1967–2009

Al Kooper
b. February 5, 1944

Steve Katz
b. May 9, 1945

Bobby Colomby
b. December 20, 1944

Jim Fielder
b. October 4, 1947

Fred Lipsius
b. November 19, 1943

Randy Brecker
b. November 27, 1945

David Clayton-Thomas
b. September 13, 1941

Dick Halligan
b. August 29, 1943

"Blood, Sweat & Tears is the best thing to happen in rock and roll so far in 1968," raved *Rolling Stone* about the group's genre-busting jazz-rock debut *Child Is Father to the Man*. Acclaim translated into success when a follow-up hit No. 1 in the U.S., clung to the Top Forty for over a year, and sold over four million copies. Rarely have bands enjoyed such a creative and successful genesis… and then managed to blow it all.

Al Kooper had played organ on Bob Dylan's "Like a Rolling Stone." When his next Blues Project band imploded, he took guitarist **Steve Katz** and teamed up with jazz drummer **Bobby Colomby** and bassist **Jim Fielder**. Influenced by *Time and Changes* by "sunshine pop" act The Buckinghams, the trio hired four horn men and started gigging, while Kooper wrote new songs. They were quickly signed to Columbia.

Their debut album yielded no hits, and Kooper quit in a dispute over the band's leadership. *Blood, Sweat & Tears* was created instead by five of the original members and four newcomers, including singer **David Clayton-Thomas**. The jazz improvisations of the first album were reined in, conjuring up radio-friendly offerings like the million-selling U.S. hit "You've Made Me So Very Happy." The new template, under Buckinghams producer James William Guercio's direction, yielded seven weeks at No. 1 in the U.S., three Grammy awards, and a then-unprecedented three gold-selling singles from one album.

The band repeated the formula, minus Guercio, for 1970's chart-topping *Blood, Sweat, & Tears 3*. But disastrous career moves saw them fritter it all away. First they agreed to tour behind the Iron Curtain (they were the first U.S. band to do so, but antipathy to Americans in the Vietnam era led to ugly scenes). This was followed by a bizarre decision to perform at a Las Vegas casino—another dubious "rock first."

As their albums became patchy and the lineup grew unstable, fans deserted the group. After 1976's *More Than Ever,* Columbia dropped them and, in the eighties, the nostalgia circuit beckoned. However, Blood, Sweat & Tears' legacy lives on: tracks such as "I Love You More Than You'll Ever Know" and "Spinning Wheel" have been sampled by rap acts including Public Enemy and the Wu-Tang Clan. **JaH**

year-by-year ■ Vocals ■ Guitar ■ Bass ■ Drums ■ Keyboards ■ Aerophones ■ Other percussion ■ Strings

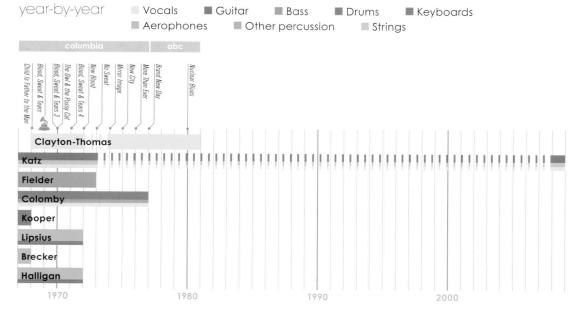

blue öyster cult 1967–present

Buck Dharma
b. November
12, 1947

Allen Lanier
b. June 25, 1946

**Albert
Bouchard**
b. May 24, 1947

**Les
Braunstein**
b. Unknown

Eric Bloom
b. December
1, 1944

**Joe
Bouchard**
b. November
9, 1948

Rick Downey
b. August 29,
1953

"Every record we do, we think, 'Right, this is gonna be it,'" mused Blue Öyster Cult's **Eric Bloom** in 1983. "So far, that hasn't quite happened!" Once contemporaries of Kiss and Black Sabbath, BÖC are indeed a cult concern, yet this only adds to the allure of their mysterious and slyly tongue-in-cheek catalog.

Inspired by svengali Sandy Pearlman, the New Yorkers united in 1967. **Les Braunstein** (vocals), Donald **"Buck Dharma"** Roeser (guitars), **Allen Lanier** (keyboards, guitars), **Albert Bouchard** (drums), and Andrew Winters (bass) were the personnel by 1969. Soon, Bloom replaced Braunstein on vocals and in 1971 **Joe Bouchard** replaced Winters on bass to create the now classic Blue Öyster Cult lineup.

In their early days, they pioneered a style of heavy metal with literate lyrics that remains the benchmark for the genre. Their debut, *Blue Öyster Cult* (1972), was a critical triumph, as were *Tyranny and Mutation* (1973) and the sublime *Secret Treaties* (1974).

BÖC became renowned for their concerts, whose blend of power and control is captured on 1975's *On Your Feet or On Your Knees*. Finally, in 1976, they hit on a marriage of creative expression and commercial success with *Agents of Fortune* (1976), thanks to its immortal hit "(Don't Fear) The Reaper."

Like *Secret Treaties*, the album boasted the talents of Lanier's girlfriend, Patti Smith. (The punk poetess also contributed lyrics to their 1984 hit "Shooting Shark.")

Spectres (1977) boasted the swaggering "Godzilla" and 1978's *Some Enchanted Evening*—the second of their five live albums—became their biggest seller. However, the burnished sheen of *Mirrors* (1979) veered slightly too far toward the pop end of the spectrum for the group's hardcore fans.

BÖC took the hint. *Cultosaurus Erectus* (1980) saw a return to their metal roots and partially revived their fortunes. The underrated *Fire of Unknown Origin* (1981) and *The Revölution by Night* (1983) contained their fair share of great songs, such as "Burnin' for You." But Albert Bouchard left the group in 1981, to be replaced by **Rick Downey**—just the start of myriad changes, including Lanier and Joe Bouchard quitting in 1985. Lanier returned in 1987, but the positions of drummer and bassist have since been filled by many. "We're practically living Spinal Tap!" marveled Bloom.

Since *Club Ninja* (1985) there have only been three albums: *Imaginos* (1988), *Heaven Forbid* (1998), and *Curse of the Hidden Mirror* (2001). Yet it is as a potent live act that Blue Öyster Cult still command considerable respect. **MiH**

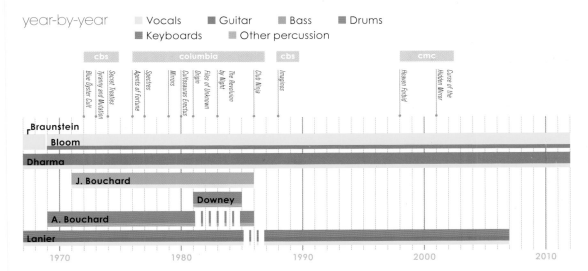

year-by-year   ▨ Vocals   ■ Guitar   ■ Bass   ■ Drums
■ Keyboards   ▨ Other percussion

blur 1989–present

B

Damon Albarn
b. March 23, 1968

Graham Coxon
b. March 12, 1969

Dave Rowntree
b. May 8, 1964

Alex James
b. November 21, 1968

As they evolved from indie darlings to survivors of the nineties Britpop scene, in a career spanning twenty-two years, there has only been one (temporary) change in Blur's lineup, when guitarist and occasional vocalist **Graham Coxon** left the group in 2002.

Coxon and front-man **Damon Albarn** met at school in Essex and bonded over a love of music. The seeds of Blur were sown from the embers of Circus, a band formed by Albarn when they were both at Goldsmith's College in London. Brought by Coxon to see them perform, **Dave Rowntree** soon found himself employed as their drummer. With another member being replaced by Coxon, two other dismissals, and the recruitment of fellow Goldsmiths student **Alex James** on bass, Circus became Seymour. Their subsequent name change to Blur in 1989 came at the request of EMI subsidiary Food Records, who loved—and signed—the group but hated the name. Their debut album, *Leisure* (1991), sold well, yet did not quite live up to the promise of the preceding Top Ten U.K. hit "There's No Other Way."

After a 1992 tour of the U.S.—during which excessive drinking nearly led to the band breaking up—Blur released *Modern Life Is Rubbish* (1993). Rather than the dreamy pop sound of much of *Leisure*, *Modern Life...* was influenced by The Kinks, The Jam, and The Small Faces, with lyrics focusing

on British eccentricities. It was a polar opposite of the then-dominant American grunge sound and formed a prequel to the quadruple platinum-selling *Parklife* (1994). Featuring hits such as the infectious title track and the hedonistic thrill of the dance-led "Girls & Boys," it fused influences as diverse as Duran Duran, punk, and music hall, and boasted cameos from actor Phil Daniels (star of the Who movie *Quadrophenia*) and Stereolab's Lœtitia Sadier.

Parklife established the band at the vanguard of Britpop—as Albarn noted, its U.K. sales outstripped a contemporary effort by EMI labelmates Pink Floyd. But while Blur won four Brit awards, they also had a public spat with a very different group who were also leading lights of the Britpop scene: Oasis. When Blur's "Country House" and Oasis's "Roll with It" were issued simultaneously in 1995, the former snared the No. 1 spot after a chart battle that made national news.

Albarn and James embraced their newfound fame and Rowntree quietly avoided it, but Coxon felt increasingly unhappy about the mainstream direction his group had taken. The pressure intensified when the phenomenal success of Oasis's *(What's the Story) Morning Glory?* led to a switch in public opinion. Oasis were seen as authentic, working-class guitar heroes; Blur were derided as being middle-class pop pretenders. The soundtrack to this unhappiness was

year-by-year   ■ Vocals   ■ Guitar   ■ Bass   ■ Drums

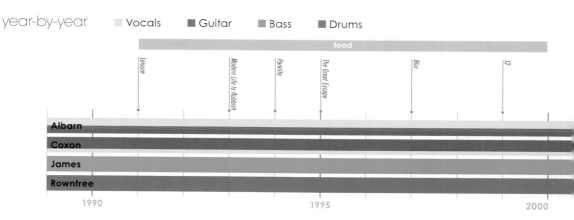

2.8M	2.2M	2.5M	1.5M
Parklife	The Great Escape	Blur	Blur: The Best of
(1994)	(1995)	(1997)	(2000)

B

the distinctly darker *The Great Escape* (1995), which blended Blur's by now customary dissections of British life and interesting characters with alien landscapes, like the beautiful "The Universal" and "Yuko and Hiro."

By 1996, tensions within the band led to Albarn's realization that something radical was needed to get them back on track. The result was *Blur* (1997), its sound influenced by U.S. groups like Pavement. *Blur* did not fare as well in the U.K. as its predecessors (although "Beetlebum" was the band's second U.K. No. 1 single), but it was an international success. In the U.S., the headbanging, woo-hooing "Song 2" became their best-known song.

With *13* (1999), Blur's evolution from the Britpop sound that had made them famous was complete. Produced by William Orbit, its experimental sound was driven by Coxon, while the lyrics were dominated by Albarn's breakup with Elastica's Justine Frischmann.

After touring *13*, Blur went on hiatus, during which Albarn and graphic artist Jamie Hewlett formed Gorillaz. This multimedia outfit promptly outsold its parent group around the world, en route to collaborating with artists including Madonna and Eminem's group D12, and enlisting Clash members Mick Jones and Paul Simonon.

Blur re-grouped in mid 2002 to begin work on *Think Tank* in Morocco. However, during the recording,

Coxon was asked to leave. "It was," he stated, "something about my attitude" (this despite him having successfully conquered alcohol addiction and depression). Simon Tong, formerly of The Verve, stepped in when they toured the album (he later played guitar with Gorillaz and alongside Paul Simonon in another Albarn project, The Good, the Bad & the Queen, in 2007). Meanwhile, the superb, Talking Heads-esque *Think Tank* (2003)—with graffiti stencil cover art by Banksy and production by Fatboy Slim—achieved their U.S. album chart peak at No. 56.

With Albarn immersed in side-projects (including the *Rocket Juice & the Moon* album, with Red Hot Chili Peppers bassist Flea), James diversifying into radio presenting and cheesemaking, Coxon enjoying solo success, and Rowntree pursuing a political career, Blur seemed finished. But, in the summer of 2009, the original quartet reunited for a joyful headlining set at the Glastonbury festival, triumphant shows in London's Hyde Park, and a series of small-scale gigs. (The band were scheduled to return to Hyde Park in 2012 for a concert marking the end of the Summer Olympics.)

In April 2012 Albarn appeared to announce a formal end to Blur as a recording and performing unit. For now, it appears that one of Britain's most imaginative, inspiring, and innovative bands of the nineties and noughties has finally called it a day. **OM**

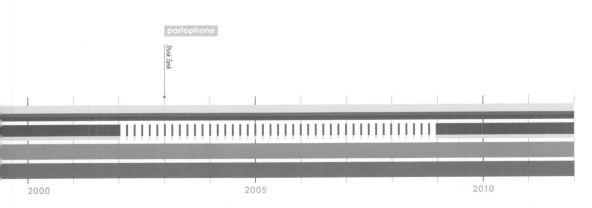

bon jovi 1983–present

B

Jon Bon Jovi
b. March 2, 1962

Richie Sambora
b. July 11, 1959

David Bryan
b. February 7, 1962

Tico Torres
b. October 7, 1953

Alec John Such
b. November 14, 1952

**Dave "The Snake"
Sabo**
b. September 16, 1964

In the absence of siblings, few bands can claim to be linked from birth. However, the history of these enduring New Jersey rockers can be traced back to long before they emerged as hirsute wannabes in Sayreville in the spring of 1983. According to rock legend, and offering up a new perspective on their 1995 single "Something for the Pain," three Bon Jovi mainstays—**Richie Sambora**, **David Bryan**, and **Jon Bon Jovi**—were delivered by the same doctor in the same Perth Amboy hospital between 1959 and 1962.

It is perhaps this bond that has kept the band rocking in harmony for almost thirty years, with only one major lineup change in that time, when bassist **Alec John Such** departed in 1994. (As a mark of respect, his replacement, **Hugh McDonald**, has never been credited as an official member.)

John Bongiovi, Jr. first hooked up with Bryan as an ambitious teenager in the band Atlantic City Expressway in 1978. After spells fronting John Bongiovi & The Wild Ones, The Lechers, and The Rest, and work at Manhattan's Power Station Studios—where he cut his first demo and the track that would give Bon Jovi their first U.S. hit ("Runaway")—the husky-voiced son of a barber and a *Playboy* bunny-turned-florist was ready to take on the world with his namesake band.

Alongside him were Bryan (keyboards), Such (bass guitar), **Tico Torres** (drums), and his neighbor, guitarist **Dave "The Snake" Sabo**. Skid Row-bound Sabo's tenure was, however, short-lived. Sambora, who had previously auditioned for Kiss, completed the classic lineup that would flourish for the next decade.

Released in 1984, Bon Jovi's self-titled debut album failed to make the Top Forty on either side of the Atlantic. Despite typically energetic live performances on tour with the Scorpions and Kiss later that same year, their sophomore set *7800° Fahrenheit*—the title of which referred to the temperature at which rock melts—fared little better. The long-overdue eruption arrived in the form of *Slippery When Wet*, America's best-selling album of 1986, which spawned the U.S. No. 1 hits "You Give Love a Bad Name" and "Livin' On a Prayer"—singles now synonymous with the mid-eighties hair rock movement, alongside Van Halen's "Jump" and Europe's "The Final Countdown."

The quartet's first transatlantic chart-topper, *New Jersey*, followed in 1988, and included five U.S. Top Ten singles. However, a punishing recording and worldwide touring schedule—and distractions such as Jon Bon Jovi and Sambora cutting their teeth as producers on Cher's album *Heart of Stone*—inevitably

year-by-year   ■ Vocals   ■ Guitar   ■ Bass   ■ Drums   ■ Keyboards

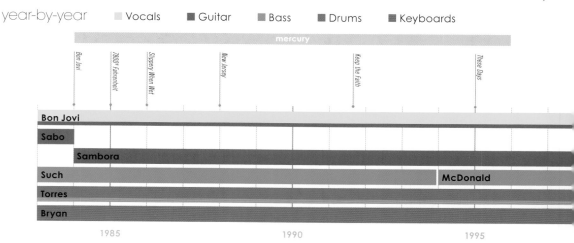

mercury

Bon Jovi | 7800° Fahrenheit | Slippery When Wet | New Jersey | Keep the Faith | These Days

Bon Jovi
Sabo
Sambora
Such   McDonald
Torres
Bryan

1985   1990   1995

26M	**18M**	**11.8M**	**20.5M**
Slippery When Wet	New Jersey	Keep the Faith	Cross Road
(1986)	(1988)	(1992)	(1994)

B

Hugh McDonald
b. December 28, 1950

took their toll on the group, resulting in the fractious members going their separate ways.

During the band's enforced downtime, Jon Bon Jovi launched a solo career (of sorts), penning the U.S. million-seller "Blaze of Glory" for the *Young Guns II* movie soundtrack. But it was not long before Bon Jovi thrust themselves back into the spotlight with the 1992 album *Keep the Faith*, followed by a well-received greatest hits package, *Cross Road*, featuring the poignant, regularly-murdered-in-karaoke-bars ballad "Always." When the wedding day favorite sold one million copies in the U.K., it ushered in a new phase for New Jersey's favorite sons. Gone were heartthrob Jon Bon Jovi's long, luscious locks (his trip to the barber even attracted national news headlines), and the group's hard rock sensibilities were watered down in favor of more mid-tempo, radio-friendly melodies.

Following Such's departure, *These Days* (1995) and *Crush* (2000) extended Bon Jovi's sequence of consecutive U.K. No. 1 albums to five and bookended renewed attempts at solo careers for both Sambora and Jon Bon Jovi during a second—and altogether more amicable—sabbatical for the band.

Lacking the critical acclaim of their earlier work and often struggling to establish a foothold on dance-driven radio, Bon Jovi in the twenty-first century have arguably produced fewer memorable musical highlights, but their ability to satisfy a loyal fan base, reinvent themselves (note the 2007 country album *Lost Highway*), consistently ride the upper reaches of the charts, and sell out stadiums worldwide has ultimately reaped handsome rewards.

It is no coincidence that Bon Jovi played the last shows at London's old Wembley Stadium and the first at the city's revamped O2 Arena, nor that awards and nominations keep coming their way. In 2004, the band scooped the American Music Award's "Award of Merit," and two years later, after "Who Says You Can't Go Home" had triumphed on country radio, they bagged their first-ever Grammy. Jon Bon Jovi and Sambora were inducted into the Songwriters Hall of Fame in 2009, and the band, who have sold 130 million albums worldwide, were recognized by *Billboard* as being the highest-grossing touring act of both 2008 and 2010.

The history of rock may be littered with tales of drug-taking, debauchery, trashed hotels, and lewd behavior, but Bon Jovi have tended to claim the moral high ground and, above all else, allowed their life-affirming music to do the talking. **MW**

■ Other percussion

island   mercury   island

Crush   *Bounce*   *Have a Nice Day*   *Lost Highway*   *The Circle*

1997   2000   2005   2010

Bon Jovi (1984)

7800° Fahrenheit (1985)

Slippery When Wet (1986)

New Jersey (1988)

Keep the Faith (1992)

These Days (1995)

Crush (2000)

Bounce (2002)

Lost Highway (2007)

The Circle (2009)

Left to right: **David Bryan**, **Alec John Such**, **Jon Bon Jovi**, **Tico Torres**, and **Richie Sambora** in their poodle-permed glory.

On tour in 1985 for the band's sophomore album *7800° Fahrenheit*.

Tempting fate in Germany as *Slippery…* shoots up the charts.

Rocking Rotterdam near the start of the *New Jersey* Syndicate Tour in November 1987.

Sambora shows California's Oakland Arena how it's done in 1993.

Bon Jovi poses in Germany, where *Crush* topped the chart.

Sambora and Bon Jovi, a musical relationship that has sustained the band for nearly thirty multi-platinum, stadium-packing years.

Sambora, Bryan, and Bon Jovi at the 2007 Bambi Awards.

Providing halftime entertainment at a Thanksgiving Day football game at Ford Field in Detroit, November 2002.

Still annoyingly handsome at forty-eight, Bon Jovi plays San José.

boston 1976–present

Tom Scholz
b. March 10, 1947

Brad Delp
b. June 12, 1951
d. March 9, 2007

Barry Goudreau
b. November 29, 1951

Fran Sheehan
b. March 26, 1949

Sib Hashian
b. August 17, 1949

Jim Masdea
b. Unknown

David Sikes
b. April 25, 1975

Doug Huffman
b. November 23, 1953

Boston exploded onto the hard rock scene with a self-titled album that remained the highest-selling debut in music history until the advent of Whitney Houston's in 1986. The group pioneered a clean metal sound of layered guitars that was to prove highly influential—a legacy of **Tom Scholz**'s crystalline production and his technical expertise. (He was even obliged to deny that he'd written the album with a computer program. "For a while," he recalled, "they even ran radio spots that said, 'Boston: better music through science.'")

The group were formed in Boston, Massachusetts, in 1976 as a vehicle for the songs of Scholz (guitars, keyboards); an accomplished engineer, he had worked on them in his home studio. **Brad Delp** (guitars and lead vocals) and **Barry Goudreau** (guitars) had played with him in groups around the city in the past. **Fran Sheehan** (bass) and **Sib Hashian** (drums) were brought in to bolster the recording and make up a touring band. Their monicker echoed a vogue for places as band names, hence the similarly critically reviled America, Chicago, Kansas, and, later, Asia.

Boston (1976) hit No. 3 on the *Billboard* album chart and went on to sell over seventeen million in the U.S. alone, a phenomenal achievement. It also reached No. 11 in the United Kingdom. The record was packed with memorable songs, not least the opening "More Than a Feeling," which became a No. 5 U.S. hit and enduring classic (Nirvana recycled its main riff on "Smells Like Teen Spirit")."Peace of Mind," "Rock & Roll Band," and "Foreplay/Long Time" kept up the tremendously high standard—one that the group would find almost impossible to surpass.

Don't Look Back (1978) stuck with a winning sonic formula, although lyrically it was more introspective, the pressures of sudden fame biting deep. The title track was another hit (U.S. No. 4) and the album raced to No. 1. Songs such as the epic "A Man I'll Never Be," "Don't Be Afraid," and the more up-tempo "Party" were worthy additions to the Boston repertoire. However, the perfectionist Scholz felt the record company had rushed out the album. "The second side is only fifteen minutes long," he complained to writer Craig Rosen. "I would have liked another six months to work on a fifth song on that side."

That was only one of many disagreements. Amid lawsuits and counter-suits, the record company demanded damages for non-delivery of material, while Scholz demanded withheld royalties. It was a wearying business but Scholz—who claimed, credibly, that his perfectionism was a strong contributory factor

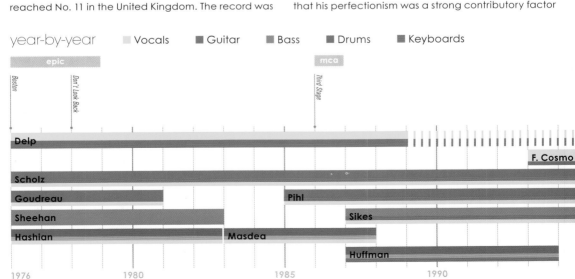

year-by-year ■ Vocals ■ Guitar ■ Bass ■ Drums ■ Keyboards

epic   mca

Boston   Don't Look Back   Third Stage

Delp
F. Cosmo
Scholz
Goudreau   Pihl
Sheehan   Sikes
Hashian   Masdea
Huffman

1976   1980   1985   1990

Fran Cosmo
b. September 3,

Curly Smith
b. January 31,
1952

Anthony Cosmo
b. Unknown

Michael Sweet
b. July 4, 1963

Gary Pihl
b. November 21, 1950

Kimberley Dahme
b. April 22

Jeff Neal
b. Unknown

Tommy DeCarlo
b. April 23, 1965

in Boston's incredible success—eventually emerged the winner and Boston moved to the MCA label.

Amid a consequent shortfall in live activity (Scholz preferred studio work anyway), Goudreau left in 1981, while Sheehan and Hashian departed in 1983. The latter was replaced by drummer **Jim Masdea**, who had played on many of the original tracks on the first album, with Scholz playing bass. Ex-Sammy Hagar sidekick **Gary Pihl** (guitars, keyboards) joined in 1985.

There was an eight-year gap until *Third Stage* (1986), but it nevertheless became their second U.S. chart-topper. The opening "Amanda" hit No. 1 too, while other fine songs included "We're Ready," "Cool the Engines," and "I Think I Like It." Although the writing did not show quite the development that might have been expected after such a hiatus, Scholz told Craig Rosen that he "did feel much better about the sound quality on *Third Stage,* compared to the first two albums. I felt that I finally learned how to make a record sound the way I wanted it to."

David Sikes (bass) and **Doug Huffman** (drums) joined in 1987, while Delp left in 1989 to join Goudreau in RTZ. No one could accuse Boston of rushing things— it was *another* eight years before *Walk On* (1994) emerged. This time, the album "only" reached No. 7

in the U.S., but went platinum in just three months. "I Need Your Love" was a minor hit. By that time, **Curly Smith** (drums) and **Fran Cosmo** (vocals) were on board and Delp returned to take part in the tour that followed. A 1997 hits set kept the fires simmering.

Naturally, eight years elapsed before *Corporate America* (2002), with **Anthony Cosmo** (guitar, vocals) and **Kimberley Dahme** (bass). The album reached No. 42 in the U.S. On drums, Anthony Citrinite and Tom Hambridge joined briefly around that time: **Jeff Neal** stayed longer and is still in the lineup (though Smith has deputized for him on tour). Both Cosmos left after a 2004 tour, and tragedy struck when Brad Delp committed suicide in 2007. The group played a benefit show in his honor, uniting all surviving members.

Michael Sweet (vocals, guitar) and **Tommy DeCarlo** (vocals, keyboards) joined, although Sweet left to focus on Christian metal band, Stryper. And a new album? "Progressing at an agonizingly slow rate," Scholz admitted in 2010, "like that would be news— but it is progressing. While I wouldn't want to give away too much about the album, it will contain both the very recognizable Boston sound plus some surprises I think everyone will appreciate—as long as you like big band swing and rap… just kidding!" **MiH**

■ Aerophones   ■ Other percussion

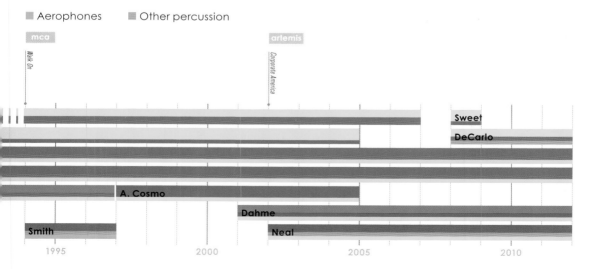

david bowie 1964–2004

B

David Bowie
b. January 8, 1947

Mick Ronson
b. May 26, 1946
d. April 29, 1993

**"Woody"
Woodmansey**
b. ca. 1951

Trevor Bolder
b. June 9, 1950

Carlos Alomar
b. January 9, 1951

Mike Garson
b. July 29, 1945

Ziggy played guitar… and so did David Jones—but, early efforts at mime aside, Bowie was never a one-man act. However, singles with the King Bees, Lower Third, and Manish Boys flopped—despite the latter's "I Pity the Fool" (1965) featuring soon-to-be star Jimmy Page. A name change to the evocative "**Bowie**" did little to improve his fortunes, though he scored a fluke hit with 1969's "Space Oddity" (featuring future Yes star Rick Wakeman, who returned on *Hunky Dory*). Unbowed, Bowie recruited producer Tony Visconti, guitarist **Mick Ronson**, bassist **Trevor Bolder** (later of Uriah Heep), and drummer **"Woody" Woodmansey**.

The Man Who Sold the World and *Hunky Dory*, coupled with provocative interviews, brought Bowie enviable press coverage but negligible sales. That ended with *The Rise and Fall of Ziggy Stardust and the Spiders from Mars*, the first of a sequence of albums from 1972 to 1977 that—for variety, innovation, and influence—is eclipsed only by The Beatles. Unleashed at a now unthinkable rate, *Aladdin Sane*, *Diamond Dogs*, *Young Americans*, *Station to Station*, and an extraordinary 1977 quartet—*Low*, *"Heroes,"* and Iggy

Pop's *The Idiot* and *Lust for Life* (both as much Bowie's work as Iggy's)—proved influential for generations. Even the throwaway *Pin Ups* hit the U.K. No. 1, while *David Live* went Top Ten on both sides of the Atlantic.

An array of musicians gave life to his music. After the dismissal of the band with whom Bowie had found fame, Ronson was replaced by **Earl Slick**, then **Carlos Alomar**, who co-wrote the star's first U.S. chart-topper, "Fame." (Alomar had been in the Harlem Apollo's house band. His replacement in that lineup was Nile Rodgers.) "Fame" was written with John Lennon, who played on it and a cover of "Across the Universe" on *Young Americans* (which also starred Luther Vandross).

Diamond Dogs featured bassist Herbie Flowers, who had played on "Space Oddity" and Lou Reed's Bowie-produced "Walk on the Wild Side," while *Aladdin Sane* and *Young Americans* showcased the piano of **Mike Garson**. The latter stayed until usurped on *Station to Station* (1976) by Springsteen keyboardist Roy Bittan and on tour by Yes man Tony Kaye.

The "Berlin trilogy"—*Low*, *"Heroes,"* and *Lodger*—ushered in new musical foils. **Brian Eno** influenced their

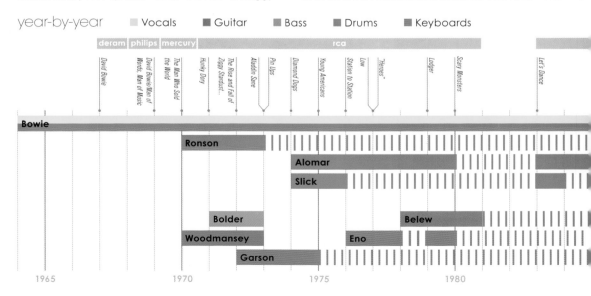

year-by-year   ■ Vocals   ■ Guitar   ■ Bass   ■ Drums   ■ Keyboards

7.5M	9.5M	2.5M	3.5M
The Rise and Fall of Ziggy Stardust... (1972)	Let's Dance (1983)	Tonight (1984)	Best of Bowie (2002)

Earl Slick
b. October 1, 1952

Brian Eno
b. May 15, 1948

Adrian Belew
b. December 23, 1949

Reeves Gabrels
b. June 4, 1956

Gail Ann Dorsey
b. November 20, 1962

experimentation, but producer Visconti was equally important, creating unique sounds such as the treated drums on *Low* and *The Idiot*. King Crimson's Robert Fripp played guitar on *"Heroes"* and Frank Zappa guitarist **Adrian Belew** featured on *Lodger* and 1978's live *Stage* (before joining Crimson in 1981). Meanwhile, Iggy's *Lust for Life* featured bassist and drummer Hunt and Tony Sales, later Tin Machine's rhythm section.

Scary Monsters—featuring Fripp, Bittan, and Pete Townshend—bookended Bowie's "classic" period. He replaced rock with acting for two years but created the splendid "Under Pressure" with Queen and "Cat People" with pioneering producer Giorgio Moroder.

By 1982, Bowie had no record deal (he had fled RCA, the label he shared with another star born on January 8: Elvis Presley) and a modest profile in the U.S. (where he last troubled the Top Ten with *Station to Station*). Accordingly, his brief to new producer Nile Rodgers (latterly of Chic) was simple: "Make hits." Blessed with a key Bowie discovery—the then-unknown guitarist Stevie Ray Vaughan—*Let's Dance* duly became his greatest commercial success.

The ensuing years saw the patchy *Tonight* and *Never Let Me Down*, the ill-fated Tin Machine, a hits-recycling 1990 tour (featuring Belew), and a reunion with Rodgers and Ronson for *Black Tie White Noise*. The latter topped the U.K. chart but failed to revive his again waning U.S. fortunes. Blissfully unconcerned, Bowie produced the beautifully uncommercial *The Buddha of Suburbia*, featuring Lenny Kravitz, and the often splendid Eno and Garson reunion, *1. Outside*.

Bowie rounded off the nineties with the dancey *Earthling* and dour *Hours*... Associates included guitarist **Reeves Gabrels**, who first appeared with him in 1988 before graduating to Tin Machine, and bassist **Gail Ann Dorsey**, a Tears for Fears alumnus. Bowie's fortunes were revived by a reunion with Visconti—exiled after *Scary Monsters*—for *Heathen* (featuring Townshend and Dave Grohl) and *Reality* (with Garson, latterly a Smashing Pumpkin). A 2003–2004 tour was cut short by ill health and may prove to have been Bowie's last. However, ecstatically received onstage cameos with Arcade Fire (2005) and David Gilmour (2006) confirmed his legend is very much intact. **BM**

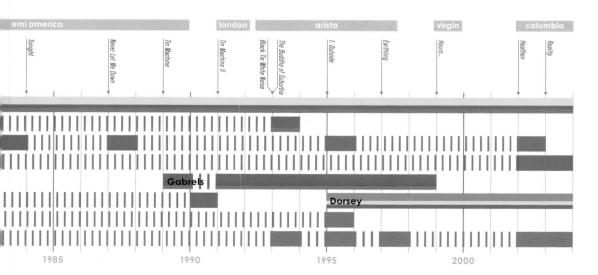

The Man Who Sold the World (1970)

Hunky Dory (1971)

The Rise and Fall of Ziggy Stardust... (1972)

Aladdin Sane (1973)

Diamond Dogs (1974)

Low (1977)

Scary Monsters (1980)

Let's Dance (1983)

Earthling (1997)

Heathen (2002)

The fresh-faced "Space Oddity" star, shortly before donning a dress.

Straight from the glitter galaxy to the heart of London, Ziggy Stardust poses in June 1972.

Entertaining DJ Rodney Bingenheimer's party guests in L.A. in 1971.

The *Aladdin Sane* look continued on the artwork for the covers collection *Pin Ups*. "A lovely man," was the verdict of supermodel Twiggy, his co-star in this shot.

Performing the anthemic "Rebel Rebel" in Holland's Top Pop Studios in February 1974.

With actress and Andy Warhol associate Monique van Vooren at a 1977 movie premiere.

At the Broadway opening of *The Elephant Man*, one of his post-*Scary Monsters* acting roles.

Bowie opens his set at Britain's Phoenix festival in July 1997 with *Hunky Dory*'s "Quicksand."

Live in London with bassist Carmine Rojas and **Carlos Alomar** on 1983's blockbuster Serious Moonlight tour.

In California, 2002, on the *Area:2* tour—a co-headliner with Moby.

(navigation tabs)

buffalo springfield 1966–2011

B

Neil Young
b. November 12, 1945

Stephen Stills
b. January 3, 1945

Bruce Palmer
b. September 9, 1946
d. October 1, 2004

Richie Furay
b. May 9, 1944

Dewey Martin
b. September 30, 1940
d. January 31, 2009

Jim Messina
b. December 5, 1947

The best sixties band never to make it big began in a traffic jam. Stuck on L.A.'s Sunset Boulevard in early 1966, ex-folkies **Stephen Stills** (a failed auditionee for The Monkees) and **Richie Furay** spotted a hearse with Ontario plates. Its driver was **Neil Young**, whom Stills knew, and his passenger was bassist **Bruce Palmer**. They hitched up, added drummer **Dewey Martin** (ex-The Dillards) within the week, and named themselves after a steamroller parked in the street where Stills and Furay lived. Seasoned musicians all, they gelled swiftly and caused a buzz in L.A., cemented by a residency at the Whisky a Go Go club and a tour with The Byrds.

Stills and Young were standout guitarists and—along with Furay—singular songwriters. A self-titled 1966 debut set was re-released in March 1967 to include Stills's "For What It's Worth"—a compelling tale of rioters clashing with cops on Sunset Strip in 1966 that provided their biggest hit (U.S. No. 7).

But cracks were already appearing. Palmer was busted in early 1967 and deported back to Canada. Sessions for the follow-up album, *Stampede*, were fractious, and it was eventually shelved. Palmer returned but then Young briefly quit; David Crosby of The Byrds filled in for him when the group played at the Monterey Pop festival in June 1967.

Remarkably, late 1967's *Buffalo Springfield Again* (U.S. No. 44) was a masterpiece, though more a "White Album"-style collection of solo works than an ensemble piece. Aided by producer Jack Nitzsche, Young created the orchestrated epics "Expecting to Fly" and "Broken Arrow"; Stills shone on "Rock'n'Roll Woman" and "Bluebird"; and Furay contributed three tracks, notably "A Child's Claim to Fame" and Motown-style belter "Good Time Boy."

Then Palmer was busted again—to be replaced by **Jim Messina**—and Young began drifting toward a solo career; the cover of their swan song *Last Time Around* (1968) showed him facing away from the others. However, the record itself contained a handful of gems, including Young's disarming "I Am a Child." After another bust in spring 1968, the band folded.

Together for just two years, Buffalo Springfield pioneered country rock and paved the way for the likes of the Eagles and Poco (featuring Furay and Messina). "That was a great group, man," Young reflected fondly in 1975. "I'd love to play with that band again, just to see if the buzz was still there." Remarkably, they did exactly that—minus Palmer and Martin, who died in 2004 and 2009, respectively—for well-received gigs in 2010 and 2011. **RD**

year-by-year   ▪ Vocals   ■ Guitar   ■ Bass   ■ Drums

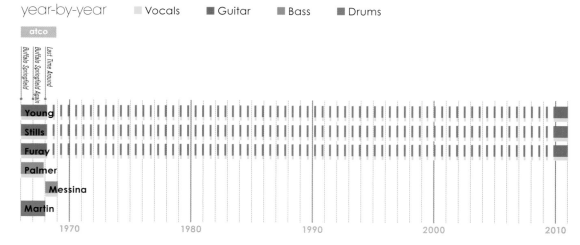

atco

Last Time Around
Buffalo Springfield Again
Buffalo Springfield

Young
Stills
Furay
Palmer
   Messina
Martin

1970   1980   1990   2000   2010

bush 1992–present

Gavin Rossdale
b. October 30, 1965

Robin Goodridge
b. September 10, 1966

Dave Parsons
b. July 2, 1965

Nigel Pulsford
b. April 11, 1963

Chris Traynor
b. June 22, 1973

Corey Britz
b. July 5, 1979

It is one of music's great mysteries: why were British rock band Bush not bigger in their home country? In 1992, when their mutual love of the Pixies got them chatting at a London club, **Gavin Rossdale** and **Nigel Pulsford** had the world in their sights. British rock fans were clamoring for homegrown talent to compete with the American grunge movement, while the charts were bursting with a conveyor belt of boy bands and female warblers. The duo formed Future Primitive with **Dave Parsons** and **Robin Goodridge**, then rebranded themselves as Bush after Shepherd's Bush, the area of London they called home.

Bush's debut, *Sixteen Stone*, failed to gain a foothold in their homeland in 1994, but it was a completely different story in America. Attracting the same passionate fans that put grunge heavyweights Nirvana and Pearl Jam on the map, and with cuts like "Comedown" and "Glycerine" in heavy rotation on radio, *Sixteen Stone* would eventually breach the Top Five and sell six million copies.

With one album, Bush had set the blueprint for modern British rock (notably Radiohead and Coldplay) to make inroads in America, although few would admit it, given the perplexing "uncool" tag stapled to Rossdale's charges in the intervening years.

The group's career peak arrived at the tail-end of 1996 and the beginning of 1997 when *Razorblade Suitcase* crowned the U.S. album chart and made

No. 4 in the United Kingdom. Regarded by some as the death knell of grunge in the aftermath of Kurt Cobain's suicide, the abrasive *Suitcase* featured "Swallowed," their only U.K. Top Ten single. (The album was knocked off the U.S. top spot by Bush's Trauma Records labelmates No Doubt, featuring Rossdale's future wife, Gwen Stefani.)

Despite bagging a fourth No. 1 on the U.S. Modern Rock Tracks chart with "The Chemicals Between Us," the post-grunge era made casualties of *The Science of Things* (1999) and *Golden State* (2001), an ill-timed attempt at a return to their riff-laden glory days. In 2002, Pulsford left and was replaced by **Chris Traynor**, who appeared on one tour before Bush disbanded.

Following the split, Rossdale showcased his vocal prowess with Institute, released a solo album (*Wanderlust*), and delved into acting. However, after a nine-year hiatus, Bush returned in 2010 with **Corey Britz** replacing Parsons. Allmusic described *The Sea of Memories* (2011) as "easily the most enjoyable collection of songs released under Bush's name."

Bush maintain an uneasy relationship with the U.K., where visitors to their website are greeted with videos that are "unavailable in your country"—but type "bush" into any search engine and they still come out ahead of Kate, George W., and all manner of shrubs. With *The Sea of Memories* hinting at a bright future, Bush should keep it that way for years to come. **MW**

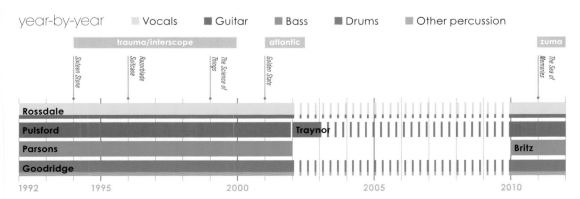

year-by-year ■ Vocals ■ Guitar ■ Bass ■ Drums ■ Other percussion

trauma/interscope   atlantic   zuma

Sixteen Stone *Razorblade Suitcase* *The Science of Things* *Golden State* *The Sea of Memories*

Rossdale
Pulsford — Traynor
Parsons — Britz
Goodridge

1992   1995   2000   2005   2010

B

buzzcocks 1976–present

Pete Shelley
b. April 17, 1955

Steve Diggle
b. May 7, 1955

Howard Devoto
b. March 15, 1952

John Maher
b. April 21, 1960

Steve Garvey
b. January 8, 1958

Mike Joyce
b. June 1, 1963

Away from the mayhem and manifestos of the mid-seventies London punk scene, a couple of hundred miles to the north was a group fronted by a helpless romantic called Shelley singing about loves lost and mislaid. In many ways, Buzzcocks were the heart of punk. And, going by their succession of spikily classic 45s, it was all too often a broken heart.

Howard Trafford and Peter McNeish knew each other from college days in the northwest of England. As **Howard Devoto** and **Pete Shelley**, they started to knock musical ideas around and made a live debut in April 1976, with Devoto on vocals, Shelley on guitar, Garth Davies on bass, and Mick Singleton on drums. But it was Sex Pistols shows—whether traveling to see the band in London, organizing a gig in Manchester (northwest England), and then even supporting them, now with **Steve Diggle** on bass and **John Maher** on drums—that were the turning point.

In January 1977, the *Spiral Scratch* EP—including "Boredom" and its wonderful two-note guitar solo—made for a powerful vinyl debut. The band had hardly got started before it was faced with the potentially fatal departure of Devoto (to form the magnificent, moody Magazine), although a Devoto co-write, "Orgasm Addict," was their riotous first major-label

release. With Diggle moving to lead guitar and Shelley taking the microphone, the bedrock on which most of Buzzcock history has been based was in place. Over the years, the rhythm section has been less stable, but **Steve Garvey** (bass) completed the quartet for the band's commercial heyday of 1977–1981.

Where the debuts of the Sex Pistols and The Clash were products of their times and tensions and have weathered accordingly, *Another Music in a Different Kitchen* is ageless in its themes. As Shelley said in 1999, rather than trying "to make a statement of the time, we were saying what was going on inside of us." That was usually relationship agonies, with song titles often posing questions—for example, the first U.K. Top Forty hit "What Do I Get?"—suggesting Shelley knew no more of the answers than anyone else. ("They had an endearingly confused quality," remarked Morrissey.)

New York's legendary Brill Building was a conveyor belt for hit singles, but it was in an Edinburgh guest house that one-man production line Shelley wrote the signature Buzzcocks song, "Ever Fallen in Love… (with Someone You Shouldn't've)." An adrenaline rush of anguish, it became the band's biggest hit: U.K. No. 12. Not that Diggle was any slouch in the songwriting department. The beguiling "Harmony in My Head"

year-by-year ■ Vocals ■ Guitar ■ Bass ■ Drums

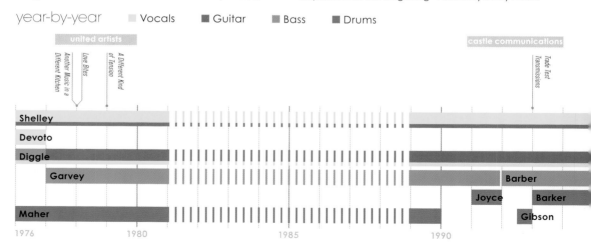

250,000	350,000	250,000	250,000
Another Music in a Different Kitchen (1978)	Love Bites (1978)	A Different Kind of Tension (1979)	Buzzcocks (2003)

Steve Gibson
b. Unknown

Tony Barber
b. April 20, 1963

Phil Barker
b. Unknown

Danny Farrant
b. Unknown

Chris Remington
b. Unknown

was the second of four Top Forty entries from the slightly underwhelming *Love Bites*, though that album, like its predecessor, went Top Twenty in the U.K.

Shelley was clearly relishing the prolific period he found himself in. "I can just sit there and go dee-da-dee-da-dee, da-dee-da-dee, put some words to it, teach the other three how to play it, go to the studio and record it, and put it out," he said in 1979.

It could not last. With over-indulgence creeping into an unceasing cycle of tours and albums, the group burned out in 1981, after the relative failure of *A Different Kind of Tension*. Shelley's solo career hit an early high with "Homosapien," while Diggle and Maher flew under their Flag of Convenience. ("I really thought Steve and everybody else would carry on as Buzzcocks without me," Shelley protested.)

The classic Shelley-Diggle-Garvey-Maher lineup reconvened in 1989, although ex-Smith **Mike Joyce** (who had "learned to play drums by banging on the back of me mum's sofa listening to the Buzzcocks") took over drums for a while, followed by **Steve Gibson**.

By the time of *Trade Test Transmissions* (1993), **Tony Barber** (bass) and **Phil Barker** (drums) were in the recording studio with Shelley and Diggle. Soon after, Kurt Cobain paid homage to the band's influence by

inviting them on a U.S. tour with Nirvana. "We got on like two peas in a pod," said Shelley.

All Set from 1996 saw the band truly back in stride, with Shelley in prime form for "Totally from the Heart" and "Without You" in an admirably consistent set. Past and present was represented on *Modern* (1999). It says something about the consistency of the songwriting that its fourteen tracks do not come off unduly damaged by a second CD of hits and highlights.

The first decade of the new millennium saw some unfinished business revisited. Two albums—a self-titled release in 2003 and the sinewy *Flat-Pack Philosophy* (2006)—were preceded by *Buzzkunst* by ShelleyDevoto, the pair working together for the first time in over two decades. For Shelley's day job, there was some unexpected and unpaid promotion. The band's name originally came from a review of a TV show *Rock Follies*, headlined "It's the buzz, cocks!" In turn, Shelley and company were now used in the title of a BBC music quiz, *Never Mind the Buzzcocks*.

Another overhaul of the backroom boys (**Danny Farrant** on drums; **Chris Remington** on bass), was followed by events coming full circle—gigs in 2012 featuring Devoto, Maher, Garvey, and the current lineup. Love never goes out of style. **CB**

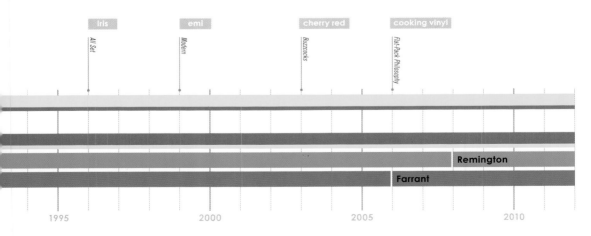

iris | emi | cherry red | cooking vinyl

All Set | *Modern* | *Buzzcocks* | *Flat-Pack Philosophy*

Remington

Farrant

1995 | 2000 | 2005 | 2010

the byrds 1964–1973

Jim (Roger) McGuinn
b. July 13, 1942

Gene Clark
b. November 17, 1944
d. May 24, 1991

David Crosby
b. August 14, 1941

Chris Hillman
b. December 4, 1944

Michael Clarke
b. June 3, 1946
d. December 19, 1993

Kevin Kelley
b. March 25, 1943
d. April 6, 2002

They were America's Beatles, matching freewheeling studio experimentation with top-notch songwriting and blissful harmonies. The Byrds' heyday lasted only from 1965 to 1968; their influence is lasting far longer.

Jim (later **Roger**) **McGuinn**, **Gene Clark**, and **David Crosby** had been folkies and initially teamed up as The Jet Set. After The Beatles hit America in 1964, though, all that changed. Invigorated by the Fabs' *A Hard Day's Night*, they briefly became The Beefeaters (an Anglophile nod to the U.K. pop invasion of the States). Joined by bassist **Chris Hillman**, whose background was in bluegrass, and drummer **Michael Clarke** (recruited because of his Brian Jones haircut), on November 26, 1964, they became The Byrds.

Initially, they grumbled over the choice of Bob Dylan's "Mr. Tambourine Man" for their first single, but mellowed when it became a worldwide No. 1. The debut album *Mr. Tambourine Man* (1965) showcased Gene Clark's songwriting skill, notably on the delirious

stomp "Feel a Whole Lot Better" and the wistful "I Knew I'd Want You." With their louche on-stage cool, McGuinn's tinted sunglasses and Crosby's whimsical grin, The Byrds swiftly became teenybop faves.

Turn! Turn! Turn! (1965) was marginally less ecstatic, though the title track secured their last U.S. No. 1 hit. But problems were brewing. There was resistance to Clark's material within the group, touring exhausted him, and he was afraid of flying. After a hit-and-miss tour of the U.K., he quit—though not before co-writing the jazz-and-raga-influenced "Eight Miles High," based on their U.K. tour and among their finest cuts.

Initially, the four-piece Byrds maintained the momentum. The diverse *Fifth Dimension* (1966) augured well, while *Younger Than Yesterday* (1967) was a triumph: studio magic sprinkled over stand-out tunes, including Crosby's divinely melancholy "Everybody's Been Burned." Alas, Crosby was now increasingly unpredictable, given to on-stage rants

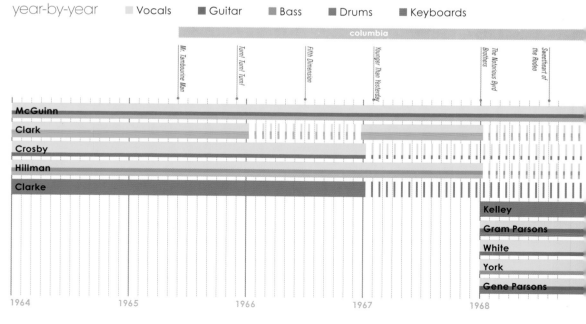

year-by-year · ■ Vocals · ■ Guitar · ■ Bass · ■ Drums · ■ Keyboards

| 3.5M | 2M | 1M | 4M |
| Mr. Tambourine Man (1965) | Turn! Turn! Turn! (1965) | Fifth Dimension (1966) | The Byrds Greatest Hits (1967) |

B

Gram Parsons
b. November 5, 1946
d. September 19, 1973

Clarence White
b. June 7, 1944
d. July 14, 1973

John York
b. August 3, 1946

Gene Parsons
b. September 4, 1944

Skip Battin
b. February 18, 1934
d. July 6, 2003

and poor playing, and engaged in a power struggle with McGuinn. *The Notorious Byrd Brothers* (1968) was another strong set but, by its release, Crosby and Clarke had been dismissed, the latter replaced by Hillman's cousin **Kevin Kelley**. Crosby went on to form Crosby, Stills and Nash (and, occasionally, Young), one of rock's most successful supergroups.

The newly recruited **Gram Parsons** led The Byrds into country music, though it had influenced their work since at least "Satisfied Mind" on *Turn! Turn! Turn!*. On *Sweetheart of the Rodeo* (1968), they embraced country ballads and standards—dismaying many fans. The willful Parsons left prior to an ill-fated tour of South Africa, and The Byrds' next incarnation saw McGuinn and Hillman joined by country guitarist **Clarence White** and bassist **John York**. The four-piece recorded *Dr. Byrds and Mr. Hyde* (1960)—country meets psychedelia—and *Ballad of Easy Rider* (1969)—which had little to do with *Easy Rider* (1969) the movie.

Hillman left to join Parsons in The Flying Burrito Brothers (with ex-Byrd Michael Clarke), and the final incarnation of the group saw drummer **Gene Parsons** (no relation to Gram) and bassist **Skip Battin** replace Kelley and York respectively. They recorded the well-received *Untitled* (1970), featuring "Chestnut Mare," a U.K. Top Twenty hit, though *Byrdmaniax* (1971) and *Farther Along* (1971) were poorly received.

The Byrds finally folded in 1973. Hopes were high when the original five-piece reunited for that year's *Byrds*, but only "Full Circle" and a cover of Neil Young's "(See The Sky) About To Rain" hinted at past magic.

Latterly, individual members performed together —and issued lawsuits against each other for touring fake "Byrds" outfits—while the original five reunited for their inauguration into the Rock and Roll Hall of Fame in 1991. Revisit their music from 1965 to 1968—then listen to jingly-jangly descendants like Tom Petty and R.E.M.—and you'll see why they matter so much. **RD**

■ Aerophones   ■ Other percussion   ■ Strings

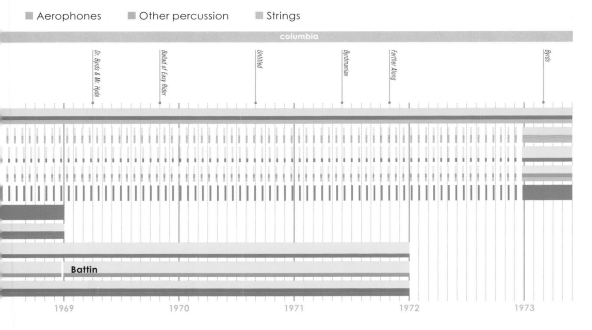

columbia

Dr. Byrds & Mr. Hyde | Ballad of Easy Rider | Untitled | Byrdmaniax | Farther Along | Byrds

Battin

1969   1970   1971   1972   1973

can 1968–1991

Holger Czukay
b. March 24, 1938

Jaki Liebezeit
b. May 26, 1939

Irmin Schmidt
b. May 29, 1937

Michael Karoli
b. Apr 29, 1948
d. Nov 17, 2001

Malcolm "Desse" Mooney
b. Unknown

Kenji "Damo" Suzuki
b. January 16, 1950

Rosko Gee
b. Unknown

"Reebop" Kwaku Baah
b. Feb 13, 1944
d. Jan 12, 1983

"I felt they had picked up the gauntlet that The Velvet Underground had thrown down," Brian Eno observed in 1997. A glowing testament—and totally warranted when, as Can did, you re-write the rules of rock.

Like the Velvets, Can had one foot in the avant-garde—**Holger Czukay** (bass) and **Irmin Schmidt** (keyboards) had even studied with classical *enfant terrible* Karlheinz Stockhausen. **Michael Karoli** (guitar), a pupil of Czukay, alerted him to Hendrix and the twisted rock of the Velvets. **Jaki Liebezeit** provided their locked beat and **Malcolm "Desse" Mooney** added spontaneous vocals and off-kilter energy.

Monster Movie (1969) was a wildly original debut; for "Yoo Do Right," Mooney sang a letter he had received from his girlfriend. Alas, a nervous breakdown obliged the singer to return to the U.S. for help. Czukay and Liebezeit found his replacement, **Kenji "Damo" Suzuki**, busking in Munich. After a highly confrontational show, only thirty of the 1,500 crowd were left—including, oddly, actor David Niven.

Having refined their sound on *Soundtracks* (1970), Can delivered their first masterpiece with *Tago Mago* (1970), produced by Conny Plank. It boasted the funky, eighteen-minute "Hallelujah" and "Augmn"—like a farther out-there "Interstellar Overdrive."

Ege Bamyasi (1972) was more approachable and featured an unlikely German No. 1 in "Spoon," while the gentle *Future Days* (1973) offered myriad delights, from the shuffling beat of the title track to the shape-shifting closer, "Bel Air." Suzuki subsequently departed to become a Jehovah's Witness; Karoli and Schmidt shared vocals on the ambient *Soon Over Babaluma* (1974) and *Landed* (1975). By now, Can's avant-garde edge had been somewhat dulled. Newcomers **Rosko Gee** (bass) and **"Reebop" Kwaku Baah** (percussion) were good musicians, but perhaps too conventional for Can, though *Flow Motion* (1976) gave the band their sole U.K. hit (No. 26) with "I Want More."

Increasingly drawn toward more left-field music making, Czukay drifted from the group and was gone by their final set, 1978's *Can* (aka *Inner Space*), by which time elements of world music had filtered in. In 1986, the five core members (including a more stable Mooney) reconvened for *Rite Time* (1989), while a 1991 reunion saw them contribute a track to Wim Wenders's 1991 movie *Until the End of the World*.

Can's brew of improvisation, hypnotic rhythms, and enigmatic vocals continues to fascinate. Those smitten have included David Bowie, Brian Eno, The Fall, The Flaming Lips, and Primal Scream. **RD**

year-by-year   ■ Vocals   ■ Guitar   ■ Bass   ■ Drums   ■ Keyboards
■ Other percussion   ■ Strings   ■ Programming

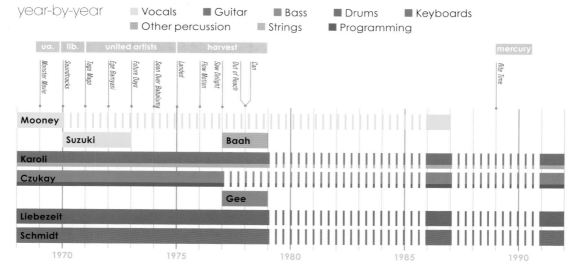

canned heat 1965–present

Bob "The Bear" Hite
b. Feb 26, 1943
d. Apr 5, 1981

Alan "Blind Owl" Wilson
b. July 4, 1943
d. September 3, 1970

Frank Cook
b. Unknown

Henry "Sunflower" Vestine
b. Dec 25, 1944
d. Oct 20, 1997

Larry "The Mole" Taylor
b. June 26, 1942

Fito de la Parra
b. February 8, 1946

Harvey "The Snake" Mandel
b. Mar 11, 1945

Dale Spalding
b. April 16, 1949

Canned Heat were five white Americans who wanted to play the blues, popularize it, and raise awareness of its black roots. The band was the brainchild of frontman **Bob "The Bear" Hite** and guitarist **Alan "Blind Owl" Wilson**, who hired drummer **Frank Cook**, former Frank Zappa guitarist **Henry "Sunflower" Vestine**, and former Jerry Lee Lewis bassist **Larry "The Mole" Taylor**. The name of the band was inspired by "Canned Heat Blues" by guitarist Tommy Johnson—"canned heat" being a colloquial term for Sterno, a cooking fuel drunk by impoverished alcohol dependents.

The band attracted attention at 1967's Monterey Pop festival even before their self-titled debut album. Their covers of long-forgotten blues numbers and almost encyclopedic knowledge of the music's roots gave them a good-time worthiness that built an appreciative audience. Canned Heat soon made headlines—not all of them desirable. They were notorious for their excesses, and a drug bust in Denver precipitated the departure of Cook. He was replaced by **Fito de la Parra**. However, *Boogie with Canned Heat* (1968) featured two transatlantic Top Twenty hits with which they remain forever associated: "On the Road Again" and "Going Up the Country."

The final year of the sixties was Canned Heat's annus mirabilis as they consolidated their fanbase with new albums and broadened it with a strong set at the Woodstock festival. In 1970, their definitive cover of "Let's Work Together"—originally by Wilbert Harrison—hit No. 2 in the U.K. and No. 26 in the U.S. But just as the band was about to embark on a British tour in September, Blind Owl died of a drug overdose, shaking the band to its core.

Now under Hite's sole direction, Canned Heat began to recover when a session with John Lee Hooker was released as 1971's *Hooker 'n Heat*, giving a welcome wake-up to the blues master's career. They would collaborate with two more blues stars in 1973: Clarence "Gatemouth" Brown (*Gate's on the Heat*) and Memphis Slim (*Memphis Heat*).

From the early seventies, as musicians came and went, the only constant was Hite. His fatal heroin-induced heart attack in 1981 seemed to spell the end of the band, but de la Parra kept it going. In the twenty-first century, Canned Heat's participation in the Heroes of Woodstock Tour, marking the fortieth anniversary of the festival, brought guitarist **Harvey Mandel** and Larry Taylor back into the fold. In 2010, the official lineup comprised Mandel, Taylor, de la Parra, and harmonica player **Dale Spalding**. They continue to tour, and the band's motto, "Don't forget to boogie!," holds as true as ever. **GL**

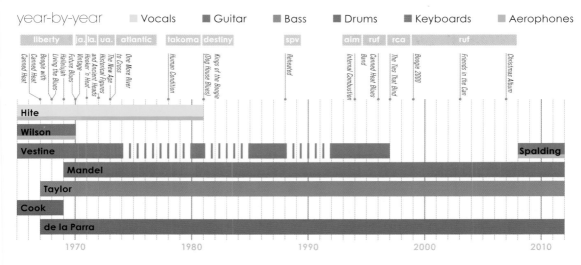

year-by-year □ Vocals ■ Guitar ■ Bass ■ Drums ■ Keyboards ■ Aerophones

captain beefheart and his magic band

**Don Van Vliet
(Captain
Beefheart)**
b. January 14, 1941
d. December 17, 2010

Ry Cooder
b. March 15, 1947

Alex St Clair
b. September 14, 1941
d. January 5, 2006

John French
b. September 29, 1948

Jerry Handley
b. Unknown

Jeff Cotton
b. May 31, 1948

In rock's pantheon of great eccentrics, Captain Beefheart stands alone. His uncompromising music has inspired successive generations; his surreal pronouncements have baffled, infuriated, and entertained. And, after abandoning music altogether, he achieved enormous success as a painter: prior to his death in December 2010, his works were among the highest priced of any living artist.

Born in Glendale, California in 1941, Don Glen Vliet was a child prodigy who, by the age of eleven, had won first prizes in sculpture and featured on local television. Although Vliet's blue-collar father was not comfortable with his son's interests, he was indulged by his mother and allowed to spend his teens sculpting, painting, and listening to blues and modern jazz, with little interruption from the outside world.

Having met Frank Zappa at high school, Vliet teamed up with him in a group known as the Soots. Vliet's deep bass Howlin' Wolf growl, Zappa's distorted electric guitar, and song titles such as "Metal Man Has Won His Wings" found the duo well adrift of the prevailing musical styles of the period. Although this collaboration was brief, Zappa would play a pivotal role in the Captain Beefheart story.

In early 1965, guitarist Alex Snouffer invited Vliet to sing with an R&B group he was assembling. With the singer now **Don Van Vliet**, they became known as Captain Beefheart and his Magic Band and signed with A&M to produce two singles in 1966, one a cover of Bo Diddley's "Diddy Wah Diddy." Unimpressed by the group's lack of success and the "negative" sound of their demos, A&M promptly dropped them.

Two important new arrivals appeared at the end of 1966. Drummer **John French** took on the critical task of interpreting "non-musician" Van Vliet's creative ideas. Meanwhile, twenty-year-old guitar prodigy **Ry Cooder** honed and rearranged the band's material for what would become their 1967 debut album, *Safe as Milk*. Recorded for the Buddah label, this contorted slab of blues-rock made little commercial impact in the U.S., but affected an influential group of musicians in Europe—not least John Lennon, who tried briefly to sign the Magic Band to the Apple label.

Cooder's tenure in the band was a brief one, **Jeff Cotton** joining in time for sessions for an album/design concept intended to be called *It Comes in a Plain Brown Wrapper*. Once again, initial recordings—more overtly "period" sounds with psychedelic audio

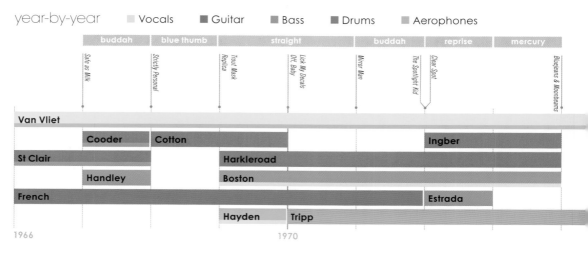

year-by-year   ■ Vocals   ■ Guitar   ■ Bass   ■ Drums   ■ Aerophones

750,000
Trout Mask Replica
(1969)

450,000
Lick My Decals Off Baby
(1970)

300,000
Mirror Man
(1971)

300,000
The Spotlight Kid
(1972)

Bill Harkleroad
b. December 12, 1948

Mark Boston
b. 1949

Victor Hayden
b. Unknown

Art Tripp
b. September 10, 1944

Elliot Ingber
b. Unknown

Roy Estrada
b. April 17, 1943

effects—were not appreciated by the pop-oriented Buddah. The Magic Band were dropped and the album emerged as *Strictly Personal* on a tiny label owned by the band's producer, Bob Krasnow.

The year 1969 proved pivotal for the Magic Band. With no record deal in place, Van Vliet's old friend Frank Zappa—now successful with the Mothers of Invention—stepped in, offering to produce an album for his own newly created Straight label. At this time, Van Vliet began to assert his domination of the group. Living communally in a rented house in a Los Angeles suburb, the Magic Band spent eight months learning Van Vliet's new music: a complex, avant-garde hybrid of blues, rock, and free jazz. A dramatic shift in compositional style came about as Van Vliet created new material at the piano, an instrument for which he had no training or knowledge. He would "play" until he found the required sounds, chords, or rhythms, which drummer French would articulate to the others.

The conditions were, claimed French, "cult-like," as the broke and starving musicians were drilled fourteen hours a day, continually berated by Van Vliet to perfect what may have sounded like a group free improvisation, yet in truth was anything

but. The double album that emerged, *Trout Mask Replica*, made no immediate impact in America and spent one week in the U.K. chart—largely on the strength of producer Zappa's involvement. But, to be appreciated, *Trout Mask Replica* requires multiple close listens. It is now revered as a landmark in rock.

The same process was matured on 1970's self-produced *Lick My Decals Off, Baby*, which provided the Magic Band with their only Top Twenty album in the United Kingdom. In spite of its predecessor's stature, Van Vliet rated *Decals* as his best work.

Throughout the seventies, Captain Beefheart, with an ever-changing Magic Band, continued to release albums that increasingly mined a more accessible, blues-oriented rock furrow. After a falling-out with Zappa, Van Vliet reunited with him for 1975's *Bongo Fury*, a blend of live and studio recordings.

Ice Cream for Crow, released in 1982, would be Van Vliet's final studio album before music finally gave way to his love of abstract expressionist painting. Wheelchair-bound with multiple sclerosis, Van Vliet made few public appearances over the two decades before his death, three weeks before his seventieth birthday, on December 17, 2010. **TB**

■ Other percussion

mercury

warner

virgin

Unconditionally Guaranteed

Shiny Beast (Bat Chain Puller)

Doc at the Radar Station

Ice Cream for Crow

1975

1980

the cars 1976–present

Ric Ocasek
b. March 23, 1949

Benjamin Orr
b. September 8, 1947
d. October 3, 2000

Elliot Easton
b. December 18, 1953

Greg Hawkes
b. October 22, 1952

David Robinson
b. April 2, 1949

The Cars were always hard to categorize, and maybe their reputation is not as high as it should be for precisely that reason. Both a singles and an albums band (when that distinction still mattered), they mixed the essentials of new wave and alternative rock with the instant hooks and catchy choruses of great pop. They were also an amalgam of opposites: they were smooth, yet jagged, they were gleaming, yet opaque.

The Cars came together in Boston, Massachusetts, in 1976, although—having met in Colombus, Ohio—**Ric Ocasek** (vocals, guitar) and **Benjamin Orr** (vocals, bass) had been playing together in various forms for over six years, during which they were joined by **Elliot Easton** (lead guitar) in Cap'n Swing. When **Greg Hawkes** (keyboards), who had been in folk outfit Milkwood with Ocasek and Orr, and **David Robinson** (drums) were brought in to replace previous jazzier incumbents, the group needed a change of name. Robinson suggested The Cars and, for its simplicity, it stuck. As Ocasek remarked, "It's so easy to spell; it doesn't have a 'z' on the end; it's real authentic. It's pop art in a sense."

Live, the group were a well-oiled machine, although the musicians tended to be somewhat statuesque in performance. It was Ocasek's songs that were the main focus. A demo pressing of "Just What I Needed" got heavy airplay on a local radio station and attracted the attention of the Elektra label, which signed the group. Roy Thomas Baker, the producer noted for his work with Queen, came in to work on their first album, *The Cars* (1978). The results were as good as could have been hoped. In addition to "Just What I Needed," the tracks "My Best Friend's Girl," "Moving in Stereo," and "Good Times Roll" were perfect pop statements and earned sales as singles to match. The album camped on the *Billboard* chart for almost three whole years.

Candy-O (1979) was a superb follow-up (and U.S. No. 3). "Let's Go," "It's All I Can Do," "Dangerous Type," and the title track showed the group were wonderfully adept at delivering Ocasek's visions, which ran the gamut from bright and breezy to dark and skewed. Robinson even managed to persuade *Playboy* cartoonist Vargas out of retirement to draw the cover art for the LP sleeve.

On the third album, *Panorama* (1980), the group allowed themselves a little more room to experiment, although without straying far from their chosen path. It was a mixed bag. The title track and "Touch and Go" were excellent, but overall doubts were starting to creep in and the self-confidence that had permeated the first two records was sometimes missing.

year-by-year   Vocals   Guitar   Bass   Drums   Keyboards

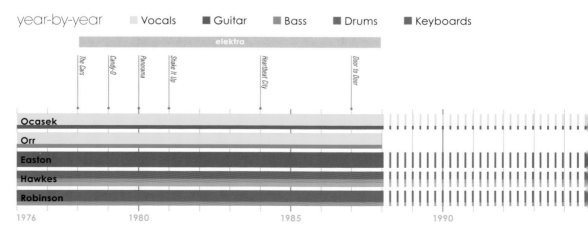

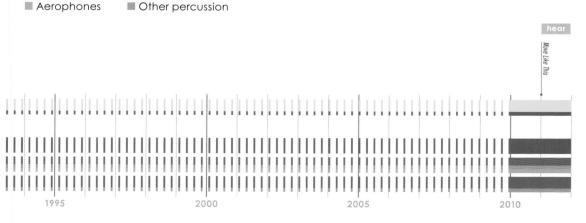

7.5M
The Cars
(1978)

6M
Candy-O
(1979)

6.8M
Heartbeat City
(1984)

8M
*The Cars
Greatest Hits*
(1985)

Perhaps the strains caused by their success were beginning to show. Although the group were back in the studio the following year for *Shake It Up*—where the mood was a little less somber with offerings such as "Since You're Gone," "Think It Over," and the up-tempo title track—some members were getting itchy feet. Ocasek and Hawkes both released solo albums before the Cars recorded again.

Now with Robert John "Mutt" Lange, fresh from Def Leppard's *Pyromania*, at the helm, *Heartbeat City* (1984) proved to be the last great flowering of their combined talents. "You Might Think," "It's Not the Night," "Magic," and "Hello Again" were all U.S. hits, as the group's spiky offerings turned out to be ideally suited to the then-booming MTV and its insatiable demand for polished product. In fact, their sound had been revved up to suit the mid-eighties fads.

Their biggest hit of all was the emotive ballad "Drive" (with lead vocals supplied by Orr), peaking at No. 3 on the U.S. *Billboard* Hot 100 and reaching the higher echelons of the singles charts in the U.K., West Germany, and Canada. "Drive" was later used as the theme song for the promotional video at the heart of the 1985 Band Aid efforts to relieve the famine in Ethiopia. The group played at the resulting Philadelphia Live Aid concert and it seemed as though their engine had been retuned. Meanwhile, proving that this single did not only impact on them commercially, Ocasek met his future wife, supermodel Paulina Porizkova, at the video shoot.

Their success was not to last. *The Cars' Greatest Hits* came out in late 1985 and helped to keep the group at the forefront (with new hit "Tonight She Comes"), but they were now running almost on empty. *Door to Door* (1987) included "You Are the Girl"—a Top Twenty single in the United States—but the songs did not quite reach Ocasek's best level and the synthesizers were becoming too dominant. The conviction had gone, and there was no sign of a compensatory desire to experiment.

The group split up in 1988 and, despite several further greatest hits packages and compilations, resisted all pleas to get back together. Ocasek went so far as to say it would never happen. The death of Benjamin Orr from cancer in 2000 seemed to have closed the book. However, in 2010, the four surviving members announced they were reforming and produced a well-received album, *Move Like This* (2011)—the title mocking their own stage inertia—that featured "Blue Tip" and the especially fine "Sad Song." The Cars supported the record with a sparkling tour of the U.S. and Canada. **MiH**

■ Aerophones   ■ Other percussion

hear

Move Like This

1995   2000   2005   2010

nick cave & the bad seeds 1984–present

Nick Cave
b. September 22, 1957

Mick Harvey
b. August 29, 1958

Blixa Bargeld
b. January 12, 1959

Barry Adamson
b. June 11, 1958

Hugo Race
b. unknown

Anita Lane
b. unknown

Thomas Wydler
b. October 9, 1959

Kid "Congo" Powers
b. March 27, 1959

Nick Cave is a writer and performer of distinctive power, whose violent, exciting, and sometimes macabre visions are unmatched in rock. The Bad Seeds have supported him with an ideal mixture of thunder, beauty, and menace through various incarnations. Cave is also an accomplished prose author with a taste for hellfire preacher tales of the old American South (which also permeate his songs).

Cave was at school in Melbourne, Australia, with multi-instrumentalist **Mick Harvey** when he formed what became The Birthday Party, an impressively incoherent group who flirted with success from 1978 to 1983. Their lineup also included **Tracy Pew** (bass), Phill Calvert (drums), and Rowland G. Howard (guitar).

After The Birthday Party imploded through the usual combination of hard drugs, drink, and brittle egos, Cave looked around for collaborators who shared, or at least understood, his world view. Cave's inner circle included Harvey and **Anita Lane**, his then girlfriend, co-writer, and muse. In late 1983 he got together with the musicians that became the Bad Seeds (not fixing on that name until 1984). As well as Harvey (guitar, drums, and just about everything else)

and the non-playing Lane, the new group featured **Blixa Bargeld** (guitar), **Barry Adamson** (guitar, piano, bass, drums), and **Hugo Race** (guitar).

They kicked off with *From Her to Eternity* (1984) but it proved to be the swan song of the affair between Cave and Lane, with the title track as their parting gift. Race also failed to stay the course. German filmmaker Christoph Dreher, Jim Thirlwell, Edward Clayton-Jones, and old Birthday Party mates Pew and Howard guested briefly in the early Bad Seeds.

The Firstborn Is Dead (1985), with the knockout American Gothic "Tupelo," still had Cave railing in opiated isolation. **Thomas Wydler** (drums) joined before *Kicking Against the Pricks* (1986), a covers LP with Biblical tales of woe. Adamson left and his versatile prowess was replaced by the infusion of **Kid "Congo" Powers** (guitar) and **Roland Wolf** (keyboards).

It was back to original songs for *Your Funeral…My Trial* (1986), and the heroin-suffused outcome was all the bleaker for that. The lashings of Grand Guignol mounted higher still on *Tender Prey* (1988) with the coruscating "The Mercy Seat" and desperate "City of Refuge." However, by the release of *The Good Son*

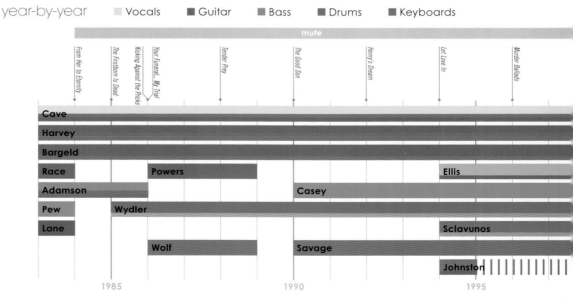

year-by-year ■ Vocals ■ Guitar ■ Bass ■ Drums ■ Keyboards

mute

From Her to Eternity · *The Firstborn Is Dead* · *Kicking Against the Pricks* · *Your Funeral…My Trial* · *Tender Prey* · *The Good Son* · *Henry's Dream* · *Let Love In* · *Murder Ballads*

Cave
Harvey
Bargeld
Race — Powers — Ellis
Adamson — Casey
Pew — Wydler
Lane — Sclavunos
Wolf — Savage
Johnston

1985 · 1990 · 1995

C

Roland Wolf
b. 1965
d. March 29, 1995

Martyn P. Casey
b. July 10, 1960

Conway Savage
b. July 27, 1960

Jim Sclavunos
b. unknown

Warren Ellis
b. 1965

James Johnston
b. 1966

Ed Kuepper
b. December 20, 1955

Tracy Pew
b. December 19, 1957
d. November 7, 1986

(1990), Cave had reached an accommodation of sorts with his demons, due to love, relocation to Brazil, and a measure of cleaning up, although his keening lyricism, such as on the title track and "The Weeping Song," still contained savage cries of longing.

Martyn P. Casey (bass) and **Conway Savage** (keyboards) fleshed out the group for *Henry's Dream* (1992) featuring the tumultuous "John Finn's Wife." However, Cave, unhappy with the production, was moved to release *Live Songs* the following year to rectify matters. *Let Love In* (1994), with the smoldering single "Do You Love Me?," was also underrated at the time, merely serving to confirm how staggeringly consistent Cave has been throughout the years, notwithstanding his addictions. **Warren Ellis** (violin) and **Jim Sclavunos** (drums) joined the group in 1994, although Ellis was listed as a guest member until 1997.

Murder Ballads (1996) was perhaps the group's biggest success because of the unlikely duet with Kylie Minogue on "Where the Wild Roses Grow" (a U.K. hit), but the album as a whole was well executed. There was a more confessional tinge to *The Boatman's Call* (1997) as Cave hinted at breakdowns in his

relationships with Polly Harvey and Viviane Carneiro: no wild shouts, just elegant, mournful resignation.

However, some of the old dynamic angst was back in *No More Shall We Part* (2001) on tracks such as "Oh My Lord." *Nocturama* (2003) presaged another parting of the ways, Bargeld leaving to be replaced by **James Johnston** on guitar.

Abattoir Blues/The Lyre of Orpheus (2004) was an artfully schizophrenic double CD, the former highlighting Cave's manic tendencies, the latter more reflective. In addition, Cave formed a side-project, Grinderman (dubbed the mini-Seeds), with Casey, Sclavunos, and Ellis, dedicated to pursuing the more raucous, carnal side of his music. They released two albums, *Grinderman* (2007) and *Grinderman 2* (2010) before deciding to split up in 2011.

After recording *Dig, Lazarus, Dig!!!* (2008), which also featured Cave's less crafted, more immediate aspects, Johnston quit. Then Harvey left the group in 2009 after a thirty-five-year creative relationship with Cave, and was replaced by **Ed Kuepper**. Crucially, Cave remains in place—one of rock's few inimitable visionaries and commanding live performers. **MiH**

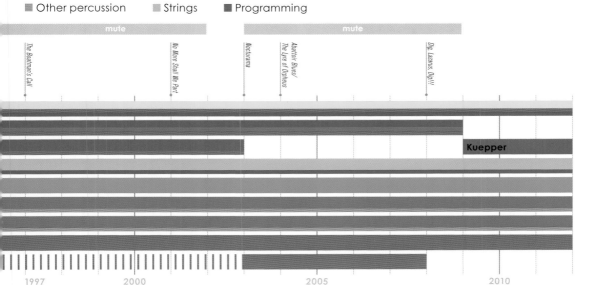

■ Other percussion   ■ Strings   ■ Programming

From Her to Eternity (1984)

Kicking Against the Pricks (1986)

Tender Prey (1988)

The Good Son (1990)

Henry's Dream (1992)

Murder Ballads (1996)

The Boatman's Call (1997)

No More Shall We Part (2001)

Abattoir Blues/The Lyre of Orpheus (2004)

Dig, Lazarus Dig!!! (2008)

Feel his pain: **Nick Cave** performs at de Meervaart in Amsterdam, the Netherlands, in 1984.

Cave mid-performance at Utrecht, the Netherlands, in 1986.

Cave onstage with **Blixa Bargeld** at London's Town and Country Club in October 1988.

A 1990 portrait of a man who transforms dark thoughts into fine songs.

Cave plays the Ritz Club, New York, in November 1986.

Cave sings with fellow dark balladeer PJ Harvey on U.K. TV show *The White Room* in 1996.

Cave outstares the camera in 2001.

Cave performs again on the U.K. TV show *The White Room* in 1997.

Cave plays Amsterdam in the Netherlands during a European tour in 2004.

Cave and the Bad Seeds appear on the U.S TV show *Late Night with Conan O'Brien* on October 3, 2008.

cheap trick 1973–present

Rick Nielsen
b. December 22, 1946

Bun E. Carlos
b. June 12, 1951

Tom Petersson
b. May 9, 1950

Robin Zander
b. January 23, 1953

Pete Comita
b. unknown

Jon Brant
b. February 22, 1955

Cheap Trick, whose beautifully textured Anglophile songs teeter on the edge of hard rock and power pop, with the occasional tinge of heavy metal, produced a series of interesting albums as well as attracting excited audiences worldwide.

In 1973, **Rick Nielsen** (guitar) and **Tom Petersson** (bass) had been touring in their group Sick Man of Europe when they reunited with **Bun E. Carlos** (drums) of hometown Rockford, Illinois, and brought in Randy Hogan (vocals) to form Cheap Trick. Hogan was soon replaced by **Robin Zander** and the classic (also current) lineup was complete.

After extensive gigging, the first album *Cheap Trick* (1977) was released, a burst of hard rock adrenaline characterized by "ELO Kiddies." The follow-up *In Color* (1977) was a more polished, quintessentially power pop album, featuring the swooning "Southern Girls." *Heaven Tonight* (1978) confirmed all the promise the group had shown thus far, the stately title track offset by the jubilant nostalgia of "Takin' Me Back" and the delirious "Surrender." But it was the live *Cheap Trick at Budokan* (1978), recorded in front of their screaming Japanese fans, that gave them their breakthrough, peaking at No. 4 in the U.S. and launching a live single of "I Want You to Want Me" to No. 7.

This success was echoed by the darkly paranoid *Dream Police* (1979), epitomized by the lush,

schizophrenic "Voices" and frenetic title track. The album reached No. 6, a position not quite matched by *All Shook Up* (1980) despite the inclusion of the epic "Stop This Game" and "World's Greatest Lover."

Petersson quit in 1980, to be replaced first by **Pete Comita** and then by **Jon Brant**. The group was unable to repeat the careless rapture of the early albums, though their work ethic was strong throughout the decade. *One on One* (1982), *Next Position Please* (1983), and *Standing on the Edge* (1985) were all perfectly sound bodies of work, even if *The Doctor* (1986) displayed symptoms of undue cynicism.

By the time of *Lap of Luxury* (1988), Petersson had returned and Cheap Trick were rewarded with their only No. 1 U.S. single "The Flame" (follow-up "Don't Be Cruel" hit No. 4) and a top placing of the LP at No. 16, their second highest for a studio recording. It proved to be a poisoned chalice, since the group felt their development was constrained by this success.

Busted (1990) repeated the formula, if not the sales, though "Can't Stop Fallin' into Love" was a U.S. No. 12. *Woke up with a Monster* (1994) could not emulate its title's wishes, although it and with *Cheap Trick* (1997), *Special One* (2003), *Rockford* (2006), and *The Latest* (2009) have all made respectable showings in the lower reaches of the charts. As a live group, Cheap Trick continue to be revered. **MiH**

year-by-year   Vocals   Guitar   Bass   Drums   Keyboards   Other percussion

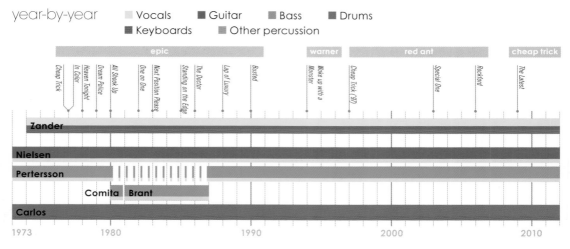

chicago 1967–present

Robert Lamm
b. October 13, 1944

Peter Cetera
b. September 13, 1944

Terry Kath
b. January 31, 1946
d. January 23, 1978

Lee Loughnane
b. October 21, 1946

James Pankow
b. August 20, 1947

Walt Parazaider
b. March 14, 1945

Daniel Seraphine
b. August 28, 1948

Bill Champlin
b. May 21, 1947

From the opening fired-up brass arrangement of "Introduction" on Chicago Transit Authority's eponymous debut, the three horn players announced "jazz rock." The rock really came from the amazing guitar feedback and rhythmic funk of **Terry Kath**— even Jim Hendrix graciously acknowledged of Chicago "your horns are one set of lungs and you know your guitar player is better than me." Listening to Kath's four-minute "Free Form Guitar" feedback and fuzz segueing into the swamp grunge of "South California Purples" you can see his point.

Chicago (they shortened the name after the threat of a law suit), along with Blood, Sweat & Tears, created the jazz rock genre—but Chicago was always a rock band with horns. Linking the bands was James William Guercio, producer and manager at varying times in their careers. He mentored them, secured a deal with Columbia, and steered them to becoming one of the most successful homegrown bands in the U.S. With current total sales of 100 million units, statistics are almost meaningless, but what was impressive was the run of five consecutive U.S. No. 1 albums between 1972 and 1975, three No. 1 singles, and being the first U.S. band to have Top Forty albums spanning five decades.

Chicago was always a tight unit chiefly because they were all friends and enjoyed remarkably few lineup changes. Guercio gave them the confidence and sheen to become the next big thing. His style could be heavy handed, however. Three double and one quadruple album in three years was over-ambitious and listening fatigue (at least with the music press) was setting in. The band pulled few musical surprises after the first album and churned out a string of highly polished, commercially successful follow-ups labeled consecutively with Roman numerals—currently up to XXXIV—and prefixed by their name as a logo in varying graphic designs by Nick Fasciano. It became corporate rock with vocalist **Peter Cetera**'s songwriting coming to the fore, exemplified by "If You Leave Me Now," his lush, Grammy-winning first No. 1 single in 1976.

They might have pulled back from the brink of being the "Mantovanis of Rock" if Kath, an avid gun collector, had not accidentally shot himself dead. After that the band really lost their way in MOR aimed at Middle America. Cetera left amid bitterness in 1985, showing his true colors with two further U.S. No. 1 ballads in 1986: "The Glory of Love" and "The Next I Fall" with Christian singer Amy Grant. **JaH**

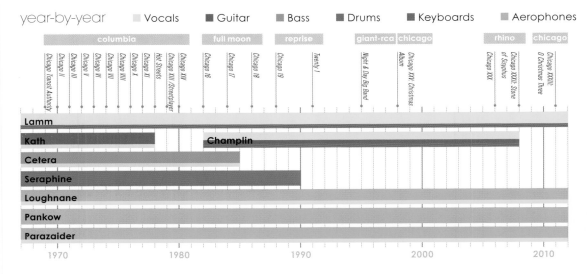

year-by-year   ■ Vocals   ■ Guitar   ■ Bass   ■ Drums   ■ Keyboards   ■ Aerophones

columbia   full moon   reprise   giant-rca   chicago   rhino   chicago

Chicago Transit Authority · Chicago II · Chicago III · Chicago V · Chicago VI · Chicago VII · Chicago VIII · Chicago X · Chicago XI · Hot Streets · Chicago XIII/Streetplayer · Chicago XIV · Chicago 16 · Chicago 17 · Chicago 18 · Chicago 19 · Twenty 1 · Night & Day Big Band · Chicago XXV: Christmas Album · Chicago XXVI · Chicago XXX · Chicago XXVII: Stone of Sisyphus · Chicago XXXIII: O Christmas Three

Lamm
Kath   Champlin
Cetera
Seraphine
Loughnane
Pankow
Parazaider

1970   1980   1990   2000   2010

the clash 1976–1986

Mick Jones
b. June 26, 1955

Joe Strummer
b. August 21, 1952
d. December 22, 2002

Paul Simonon
b. December 15, 1955

Terry Chimes
b. July 5, 1956

Keith Levene
b. July 18, 1957

Rob Harper
b. Unknown

Purveyors of muscular, exciting punk rock, The Clash were the most political of all the major groups of the era. As Pete Townshend of The Who put it, "When you listen to The Clash, you're facing up to life, and at the same time being given strength to deal with it."

The Clash formed in London in 1976. Guitarist **Mick Jones**'s manager, Bernie Rhodes, who had already recruited **Paul Simonon** so that Jones could teach him to play bass, brought in **Joe Strummer** from pub rock stalwarts The 101'ers on vocals. Guitarist **Keith Levene** (who later joined John Lydon in Public Image Ltd) and drummer **Terry Chimes** completed the lineup, although Levene was soon fired.

If 1976 was the year that changed the direction of rock music because of the punk explosion, then the principal U.K. providers of the dynamite were The Clash and Sex Pistols. One of punk's credos was that boring "musicianship" led to earnest navel-gazing of the "multiple concept album with endless solos" variety. So punk championed a DIY "pick up and play" ethos in response, with sometimes rudimentary results. Yet the members of The Clash could play.

After a premature opening gig supporting the Sex Pistols, they rehearsed furiously before going on an infamous tour with the same headliners, where nearly every other concert was called off. Chimes quit, disgusted by the punk habits of spitting and bottle throwing, to be replaced by **Rob Harper**, although he returned to play on their first album. Soon afterwards **Nicky "Topper" Headon** took over on drums.

Their debut LP *The Clash* came out in the U.K. in 1977. It was an instant hit in their homeland, the adrenaline rush of the opening lyrics to the first track "Janie Jones" ("he's in love with a rock 'n' roll world") never letting go of the listener. Not released in the U.S., allegedly because of the lack of radio-friendly songs, the album eventually came out there in 1979 after it had become the highest ever seller on import. *Give 'Em Enough Rope*—produced by Sandy Pearlman, best known for his work with New York's sophisticated heavy metal outfit Blue Öyster Cult—followed in 1978 and solidified the group's appeal.

The Clash's third (double) album came out in December 1979 in the United Kingdom and a month later in the United States. Heralded by its anthemic title track, *London Calling* was produced by Guy Stevens, who had guided the early career of Mott the Hoople. It was a break-out hit in the U.S. after

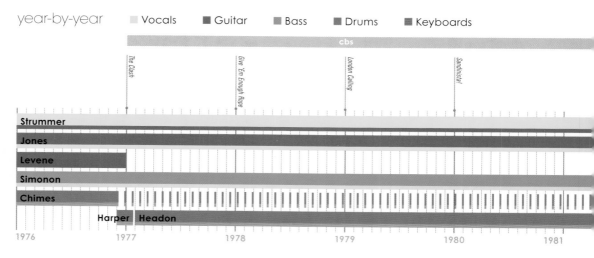

year-by-year   ▪ Vocals   ▪ Guitar   ▪ Bass   ▪ Drums   ▪ Keyboards

cbs

The Clash

Give 'Em Enough Rope

London Calling

Sandinista!

Strummer

Jones

Levene

Simonon

Chimes

Harper   Headon

1976   1977   1978   1979   1980   1981

1.4M	750,000	2.1M	3.7M
The Clash (1977)	Give 'Em Enough Rope (1978)	London Calling (1979)	Combat Rock (1982)

Nicky "Topper" Headon
b. May 30, 1955

Pete Howard
b. Unknown

Nick Sheppard
b. 1960

Vince White
b. 1960

receiving extravagant praise, and is still regarded as their most artistically successful statement. By contrast, *Sandinista!*, released at the end of 1980 in the U.K. (and, again, a month later in the U.S.) was more diffuse and experimental. The irony that this was a triple album was not lost on diehard and former punks, although the sprawling record contained many good songs. In typical fan-friendly style, both these albums cost only the price of a single LP.

Years of constant touring were beginning to take their toll. Headon was fired in April 1982 because of his addiction to heroin. Chimes, perhaps relieved that bottles and spitting were no longer prevalent, briefly returned. The group's fifth album, *Combat Rock*, was released later that same year. It turned out to be their most successful commercially and also spawned two hits, "Rock the Casbah" and "Should I Stay or Should I Go?" Jones confessed that the latter song, which would go on to become the band's only chart-topping record, described his tempestuous relationship with American singer Ellen Foley.

However, tensions between the two chief songwriters had been steadily rising and something had to give. Jones left The Clash in 1983 and formed

Big Audio Dynamite two years later, after dabbling with the group General Public. Chimes quit for the final time; Strummer and Simonon recruited **Pete Howard** on drums, and **Nick Sheppard** and **Vince White** on guitars, to carry on.

Despite some belligerence on behalf of the miners in 1984 (there was a huge U.K. strike), the best days of the group were now over. After a chaotic recording schedule, *Cut the Crap* came out in 1985—it turned out to be The Clash's final studio album. Although they put on The Busking Tour to support its release, the material was not as strong as in their heyday. The Clash had always relied more than most on fire and brimstone, and Strummer and Simonon no longer had the will to keep going. The group split in 1986, leaving a body of work remarkable for its consistency and memories of a tremendous stage presence. Their reputation has grown in the years since then.

Strummer died from heart complications in 2002. That same year, the group and director Don Letts received a Grammy for *Westway to the World* in the Best Long Form Video category, followed by Rock and Roll Hall of Fame induction a year later—belated recognition for their enduring popularity. **MiH**

■ Other percussion

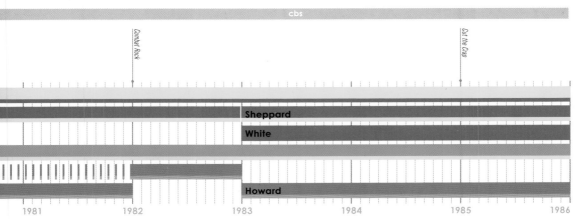

The Clash (1977)

Give 'Em Enough Rope (1978)

London Calling (1979)

Sandinista! (1980)

Combat Rock (1982)

Cut the Crap (1985)

Left to right **Paul Simonon, Joe Strummer, Topper Headon,** and **Mick Jones** in 1977.

Jones, Strummer, and **Simonon** hold the frontline at Rafters, Manchester, on July 3, 1978.

Strummer plays the New York Palladium on September 20, 1979.

London posing: The Clash outside the city's Notre Dame Hall off Leicester Square.

Doing the business: **Jones, Strummer,** and **Simonon** set things to rights in 1980.

Jones and **Strummer** at the Warfield Theater, San Francisco, on March 2, 1980.

Jones, Simonon, Terry Chimes, and **Strummer** at JFK Stadium, Philadelphia, in 1982.

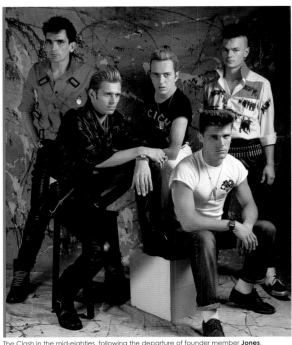

The Clash in the mid-eighties, following the departure of founder member **Jones**.

joe cocker 1959–present

Joe Cocker
b. May 20, 1944

Chris Stainton
b. March 22, 1944

Alan Spenner
b. May 7, 1948

Neil Hubbard
b. Unknown

Henry McCullough
b. July 21, 1943

Bruce Rowland
b. May 22, 1941

Leon Russell
b. April 2, 1942

Standing still while whirling his arms has made this Yorkshireman's performing style widely parodied, but his gritty vocals are inimitable and unforgettable—and his soulful delivery was credited with raising Beatles material to an even more exalted plane.

Cocker formed his first band in 1959. By the early sixties they were playing pubs in his native Sheffield as Vance Arnold and The Avengers. Signed by Decca in 1964, their debut single—a cover of The Beatles' "I'll Cry Instead" (featuring session guitarist Jimmy Page)—was a flop. Cocker, having given up his day job as a gas fitter, opted to try his luck in London. There, he and keyboardist **Chris Stainton**, a fellow Sheffield lad, formed The Grease Band—also featuring bassist **Alan Spenner**, guitarists **Neil Hubbard** and **Henry McCullough**, and drummer **Bruce Rowland**—then co-wrote "Marjorine," a minor U.K. hit.

The breakthrough came with their version of Lennon and McCartney's "With a Little Help from My Friends" (featuring Page and Steve Winwood), which hit No. 1 in the U.K. An album of the same name reached the U.S. Top Forty, then a stunning performance at the 1969 Woodstock festival propelled a second album, *Joe Cocker!* (featuring **Leon Russell**), to No. 11. Another Beatles song, "She Came in Through

the Bathroom Window," was a Top Thirty hit in the U.S., while the live *Mad Dogs and Englishmen* got to No. 2.

As Cocker's career took off, his health deteriorated, mainly through alcohol abuse, and his decline enabled Russell to steal the show when on tour. After 1974's *I Can Stand a Little Rain*, sales waned, and Cocker became notorious for vomiting on stage. Having returned home to live quietly with his family, he had got his act together by the early eighties. He re-established himself with an Oscar-winning, platinum-selling duet with Jennifer Warnes—"Up Where We Belong" (from the soundtrack of the 1982 movie *An Officer and a Gentleman*)—which topped the U.S. chart in 1982. His troubles seemingly behind him and his vocal power undiminished, Cocker, now popular globally, has enjoyed even greater success the second time around.

In 1996 he released *Organic*, a Don Was-produced album of new material, with contributions from a host of big-name guests, including Jim Keltner, Billy Preston, and Randy Newman. Cocker has since continued to do what he does best—interpreting great pop, blues, and soul and making them sound sublime. His admirers agree that, no matter how good the original version of any song, Joe Cocker's is even better. **GL**

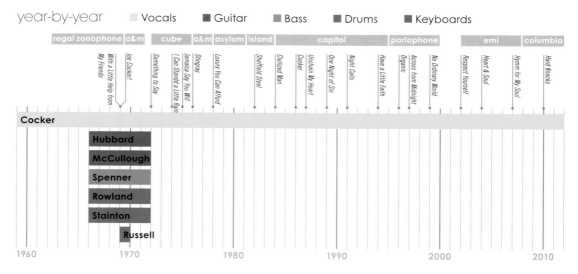

year-by-year ▪ Vocals ▪ Guitar ▪ Bass ▪ Drums ▪ Keyboards

cold chisel 1973–present

Jimmy Barnes
b. April 28, 1956

Don Walker
b. November 29, 1951

Ian Moss
b. March 20, 1955

Phil Small
b. Unknown

Ray Arnott
b. Unknown

Les Kaczmarek
b. 1955
d. December 5, 2008

Steve Prestwich
b. March 5, 1954
d. Jan 16, 2011

Cold Chisel evolved as the ultimate hardworking, hard-drinking, hard-rocking Aussie bar band. Largely unknown to non-Antipodean audiences, they are a national institution in their home country. Formed in Adelaide in 1973, Cold Chisel began life as a blues-rock cover band. They gigged relentlessly, relocating first to Melbourne, then Sydney, but found little success until 1977 when they were signed by WEA.

The band's self-titled debut appeared a year later. Ranging from jazz- and blues-based ballads to hard pub rock, it scraped into the Top Forty. The first single, **Don Walker**'s "Khe Sanh," was named after a battle in the Vietnam War and detailed the struggles of an Australian veteran returning home. It should have been a major hit, but was thwarted by Australian censors deeming it unfit for airplay because of its sex and drugs references. It struggled to reach No. 48 in the chart at the time, but in 2001 was voted No. 8 in a list of the greatest Australian songs.

Breakfast at Sweethearts (1979) gave Cold Chisel their commercial breakthrough. A new, radio-friendly sound helped take the album into the Top Five, but the band disliked its smooth production. Bluff frontman **Jimmy Barnes** was characteristically forthright: "*Breakfast at Sweethearts* stunk—and you can spell that F-U-C-K-E-D!"

East (1980) was notable as the first album on which the whole band contributed to the songwriting—every member would eventually write one of their hits. *East* was also the first album on which Cold Chisel were able to achieve a commercial sound that retained the raw edge of their powerful live shows. It was the biggest-selling album of the year in Australia and provided them with their only overseas success, briefly scraping into *Billboard*'s Top 200. By 1981 Cold Chisel were enormously popular, but they were notorious for their unruly behavior: live on TV, they smashed up the stage at that year's music business *Countdown* award show.

Circus Animals (1982) was another massive success at home, yielding three hits. But continued lack of success outside of Australia and New Zealand fed a mood of growing despondency and, by 1984's *Twentieth Century*, the band were barely on speaking terms. Although the album shot straight to the top of the chart, Cold Chisel announced their break-up.

In the aftermath, Barnes enjoyed a solo career that, commercially speaking, eclipsed his old band, with nine chart-topping albums. Personality issues having thawed over time, in 1998 Cold Chisel re-formed to record *The Last Wave of Summer*, which, supported by a tour, once more topped the chart. **TB**

year-by-year

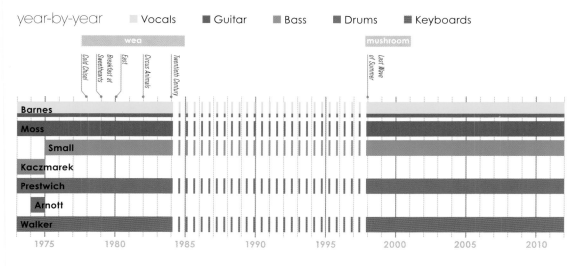

coldplay 1998–present

Chris Martin
b. March 2, 1977

Jonny Buckland
b. September 11, 1977

Guy Berryman
b. April 12, 1978

Will Champion
b. July 31, 1978

From tentative, daydreamy roots at University College London in 1996, Coldplay have become one of the biggest bands in the world. They have effortlessly filled arenas and soundtracked lives all over the globe with their universal but increasingly ambitious music. Only five albums into their career, they stand shoulder to shoulder with U2 and have in truth taken even less time to achieve world domination than Bono and company—Bono said of singer **Chris Martin**, "Chris is a songwriter in the high British line of Paul McCartney, Ray Davies, and Noel Gallagher."

Chris Martin and guitarist **Jonny Buckland** met at UCL in the mid-nineties and kicked around the idea of forming a band from the first moment. Shaky starts as Pectoralz and Starfish were soon brushed under the carpet as bassist **Guy Berryman**, then drummer **Will Champion**, joined in 1998 to form a unit that has remained rock solid ever since.

Their debut release, the *Safety* EP in 1998, was a limited issue designed to reach out to labels, but their break soon came when they performed at the Falcon pub in Camden, London, that December. In attendance, Fierce Panda Records chief Simon Williams was seriously impressed and the young band were signed up to record their *Brothers and Sisters* EP in the new year. That release tickled the U.K. Top 100 and—completing an extraordinary trajectory—

Coldplay signed to Parlophone within a few months, pausing only briefly to finish their university degrees.

Another EP—*The Blue Room*—followed, as well as a debut performance at the Glastonbury festival, an event that they would come to dominate, before they recorded debut album *Parachutes*. Their first proper single, "Shiver," made the lower reaches of the U.K. Top Forty in spring 2000, but it was the follow-up "Yellow" that got them noticed, becoming Coldplay's first Top Ten hit. The groundwork was complete for *Parachutes*, which duly topped the U.K. chart, stopped just short of the Top Fifty in the U.S., and was later nominated for the U.K.'s Mercury Prize.

Parachutes' worldwide success was initially a source of pressure, but a strong work ethic and early satisfaction with what would be its first single, "In My Place," kept the band focused on the second album *A Rush of Blood to the Head* (2002). They trailed its release with a feverishly received Glastonbury headline slot, where they aired their new, assured songs—including the stunningly melodic "Clocks" and piano ballad "The Scientist"—to a wider TV audience for the first time. The band's fresh confidence was well placed. On its August release, the muscular, stadium-filling material propelled *A Rush of Blood to the Head* to the top spot in the U.K., Top Five in the U.S., and multi-million global sales in a few months.

year-by-year ■ Vocals ■ Guitar ■ Bass ■ Drums ■ Keyboards

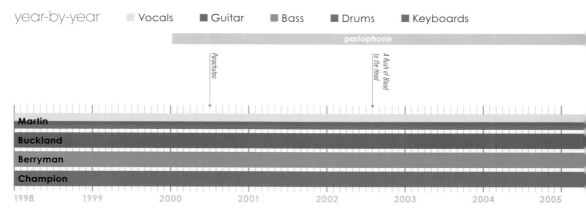

8.2M
Parachutes
(2000)

12.4M
A Rush of Blood to the Head
(2002)

10.8M
X&Y
(2005)

7.6M
Viva La Vida or Death and All His Friends
(2008)

Then there were the awards: Best British Album at the Brits, Best Alternative Music Album at the Grammys, and further Grammys for the singles "In My Place" and "Clocks." If the hardworking Coldplay had not quite conquered all before them in 2000, they certainly had now. Marking the end of their relentless tour cycle, Martin was to cap his rise to super-stardom when he married Hollywood actress Gwyneth Paltrow in December 2003.

When the hectic schedule let up for a year, Coldplay cooked up a third album. *X&Y* (2005) topped the chart in every territory and became the best-selling album worldwide that year. A good thing, too—the story was that EMI's share price depended on it—but critics did not give it an easy ride. There was fierce scrutiny of Martin's everyman style of lyric, and disquiet at a perceived lack of killer tunes (despite the inclusion of the anthemic "Fix You," which reached the Top Five in the U.K. and the Top Twenty in the U.S. Martin was unsettled, too, by EMI's obsession with its bottom line: "Shareholders, stocks—all that stuff—it has nothing to do with me." Still, EMI were undoubtedly delighted with the results.

But something must have stung because, next time out, Coldplay went for a change of direction. Taking the well-worn U2 route, they co-opted super-producer Brian Eno to add magic dust to *Viva La Vida or Death and All His Friends* (2008) and the results were dramatic. The more ordinary lines of their mass-appeal rock were bent out of shape, songs were extended, risks taken—and the audience went with them. The title track went to No. 1 in the U.K. on downloads alone when released exclusively via iTunes; it would later achieve a kind of notoriety after American virtuoso guitarist Joe Satriani claimed it had appropriated portions of his "If I Could Fly." That case was eventually settled, and the song went on to gain two Grammy awards. The bold move to bring in Eno certainly paid off, as once more Coldplay topped album charts all over the world.

Similar accolades greeted 2011's *Mylo Xyloto*, another Eno collaboration, which delved further into a brighter pop style and included a duet with R&B star Rihanna (Martin had long professed a love of pop—Jay-Z and Girls Aloud supported Coldplay in the U.K. in 2009). The album's path was eased by the sparkling single "Every Teardrop Is a Waterfall" in the summer and a return to top billing at Glastonbury, and Coldplay dominated the global charts yet again. Martin coquettishly hinted that it might be Coldplay's last album, perhaps in the belief that their stock might never be higher. A pity if that were to be the case, though, because there appear to be many more classic tunes still to come. **MaH**

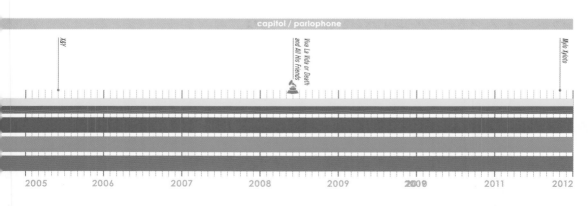

Parachutes (2000)

A Rush of Blood to the Head (2002)

X&Y (2005)

Viva La Vida or Death and All His Friends (2008)

Mylo Xyloto (2011)

Ivy-clad Coldplay (left to right) **Guy Berryman**, **Will Champion**, **Chris Martin**, and **Jonny Buckland** in July 2000.

Champion, **Martin**, and **Berryman** at the KROQ-FM Almost Acoustic Xmas XI annual concert at Universal City, California, on December 16, 2000.

Buckland, **Martin**, **Champion**, and **Berryman** perform in October 2002 beneath large images for the benefit of those at the back.

Champion swaps drums for piano during a special hour-long concert performed for the *Austin City Limits* TV program on December 13, 2005.

Martin plays piano at the Manchester Evening News Arena on December 11, 2008.

Martin and **Buckland** perform in a paper storm at Cologne, Germany, in December 2011.

alice cooper 1968–present (solo)

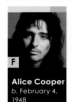

Alice Cooper
b. February 4, 1948

Glen Buxton
b. Nov 10, 1947
d. Sept 19, 1997

Michael Bruce
b. March 16, 1948

Dennis Dunaway
b. December 8, 1946

Neal Smith
b. September 23, 1947

Dick Wagner
b. December 14, 1943

Steve Hunter
b. June 14, 1948

Kip Winger
b. June 21, 1961

Alice Cooper (born Vincent Damon Furnier), the world famous solo star, has far outlived Alice Cooper the group. Both will always be associated with the vivid horror-inspired theatricality of their stage shows, but the original band were also a superb outfit, pitched between hard rock and heavy metal. Their singer (who kept the name after the band split) has maintained both traditions over the ensuing decades.

The group formed in Phoenix, Arizona, in 1968, when Furnier (vocals and harmonica), **Glen Buxton** (lead guitar), **Michael Bruce** (rhythm guitar and keyboards), **Dennis Dunaway** (bass), and **Neal Smith** (drums) were known as The Nazz. They needed a new name to avoid clashing with Todd Rundgren's psychedelic garage rockers, Nazz, so Furnier—alive to a gimmick even then—chose Alice Cooper. The group moved to Los Angeles, where they were seized upon by Frank Zappa and signed to his Straight label.

When the Pink Floyd-influenced *Pretties for You* (1969) and *Easy Action* (1970) sank without a trace, the group decamped to Detroit, Furnier's birthplace, in search of inspiration. They found it—and Canadian producer Bob Ezrin, whose sonic ambitions matched perfectly their warped cinematic visions.

With *Love It to Death* (1971), the group began to reap the rewards of their planning—"I'm Eighteen" and "The Ballad of Dwight Fry" were magnificent calling cards. *Killer* (1971) gave a closer approximation of their mock-execution stage shows. The crunching "Under My Wheels" and epic "Halo of Flies," coupled with the title track and "Dead Babies," took them to the cusp of stardom. Then *School's Out* (1972) sent them into the stratosphere; plundering *West Side Story* for material, it introduced axe hero **Dick Wagner** on "My Stars," and yielded an evergreen anthem in the form of its U.K. chart-topping title track.

Those few years were a time of staggering success for Alice Cooper. Their shows were the most eagerly awaited demonstrations of stagecraft on the planet (the embryonic Kiss took notes when Alice played New York's Madison Square Garden). *Billion Dollar Babies* (1973) topped the charts on both sides of the Atlantic and was crammed with gems, including "No More Mr. Nice Guy." But the group was beginning to fall apart. Buxton was hospitalized with drug problems and needed cover from guitar gods Wagner and **Steve Hunter**, whose dueling had been perfected in defunct Detroit hard rock group Frost. *Muscle of Love* (1973) betrayed the band's state, and Cooper was never without a drink in his hand. The prophetic single "Teenage Lament '74" proved to be their swan song.

With the group further torn between theater and music, the inevitable break-up came in 1974. The four musicians formed Billion Dollar Babies until litigation

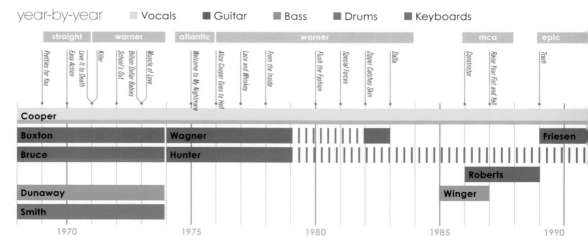

year-by-year ░ Vocals ■ Guitar ■ Bass ■ Drums ■ Keyboards

| straight | warner | atlantic | warner | mca | epic |

Albums (timeline): Pretties for You · Easy Action · Love It to Death · Killer · School's Out · Billion Dollar Babies · Muscle of Love · Welcome to My Nightmare · Alice Cooper Goes to Hell · Lace and Whiskey · From the Inside · Flush the Fashion · Special Forces · Zipper Catches Skin · DaDa · Constrictor · Raise Your Fist and Yell · Trash

Cooper
Buxton — Wagner — Friesen
Bruce — Hunter
Roberts
Dunaway — Winger
Smith

1970   1975   1980   1985   1990

C

Kane Roberts	Pete Friesen	Eric Singer	Ryan Roxie	Eric Dover	Damon Johnson	Keri Kelli	Orianthi
b. unknown	b. November 19, 1965	b. May 12, 1958	b. December 1, 1965	b. January 19, 1967	b. July 13, 1964	b. September 7, 1961	b. January 22, 1985

forced them to drop the name, while Furnier stayed as Alice Cooper and launched his solo career. The concept album *Welcome to My Nightmare* (1975) continued in the great tradition, underpinned by the brooding "Only Women Bleed." Hunter and Wagner, fresh from a towering stint together with Lou Reed, joined his backing band.

The prolific Cooper issued two albums in 1976—*Alice Cooper Goes to Hell* and *Lace and Whiskey*—and toured with ever more theatrical extravaganzas. But, by 1977, his heavy drinking had lurched into full-blown alcoholism. He checked himself into a New York clinic and dried out—typically, even this resulted in an album (co-written by Elton John's lyricist Bernie Taupin) based on his experiences and the people he met in rehab: 1978's *From the Inside* (1978). That same year, unlikely praise came from Bob Dylan: "I think Alice Cooper is an overlooked songwriter."

Experimenting in style with varying degrees of success on *Flush the Fashion* (1980) and *Special Forces* (1981), Cooper rushed out four albums in three years before returning to treatment for his revived alcoholism—he claims he cannot recall recording either *Zipper Catches Skin* (1982) or *Dada* (1983). After emerging sober, Cooper left Los Angeles for Phoenix in 1984, to avoid a "Hollywood social scene [that] was nothing but drinking and partying every night."

Constrictor (1986) and *Raise Your Fist and Yell* (1987), and their accompanying tours, revived the live spectaculars for a new generation. With his profile raised, Cooper went for the jugular with 1989's *Trash* (1989). Featuring guests from Bon Jovi and Aerosmith, it included the hit "Poison" and went Top Twenty on both sides of the Atlantic. *Hey Stoopid* (1991) maintained the momentum, its success leading to Cooper's ambitious *The Last Temptation* (1994).

Touring filled the ensuing years, before a renewed burst of creativity. The industrial-flavored *Brutal Planet* (2000) and *Dragontown* (2001) preceded the "classic Alice" sounds of *The Eyes of Alice Cooper* (2003), *Dirty Diamonds* (2005), *Along Came a Spider* (2008), and *Welcome 2 My Nightmare* (2011). The latter—a reunion with Bob Ezrin—featured contributions from electropop singer Ke$ha and country legend Vince Gill. Cooper has also worked with a variety of notable metal names in more recent years, including future Kiss drummer **Eric Singer**, Rob Zombie, and Slash (Cooper re-recorded "Under My Wheels" with Guns N'Roses in 1988 and appeared on *Use Your Illusion I* in 1991). Cooper's shows are still spectacular—**Orianthi**, Michael Jackson's guitarist on his aborted final tour, joined his live band in 2011—and, in belated tribute, the original Alice Cooper group were inducted into the Rock and Roll Hall of Fame in 2011. **MiH**

■ Aerophones

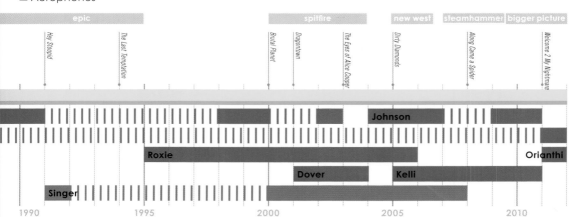

Love It to Death (1971)

Killer (1971)

School's Out (1972)

Billion Dollar Babies (1973)

Welcome to My Nightmare (1975)

Constrictor (1986)

Trash (1989)

The Last Temptation (1994)

Along Came a Spider (2008)

Welcome 2 My Nightmare (2011)

Alice Cooper goes into a typically arresting "straitjacket" routine in 1971.

Cooper with (left to right) **Dennis Dunaway, Glen Buxton, Michael Bruce,** and **Neal Smith.**

Cooper addresses his audience from an "electric chair" in 1971.

Cooper about to apply his career-enhancing eye makeup.

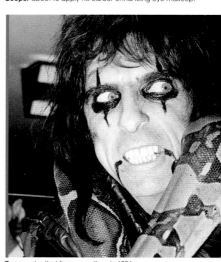

Cooper plus that famous python in 1986.

Cooper makes a theatrical entrance in a 1975 stage show, aided by an assortment of helium-filled balloons.

Taking prisoners in 1989.

Cooper plays the Olympiahalle in Munich, Germany, in November 2008.

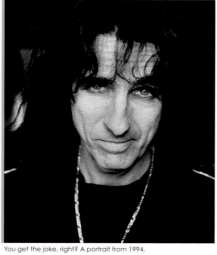

You get the joke, right? A portrait from 1994.

Still scary after all these years at the Cobb Energy Center, Atlanta in December 2011.

julian cope / the teardrop explodes

C

Julian Cope
b. October 21, 1957

Paul Simpson
b. Unknown

Mick Finkler
b. Unknown

Dave Balfe
b. October 2, 1958

Gary Dwyer
b. 1958

Ged Quinn
b. Unknown

Alan Gill
b. Unknown

Jeff Hammer
b. Unknown

A product of Liverpool's thriving post-punk scene, The Teardrop Explodes were put together by **Julian Cope**, a bass-playing art student from Tamworth, Staffordshire, and drummer **Gary Dwyer** in 1978. They recruited keyboardist **Paul Simpson** and guitarist **Mick Finkler** to complete the original lineup. Cope took the name from a caption in a Marvel comic book.

Signing to local independent Zoo Records early in 1979, they came under the management auspices of label co-owners **Dave Balfe** and Bill Drummond. After "Sleeping Gas," the first of three singles for Zoo, Simpson left because of onstage rivalry with Cope. He was replaced briefly by **Ged Quinn** and, on a long-term basis, by Balfe. The Teardrop Explodes' final single for Zoo, "Treason (It's Just a Story)," was produced by rising stars Alan Langer and Clive Winstanley, paving the way for a transfer to major label Fontana in 1980.

During the sessions for the debut album, the pop-psychedelic *Kilimanjaro* (1980), Cope dismissed Finkler and recruited **Alan Gill**. Gill turned Cope onto LSD and marijuana, which were to have a big influence on both the band's music and Cope's lifestyle. Disillusioned with touring, Gill quit in November 1980 after the band recorded "Reward," which, in 1981,

became their breakthrough hit in the U.K., reaching No. 6. A re-release of "Treason" followed it into the Top Twenty and, for a while, the band looked set to become unlikely pop stars. Meanwhile, Gill was replaced by **Troy Tate** and Balfe relinquished keyboard duties while retaining co-manager status. For live work, keyboardist **Jeff Hammer** was recruited alongside bass guitarist **Alfie Agius**, but both were fired after a disastrous U.S. tour, leading to Balfe's reinstatement.

"Passionate Friend" in 1981 was to be their last brush with the U.K. Top Forty singles chart. An ambitious second album, *Wilder*, was released in November 1981 but performed less well. Bassist **Ron Francois** and trumpeter **Ted Emmett** joined for live dates, but by early 1982 the Teardrops had shrunk to a trio of Balfe, Cope, and Dwyer. Sessions for a third album were abandoned after Cope and Balfe both tried to impose their wildly divergent visions of the band. They split up in November 1982, and a posthumous EP, "You Disappear from View," emerged in February 1983. Along with tracks intended for the aborted third album, it formed the basis of *Everybody Wants to Shag… The Teardrop Explodes* in 1990. A CD, *Zoology*, was issued via Cope's website in 2004.

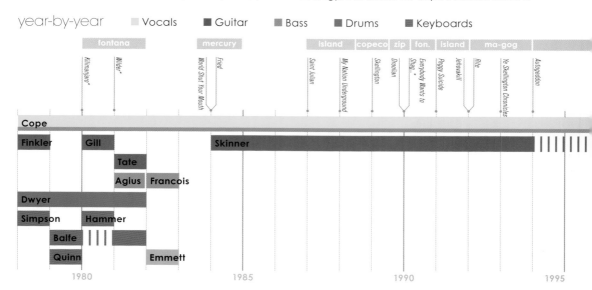

year-by-year   ▢ Vocals   ■ Guitar   ■ Bass   ■ Drums   ■ Keyboards

fontana   mercury   Island   copeco   zip   fon.   Island   ma-gog

Kilimanjaro*   Wilder*   World Shut Your Mouth   Fried   Saint Julian   My Nation Underground   Skellington   Droolian   Everybody Wants to Shag…*   Peggy Suicide   Jehovahkill   Rite   Ye Skellington Chronicles   Autogeddon

Cope
Finkler   **Gill**   **Skinner**
Tate
Agius   **Francois**
Dwyer
Simpson   **Hammer**
Balfe
Quinn   **Emmett**

1980   1985   1990   1995

300,000
Kilimanjaro
(1980)

250,000
Wilder
(1981)

300,000
Saint Julian
(1987)

100,000
Floored Genius
(1992)

C

Alfie Agius
b. Unknown

Ron Francois
b. Unknown

Ted Emmett
b. September 9, 1957

Troy Tate
b. Unknown

Donald Ross Skinner
b. Unknown

Cope's reputation for extreme behavior would threaten to overshadow his post-Teardrops career, particularly as his first solo work, *World Shut Your Mouth*, did not emerge until 1984. Its similarity to The Teardrop Explodes led to accusations that he was treading water, and Cope adopted a more visceral approach for *Fried*, released six months later.

Saint Julian (1987) was a collection of relatively straightforward rock songs and spawned his only Top Twenty hit, "World Shut Your Mouth." Cope was unhappy with 1988's *My Nation Underground*, believing it unrepresentative of his art. In 1989 he recorded the lo-fi *Skellington*, which was issued independently. The conflict between Cope's artistic ambitions and hard commercial realities was to become a recurring theme as the spontaneous, one-take approach he now favored set him at odds with his label, Island, who wanted a more polished final product. A second lo-fi album, *Droolian*, was originally released only in Texas in 1990 as a fundraiser for Cope's incarcerated hero Roky Erickson, former leader of 13th Floor Elevators.

Patching up relations with Island, Cope delivered the career-defining *Peggy Suicide* (1991) which retained MC5-influenced looseness while introducing such personal obsessions as the occult and ecology.

Cope combined mainstream major label releases *Jehovakill* (1992) and *Autogeddon* (1994) with a variety of eclectic projects on his own imprints. *Rite* (1993) was an instrumental collaboration with long-term musical foil **Donald Ross Skinner**. *20 Mothers* (1995) saw the artist broaden his musical palate again and, after 1996's *Interpreter*, Cope went fully independent via his Head Heritage organization.

Liberated from commercial constraints, Cope gave free rein to his experimental side, unleashing such projects as *Odin* (1999), plus three albums by his ironically theatrical heavy metal outfit Blood Donor. Prolific as ever, he kept the music coming—two challenging albums in 2005, *Citizen Cain'd* and *Dark Orgasm*, and the more accessible *You Gotta Problem with Me* (2007) and *Black Sheep* (2008) .

A renaissance man and true British eccentric, Cope is a respected antiquarian, having authored two best-selling books on ancient monuments. He has also penned two volumes of autobiography plus engaging musical guides to German krautrock and experimental Japanese rock. **MHe**

■ Aerophones

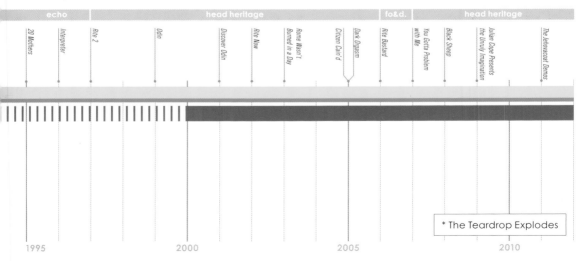

echo | head heritage | fo&d. | head heritage

20 Mothers · Interpreter · Rite 2 · Odin · Discover Odin · Rite Now · Rome Wasn't Burned in a Day · Citizen Cain'd · Dark Orgasm · Rite Bastard · You Gotta Problem with Me · Black Sheep · Julian Cope Presents the Unruly Imagination · The Jehovanoal Demos

* The Teardrop Explodes

1995   2000   2005   2010

elvis costello 1977–present

Elvis Costello
b. August 25, 1954

Steve Naïve
b. February 19, 1958

Bruce Thomas
b. August 14, 1948

Pete Thomas
b. August 9, 1954

Davey Faragher
b. August 18, 1957

Elvis Costello has rarely remained in one place for very long. The son of big band vocalist Ross MacManus, he learned the ropes with mid-seventies pub rockers Flip City, before going solo as D.P. Costello. In 1977, a demo tape secured a contract with Stiff Records, one of a new breed of pioneering British independents. Label co-founder Jake Riviera became the singer's manager, suggesting the irreverent appropriation of the king of rock 'n' roll's given name, largely for publicity purposes.

Costello's debut album *My Aim Is True* was released in July 1977 at the height of the British punk explosion. Although it shared some of the movement's anger and energy, the album's lyrical stance and musical styling set it apart. Costello was backed by U.S. country rockers Clover, whose ranks included Huey Lewis. Later in 1977, the Attractions—comprising **Steve Naïve** (keyboards), **Bruce Thomas** (bass), and **Pete Thomas** (no relation, drums)—were recruited, although only Naïve featured on his first hit "Watching the Detectives" (U.K. No. 15). The Attractions were not jointly credited on 1978's *This Year's Model* but their taut new wave sound was a major factor in its success.

Costello was one of a select few British new wavers to break through in the U.S. and *Armed Forces* (1979) was his biggest success to date, going Top Ten. The following year, however, was to be a problematic

one. Label problems delayed the release of *Get Happy!!*, a twenty-track soul-infused affair, and, while touring the U.S. to promote the album, Costello was involved in a bar room brawl in Columbus, Ohio, with fellow musicians Bonnie Bramlett and Stephen Stills. Costello allegedly used offensive racial slurs, and the resulting negative publicity hampered his career in America for several years.

In 1981 came the drug-fueled *Trust*, then *Almost Blue,* a collection of country and western covers recorded in Nashville. The surprise factor was underlined by cover stickers warning that the record "may cause offense to narrow-minded listeners." Normal service was resumed with the expansive *Imperial Bedroom* (1982), produced by Beatles engineer Geoff Emerick. Brass and female backing vocalists were added on *Punch the Clock* (1983), and "Everyday I Write the Book" became his first U.S. hit single. After 1984's somewhat lackluster *Goodbye Cruel World*, Costello dispensed with the Attractions for all but one track on *King of America* (1986)— relying instead on top session musicians, including Elvis Presley's former guitarist James Burton. The band returned later in 1986 for the splenetic *Blood & Chocolate*, their last collaboration for eight years.

The first two albums of his renewed "solo" career, *Spike* (1989) and *Mighty Like a Rose* (1991), featured

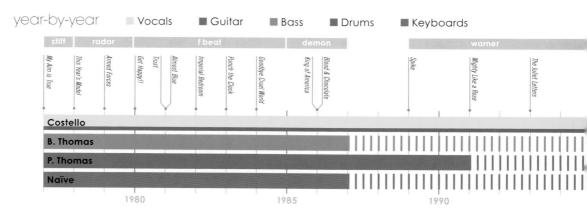

year-by-year   ▪ Vocals   ▪ Guitar   ▪ Bass   ▪ Drums   ▪ Keyboards

| stiff | radar | | f beat | | | demon | | warner | | |

My Aim is True · *This Year's Model* · *Armed Forces* · *Get Happy!!* · *Trust* · *Almost Blue* · *Imperial Bedroom* · *Punch the Clock* · *Goodbye Cruel World* · *King of America* · *Blood & Chocolate* · *Spike* · *Mighty Like a Rose* · *The Juliet Letters*

Costello

B. Thomas

P. Thomas

Naïve

1980   1985   1990

3M	1.5M	2.5M	1M
My Aim Is True (1977)	Armed Forces (1979)	The Best of Elvis Costello (1985)	Spike (1989)

C

some of the fruits of Costello's temporary songwriting partnership with Paul McCartney, including the 1989 single "Veronica," which featured the ex-Beatle on bass and was Costello's biggest U.S. hit. His next major work, *The Juliet Letters* (1993), marked another radical switch in direction. A joint venture with the Brodsky Quartet, the album fused classical and rock.

In 1994, Costello reverted to familiar territory, reuniting with the Attractions for *Brutal Youth*. In rapid succession there followed *Kojak Variety* (1995), a collection of cover versions recorded five years earlier, and an album of songs composed for other artists, *All This Useless Beauty* (1996). The original Attractions lineup completed a final tour in 1996, during which the strained relationship between Costello and Bruce Thomas—exacerbated by the latter's unflattering portrayal of the singer in his 1990 book *The Big Wheel*—reached breaking point. The pair would not work together again.

Moving on, Costello worked with legendary sixties songwriter Burt Bacharach on 1998's *Painted from Memory*. Its lyrics reflected on the breakup of his sixteen-year marriage to former Pogues bassist Cait O'Riordan. In 2002, he debuted a new band, The Imposters, featuring Steve Naïve and Pete Thomas along with bassist **Davey Faragher** on *When I Was Cruel*. The year also saw him achieve the ultimate

accolade with a cameo on *The Simpsons*, starring as himself. The singer's love life again inspired an album, *North* (2003)—a collection of piano ballads drawing on both the end of his previous marriage and his new love, Canadian jazz singer and pianist Diana Krall.

The following year, Costello's classical symphony *Il Sogno* was performed by the London Symphony Orchestra and was issued on CD on the same day as his second album with The Imposters, *The Delivery Man*. Their next work, *Momofuku* (2008), originally available on vinyl and download only, was a quickly recorded back-to-basics exercise. In between, Costello had worked, separately, with jazz musicians Alain Toussaint and Marian McPartland. *Secret, Profane & Sugarcane*, released in 2009, was a largely acoustic affair featuring pieces originally composed for *Secret Songs*, an unfinished chamber opera commissioned by the Danish Royal Opera. The Imposters were back on the sequel, *National Ransom*, which arrived in quick succession in 2010.

Eclectic to a fault, Costello's journey from angry outsider to genial elder statesman (witness his fleeting, self-mocking cameo in the Spice Girls' movie *Spiceworld*) has never been less than entertaining. As fan and U.S. singer-songwriter Liz Phair enthused to *Rolling Stone*, "All of his music tells you, 'You could come along for the ride—but I'm not stopping.'" **MHe**

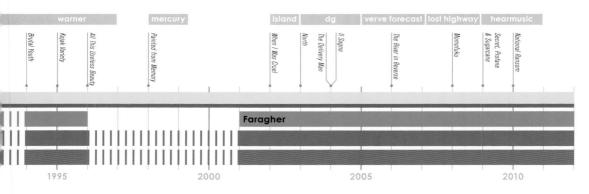

My Aim Is True
(1977)

This Year's Model
(1978)

Armed Forces
(1979)

Get Happy!! (1980)

Imperial Bedroom
(1982)

King of America
(1986)

Spike (1989)

**All This Useless
Beauty** (1996)

The Delivery Man
(2004)

National Ransom
(2010)

Elvis Costello with Attractions bassist **Bruce Thomas** in England, October 1977.

Attractions **Steve Naïve, Pete Thomas,** and **Bruce Thomas,** with **Costello,** on tour in the U.S. in 1979.

Richard Hell and **Costello** at New York's CBGB club in October 1978.

Costello performs live onstage in Boston, Massachusetts, 1980.

Costello in New York as part of an extensive world tour.

On tour in the Netherlands in April, 1996.

With Cait O'Riordan, former Pogue and his then-wife, in London, 1986.

Nick Lowe, June Carter Cash, and Johnny Cash, join **Costello** onstage in London, 1989.

With Dave Grohl and Bruce Springsteen at the Grammys, shortly before recording *The Delivery Man*.

A relaxed **Costello** with Norah Jones in 2010.

counting crows 1991–present

Adam Duritz
b. August 1, 1964

David Bryson
b. November 5, 1961

Charlie Gillingham
b. January 26, 1960

Matt Malley
b. July 4, 1963

Steve Bowman
b. January 14, 1967

Ben Mize
b. February 2, 1971

When California dreamers The Himalayans sat down to write "Mr. Jones" as struggling musicians in the early nineties, they did not know that the song's final line would shortly come true for one of its close-to-home subjects. As prophecies go, the lyric "Mr. Jones and me, we're gonna be big stars" would sadly prove to be wide of the mark for the unfortunate Mr. Jones, The Himalayans' bass player and **Adam Duritz**'s childhood buddy Marty Jones. However for the comically coiffured Duritz ("me"), it was a different story. Blessed with an inimitable, richly toned voice, Duritz left The Himalayans to scale the heights with Counting Crows, an alternative rock group from Berkeley, California, that has sold more than 20 million albums.

Duritz formed the Crows as an acoustic duo with guitarist and songwriter **David Bryson**, who produced three songs on The Himalayans' only album, *She Likes the Weather* (1991). Joined by drummer **Steve Bowman**, keyboard player **Charlie Gillingham**, and bassist **Matt Malley**, and drawing on a handful of demos recorded by The Himalayans ("Rain King," "Omaha," "Mr. Jones"), the Crows set about piecing together *August and Everything After* (1993).

It opened with the live favorite "Round Here," a version of a track that first appeared on *She Likes the Weather*. Impressively, *August and Everything After* boasted a supporting cast that included "Show Me Heaven" hitmaker Maria McKee, Jayhawks Mark Olson, and Gary Louris, unofficial (at the time) Crow **David Immerglück**, and producer/musician of note T-Bone Burnett. No surprise, then, that *August* had been certified seven times platinum by 1996.

Counting Crows toured extensively in support of *August*, sharing stages with The Rolling Stones and Bob Dylan. But, as he launched into "Mr. Jones" night after night, an ever more introspective Duritz began to live the track's tortured message. The lyrics "When everybody loves you, you can never be lonely" and "Believe in me, 'cause I don't believe in anything" prefaced a widely publicized nervous breakdown.

Kurt Cobain's death in April 1994 shook Duritz and forced him to admit that "things in my life are getting so out of control." He began his rehabilitation by pouring his turmoil into the U.S. No. 1 *Recovering the Satellites*, a sturdier, Gil Norton–produced album that also offered glimpses of happier times ahead.

year-by-year ■ Vocals ■ Guitar ■ Bass ■ Drums ■ Keyboards

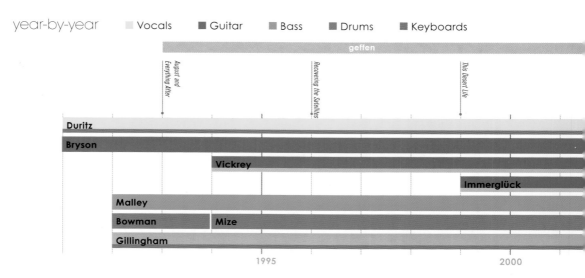

geffen

August and Everything After

Recovering the Satellites

This Desert Life

Duritz

Bryson

Vickrey

Immerglück

Malley

Bowman   Mize

Gillingham

1995   2000

9.9M
*August and
Everything After*
(1993)

3.4M
*Recovering the
Satellites*
(1996)

2M
This Desert Life
(1999)

2M
Hard Candy
(2002)

C

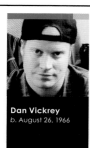

Dan Vickrey
b. August 26, 1966

David Immerglück
b. May 3, 1961

Jim Bogios
b. 1968

Millard Powers
b. December 24, 1965

Satellites-era Crows featured **Dan Vickrey** on lead guitar and Bowman's replacement **Ben Mize** on drums. By the time *This Desert Life* surfaced in 1999—the year they appeared at the controversial Woodstock festival—multi-instrumentalist Immerglück had been persuaded to join the group full-time.

The late nineties also saw the release of *Across a Wire—Live in New York*, an album of tracks culled from their first two studio albums that capitalized on their reputation for energetic, passionate stage shows that frequently featured crowd-pleasing dissections or re-interpretations of familiar Crows hits, their lyrics interpolated with those of other acts. When it comes to songcraft, Duritz is the master craftsman.

As Counting Crows attempted to replicate past glories in the 2000s, they found a faithful ally in movie soundtracks, namely *Cruel Intentions* (*This Desert Life*'s "Colorblind"), *Two Weeks Notice* (*Hard Candy*'s much-derided "Big Yellow Taxi"; Duritz once admitted his greatest extravagance was owning nine copies of Joni Mitchell's *Blue*, so how could she refuse him permission to cover the track?), and *Shrek 2* (the breezy, Oscar-nominated "Accidentally in Love").

The release of a greatest hits package in 2003 was followed by the group's fifth studio album, *Saturday Nights & Sunday Mornings*, which maintained their career-long presence in the U.S. Top Ten and the U.K. Top Twenty, this time with **Jim Bogios** on drums and **Millard Powers** on bass. The album returned the Crows to their acoustic roots with the subdued, country-tinged *Sunday Mornings* half acting as the perfect antidote to the rockier *Saturday Nights*.

Counting Crows ended their eighteen-year association with Geffen in 2009 but remained a live draw, heading out on the ambitious "Saturday Night Rebel Rockers Traveling Circus and Medicine Show" tour with Michael Franti's Spearhead and Augustana, a trek replicated in 2010 with rapper NOTAR.

Since 2010, Duritz, Vickrey, and Bogios have indulged in a number of side projects. But after Duritz recovered from "several prescription drug addictions," attention turned to the group's intriguing covers album *Underwater Sunshine (or What We Did on Our Summer Vacation)*, featuring songs by Bob Dylan, Gram Parsons, Madonna, The Faces, Big Star, and Vickrey and Bogios's *Tender Mercies*. **MW**

■ Aerophones   ■ Strings

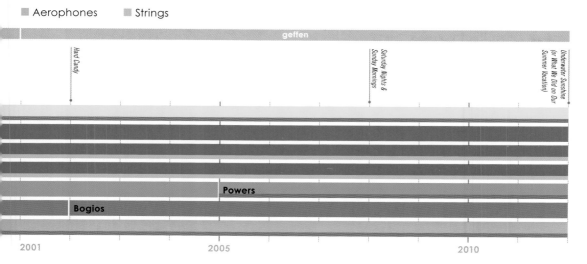

geffen

Hard Candy

Saturday Nights &
Sunday Mornings

Underwater Sunshine
(or What We Did on Our
Summer Vacation)

Powers

Bogios

2001   2005   2010

cream / eric clapton 1966-present

Eric Clapton
b. March 30, 1945

Jack Bruce
b. May 14, 1943

Ginger Baker
b. August 19, 1939

Steve Winwood
b. May 12, 1948

Albert Lee
b. December 21, 1943

Chris Stainton
b. March 22. 1944

"We set out to change the world," **Eric Clapton** noted of the band that confirmed his star status, "to upset people, and to shock them… Our aim was to get so far away from the original line that you're playing something that's never been heard before."

Cream were arguably the first and the finest, and undoubtedly the most lauded, of all the supergroups. Their name perfectly evoked their individual prowess, and their fusing of blues and jazz roots created a new kind of powerhouse rock. The trio was born when Eric Clapton (who had quit The Yardbirds) and John Mayall's Bluesbreakers joined up with Bluesbreakers bassist **Jack Bruce** (who arrived after a short stint with Manfred Mann) and **Ginger Baker**, who had drummed alongside Bruce in bands fronted by Alexis Korner and Graham Bond.

The group made their live debut at Manchester's Twisted Wheel nightclub in on July 29, 1966, ahead of their formally advertised debut two days later at the Windsor Jazz & Blues Festival. Signed to entrepreneur Robert Stigwood's Reaction label (and to Atlantic in the U.S.), they debuted on vinyl with the U.K. Top Forty hit "Wrapping Paper," written by Bruce and rock and folk poet Pete Brown (and, according to Baker, "the most appalling piece of shit I've ever heard"). Around this time, Clapton had become the must-see

guitarist about town, but met his match at a London Polytechnic College gig in October 1966 when newly arrived U.S. guitarist Jimi Hendrix joined Cream for an unannounced and memorable blues jam.

The group's debut album, *Fresh Cream* (1966) shot to No. 6 in the U.K., establishing the band's blend of high-volume blues and rock at the forefront of the music scene. A second Bruce/Brown composition, "I Feel Free," was another hit in early 1967. Meanwhile, Stateside shows—featuring loud and massively extended versions of album tracks—eventually propelled *Fresh Cream* into the U.S. Top Forty.

Cream rose to new heights with *Disraeli Gears*, released in November 1967. It charted at No. 5 in the U.K., went one better in the U.S. (where it went on to sell a million copies), and spawned classics such as "Strange Brew" (U.K. No. 17) and "Sunshine of Your Love" (U.S. No. 5). But, by early 1968, there were stories of strife within the band—particularly between Bruce and Baker—and a split looked inevitable.

Despite the rumors, 1968's double *Wheels of Fire*— the live half of which was recorded at San Francisco's Fillmore West, and included Baker's seventeen-minute drum showcase "Toad"—earned Cream their sole U.S. No. 1. "The band probably was dead already, but it didn't know it," Bruce admitted to author Craig Rosen.

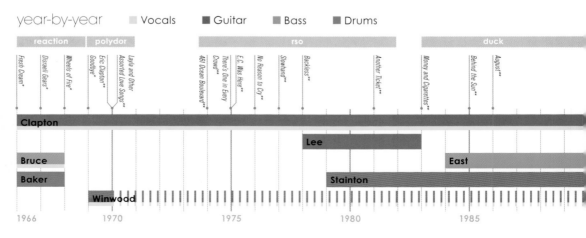

year-by-year   ■ Vocals   ■ Guitar   ■ Bass   ■ Drums

reaction | polydor | rso | duck

Fresh Cream* | Disraeli Gears* | Wheels of Fire* | Eric Clapton/ Goodbye** | Layla and Other Assorted Love Songs** | 461 Ocean Boulevard** | There's One in Every Crowd** | E.C. Was Here** | No Reason to Cry** | Slowhand** | Backless** | Another Ticket** | Money and Cigarettes** | Behind the Sun** | August**

Clapton

Lee

Bruce

East

Baker

Stainton

Winwood

1966 | 1970 | 1975 | 1980 | 1985

6.2M
Slowhand
(1977)

11.8M
Time Pieces
(1982)

24M
Unplugged
(1992)

6.6M
From the Cradle
(1994)

Nathan East
b. December 8, 1955

Andy Fairweather Low
b. August 2, 1948

* Cream
** Eric Clapton

C

"There were things going down through those sessions that probably led to the demise of Cream… Eric didn't do very much writing, and I didn't do much more."

In September the band finally made their much-anticipated "Cream split" announcement after little more than two years together. A farewell U.S. tour, during which "White Room" hit No. 6, was followed by two sign-off shows at London's Royal Albert Hall in November 1968, at which 10,000 fans paid homage. The band's final studio set, *Goodbye,* turned out to be their first and only British No. 1 (U.S. No. 2), aided by the George Harrison co-write "Badge."

Life after Cream saw a series of live sets and compilations surface throughout the seventies and eighties, while Clapton and Baker teamed up with Steve Winwood and Ric Grech to form the album chart-topping supergroup Blind Faith. Bruce forged an enduring solo career, co-founding West, Bruce, and Laing and BLT along the way. Baker went on to form Airforce, followed by the Baker-Gurvitz Army, and Clapton went spinning off into a host of hugely successful ventures involving Delaney and Bonnie and Friends, Derek and the Dominos, and a host of hugely successful solo recordings.

The man known to the rock fraternity as "God" and "Slowhand" survived addiction to drink and drugs while adding to his catalog of classics with the imperious "Layla," the reggaefied "I Shot The Sheriff," and the emotional "Tears in Heaven." *461 Ocean Boulevard* (1974) topped the U.S. chart and hit the U.K. Top Three, while 1980's live *Just One Night* and 1991's *Journeyman* continued his success into new decades. The Grammy-winning *Unplugged* (1992) topped the U.S. chart, and a collection of blues standards, 1994's *From the Cradle,* hit No. 1 on both sides of the Atlantic. More recently, rock albums such as *Pilgrim* (1998) and *Reptile* (2001) have punctuated journeys back to the blues, like *Riding with the King* (a 2000 collaboration with B.B. King) and *Me and Mr. Johnson* (2004).

In 1993, Cream were inducted into America's Rock and Roll Hall of Fame, with all three members reunited for the first time in decades. Bruce and Baker teamed up with guitarist Gary Moore for the faux-Cream of *Around the Next Dream* (1994), but a more serious comeback occurred in May 2005 when Clapton, Bruce, and Baker returned to the Royal Albert Hall to play four shows—all sold out in less than an hour. They completed the revival with three dates in New York's Madison Square Garden in October, to critical acclaim and a rapturous reception from fans. A year later, the trio earned the Lifetime Achievement Grammy for their all too brief period as Cream. **BS**

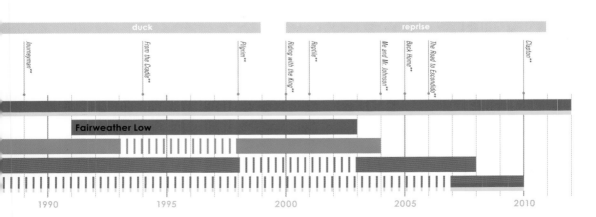

duck

reprise

Journeyman**

From the Cradle**

Pilgrim**

Riding with the King**

Reptile**

Me and Mr. Johnson**

Back Home**

The Road to Escondido**

Clapton**

Fairweather Low

1990   1995   2000   2005   2010

Fresh Cream
(1966)

Disraeli Gears
(1967)

Wheels of Fire
(1968)

Left to right: **Eric Clapton, Jack Bruce, Ginger Baker** in October 1966.

Cream on the streets of London in 1967.

Goodbye (1969)

Cream pose for a portrait in Central Park, New York, in November 1968.

**461 Ocean
Boulevard** (1974)

August (1986)

Clapton chills with *461 Ocean Boulevard* in 1974.

Journeyman
(1989)

From the Cradle
(1994)

Studio portrait taken in 1969 featuring, from left to right, **Clapton, Baker,** and **Bruce.**

Pilgrim (1998)

**Me and Mr
Johnson** (2004)

Clapton gets lost in a guitar solo in 1986.

Clapton with Ozzy Osbourne and Grace Jones in 1989.

Bonnie Raitt joins **Clapton** onstage at Birmingham NEC Arena on October 13, 1998.

A live TV performance for *Saturday Night Live* in 1994.

Clapton with bassist Nathan East, in Barcelona in 2004, on the *Me and Mr. Johnson* tour.

creedence clearwater revival 1967–1972

C

John Fogerty
b. May 28, 1945

Tom Fogerty
b. November 9, 1941
d. September 6, 1990

Stu Cook
b. April 25, 1945

Doug "Cosmo" Clifford
b. April 24, 1945

Rock has seen extreme bursts of notable productivity. Buddy Holly's all too brief career and The Beach Boys from 1963 to 1965 are just two examples. Arguably, however, nothing tops the run of creativity that Creedence Clearwater Revival enjoyed during their original four-year stint on the charts. During that time, the roots rock band from El Cerrito, California, notched fourteen Top Forty singles in the U.S. and released seven albums, all of which would eventually be certified gold or platinum. In 1969 alone, Creedence Clearwater Revival put out three albums—*Bayou Country*, *Green River*, and *Willy and the Poor Boys*. Each is cherished by fans to this day.

The band had more in common with Buddy and The Beach Boys than just productivity—the reason CCR were enshrined in the Rock and Roll Hall of Fame in 1993 had everything to do with their notable success as a singles act. The songs **John Fogerty** wrote and sang, including such classic rock staples as 1969's "Bad Moon Rising" and 1970's "Travelin' Band," overshadowed their parent albums. (In the view of Pavement main-man Stephen Malkmus, "Fogerty wrote more classic songs in a three-year stretch than anyone other than The Beatles.") That went against the grain at the time, especially in the band's native San Francisco Bay Area, where the full-length album was king. Fogerty seemingly had no interest in

trying to "out jam" local acts the Grateful Dead and Quicksilver Messenger Service—although he proved on tracks like "Susie Q" that he could operate in the psychedelic realm. Fogerty's specialty—and one he would stick to throughout his solo career—was to draw influences from country and rock 'n' roll to create concise, contemporary pop. "Creedence wasn't the hippest band in the world," observed Bruce Springsteen, when he inducted them into the Rock and Roll Hall of Fame, "but they were the best."

Fogerty's talent was so undeniable that it is hard to understand how his bandmates denied it for so long. Chalk that one up to sibling rivalry, perhaps. John's brother **Tom Fogerty** was the primary vocalist on the first recordings the band made, under the very sixties name the Golliwogs. It was not until the quartet switched monikers—to one reportedly inspired by Tom's friend, Credence Nuball; allegedly the inclusion of Clearwater comes from a beer commercial—and, more importantly, changed singers that CCR took flight in 1967. With John at the helm, the band inked a deal with Saul Zaentz's local label Fantasy Records and entered the studio to cut their self-titled debut. The record made some noise on the charts, thanks to an extended workout on Dale Hawkin's swamp rock classic "Susie Q" and a convincing take on Screamin' Jay Hawkins's "I Put a Spell on You."

year-by-year   ■ Vocals   ■ Guitar   ■ Bass   ■ Drums

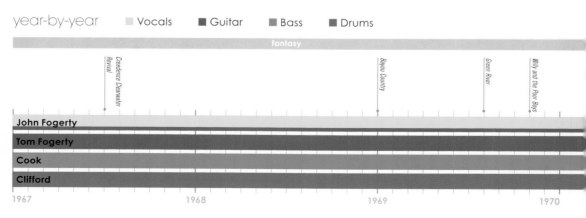

5.7M	**4.1M**	**6.7M**	**11.8M**
Green River	Willie and the	Cosmo's Factory	Chronicle
(1969)	Poor Boys	(1970)	(1976)
	(1969)		

Their sophomore effort, *Bayou Country*, released in January 1969, produced the first Fogerty-penned classics, "Born on the Bayou" and "Proud Mary." The latter would give Creedence Clearwater Revival a No. 2 hit in the U.S.—as high a ranking as they would ever achieve. (CCR holds the distinction of being the band with the most No. 2 singles, without ever scoring a chart topper—it had five second-place finishes.)

Green River, released in August 1969, hit No. 1 in the U.S., thanks to such Fogerty gems as "Bad Moon Rising"—which went on to feature in the soundtrack of at least ten movies, perhaps most memorably 1981's *An American Werewolf in London*—and the title song (both were No. 2 hits). "Out of all the albums I've done," Fogerty reflected to writer Craig Rosen over two decades later, "*Green River* is my favorite."

Creedence finished 1969 by delivering *Willy and the Poor Boys* in November, which included two of Fogerty's most memorable compositions—the rollicking "Down on the Corner" and the Vietnam protest anthem "Fortunate Son," which was ranked No. 99 on *Rolling Stone*'s list of "500 Greatest Songs of All Time" (and covered by U2, among many others).

Those three albums, as well as a heavy tour schedule that included a high-profile late-night set at Woodstock, quickly transformed Creedence into one of America's biggest bands. The momentum was further boosted by another excellent batch of singles, including "Up Around the Bend" in April 1970 and "Lookin' Out My Back Door" in July the same year. The group's fifth album, *Cosmo's Factory* (named after drummer **Doug "Cosmo" Clifford**), duly vaulted to the top of the U.S. charts. *Pendulum*, containing the stand-outs "Have You Ever Seen the Rain?" and "Hey Tonight," followed a few months later, eventually peaking at No. 5. Fogerty's success as the main—perhaps, sole—driving force behind the music, however, had a downside. Clifford, bassist **Stu Cook**, and, especially, brother Tom resented being shut out of the creative process and Tom quit the band in 1971.

John called on his two remaining bandmates to contribute songs to 1972's *Mardi Gras*—Creedence's seventh and final studio recording. The result was a commercial disappointment by the band's now high standards, failing to break into the U.S. Top Ten. It was slammed by critics, who were shocked at the album's dearth of memorable songs. *Mardi Gras* proved to be Creedence's last party—the band announced their breakup six months after its release. Fogerty went on to a lengthy and successful solo career (including penning "Rockin' All Over the World," as immortalized by British rockers Status Quo), albeit one that has always been overshadowed by the work he accomplished during four years with CCR. **JiH**

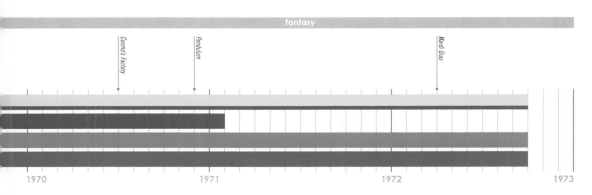

fantasy

Cosmo's Factory | Pendulum | Mardi Gras

1970 | 1971 | 1972 | 1973

crosby, stills, nash & young 1968–present

David Crosby
b. August 14, 1941

Stephen Stills
b. January 3, 1945

Graham Nash
b. February 2, 1942

Neil Young
b. November 12, 1945

Dallas Taylor
b. April 7, 1948

Greg Reeves
b. 1955

Johnny Barbata
b. April 1, 1945

Calvin "Fuzzy" Samuels
b. Unknown

"Not a group, just one aggregate of friends" was how **David Crosby** once described this collective, named like a law firm. **Graham Nash** recalls a more volatile Crosby description: "It's like juggling four bottles of nitroglycerin. If you drop one, they all go up."

When Californian Crosby and Texan **Stephen Stills** persuaded Englishman Nash to join them in a new group—born with a confidence based on their former respective roles in The Byrds, Buffalo Springfield, and The Hollies—they created something revolutionary. In a period when artists were wresting power from the business, the trio made music together on their terms and tested it on their peers around the poolsides and verandas of Laurel Canyon and then in a tiny flat in London. They had the songs and wanted a record deal but would not be rushed. When the Beatles' Apple label came calling and declined to sign them they bided their time and went with Atlantic Records, who provided them with the support they needed to release their sparkling 1969 debut album *Crosby, Stills, & Nash*. The songs were radio friendly, (Nash's "Marrakesh Express"), beautifully understated

(Crosby's "Guinevere"), and intricate (Stills' love song to folkie Judy Collins, "Suite: Judy Blue Eyes").

Before the album was released, **Neil Young**—like Stills, formerly of Buffalo Springfield—had joined, primarily to beef up the sound for shows like their second booking, Woodstock. The *Billboard* chart-topping *Déjà Vu* (1970) carried the names of Crosby, Stills, Nash, & Young, bassist **Greg Reeves**, and drummer **Dallas Taylor** on a cover depicting all six as American Civil War characters. Less reliant on the acoustic side, the album rocked on tracks like Crosby's "Almost Cut My Hair" and Joni Mitchell's "Woodstock." Young began to assert his authority and, soon after *Déjà Vu*, called CSN&Y to a one-day recording session to cut the hit "Ohio"—an instant response to the National Guard shooting dead four Kent State students who protested at the Nixon presidency and the U.S. role in Vietnam.

CSN&Y had never planned to stay together and duly went their separate ways in 1970, all producing stunning solo albums. The CSN&Y void was filled by the live *4 Way Street*, which shot to No. 1 in 1971.

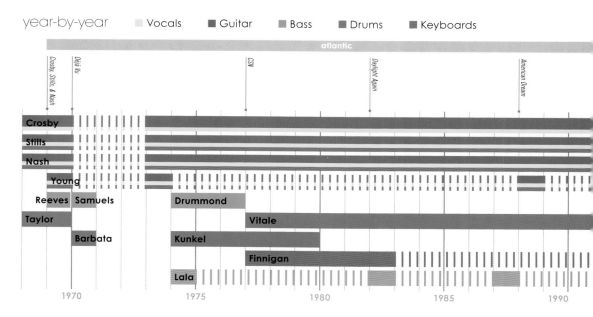

year-by-year ■ Vocals ■ Guitar ■ Bass ■ Drums ■ Keyboards

atlantic

Crosby, Stills, & Nash
Déjà Vu
CSN
Daylight Again
American Dream

Crosby
Stills
Nash
Young
Reeves Samuels Drummond
Taylor Vitale
Barbata Kunkel
Finnigan
Lala

1970   1975   1980   1985   1990

6.8M	**13.5M**	**10M**	**5.9M**
Crosby, Stills, & Nash (1969)	*Déjà Vu* (1970)	*So Far* (1974)	*CSN* (1977)

C

Tim Drummond	**Russell Kunkel**	**Joe Lala**	**Michael Finnigan**	**Joe Vitale**	**Spooner Oldham**	**Donald "Duck" Dunn**
b. April 20, 1941	*b.* September 1, 1948	*b.* March 11, 1947	*b.* 1945	*b.* 1949	*b.* June 14, 1943	*b.* Nov 24, 1941 *d.* May 13, 2012

The four went back to "the mothership," as they called it, for a lucrative 1974 tour, ending triumphantly at Britain's Wembley Stadium. Once content to take a back seat, Young was now the focal point of attention, but simmering tensions got in the way of any recorded output. By 1977, four had become three again, touring for the first time as a trio and releasing the well-received *CSN*. In 1982, *Daylight Again* also had its moments—"Wasted on the Way" showed Nash was still a master of hits—but the magic was missing.

The eighties became a nightmare for Crosby. He was hospitalized and occasionally suicidal owing to drug addiction, preventing any consistently good music from CSN. On the run in 1986, the inevitable happened: Crosby was arrested and sentenced to a lengthy stay in Huntsville State prison in Texas. The stoical support of his bandmates (particularly the long suffering Nash) was boosted by Neil Young's move to get CSN&Y back in the studio to aid Crosby's rehabilitation. *American Dream* (1988) was the result, which had Young's bouncy title track and Crosby's compelling "Compass" to commend it.

Out of fashion in the nineties, CSN were rebels without much of a cause, and lost their raw appeal on the over-produced *Live It Up* (1990) and *After The Storm* (1994). Back into the frame came Young once again for *Looking Forward* in 1999, notable for decent Young songs enhanced by CSN's terrific harmonies on "Slowpoke" and the title track. All four headed out on a thirty-five-city CSNY2K tour of the states. They gave 551,000 adoring fans what they wanted with lengthy gigs featuring a wealth of band and solo material. Buoyed by the response, they went out again in 2002.

The twenty-first century may have produced little new CSN&Y music, but their live appearances have been extraordinary. When Young toured his *Living with War* album, its anti-Iraq war sentiments proved a perfect fit for his old bandmates. They toured in 2006 and made headlines for their controversial performances, captured in the movie *Déjà Vu*, which brought them full circle from their Nixon-bashing in 1970. Four volatile egos had found an almost brotherly love and the various permutations—C&N, CS&N, CSN&Y—seem set to perform live until they drop. **DR**

■ Other percussion

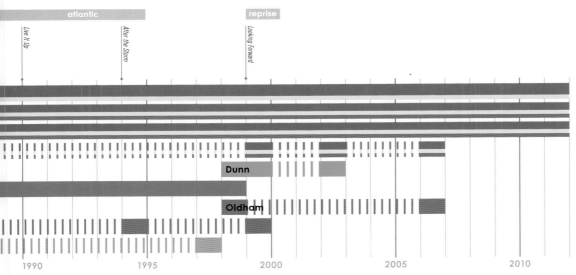

Crosby, Stills, & Nash (1969)

Déjà Vu (1970)

4 Way Street (1971)

So Far (1974)

CSN (1977)

Daylight Again (1982)

American Dream (1988)

Live It Up (1990)

After the Storm (1994)

Looking Forward (1999)

At Stephen Stills' house in Los Angeles, the **Crosby**, **Stills**, **Nash** & **Young** *Déjà Vu* lineup in 1969, augmented by drummer **Dallas Taylor** (far left) and bassist **Greg Reeves** (far right).

Joni Mitchell guests with **Crosby** and **Nash** at Wembley Stadium, London, in 1971.

Nash, Crosby (fingers crossed it works, man), and **Stills** rehearse backstage before a concert in 1970.

CSN&Y with drummer **Johnny Barbata** in 1970, the year they taped the live *4 Way Street*.

"Captain Manyhands" **Stills** at Berkeley's Bread & Roses Festival, 19

Nash steps up to the mike in November 1982.

Foreground, left to right: **Nash**, **Crosby**, and **Stills** perform for Atlantic Records' 40th Anniversary Celebration at Madison Square Garden, New York, in May 1988.

Left to right **Crosby**, **Young**, **Nash**, and **Stills** play at a concert held to benefit the California Environmental Protection Initiative in April 1990.

Crosby performs at Woodstock II in 1994.

Looking Forward: (clockwise from top left) **Young**, **Stills**, **Nash**, and **Crosby** in April 2000.

crowded house 1985–present

Neil Finn
b. May 27, 1958

Nick Seymour
b. December 9, 1958

Paul Hester
b. January 8, 1959
d. March 26, 2005

Tim Finn
b. June 24, 1947

Mark Hart
b. July 2, 1953

Liam Finn
b. September 24, 1983

To paraphrase the song, "Everywhere you go, you always take a Crowded House song with you." Or so it seemed in the early nineties when the New Zealand band seemed to dominate the international airwaves. Five singles from their third album, 1991's *Woodface*—"Fall at Your Feet," "Chocolate Cake," "Weather with You," "It's Only Natural," and "Four Seasons in One Day"—were automatic playlist choices for radio stations.

Woodface was a family affair—and not the first. When bandleader **Neil Finn** had his first batch of songs turned down by the record company, he asked elder brother **Tim Finn** if he could use the tracks they had written together for a prospective Finn Brothers project. Tim agreed, on condition he could join the band. "Why not?" thought Neil. After all, thirteen years earlier Tim had let Neil join *his* band.

That was 1977, when Neil, still mastering the guitar, was invited to replace Phil Judd in Tim's band Split Enz. Finn Jr.'s stage antics slotted comfortably into the over-the-top glam/art rock theatrics of his new friends. His arrival also marked a stylistic change as the Enz' *Dizrythmia*, took a simplified, more "pop" approach to the earlier Australasian-only *Mental Notes* (1974) and *Second Thoughts* (1976—confusingly released outside Australasia as *Mental Notes*).

Originally formed as Split Ends in 1972 by Tim and school pal Mike Chunn, the name-change a few years later was a rare blast of patriotism from guys so young, with "NZ" added to make it clear to the world that they were *not* Australians.

Early elaborate—or chaotic—performances won as many raised eyebrows as fans, and one of the most notable aspects of Split Enz was the high turnover of personnel. The original acoustic lineup of Finn, Mike Chunn, Judd, Miles Golding, and Mike Howard did not last long. Golding and Howard's departures, either side of the release of their NZ first single—"For You"/"Split Ends"—saw the group go electric, thanks to new boys Paul "Wally" Wilkinson, Geoff Chunn, and Robert Gillies. Geoff Chunn and Gillies left in 1974, with Emlyn Crowther picking up the sticks. But it was the arrival of Eddie Rayner (attracted by the band's impressive performance on TV talent show *New Faces*) and Noel Crombie (as much for theatrical input as his talent on the spoons) that made a difference.

By the time the revolving door had finished spinning in 1977, not only had Mrs. Finn's younger boy joined his brother, but Mike Chunn had been replaced by Nigel Griggs, while Malcolm Green—the first non-NZ member—was behind the drums. Astonishingly, this lineup made a tour and the subsequent album

year-by-year ■ Vocals ■ Guitar ■ Bass ■ Drums ■ Keyboards

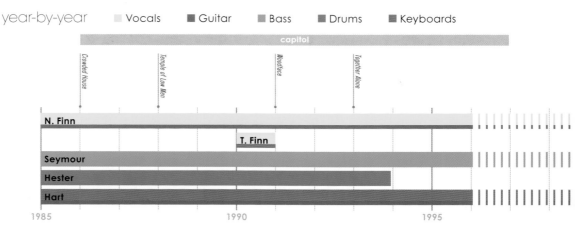

capitol

Crowded House

Temple of Low Men

Woodface

Together Alone

N. Finn

T. Finn

Seymour

Hester

Hart

1985　　　　　　　　1990　　　　　　　　1995

C

Matt Sherrod
b. July 11, 1968

Frenzy (1979), and survived to enjoy true (if short-lived) commercial success via 1980's *True Colours*. Tellingly, this was the first time the fraternal partnership at the heart of the band really came into its own, with Neil's "I Got You" reaching No. 1 at home and Australia.

Crombie took over main drumming duties for *Time and Tide* (1981) and *Conflicting Emotions* (1983) but, for a tour, **Paul Hester** was brought in. With Tim distracted by his debut solo album, writing credits on *Emotions*—including the hit "Message to My Girl"— were dominated by Neil. It was the same story the following year on *See Ya Round*, except by this time Tim had actually quit. The Enz was nigh.

While Tim was enticed back for the band's final tour, of more importance was a chance meeting with bassist **Nick Seymour** after one of the gigs. From the ashes of Split Enz a new group was formed with Seymour, Neil, Hester, and guitarist Craig Hooper at its heart. And that group was... The Mullanes.

By the time the group's first album appeared in June 1986, they were called Crowded House—just like the record. And what a record. Thanks to Neil's "Don't Dream It's Over" topping worldwide charts and making No. 2 in America, the album was still riding high a year later. The downside was that 1988's *Temple of Low Men* had a hard act to follow. However,

only in America did the group suffer: *Woodface* (1991) and *Together Alone* (1993)—and singles including "Distant Sun," "Private Universe," and "Pineapple Head"—achieved phenomenal sales elsewhere.

Tim Finn was replaced by **Mark Hart**, but he and Neil united as the Finn Brothers for *Finn* (1995). Then, after the best-of *Recurring Dream*, Crowded House (now with Peter Jones on drums) bowed out with a 1996 show at the Sydney Opera House (issued a decade later as *Farewell to the World*). Neil's solo career yielded the greatest successes, notably five shows in Auckland in 2001. A star-studded roster included Eddie Vedder, Tim Finn, Lisa Germano, The Smiths' Johnny Marr, and Radiohead's Ed O'Brien and Phil Selway. The results were issued as *7 Worlds Collide* (2001), which became the name for a project that yielded a second album, *The Sun Came Out*, in 2009. This time the lineup included Neil and Tim, alongside Marr, O'Brien, Selway, Germano, and others including singer-songwriter KT Tunstall and Wilco's Jeff Tweedy.

In 2006, something odd happened to Finn's third solo album on its way from the studio: it became *Time on Earth*, the first Crowded House material for a decade. With *Intriguer* following in 2010 and even Split Enz stepping out for reunion appearances, the Finn brothers still seem to be "everywhere you go." **JeH**

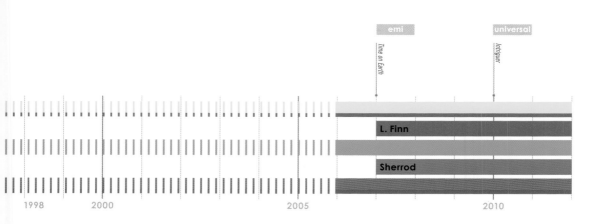

cui jian 1984–present

Cui Jian
b. August 2, 1961

Liu Yuan
b. January 1, 1960

**Eddie Ran-
driamampi-
onona**
b. Unknown

Bei Bei
b. Unknown

Liu Yue
b. Unknown

**Zhang
Yongguang**
b. Unknown

Kassai Balazs
b. Unknown

Cui Jian, a Beijing-born singer-songwriter and multi-instrumentalist, is the founding father of Chinese rock. He has sold more than ten million albums in Asia, and spent much of his career in conflict with the Chinese authorities owing to the political content in his music.

Cui's musical career began in 1981, as a trumpet player in the Beijing Philharmonic Orchestra. In 1984 he formed his first pop band, Seven-Ply Board, which mostly played sentimental ballads and covers of songs from the West. He issued a crudely made album in this vein on cassette in China and vinyl in Korea.

In 1986, Cui found fame thanks to a televised Beijing concert at which he sang his own "Nothing to My Name." The following year, he left the orchestra to concentrate on working with his new band ADO, which included two musicians with day jobs in foreign embassies: Hungarian bassist **Kassai Balazs** and Madagascan guitarist **Eddie Randriamampionona**. The band's music reflected its multinational membership, drawing on Western musical genres from punk to jazz as well as Chinese folk music.

Cui Jian's popularity and influence peaked in 1989, the year of what he described as his real debut album: *Rock 'n' Roll on the New Long March*. "Nothing to My Name" is a love song about a young man rejected because of his poverty, but its yearning tone and theme of deprivation made it an anthem for student protesters in Tiananmen Square. Cui joined the students there on several occasions before the government suppressed the protests. This crackdown forced Cui into brief exile in the Chinese provinces.

In 1990, a national tour was cut short when a government official objected to Cui performing the overtly political "Piece of Red Cloth" while wearing a red blindfold. The rest of the tour was canceled by the authorities, and Cui was banned from airplay on the Chinese media. He was also refused permission to play in Beijing's major venues, but maintained his popularity by means of shows away from the capital and in smaller Beijing venues. He also ventured into acting and starred in the gritty film drama *Beijing Bastards* (1993), playing a troubled rock star.

Balls Under the Red Flag (1995) contained more outspoken lyrics and a sound strongly influenced by American alternative rock, but also prominently featuring traditional Chinese percussion. *The Power of the Powerless* (1999) introduced rap-rock into Cui's mix, earning comparisons to Rage Against The Machine. He toured extensively during the nineties, making repeated visits to Europe and the U.S.

In 2001 Cui composed the music for a modern dance production, *Show Your Colors*. A concept album of the same name in 2005 failed to match his earlier sales. However, he remained a hugely popular live performer, and continued his acting career with the award-winning drama *Dooman River* (2010). **DJ**

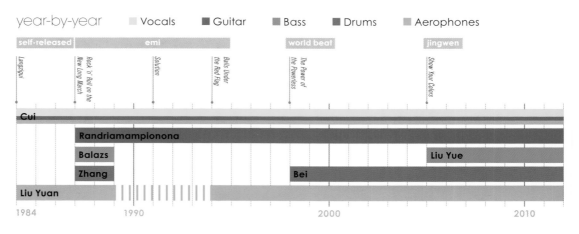

year-by-year   ■ Vocals   ■ Guitar   ■ Bass   ■ Drums   ■ Aerophones

self-released   emi   world beat   jingwen

Langziqui   Rock 'n' Roll on the New Long March   Solution   Balls Under the Red Flag   The Power of the Powerless   Show Your Colors

Cui

Randriamampionona

Balazs

Zhang

Liu Yuan

Liu Yue

Bei

1984   1990   2000   2010

the cult 1983–present

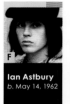

Ian Astbury
b. May 14, 1962

Billy Duffy
b. May 12, 1961

Jamie Stewart
b. 1964

Ray Mondo
b. Unknown

Nigel Preston
b. April 4, 1959
d. April 1, 1992

Les Warner
b. Unknown

Matt Sorum
b. November 19, 1960

Indomitable U.K. band The Cult had a slow gestation, shedding elements of their name before settling into place as the eighties goth/rock act par excellence. All crucifixes and chains, they broke through at the midpoint of the decade before morphing into hard-riffing rock monsters and demonstrating a staying power beyond less adaptable rivals.

Their earliest incarnation was Southern Death Cult, formed in 1981. The name was drawn from Native American mythology, a hardy obsession for singer **Ian Astbury** and one that continued to inform his imagery—and, indeed, image. But the crucial shift came when Southern Death Cult split in spring 1983 after a tour with Bauhaus. Astbury soldiered on, recruiting guitarist and long-term creative partner **Billy Duffy** for a band called Death Cult. The "Death" would slip within a year, just in time for "Dreamtime," The Cult's first single. By this point, **Jamie Stewart** was on bass and **Nigel Preston** had replaced original drummer **Ray Mondo**. At breakneck pace, they ruled the U.K.'s independent charts with "Spiritwalker" and their full debut album *Dreamtime*, released in 1984.

The Cult crashed the mainstream with 1985's *Love*, a startling U.K. Top Five hit heralded by the enduring anthem "She Sells Sanctuary." "You write a song like that where everything comes together far beyond what you could've expected," Astbury admitted to guestlisted.blogspot.com, "and then you spend the rest of your life trying to write another one as good."

The gothic darlings' next step was to grab rock by the throat. Shipping in producer Rick Rubin, they surged back with 1987's *Electric*, a masterpiece of gonzo metal and a masterclass in repositioning. The Cult, glorying in a Top Five U.S. hit album, planted their cowboy boots into the middle of the hard rock scene.

The run-up to 1989's transatlantic Top Ten album *Sonic Temple* saw The Cult lose drummers at a rate of knots: **Les Warner**, who played on *Electric*, was out. Eventually, Mickey Curry played on the album, but was soon replaced by future Guns N' Roses sticksman **Matt Sorum**, who would also come and go over the years. *Ceremony* (1991) was damaged by Astbury and Duffy's increasingly fractious relationship but the hits set *Pure Cult* (1993) gave them a first No. 1 in Britain.

With Craig Adams (ex-Mission) on bass, the band limped to an end with *The Cult* (1994) and split after an abortive South American tour. However, solo ventures had little impact and, in 1999, Astbury and Duffy buried the hatchet and rebooted The Cult with Sorum and Porno for Pyros bassist Martyn LeNoble. *Beyond Good and Evil* (2001) underperformed and The Cult took another break while Astbury enjoyed a stint as a new-generation Jim Morrison in a re-formed Doors.

The Cult were back on the road in 2005 with yet another new lineup—featuring former Rob Zombie drummer John Tempesta and Ozzy Osbourne bassist Chris Wyse—and plowed ahead with *Born Into This* (2007) and *Choice of Weapon* (2012). **MaH**

year-by-year ■ Vocals ■ Guitar ■ Bass ■ Drums

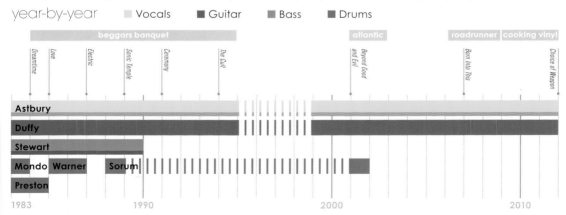

the cure 1976–present

Robert Smith
b. April 21,1959

Laurence "Lol" Tolhurst
b. February 3, 1959

Porl Thompson
b. November 8, 1957

Michael Dempsey
b. November 29, 1958

Simon Gallup
b. June 1, 1960

Matthieu Hartley
b. February 4, 1960

Like few other bands to emerge from the wreckage of the punk years, The Cure have proved surprisingly durable. The band's gloomy, gothic image sometimes masks an unexpected diversity in sound and leader **Robert Smith**'s undervalued way with a pop tune.

Formed in Crawley, a small town outside London, the Easy Cure were formed in 1976 by schoolmates Smith (vocals, guitar), **Michael Dempsey** (bass), and **Laurence "Lol" Tolhurst** (drums). In December 1978, as The Cure, they released "Killing an Arab" on the tiny Small Wonder label, before signing to Fiction.

The Cure's debut album, *Three Imaginary Boys*, emerged in 1979, and an upbeat follow-up, "Boys Don't Cry," added to their repertoire of early classics. That same year, The Cure supported Siouxsie and the Banshees on tour. When the headliners' guitarist quit unexpectedly, Smith stood in for the remaining dates. "I'd wanted us to be like the Buzzcocks or Elvis Costello," he recalled of The Cure. "Being a Banshee really changed my attitude." His new songs marked a departure that didn't sit well with bassist Dempsey, who left the band to be replaced by **Simon Gallup**.

So different was *Seventeen Seconds* (1980) from its predecessor that it might have been an entirely different band at work. Gone were the pop tunes; in their place, stark, downbeat pieces. It nevertheless gave The Cure a first glimpse of the U.K. Top Twenty.

Faith (1981) and *Pornography* (1982) mined a similarly oppressive, doom-laden seam, yet the latter sailed the band into the Top Ten. Meanwhile, touring in 1982, Smith abandoned his previous "anti-image" stance and concocted the towering black hair and smeared red lipstick that made him a goth icon.

The ensuing year saw an unexpected *volte-face*: with no album ready for release, Smith came up with a trio of upbeat pop singles: "Let's Go to Bed," "The Walk," and "The Love Cats." But with the group under strain—not least owing to drink and drugs—Gallup quit and Smith played most of the instruments on 1984's psychedelic *The Top*. The bassist returned a year later and The Cure made *The Head on the Door*, a triumphant blend of both facets of their sound.

The group grew in international stature with each new release. The sprawling, superb *Kiss Me Kiss Me*

year-by-year ◻ Vocals ◼ Guitar ◼ Bass ◼ Drums ◼ Keyboards

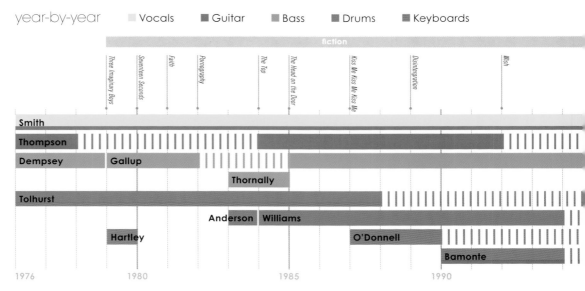

Andy Anderson
b. January 30, 1951

Phil Thornally
b. January 5, 1960

Boris Williams
b. April 24, 1952

Roger O'Donnell
b. October 29, 1955

Perry Bamonte
b. September 3, 1960

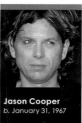
Jason Cooper
b. January 31, 1967

Kiss Me took them into the U.S. Top Forty, as did its enduringly gorgeous hit "Just Like Heaven."

At the same time, Smith reluctantly forced founder member and close friend Tolhurst out of the band when personal issues began to affect his drumming. A return to the moody, gothic atmospherics of their earlier work on 1989's *Disintegration* was met with resistance from the band's U.S. label, Elektra, who considered that Smith was being "willfully obscure." Refusing to compromise, The Cure delivered their best-selling non-compilation album, and an ensuing tour saw them playing 40,000-seater stadiums in the U.S. Unable to comprehend the scale of this success, Smith maintained a low profile for the next two years.

Wish (1992) established The Cure as one of the world's most popular groups, topping the U.K. and Australian charts and peaking across the Atlantic at No. 2. The hit "Friday I'm in Love" illustrated once more that Smith was more than adept at writing classic hits.

The kaleidoscopic *Wild Mood Swings* (1996) and *Disintegration*-esque *Bloodflowers* (2000) continued to illustrate their mastery of skewed pop and gothic grandeur. They were also cited as an influence by a growing number of alternative bands—from Dinosaur Jr. to My Chemical Romance—making it marginally less surprising that Slipknot producer Ross Robinson helmed their rockiest album to date, 2004's *The Cure*.

Both sides of their sound were represented at increasingly lengthy shows, which characteristically clocked in at around three hours. None of their live albums—*Concert* (1984), *Entreat* (1991), *Show* (1993), *Paris* (1993), and *Bestival Live 2011* (2011)—quite do justice to these epic events, although all have their charms. The live *Trilogy* DVD of 2003 perhaps comes closest, with its full-length performances of *Pornography*, *Disintegration*, and *Bloodflowers*.

The torturous conception of *4:13 Dream* (2008)— during which it was chopped from a double to single album—and lackluster promotion led to the band's poorest sales in decades. More excitement was generated by the return of Tolhurst for a series of retrospective shows, and—like their alternative compadres Depeche Mode—The Cure continue to be a mammoth live draw around the world. **TB/BM**

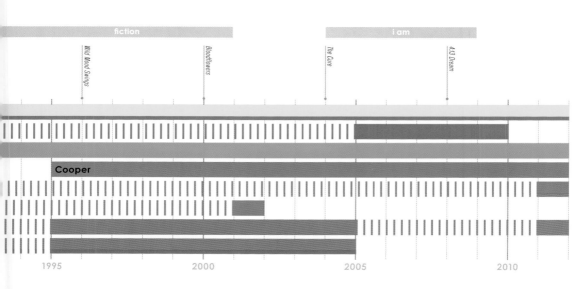

fiction
i am

Wild Mood Swings
Bloodflowers
The Cure
4:13 Dream

Cooper

1995   2000   2005   2010

Three Imaginary Boys (1979)

Seventeen Seconds (1980)

Faith (1981)

The Top (1984)

The Head on the Door (1985)

Kiss Me Kiss Me Kiss Me (1987)

Disintegration (1989)

Wish (1992)

Bloodflowers (2000)

The Cure (2004)

Robert Smith at Birmingham Odeon, England, in September 1979.

Smith and **Lol Tolhurst** with Blondie's Debbie Harry in New York, in April 1980.

Simon Gallup, Smith, and Tolhurst in the U.S. in mid 1981.

Implausible pop stars The Cure in all their backcombed glory in November 1984.

Bringing *The Head on the Door* to Rotterdam in November 1985.

Gallup, Smith, Tolhurst, **Boris Williams** (on floor), and **Porl Thompson** in Brazil in March 1987.

Smith on the road in the U.S. on 1992's Wish tour.

Smith in Chicago on the Prayer tour in 1989.

The Cure bring *Bloodflowers* to Brisbane in October 2000.

Roger O'Donnell, Smith, Gallup, and **Perry Bamonte** perform live in London in September 2004.

the damned 1976–present

Dave Vanian
b. October 12, 1956

Captain Sensible
b. April 24, 1954

Rat Scabies
b. July 30, 1955

Brian James
b. February 18, 1955

Roman Jugg
b. July 25, 1957

Stu West
b. December 24, 1964

Pinch
b. September 5, 1965

Monty Oxy Moron
b. September 27, 1961

British punk milestones for The Damned flew by at the same breakneck speed as the songs they spewed out: first to release a single, first to release an album, first to tour the U.S., first to split, all in eighteen amphetamine-fueled months. This was after **Brian James** met drummer **Rat Scabies** at an unsuccessful audition for the London SS, which included Mick Jones. Scabies knew a south London janitor who swapped his toilet brush for bass guitar and the name Ray Burns for **Captain Sensible**. Cemetery worker **Dave Vanian** rose from the grave to lend vampiric vocals.

Damned, Damned, Damned (1977) was recorded in a blur, with Sensible recalling that producer Nick Lowe bought them "bottle after bottle of scrumpy cider." Time was not wasted on the introductory single "New Rose." "The whole thing was written in fifteen minutes," said James. In the studio, Scabies "smashed his drum kit apart." U.K. punk was born.

Syd Barrett was mooted to produce the follow-up. In the end, Nick Mason oversaw Music for Pleasure. Right Floyd, wrong member. Among the touring replacements for the departed Scabies was future Culture Clubber Jon Moss, but the band fell apart. Individual projects did not ignite, so Sensible, Scabies, and Vanian re-united, with Algy Ward on bass and Sensible replacing James as guitarist/songwriter. Speed remained key on Machine Gun Etiquette, but psychedelia weighed heavier than garage rock.

Those interests were further explored on The Black Album (1980), a seductive delight whose highlight was "Curtain Call." Ex-Eddie and the Hot Rods bassist Paul Gray stayed through this and Strawberries (1982) as the band pulled ahead of their 1976 contemporaries.

With Sensible unable to juggle band commitments with his solo career (including 1982's U.K. No. 1 "Happy Talk"), **Roman Jugg** moved from keyboards to guitar, recommending Bryn Merrick for bass. Success arrived with the ghoulish goth of Phantasmagoria in 1985 and single "Eloise," a U.K. No. 3. But in the world The Damned inhabit, good times rarely last. Anything (1986) was a critical and commercial disappointment.

Scabies and Vanian were the only founder members on I'm Alright Jack & the Beanstalk (U.S. title Not of This Earth), which drew on ex-members of New Model Army and The Godfathers. Keeping track of comings and goings was a full-time job. Out: Scabies, Moose, Kris Dollimore, Allan Lee Shaw. In: Patricia Morrison, **Monty Oxy Moron**, **Pinch**. Back in: Sensible. Offspring frontman Dexter Holland bankrolled Grave Disorder, which was more like peak-period Damned. Morrison—aka Mrs Vanian—handed bass duties to **Stu West**, who featured on So, Who's Paranoid? (2008). Its singular sound summed up The Damned's bloodyminded attitude. Recalled Sensible: "We were just doing what we wanted to hear, because there was nothing around at the time that we liked." **CB**

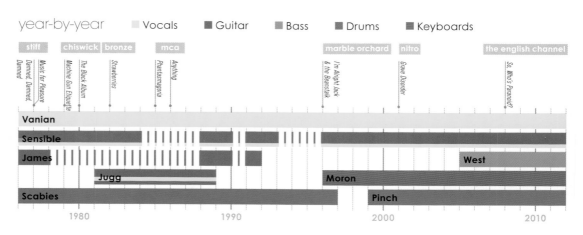

year-by-year ■ Vocals ■ Guitar ■ Bass ■ Drums ■ Keyboards

stiff   chiswick   bronze   mca   marble orchard   nitro   the english channel

Damned, Damned, Damned
Music for Pleasure
Machine Gun Etiquette
The Black Album
Strawberries
Phantasmagoria
Anything
I'm Alright Jack & the Beanstalk
Grave Disorder
So, Who's Paranoid?

Vanian

Sensible

James

Jugg

Moron

West

Scabies

Pinch

1980   1990   2000   2010

dead kennedys 1978–present

East Bay Ray
b. November
17, 1958

**Klaus
Flouride**
b. May 30, 1949

Jello Biafra
b. June 17, 1958

D.H. Peligro
b. July 9, 1959

Ted
b. unknown

6025
b. unknown

One of the greatest U.S. punk bands was formed in the former hippie haven of San Francisco in 1978. Dead Kennedys started out as a quintet, all adopting *noms de guerre*. Frontman Eric Boucher became **Jello Biafra.** He was joined by **East Bay Ray** (aka Raymond Pepperell) on lead guitar, **Klaus Flouride** (Geoffrey Lyall) on bass, **Ted** (Bruce Slesinger) on drums, and **6025** (Carlos Cadona) on second guitar.

6025 left before the June 1979 release of debut single, "California Über Alles," a withering attack on Californian governor Jerry Brown. Their follow-up "Holiday in Cambodia," was a roller-coaster of a song that lampooned Communist totalitarianism and the delusions of privileged Americans with equal venom. Next came critically lauded *Fresh Fruit for Rotting Vegetables* (1980), on which pure punk sonic assault met speeded-up surf pop and scathing social satire.

Ted left at the end of 1980 to be replaced by future Red Hot Chili Peppers drummer **D.H. Peligro** (Darren Henley). The new lineup debuted with "Too Drunk to Fuck," which reached the U.K. Top Forty despite predictable airplay restrictions. December 1981 brought the *In God We Trust Inc.* EP, dominated by full-tilt hardcore punk. *Plastic Surgery Disasters* (1982) was a more varied collection, the lyrics becoming even more caustic as the music diversified.

Dead Kennedys then took an extended break from recording as Biafra and Ray developed their

Alternative Tentacles label into a home for a variety of underground acts. They returned with the well-received *Frankenchrist* (1985), but the melodically menacing music on the album was overshadowed by obscenity charges arising from a free print included in its packaging: *Penis Landscape*, an image of rows of copulating genitalia, created by *Alien* artist H.R. Giger. Biafra vigorously contested the charges and was eventually acquitted, but the lengthy legal proceedings—coupled with growing disillusionment with the hardcore punk scene—drained energy from the band. They split before the November 1986 release of their swansong album, *Bedtime for Democracy*. A gold-selling compilation of non-album tracks, *Give Me Convenience or Give Me Death*, followed in 1987.

In the late nineties Biafra was successfully sued by Flouride, Ray, and Peligro over underpayment of royalties. The resultant bad feeling was one of the reasons that Biafra declined to join in the Dead Kennedys reunion instigated by his former colleagues in 2001. Even without Biafra, however, Dead Kennedys remained a popular live act. Their first new front-man was former child actor Brandon Cruz, followed by Jeff Penalty and then Skip McSkipster. In 2011, Flouride declared that their original singer could return if he wished, but instead Biafra has devised new variations on the Dead Kennedys sound with his own band, Jello Biafra and the Guantanamo School of Medicine. **DJ**

year-by-year ■ Vocals ■ Guitar ■ Bass ■ Drums

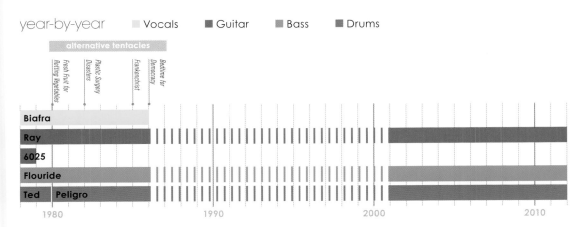

deep purple 1968–present

Ian Paice
b. June 29, 1948

Jon Lord
b. June 9, 1941

Ritchie Blackmore
b. April 14, 1945

Nick Simper
b. November 3, 1945

Rod Evans
b. January 19, 1947

Ian Gillan
b. August 19, 1945

Roger Glover
b. November 30, 1945

Glenn Hughes
b. August 21, 1952

Although Deep Purple helped lay the foundations for heavy metal, their consummate musicianship meant they also transcended the genre. Indeed they began as a progressive rock group with their eyes, unusually, on the singles market. Yet they certainly rocked, as their shows from the earliest days conclusively proved.

The group's roots extend to 1967, when Chris Curtis, latterly of Merseybeat band The Searchers, enlisted **Ritchie Blackmore** (guitar) and **Jon Lord** (keyboards) for a new band called Roundabout. By April 1968, Curtis was out, and **Ian Paice** (drums), **Nick Simper** (bass), and **Rod Evans** (vocals) were in. One name change later, they cut *Shades of Deep Purple* (1968), which rose to No. 24 in the U.S., thanks to the Top Five success of their single, a cover of Joe South's "Hush."

The Book of Taliesyn (1968) was less successful, despite an attempt to repeat the hit trick with Neil Diamond's "Kentucky Woman." Problems at the band's U.S. record label delayed the release of *Deep Purple* (1969), effectively sinking its chances. However, the group were already contemplating a change to a much harder, rockier sound. **Ian Gillan** (vocals) and **Roger Glover** (bass) from Episode Six were enlisted to replace the more pop-oriented Evans and Simper.

Before this change of direction could bear fruit, *Concerto for Group and Orchestra* (1969)—a live recording inspired by Lord's classical training—gave Purple their U.K. chart debut. This prepared the way for their breakthrough: with Blackmore rather than Lord in charge, *Deep Purple in Rock* (1970)—featuring the mighty anthems "Child in Time" and "Speed King"—crashed the U.K. Top Five. The group had now drawn up their own heavy rock blueprint: thunderous rhythm section, virtuoso guitar, swooping vocals, and dynamic organ. But unlike contemporaries such as Led Zeppelin and Pink Floyd, they were not above playing the hit singles game: hence the U.K. Top Ten smashes "Black Night" and "Strange Kind of Woman."

Fireball (1971), boasting a hectic, hit title track, and *Machine Head* (1972), featuring "Highway Star," topped the U.K. chart. The latter also revived their significant U.S. success: it stomped into *Billboard*'s Top Ten, and—thanks to the hit "Smoke on the Water"—earned Purple their first of nine U.S. gold albums. The double live *Made in Japan* (1972) was another big-selling triumph, with its admirers including future stars of Metallica, Def Leppard, and Dream Theater (the latter act covered the complete album live in 2006).

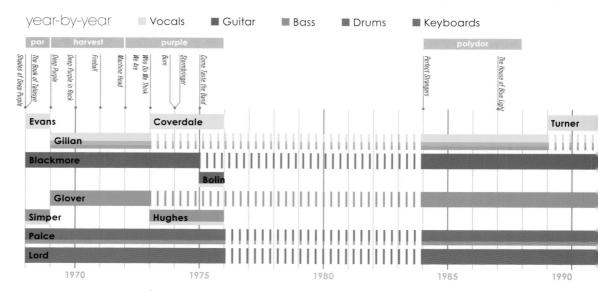

○ 4M
Machine Head
(1972)

○ 3M
Made in Japan
(1972)

○ 2.5M
Deepest Purple
(1980)

○ 2.5M
Perfect Strangers
(1984)

D

David Coverdale
b. September 22, 1951

Tommy Bolin
b. August 1, 1951
d. December 4, 1976

Joe Lynn Turner
b. August 2, 1951

Joe Satriani
b. July 15, 1956

Steve Morse
b. July 28, 1954

Don Airey
b. June 21, 1948

However, *Who Do We Think We Are* (1973)—which included the rampant "Woman from Tokyo"—proved a turning point. The album's success, coupled with that of its two predecessors, made Purple the biggest-grossing act of 1973 in the U.S. But constant touring caused illness and friction, often expressed in arguments with Blackmore over musical direction. That summer, Gillan and Glover quit, replaced by **Glenn Hughes** (bass) and **David Coverdale** (vocals).

It was the beginning of the end, although sales of *Burn* and *Stormbringer* (both 1974) held up well. Songs such as "Burn" and "Soldier of Fortune" carried their old attack and it seemed fans were ready to accept the changes. But Blackmore had fallen out with the rest of the group, and quit to found Rainbow. His place was taken by **Tommy Bolin**, most recently Joe Walsh's successor in The James Gang. The group recorded *Come Taste the Band* (1975) before splitting up early the following year. In a tragic coda, Bolin died soon afterwards as a result of his drug problems.

Coverdale, Lord, and Paice enjoyed success in Europe with Whitesnake, as did Gillan with a band named after himself. After an abortive attempt at a Purple reunion, Gillan briefly joined Black Sabbath.

However, the classic "Mark II" lineup—Paice, Lord, Blackmore, Glover, and Gillan—triumphantly reconvened in 1984, unleashing the platinum-selling *Perfect Strangers*. The follow-up, 1987's *The House of Blue Light*, was an interesting semi-departure as the group tried to come to terms with a changed musical landscape. However, internal feuds were rekindled and Gillan again lost out to Blackmore. By *Slaves and Masters* (1990), the singer had been replaced by former Rainbow front-man **Joe Lynn Turner**.

Gillan was back in time for *The Battle Rages On...* (1992), but it was Blackmore's turn to quit again well before *Purpendicular* (1996). **Joe Satriani** replaced him on tour, then **Steve Morse** came in to work on the record. The same personnel created *Abandon* (1998). The final change to the lineup occurred when Lord left in 2002 to pursue his classical work. Former Rainbow/Whitesnake keyboard player **Don Airey** joined and the group, stable for the past decade, made *Bananas* (2003) and *Rapture of the Deep* (2005).

Purple remain a strong live draw and, in 2012, began work on a new album with producer Bob Ezrin. "There's nothing wrong with nostalgia," Glover told *Kerrang!*, "as long as its not *all* nostalgia." **MiH**

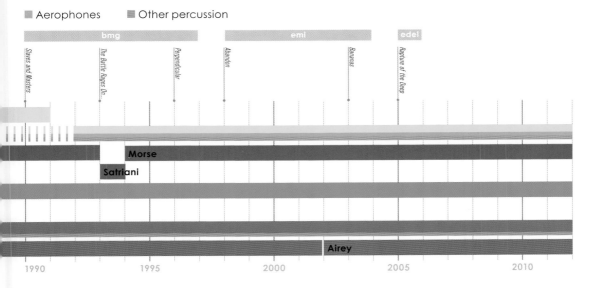

■ Aerophones ■ Other percussion

bmg   emi   edel

Slaves and Masters
The Battle Rages On...
Perpendicular
Abandon
Bananas
Rapture of the Deep

Morse

Satriani

Airey

1990   1995   2000   2005   2010

Shade of Deep Purple (1968)

In Rock (1970)

Fireball (1971)

Machine Head (1972)

"Who Do We Think We Are" (1973)

Burn (1974)

Come Taste the Band (1975)

Perfect Strangers (1984)

Slaves and Masters (1990)

Abandon (1998)

Mark I: **Rod Evans**, **Jon Lord**, **Ritchie Blackmore**, **Nicky Simper** and **Ian Paice** in London.

Mark II: **Roger Glover**, **Ian Gillan**, **Blackmore**, **Paice**, and **Lord**.

Blackmore and **Glover** at work on *Fireball* in London in September 1970.

Gillan unleashes his earthshaking voice in Denmark in March 1972.

The Mark II lineup rocks the Rainbow in London, February 1973.

Mark III: **Lord,** singer **David Coverdale,** bassist **Glenn Hughes, Blackmore,** and **Paice** in 1974.

Blackmore at the Mark II's U.K. comeback show at the Knebworth Fayre, in 1985.

Tommy Bolin, Blackmore's brilliant but doomed successor, in 1975. Less than five months after Purple disbanded in 1976, the guitarist died of a drug overdose, aged twenty-five.

Former Rainbow bandmates **Joe Lynn Turner** and **Blackmore** reunited in Purple.

Blackmore's second successor, **Steve Morse,** performs live in Melbourne, Australia.

def leppard 1977–present

Joe Elliott
b. August 1, 1959

Rick Savage
b. December 2, 1960

Pete Willis
b. February 16, 1960

Steve Clark
b. April 23, 1960
d. January 8, 1991

Rick Allen
b. November 1, 1963

Phil Collen
b. December 8, 1957

A supercharged blend of twin guitars and soaring harmonies, Def Leppard has been one of the most successful rock acts of the past thirty years. The group was formed in Sheffield, England, in 1977 by singer **Joe Elliott**, bassist **Rick Savage**, drummer Tony Kenning, and guitarist **Pete Willis**, and joined in 1978 by second guitarist **Steve Clark**, giving them their classic sound. At the end of that year—after the recording of their self-titled debut EP with temporary drummer Frank Noon—the drum stool was taken by **Rick Allen**.

Championed by BBC DJ John Peel and the music paper *Sounds,* Leppard were lumped in with the likes of Iron Maiden and Saxon in the new wave of British heavy metal. In truth, their sound had a more American sheen, hence the Stateside success of their debut album *On Through the Night* (1980), which fell just short of *Billboard*'s Top Fifty. At home, it hit No. 15, although Leppard soon found themselves victims of a backlash by British audiences, who regarded their extraordinary international ambition as selling out.

Now signed to the same management team as AC/DC, Leppard recruited that band's producer, Robert John "Mutt" Lange, to helm *High 'n' Dry* (1981). Their domestic success plummeted, but MTV's adoption of "Bringin' on the Heartbreak" pushed the album to gold sales in the U.S. The following year, Girl

guitarist **Phil Collen** replaced Willis to provide a key boost and Leppard, as Elliott reflected, "set out to make our version of *Sgt. Pepper's.*"

Pyromania (1983) fell short of that lofty ambition, but nonetheless lit the fire as they had hoped. Lange polished their driving sound, and the magnificent results—including "Foolin'," "Photograph," and "Rock of Ages"—ensured the album stayed in the U.S. chart for nearly two years. Hugely influential on a new crop of bands—not least Bon Jovi—*Pyromania* was kept off the No. 1 spot only by Michael Jackson's *Thriller.*

Now out to conquer the world, Leppard "sat in the studio," recalled Elliott to BBC Radio 1, "and said… Tell me one good reason why a white English rock band can't sell ten million albums." This time, their ambition would be realized, but only after fruitless work with Meat Loaf collaborator Jim Steinman in 1984 and, on New Year's Eve, a car crash in which Allen lost an arm. Though the drummer worked hard to regain his chops, the album only took shape when producer Lange (who had originally cried off, citing exhaustion) came back on board in the summer of 1985. Collen recalled, "[He] said to us, 'We have to make Def Leppard sound different than other rock bands. Let's cross Queen with AC/DC.'" A year later, Leppard restored their domestic reputation at Britain's Monsters of Rock

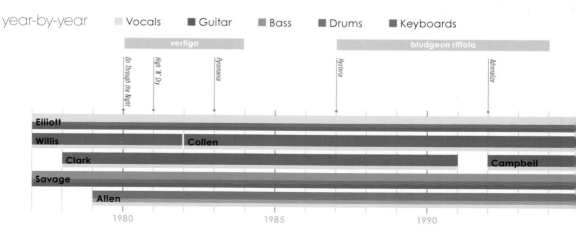

year-by-year ■ Vocals ■ Guitar ■ Bass ■ Drums ■ Keyboards

vertigo

bludgeon riffola

On Through the Night

High 'N' Dry

Pyromania

Hysteria

Adrenalize

Elliott

Willis   Collen

Clark   Campbell

Savage

Allen

1980   1985   1990

13.5M *Pyromania* (1983)	19.2M *Hysteria* (1987)	5.5M *Adrenalize* (1992)	7M *Vault* (1995)

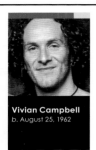

Vivian Campbell
b. August 25, 1962

festival. (When Elliott introduced "my mate, Rick Allen," every hand shot in the air and the drummer, in his own words, "burst into tears.") A year after that, *Hysteria* (1987) entered the U.K. chart at No. 1.

Even this overdue domestic achievement paled beside *Hysteria*'s U.S. success. Thanks to seven hits—notably the gold-selling "Pour Some Sugar on Me" and chart-topping "Love Bites"—the album hit No. 1 in 1988, en route to selling twelve million copies in the U.S. alone. By the end of the eighties, Def Leppard was one of the biggest bands in the world.

Such success brought pressures. Clark used drink and drugs to cope (hence Lange mostly using Collen for guitar parts on *Hysteria*) and he was given a leave of absence to clean up. Sadly, it did not help—he died in his London flat in February, 1991, the victim of prescription drugs and alcohol. But, again, the group rebounded from tragedy: despite Lange being relegated to "executive producer," *Adrenalize* (1992) topped the charts on both sides of the Atlantic, beating new releases by Bruce Springsteen.

To maintain the magnificent onstage interplay Collen had enjoyed with Clark, the band hired **Vivian Campbell**, formerly of Dio and Whitesnake. Although Campbell, by his own admission, plays second fiddle to Collen, the lineup has remained stable ever since.

After the multi-platinum compilations *Retro Active* (1993) and *Vault* (1995), Leppard reinvented their sound on 1996's somber *Slang* (1996). It went gold in the U.K. and U.S. but was judged a flop, and *Euphoria* (1999) marked a retreat to their classic formula.

Thereafter, the band eased into middle age with respectably charting albums— *X* (2002), the covers set *Yeah!* (2006), *Songs from the Sparkle Lounge* (2008), and the live *Mirrorball* (2011)—and well-attended tours (the latter co-headlined by Whitesnake in 2008, Heart and Mötley Crüe in 2011, and Poison in 2012). Leppard's anthemic "Rock of Ages" became the title of a musical and movie that affectionately pastiche the era in which they shot to fame (the movie also features Tom Cruise singing "Pour Some Sugar on Me"). Meanwhile, the band members have indulged in various solo projects, notably Elliott's founding of Down 'n' Outz to record and play music by Mott the Hoople and other Ian Hunter-fronted acts.

The quintet's resilience has been remarkable, and only four other acts can match their achievement of consecutive studio albums selling ten million in the U.S. At their very best—and they were up there for years—they proved that the awesome attack of hard rock could be allied to the sheen and hooks of great pop, with results enjoyed by several generations. **MiH/BM**

■ Other percussion

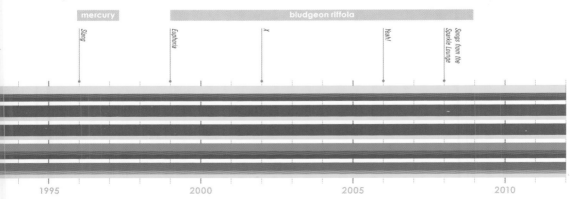

On Through the Night (1980)

High 'n' Dry (1981)

Pyromania (1983)

Hysteria (1987)

Adrenalize (1992)

Slang (1996)

Euphoria (1999)

X (2002)

Yeah (2006)

Songs from the Sparkle Lounge (2008)

Leppard's **Joe Elliott** at the U.K.'s Reading Festival in August 1980.

Rick Savage, **Elliott**, **Pete Willis**, **Rick Allen**, and **Steve Clark** in July 1981.

Savage, **Clark**, new recruit **Phil Collen**, and **Elliott** storm the stage on the *Pyromania* tour.

The resilient thunder god **Allen** onstage in 1987 with his specially adapted drum kit.

Elliott at the Freddie Mercury tribute show in London, in 1992.

Elliott and Collen during a tour promoting the group's sadly underrated *Slang* album.

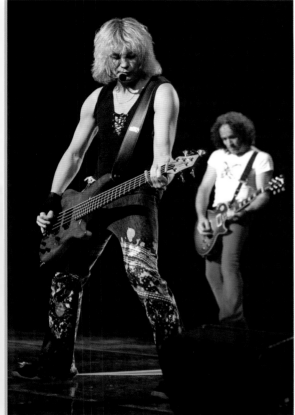

Savage and Vivian Campbell continue to proudly defy fashion.

Campbell, once a protégé of Ronnie James Dio, now firmly established in Leppard.

Leppard's resident teetotaler Collen rocks Britain's Bournemouth on the *Euphoria* tour.

Elliott onstage at London's Wembley Arena during a co-headlining tour with Whitesnake.

dinosaur jr. 1984–present

J. Mascis
b. December 10, 1965

Lou Barlow
b. July 17, 1966

Murph
b. December 21, 1964

Mike Johnson
b. 1965

George Berz
b. Unknown

D

Combining an insouciant cool with explosions of pure guitar noise, Dinosaur Jr. was a band that paved the way for the grunge explosion of the early nineties.

J. (Joseph) **Mascis** and **Lou Barlow** first united as the drummer and bassist for short-lived hardcore punks Deep Wound, based in their home town of Amherst, Massachusetts. When that band split in 1983, they recruited drummer **Murph** (Emmett Murphy) to form Dinosaur. Mascis switched to vocals and guitar, although Barlow was the main singer in the early days.

The trio's deafening shows earned them a cult following, and in 1985 they released a self-titled debut album. However, *Dinosaur* came to the attention of veterans of a sixties band of the same title. Their legal threats prompted Mascis, Barlow, and Murph to add "Jr." to their band's name.

You're Living All Over Me (1987) brought Dinosaur Jr. greater media attention, and established Mascis's trademarks of drawled, laconic vocals and furious guitar pyrotechnics. The immortal "Freak Scene" (1988) was a perfect blend of vulnerable voice, poppy melody, and full-on guitar assault. Its popularity ensured a sizeable audience for *Bug* (1988), consolidated by a 1989 version of The Cure's "Just Like Heaven" (acclaimed by composer Robert Smith as his favorite Cure cover). However, tensions within the band—largely due to Mascis's ever-increasing insistence on complete control of their creative output—culminated in the ousting of Barlow in 1989.

Green Mind (1991) was the first Dinosaur Jr. album on a major label, but was essentially a solo effort by Mascis—he even played drums on all but three tracks. **Mike Johnson** was recruited to play bass on the tour to promote the album, on which the support act was Nirvana. By the time *Where You Been* was released in 1993, Nirvana were global stars, and the musical climate was more favorable for noisy alternative acts. *Where You Been*—the source of the splendid "Start Choppin'"—duly hit the U.K. Top Ten and U.S. Top Fifty.

That album had been an authentic group effort, but Mascis assumed total dominance again for 1994's *Without a Sound*. Murph did not appear on the album and subsequently left, to be replaced by **George Berz** for live work. In 1995 Mascis toured as a solo acoustic act, hence the following year's live *Martin & Me*. After one more album under the Dinosaur Jr. name, *Hand It Over* (1997), he announced the group's demise.

In the following years Mascis issued albums under the name of J. Mascis and the Fog, while Barlow won cult status with Sebadoh and The Folk Implosion. By 2002 the two were sufficiently friendly to attend each other's gigs—and, when Mascis regained the rights to the first three Dinosaur Jr. albums in 2004, they decided to re-form the band, with Murph back on drums. They have since released *Beyond* (2007) and *Farm* (2009), both genuine group creations that achieved the rare feat of being just as excellent as the albums that had made them famous. **DJ**

year-by-year   ■ Vocals   ■ Guitar   ■ Bass   ■ Drums

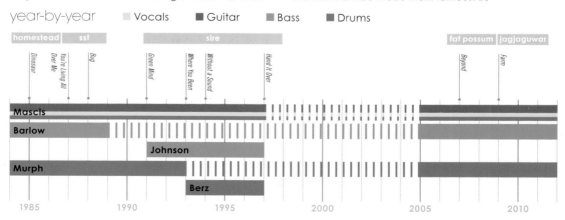

dire straits 1977–1991

Mark Knopfler
b. August 12, 1949

David Knopfler
b. December 27, 1952

John Illsey
b. June 24, 1949

Pick Withers
b. April 4, 1948

Hal Lindes
b. June 30, 1953

Alan Clark
b. March 5, 1952

Terry Williams
b. 11 January, 1948

Guy Fletcher
b. 24 May 1960

Timing, they say, is everything and the meteoric rise of the already popular Dire Straits at the dawn of the CD era illustrates the point. *Brothers in Arms* still sounds good, but its statistics are arguably more eye-opening than its music, with estimated sales of thirty million.

Brothers **Mark** and **David Knopfler** learned guitars as teenagers but had not played together until David moved to London. With a flatmate, **John Illsey**, on bass and a session drummer, **Pick Withers**, they recorded a five-song demo, and Withers named the band Dire Straits. "Sultans of Swing" nailed the sound that would make them famous and, when the BBC played it, the group received calls from A&R men. They signed with Philips' progressive label, Vertigo.

Their self-titled 1978 debut album made No. 2 in the U.S. chart, a better showing than in the U.K. and a real achievement in the midst of disco fever. When the band toured the U.S., Bob Dylan invited Mark and Pick to play on his *Slow Train Coming*. "Mark," he commented, "does me better than anybody."

Irritated that his own songs were not considered for *Communiqué* (1979), David left during the sessions for *Making Movies* (1980) and his parts were re-recorded by session musician Sid McGinnis. The album, arguably their best, included the U.K. Top Ten hit "Romeo and Juliet." **Hal Lindes** replaced David on rhythm guitar and **Alan Clark** joined on keyboards.

Love Over Gold (1982)—their first domestic No. 1—featured just five tracks, including the epic "Telegraph Road" and the spellbinding "Private Investigations." Big-selling albums led to larger concert venues—and 1984's live *Alchemy*—but Withers was uncomfortable with rearranging the songs for arenas. He left in 1983, to be replaced by **Terry Williams** from Man.

In 1985 came the international No. 1 *Brothers in Arms*, which Philips used to promote the recently-launched compact disc format. One selling point was that *Brothers in Arms* lasted fifty-four minutes with no loss in sound quality, and sell it did: the album was the first to shift a million copies in the new format.

By *On Every Street* (1991), Knopfler had set his sights beyond Dire Straits. In 1990, his Notting Hillbillies hit U.K. No. 2 with *Missing... Presumed Having a Good Time*. He has since made solo albums, and recorded with Chet Atkins and Emmylou Harris. The live *On the Night* (1993) became the group's epitaph.

With Knopfler uninterested in a reunion, Alan Clark and six sidemen (including Tom Petty's drummer Steve Ferrone) took to touring as The Straits. Meanwhile, paleontologists listening to Dire Straits discovered a new species of dinosaur in 2001 and called it *Masiakasaurus Knopfleri* in Knopfler's honor. "The fact that it's a dinosaur is certainly apt," he said, "but I'm happy to report that I'm not in the least bit vicious." **SL**

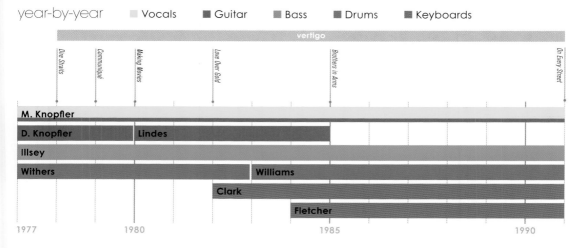

year-by-year ■ Vocals ■ Guitar ■ Bass ■ Drums ■ Keyboards

the doobie brothers 1970–present

John Hartman
b. March 18, 1950

Tom Johnston
b. August 15, 1948

Dave Shogren
b. Unknown
d. 1999

Patrick Simmons
b. January 23, 1950

Tiran Porter
b. September 26, 1949

Michael Hossack
b. Sept 17, 1946
d. Mar 12, 2012

Keith Knudson
b. October 18, 1952
d. 2005

Bill Payne
b. March 12, 1949

It has been a Long Train Runnin' (as the Doobies' thirty-year retrospective box set aptly called it) for a band who garnered two U.S. No. 1 singles (five years apart), one U.S. No. 1 album, and considerable personnel and stylistic changes along the way. But perhaps the greatest accolade is an unlikely namecheck by arch funksters Parliament in their "P.Funk (Wants to Get Funked Up)" song, which notes that listening to the band is "cool—but can you imagine Doobiein' your funk?" Recreational drugs were the lifeblood of seventies California, so a band name based on slang for a marijuana joint seemed cool—and the vibe felt like they were brothers even though they weren't.

Drummer **John Hartman**—still leading the band today—had come to San José to re-form Moby Grape with guitarist Skip Spence. Instead, he formed a power trio, Pud, with lead guitarist **Tom Johnston** and bassist Gregg Murphy. With the replacement of the latter by **Dave Shogren**, and the addition of singer and bluegrass-influenced guitarist **Patrick Simmons**, the quartet became The Doobie Brothers.

They started as a roadhouse boogie band popular with Hells Angels, but their musical direction was steered by the pristine production of Ted Templeman. His vocals on the 1967 hit "59th Street Bridge Song (Feelin' Groovy)" by Harpers Bizarre gave few future pointers, but his drumming abilities injected impetus into the Doobies, as did his cooperative style of producing. As a producer at Warner Bros., he heard the Doobies' demo tape and persuaded his boss Larry Waronker to sign them. Their self-titled 1971 debut album was a dud—but, with Templeman having refined his production skills on Van Morrison's Tupelo Honey, he was ready to roll on the second Doobies set, Toulouse Street. The band now had a second drummer, **Michael Hossack**, and a new bassist, **Tiran Porter**. The radio-friendly "Listen to the Music"—with its then-novel flanging effect on the vocals—became their first hit, reaching No. 11 in the U.S.

Templeman twiddled the knobs on all their studio albums until 1980 (and returned for 2010's World Gone Crazy). He helped create a Spector-esque "wall

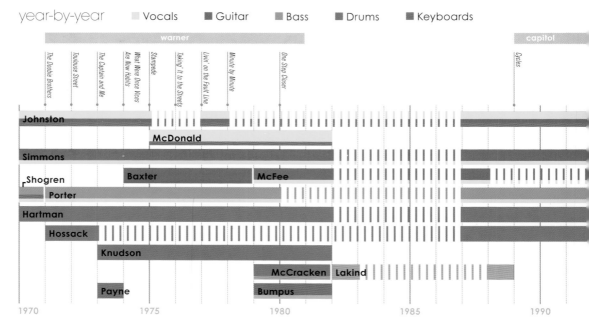

year-by-year   ■ Vocals   ■ Guitar   ■ Bass   ■ Drums   ■ Keyboards

warner   capitol

The Doobie Brothers
Toulouse Street
The Captain and Me
What Were Once Vices Are Now Habits
Stampede
Taking It to the Streets
Livin' on the Fault Line
Minute by Minute
One Step Closer
Cycles

Johnston
McDonald
Simmons
Shogren   McFee
Porter
Hartman
Hossack
Knudson
McCracken   Lakind
Payne   Bumpus

1970   1975   1980   1985   1990

Jeff "Skunk" Baxter
b. December 13, 1948

Michael McDonald
b. February 12, 1952

John McFee
b. November 18, 1953

Chet McCracken
b. July 17, 1952

Cornelius Bumpus
b. January 13, 1952
d. 2004

Bobby Lakind
b. April 28, 1945
d. June 14, 1992

D

of sound" (double power drumming, interlocking guitars, and high-rise vocals) that hit the listener full-on with their third album and finest hour, *The Captain and Me* (1973). Every track is a standout, but "Without You" and "Dark Eyed Cajun Woman"—with **Jeff "Skunk" Baxter** guesting on pedal steel guitar (he later joined full-time after leaving Steely Dan) are pure uncut Doobies. An obvious chart-topper eluded them, however; instead, *What Were Once Vices Are Now Habits* (1974) gave the band their first U.S. No. 1 in "Black Water," a country rock oddity. Originally relegated to a B-side, this part *a capella* song (**Keith Knudson** had joined the band on vocals) unravels slowly with drums overdubbed onto a rhythm machine (and not very well either). But Southern U.S. music stations picked it up and the Mississippi-inspired song grabbed the airwaves nationally.

The *...Vices...* album title was misleading, as the band played it safe with this and 1975's countrified *Stampede*. What did change was the influence of versatile guitarist Jeff Baxter and, crucially, the arrival

of another Steely Dan dropout, keyboardist **Michael McDonald**, for 1976's *Takin' It to the Streets*. Its title track revealed that McDonald had one of the planet's best blue-eyed soul falsettos. His songwriting skills hit paydirt in 1979 with the U.S. chart-topping "What a Fool Believes." Thanks to McDonald's mellifluous vocals and the band willingness to stretch out under the guiding light of Templeman, The Doobie Brothers became polished purveyors of a more urbane, light soul-funk—more Steely Dan than Allman Brothers. The set that spawned "What a Fool Believes," *Minute by Minute*, became the band's only U.S. No. 1 album, reigning at the summit for five consecutive weeks in 1979. (Oddly, it failed to chart at all in the U.K.)

The Doobies were now pretty much Michael McDonald's backing band. His star was in the ascendancy, but Simmons's guitar-led songs had nowhere to go, and the group split in 1982 with their *Farewell Tour* live album. After a five-year hiatus, they re-formed under Johnston but without McDonald. The good time boogie band was back. **JaH**

■ Aerophones   ■ Other percussion

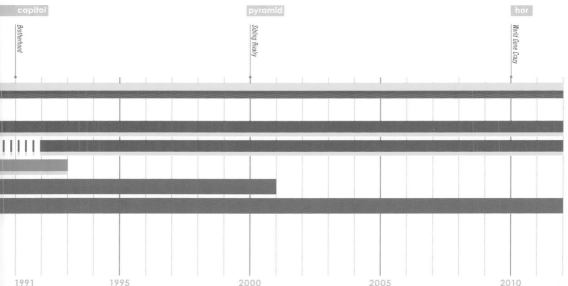

the doobie brothers 159

the doors 1965–1973

Jim Morrison
b. December 8, 1943
d. July 3, 1971

Ray Manzarek, Jr.
b. February 12, 1939

John Densmore
b. December 1, 1944

Robby Krieger
b. January 8, 1946

Few bands polarize opinion like The Doors. For some, the six studio albums they released between 1967 and 1971 burn with a seductive fire of hallucinatory imagery, paeans to sex and incitements to riot. For others, they represent an overrated grab-bag of proto-prog rock pretension. How you feel about the band's singer tends to decide which side you are on.

In 1965, The Doors—formed in Los Angeles—were just another group playing mostly cover versions in clubs. Drummer **John Densmore** provided supple, jazz-inflected rhythms. **Robby Krieger**'s sinuous guitar lines drew on flamenco, blues, and tough rock 'n' roll. **Ray Manzarek**'s chirpy Vox Continental keyboards gave the band its signature sound (he used another keyboard, a Fender Rhodes piano bass, to provide bass lines in concert). What ultimately distinguished them, though, was **Jim Morrison**: strikingly handsome; gifted with a versatile baritone that could rise from a sonorous croon to a startling blues shriek; and a poet to boot. Morrison's lyrics were informed by his voracious reading (Existentialist philosophy, French Symbolism, the Beats, avant-garde theater)—and by drugs, particularly LSD.

Having built a fearsome live reputation—the intrinsically shy Morrison developed into a powerful, if unpredictable, front-man—the band were signed to the Elektra label in August 1966. Their assured

debut album *The Doors* (1967) featured a wealth of Morrison's trademark dark visions, none darker than the shocking, Oedipal-themed "The End." But it was the jazzy "Light My Fire," written mostly by Krieger, that launched the band. Edited down from the seven-minutes-plus album version, it topped the *Billboard* Hot 100 in April 1967. The follow-up, *Strange Days* (1967), explored similar territory, and included the haunting "People Are Strange" and the lengthy, apocalyptic workout "When the Music's Over." Krieger's slide guitar scintillated on "Moonlight Drive."

The Doors were banned from Hollywood club the Whisky a Go Go after Morrison littered "The End" with profanities, while an on-stage rant against local cops in New Haven, Connecticut, saw him jailed. Increasingly untogether, he made the sessions for *Waiting for the Sun* (1968) hard work for everyone, and the album suffered accordingly. "Hello, I Love You" (another U.S. No. 1) sounded too poppy for the Nietzschean Doors—and a little too like The Kinks' "All Day and All of the Night." However, their originality still shone out on the anti-war "The Unknown Soldier" and the strident Us vs. Them call-to-arms "Five to One."

The Soft Parade (1969) added strings and brass, but lacked inspiration. "Touch Me" returned the band to the U.S. Top Three, but lightweight efforts ("Easy Ride"), inoffensive singalongs ("Tell All the People"),

year-by-year   ▧ Vocals   ■ Guitar   ■ Drums   ■ Keyboards

| | | | elektra | | |
| | | *The Doors* | *Strange Days* | | *Waiting for the Sun* |

	1965	1966	1967	1968	1969
Morrison					
Krieger					
Densmore					
Manzarek					

and the long, lackadaisical title track further dented the band's image. A drunken, bearded, chubbier Morrison may or may not have exposed himself on stage at an overheated Miami concert in 1969—but, either way, the result was disastrous for the band, with panicked venues pulling engagements. Morrison now had a court case hanging over him. (He was finally pardoned, posthumously, in 2010.)

Morrison Hotel (1970) saw a return to form, the band embracing a hard, funky edge on "Roadhouse Blues" and the stark "Peace Frog," and sounding positively bouncy on "Ship of Fools" and "Land Ho!" The same year, *Absolutely Live* confirmed that The Doors could be a supple and powerful live act.

L.A. Woman (1971) maintained the momentum. Strong material—from the blues (including John Lee Hooker's "Crawling King Snake") to the boogie-friendly "The WASP"—earned it their eighth gold album in a row (including 1970's hits set *13*). Two longer tracks dominate: the chug-along title track and the muted, melancholy closer, "Riders on the Storm," highlighted by Manzarek's brooding keyboards. Morrison's vocals are ragged but riveting throughout, though heavy smoking had shredded his voice.

Shortly before its release in April 1971, Morrison left for Paris with his partner, Pamela Courson. Three months later he was dead—probably of a heart attack while bathing, although the myth surrounding his demise endures to this day. The remaining three Doors struggled on for two years—issuing *Other Voices* and *Full Circle* (on which Manzarek and Krieger sang lead vocals)—and reunited in 1978 to set some of Morrison's poetry to music for *An American Prayer*.

The music was not over, though. Francis Ford Coppola's atmospheric use of "The End" in *Apocalypse Now* (1979), and the following year's uncritical but enjoyable Morrison biography *No One Here Gets Out Alive* by Jerry Hopkins and Danny Sugarman, sparked renewed interest in The Doors in the eighties. In 1981, Morrison graced a *Rolling Stone* cover—its headline, "Jim Morrison: He's hot, he's sexy and he's dead." The live compilation *Alive, She Cried* (1983) garnered strong sales and reviews. Oliver Stone's movie *The Doors* (1991)—featuring a startlingly convincing performance by Val Kilmer as Morrison—also did much to keep the flame alive. Manzarek and Krieger even toured as "The Doors of the 21st Century," with Ian Astbury of The Cult on vocals, and The Police's Stewart Copeland, then Ty Dennis, on drums.

More than forty years after Morrison's death, the band has shifted around 100 million albums worldwide (A 2007 hits set gave them their first Australian No. 1). It seems songs about sex and death will always sell—when the band is as good as The Doors. **RD**

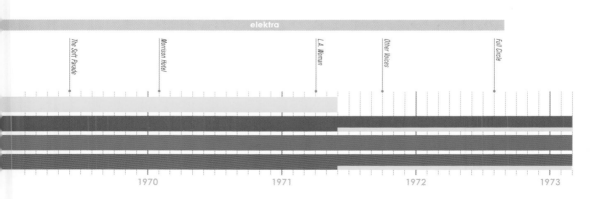

bob dylan 1959–present

Bob Dylan
b. May 24, 1941

Mike Bloomfield
b. July 28, 1943
d. February 15, 1981

Al Kooper
b. February 5, 1944

Ken Buttrey
b. April 1, 1945
d. September 12, 2004

Charley McCoy
b. March 28, 1941

Robbie Robertson
b. July 5, 1943

Levon Helm
b. May 26, 1940
d. April 19, 2012

Garth Hudson
b. August 2, 1937

The greatest works of art are those you can never completely comprehend—they keep some element of mystery about them. Great artists are like that too.

One of the greatest was born in Minnesota, on May 24, 1941, as Robert Allen Zimmerman. He began playing folk clubs as a college student in Minneapolis, where he renamed himself **Bob Dylan** (possibly after TV sheriff Matt Dillon; perhaps after Welsh poet Dylan Thomas). Leaning initially on the gutsy, plain-speaking style of Woodie Guthrie, Dylan honed his act, heading for the folk circuit of New York's Greenwich Village in the cruel winter of 1961.

A glowing review by *New York Times* critic Robert Shelton helped secure a deal with Columbia, though Dylan's self-titled debut album, featuring just two original songs, sold poorly. *The Freewheelin' Bob Dylan* (1963), however, was a revelation, from the vitriolic "Masters of War" and apocalyptic "A Hard Rain's a-Gonna Fall" to the pointed "Don't Think Twice, It's All Right." "Blowin' in the Wind" was embraced by the protest movement in the U.S., and Peter, Paul & Mary made it a hit. Dylan also gained a high-profile champion (and lover) in folk pin-up Joan Baez.

The Times They Are a-Changin' (1964) tackled injustice and civil rights, notably on "Only a Pawn in their Game" and "The Lonesome Death of Hattie Carroll," while the title track captured the zeitgeist. Resentful of the role of spokesperson thrust on him, however, Dylan created a less strident set in *Another Side of Bob Dylan* (1964). His consciously ramshackle appearance, topped by signature peaked cap, went too, to be replaced by skinny jeans, ankle boots, and an increasingly wayward head of hair.

Bringing It All Back Home (1965) marked another re-mapping of Dylan's musical geography, side one kicking off with garage-band proto-rap "Subterranean Homesick Blues" and ending with the hilarious "Bob Dylan's 115th Dream." The all-acoustic side two was even more remarkable, highlighted by the transcendent "Mr Tambourine Man." Covered by The Byrds, it became a No. 1 on both sides of the Atlantic. Bringing his newly electrified sound back home to the folkies proved a struggle, though, as an infamous set at the 1965 Newport Folk Festival showed.

Highway 61 Revisited (1965) boasted "Like a Rolling Stone"—a six-minute giant led by **Al Kooper**'s

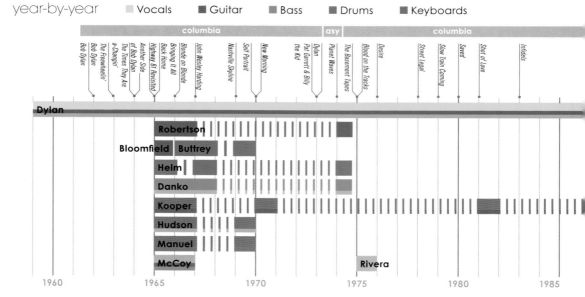

year-by-year ▪ Vocals ▪ Guitar ▪ Bass ▪ Drums ▪ Keyboards

Rick Danko
b. December
29, 1942
d. December
10, 1999

**Richard
Manuel**
b. April 3, 1943
d. March 4, 1986

**Scarlet
Rivera**
b. Unknown

Tony Garnier
b. August 18,
1956

Stu Kimball
b. December
21, 1956

**Charlie
Sexton**
b. August 11,
1968

**George
Recili**
b. Unknown

**Donnie
Herron**
b. 1962

D

joyous organ riff—plus the unsettling "Ballad of a Thin Man," and startling acoustic closer "Desolation Row." *Blonde on Blonde* (1966), characterized by what Dylan dubbed "that thin, that wild mercury sound," was another career peak: a set of surreal, beguiling songs such as "Visions of Johanna," and the side-long "Sad Eyed Lady of the Lowlands" for new wife Sara Lownds.

Backed by bar band The Hawks, Dylan aired his new sound on tour—often to audiences of angry folk purists. A motorcycle crash in July 1966 paradoxically provided a welcome enforced rest. His recuperation at home in Woodstock, New York, yielded a wealth of rootsy Americana, worked up with The Band (née The Hawks). Widely bootlegged, it was eventually released as *The Basement Tapes* in 1975. In an era of psychedelic excess, Dylan offered spare country-folk on *John Wesley Harding* (1967)—whose "All Along the Watchtower" was exuberantly transmogrified by Jimi Hendrix. *Nashville Skyline* (1969), with Johnny Cash, continued in a countrified vein and provided a transatlantic Top Ten hit in "Lay Lady Lay."

After the rapid-fire prolificacy of the sixties, Dylan's early seventies releases met with a lukewarm reception, though the gospel-tinged "Knockin' on Heaven's Door" became yet another standard. It was not until *Blood on the Tracks* (1975)—drawing on the trauma of his disintegrating marriage—that he produced his next masterpiece. *Desire* (1976) was another strong set, distinguished by **Scarlet Rivera**'s sinuous violin. But quality control dipped on subsequent releases, and a late-seventies conversion to Christianity baffled many. By the eighties, Dylan seemed directionless, given to erratic performances on what became known as his "Never Ending Tour." Perplexingly, some of his best work, such as the spell-binding "Blind Willie McTell," went unheard for years.

Oh Mercy (1989) signaled a recovery, and a late-career trilogy of *Time Out of Mind* (1997), "*Love and Theft*" (2001), and *Modern Times* (2006, his first U.S. No.1 since *Desire*) represented a genuine renaissance. Humor, passion, and reflections on mortality, sung in a hoarse husk of a voice, resonate throughout. Add his unlikely success as a DJ on *Theme Time Radio Hour*, and his absorbing autobiography *Chronicles, Volume One* (2004), and Bob Dylan's knack of confounding expectations appears remarkably intact. **RD**

■ Aerophones ■ Other percussion ■ Strings

columbia

Empire Burlesque
Knocked Out Loaded
Down in the Groove
Oh Mercy
Under the Red Sky
Good as I Been To You
World Gone Wrong
Time Out of Mind
"*Love and Theft*"
Modern Times
Together Through Life
Christmas in the Heart

Kimball

Sexton

Recill

Garnier

Herron

1985   1990   1995   2000   2005   2010

**The Freewheelin'
Bob Dylan** (1963)

**The Times They
Are a-Changin'**
(1964)

**Highway 61
Revisited** (1965)

**Bringing It All Back
Home** (1965)

Blonde on Blonde
(1966)

**Blood on the
Tracks** (1975)

Desire (1976)

Oh Mercy (1989)

Time Out of Mind
(1997)

Modern Times
(2006)

A fresh-faced **Dylan** in 1963.

Sporting arguably his most iconic look at a 1966 press conference.

Performing at the Newport Folk Festival in 1964.

Dylan plays both harmonica and piano while recording in 1965.

Playing a Fender Jazz bass while recording *Bringing It All Back Home*.

At Kezar Stadium in San Francisco, California, 1975.

With Joan Baez in Houston on 1976's Rolling Thunder Revue tour.

Cruising the amps at Palau d'Esports in Barcelona, Spain, in 1989.

With The Band's **Rick Danko** (left) at the Oakdale Theatre in Connecticut.

At the New Orleans Jazz and Heritage Festival in 2006.

eagles 1971–present

Don Henley
b. July 22, 1947

Glenn Frey
b. November 6, 1948

Bernie Leadon
b. July 19, 1947

Randy Meisner
b. March 8, 1946

Don Felder
b. September 21, 1947

Joe Walsh
b. November 20, 1947

In the beginning, there was country. Then there was rock. And the two genres were merely kissing cousins through the fifties and sixties, occasionally mingling, in a variety of ways, on a rare hit song or two. It was not until the early seventies—after much groundwork was laid by such acts as Gram Parsons, Buffalo Springfield, and Bob Dylan—that a true hybrid sound would crystallize and country rock, as we know it today, would become a big-time player on the charts. For in 1972, the subgenre would find its greatest champion— the Eagles, the California band that would do for country rock in the seventies what British groups like Cream did for blues rock in the preceding decade.

Not a bad accomplishment for players who first came together as a backup band in 1971. The gig was with Linda Ronstadt, who was looking for support both in the studio and on a summer tour. She found four ringers in session musicians **Don Henley** and **Glenn Frey**, former Poco founder **Randy Meisner**, and Flying Burrito Brothers veteran **Bernie Leadon**. The band played on Ronstadt's self-titled 1971 debut, but only backed her at one concert—a July date that year at Southern California's Disneyland. The band quickly stepped out of Ronstadt's shadow, signed a deal with David Geffen's fledgling Asylum label, and began recording their eponymous debut in London in 1971.

Guided by producer Glyn Johns, the Eagles soared in the studio, mixing country and rock more cohesively than anyone who had come before. The production had a certain "Peaceful Easy Feeling"—to borrow a track title from the album—and charmed both record buyers and DJs. The instrumentation was uncommonly warm and earthy, thanks in large part to Leadon's banjo and mandolin work, and harmonies reminiscent of Crosby, Stills & Nash. *Eagles* yielded three hits—notably "Take It Easy," co-written by Jackson Browne— and peaked at No. 22 in the U.S.

They nested in the same sound and vibe on their sophomore record—1973's *Desperado*, which charted lower (No. 41)—and stayed on course through 1974's *On the Border*. The latter provided the group's first U.S. chart-topper, "Best of My Love," and cleared the way for the Eagles to become one of rock's biggest bands.

One of These Nights, released in 1975, was the first of four consecutive U.S. No. 1 albums. It delivered three singles—the title track, "Lyin' Eyes" and "Take It to the Limit"—all of which reached the Top Five.

However, as Henley told *Billboard* writer Craig Rosen, "There was a lot of tension in the band at that point." Leadon left the band after *One of These Nights*, making his exit in spectacular fashion by pouring a beer over Frey's head, and was replaced

year-by-year   ■ Vocals   ■ Guitar   ■ Bass   ■ Drums

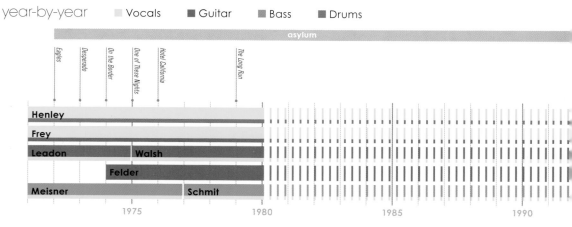

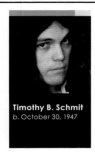

Timothy B. Schmit
b. October 30, 1947

by former James Gang guitarist **Joe Walsh**. "The party line on Joe joining the group was that it made us a strong rock 'n' roll band," observed Henley—but, as the drummer noted, Walsh in fact "presented ballads with a lot of harmonies." The Eagles were free to expand their horizons well beyond country rock, which is exactly what happened on the next album.

Hotel California is one of rock's most legendary records, full of mystery, intrigue, and anthems. The title track from that 1976 album was nothing less than an opus—detailing what Henley once described as "the dark underbelly of the American Dream" and boasting one of the greatest dueling guitar leads ever recorded—and its hold on listeners has not slipped over the years. The album helped redefine the term "blockbuster," eventually going on to sell more than 16 million copies in the U.S. alone.

The thought of following such a commercial and artistic triumph must have been terrifying. The band duly slipped from its one-record-per-year routine and held off until 1979 before releasing *The Long Run* (which they dubbed "The Long One"). Inevitably, it charged to No. 1 in the U.S., but the run was just about over. Drawing headlines for bickering on the ensuing tour, the Eagles called it a night in 1980. "I started a band," Frey noted, "I got tired of it, and I quit."

Walsh and Frey would enjoy mildly successful solo careers, though both would be eclipsed by Henley's *I Can't Stand Still* (1982), *Building the Perfect Beast* (1984), boasting the classic "The Boys of Summer," and 1989's *The End of the Innocence,* one of the finest albums of his career, whose guests included Axl Rose.

But the Eagles legend could not be stopped. The band would only grow more popular during the breakup—as *Their Greatest Hits (1971–1975)* surpassed 30 million in sales worldwide, eventually ranking as the best-selling album of the century in the U.S.

Fans' ecstatic reaction to the 1993 tribute album *Common Thread*—and Henley, Frey, Felder, Walsh, and Schmit's appearance in the video for Travis Tritt's cover of "Take It Easy"—proved the market was alive and well. The quintet duly reunited for a blockbuster tour and an MTV special issued as *Hell Freezes Over*, a title that played off Henley's famous quote that the Eagles would regroup "when hell freezes over."

It must still be cold in hell, as the regenerated band—which has outlasted the first—is still touring. They were inducted into the Rock and Roll Hall of Fame in 1998 and—minus Felder, who was fired in 2001—finally put out a seventh studio album. *Long Road Out of Eden* (2007) brought the Eagles back to familiar ground: No. 1 on the U.S. album chart. **JiH**

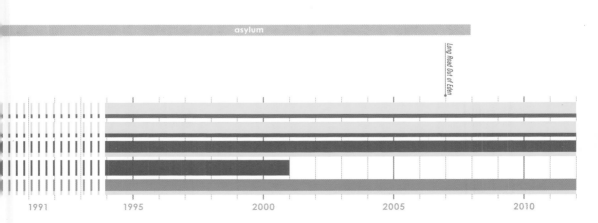

Eagles (1972)

Desperado (1973)

On the Border (1974)

One of These Nights (1975)

Hotel California (1976)

The Long Run (1976)

Glenn Frey, Don Felder, Bernie Leadon, and, on drums, Don Henley perform in 1972.

Randy Meisner, Leadon, Henley, and Frey endure a photoshoot in 1973.

Henley captured during the On the Border tour in 1974.

Long Road Out of Eden (2007)

Leadon swaps his guitar for a banjo in 1975.

Henley, Felder, Meisner (kneeling), Leadon, and Frey in 1976.

Felder, Henley, Joe Walsh, Frey, and Meisner in 1976.

Walsh solos on stage in New York in October 1979.

Frey at the Day on the Green concert in Los Angeles, in 1977.

Frey, Walsh, and Henley are reunited in 2007.

A new Eagles frontline of Timothy B. Schmit, Henley, Frey, and Walsh plays at the IndigO2 in London on October 31, 2007—an intimate show to launch Long Road Out of Eden.

einstürzende neubauten 1980–present

Blixa Bargeld
b. January 12, 1959

Alexander Hacke
b. October 11, 1965

N.U. Unruh
b. June 9, 1957

F.M. Einheit
b. December 18, 1958

Mark Chung
b. June 3, 1957

Jochen Arbeit
b. June 26, 1961

"You must draw on the musical past," said Billy Bragg in 1984. "You can't just spring out of nowhere. Unless you're Einstürzende Neubauten." Or, as a review in U.K. music paper *Sounds* put it: "I have seen the death of rock and roll and its name is Einstürzende Neubauten."

March 7, 1983 saw London's Lyceum Ballroom hosting the debut British concert by this largely unknown band of noise terrorists, who had spent the previous two years playing small art venues in their native Berlin. Strangled and screamed vocals, slow throbbing bass, and discordant guitar feedback were the only vague nods to rock convention: the rest of the performance was filled with sheets of metal, gigantic aluminum duct pipes, industrial springs, chains, slabs of concrete, and a pneumatic drill. Reports of the band's exploits attracted a large crowd, eager for a first taste of "industrial" music.

Formed by Berlin school friends **Blixa Bargeld** (Hans Christian Emmerich) and **N.U. Unruh** (Andrew Chudy), Einstürzende Neubauten—which translates as "collapsing new buildings"—played their first show on April Fools' Day, 1980. Adding **Mark Chung, F.M. Einheit** (Frank Martin Strauß), and **Alexander Hacke** (a.k.a. Alexander von Borsig)—a stable lineup for the next fifteen years—the band abandoned drums in favor of the loud crash of "found" metal percussion.

Their earliest recordings were cassettes. "The battery-operated tape recorder was an indispensable gadget…" wrote Bargeld. "We recorded discussions, music improvisation, TV, day to day noises—we yelled, looped, we kissed the microphone and threw it on long suspenders across the Wall…"

The Neubauten sound is well represented on 1981's debut album *Kollaps* ("Collapse"), issued before they had been heard outside of Berlin's post-punk scene. However, *Zeichnungen des Patienten O.T.* ("Drawings of Patient O.T.")—emerging in 1983 during their first flush of notoriety, when they were banned from venues (including Manchester's Haçienda club) because of the damage they unleashed—indicated a desire to progress beyond beating metal.

Controversy surrounding Neubauten peaked in January 1984 when they played *Concerto for Voice and Machinery* at the ICA—London's leading venue in the promotion of cutting-edge art. Before a disbelieving (albeit appreciative) crowd, the band attacked the concrete stage with jackhammers and pneumatic drills. Twenty years later, Hacke claimed the plan had been "to dig through the stage into the tunnel system underneath the venue," rumored to link up with the nearby Buckingham Palace. Officials pulled the plug after twenty minutes, but tens of

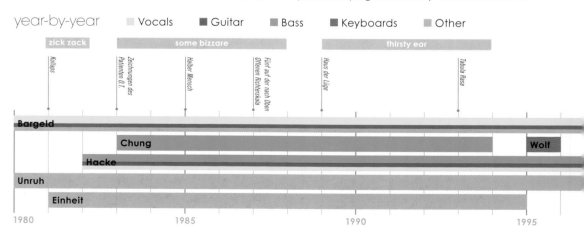

100,000
Zeichnungen des Patienten O. T.
(1983)

100,000
Halber Mensch
(1985)

100,000
Haus der Lüge
(1989)

100,000
Tabula Rasa
(1993)

E

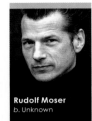

Rudolf Moser
b. Unknown

Roland Wolf
b. 1965
d. March 29, 1995

thousands of pounds' worth of damage had already been incurred. The event duly received coverage well outside of the weekly music press. (*Concerto for Voice and Machinery* gradually acquired such a legendary status that, in 2004, the venue staged a reconstruction —albeit one with a less drastic outcome.)

By 1985, Neubauten were undisputed leaders of an industrial scene that had spawned many imitators, most inspired by the band's percussive proclivities. (Depeche Mode's live sets were clearly influenced by the German band. "Hitting bits of metal," observed Martin Gore, "is very visual.") But industrial hammering was a diminishing component of their sound, which shifted toward more conventional structures, most evident in Bargeld's newly restrained vocals and lyrics. This new approach was illustrated in the 1986 movie *Halber Mensch* ("Half Men"), which documented the band's successful visit to Japan. The same period saw Neubauten visiting the United States, where *Fünf auf der nach Oben Offenen Richterskala* ("Five on the Open-Ended Richterscale") and *Haus der Lüge* ("House of the Lie") enjoyed cult success.

The nineties saw a further softening of the band's industrial sound, with 1993's *Tabula Rasa* heralding a greater use of electronic sounds. The same year, Neubauten provided unlikely support on U2's Zoo TV tour. Received with extreme hostility, their tenure lasted for one performance, ending when an iron bar was allegedly thrown from the stage into the booing crowd. For the remainder of the decade, an ever-shifting personnel—revolving around the hub of Bargeld, Unruh and Hacke—saw Neubauten maintain a diehard following in Europe, America, and Japan.

The new millennium witnessed Neubauten issuing a series of subscriber albums and DVDs. This approach was extended in 2005 with the launch of the *Musterhaus* project, a series of quarterly album releases intended to "give the band an outlet for more experimental impulses and exploration."

In addition to this prolific output, individual members continued a wide array of side interests and collaborations. Notably, Bargeld gave speech-based solo performances and was a long-standing guitarist with Nick Cave and the Bad Seeds.

In 2010, Einstürzende Neubauten celebrated the thirtieth anniversary of their first performances in Berlin with a sold-out tour of Europe (a U.S. leg was abandoned owing to visa problems). Few who witnessed those early venue-crushing events would have predicted such a vibrant and varied career for what is one of the most influential bands to have emerged from Europe in the past three decades. **TB**

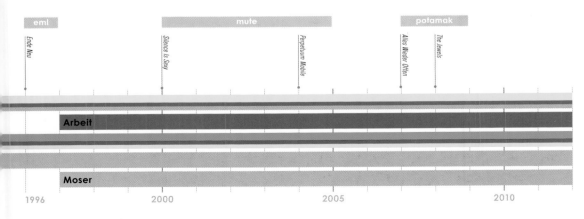

emi   mute   potamak

Ende Neu   Silence Is Sexy   Perpetuum Mobile   Alles Wieder Offen   The Jewels

Arbeit

Moser

1996   2000   2005   2010

electric light orchestra 1970–2001

Jeff Lynne
b. December 30, 1947

Roy Wood
b. November 8, 1946

Bev Bevan
b. November 24, 1944

Richard Tandy
b. March 26, 1948

Mike De Albuquerque
b. June 24, 1947

Kelly Groucutt
b. September 8, 1945
d. February 19, 2009

England's second city, Birmingham, has always made for something of a low-key cultural center. During the sixties, while London swung and Liverpool and Manchester produced a seemingly endless supply of chart acts, the "Brum Beat" scene was altogether more insular. The first breakout band was The Move, founded by **Roy Wood**, former guitarist with the city's leading beat group, The Nightriders. The Move hit the charts with such delightful slabs of period pop psychedelia as "I Can Hear the Grass Grow."

In 1970, with that band in decline, Wood and another former Nightrider, **Jeff Lynne**, conceived a new project that took as its template the baroque string sounds of The Beatles' "Eleanor Rigby." With Lynne joining Wood and drummer **Bev Bevan** for the final days of The Move, the trio began recording as the Electric Light Orchestra. Replete with violins, cellos, and horns overdubbed by Wood, a self-titled debut album (re-christened No Answer in the U.S.) emerged a year later. Tensions, however, appeared from the start, and Wood stepped back: he went on to enjoy an illustrious pop career of his own.

The new-look ELO—now including classically trained keyboard player **Richard Tandy**—emerged at the start of 1973 with ELO II. A rather unsatisfying, schizophrenic affair, its long, symphonic passages of progressive rock were interrupted by a rendition of Chuck Berry's "Roll Over Beethoven." As a single this was a sizable hit in the U.K., but it ensured that ELO would struggle to be treated as a serious entity in their homeland. Nine months later, On the Third Day appeared. On an album of shorter pieces, the same symphonic rock gestures were in place—violins and cellos, classical piano and Moog synthesizers—but the overall effect was this time far more cohesive. Significantly, though, it was their first album to achieve a chart placing in the U.S.

Consolidating this success with a heavy touring schedule, 1974's Eldorado (the source of "Can't Get It Out of My Head") and 1975's Face the Music impressed American critics and audiences, earning their first U.S. gold albums. These were also the first ELO albums to feature a full orchestra and choir, with arranger Louis Clark playing a key role in the sound.

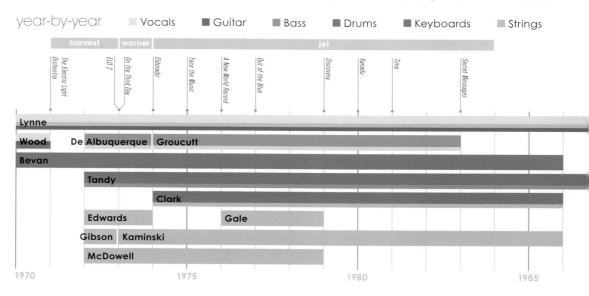

year-by-year ▪ Vocals ▪ Guitar ▪ Bass ▪ Drums ▪ Keyboards ▪ Strings

5.5M	4.1M	6.9M	3.7M
A New World Record (1976)	Out of the Blue (1977)	ELO's Greatest Hits (1979)	Discovery (1979)

Mike Edwards
b. May 31, 1948
d. September 3, 2010

Wilf Gibson
b. February 28, 1945

Mik Kaminski
b. September 2, 1951

Hugh McDowell
b. July 31, 1953

Louis Clark
b. February 27, 1947

Melvyn Gale
b. January 15, 1953

E

A New World Record (1976) saw the emergence of a global phenomenon. A magnificent symphonic pop set, the album oozed confidence, and—thanks to the hit "Livin' Thing"—gave them a first U.K. Top Ten entry.

Now on a creative roll, Lynne took the potentially dangerous step of consolidating his band's popularity with a double album. Emerging in the fall of 1977, *Out of the Blue* turned out to be an album that had fans struggling to find adequate praise. A monumental hit—advance orders alone ensured a platinum award on its release in the U.S.—it yielded four international hits, among them the enduring "Mr Blue Sky."

To support the album, ELO set out on an epic nine-month world tour, accompanied by an opulent stage show. Billed in the U.S. as *The Big Night*, it became the highest grossing concert series up to that time. *Out of the Blue* remains ELO's benchmark achievement, and is regarded as one of *the* pop albums of the decade, not least by Axl Rose, who told *Kerrang!*, "I'm an ELO fanatic! *Out of the Blue* is an awesome album."

It would prove a tough act to follow. While 1979's *Discovery* topped the U.K. chart, it received criticism,

especially for the disco feel of several tracks. Yet "Last Train to London" showed that few writers mastered the art of the irresistible hook as well as Lynne.

The group worked with Olivia Newton-John on the soundtrack of the film *Xanadu*, then 1981's *Time* saw ELO stepping back from overt commercialism with a concept album about a time-traveler from the eighties stuck a century in the future. Despite its gentle prog-rock—well out of sync with what was then fashionable—*Time* was the year's sixth-biggest seller.

Commercial success began to recede with *Secret Messages* in 1983. Conceived as a double album but forcibly cut back by the record label, it sounded tired and half-hearted. It would be a further three years before the "contractual obligation" of *Balance of Power* confirmed ELO as a spent force.

Zoom (2001) was essentially a Lynne solo album (albeit with cameos by Tandy, Ringo Starr, and George Harrison), rather than the ELO it purported to be. Bevan founded ELO Part Two—effective as a tribute band but a rather hollow experience without the man who wrote and sang the songs. **TB**

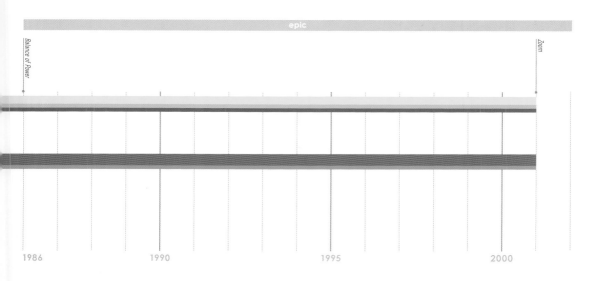

epic

Balance of Power

Zoom

1986	1990	1995	2000

emerson lake & palmer 1970–2010

E

Keith Emerson
b. November 1, 1944

Greg Lake
b. November 10, 1948

Carl Palmer
b. March 20, 1950

Cozy Powell
b. December 29, 1947
d. April 5, 1998

Robert Berry
b. Unknown

Emerson Lake & Palmer came to epitomize everything that was brilliantly cutting edge and bombastically boorish about progressive rock. Singer-songwriters ran for cover in the early seventies as ELP fired rockets, spun grand pianos thirty feet in the air, flashed banks of wired-up Moogs, and unleashed twenty-minute drum solos in an awesome and crushing display of techno-wizardry and classically trained virtuosity.

The band emerged after **Keith Emerson** (keyboard virtuoso in the English jazz-classical-rock combo The Nice) and **Greg Lake** (bassist and singer with progressive rockers King Crimson) hit it off at a 1969 soundcheck where both acts were performing. To complete the trio, Cream's manager Robert Stigwood suggested **Carl Palmer**, who had drummed up a storm with Atomic Rooster and The Crazy World of Arthur Brown. ("The press got a hold of the story that we might jam with Jimi Hendrix," Lake told the *Phoenix New Times,* "and speculated that the group would be called HELP. But, alas, it was just a rumor.")

The portents were all there at the supergroup's second gig on August 29, 1970, at the U.K. Isle of Wight festival (a few days after their live debut at Portsmouth Guildhall). They played a twenty-two-minute rendition of Mussorgsky's *Pictures at an Exhibition,* complete with real firing cannons and Emerson stabbing his keyboard with a knife (actually to wedge down the

keys). The knives really did come out: BBC DJ John Peel called it "A waste of talent and electricity." But the audience were pummeled into submission.

Their music was loud (albeit with acoustic segues), classically referenced, jazz-tinged rock, played with sophisticated signature and tempo changes, always tapping into the latest recording technologies. Emerson was influenced by Walter Carlos's use of the new Moog synthesizer in his experimental 1968 album *Switched-on Bach,* and he became the first artist to tour with a Moog, with help from its inventor, Dr Robert Moog. On their self-titled debut album, Emerson used London's massive Festival Hall organ for the first movement of "The Three Fates (Clotho)," and now fans listening on headphones or speakers on the new and affordable hi-fi systems could be transported there.

With Yes's producer Eddie Offord as engineer, the album also made the most of overdubs, phasing, switching channels left to right, and other multitrack tricks. Critically, ELP were able to replicate this aural experience live; quadraphonic sound and spectacular lighting and laser effects were used to highlight the band's theatrical showmanship.

The album made No. 4 in the U.K. and No. 18 in the U.S. The follow-up, 1971's *Tarkus,* included a side-long conceptual piece about an armored tanklike armadillo versus a mythical beast called a manticore.

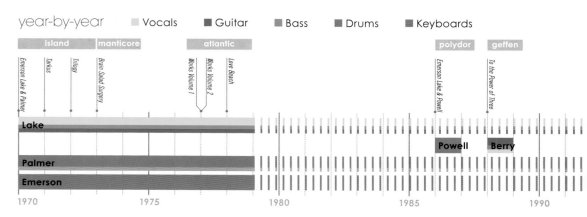

year-by-year   ■ Vocals   ■ Guitar   ■ Bass   ■ Drums   ■ Keyboards

island | manticore | atlantic | polydor | geffen

Emerson Lake & Palmer | Tarkus | Trilogy | Brain Salad Surgery | Works Volume 1 | Works Volume 2 | Love Beach | Emerson Lake & Powell | To the Power of Three

Lake

Palmer   Powell   Berry

Emerson

1970   1975   1980   1985   1990

1M	1.5M	1.8M	1.1M
Tarkus (1971)	*Pictures at an Exhibition* (1971)	*Brain Salad Surgery* (1973)	*Works Volume 1* (1977)

E

The result was ELP's first U.K. No. 1 (and first Top Ten hit in the U.S.). But it was on 1972's *Trilogy*—the cover of which featured pictures of the trio for the first time—that all their dynamic styles were best encapsulated. It duly ascended into the U.S. Top Five. Further chart success came with 1973's *Brain Salad Surgery* (by now on their own label Manticore), featuring surreal artwork by Swiss artist H.R. Giger (later of *Alien* and Debbie Harry's *Koo Koo* fame).

ELP's status as one of rock's biggest bands came through relentless touring (including Japan, where they filled stadiums), performing about 180 concerts a year with twenty-five roadies, more than thirty sound cabinets, and thirty tons of equipment, which included revolving drum kits. Having performed for two million fans, they released the live *Welcome Back My Friends to the Show That Never Ends… Ladies and Gentlemen, Emerson, Lake & Palmer* in 1974. This production remains one of only a few triple albums to hit the U.S. Top Ten.

A two-year break in group proceedings yielded Lake's solo festive perennial "I Believe in Father Christmas" (1975). ELP's artistic meandering continued on the double album *Works Volume 1* (1977), with a side for each member's solo efforts and a final one for the band. From the latter, a Hammond organ-driven interpretation of Aaron Copeland's "Fanfare for the

Common Man" was an unlikely U.K. hit. But their next live venture, to take a unionized symphony orchestra and choir on the road, was a step too far. Poor ticket sales saw the orchestra dropped. ELP plummeted even further with the contractually obligated *Love Beach*, on the cover of which they posed as Bee Gee-esque lotharios. It marked the end of Emerson Lake & Palmer for twelve years.

Palmer joined Steve Howe of Yes in new supergroup Asia in 1981, whose first album spent nine weeks at No. 1 in the U.S. the following year. In 1985, Emerson and Lake teamed up with drummer **Cozy Powell** to revive the "ELP" franchise, and with **Richard Berry** in a trio called 3, but both projects flopped.

With Palmer back in the fold, the 1992 comeback *Black Moon* kept the cauldron bubbling, and a successful world tour followed in 1992–1993. However, nerve damage in Emerson's right hand meant that his keyboard playing was compromised, and tension between him and Lake over the direction of the band's music led to 1994's disjointed and poorly received *In the Hot Seat*. While the reconciled Lake and Emerson later toured together, the album proved the last work by the trio until they reunited one final time for a show at London's Victoria Park in 2010—their fortieth anniversary. "It seemed a great way to finish things," said Palmer. "Let's just leave it there." **JaH**

■ Other percussion

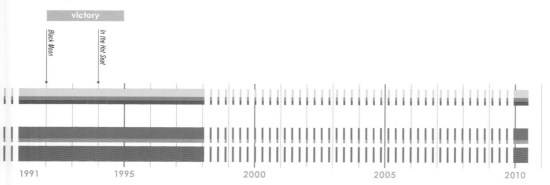

eurythmics 1980–2005

Annie Lennox
b. December 25, 1954

Dave Stewart
b. September 9, 1952

The British charts of the early eighties were flooded with synthesizer-dominated bands, as fashion turned against the guitar groups that had ruled during the preceding punk and new wave boom. Singer **Annie Lennox** and multi-instrumentalist **Dave Stewart** met in 1976 through a mutual friend and began a personal relationship while playing in one such guitar-pop band. They started out as The Catch before enjoying moderate success as The Tourists between 1977 and 1980, notably with a cover of Dusty Springfield's "I Only Want to Be with You."

The Tourists disbanded at the start of the eighties, and Lennox and Stewart ended their romantic relationship but decided to maintain their musical partnership. They named their new act Eurythmics after a method of classical musical tuition that Lennox had undergone as a child, and went to Cologne, Germany, to work on their debut album. The result was *In the Garden* (1981): a mix of psychedelic, krautrock, and electropop elements featuring contributions from Blondie drummer Clem Burke (who later toured with the duo), and Can's Holger Czukay and Jaki Liebezeit. It was warmly reviewed but sold slowly. Meanwhile, another Dave Stewart enjoyed short-lived U.K. chart success, prompting the Eurythmics' founding member to begin styling himself as David A. Stewart.

Sweet Dreams (Are Made of This), released in January, 1983, was recorded in the more humble surroundings of the duo's own tiny eight-track studio in Chalk Farm, London, though this was not apparent

from the glossy production. "Love Is a Stranger" explicitly dealt with erotic obsession and took the duo to No. 6 in the British singles chart, but it was the brooding title track that brought Eurythmics their international breakthrough.

Built around a staccato synthesizer riff, "Sweet Dreams" (later covered by artists from Marilyn Manson to Leona Lewis) darkly reflected on the manipulative and masochistic elements in human interaction. It was accompanied by a startling video in which Lennox appeared in a man's suit, her hair cropped short and dyed bright orange. Heavy MTV rotation followed, helping to push the single to No. 1 in the U.S. Lennox's striking androgynous styling became her trademark and soon promoted her to pop icon status. Her image went on to grace numerous magazine covers, including *Rolling Stone*.

The video for "Who's That Girl?," the lead single from *Touch* (1983), saw Lennox take the gender-bending a stage further. She appeared as a blonde chanteuse in a club attended by Stewart, who was seen swilling champagne with a succession of different female companions, several of whom were British music stars of the time. In the video, Lennox also portrayed a moody male customer, complete with greasy rocker's haircut and stubbly chin. The two Lennoxes finally leave together, and slick editing allowed them to kiss. *Touch* yielded two more hits: the dramatic orchestral ballad "Here Comes the Rain Again" and the atypically joyous "Right by Your Side."

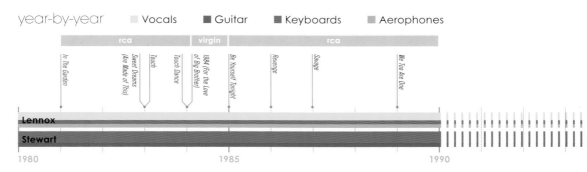

year-by-year ■ Vocals ■ Guitar ■ Keyboards ■ Aerophones

rca | virgin | rca

In The Garden · Sweet Dreams (Are Made of This) · Touch · Touch Dance · 1984 (for the Love of Big Brother) · Be Yourself Tonight · Revenge · Savage · We Too Are One

Lennox
Stewart

1980   1985   1990

3.7M
Touch
(1983)

4.1M
Be Yourself Tonight
(1985)

3.4M
Revenge
(1986)

8.9M
Greatest Hits
(1991)

E

Controversy attended two Eurythmics releases in 1984. *Touch Dance* was a remix album assembled with little input from the duo; Lennox admitted to disliking it. *1984 (For the Love of Big Brother)* was a soundtrack for Michael Radford's film, based on George Orwell's dystopian novel. Eurythmics' music was commissioned by Virgin without Radford's approval—the director wanted to use an orchestral score, and publicly voiced his anger when the studio insisted on using some of Eurythmics' music in his film. The hits, however, continued with "Sexcrime (Nineteen Eighty-Four)."

Be Yourself Tonight (1985) moved away from electronica toward soul and yielded the duo's only U.K. No. 1 single: "There Must Be an Angel (Playing with My Heart)" for which Stevie Wonder provided a harmonica solo. Lennox duetted with Aretha Franklin on another international hit, the cautiously pro-feminist "Sisters Are Doin' It for Themselves."

Revenge (1986) continued Eurythmics' progress toward commercial pop-rock, with big choruses that suited the world tour the duo undertook in its support. The fans' favorite, *Savage* (1987), returned to a more experimental sound and saw a sharper feminist focus in Lennox's lyrics. *We Too Are One* (1989) did much to reinstate Eurythmics' commercial pop gloss and sold strongly despite its lack of major hits. The title proved ironic: though Eurythmics never formally disbanded, *We Too Are One* preceded a decade-long hiatus.

Greatest Hits (1991), featuring smashes from 1982 to 1990, went triple platinum in America and sextuple

platinum in the U.K. The duo had, however, effectively split and embarked on a lengthy hiatus. Lennox launched herself as a solo singer in spectacular style in 1992 with *Diva*, which received Best British Album at the 1993 Brit Awards and three Grammy nominations, while earning the singer quadruple platinum in the U.K. and double platinum awards in the U.S.

Stewart formed Dave Stewart and the Spiritual Cowboys in 1990, with whom he recorded two albums before embarking on a solo career. (A parallel career as a producer has included Tom Petty's *Southern Accents* in 1985, Mick Jagger's *Primitive Cool* in 1987, Jon Bon Jovi's *Destination Anywhere* in 1997, and Stevie Nicks' *In Your Dreams* in 2011.)

Eurythmics finally reunited for *Peace* (1999), a lushly orchestrated collection and final album marked by a wistful, reflective atmosphere. The duo went on a worldwide tour to promote it, donating all profits to Amnesty International and Greenpeace.

A further reunion took place in 2005 when Lennox and Stewart recorded two new songs—"I've Got a Life" and "Was It Just Another Love Affair?"—for a new hits compilation, *The Ultimate Collection*. "I've Got a Life" is a song of defiance in the face of life's cruelties, featuring a particularly powerful vocal performance from Lennox. For the accompanying video, she once again donned a man's business suit, shirt, and tie, returning to the androgynous image that did much to launch the extraordinary career chronicled on *The Ultimate Collection*. **DJ**

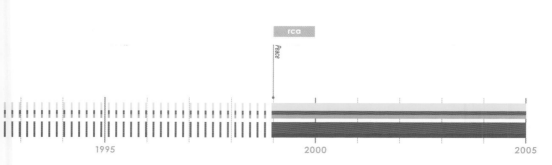

rca

Peace

1995

2000

2005

extreme 1985–present

Gary Cherone
b. July 26, 1961

Nuno Bettencourt
b. September 20, 1966

Pat Badger
b. July 22, 1967

Kevin Figueiredo
b. January 12, 1977

Paul Geary
b. July 24, 1961

Mike Mangini
b. April 18, 1963

Not quite fitting into the late-eighties wave of glam-metal but never straying that far from it either, thanks to their pretty cheekbones and penchant for tight stagewear, Massachusetts quartet Extreme scored two memorable hits in 1990 and 1991... then sank into relative obscurity. However, their reformation in recent years is testament to their impressive songs—after all, their hits still soundtrack weddings to this day—and also demonstrates the band's position somewhere outside the usual genre categories. While most glam bands of the eighties (Warrant, Cinderella, Britny Fox, we are looking at you) sound as relevant today as The Sweet, "More Than Words" and "Hole Hearted" receive as much airplay now as in those far-off days.

And let us be clear: ninety percent of Extreme's reputation rests on those two songs. Although their four first-round albums contain plenty of singable compositions, and their comeback album from 2008 is a solid effort, "More Than Words" and "Hole Hearted" define Extreme. Neither song conforms to the lightweight, diet-metal parameters established in the mid-eighties by the many hairsprayed acts whose dearest wish was to be the next Guns N' Roses or Mötley Crüe. Both songs avoided those clichés—the former because it was a wholly acoustic ballad; the

latter because it was effectively a chunk of folk rock: slide solos, twelve-string acoustic guitars, and all.

Indeed, guitars were the key ingredient in Extreme's approach. Portugal-born guitarist and founder member **Nuno Bettencourt** was and remains an awe-inspiringly gifted master of his instrument, delivering a range of styles from country picking to all-out metallic shredding at world-class standards. Nowadays he is a regular feature of guitar magazines rather than rock publications, which reveals much about the nature of Extreme's appeal to its followers.

His early band Sinful first came into contact with The Dream, featuring vocalist **Gary Cherone** and drummer **Paul Geary**, on the local rock-club scene of Malden, Massachusetts. After adding bassist **Pat Badger**, the new band was formed. Its name was derived from "ex-Dream," and inevitably, given that this took place in an era when thrash metal was at its peak, the new foursome were often thought to be an extreme metal band. Nothing could be further from the truth: Extreme's primary influences were Queen and Van Halen, with Bettencourt's clean, melodic guitar sound directly shaped by that of the former's guitarist Brian May, and his virtuoso fusillades of notes an obvious nod to Eddie Van Halen.

year-by-year ■ Vocals ■ Guitar ■ Bass ■ Drums

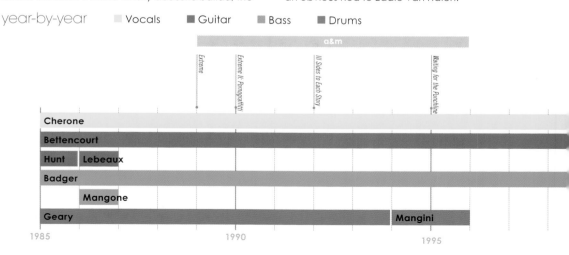

Peter Hunt
b. Unknown

Hal Lebeaux
b. Unknown

Paul Mangone
b. Unknown

A self-titled debut album came and went in 1989 without attracting much attention in the saturated rock scene. However, when Bettencourt extended his songwriting chops for its follow-up, *Extreme II: Pornograffitti* (1990), audiences responded en masse to its catchy, funky melodies and choruses—such as the saucy "Get the Funk Out." The stars aligned for the two hits, released in 1990 and 1991, which conquered charts with ease. Fans responded to the simple, heartfelt sentiments of "More Than Words" (a U.S. chart topper and No. 2 in the U.K.) and enjoyed the sly humor of its video, in which the temporarily redundant Badger and Geary lounged around with nothing to do. As for "Hole Hearted," its brisk, energetic riffage and layers of infectious vocals were difficult to resist.

Extreme were among the star attractions at 1992's Freddie Mercury Tribute Concert in London, and *III Sides to Every Story* (on which Geary was replaced by ex-Annihilator drummer **Mike Mangini**) hit Top Tens in the U.S., the U.K., and Japan. *Waiting for the Punchline* (1995), however, struggled to secure a foothold in an era when grunge, alternative rock, and the nascent nü-metal movement were occupying consumers. Even a knowing single from 1995 titled "Hip Today" could not slow the band's slide. The same year,

Cherone joined Van Halen, a move that endeared him to neither VH fans nor his own followers. "It was," he admitted, "very intimidating." By the time he quit in 1999, Extreme were long gone, with Bettencourt forming a series of low-key side projects. His collaboration with Perry Farrell of Jane's Addiction—Satellite Party's *Ultra Payloaded*—saw the light in 2007.

A reformation in 2004 was greeted with enthusiasm, and Extreme (now featuring drummer **Kevin Figueiredo**, another Satellite Party veteran) found themselves a niche once more. Their 2008 studio album *Saudades de Rock* (which, roughly translated from Portuguese, means "rock nostalgia") was never likely to match up to their early work, but respect for the band remains high and Extreme seem likely to be able to make a living as a touring and festival band for the foreseeable future.

Perhaps the best way to approach Extreme nowadays is on stage, where Bettencourt's guitar pyrotechnics can most easily be appreciated: happily, *Take Us Alive*—recorded at Boston's House of Blues in August 2010—was released for that very purpose. "We really live to challenge ourselves and challenge our audience," said Cherone, "and it happens every time we hit the stage." **JM**

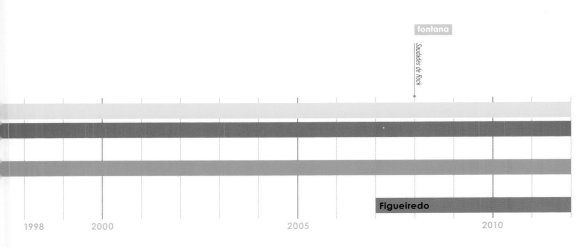

fairport convention 1967–present

Ashley Hutchings
b. January 26, 1945

Simon Nicol
b. October 13, 1950

Richard Thompson
b April 3, 1949

Judy Dyble
b. February 13, 1949

Iain Matthews
b. June 16, 1946

Martin Lamble
b. August 28, 1949
d. May 12, 1969

Dave Mattacks
b. March 13, 1948

Sandy Denny
b. January 6, 1947
d. April 21, 1978

The highly influential Fairport convened in London in 1967 with bassist **Ashley Hutchings**, guitarists **Simon Nicol** and **Richard Thompson**, and, succeeding the short-stayed Shaun Frater, drummer **Martin Lamble**. With the addition of vocalist **Julie Dybble**, they became a regular fixture of the burgeoning London scene and came to the attention of Pink Floyd producer Joe Boyd, who got them signed to the Polydor label.

Iain Matthews (vocals) joined for the recording of *Fairport Convention* (1968), influenced by the emerging American West Coast sound and the folk rock of Bob Dylan and Joni Mitchell. The album sold poorly but, with folk singer **Sandy Denny** replacing Dyble, they signed to Island and issued *What We Did on Our Holidays* (1969) to much acclaim. Denny was a singer beyond compare, while Thompson was starting to shine as a writer and, in the words of Robert Plant (who, after all, should know), "a superlative guitarist."

Matthews left the band during the sessions for *Unhalfbricking* (1969) and, a few weeks before the album was released, tragedy struck. The band's tour van crashed after a concert in Birmingham, England, killing both Lamble and Thompson's girlfriend. As they tried to cope with their injuries and sad losses, the band's future was in doubt.

Ultimately, Fairport Convention decided to continue, bringing in the brilliant **Dave Mattacks** on drums, while violinist **Dave Swarbrick**, who had appeared on *Unhalfbricking*, joined as a full member. On *Liege & Lief* (1969), they embraced the traditional folk songs Denny had introduced to the band (and Hutchings had enthusiastically researched thereafter) to create a groundbreaking work and pioneer a new musical genre—electric folk. Soon after this legendary album's release, Denny left to form the short-lived Fotheringay, and Hutchings departed to start-up Steeleye Span. With Denny proving virtually irreplaceable, **Dave Pegg** joined on bass. Their third U.K. Top Twenty album, 1970's *Full House*, coincided with a period in which the band staged particularly powerful live performances. But Thompson's departure in July, to pursue a solo career with his wife Linda Thompson, came at a time when Fairport Convention were peaking as a true musical force.

In 1971, *Angel Delight* bagged a No. 8 placing but the ambitious *Babbacombe Lee* failed to trouble the chart at all. Mattacks and the last remaining founder, Nicol, were gone by the end of 1971, and the next couple of years saw a bewildering number of short-lived lineups. Mattacks returned in 1973, alongside

year-by-year

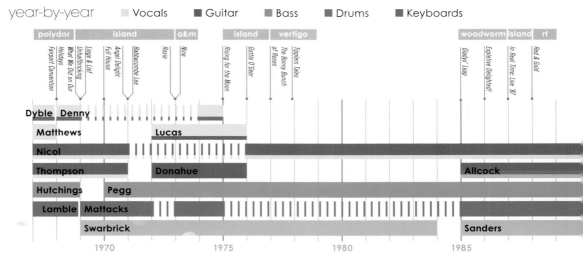

Vocals Guitar Bass Drums Keyboards

1M	1.5M	1M	1M
Unhalfbrickling (1969)	*Liege & Lief* (1969)	*Full House* (1970)	*Angel Delight* (1971)

Dave Swarbrick
b. April 5, 1941

Dave Pegg
b. November 2, 1947

Trevor Lucas
b. December 25, 1943
d. February 4, 1989

Jerry Donahue
b. September 24, 1946

Ric Sanders
b. December 8, 1952

Maartin Allcock
b. January 5, 1957

Chris Leslie
b. December 15, 1956

Gerry Conway
b. September 11, 1947

two members of folk-rockers Fotheringay (who had split after just one album): **Trevor Lucas** (vocals/guitar) and American lead guitarist **Jerry Donahue**. *Rosie* and *Nine* (both released in 1973) were the results.

To high expectations, it was announced that Denny—following fine solo albums on which her writing had blossomed—was returning. After a world tour and the replacement of Mattacks by Bruce Rowland, they issued *Rising for the Moon* (1975). But it sold poorly and Lucas and Donahue departed, to be followed in 1976 by Denny. She recorded one last solo album but her alcoholism and drug problems proved to be out of control. In March 1978, she fell down a flight of stairs and died a few days later of a cerebral hemorrhage, aged just thirty-one.

The remaining three members adapted sessions for a Swarbrick solo album into *Gottle O'Geer* (1976), Fairport's final album for Island. With Nichol returned, they signed to Vertigo for *The Bonny Bunch of Roses* (1977) and *Tipplers Tales* (1978), but plunging sales and folk rock being out of fashion saw them dropped.

After a farewell tour that culminated in an outdoor concert in Cropredy, the Oxfordshire village where Pegg resided, Fairport Convention disbanded. Pegg, Nicol, and Mattacks—having served as members of Richard and Linda Thompson's backing band through the decade—continued to do so into the eighties.

Regular reunion shows in Cropredy village turned into an annual festival, with ex-members and guests such as Robert Plant (with whom Denny had duetted on Led Zeppelin's "The Battle of Evermore"). Pegg started his own label, Woodworm Records, to release recordings of these shows as well as occasional new studio albums made by the band.

With Swarbrick departing in the mid-eighties, **Ric Sanders** (violin) and multi-instrumentalist **Maartin Allcock** joined Mattacks, Pegg, and Nicol in a lineup that lasted for the next ten years, touring and releasing a string of well-received albums. Meanwhile, their influence was clear on new acts like Midlake.

Allcock left in 1997, to be replaced by **Chris Leslie**, and Mattacks departed in 1998— former Fotheringay drummer **Gerry Conway** took his place. This lineup continues to tour and record to this day. At Cropredy, to mark their fortieth anniversary in 2007, the classic *Liege & Lief* lineup—with Chris While (ex-Albion Band) singing Sandy Denny's parts—performed the band's most revered album in its entirety. "What is it that's given Fairport its longevity?" said Sanders. "My answer is always the same: the audience." **MD**

■ Strings

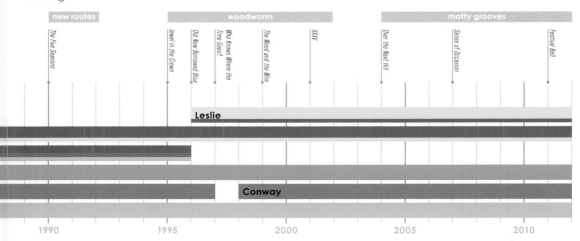

| | 1990 | 1995 | 2000 | 2005 | 2010 |

faith no more 1982–present

Mike "Puffy" Bordin
b. November 27, 1962

Roddy Bottum
b. July 1, 1963

Billy Gould
b. April 24, 1963

Mike Patton
b. January 27, 1968

Jon Hudson
b. April 13, 1968

Chuck Mosely
b. January 27, 1958

Faith No More covers Black Sabbath's "War Pigs." A musical pigeonhole is immediately identified for the band to fill, especially after tours with Metallica and Guns N' Roses. But the ever-restless outfit finds the metal label restrictive. "We were being packaged into something we weren't," says bassist **Billy Gould**. The obvious solution is found, naturally enough, at a bar. "Easy" by the Commodores plays. "We looked at each other and said, 'That's it! This'll get us out of this mess.'" Among fans, much head-scratching ensues.

It was ever thus with these brilliantly perverse Californians, a group that started in the early eighties in San Francisco, coming together around the nucleus of Gould, **Roddy Bottum** on keys, and drummer **Mike "Puffy" Bordin**. The inhabitants of other roles within the band were originally regarded as interchangeable from show to show. One of the many who came and went in the early days was future Hole frontwoman **Courtney Love**, demonstrating early signs of a devotion to the spotlight that was so apparent later on. "When we played a show and there was only five people in the audience," said Gould, "she'd make sure they were all paying attention to her."

Chuck Mosely lasted longer than anyone else at this stage as front-man, while an icon of sorts came

to them recommended by Metallica bassist Cliff Burton: **Jim Martin**—heavy of guitar and big of beard. "Subtlety is for old people," he rumbled to *Kerrang!* magazine. "Subtlety is for people who blow their noses into handkerchiefs in the bathroom."

The title track of 1985 studio album *We Care a Lot* caused ripples as it ticked off most boxes in its anti-everything stance. That and the pockets of intensity and invention elsewhere on the band's debut release were enough for a step over from an independent to a major label. "We Care a Lot" was re-recorded for *Introduce Yourself* (1987). The release was another leap forward ("Anne's Song" is a twisted highlight) but Mosely sometimes had trouble carrying a tune, and had a similar lack of control with his substances.

For all the promise shown so far, Faith No More needed something to set the band apart from the pack. Enter **Mike Patton**. His larynx was much more elastic than the departed Mosely's, switching lanes from style to style, while his lyrics were often things of dark beauty. It required the rock-rap crossover "Epic" to go Top Ten for America to wake up to *The Real Thing* (1989), after which record buyers discovered that they dug albums that sounded like being caught up in propeller blades.

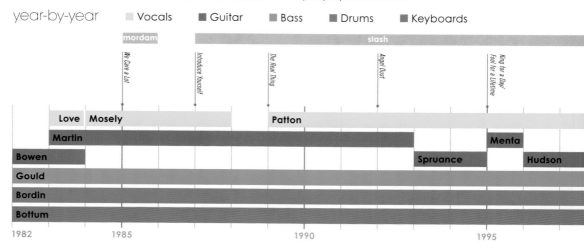

year-by-year   ■ Vocals   ■ Guitar   ■ Bass   ■ Drums   ■ Keyboards

mordam   slash

We Care a Lot   Introduce Yourself   The Real Thing   Angel Dust   King for a Day / Fool for a Lifetime

Love   Mosely   Patton

Martin   Menta

Bowen   Spruance   Hudson

Gould

Bordin

Bottum

1982   1985   1990   1995

Jim Martin
b. July 21, 1961

Trey Spruance
b. August 14, 1969

Dean Menta
b. Unknown

Courtney Love
b. July 9, 1964

Mark Bowen
b. Unknown

At this point, one of the biggest bands in the rock world switched to the status of one of the most interesting groups in any genre. "We can't go where we've been before," said Patton, referring to 1992's genre-bending *Angel Dust*. "It's boring and it's insulting." What one reviewer called "a baroque pomp-punk brew closer to Rush on acid than the acerbic funk-thrash fans had come to expect" included the tracks "Caffeine" and "Land of Sunshine," which benefited from a self-imposed sleep-deprivation experiment undergone by Patton.

The band and Martin parted—not on the best of terms—in 1993. Gould's reflective comment "people get tired of compromising with each other" was probably the most diplomatic way of summing up a difficult time internally. Much of it allegedly centered around a clash between Patton and Martin—ironic since the latter had recommended the former for the band in the first place, after hearing his work with the uncategorizable experimental band Mr. Bungle. To complicate things further, it was that band's **Trey Spruance** who came in to take Martin's place on 1995's *King for a Day/Fool for a Lifetime*, an album that might have lacked the out-there feel of its predecessor but conceded nothing in quality.

As far as Patton was concerned, Spruance's CV would read "great guitarist lacking any sense of responsibility." To go out on a seven-month world tour, **Dean Menta**—previously part of Faith No More's interchangeable backup team—was viewed as a safer bet for on-the-road guitarist. What was needed, however, was someone to work both on stage *and* in the studio. Gould's compadre, **Jon Hudson**, came in for 1997's *Album of the Year*. Such a title invites accusations of overarching ambition, but "Last Cup of Sorrow," "Ashes to Ashes," and the threatening electronica of "Stripsearch" made it a contender for the crown, if not the outright winner.

The band's effect on the world was good, bad, and obviously completely out of its hands. The likes of Limp Bizkit aped the style of the pioneering "Epic" but pretty much missed the point completely, so it was eleven long years before Faith No More returned in 2009—with the *Album of the Year* lineup—to show the young pretenders how it should be done. But how to reintroduce Faith No More onstage in Brixton, south London (the location used for the group's 1991 live album) for their first gig since 1998? With none other than an easy-listening U.S. No. 1 from 1978: "Reunited" by Peaches & Herb. **CB**

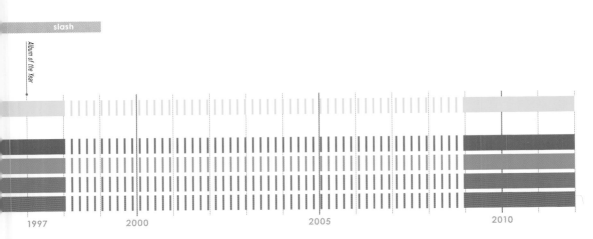

slash

Album of the Year

1997   2000   2005   2010

faith no more 183

the fall 1976–present

Mark E. Smith
b. March 5, 1957

Tony Friel
b. May 4, 1958

Una Baines
b. April 1957

Martin Bramah
b. September 18, 1957

Karl Burns
b. 1958

Marc Riley
b. July 10, 1961

Steve Hanley
b. May 29, 1959

Craig Scanlon
b. December 7, 1960

Where to start with **Mark E. Smith**'s revolving-door employment exchange? Instead of former members of The Fall, it is probably better to think of casualties of war. Those who have passed through—and, to date, that number exceeds fifty—often talk like battle-scarred veterans returned from tours of duty. They have escaped with their lives, but not always their sanity. In the same breath, many speak of unforgettable creative experiences.

At the center of this maelstrom is Smith. While seminal Sex Pistols shows inspired many to form bands, Smith saw it differently: "Whatever I did would have to be better than most of the so-called punk shite."

Named after a novel by French philosopher Albert Camus, The Fall's lineup included **Martin Bramah** (guitar), **Tony Friel** (bass), and **Una Baines** (keyboards). A drummer not around long enough for anyone to remember his name—posthumously identified as Steve Ormrod—was ejected for writing a song praising British prime minister Margaret Thatcher. Enter **Karl Burns** for the first of several stints. And, when it was time to refresh the lineup, musical proficiency was not a prerequisite. "It's like, 'You're on bass, so get cracking,'" Smith told *The Guardian*. "Seems to work."

The Fall's music is a distillation of Smith: lacerating, cruel, darkly humorous, compelling. The group's debut album, 1979's *Live at the Witch Trials*—not, in fact, live—was recorded in a single day, with future BBC DJ **Marc Riley** on bass (later guitar). A pivotal addition was **Steve Hanley**, on bass from 1979's second album, *Dragnet*. In a rare example of Smith mentioning a band member for reasons other than reminding them of their disposability, he said: "He is the Fall sound."

With *Hex Enduction Hour* (1982), the band became a chart concern, albeit a minor one. Having joined in 1983, **Brix Smith** brought qualities thus far unfamiliar to the band (and became Smith's first wife). Early Fall songs were memorable for punching holes in your brain. Now the same effect was achieved by melody. *The Wonderful and Frightening World of...* (1984), *This Nation's Saving Grace* (1985), and *Bend Sinister* (1986) are classics, with tunes to match the band's attack.

Comings and goings were relatively rare at this time. **Craig Scanlon** was a guitar rock, although the departure of **Paul Hanley** took away the pulverizing double-drummer assault at gigs. He lasted five years, commendable in itself, but still short of the nineteen years eventually served by his brother, Steve.

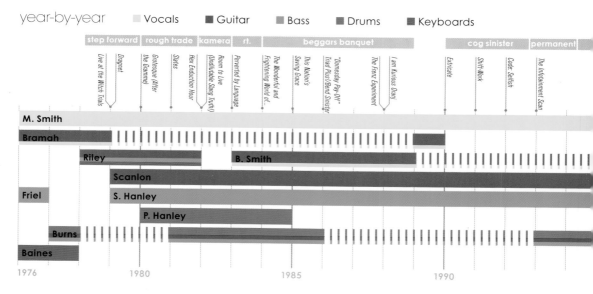

year-by-year   ☐ Vocals   ■ Guitar   ■ Bass   ■ Drums   ■ Keyboards

Paul Hanley
b. February 18, 1964

Brix Smith
b. November 12, 1962

Spencer Birtwistle
b. Unknown

Ben Pritchard
b. Unknown

Elena Poulou
b. Unknown

Steve Trafford
b. February 12, 1976

Tim Presley
b. Unknown

There were even charting singles, including covers of "Victoria" by The Kinks and R. Dean Taylor's "There's a Ghost in My House." In 1993, *The Infotainment Scan* gave the band what is likely to be its only U.K. Top Ten album. Divorce did not prevent Brix from reappearing for a couple of albums in the mid-nineties, while Bramah also made a brief return. Scanlon was dismissed for his "slovenly appearance" at the end of 1995, but more serious meltdowns followed.

New York, 1998: at Brownies, on April 7, Smith's noted tendency to mess with band members' instruments was taken too far for Karl Burns's liking. The drummer had allegedly been set on fire in Public Image Ltd by bass guitarist Jah Wobble, but even he had his breaking point. According to one eyewitness, he "grabbed Mark's head, which he looked like he was completely capable of crushing." Backstage, Smith was arrested, and the group packed their bags.

With Steve Hanley, guitarist Tommy Crooks, and Burns out, the fresh meat for *The Marshall Suite* (1999) included drummer Tom Head, guitarist Neville Wilding, and bassists Karen Leatham and Adam Helal. As BBC DJ—and Fall evangelist—John Peel commented: "I don't know if Smith is killing them or what."

Smith reserved special contempt for sticksmen. "You are only a drummer. I am Mark Smith," he told **Spencer Birtwistle**. The Chemical Brothers' manager Nick Dewey was drafted in at minutes' notice to play Britain's Reading festival in 1999. "After a while in The Fall, you're no longer normal," said Steve Hanley. Launching a sort of defense, guitarist **Ben Pritchard** said: "I have nightmares, but it's never boring."

There have been more Fall fallouts and walkouts (Birtwistle, **Steve Trafford**, and Pritchard left in 2006, again in the U.S.) but Mrs. Smith No. 3 (after a doomed second marriage to Safron Pryor and relationship with keyboardist Julia Nagle) arrived in the shape of **Elena Poulou**. Three releases from 2008—*Imperial Wax Solvent*, *Your Future Our Clutter*, and *Ersatz GB*—all feature guitarist Peter Greenway, Dave Spurr on bass, drummer Keiron Melling, and Poulou on keyboards.

The albums continue to divide the world: those who believe, as John Peel said, that The Fall is "the band against which all others are judged," and those for whom any charms stay hidden. It is fair to say that one group is larger than the other, but plowing a middle ground has never been an option. As Hanley observed: "Smith doesn't do average." **CB**

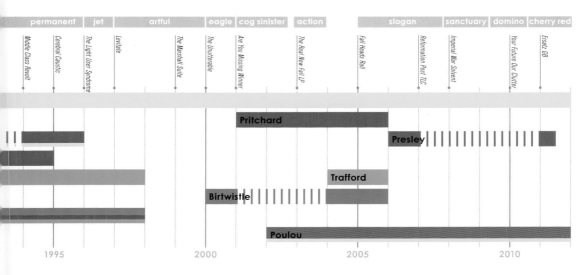

fall out boy 2001–2009

Patrick Stump
b. April 27, 1984

Pete Wentz
b. June 5, 1979

Joe Trohman
b. September 1, 1984

T.J. "Racine" Kunasch
b. Unknown

Andy Hurley
b. May 31, 1980

By 2005, pop-punk was in trouble. Blink-182 were falling apart, Simple Plan had split, and pioneers New Found Glory were battling comparisons to bandwagon-jumpers Good Charlotte. Green Day had reinvented themselves as a twenty-first-century version of The Who, and the genre's youthful angsty zest was being swamped by corporate soundalikes.

Happily, saviors awaited in the forms of Paramore, who hit with *All We Know Is Falling,* and Fall Out Boy, who scored a double platinum U.S. smash with "Sugar We're Going Down." Having pin-ups in their ranks— Hayley Williams in Paramore, bassist **Pete Wentz** in Fall Out Boy—did not hurt, and neither did the fact that they were not much older than many of the fans.

Wentz and guitarist **Joe Trohman** first united in Chicago, recruiting drummer Mike Pareskuwicz and singer **Patrick Stump**. Their name referred to a comic strip character in *The Simpsons*—in Wentz's self-deprecating view, said Stump, the band would "always be the Fall Out Boy to somebody else's Radioactive Man." Their first full-length release— *Fall Out Boy's Evening Out with Your Girl*—indeed troubled no charts, but secured them a deal with Florida indie label Fueled by Ramen (the home of Paramore). It also attracted major label Island, who bankrolled 2003's *Take This to Your Grave* (featuring a

new drummer, Wentz's friend **Andy Hurley**). Touring, coupled with airplay for *Grave*'s "Grand Theft Autumn/Where Is Your Boy" and "Saturday" laid the groundwork for 2005's *From Under the Cork Tree.* The album smashed into the U.S. Top Ten, as did "Sugar We're Going Down" and "Dance Dance." The band earned a Grammy nod, and toured with Wentz's protégés Panic! at the Disco. The latter were signed to the bassist's label Decaydance, also home to Gym Class Heroes, on whose "Cupid's Chokehold" Stump appeared (he bolstered his hip-hop discography with cameos on cuts by The Roots, Lupe Fiasco, and Tyga).

Now fully fledged stars, Fall Out Boy scored a U.S. No. 1 and global smash with 2007's *Infinity on High.* The ensuing tour was commemorated by **** *Live in Phoenix,* featuring a cover of Michael Jackson's "Beat It." However, ambition bested them on 2008's *Folie à Deux.* Featuring Elvis Costello, Pharrell Williams, and Blondie singer Debbie Harry, it left all but the most devoted fans cold. With Wentz's marriage to pop star Ashlee Simpson attracting more interest than his music, Fall Out Boy were put on ice in 2009. Fans hoping for a reunion should not hold their breath: "It'll have to be when we all genuinely want to do it again," Wentz told MTV. "When you do it for seven years straight, you start grating on each other." **BM**

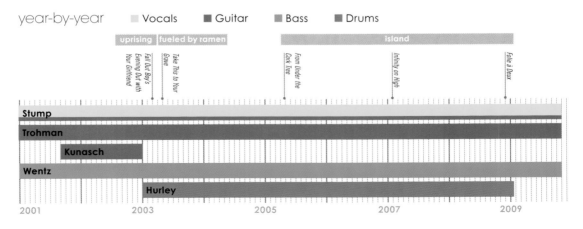

year-by-year   ■ Vocals   ■ Guitar   ■ Bass   ■ Drums

uprising | fueled by ramen | island

Fall Out Boy's Evening Out with Your Girlfriend
Take This to Your Grave
From Under the Cork Tree
Infinity on High
Folie à Deux

Stump
Trohman
Kunasch
Wentz
Hurley

2001   2003   2005   2007   2009

faust 1971–present

Uwe Nettelbeck
b. August 7, 1940
d. January 17, 2007

Werner "Zappi" Diermaier
b. Unknown

Hans Joachim Irmler
b. 1950

Jean-Hervé Péron
b. Unknown

Rudolf Sosna
b. Unknown

Gunter Wüsthoff
b. Unknown

In 1973, before his empire ballooned, record label owner Richard Branson introduced avant-garde German rock to the masses by selling an LP for the price of a single. As a marketing idea it was a triumph: more than 100,000 paid pennies for *The Faust Tapes*. Many buyers doubtless got no further than ten minutes into side one before consigning the record to its jacket, never again to be disturbed. But for a minority it was a life-changing entry point to an alien universe.

Faust were formed in 1971 in the rural German town of Wümme by producer and "overseer" **Uwe Nettelbeck** and musicians **Hans Joachim Irmler, Jean-Hervé Péron, Werner "Zappi" Diermaier, Rudolf Sosna, Gunther Wüsthoff**, and Armulf Meifert. Nettelbeck negotiated an advance from the Polydor label to convert a schoolhouse into a studio. The *modus operandi* was initially simple: Faust would experiment and record at their leisure, without being charged by the hour. The results would be studied and tapes chopped labor-intensively into musical fragments, to create the band's noisy sound collages.

Faust's self-titled 1971 debut LP, pressed on clear vinyl, sold poorly but won the group a passionate cult following. *Faust So Far* (1972) was another commercial failure that lost the band its existing deal but earned a new one as an early signing to Branson's Virgin label.

As a condition of the new contract, as negotiated by Nettelbeck, Faust gave an album to Branson free of charge on the condition that it was sold as cheaply as possible. Hence 1973's *The Faust Tapes* became arguably the biggest-selling avant-garde rock album of all time, and earned the band not a single pfennig.

That same year, Faust collaborated at their studio in Wümme with American avant-garde musician and filmmaker Tony Conrad on the minimalist classic *Outside the Dream Syndicate*. Meanwhile, hoping to capitalize on the wide circulation of *The Faust Tapes*, Virgin issued *Faust IV*. Sales suggested that few buyers desired a second helping: Faust were dropped from Branson's growing roster and disbanded.

Little more was heard until, in 1990, Irmler, Péron, and Diermaier re-formed for European performances and, in 1993, their first U.S. shows, with old friend Tony Conrad. New releases *Rien* and *You Know FaUSt* were hailed as the return of genuine musical pioneers.

Faust continue to function, albeit as two bodies: one headed by Irmler, the other by Péron and Diermaier. Both remain worthy of investigation. **TB**

year-by-year   ■ Vocals   ■ Guitar   ■ Bass   ■ Drums   ■ Keyboards   ■ Aerophones   ■ Programming   ■ Other

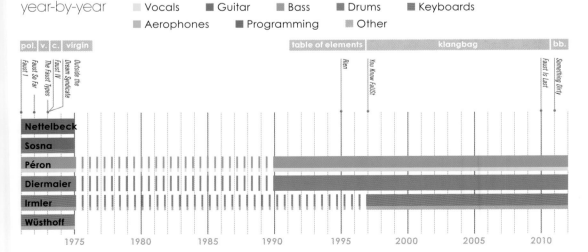

the flaming lips 1983–present

Wayne Coyne
b. January 13, 1961

Michael Ivins
b. March 17, 1963

Richard English
b. Unknown

Nathan Roberts
b. Unknown

Jonathan Donahue
b. May 6, 1966

Ronald Jones
b. November 26, 1970

"If you think you're going to hear an utterly original, powerful, and freaky record when you put on *Nevermind…*" **Wayne Coyne** complained to *The Guardian*, "Christ, you're going to be disappointed. You're going to think, 'Who is this band that sounds like Nickelback? What are these drug addicts going on about?'" This desire to buck prevailing trends has clearly informed his own band, who blazed a Technicolor trail for acts like MGMT and Passion Pit.

The Flaming Lips are the premier purveyors of modern psychedelia, employing colorful and eccentric methods of making and presenting music. They formed in Oklahoma City in 1983 as a trio: Coyne on guitar, his brother Mark Coyne on vocals, and bassist **Michael Ivins**. Their first regular drummer, **Richard English**, joined in 1984, in time to feature on a self-titled debut EP. Wayne took over as singer after his sibling quit in 1985, and the lineup produced three albums that moved from straightforward indie rock to something stranger: *Hear It Is* (1986), *Oh My Gawd!!!* (1987), and 1989's *Telepathic Surgery*.

In 1989, English was replaced by drummer **Nathan Roberts** and the Lips were joined by guitarist **Jonathan Donahue**, also a member of Mercury Rev. *In A Priest Driven Ambulance* (1990) introduced the fragile falsetto that became one of Coyne's vocal trademarks, earning comparisons to Neil Young.

Signed to Warner, the Lips made their major-label debut in 1991 with an EP whose title hardly suggested corporate compromise: *Yeah I Know It's a Drag… But Wastin' Pigs Is Still Radical*. The album *Hit to Death in the Future Head* followed in 1992, after a delay caused by clearing the use of a sample. By the time it hit stores, Donahue and Roberts had been replaced by guitarist **Ronald Jones** and drummer **Steven Drozd**. (Donahue returned to Mercury Rev, whose drummer Dave Fridmann produced many of the Lips' albums.)

The band's first commercial success came when MTV's *Beavis and Butt-head Show* belatedly picked up on the jokey single "She Don't Use Jelly," from 1993's *Transmissions from the Satellite Heart*. It took The Flaming Lips into the *Billboard* Hot 100 for the first and only time, and earned them an improbable guest spot on the teen drama *Beverly Hills 90210*.

After *Clouds Taste Metallic* (1995) sold less well despite positive reviews, Jones quit. Drozd began to contribute guitar and keyboards as well as drums and, with Coyne and Ivins, embarked on sonic experiments that culminated in *Zaireeka* (1997), a set of four CDs intended to be played simultaneously.

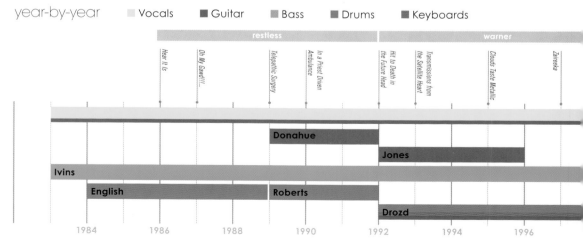

year-by-year   Vocals   Guitar   Bass   Drums   Keyboards

restless   warner

Hear It Is
Oh My Gawd!!!
Telepathic Surgery
In a Priest Driven Ambulance
Hit to Death in the Future Head
Transmissions from the Satellite Heart
Clouds Taste Metallic
Zaireeka

Donahue

Jones

Ivins

English   Roberts

Drozd

1984   1986   1988   1990   1992   1994   1996

Steven Drozd
b. June 11, 1969

Kliph Scurlock
b. June 16, 1973

The Soft Bulletin (1999) boasted lush, symphonic arrangements that drew comparisons to The Beach Boys' *Pet Sounds*. The Lips expanded their live show into a colorful carnival involving dancers in animal costumes, special effects, video screens, and confetti.

Yoshimi Battles the Pink Robots (2002) added more electronica and weightier words. After its release, the band toured with Beck both as the opening act and as Beck's backing musicians. "Do You Realize??" and part one of the title track both became U.K. hits, and in 2003 the Lips collected the Grammy for Best Rock Instrumental performance for "Approaching Pavonis Mons by Balloon (Utopia Planitia)." *At War with the Mystics* (2007) featured simpler, poppier music, allied to direct and sometimes polemical lyrics. It received a mixed response but earned two more Grammys.

Typically, the Lips reacted to this acceptance by becoming outré again. In 2008, they premiered the quirky, low-budget, sci-fi movie *Christmas on Mars* that they had worked on since 2001. Then came the often cacophonous *Embryonic* (2009), on which jazz-influenced freak-outs were more in evidence than psychedelic pop. Later the same year, they teamed up with another Oklahoma band, Stardeath and White Dwarfs, plus electroclash queen Peaches and

hardcore legend Henry Rollins to remake Pink Floyd's *Dark Side of the Moon*. ("Pink Floyd were always a group of great creative minds," Coyne told *Rolling Stone*, "who did whatever the fuck they wanted"—a verdict that could easily be applied to his own band.)

The Lips spent 2011 releasing new songs in bizarre formats, such as flash drives encased in a jelly fetus or a jelly skull. In September 2011, they issued *Strobo Trip*, a package consisting of three songs—including the six-hour-long "I Found a Star on the Ground"—and a set of discs that produced visual effects when spun and lit with an enclosed strobe.

For Halloween, the Lips went to a new extreme: a twenty-four-hour song on a hard drive inside a real human skull. Only five of these macabre packages were created, but the day-long track soon found its way online. In the same highly productive year, the band issued a series of limited-edition collaborative EPs. Four tracks from these releases were included on 2012's vinyl-only double album *The Flaming Lips and Heady Fwends*. It included collaborations with Coldplay's Chris Martin, Ke$ha, Yoko Ono, Nick Cave, and Erykah Badu—an impressive list reflecting the widespread respect that this most unpredictable of bands enjoys worldwide. **DJ**

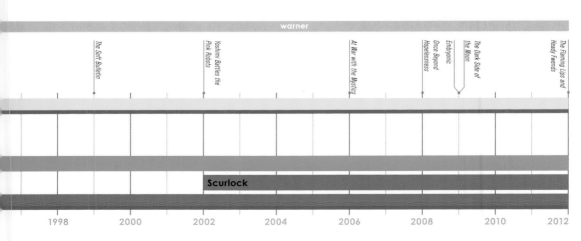

fleetwood mac 1967–present

Mick Fleetwood
b. June 24, 1947

Peter Green
b. October 29, 1946

Jeremy Spencer
b. July 4, 1948

Bob Brunning
b. June 29, 1943
d. October 18, 2011

John McVie
b. November 26, 1945

Danny Kirwan
b. May 13, 1950

Christine McVie
b. July 12, 1943

Bob Welch
b. August 31, 1945
d. June 7, 2012

Perhaps "Fleetwood Macs" would be nearer the mark than "Fleetwood Mac," for there have been many incarnations through the years. Drummer **Mick Fleetwood** had joined John Mayall's Bluesbreakers in 1967. **Peter Green** was part of that band (having replaced Eric Clapton in 1966) but, within a month of Fleetwood joining, Mayall fired him and Green. The duo promptly formed their own outfit, with Green on vocals and lead guitar, alongside guitarist **Jeremy Spencer** (ex-The Levi Set). **Bob Brunning** played bass, until he left to form The Brunning Sunflower Blues Band in September 1967, to be replaced by another former Bluesbreaker, **John McVie** (Mayall had fired him, too).

Joined in mid-1968 by third guitarist **Danny Kirwan** (ex-Boilerhouse), the quintet became shining lights of the U.K.'s blues boom, aided by Green's outstanding musicianship and songwriting chops. From 1968, they enjoyed a run of hit albums, including Top Tens *Fleetwood Mac*, *Mr. Wonderful* (featuring Chicken Shack's Christine Perfect, the future Christine McVie), and *Then Play On*. The Peter Green-penned "Albatross," "Man of the World," "Oh Well," and "The Green Manalishi (with the Two-Prong Crown)" (later covered by Judas Priest) were also British Top

Ten hits, though their melancholic tinge suggested their composer was not a happy man. Unsettled by their success and destabilized by LSD use, Green announced his departure from the group in 1970, withdrawing from the world and releasing only the occasional solo album before reappearing with his Splinter Group in the late nineties (he left them in 2004 and joined The British Blues All Stars). More positively, however, keyboard player **Christine McVie** joined.

On a U.S. tour in 1971, Spencer went out for a newspaper and never returned; he had joined a cult, The Children of God. (He later released a 1979 album, *Flee*, with the Jeremy Spencer Band.) His replacement was guitarist **Bob Welch**, who, with Christine McVie, helped steer the band in a more melodic direction.

The Mac played across the U.S. in the early seventies, with frequent lineup changes. The unreliable Kirwan was fired in 1972, to be replaced by **Dave Walker** (formerly of The Idle Race, and Savoy Brown) and **Bob Weston**, though they only lasted one album—1973's *Penguin*. (Walker went on to form Hungry Fighter with the ejected Kirwan, then to join Raven and Mistress, and was briefly a contender to replace Ozzy Osbourne in Black Sabbath.) Meanwhile, an affair with

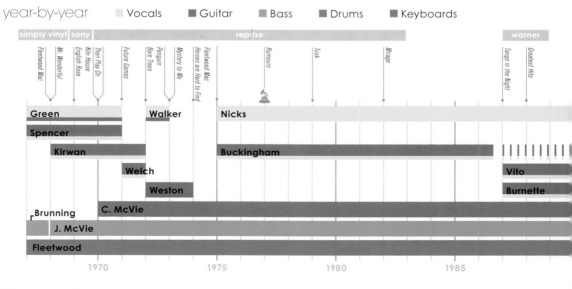

Dave Walker
b. January 25, 1945

Bob Weston
b. Nov 1, 1947
d. January 3, 2012

Lindsey Buckingham
b. October 3, 1949

Stevie Nicks
b. May 26, 1948

Rick Vito
b. October 13, 1949

Billy Burnette
b. May 8, 1953

Bekka Bramlett
b. April 19, 1968

Dave Mason
b. May 10, 1946

Fleetwood's wife Jenny saw Weston fired in September 1973. Then, toward the end of 1974, Welch departed to form Paris and embark on a successful solo career.

With Fleetwood and the McVies now settled in California, the drummer's interest was piqued by a tape of an album by **Lindsey Buckingham** and **Stevie Nicks**. The duo were invited to join the band, creating the band's tenth and most successful incarnation.

After a slow climb, the West Coast-flavored *Fleetwood Mac* made No. 1 in the U.S. in 1976. By the next year, the relationships between Fleetwood and his wife, the McVies, and Nicks and Buckingham were collapsing. "A complete disaster zone..." Fleetwood told writer Craig Rosen. "Emotional hell laced with musical pleasure." Despite (and even inspired by) their friction and cocaine habits, 1977's melodic *Rumours* became one of rock's all-time best-sellers.

Eager to avoid making *Rumours Pt II*, Buckingham pushed for an experimental approach for *Tusk* (1979). The title track and "Sara" were both hits, but the band returned to less controversial waters for *Mirage* (1982).

With Nicks having launched a platinum-selling solo career with 1981's *Bella Donna*, the Mac went their separate ways for three years. They re-formed in late 1985 to create *Tango in the Night* (1987), which proved another huge hit. However, plans for a tour broke down and Buckingham quit, to be replaced by guitarist **Rick Vito** and vocalist **Billy Burnette** (who had played with Fleetwood in the latter's band The Zoo).

The six-strong lineup cut 1990's *Behind the Mask*, but Nicks and McVie quit at the end of the year. The full return of the Mac came in 1993, at the request of President Bill Clinton: Buckingham, Nicks, Fleetwood, and the McVies performed *Rumours'* "Don't Stop" at his inauguration party. However, it proved a one-off—instead, Fleetwood and the McVies recruited vocalist **Bekka Bramlett** and former Traffic guitarist **Dave Mason** for 1995's disappointing *Time*.

The famous five re-grouped again for 1997's live *The Dance* (1997). Coupling originals with old hits, it returned them to the multi-platinum status of old, and preceded a spectacularly successful reunion tour.

Christine McVie departed again in 2003, but the remaining four produced that year's *Say You Will* (despite renewed tension between Buckingham and Nicks) and mounted a hits tour in 2009. "I don't believe Fleetwood Mac will ever tour again," Fleetwood told *Playboy* in 2012, "but I really hope we do." **RD**

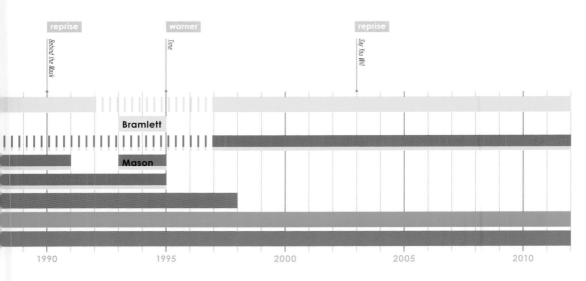

reprise

warner

reprise

Behind the Mask

Time

Say You Will

Bramlett

Mason

1990 1995 2000 2005 2010

Mr. Wonderful
(1968)

Then Play On
(1969)

Bare Trees (1972)

Mystery to Me
(1973)

Fleetwood Mac
(1975)

Rumours (1977)

Tusk (1979)

Tango in the Night
(1987)

Behind the Mask
(1990)

Say You Will (2003)

Left to right: **Mick Fleetwood, Jeremy Spencer, John McVie,** and **Peter Green** in 1968.

Danny Kirwan (bottom left) with Fleetwood Mac in 1969.

Fleetwood plays at the Sundown, a converted cinema in Mile End, London, in 1972.

From top: **Fleetwood, Bob Weston, Bob Welch, Dave Walker, John McVie,** and **Christine McVie** in 1973.

John McVie, Lindsey Buckingham, Christine McVie, Stevie Nicks, and **Fleetwood**—Fleetwood Mac's most commercially successful lineup—in 1975.

McVie performs onstage with **Buckingham** in 1977.

Nicks, Fleetwood, Rick Vito, Christine McVie, John McVie, and **Billy Burnette**—the lineup that took *Tango in the Night* on the road after Buckingham declined to tour.

Nicks wearing characteristically other-worldly finery in 1979.

Christine McVie, Fleetwood, Nicks and **Burnette** in 1990.

Fleetwood performs with his band on *The Tonight Show with Jay Leno* in April 2003.

the flying burrito brothers 1968–2000

Gram Parsons
b. November 5, 1946
d. September 19, 1973

Chris Hillman
b. December 4, 1944

Michael Clarke
b. June 3, 1946
d. December 19, 1993

Sneaky Pete Kleinow
b. Aug 20, 1934
d. January 6, 2007

Chris Ethridge
b. February 10, 1947
d. April 23, 2012

Bernie Leadon
b. July 19, 1947

John Beland
b. July 24, 1949

Gib Guilbeau
b. September 26, 1937

When the experimental International Submarine Band petered out owing to a lack of success, bassist Ian Dunlop dreamed up a name for a new band (featuring ex-ISB drummer Mickey Gauvin) that reflected the soul, jump, rock 'n' roll, and western swing they wanted to play. The Flying Burrito Brothers were born, but the name was soon adopted by another two former ISB members, **Gram Parsons** and the short-stayed John Nuese. Parsons buried old animosity with **Chris Hillman** (with whom he had played in The Byrds) and the two set about writing the country rock classic *The Gilded Palace of Sin* in 1968.

The Parsons/Hillman partnership flourished at a house—nicknamed "Burrito Manor"—shared by the two in L.A. An A&M contract followed and *The Gilded Palace of Sin*, despite only minor chart success in 1969, proved to be an album of enduring quality, reflected by its rank in the top half of *Rolling Stone*'s 500 Greatest Albums of All Time list. "Christine's Tune (Devil in Disguise)" was typical of the Burritos' souped-up country music. Parsons' laidback interpretation and persistent love of the genre extended to the band's extraordinary stage apparel: Nudie suits boasting traditional embroidery, with Gram's depicting marijuana leaves and naked women.

Another ex-Byrd, **Michael Clarke** joined and, before the end of 1969, **Chris Ethridge** left. Guitarist

Bernie Leadon arrived ahead of *Burrito Deluxe* (1970). The harmony Hillman and Parsons had enjoyed was now compromised by the latter's drug dependency. Parsons went solo, and Rick Roberts joined for *The Flying Burrito Bros* (1971). The revolving door hadn't stopped yet: **Sneaky Pete Kleinow** left, replaced by pedal steel legend Al Perkins. Kenny Wertz filled the void left by Leadon, who hooked up with the new kids in town, the Eagles. The live *Last of the Red Hot Burritos* (1972) seemed to signal the end, leaving Hillman to close down the band. Rick Roberts soldiered on with a Burritos tour of Europe in 1973 while 1974's *Close Up the Honky Tonks* compilation kept the flag flying.

The death of Parsons in 1973 heightened interest in his past recordings, and a reconvened band—featuring the returning Kleinow and Ethridge, with new additions Gene Parsons, **Gib Guilbeau**, and Joel Scott Hill—released the appropriately titled *Flying Again* (1975). A year later, *Airborne* saw former Byrd Skip Battin replacing Ethridge. A less rock-oriented, more countrified Burritos wowed fans and critics.

With Guilbeau and newly joined **John Beland**, supported by veteran Burrito Kleinow (and a long line of the finest country musicians), they soared toward a *Billboard* award in 1981 for Best New Country crossover group—exactly what early Burritos Parsons and Hillman had been striving for in 1968. **DR**

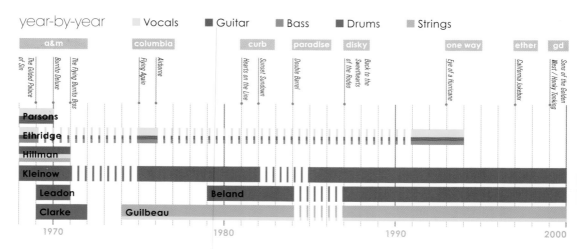

year-by-year · Vocals · Guitar · Bass · Drums · Strings

a&m · columbia · curb · paradise · disky · one way · ether · gd

The Gilded Palace of Sin · Burrito Deluxe · The Flying Burrito Bros · Flying Again · Airborne · Hearts on the Line · Sunset Sundown · Double Barrel · Back to the Sweethearts of the Rodeo · Eye of a Hurricane · California Jukebox · Sons of the Golden West / Honky Tonking

Parsons
Ethridge
Hillman
Kleinow
Leadon · Beland
Clarke · Guilbeau

1970 · 1980 · 1990 · 2000

focus 1969–present

Thijs van Leer
b. March 31, 1948

Jan Akkerman
b. December 24, 1946

Hans Cleuver
b. Unknown

Pierre van der Linden
b. February 19, 1946

Cyril Havermans
b. Unknown

Bert Ruiter
b. November 26, 1946

David Kemper
b. 1947 or 1948

A talented bunch of progressive jazz-rockers, the Dutch group Focus came together in 1969, comprising **Thijs van Leer** (keyboards, flute, vocals), **Jan Akkerman** (guitar), Martin Dresden (bass), and **Hans Cleuver** (drums). The alternative title of *Focus Plays Focus,* their 1970 debut—*In and out of Focus*—proved prophetic: Akkerman promptly left to play with **Cyril Havermans** (bass) and **Pierre van der Linden** (drums). But when Dresden and Cleuver also departed, van Leer swiftly teamed up with Akkerman's trio to form a new Focus.

This lineup recorded *Focus II*—also known as *Moving Waves.* It bore a surprise hit in the exhilarating, yodeling "Hocus Pocus," which rose to No. 9 in the U.S., balanced by the classically inspired, sidelong "Eruption." The album peaked at No. 2 in the U.K.

Havermans then left to be replaced by bassist **Bert Ruiter.** *Focus 3* (1972), a U.K. No. 6, featured another hit, "Sylvia," a U.K. No. 4, as well as another full-length workout, "Anonymous II." The live *At the Rainbow* (1973) caught Focus near the group's zenith.

British drummer Colin Allen replaced van der Linden before their next studio recording, *Hamburger Concerto* (1974). It boasted a lengthy title track based on a Brahms variation on a Haydn theme, yet still made the U.K. Top Twenty. The lighter, poppier *Mother Focus* (1975) followed with twelve radio-friendly songs,

with **David Kemper** now on drums. *Ship of Memories* was released in 1976, although all the tracks had been originally recorded for release in 1973 and 1974.

Akkerman, who apparently never liked those sessions, departed once more, with guitarists Philip Catherine and Eef Albers coming in to play on the next album, as did drummer Steve Smith. Never a predictable group, Focus then united with flamboyant American singer P.J. Proby for *Focus con Proby* (1977).

Van Leer and Akkerman created *Focus*—confusingly, not a group album—in 1985 and briefly reunited with Ruiter in 1990. After 1994's *The Best of Focus: Hocus Pocus,* van Leer made another attempt at re-forming the group in 1999, with Ruiter, Cleuver, and new guitarist Menno Gootjes. It did not last.

Finally, van Leer successfully re-formed the group in 2001, with Jan Dumeé (guitar), Bobby Jacobs (bass), and Ruben van Roon (drums), although the latter was soon replaced by Bert Smaak. This new incarnation recorded *Focus 8* (2002) and toured extensively—hence 2003's *Live in America* and 2004's *Live in South America*—before van der Linden returned in place of Smaak. Nils van der Steenhoven came in on guitar for Dumeé to record *Focus 9/New Skin* (2006) to the group's satisfaction, although Gootjes reappeared to oust him in 2010. In and out of Focus, indeed! **MiH**

year-by-year

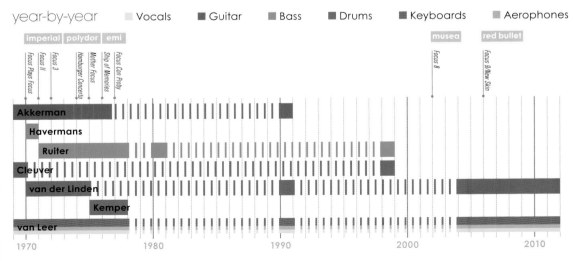

foo fighters 1994–present

Dave Grohl
b. January 14, 1969

Nate Mendel
b. December 2, 1968

Pat Smear
b. August 5, 1959

William Goldsmith
b. July 4, 1972

Franz Stahl
b. October 30, 1962

Taylor Hawkins
b. February 17, 1972

Born from the ashes of a phenomenon, Foo Fighters powered into the mainstream in 1995, led by Nirvana's ex-drummer **Dave Grohl**. In fact, Grohl was the sole official member when Foo Fighters' self-titled debut was recorded in 1994. (The only other musician on the album was The Afghan Whigs' Greg Dulli). Bandmates were soon recruited, however, in the form of former Sunny Day Real Estate bassist **Nate Mendel** and drummer **William Goldsmith**, plus guitarist **Pat Smear**, with whom Grohl had briefly played in Nirvana.

The Foos were an instant smash, particularly in the U.K. But when Goldsmith and then Smear left within two years, Grohl must have wondered why he did not just go it alone. *The Colour and the Shape* (1997) featured Smear, but Grohl re-recorded its drums himself when Goldsmith's standards did not match his own. The disruption did not appear to affect the album's success: it made No. 10 in the U.S. and No. 3 in the U.K. The throat-shredding hit "Monkey Wrench" dealt with the painful end of Grohl's marriage.

Alanis Morissette's drummer **Taylor Hawkins** took Goldsmith's position, while Smear's shoes were briefly filled by **Franz Stahl**, formerly of Grohl's pre-Nirvana hardcore band Scream, but he left before the band recorded *There Is Nothing Left to Lose* (1999). The

remaining trio's results proved successful, hitting the Top Ten in the U.S. and U.K., and spawning the U.S. hit, "Learn to Fly." Guitarist **Chris Shiflett** joined the band for a tour to promote the album.

Despite achieving what seemed like a settled lineup, the Foos fell apart in the studio. To his band's dismay, Grohl abandoned their sessions and joined Queens of the Stone Age for 2002's *Songs for the Deaf* and a tour. When the Foos regrouped, it was made clear that Grohl, for all his happy-go-lucky public persona, would be the one who called the shots.

With this tension kept from their fans, the band's success was undiminished: *One by One* topped the U.K. chart in 2002. "All My Life" announced the album in style, while "Times Like These"—featuring an opening riff instantly familiar to fans of The Cult's "She Sells Sanctuary"—became one of their best-loved hits.

Stable at last, the Foos tried something different with *In Your Honor* (2005). Its first disc was packed with roaring rock; its second with acoustic tracks. A duet with easy-listening star Norah Jones on "Virginia Moon" turned a few heads, but it was a tribute to their versatility. The fans voted with their wallets, and *In Your Honor* reached No. 2 in the U.S. (becoming Foo Fighters' highest-charting album to date).

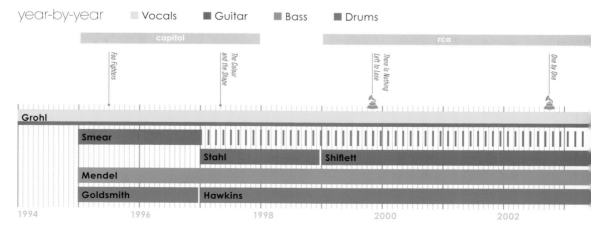

year-by-year ■ Vocals ■ Guitar ■ Bass ■ Drums

capitol

rca

Foo Fighters

The Colour and the Shape

There Is Nothing Left to Lose

One by One

Grohl

Smear

Stahl   Shiflett

Mendel

Goldsmith   Hawkins

1994   1996   1998   2000   2002

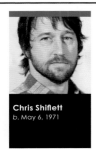

Chris Shiflett
b. May 6, 1971

F

In Your Honor's introductory "Best of You" became the Foos' first platinum single at home and hit No. 2 in the U.K., where they played to 85,000 fans in London's Hyde Park in the summer of 2006. Supported by The Strokes and Motörhead, and featuring cameos by Queen's Brian May and Roger Taylor, the show—issued on DVD alongside the live acoustic album *Skins and Bones*—was a crowning achievement for the band, cementing their place among rock's elite.

After a two-year gap, Foo Fighters returned with a bang in 2007 with "The Pretender," a rock anthem that hit No. 8 in the U.K. and went Top Forty in the U.S. It came from *Echoes, Silence, Patience & Grace*, which made No. 3 in the U.S. and once more topped the U.K. chart. Another highlight was "Long Road to Ruin," released in December 2007, whose accompanying video depicted the band lampooning old U.S. soap operas with a hilarious seventies-themed hospital drama. The video became a cult classic in the same vein as 1999's "Learn to Fly," quickly clocking up more than seven million views on YouTube.

More importantly, however, 2007 saw the band graduate to stadium stars. Instructed by their manager to be "better than Metallica" (a tall order, as Grohl admitted to listening to the metal legends even more than he did to the Pixies, The Beatles and Led Zeppelin), the Foo Fighters stole the show at the globally televised Live Earth extravaganza at London's Wembley Stadium. This set the scene for their own pair of sell-out shows at the same venue in 2008, at the second of which they were joined by Led Zeppelin's Jimmy Page and John Paul Jones.

With six albums and 2009's *Greatest Hits* under their belt, the band could have hung up their guitars with no regrets. Indeed, Grohl promptly formed Them Crooked Vultures with John Paul Jones and Queens of the Stone Age's Josh Homme, while Hawkins recorded with his troupe, the Coattail Riders.

However, the Foos returned in 2011 with *Wasting Light*. With Pat Smear back in the fold, production by *Nevermind*'s Butch Vig, and cameos by Nirvana's Krist Novoselic and Grohl's most obvious influence, Hüsker Dü's Bob Mould, an old-school feel was assured. It was just what fans wanted, becoming a global chart-topper (including an overdue U.S. No. 1). Despite airing their dirty laundry in the accompanying documentary *Back and Forth*, the Foos seem able to do no wrong. "All we are is a rock 'n' roll band, man," Hawkins told *Classic Rock* in 2011. "It's simple as that. We don't claim to be anything more." **DH**

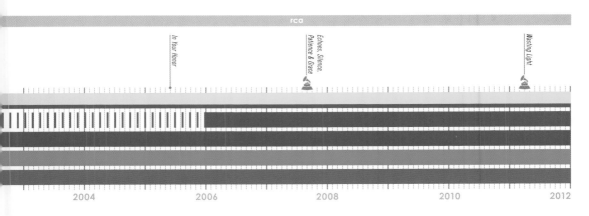

foreigner 1976–present

Lou Gramm
b. May 2, 1950

Mick Jones
b. December 27, 1944

Ian McDonald
b. June 25, 1946

Ed Gagliardi
b. February 13, 1952

Al Greenwood
b. October 20, 1951

Dennis Elliott
b. August 18, 1950

Rick Wills
b. December 5, 1947

Mark Rivera
b. Unknown

More than three decades into their lifespan, Foreigner have enjoyed one constant—guitarist **Mick Jones**. The Londoner was a veteran of Spooky Tooth and Nero and The Gladiators (minor U.K. chart visitors in the early sixties) by the time Foreigner formed. He struck up a plan with former King Crimson multi-instrumentalist **Ian McDonald** to assemble a band that would place a marker in mainstream rock. The duo were joined by New Yorkers **Lou Gramm** (vocals), **Ed Gagliardi** (bass), and **Al Greenwood** (keyboards), and another Londoner, **Dennis Elliott** (drums). Their name arose from the varying backgrounds of their members.

Experience shone through from the outset, with a self-titled debut album (1977) showing off their combined, accomplished musicianship. It went on to sell four million copies in the United States alone, and produced the hits "Feels Like the First Time," "Long, Long Way from Home," and—most notably—"Cold as Ice," which would enjoy a second lease of life decades later as the basis for hip-hop duo M.O.P.'s own "Cold as Ice" in 2001. A year-end poll in *Rolling Stone* magazine saw the group voted top new artists, establishing them as contenders from the outset.

In 1978, Foreigner appeared with Aerosmith at the huge California Jam II festival. Then *Double Vision*

trumped its predecessor's feats, shifting five million units in the United States alone and yielding two Top Three U.S. hits with "Hot Blooded" and the title track.

The band's personnel was rearranged prior to their third album as Gagliardi was replaced on bass by another Englishman, ex-Roxy Music member **Rick Wills**. *Head Games* (1979) saw no let-up in Foreigner's success, spawning more hits in the title track and "Dirty White Boy." However, Gramm told writer Craig Rosen, "No one was really satisfied with *Head Games*. That was the album that got away."

In 1980, McDonald and Greenwood left, the latter hooking up with Gagliardi to form rival band Spys. The remaining quartet—augmented by multi-instrumentalists **Bob Mayo** and **Mark Rivera** and with guest spots by British eighties production guru Thomas Dolby and saxophonist Junior Walker—labored for eight months on a new album with producer "Mutt" Lange. "It was very heavy between us and him at times…," Jones told *Kerrang!* magazine. "He's very straightforward, though—no bullshit. And he really wanted to help us make a tremendous album."

The hard work paid dividends. *4* (1981) topped the U.S. chart for ten weeks and went platinum six times. Its best-known single, "Waiting for a Girl Like

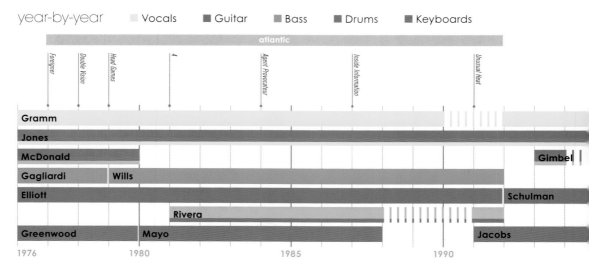

year-by-year   ▨ Vocals   ■ Guitar   ■ Bass   ■ Drums   ■ Keyboards

atlantic

Foreigner   *Double Vision*   *Head Games*   *4*   *Agent Provocateur*   *Inside Information*   *Unusual Heat*

Gramm

Jones

McDonald · Gimbel

Gagliardi | Wills

Elliott · Schulman

Rivera

Greenwood | Mayo · Jacobs

1976   1980   1985   1990

Bob Mayo
b. Aug 25, 1951
d. February 23, 2004

Jeff Jacobs
b.1962

Mark Schulman
b. Unknown

Thom Gimbel
b. Unknown

Brian Tichy
b. August 18, 1968

Jeff Pilson
b. January 19, 1959

Kelly Hansen
b. April 18, 1961

Michael Bluestein
b. Unknown

F

You," spent ten weeks at No. 2 in the *Billboard* Hot 100 and provided Foreigner with their first U.K. Top Ten hit. Dolby's anthemic keyboard line alone represented a bridge between rock and pop that would define the MTV-led mainstream of the decade to come.

Even greater achievements were waiting in the wings as Foreigner embraced the softer style that had such an impact on the charts. After a smash greatest hits with *Records* (1982), the band extended their global reach with *Agent Provocateur* (1984) and its most effective weapon, the power ballad "I Want to Know What Love Is." This momentous hit was a career peak, topping charts on both sides of the Atlantic and providing an evergreen radio favorite with its grand sentiment and song-stealing turn from the New Jersey Mass Choir. "I'm quite proud of writing music that is popular, as opposed to 'pop music'," Jones remarked.

Later years brought a whirl of personnel changes and band side-projects. Crucially, singer Gramm scored a U.S. Top Ten hit with 1987's "Midnight Blue" (from the Top Thirty album *Ready or Not*). The band reconvened that same year for *Inside Information*—a million-selling success, modest by their standards—but the writing was on the wall. Gramm released another solo album—1989's *Long Hard Look*—before fulfilling

predictions and leaving Foreigner the next year to form Shadow King with former Whitesnake (and future Def Leppard) guitarist Vivian Campbell.

Jones would not be deterred, enlisting former King Kobra singer Johnny Edwards to take over vocals for the flop *Unusual Heat* (1991). But by the time of 1992's *The Very Best... and Beyond,* Gramm had returned, Wills had left for Bad Company (to be replaced by bassist Bruce Turgon, who had enjoyed a brief stint in Shadow King with his friend Gramm), and Edwards had been followed by drummer **Mark Schulman**.

With keyboard player **Jeff Jacobs**, *Mr. Moonlight* (1994) fared even worse than *Unusual Heat*. Foreigner hit the nostalgia touring circuit with the likes of The Doobie Brothers, Cheap Trick, and REO Speedwagon, before Gramm was successfully treated for a brain tumor in 1997. He left again in 2003, but Foreigner forged ahead with **Kelly Hansen** (ex-Hurricane) on vocals and John Bonham's son Jason on drums.

Escalating appreciation for the type of classic rock once spearheaded by Foreigner provided an audience for 2009's *Can't Slow Down*, their first new album in fifteen years. Produced by Mark Ronson—Jones's stepson—it returned them to the *Billboard* Top Thirty after a twenty-one-year absence. **MaH**

■ Aerophones

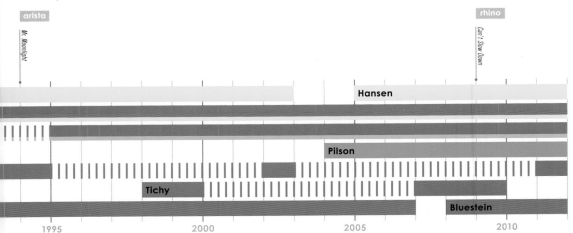

free 1968–1973

Paul Rodgers
b. December
17, 1949

Paul Kossoff
b. Sept 14, 1950
d. March 19,
1976

Andy Fraser
b. July 3, 1952

Simon Kirke
b. July 28, 1949

**John
"Rabbit"
Bundrick**
b. Nov 21, 1948

**Tetsu
Yamauchi**
b. October 21,
1946

**Wendell
Richardson**
b. Unknown

F

Free had a short lifespan but their reputation as bluesy hard rockers was forever sealed before their demise. **Paul Rodgers** (vocals), **Paul Kossoff** (guitar), **Andy Fraser** (bass), and **Simon Kirke** (drums) united in London in 1968 as teenagers. Rodgers had come south from Middlesbrough in search of fame, and met Kossoff and Kirke of blues-rockers Black Cat Bones. They were named Free by bluesman Alexis Korner, who introduced them to Fraser, a veteran of John Mayall's Bluesbreakers.

Free's debut album *Tons of Sobs* (1968) showed the group's unmistakable promise. Fine Fraser-Rodgers compositions such as "I'm a Mover" and "Wild Indian Woman" were buttressed by the laconic Booker T song, "The Hunter." *Free* (1969) was more technically proficient and garnered higher U.K. sales. "I'll Be Creeping," "Woman," and "Songs of Yesterday" were splendid examples of the group's strengths: loping bass, ruthless drumming, powerful, brooding vocals, and a beautiful guitar tone.

Fire and Water (1970) proved their breakthrough, boosted by the transatlantic hit "All Right Now." The album's title track, "Oh I Wept," and "Mr. Big" all brought the self-confidence of their playing to a brash crescendo that perfectly suited four young musicians on the brink of international success. The album rose to U.K. No. 4 and was Free's only U.S. Top Twenty hit.

Oddly, *Highway* (1970) failed to repeat these triumphs, perhaps because three of the group had relaxed after achieving their goals, whereas Kossoff was feeling greater pressure. Certainly, "The Stealer," "Be My Friend," and "The Highway Song" deserved better—but internal fissures deepened. "My Brother Jake" (1971) brought them renewed U.K. success, but was released after Free had split. In time-honored fashion, their record company kept the pot bubbling during the hiatus with *Free Live!*

With the split lasting just seven months, *Free at Last* was the reunited group's attempt to save the troubled Kossoff, who was spiraling into the drug addiction that was to cause his death in 1976. "Soldier Boy," "Sail On," and "Little Bit of Love" were poignant pleas.

Fraser now had had enough and quit again, with **Tetsu Yamauchi** coming in on bass. A keyboard player was needed to boost the sound and, after a brief stint with Leigh Webster, in jumped John **"Rabbit" Bundrick**. Kossoff's problems, masked in the studio, became all too clear when the group went on tour. Eventually, he was replaced by **Wendell Richardson** from Osibisa, but their styles were so different that the experiment was not a success. *Heartbreaker* (1973) proved to be the group's swansong. Nonetheless, "Wishing Well," "Come Together in the Morning," and the title song were excellent epitaphs for a much-loved group. **MiH**

year-by-year   ■ Vocals   ■ Guitar   ■ Bass   ■ Drums   ■ Keyboards

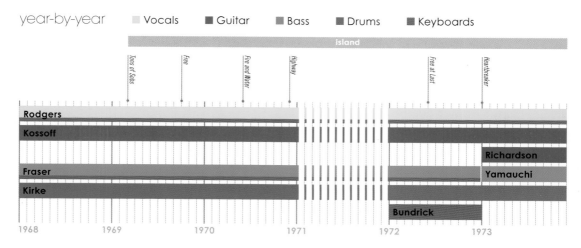

island

Tons of Sobs · *Free* · *Fire and Water* · *Highway* · *Free at Last* · *Heartbreaker*

Rodgers
Kossoff
Richardson
Fraser
Yamauchi
Kirke
Bundrick

1968   1969   1970   1971   1972   1973

the j. geils band 1967–present

J. Geils
b. February 20, 1946

Danny Klein
b. May 13, 1946

Magic Dick
b. May 13, 1945

Peter Wolf
b. March 7, 1946

Stephen Jo Bladd
b. July 14, 1942

Seth Justman
b. January 27, 1951

Ultimate Spinach and other proponents of the manufactured "Bosstown sound" failed to put the city of Boston on the map. Instead, that task fell to what rock writer Robert Christgau dubbed a "gritty Jewish R&B band." Years before local boys Aerosmith blasted to fame, The J. Geils Band became Boston's best rock 'n' rollers and one of America's finest live attractions.

Guitarist John **"J." Geils**, bassist **Danny** "Dr Funk" **Klein**, and harmonica player Richard **"Magic Dick"** Salwitz first convened as a country blues trio. With DJ-turned-singer **Peter Wolf** and drummer **Stephen Jo Bladd**, they became The J. Geils Blues Band, and earned a live reputation that won them a contract with Atlantic. (It also got them an invitation to play at the Woodstock festival, which they declined.)

With fan and keyboard player **Seth Justman** on board, and the "Blues" dropped from their name, a self-titled debut album crept into the U.S. chart. *Rolling Stone* named them as the "most promising new band," then *The Morning After* (1971) and a cover of Bobby Womack's "Looking for a Love" provided their first Top 100 chart entries. They capitalized on their reputation with 1972's thrilling *"Live" Full House*. (Further well-received live sets followed in the form of 1976's *Blow Your Face Out* and 1982's *Showtime!*)

Bloodshot (1973) hit the U.S. Top Ten and earned their first gold award. However, *Ladies Invited* (1973) saw the band moving closer to rock than R&B, and marked the beginning of the end of their relationship with Atlantic. By *Monkey Island* (1977), they were generating more attention for Wolf's marriage to movie star Faye Dunaway than for their stagnating and increasingly debt-ridden career.

Jumping ship to EMI, the band enjoyed revived fortunes with *Sanctuary* (1978) and *Love Stinks* (1980). "And then," Wolf remarked drily, "*Freeze Frame* made us an overnight success." The 1981 album was a high-tech take on R&B, and marked Justman's takeover of the band's direction. It earned the band their only platinum award, thanks to three hits including the U.S. chart-topping "Centerfold."

However, after a British tour with The Rolling Stones, "miscommunication and disharmony" forced Wolf out of the group in 1983. The band staggered on—Justman and Bladd sharing vocals on *You're Gettin' Even While I'm Gettin' Odd*—but were eclipsed by Wolf's solo career and split in 1985.

A 1999 reunion saw Henry Rollins's drummer Sim Cain deputizing for Bladd, while further shows in 2009 saw the drum stool occupied by Marty Richards. Wolf threatened that a 2010 Boston benefit show would be their last—but, with further dates (including one with old rivals Aerosmith) that year and the next, the group's story still has a few pages left to write. **BM**

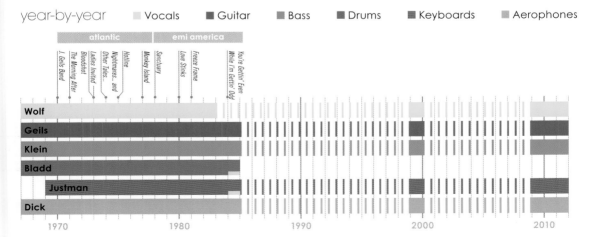

year-by-year   ■ Vocals   ■ Guitar   ■ Bass   ■ Drums   ■ Keyboards   ■ Aerophones

genesis 1967–present

Peter Gabriel
b. February 13, 1950

Tony Banks
b. March 25, 1950

Mike Rutherford
b. October 2, 1950

Chris Stewart
b. 1950

Anthony Phillips
b. December 23, 1951

John Silver
b. 1950

John Mayhew
b. Mar 27, 1947
d. Mar 26, 2009

Steve Hackett
b. February 12, 1950

"Rebellious, restless, constantly striving for something more than the obvious," was Phish front-man Trey Anastasio's view of Genesis when he inducted them into the Rock and Roll Hall of Fame—an appropriate summation of a band as cherished for early, theatrical epics as for million selling pop gems of latter years.

Genesis were formed in 1967 as a songwriting project by students at the Charterhouse school in Surrey, England: **Peter Gabriel** (vocals), **Tony Banks** (keyboards/guitars), **Mike Rutherford** (bass/guitars), and **Anthony Phillips** (guitar). Former Charterhouse student and pop impresario Jonathan King won them a deal with the Decca label, and masterminded 1969's From Genesis to Revelation (by the recording of which **John Silver** had replaced first drummer **Chris Stewart**). This blandly orchestrated, light folk-pop affair sold poorly, but the band refused to give up.

For a new direction they looked to the progressive rock being pioneered by the likes of King Crimson and Yes. Signed to the Charisma label in 1970, Genesis cut Trespass with drummer **John Mayhew**. But Phillips quit before its release, to be replaced fleetingly by Mick Barnard, then, in December 1970, by **Steve Hackett**. With drummer **Phil Collins** having replaced Mayhew in September, the classic lineup was born.

Mixing complex epics, shorter melodic songs, and eccentric lyrics, the group were uniquely English in sound and style. Nursery Cryme (1971), Foxtrot (1972), and Selling England by the Pound (1973) duly sold well and cemented their reputation as one of the best progressive bands. Bringing a theatrical element to their performances, Gabriel's increasingly elaborate stage costumes—including fox-head and flower-petal masks—gave the band a quirky visual edge.

The highly ambitious concept album The Lamb Lies Down on Broadway (1974), driven by Gabriel and performed in its entirety on the long tour that followed, divided the band. This culminated in the shock announcement that Gabriel was leaving to pursue what would become a successful solo career. (He would reunite with Genesis for a one-off show at Britain's Milton Keynes Bowl in October 1982.)

Having auditioned innumerable replacements, Genesis chose Collins—who had already contributed distinctive backing and occasional lead vocals—to be the new front-man. Dropping the theatrical side but keeping the progressive element, the new lineup recorded A Trick of the Tail (1976). The loss of Gabriel, at the time considered fatal, proved to be no bar to their continued success: Wind and Wuthering (1976)

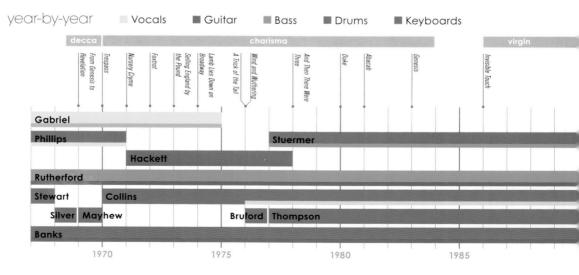

year-by-year   ■ Vocals   ■ Guitar   ■ Bass   ■ Drums   ■ Keyboards

decca | charisma | virgin

From Genesis to Revelation | Trespass | Nursery Cryme | Foxtrot | Selling England by the Pound | Lamb Lies Down on Broadway | A Trick of the Tail | Wind and Wuthering | And Then There Were Three | Duke | Abacab | Genesis | Invisible Touch

Gabriel

Phillips | Stuermer

Hackett

Rutherford

Stewart | Collins

Silver | Mayhew | Bruford | Thompson

Banks

1970   1975   1980   1985

5.5M
Abacab
(1981)

9.5M
Genesis
(1983)

14.5M
Invisible Touch
(1986)

13.5M
We Can't Dance
(1991)

Phil Collins
b. January 30, 1951

Bill Bruford
b. May 17, 1949

Daryl Stuermer
b. November 27, 1952

Chester Thompson
b. December 11, 1948

Ray Wilson
b. September 8, 1968

maintained the U.K. Top Ten placings that continued until 1993, and took them into the U.S. Top Thirty for the first time. To free Collins onstage, they brought in a second drummer for concerts: first, in 1976, **Bill Bruford** (of Yes and King Crimson); then, for much of the rest of their career, **Chester Thompson** (ex-Frank Zappa).

Hackett, feeling increasingly marginalized, left in 1977 and went solo. Rutherford took over guitar duties in the studio for the more commercial *And Then There Were Three* (1978), which yielded the American hit "Follow You, Follow Me." The album itself duly became their first to go gold in the U.S., while American guitarist **Daryl Stuermer** came on board for live work.

In 1979, Collins toured with his jazz-rock act Brand X, while Rutherford and Banks cut *Smallcreep's Day* and *A Curious Feeling*, respectively, both of which made the U.K. Top Thirty. Genesis returned with 1980's fabulous *Duke*: their first U.K. chart-topping album and the start of their most commercially successful phase. Unlike contemporaries such as Yes and Emerson Lake & Palmer, Genesis easily hurdled the transition from the progressive seventies to the poppy eighties—and the gentlemanly Rutherford and Banks were unfazed by Collins's explosive solo success (beginning with 1981's U.K. chart-topping *Face Value*).

Abacab (1981) and *Genesis* (1983) were platinum-selling blends of hits (notably 1983's creepy "Mama") and fan favorites (such as "Home by the Sea"). But both were commercially eclipsed by *Invisible Touch* (1986) and *We Can't Dance* (1991), which transformed Genesis into stadium-filling MTV staples.

When Collins departed amicably in 1996 to focus on his solo career, Banks and Rutherford enlisted Stiltskin vocalist **Ray Wilson**. *Calling All Stations* (1997) was a modest success in Europe, but U.S. dates on an ensuing tour—for which Stuermer and Thompson (both now in Collins's band) were replaced by guitarist Anthony Drennan and drummer Nir Zidkyahu (drums)—were canceled owing to poor sales. Genesis were put on indefinite hold.

An oft-mooted reunion of the classic seventies lineup, with Hackett and Gabriel, ultimately yielded only a gorgeous 1999 re-recording of *The Lamb Lies Down on Broadway*'s "The Carpet Crawlers." Instead, Collins, Rutherford, Banks, Thompson and Stuermer mounted a huge, and apparently final, tour in 2007. Since then, health problems have forced Collins to retire altogether, making any future reunion unlikely. Their legacy, however, is one of the best-selling and most idiosyncratic among British rock acts. **MD**

■ Aerophones

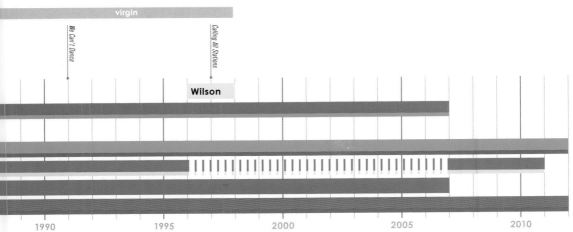

virgin

We Can't Dance

Calling All Stations

Wilson

1990   1995   2000   2005   2010

F

Nursery Cryme (1971)

Foxtrot (1972)

Selling England by the Pound (1973)

The Lamb Lies Down on Broadway (1974)

A Trick of the Tail (1976)

And Then There Were Three (1978)

Abacab (1981)

Invisible Touch (1986)

We Can't Dance (1991)

Calling All Stations (1997)

Peter Gabriel's sense of theater helped draw attention to Genesis.

The classic incarnation in concert in the early seventies, now with **Phil Collins** on drums.

Peter Gabriel and **Mike Rutherford** on the *Lamb* tour.

Steve Hackett appears with Genesis at Newcastle City Hall, England, in October 1973.

In New York in 1976: **Hackett, Phil Collins**, King Crimson drummer **Bill Bruford** (who guested for the A Trick of the Tail tour), **Tony Banks**, and **Rutherford**.

Rutherford silhouetted against **Collins** in Rotterdam, The Netherlands, in September 1978.

Collins and **Banks** at The Spectrum, Philadelphia, on the *Abacab* tour, in November 1981.

Genesis take a bow at Wembley Stadium, London, on July 3, 1987. Left to right **Collins**, **Chester Thompson**, **Banks**, **Rutherford**, and **Daryl Stuermer**.

Collins sings in 1992; he took over vocal duties from **Gabriel** in 1975.

Ex-Stiltskin vocalist **Ray Wilson** performs with Banks in 1997.

gilberto gil 1964–present

Gilberto Gil
b. June 26, 1942

Caetano Veloso
b. August 7, 1942

Maria Bethânia
b. June 18, 1946

Gal Costa
b. September 26, 1945

Tom Zé
b. October 11, 1936

One of the giants of Brazilian music, singer, songwriter, and guitarist **Gilberto Gil** established a reputation for innovation that began with his central role in the Tropicália movement. He eventually emerged as one of the country's biggest-selling artists, incorporating an eclectic range of influences, including rock, samba, bossa nova, reggae, and music from Africa. Gil's lifelong commitment to Brazilian politics saw him first exiled by the country's military leadership in the seventies and then, thirty years later, taking a senior ministerial position in the government of President Luiz Inácio Lula da Silva.

Gilberto Gil was born in Salvador, an industrial city in the northeast of Brazil. He came from a solidly middle-class background: his father was a doctor and his mother a school teacher. Gil was prodigiously talented—by the age of ten he was already playing the drums and trumpet, as well as studying classical accordion. At high school, Gil joined his first band, Os Desafinados ("The Out of Tunes"), but hearing guitarist João Gilberto led him to abandon the accordion and learn to play bossa nova on the acoustic guitar. (Fellow vocalist Robert Palmer later described him as "the most tender of all the bossa nova singers.")

In 1963, while a business student at the Federal University of Bahia in Salvador, Gil met singer and guitarist **Caetano Veloso**. A year later, with Veloso, **Maria Bethânia**, **Gal Costa**, and **Tom Zé**, Gil took part in *Nos Por Exemplo* ("Us, For Example"), a show of bossa nova and traditional Brazilian songs, eventually becoming its musical director. This collective, under the leadership of Gil and Caetano, came together once again on the landmark *Tropicália: Ou Panis et Circensis* ("Tropicália: Or Bread and Circuses") in 1968, one of Brazilian music's most important albums, and, according to Gil, the birth of Tropicália, an artistic movement based on the idea of *antropofagia*—the taking of cultural influences from different genres to create something unique. The stars of Tropicália, among them Os Mutantes, would play a dominant role in Brazilian culture over the coming decades.

Gil enjoyed his first personal success in 1965 when singer Elis Regina had a hit with his song "Louvação." He also began to establish a name for himself as a protest singer at this time, and in 1967 he recorded his debut album, also called *Louvação*. A year later, he produced a characteristic Tropicália follow-up with his second album, *Gilberto Gil*, which blended traditional Brazilian styles such as samba and bossa nova with electric rock music provided by Os Mutantes.

The antics of the Tropicálistas did not sit well with Brazil's right-wing military regime, and in February 1969

year-by-year   ▪ Vocals   ▪ Guitar   ▪ Keyboards

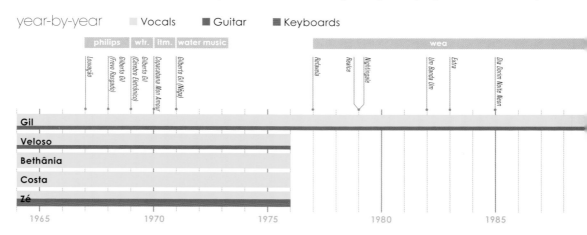

250,000	250,000	250,000	250,000
Tropicália ou Panis et Circensis (1968)	*Gilberto Gil* (1968)	*Expresso 2222* (1972)	*Doces Báraros* (1976)

both Gil and Veloso were arrested; they spent three months in prison and a further four under house arrest. No official reasons were ever given but Gil would maintain that the authorities saw the emergence of their new culture as a threat.

Released from custody, Gil, Veloso, and their wives were exiled to London, where they remained for three years. (They lived in Chelsea with singer Terry Reid, and the Tropicália influence can be clearly heard on his 1973 album *River*.) As a songwriter, this period gave Gil plenty of ammunition for his new material and, while in London, Jimmy Cliff and Burning Spear also provided his first exposure to reggae, which would have a profound effect on his future music.

Returning to Brazil in 1972, Gil recorded *Expresso 2222*—which yielded two major hits, "Back in Bahia" and "Oriente"—before beginning a period of collaborations. This culminated in a 1976 "supergroup" tour with Veloso, Costa, and Bethânia—by then three of the biggest stars in Brazilian musical history—documented on the massive-selling live album *Doces Báraros*. During the seventies and eighties, much of Gil's work followed contemporary trends and production methods, and it can sound rather dated. Songs from this period are generally better appreciated on his many live recordings.

Until 1977, Gil's success had largely been restricted to his homeland. An international deal with the WEA group of labels enabled him to establish a broader following, touring extensively throughout the U.S., his albums no longer restricted to the specialist import bins. In 1982 he enjoyed a huge crossover success with the joyous, sophisticated jazz funk of "Palco," a dance hit that led to greater exposure of his music in Europe.

Back in Brazil, Gil had become increasingly politically active as a prominent spokesman for black rights within his country. He was also largely responsible for the introduction of reggae to Brazil when his 1980 cover of Bob Marley's "No Woman No Cry" topped the chart, selling over 750,000 copies.

During the nineties, Gil found increasing support for his growing involvement in social and political causes, and he was elected to office in his hometown, Salvador. In 2003, he became Brazil's Minister of Culture, before stepping down in 2008, citing health reasons. His music had taken a back seat during this period, but in 2010 he signaled a return with *Fé Na Festa*—an album of original songs performed in traditional forró style—marking the São João festival celebrated in his native northeast Brazil.

Gil continues to tour, and features in Spike Lee's 2012 documentary, *Go Brazil, Go!* **TB**

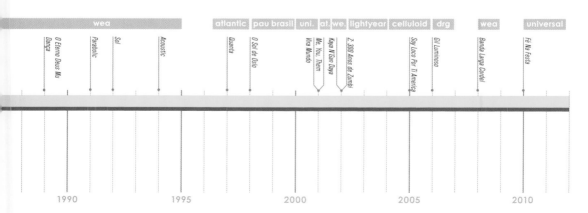

grateful dead 1965–1995

Jerry Garcia
b. August 1, 1942
d. August 9, 1995

Bob Weir
b. October 16, 1947

Phil Lesh
b. March 15, 1940

Ron "Pigpen" McKernan
b. September 8, 1945
d. March 8, 1973

Bill Kreutzmann
b. May 7, 1946

Mickey Hart
b. September 11, 1943

Of all the groups to emerge from America's West Coast in the sixties, The Grateful Dead managed to combine different musical styles with long-lasting success better than any, while epitomizing with panache what the hippie counter-culture stood for.

Jerry Garcia (guitar), **Bob Weir** (guitar), **Phil Lesh** (bass), **Ron "Pigpen" McKernan** (keyboards), and **Bill Kreutzmann** (drums) formed The Warlocks in San Francisco in early 1965, becoming the Grateful Dead a year later. Ken Kesey's contemporary Robert Hunter, who was to become lyricist for many of the group's songs, was partly instrumental in bringing them together. From their commune in Haight-Ashbury, San Francisco, the band's reputation—based on lengthy, improvisational live shows and their enthusiastic espousal of psychedelic drugs—grew rapidly.

The Grateful Dead (1967) was a solid debut, although the group felt it was not fully representative of their free-form spirit. **Mickey Hart** (drums) joined later in 1967, and **Tom Constanten** (keyboards) was added before *Anthem of the Sun* (1968). It was rather too experimental for commercial success (and is the

only one of their early albums yet to go gold) but, artistically, the group were happy with it. *Aoxomoxoa* (1969), including "St. Stephen," featured further interesting experimentation and the Dead were now established as an outstanding live draw.

Live/Dead (1969) proved their unrivaled ability to improvise on blues rock and acid rock themes, with Garcia's extended lead solos and Weir's sympathetic interplay to the fore. Constanten left at the start of 1970, which was to prove the *annus mirabilis* of their studio output. *Workingman's Dead* (1970) was another change in direction, with more succinct songs in a country rock vein, and gave the Dead their first taste of the U.S. Top Thirty. *American Beauty* came out later the same year, broke into the Top Thirty again, and gave the band their highest U.K. chart placing, No. 27.

Typically, the group followed these triumphs with a bout of solo projects and further upheavals. Hart left—possibly because his father, who had been the Dead's manager, absconded with a lot of their cash. Around the same time, Pigpen's narcotic and alcohol habits were causing problems and the jazz-leaning

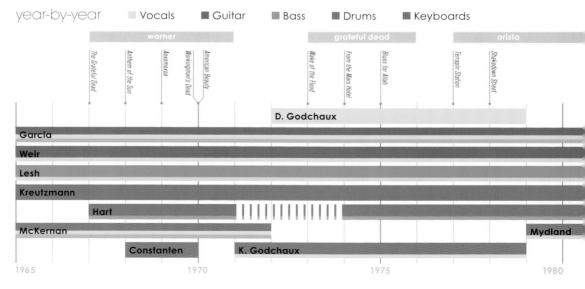

year-by-year ■ Vocals ■ Guitar ■ Bass ■ Drums ■ Keyboards

Tom Constanten
b. March 19, 1944

Keith Godchaux
b. July 19, 1948
d. July 23, 1980

Donna Godchaux
b. August 22, 1947

Brent Mydland
b. October 21, 1952
d. July 26, 1990

Vince Welnick
b. February 21, 1951
d. June 2, 2006

Bruce Hornsby
b. November 23, 1954

Keith Godchaux joined as another keyboard player. Two more live albums emerged, the second of which, *Europe '72*, reached No. 12 in the U.S. By this time, **Donna Godchaux** (vocals) had joined her husband in the group. Meanwhile, Pigpen quit the band; he died from liver complications in 1973.

Wake of the Flood, released just afterward, was the group's first studio album for three years, and reached No. 18 on the *Billboard* chart. *From the Mars Hotel* (1974) went one place better and Hart rejoined in time for *Blues for Allah* (1975), a U.S. No. 12.

The lush *Terrapin Station* (1977), featuring "Estimated Prophet" and the long title track, and *Shakedown Street* (1978), produced by Little Feat's Lowell George, fell short of the Top Twenty, although both subsequently reached gold status. With the pressures of endless touring, they increasingly turned to harder drugs. Keith and Donna Godchaux left, replaced by **Brent Mydland** (keyboards) in 1979.

Go to Heaven (1980) was the Dead's last studio album for seven years, while they continued to play live and wrestle with their demons. Garcia became

so seriously ill in 1985 that he was forced to clean up. Their comeback album, *In the Dark* (1987), was their biggest seller, reaching No. 6. Its single, "Touch of Grey," became their only Top Forty single, peaking at No. 9 as they toured with Bob Dylan (hence 1989's gold-selling but rotten live album *Dylan & the Dead*).

Built to Last (1989) proved to be the Dead's final studio album: Mydland died in 1990, replaced by **Vince Welnick**, formerly of The Tubes; **Bruce Hornsby** also played piano from 1990 to 1992. The Dead were inducted into the Rock and Roll Hall of Fame in 1994, but the end was near. Garcia died in 1995, and the rest of the group called it a day, although there have been various revivals since. The band's numbers were further depleted when Welnick tragically took his own life in 2006. As a belated testimonial, the surviving members of the Grateful Dead were given a Grammy Lifetime Achievement Award in 2007. "The Dead," observed Warren Haynes (who has played with later versions of the band), "redefined success. They created this following that grew and grew, and they did it without compromising themselves." **MiH**

■ Aerophones　　■ Other percussion

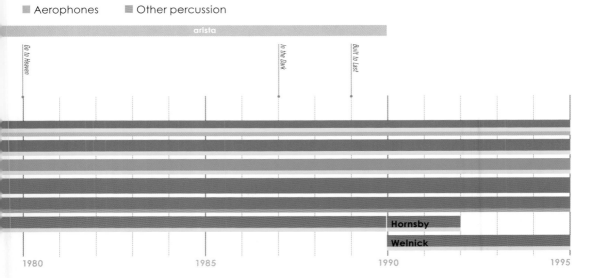

green day 1987–present

Billie Joe Armstrong
b. February 17, 1972

Mike Dirnt
b. May 4, 1972

Al Sobrante
b. July 11, 1969

Tré Cool
b. December 9, 1972

Green Day helped drive the rebirth of U.S. punk in the nineties, and evolved in the twenty-first century to appeal to a whole new generation of fans. The band began as a hobby of Californian teens **Billie Joe Armstrong** and Mike Pritchard (known to his friends as **Mike Dirnt**) in 1987, at a time when bands like Guns N' Roses and Mötley Crüe were the characters—and performers—that most kids like them were idolizing. But Armstrong and Dirnt preferred punk heroes, in particular fellow Californians Rancid, a punk outfit set up by Tim Armstrong and Matt Freeman, and set about forming a group in the same vein, originally known as Sweet Children. Billie Joe assumed vocal duties and guitar while Mike took up bass.

A year later, they met drummer John Kiffmeyer, better known as **Al Sobrante** (the nickname was a reference to his hometown of El Sobrante, California), who was a couple of years older and assumed the role of manager. A party derailed by snow would prove to be the band's big break. Scheduled to play with fellow local band, the Lookouts, adverse weather conditions saw Sweet Children playing to a handful of friends. Lookouts' singer Larry Livermore was impressed and signed them to his independent label for their first EP, *1,000 Hours*, released in April 1989.

Renamed Green Day, the band issued their debut album *39/Smooth* in 1990. "They were in bands when they were fourteen and put out their own record when the lead singer was seventeen…" observed

R.E.M.'s guitarist Peter Buck, admiringly. "They're heirs to a tradition: you're sixteen, you write punk songs, you make your own record on a small label, you tour."

Sobrante's college commitments saw him leave the band in 1990, with Lookouts' drummer **Tré Cool** (born Frank Edwin Wright III) stepping in. With him, Green Day's sophomore album, *Kerplunk!*, released in April 1992, featured an early version of their signature song "Welcome to Paradise." The trio's underground momentum was building, and they opted to sign to Reprise, a subsidiary of Warner.

Backed by a major label, Green Day hit the big time with *Dookie* (1994), as the trio became poster boys for the emerging punk generation (even old hands like Elton John and Patti Smith expressed their liking for them). Tracks such as "When I Come Around," "Longview," and "Basket Case" helped *Dookie* to No. 2 in the U.S. chart and No. 13 in the U.K., with sixteen million copies eventually shifted worldwide. A mudfight with the audience at August 1994's Woodstock II festival provided one of the event's most memorable performances.

Insomniac followed a year later, and equaled *Dookie's* U.S. position of No. 2 (U.K. No. 8). The album—whose working title, Armstrong later claimed, was *Jesus Christ Supermarket*—could not match the runaway success of its predecessor, but nonetheless went double platinum on the back of tracks like "Geek Stink Breath" and "Walking Contradiction."

year-by-year   ▨ Vocals   ▪ Guitar   ▪ Bass   ▪ Drums

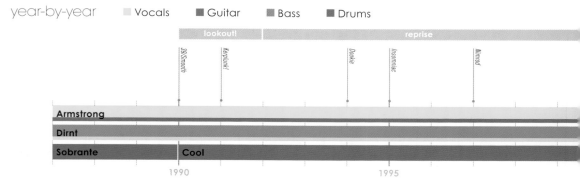

16M	6M	14M	4.5M
Dookie (1994)	Nimrod (1997)	American Idiot (2004)	21st Century Breakdown (2009)

With a loyal fanbase sustaining the group once the hype had dissipated, *Nimrod* (1997) made the U.S. Top Ten (U.K. No. 11). The album is notable for the acoustic gem "Good Riddance (Time of Your Life)," which became a lighter-raising moment at live shows.

Warning (2000) proved a watershed for Green Day. After a three-year gap between albums, it rocketed to No. 4 in both the U.S. and the U.K., but sales were no match for previous efforts. Critics were beginning to sharpen their pens, with *NME* describing the album as "the sound of a band losing its way." More embarrassingly, in 2002, Green Day found themselves supporting Blink-182, a punk trio who had originally followed in their footsteps.

The band busied themselves with *Money Money 2020*, recorded with friends and issued under the band name The Network in 2003, and a new album, *Cigarettes and Valentines*. When the latter began to look like just another entry in their dwindling career, they abandoned it and instead, with producer Rob Cavallo, created the greatest album of their career.

With a new image and sound, the unashamedly grandiose *American Idiot* (2004) was a rock opera whose energy never flagged—even with two tracks, "Jesus of Suburbia" and "Homecoming," clocking in at over nine minutes each and split into "acts." *American Idiot* rocketed to No. 1 in both the U.S. and the U.K., ultimately becoming the band's second-biggest seller. Five of its songs were hits, with "Boulevard of Broken Dreams" and "Wake Me Up When September Ends" both making the U.S. Top Ten (and, in the former's case, going double platinum).

American Idiot earned a Grammy nomination for album of the year. Ultimately, it picked up the trophy for best rock album, while "Boulevard of Broken Dreams" took the prestigious Record of the Year award (its video won six trophies at the MTV Video Music Awards in 2005). The album even spawned a musical of the same name—a move into the mainstream that emphasized the gulf between Green Day and their former contemporaries. The *American Idiot* tour was commemorated by *Bullet in a Bible*, a 2005 CD/DVD set recorded at massive shows in Britain.

The follow-up would always be a big ask, but Green Day cemented their position in punk and rock history with *21st Century Breakdown* in 2009. Despite the longest gap between albums of the trio's career, it picked up where *American Idiot* left off, hitting No. 1 around the world. (The ensuing stadium tour was cherry-picked to create another CD/DVD set, 2011's modestly monickered *Awesome as F**k*.)

Carrying on its predecessor's social commentary, *21st Century Breakdown*—their fifth Grammy-winner— underlined Green Day's position as a band with something to say and an audience that would listen. Grandiose plans for the future include a trilogy of albums: *¡Uno!*, *¡Dos!*, and *¡Tré!* A long way from two kids with a dream in a Californian garage. **DH**

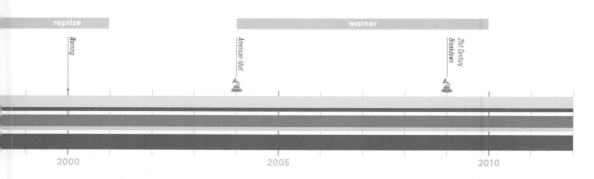

reprise warner

Warning | American Idiot | 21st Century Breakdown

2000 | 2005 | 2010

39/Smooth (1990)

Kerplunk! (1991)

Dookie (1994)

Insomniac (1995)

Nimrod (1997)

Warning (2000)

American Idiot
(2004)

21st Century Breakdown (2009)

Billie Joe Armstrong at one of Green Day's formative punk shows.

Mike Dirnt, **Armstrong**, and **Tré Cool** make their punk roots clear in a promotional shot.

Continuing to deplete California's hair dye reserves at the Shoreline Amphitheater in 1994.

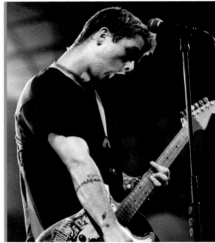

Armstrong rocks the Lowlands festival in the Netherlands, in 1995.

Armstrong and **Dirnt** live in L.A., shortly before the release of *Nimrod*.

Dirnt defies their decline as the twenty-first century dawns.

Say cheese: **Dirnt**, **Cool**, and **Armstrong** circa *Warning*.

Displaying a new sense of purpose as the *American Idiot* era begins.

The trio take punk's "do it yourself" edict the wrong way in Ireland in 2004.

At 2009's American Music Awards, where the trio played *21st Century Breakdown*'s opening hit, "21 Guns."

guitar wolf 1987–present

Guitar Wolf
b. September 22, 1963

Bass Wolf
b. January 8, 1967
d. March 31, 2005

Drum Wolf
b. August 29, 1969

U.G.
b. Unknown

G

The fabulously named Guitar Wolf are a three-piece garage power-punk band originating from Nagasaki, Japan. They coined the term "jet rock 'n' roll" to describe their own brand of music, which features extremely high-volume, piercing vocals, and much deliberate distortion, noise, and feedback. Easy listening they ain't—but their energy on stage and recorded work is infectious. Love them or loathe them, once seen and heard they are not easily forgotten.

Guitar Wolf were formed in 1987 by Seiji and Billy, two young men who originally got to know each other through their jobs—the former worked in a clothing store close to Harajuku Station in Tokyo, the latter in a nearby punk rock shop. Their conversations revealed shared musical tastes, plus the determination, dedication, and desire to produce a new sound all their own. The problem was they both played guitar and therefore needed a drummer, so they persuaded Seiji's work colleague Narita to join them.

With the cast in place, they set about forging an identity. "My great-grandma was a wolf," claimed Seiji. "The band name came from that." Using the Ramones as their model, they decided to adopt the same surname: they would all be "Wolf"—Seiji became **Guitar Wolf**; Billy became **Bass Wolf**; and Narita became **Drum Wolf**.

Before long, Narita left to pursue other interests—according to some accounts he became a fortune teller—and new recruit Toru became Drum Wolf. He

was recommended to Seiji and Billy by one of their heroes, Rockin' Enocky "Papa Burger" "Thunderbolt" Enomoto, charismatic lead guitarist of the Japanese surf band Jackie & The Cedrics.

In this revised lineup, the threesome worked feverishly on their sound, which soon turned out to be a lot harder to describe than to label. Taking the line of least resistance, Seiji named their style after Runaway turned solo star Joan Jett, his proclaimed idol and greatest influence. Guitar Wolf later took to billing themselves as "The World's Greatest Jet Rock 'n' Roll Band," fully mindful that, since they had no imitators, they were—and, at the time of writing, still are—the only known exponents of this genre.

Six years after the band's formation came their first album, *Wolf Rock!* (1993). Recorded, according to Seiji, on "a four-track and Walkman," its twelve songs conjured up the black vinyl spirit of garage punk (as one online reviewer remarked approvingly, "You can hear the needle").

Success in Japan emboldened the band, who undertook a tour of the U.S. A set at the Garageshock festival in Memphis attracted the attention of Eric Friedl of U.S. punk band Oblivians, who decided to release *Wolf Rock!* on a label he founded specially for the purpose, Goner Records. (The original version was digitally remastered, as its lo-fi quality was not considered acceptable.) After 1994's *Run Wolf Run* and 1995's *Missile Me!*, both released on the Japanese

year-by-year ■ Vocals ■ Guitar ■ Bass ■ Drums

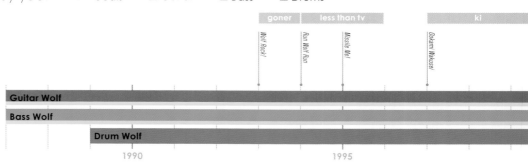

Less Than TV label, a lucky breakthrough occurred in 1996. An executive from New York record label Matador happened to see Guitar Wolf give an in-store performance at a record shop in that city. Blown away by their power and energy, he offered the band a contract on the spot and *Planet of the Wolves* (essentially a slightly tweaked version of 1997's *Ookami Wakusei*) and *Jet Generation* (1999) both came out on that label. The latter featured a prominent sticker that warned, "This is the loudest album ever recorded. Playing at normal volume may cause irreparable damage to stereo equipment. Use at your own risk."

During their time with Matador, Guitar Wolf diversified into movies. They worked twice with writer/producer/director John Michael McCarthy: all three band members appeared as "mysterious strangers" in his *The Sore Losers* (1997)—which boasted the thought-provoking tagline "They wanted meat so they ate the flower children!"—then McCarthy directed the video for their "All Night De Buttobase!! (Roaring All Night!!)." The trio starred as themselves in 2000's *Wild Zero* (tagline—"Trash and chaossss!!!!"), a Japanese rock 'n' roll zombie horror movie directed by Tetsuro Takeuchi. ("The population of zombies has been increasing recently," Seiji mused eight years later. "We have to kill them in *Wild Zero II*.")

Guitar Wolf's later output found an international audience via Narnack Records. The independent New York label released *Rock 'n' Roll Etiquette* and

Live! (both 2000), *UFO Romantics* (2002), and *Loverock* (2004). By this time the Guitar Wolf back catalogue had grown sufficiently for an album of greatest hits—2005's *Golden Black*—but tragedy was about to strike their seemingly unstoppable progress.

Returning to Japan at the end of a successful U.S. tour, Billy/Bass Wolf had a heart attack and died in Tokyo. Only then did his personal details and circumstances become public: his real name was Hideaki Sekiguchi, he was only thirty-eight years old, and he left a wife and two children. Six months after Billy's funeral, Guitar Wolf played their first gig with a new bassist, known to the outside world only as **U.G.**

Stories about the band—such as touring the U.S. on Harleys with guitars strapped to their backs—do much to promote their rockin' rep. But they have to be seen live to be believed. Guitar Wolf shows have plenty of everything: endurance-testing volume, wild lightshows, ridiculously over-sized speakers, fire-spitting microphones, and—above all—boundless energy. The band—whose sunglasses, they claim, allow them to see "only cute and sexy girls"—often play nonstop, with no breaks between numbers.

As an intro to their oeuvre, check out their take on The Rolling Stones' "(I Can't Get No) Satisfaction" (on *Planet of the Wolves*). It is a mess, certainly, but it is meant to be. And what does the future hold for the band? According to the ever-optimistic Seiji, "scandals with Hollywood actresses." **GL**

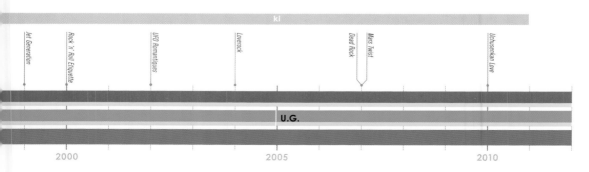

guns n' roses 1985–present

W. Axl Rose
b. February 6, 1962

Slash
b. July 23, 1965

Izzy Stradlin
b. April 8, 1962

Duff McKagan
b. February 5, 1964

Steven Adler
b. January 22, 1965

Gilby Clarke
b. August 17, 1962

Tommy Stinson
b. October 6, 1966

Dizzy Reed
b. June 18, 1963

Alongside their Los Angeleno compadres Mötley Crüe, Guns N' Roses were the only major group to emerge from the hair-metal movement of the eighties with full credibility and full wallets. At the peak of their commercial profile, the band co-headlined a tour with Metallica, metal's biggest act. Like that band, Guns N' Roses continue to tour regularly, often causing controversy and occasionally mayhem. But unlike Metallica, GN'R have been plagued by the hopes of fans that the group's classic lineup will re-form, tour, and scoop multi-million ticket sales.

All of this is a long way from the band's early days, when they were starving longhairs whose only income was a few dollars a day from their stripper girlfriends. Singer **W. Axl Rose** (born William Bailey), who had moved to L.A. from rural Indiana in 1982, formed a group called Hollywood Rose with his childhood friend and guitarist **Izzy Stradlin** (Jeffrey Isbell), who had also moved to the city. The other members—guitarist **Tracii Guns** (Tracy Ulrich), bassist Ole Beich, and drummer Rob Gardner—were soon replaced by local guitar hero **Slash** (Saul Hudson), Seattle-raised punk **Duff** (Michael) **McKagan** and Slash's high-school pal **Steven Adler** (Michael Coletti), respectively. The band

had been renamed when Guns and Rose combined their surnames, and the classic quintet first played together in June 1985. "Playing the first few chords," said McKagan, "was like… lightning had hit the room."

As Slash, Adler, and McKagan have recalled in their autobiographies, GN'R's early days were debauched but tough, with the self-styled "most dangerous band in the world" struggling to make a local impact, let alone a national or international one. However, after building a following in L.A. and attracting sufficient record label interest to start a minor bidding war, they signed to Geffen, thanks to the negotiations of A&R executive Tom Zutaut (also the man behind the Crüe). While recording their debut album, they whetted fans' appetites with the *Live ?!*@ Like a Suicide* EP, issued on a fake independent label and distributed by Geffen.

Appetite for Destruction (1987) originally emerged to what Slash recalled as "little or no fanfare at all" outside of the metal press. However, after GN'R toured with The Cult and the Crüe—and, crucially, after MTV began airing "Welcome to the Jungle"— their profile exploded. By the fall of 1988, they had upstaged touring partners Aerosmith, seen *Appetite* and "Sweet Child o' Mine" top the U.S. charts, and

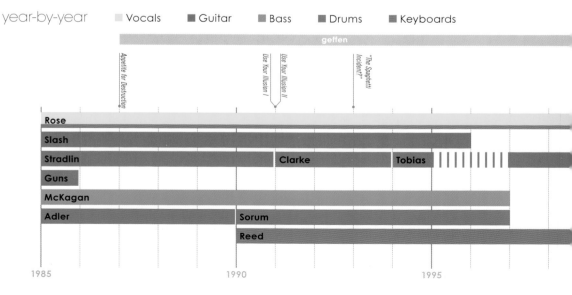

year-by-year ■ Vocals ■ Guitar ■ Bass ■ Drums ■ Keyboards

29.5M
Appetite for Destruction
(1987)

17.8M
Use Your Illusion I
(1991)

18.6M
Use Your Illusion II
(1991)

11M
Greatest Hits
(2004)

Matt Sorum
b. November 19, 1960

Chris Pitman
b. November 16, 1961

Richard Fortus
b. November 17, 1966

Ron "Bumblefoot" Thal
b. Sept 25, 1969

Frank Ferrer
b. 1966

Tracii Guns
b. January 20, 1966

Buckethead
b. May 13, 1969

Paul Tobias
b. August 1963

become the most popular band in the U.S. "It's gonna be interesting to watch them now..." observed Eagles man Don Henley (on whose *The End of the Innocence* Axl guested, and who drummed with GN'R at an award show), "Selling eight million copies of your first album will mess you up." Indeed, all bar Rose (who had self-destructive psychological issues) would have battles with substances, from booze to heroin. While the band struggled to get to grips with their success, *GN'R Lies* (1990) twinned the *Live ?!*@ Like a Suicide* tracks with new acoustic numbers, including the racist and homophobic "One in a Million."

After the heroin-addicted Adler was replaced by ex-Cult drummer **Matt Sorum**, and keyboard player **Dizzy Reed** was enlisted, GN'R issued two albums on September 17, 1991. Stradlin quit shortly afterward (to be replaced by **Gilby Clarke**), but *Use Your Illusion I* and *II* (whose guests included Mike Monroe of GN'R's antecedents Hanoi Rocks) became an inescapable presence in the last years of metal's first reign. When grunge broke later that year and the overblown hair-metal scene became obsolete overnight, GN'R survived—and could reasonably have claimed to be the most popular band then active in the world.

However, a tour lasting more than two years tore the band apart, as Axl asserted control, and his bandmates lost themselves in booze and drugs (McKagan's pancreas exploded from years of abuse). After a covers album, 1993's *"The Spaghetti Incident?"*, and a hit cover of the Stones' "Sympathy for the Devil" in 1994, the core members peeled away. (Slash, McKagan, and Sorum formed Velvet Revolver with Stone Temple Pilots' Scott Weiland.) By 1999, when GN'R issued "Oh My God" on the *End of Days* soundtrack, only Rose remained of the original band.

After years of producers and guests (including Brian May, Moby, and Killing Joke's Youth) coming and going, *Chinese Democracy* finally appeared in 2008, but its inconsistency betrayed the songs' overlong gestation. It was largely dismissed by GNR's fanbase, although Rose continues to tour, his band variously including the KFC-capped **Buckethead** and his six-string successor **Ron "Bumblefoot" Thal**, former Replacements bassist Tommy Stinson, Nine Inch Nails guitarist Robin Finck, and the long-serving Dizzy Reed.

Stradlin and McKagan have jammed with Rose onstage, but, regarding Slash, Rose remarked in 2009, "One of the two of us will die before a reunion." **JM**

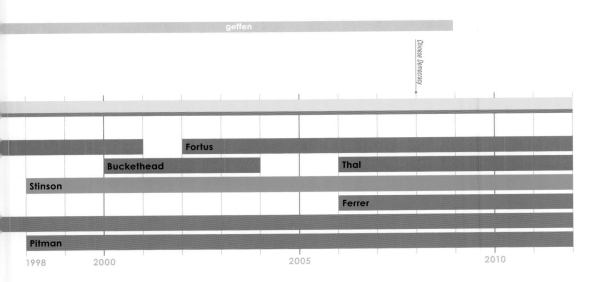

geffen

Chinese Democracy

Fortus

Buckethead

Thal

Stinson

Ferrer

Pitman

1998   2000   2005   2010

Appetite for Destruction (1987)

Use Your Illusion I (1991)

Use Your Illusion II (1991)

"The Spaghetti Incident?" (1993)

Chinese Democracy (2008)

Duff McKagan and **Slash** rock the Ritz club in New York: a 1988 concert shown on MTV.

Axl Rose, possibly still a farm-boy from Indiana at heart, in 1987.

Still standing—just—after a series of dates supporting Mötley Crüe in late 1987, the classic line-up of **McKagan**, **Slash**, **Rose**, **Izzy Stradlin**, and **Steven Adler**.

They haven't had many good things to say about each other in the past two decades—but, at their peak, **Rose** and **Slash** were rock's most exciting double act.

McKagan, **Slash**, **Rose**, and **Gilby Clarke** at 1992's Freddie Mercury tribute show, at Wembley Stadium.

Axl with Adler's replacement, former Cult drummer **Matt Sorum**, at the Freddie Mercury tribute show.

Slash handled most press promotion for *"The Spaghetti Incident?"*.

Reunited with **Stradlin** (and Ronnie Wood) in Britain in 1993.

Rose: still nuts and still incapable of arriving onstage on time, but still packing in the crowds.

Ron "Bumblefoot" Thal, in Ottawa, Canada, 2010.

george harrison 1968–2001

George Harrison
b. February 25, 1943
d. November 29, 2001

Jim Keltner
b. April 27, 1942

Billy Preston
b. September 2, 1946
d. June 6, 2006

Gary Wright
b. April 26, 1945

Dhani Harrison
b. August 1, 1978

For **George Harrison**, being a Beatle came to be frustrating. Often overlooked as a songwriter by his bandmates, he was also uncomfortable with the demands on his time and privacy that came with life as a star, and unhappy with touring and the screaming that drowned out the group's shows.

When the Fab Four gave up touring in 1966, he remarked, "That's it. I don't have to be a Beatle anymore." In 1968, Harrison became the second (after Paul McCartney) to issue material outside the group; his soundtrack *Wonderwall Music* (1968), the first album on The Beatles' Apple label, hit the U.S. Top Fifty. This sparked Harrison's desire for greater personal recognition; he released the experimental *Electronic Sound* (1969), and produced the London Radha Krishna Temple and other Apple acts such as Badfinger and Billy Preston. (The latter was one of a handful of musicians who regularly contributed to Harrison's later solo albums, alongside drummer Jim Keltner and keyboard player Gary Wright.)

In 1970, a year after he tasted success as a songwriter for The Beatles with "Something," Harrison went on the road with Delaney and Bonnie & Friends (including Eric Clapton). He also began work on *All Things Must Pass*. This Phil Spector-produced triple album, whose length alone illustrated his frustration with his input into The Beatles, hit U.S. No. 1 and made him the first of the four to top the charts as a solo artist. The single "My Sweet Lord" also made him the first solo Beatle to top the U.K. and U.S. singles charts, although he was accused of plagiarism by the publishers of The Chiffons' 1963 hit "He's So Fine."

Asked by his friend and sitar teacher Ravi Shankar to help victims of war and famine in Bangladesh, Harrison organized the Concert for Bangladesh. Held at New York's Madison Square Garden in August 1971, six months after The Beatles' official split, it featured the likes of Bob Dylan, Clapton, and Ringo Starr. The two shows resulted in a Grammy award-winning triple live album (U.K. No. 1 and U.S. No. 2).

In 1973, Harrison's *Living in the Material World* (another U.S. chart-topper) included the hit "Give Me Love (Give Me Peace on Earth)" and heralded the formation of his own Dark Horse record label, which featured Shankar and the group Splinter. Before the year was out, he became the first Beatle to undertake a solo tour, making a thirty-date trek while his new album *Dark Horse* (1974) hit U.S. No. 4 but flopped in Britain. Having been with EMI since 1962, Harrison ended his long association with the company with the 1975 release of *Extra Texture (Read All About It)*.

With his Dark Horse label now distributed by Warner, Harrison issued the modestly successful *Thirty-Three & 1/3* (1976), featuring six songs written

year-by-year ▪ Vocals ▪ Guitar ▪ Drums ▪ Keyboards

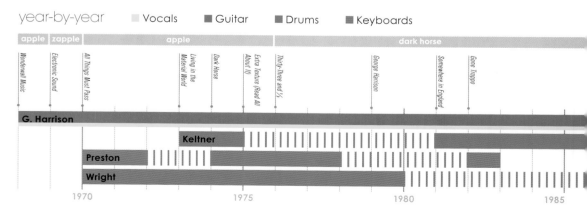

during his time with The Beatles. Divorced from his first wife Patti Boyd (who wound up with Clapton), Harrison married former A&M and Dark Horse assistant Olivia Arias in 1978, just ahead of the 1979 release of the album *George Harrison*.

However, newfound interest in Formula One motor racing and his movie company Handmade Films—which gave much-needed support to the Monty Python film *Life of Brian* (1979) and movies such as *The Long Good Friday* (1980), *Time Bandits* (1981), and *A Private Function* (1984)—kept him away from music. His film career also encompassed a cameo in Python member Eric Idle's Beatles spoof *The Rutles: All You Need Is Cash* (1978). And as executive producer of Madonna's doomed movie *Shanghai Surprise* (1986), he acted as peacemaker between the star, her husband Sean Penn, and a near-mutinous film crew.

Somewhere in England (1981) featured the hit "All Those Years Ago," a tribute to the murdered John Lennon featuring both McCartney and Starr. But with his enthusiasm for the music business at an all-time low, the contract-fulfilling *Gone Troppo* (1982) was Harrison's last album for five years. Even so, he performed with his early heroes, the rock 'n' roll pioneers Carl Perkins and Duane Eddy, before turning up to play guest spots alongside the likes of Robert Plant, Dylan, Elton John, and Bryan Adams.

The Jeff Lynne-produced *Cloud Nine*—featuring Clapton, Elton John, and Ringo Starr—restored him to Top Tens on both sides of the Atlantic in 1987, while his version of James Ray's song "Got My Mind Set on You" returned him to No. 1 in the U.S.

Heartened by this success, Harrison and Lynne joined Dylan, Tom Petty, and Roy Orbison in The Traveling Wilburys. Their 1988 debut album was a million-seller, spawning a sequel in 1990. A solo tour of Japan in 1991 with Clapton—resulting in the successful album *Live in Japan* (1992)—was followed by *Billboard* presenting him with their inaugural Century Award. Collecting the prize, Harrison finally admitted that, "Being a Beatle was no hindrance on my career."

In 1999, Harrison survived a knife attack at his home, but he was, sadly, to die of cancer in 2001. His last album, *Brainwashed* (2002)—a U.S. Top Twenty hit—was completed by his son **Dhani** and Jeff Lynne, who were also instrumental in arranging the 2002 Concert for George in honor of the man they dubbed "the quiet Beatle." Held at London's Royal Albert Hall, the show featured Clapton, Petty, members of Monty Python, Tom Hanks, Jools Holland, and George's fellow ex-Beatles Starr and McCartney. Eight years later, in 2011, the much-missed star was commemorated by Martin Scorsese's loving film biography, *Living in the Material World*. **BS**

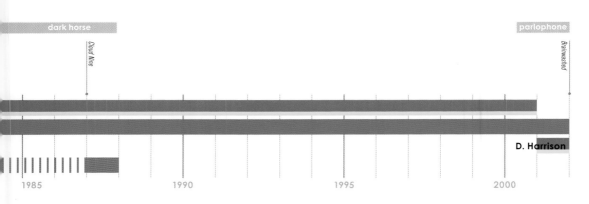

hawkwind 1969–present

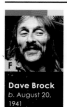

Dave Brock
b. August 20, 1941

Nik Turner
b. August 26, 1940

Michael "Dik Mik" Davies
b. 1943

Terry Ollis
b. April 11, 1952

Huw Lloyd-Langton
b. February 6, 1951

Del Dettmar
b. April 20, 1947

Robert Calvert
b. April 9, 1944
d. Aug 14, 1988

Simon King
b. 1950

Hawkwind have had a huge influence on acid rock, psychedelic rock, and trance music. The group was formed when **Dave Brock** (vocals, guitar) and Mick Slattery (guitar) came together with **Nik Turner** (saxophone, flute) in 1969 as Group X to play at All Saints Hall in London's Ladbroke Grove. With **Dik Mik** (keyboards, synthesizers), John Harrison (bass), and **Terry Ollis** (drums), they became Hawkwind.

Hawkwind (1970) was produced by Pretty Things guitarist (and former Rolling Stone) Dick Taylor, who decided to record the group live in the studio. It was a portent of things to come. The group were constantly on the road and a free concert outside the (relatively expensive) Isle of Wight festival in 1970 established their credentials. For the next five years, it was near-impossible to attend a free festival without seeing Hawkwind and their voluptuous dancer, Stacia.

The other reliable thing about Hawkwind was constantly changing personnel. Slattery left, replaced briefly by **Huw Lloyd-Langton** (guitar), while Thomas Crimble then Dave Anderson took over from Harrison on bass. By the next album, **Del Dettmar** had joined

to add more synthesizers. *In Search of Space* (1971) created an even trippier sound than their debut, and rose to No. 18 in the U.K. **Robert Calvert** joined as vocalist and lyricist, **Simon King** took over from Ollis, and **Ian "Lemmy" Kilmister** replaced Anderson.

The excellent *Doremi Fasol Latido* (1972) continued their upward trajectory, hitting No. 14. An astonished Hawkwind had already scored an unlikely smash when "Silver Machine," sung by Lemmy, soared to No. 3 in Britain earlier that year. However, they seemed unconcerned about following it up and this remained their only brush with mainstream commercial success.

The thunderous live set *Space Ritual* (1973) became Hawkwind's only Top Ten album. The first of multiple live recordings, it was a fair reflection of the overwhelming experience on offer. Shortly after their debut show in the U.S., it snuck into *Billboard*'s Top 200.

The studio-borne *Hall of the Mountain Grill* (1974) was one of the group's definitive musical statements (classically trained keyboard player **Simon House** gave them a boost) and they continued to unleash idiosyncratic albums. *Warrior on the Edge of Time*

year-by-year ■ Vocals ■ Guitar ■ Bass ■ Drums ■ Keyboards

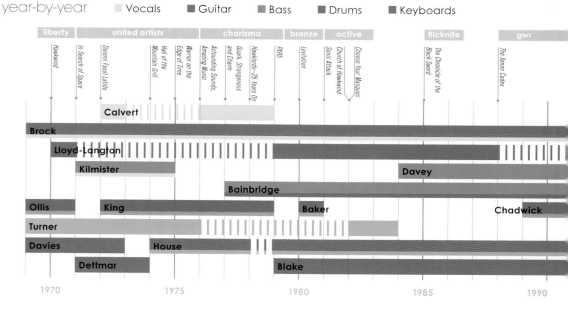

| 250,000 | 250,000 | 250,000 | 250,000 |
| In Search of Space (1971) | Doremi Farsol Latido (1972) | Space Ritual (1973) | Live Seventy Nine (1980) |

Ian "Lemmy" Kilmister
b. December 24, 1945

Harvey Bainbridge
b. September 24, 1949

Ginger Baker
b. August 19, 1939

Alan Davey
b. September 11, 1963

Tim Blake
b. February 6, 1952

Richard Chadwick
b. Jan 30, 1957

Ron Tree
b. 1963

Simon House
b. August 29, 1948

(1975), *Astounding Sounds, Amazing Music* (both 1976), and *Quark, Strangeness and Charm* (1977) had many admirers, but after that they somewhat lost their way. The group even changed their name to Hawklords for the album *Hawklords—25 Years On* (1978), but were Hawkwind once again for *PXR5* (1979).

Meanwhile Dik Mik, Dettmar, and Lemmy had gone, the latter replaced by Paul Rudolph, then **Harvey Bainbridge**. The virtuoso **Ginger Baker** took over from King, starting a run of many drummers, and Lloyd-Langton returned on guitar. Calvert also left, to die tragically young in 1988. The new decade brought a flurry of varied albums: *Levitation* (1980), *Sonic Attack* (1981), and *Church of Hawkwind* and *Choose Your Masques* (both 1982). The group next adapted *The Chronicle of the Black Sword* (1985) from stories by Michael Moorcock. By now, **Alan Davey** was on bass.

A brief silence fell until *The Xenon Codex* (1988)—the second album on which Danny Thompson Jr., son of the legendary Pentangle bassist, played drums before **Richard Chadwick** joined. *Space Bandits* (1990) featured Bridget Wishart, Hawkwind's solitary female

lead vocalist. By *Electric Tepee* (1992), the group were down to a trio: Brock, Chadwick, and Davey. The same trio recorded *It Is the Business of the Future to Be Dangerous* (1993), covering "Gimme Shelter" and removing the lead vocals of unlikely collaborator Samantha Fox (the glamor model turned pop star).

White Zone (1995) was credited to the Psychedelic Warriors because it contained more electronica than rock, although Hawkwind reverted to name (and type) for *Alien 4*, adding **Ron Tree** (vocals) and Jerry Richards (guitar). Tree took over on bass when Davey left on sabbatical before *Distant Horizons* (1997). *In Your Area* (1999) was only half a studio album—six tracks were recorded live.

A five-year hiatus ensued while Brock put out one solo (*Spacebrock*, issued under the Hawkwind name) and several live albums, before *Take Me to Your Leader* (2005) and *Take Me to Your Future* (2006). Just after the group celebrated their fortieth anniversary, they released *Blood of the Earth* (2010). No one can accuse Hawkwind of not being prolific, and they remain an exciting live act. **MiH**

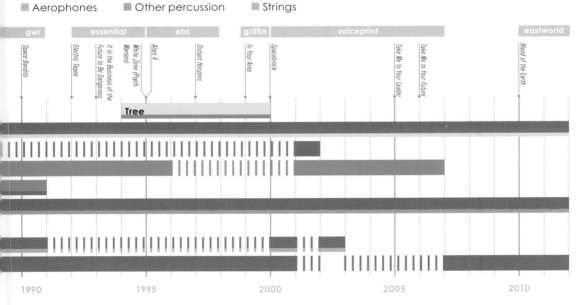

■ Aerophones   ■ Other percussion   ■ Strings

jimi hendrix 1966–1970

Jimi Hendrix
b. November 27, 1942
d. September 18, 1970

Noel Redding
b. December 25, 1945
d. May 11, 2003

Mitch Mitchell
b. June 9, 1947
d. November 12, 2008

Buddy Miles
b. September 5, 1947
d. February 26, 2008

Billy Cox
b. October 18, 1941

Larry Lee
b. March 7, 1943
d. October 30, 2007

Born in Seattle, Washington, Johnny Allen Hendrix arrived in Britain in 1966 and began his transformation from a side player on the "chitlin' circuit"—the venues at which African American acts played—to the guitar wielding, global superstar known as **Jimi Hendrix.**

After leaving the U.S. Army in 1962, he toured with Little Richard, Ike and Tina Turner, and the Isley Brothers. In 1965, Hendrix cut his first records for PPX Productions, which resulted in a five-year legal dispute. While playing around New York as Jimmy James & the Blue Flames, Hendrix was spotted by Chas Chandler, bassist with British band The Animals, who suggested that he become part of London's swinging sixties scene. Hendrix adopted the name Jimi, reportedly en route to the U.K., and in October 1966 recruited bassist **Noel Redding** and drummer **Mitch Mitchell** to create The Jimi Hendrix Experience.

Having signed a deal with the new Track label, their debut single "Hey Joe" peaked at No. 6 in early 1967. Following a series of club gigs in Europe, the Experience joined The Walker Brothers on a tour around Britain, during which Hendrix was criticized for setting fire to his guitar and for his "erotic" stage act.

Now a fully-fledged sensation in Britain, the band scored Top Three hits with "Purple Haze" and *Are You Experienced*, despite the latter including neither of their British hit singles. The album was, however, packed with classics, like "Fire," "Foxy Lady," "Manic Depression," and "3rd Stone from the Sun."

Ten months after leaving America, Hendrix returned to the States when The Experience played at the Monterey International Pop Festival alongside The Who and the Grateful Dead. The band were also booked to support pop sensations The Monkees on a U.S. tour—but, after eight shows, they departed amid protests about the guitarist's act. "Hendrix would be up there belting out 'Foxy Lady'," marveled drummer Micky Dolenz to *Livewire*, "and the kids would be screaming for The Monkees. It was kinda strange!"

After "The Wind Cried Mary" and "Burning of the Midnight Lamp" provided further British hits, Hendrix made his U.S. chart debut with "Purple Haze." Then *Are You Experienced?* began a 100-week run on the *Billboard* chart, including sixty weeks in the Top Ten.

After a British tour (on which Motörhead's Lemmy was a roadie) supported by The Move, The Nice, and

year-by-year   ■ Vocals   ■ Guitar   ■ Bass   ■ Drums   ■ Other percussion

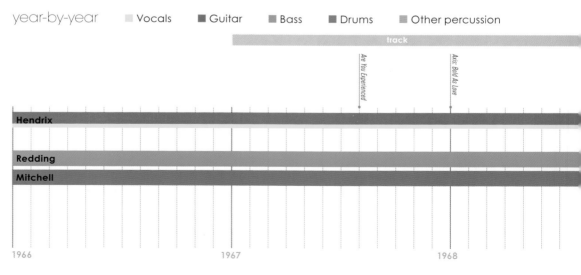

Juma Sultan
b. April 13, 1942

Jerry Velez
b. August 15, 1947

Pink Floyd, the band scored another Top Five hit on both sides of the Atlantic with *Axis: Bold as Love* (1967). Its clutch of classics included the lovely "Little Wing," "Wait Until Tomorrow," and "Castles Made of Sand," although its only (minor) hit was "Up from the Skies."

Hendrix relocated to New York to develop his career in America with a series of tours and a third album, *Electric Ladyland*. Reaching No. 6 in the U.K.—where the original sleeve featured twenty naked women—it hit No. 1 in the U.S., where the cover was changed to a less controversial psychedelic design.

The compilation *Smash Hits* reached the U.K. Top Five in 1968. A year later, a different collection of the same name—featuring the Experience's first U.S. hit single, an acclaimed cover of Bob Dylan's "All Along The Watchtower"—hit the U.S. Top Ten.

Hendrix, Redding, and Mitchell played a last show together in Denver, in June 1969. While Redding formed the band Fat Mattress, Mitchell continued to support Hendrix—including a dramatic closing spot that summer at the legendary Woodstock festival with guitarist **Larry Lee**, bassist **Billy Cox**, and percussionists **Juma Sultan** and **Jerry Velez**. This temporary band—

dubbed Gypsy Sun & Rainbows—evolved into Band of Gypsys (Hendrix, Cox, and drummer **Buddy Miles**) for the live album *Band of Gypsys*. (Miles resurfaced as lead vocalist for TV sensation the California Raisins.)

In August 1970, Hendrix returned to Britain for only the second time in three years to play the Isle of Wight festival (for which his sound was mixed by Pink Floyd's David Gilmour). But after jamming with Eric Burdon at a London club on September 17, he returned to his girlfriend's flat, where he was found unconscious and rushed to hospital. He died, aged just twenty-seven, as a result of inhalation of vomit caused by barbiturate intoxication. Two months later, he topped the U.K. singles chart with "Voodoo Child." In early 1971, his final official studio album, *The Cry of Love*, was a Top Three hit in both America and Britain.

The ensuing decades saw a slew of live albums, and compilations of archive material—with 2010's *Valleys of Neptune*, featuring unreleased tracks spanning 1967 to 1970, billed as a "lost" studio album.

Despite myriad guitar heroes emerging in his wake, Hendrix remains the ultimate. "He did things," observed Pete Townshend, "which were magical." **BS**

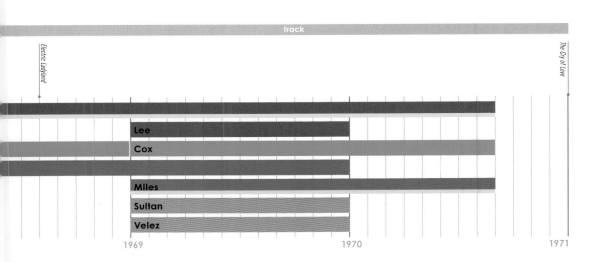

Are You Experienced
(1967)

Axis: Bold as Love
(1967)

Electric Ladyland
(1968)

The Cry of Love
(1971)

Jimi Hendrix finding his groove at the Star Club, Hamburg, 1967.

The Jimi Hendrix Experience: **Mitch Mitchell**, **Hendrix**, and **Noel Redding**.

In the midst of psychedelia in 1967.

Performing a trademark **Hendrix** move in the late sixties.

Hendrix, Mitchell, and **Redding** at London's legendary Marquee Club in London, 1967.

Making history at the Woodstock festival, where he was the highest-earning performer.

The guitar hero rocks London's Royal Albert Hall in February 1969.

Playing in his last concert, at the Isle of Fehmarn, Germany, in September 1970.

Rock and roll and afros. Left to right **Mitchell**, **Hendrix**, and **Redding**.

los hermanos 1997–present

Marcelo Camelo
b. April 2, 1978

Rodrigo Amarante
b. September 6, 1976

Bruno Medina
b. August 10, 1978

Rodrigo Barba
b. January 23, 1979

Patrick Laplan
b. Unknown

Los Hermanos is a multi-faceted quartet based in Rio de Janeiro. They started out in 1997 as an indie-rock band with punk and ska influences and a tendency to concentrate on romantic matters in their lyrics, drawing comparisons to U.S. acts such as Weezer. Despite their Brazilian origins, the group's name is Spanish for "the brothers." The first stable lineup consisted of singer/guitarists **Marcelo Camelo** and **Rodrigo Amarante**, keyboard player **Bruno Medina**, drummer **Rodrigo Barba**, and bassist **Patrick Laplan**.

Appearances at some of Brazil's biggest music festivals won Los Hermanos a reputation as a powerful live act and a contract with Sony BMG followed. Their self-titled debut album, released in 1999, was propelled by the hit "Anna Júlia," a melodic slice of indie-pop whose huge success overshadowed their career. The song was covered by artists including Jim Capaldi, whose English version featured guitar by George Harrison—one of his last recordings.

Bloco do Eu Sozinho (2001) established a fresh direction: moving away from the noisier elements of their debut and incorporating samba rhythms. The brooding, musically complex single "Todo Carnaval Tem Seu Fim" ("Every Carnival Has Its End") was a world away from the chirpy pop of "Anna Júlia." The album was positively reviewed, but the lack of a major hit meant it failed to match the success of their debut.

Minus Laplan (who resurfaced as a member of the dance act Eskimo), 2003's *Ventura* further developed Los Hermanos' distinctive Brazilian identity, adding choro and bossa nova to the rhythmic mix. The album earned further critical acclaim and expanded their following in their homeland. However, they alienated some fans and reviewers with the melancholy mood of their fourth album, released in 2006 and simply titled *4*. By this point Los Hermanos were seen as leading lights of MPB (Musica Popular Brasiliera), a loosely knit cultural movement encompassing all popular music with traditional Brazilian characteristics.

Los Hermanos toured extensively over the next two years, and the compilation *Perfil* was released to healthy sales in 2006. Then, in April 2007, Los Hermanos announced that they would be going on hiatus after a series of homecoming dates in Rio de Janeiro in June. The band explained that the split was entirely amicable, prompted by nothing more than the need for a break. Accordingly, they reunited in 2009 for two festival dates in Rio and São Paulo. Another short series of shows in their home nation followed in 2010.

As the fifteenth anniversary of their formation approached, the group revealed that they would be marking the occasion with a full tour of Brazil in April and May 2012. The public response demonstrated that they remained among Brazil's most beloved bands. **DJ**

year-by-year ▫ Vocals ■ Guitar ■ Bass ■ Drums ■ Keyboards

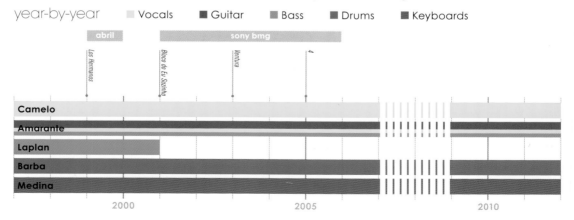

héroes del silencio 1984–2007

Enrique Bunbury
b. August 11, 1967

Juan Valdivia
b. December 3, 1965

Joaquin Cardiel
b. June 2, 1965

Pedro Ardreu
b. April 15, 1966

Alan Boguslavsky
b. May 18, 1965

Gonzalo Valdivia
b. October 3, 1972

Héroes del Silencio were one of the most successful rock bands ever to emerge from continental Europe. Formed in Zaragoza, Spain, in 1984, their loyalty to their native tongue made them major contributors to the Rock en Español movement of the nineties. Their dramatic, bombastic style brought them lasting popularity in Europe and Latin America, their Goth-tinged sound and visual image drawing comparisons to British post-punk acts like The Cult and The Mission.

Guitarist **Juan Valdivia** and singer **Enrique Bunbury** first performed together in another Zaragoza-based band, Zumo de Vidrio ("Glass of Juice"). Born Enrique Ortiz de Landázuri Izardui, Bunbury took his stage name from a character in the Oscar Wilde play *The Importance of Being Earnest*. The first HDS lineup was completed by Juan's drummer brother Pedro, with Bunbury on bass. By the end of 1985, the former had been replaced by **Pedro Andreu** and the band had expanded to a quartet with bassist **Joaquin Cardiel**.

Their debut was the well-received EP *Héroe de Leyenda*, released in 1988. The four tracks on the EP included "El Mar No Cesa," also the title of the Héroes' first full-length album, although the eponymous song does not appear on the album. By the time of that debut album's release in February 1989, HDS had built up a sizable following via extensive touring. *El Mar No Cesa* proved to be a platinum-selling hit in Spain.

Produced by Roxy Music guitarist Phil Manzanera, *Senderos de Tración* (1990) became their greatest commercial success, selling more than two million copies. It also drew positive reviews from the Spanish music press, who were not always supportive of HDS's efforts. "Entre Dos Tierras" became an international hit and the band's best known song, aided by a sepia-toned video in which their performance was intercut with scenes of domestic violence.

El Espíritu del Vino followed in 1993, with Manzanera again producing. Second guitarist **Alan Boguslavsky** was added to the lineup for the tour that followed its release. Another hit album arrived in the form of 1995's *Avalancha*, produced by Bob Ezrin.

A decade of touring led to increasing tensions within the band, and they went on hiatus in October 1996. The final date on their farewell tour came to an ignominious end when the band was forced off stage in Los Angeles by missiles thrown by the audience.

In the years that followed, Bunbury launched a successful solo career, and various compilations and live albums have enjoyed healthy sales. The group reunited in 2007 for a tour that took them to South America and the U.S. before concluding with a triumphant homecoming in Spain. A CD and DVD taken from the tour, titled simply *Tour 2007,* were released just in time for Christmas of that year. **DJ**

year-by-year ▢ Vocals ■ Guitar ■ Bass ■ Drums

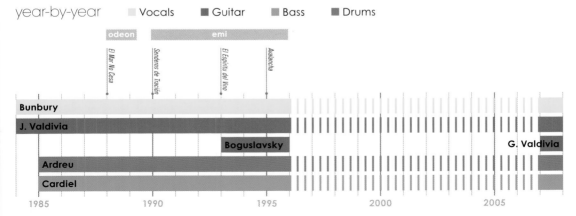

hole 1989–present

Courtney Love
b. July 9, 1964

Eric Erlandson
b. January 9, 1963

Caroline Rue
b. Unknown

Jill Emery
b. May 1, 1962

Patty Schemel
b. April 24, 1967

Kristen Pfaff
b. May 26, 1967
d. June 16, 1994

"She's almost a genius," remarked Smashing Pumpkins figurehead Billy Corgan of **Courtney Love**, "in an insane kind of way." This insane genius had graced the cover of the Grateful Dead's *Aoxomoxoa* (via her father, Hank Harrison, briefly the Dead's manager), hung out with Julian Cope and The Teardrop Explodes, fronted Faith No More in 1982, and formed Sugar Babydoll with Jennifer Finch and Kat Bjelland (latterly of L7 and Babes in Toyland, respectively).

After Love's heroin use caused Sugar Babydoll to implode, she moved on to movie work, starring in Alex Cox's *Sid & Nancy* (1986) and *Straight to Hell* (1987), the latter also featuring Joe Strummer. Neither project made her famous, and Love returned to an intermittent stripping career. In 1989, she settled in L.A. for a final stab at stardom. Thanks to an ad declaring, "My influences are Big Black, Sonic Youth, and Fleetwood Mac," she snared guitarist **Eric Erlandson**.

Dubbing themselves Hole, the duo enlisted bassist Lisa Roberts, drummer **Caroline Rue**, and guitarists Mike Geisbrecht and Errol Stewart. In 1990, the band solidified with Love, Erlandson, Rue, and bassist **Jill Emery**. Abrasive singles foreshadowed *Pretty on the Inside*, released in 1991 and co-produced by Sonic Youth's Kim Gordon. Despite including a cover of Joni Mitchell's "Clouds," the album was, Erlandson noted, "really obnoxious and in your face and noisy."

On tour in 1991, Hole played Leadbelly's "Where Did You Sleep Last Night?"—an idea that clearly resonated with Love's soon-to-be boyfriend, Kurt Cobain (whom she met after a liaison with Corgan). Love and Cobain married in February 1992, Emery quit Hole, and Rue was reportedly fired. Hole regrouped with drummer **Patty Schemel** and temporary bassist Leslie Hardy, although producer Jack Endino played bass on their next single, "Beautiful Son."

Songs for Hole's sophomore album were road-tested in 1993 with new bassist **Kristen Pfaff**. But, with tragic timing, *Live Through This* was released just days after Cobain's suicide in April 1994. The nightmare was compounded by Pfaff's fatal overdose in June.

Corgan recommended Hole's new bassist, **Melissa Auf der Maur**. "I am gonna enter the dark side," she acknowledged, "and be living in close proximity to people who play with death." The new lineup debuted, messily, at Britain's Reading festival, then toured the U.S. with Nine Inch Nails. Love's criticism of NIN, and an alleged fling with their leader Trent Reznor, sparked an undying war between the two.

In 1995, Love oversaw the *Tank Girl* film soundtrack and, on Valentine's Day, Hole performed tellingly dark cuts such as Donovan's "Season of the Witch" and The Crystals' "He Hit Me (and It Felt Like a Kiss)" for MTV's *Unplugged*. Amid a controversy-plagued tour, Love

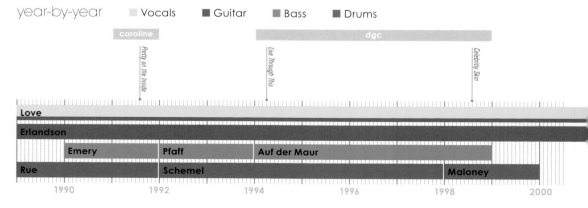

year-by-year   ■ Vocals   ■ Guitar   ■ Bass   ■ Drums

caroline

dgc

Pretty on the Inside

Live Through This

Celebrity Skin

Love

Erlandson

Emery | Pfaff | Auf der Maur

Rue | Schemel | Maloney

1990   1992   1994   1996   1998   2000

Melissa Auf der Maur
b. March 17, 1972

Samantha Maloney
b. December 11, 1975

Micko Larkin
b. October 13, 1986

Stuart Fisher
b. circa 1975

Shawn Dailey
b. Unknown

conceived the artwork for the archive-plundering EP *Ask for It:* a woman's slashed wrists.

Reinvention came in 1996. While Hole covered Fleetwood Mac's "Gold Dust Woman"—produced by Cars singer Ric Ocasek—for the soundtrack of *The Crow: City of Angels,* Love starred in the movies *Feeling Minnesota* and *The People Vs. Larry Flynt.* As Hollywood embraced her, further archive releases plugged the gap in Hole's output: 1997's *The First Session* and *My Body, the Hand Grenade.*

To complete a love letter to the West Coast, Hole undertook a writing project with Billy Corgan. The result was *Celebrity Skin* (1998), which turned platinum three times faster than *Live Through This.* However, as Auf der Maur observed, "A lot of blackness went into it." At producer Michael Beinhorn's behest, Schemel's parts were played by former Bad English (and future Journey) drummer Deen Castronovo. Although pictured on the album's artwork, Schemel quit in protest. Hole hired a lookalike for the "Celebrity Skin" video, then installed drummer **Samantha Maloney**.

After the ensuing tour, including a rancorous stint with Marilyn Manson, Auf der Maur joined The Smashing Pumpkins and Maloney jumped ship to Mötley Crüe. Then Love and Erlandson fell out, finally declaring Hole defunct in 2002. In the interim, Love formed "punk rock femme supergroup" Bastard with

Schemel and Veruca Salt's Louise Post and Gina Crosley. The project collapsed amid, Post reported, "unhealthy and unprofessional working conditions."

With her life in freefall, Love assembled the sadly underrated solo album *America's Sweetheart* (2004) with producer Linda Perry. Contributions came from Elton John's lyricist Bernie Taupin and members of the Distillers, the Pixies, and Girls Against Boys. None could save it from barbed reviews and poor sales.

Finally, after years in which her personal notoriety eclipsed her music, including an attempted second solo album (with Corgan and Perry), Love revived the Hole banner—to the absent Erlandson's annoyance—for *Nobody's Daughter* (2010). Guitarist **Micko Larkin**, formerly of British band Larrikin Love, headed the new lineup. (Former Red Hot Chili Peppers/Pearl Jam drummer Jack Irons also contributed.)

Hopes for a genuine reunion were raised when Love, Erlandson, and Auf der Maur attended a 2011 screening of *Hit So Hard,* P. David Ebersole's documentary about Patty Schemel—essential viewing for Hole and Nirvana fans.

Regarding Hole, Erlandson admitted that "Nothing has been resolved, but I'm open to all possibilities." With customary defiance, Love declared, "Madonna wakes up every day and someone wants to be her. Nobody wants to be me. Which is awesome!" **BM**

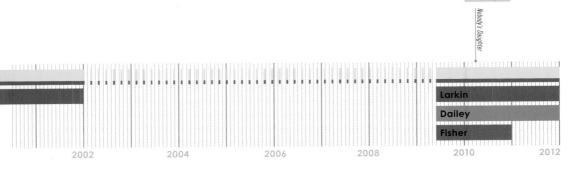

mercury

Nobody's Daughter

Larkin
Dailey
Fisher

2002   2004   2006   2008   2010   2012

buddy holly & the crickets 1957–1959

Buddy Holly
b. September 7, 1936
d. February 3, 1959

Niki Sullivan
b. June 23, 1937
d. April 6, 2004

Jerry Allison
b. August 31, 1939

Joe B. Mauldin
b. July 8, 1940

Sonny Curtis
b. May 9, 1937

Buddy Holly was one of the most prolific musicians to emerge during America's fifties rock 'n' roll boom. Born in Texas, he began performing at thirteen with his school pal Bob Montgomery—as Buddy & Bob, they graced local country/bluegrass concerts. After adding bass player Larry Welborn, Buddy & Bob supported Bill Haley & His Comets and found themselves doing the same for Elvis Presley in 1955.

In 1956, Holly was offered a solo deal by Decca and recruited guitarist **Sonny Curtis**, bassist Don Guess, and drummer **Jerry Allison**. As Buddy Holly & The Three Tunes, they released "Blue Days, Black Nights" and "Modern Don Juan" before Decca let them go.

In 1957, with Allison, Welborn, and guitarist **Niki Sullivan**, Holly recorded "That'll Be the Day" with producer Norman Petty. With **Joe B. Mauldin** replacing Welborn, they took on the name The Crickets and were assigned to Brunswick, which issued the single. It reached No. 1 in the U.S. and the U.K.

The group came to Britain in March 1958 for a twenty-five-date tour, which made hits of "Listen to Me" and "Maybe Baby." But in October that year, Holly left The Crickets to pursue a solo career. (His first single—"Early in the Morning"—had been released in August.) The twenty-two-year-old moved to New York. He ended his association with Petty and passed rights to the Crickets name to Allison and Mauldin.

(Their career as The Crickets would extend well into the nineties, and include collaborative efforts such as 1962's *Bobby Vee Meets the Crickets* and, with singer Nanci Griffith, 1996's *Too Much Monday Morning*).

Holly recorded in Coral's studios in New York in 1958 and entered the charts with "Heartbeat" on the eve of a U.S. tour with The Big Bopper, Richie Valens, and Dion & The Belmonts. On February 2, 1959, Holly played in Iowa then, with Valens and the Big Bopper, boarded a plane to fly to North Dakota. Minutes after takeoff, the plane crashed, killing all three stars.

Within two months of his death, a track from his last session in November 1958—Paul Anka's "It Doesn't Matter Anymore"—hit No. 13 in the U.S. and topped the U.K. charts. During his ten years as a professional musician Holly made over 120 recordings—releasing less than fifty of them in his lifetime. Two years after his death, *That'll Be the Day*—a collection of his early Decca recordings—charted in the U.K. at No. 5. It was among a host of compilations that have appeared since 1959, with both *20 Golden Greats* (1978) and *Words of Love* (1993) topping the U.K. chart.

"He was one of the first to get away from the Tin Pan Alley songwriting factory and communicate directly, honestly with his audience," observed John Mellencamp in *Rolling Stone*. "The magic that Buddy Holly created was nothing short of a miracle." **BS**

year-by-year   ▪ Vocals   ▪ Guitar   ▪ Bass   ▪ Drums

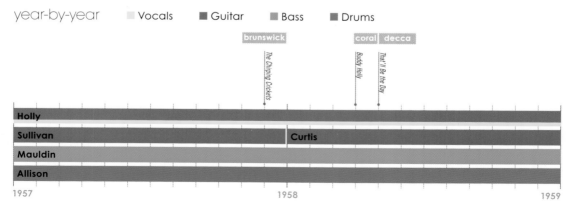

hootie & the blowfish 1986–present

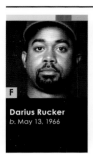
Darius Rucker
b. May 13, 1966

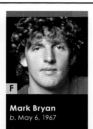
Mark Bryan
b. May 6, 1967

Dean Felber
b. June 9, 1967

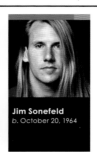
Jim Sonefeld
b. October 20, 1964

If you are one of the sixteen million Americans who bought a copy of *Cracked Rear View*, you will need no introduction to Hootie & the Blowfish. If you live anywhere else in the world, you might be forgiven for asking "Who's Hootie?" or "What's a blowfish?"

Hootie & the Blowfish (**Darius Rucker**, **Mark Bryan**, **Dean Felber**, and **Jim Sonefeld**, who replaced Brantley Smith in 1989) were one of a number of feel-good, melody-driven rock groups to emerge in the early nineties—alongside the Dave Matthews Band, Gin Blossoms, Blues Traveler, and Hootie's rivals in nominal daftness, Toad the Wet Sprocket.

The band were named after friends of Rucker: Hootie (nicknamed on account of his round face and glasses making him look like an owl) and Blowfish (whose chubby cheeks inspired his pseudonym). Having formed in 1986 in South Carolina, they issued the self-released EP *Kootchypop* in 1993; "We sold so many copies…" Rucker told *Billboard* writer Craig Rosen, "people couldn't believe it."

But it was their debut album that really shook the music industry to its core. *Cracked Rear View* (1994) has been outsold by only fifteen albums in U.S. chart history, and it yielded a string of hits that radio could not get enough of. "Hold My Hand" (featuring backing vocals by David Crosby), "Let Her Cry," "Only Wanna Be with You," and "Time"—all of which had originally appeared on *Kootchypop*—cracked the Top Twenty, with "Let Her Cry" winning a Grammy.

The quartet appeared on the soundtrack to the sitcom *Friends* with "I Go Blind" after being named in an episode (Courteney Cox's character, having met the band, admits a love-bite is "the work of a Blowfish"). They also contributed to the 1995 Led Zeppelin tribute album *Encomium*.

After founding the short-lived Breaking Records label, they released their second U.S. No. 1, *Fairweather Johnson*, featuring the hits "Old Man & Me (When I Get to Heaven)" and "Tucker's Town."

In 1998, Hootie released some of their finest work on the platinum-selling *Musical Chairs*—namely the single "I Will Wait" and the glorious ballad "Only Lonely." Then they drifted off into relative obscurity with the covers album *Scattered, Smothered & Covered* (2000) and two further studio sets, *Hootie & the Blowfish* (2003) and *Looking for Lucky* (2005).

Rucker reinvented himself as a country singer in 2008—six years after his R&B album *Back to Then*—and has two chart-topping albums (*Learn to Live* and *Charleston, SC 1966*) and five No. 1 country singles to his credit. While his solo projects seemed to mark the end of the Blowfish and their exhaustive charity work, the versatile singer-songwriter has hinted at a revival of the band "some time down the road." **MW**

year-by-year   ◻ Vocals   ◼ Guitar   ◼ Bass   ◼ Drums   ◼ Keyboards
◼ Aerophones   ▨ Other percussion

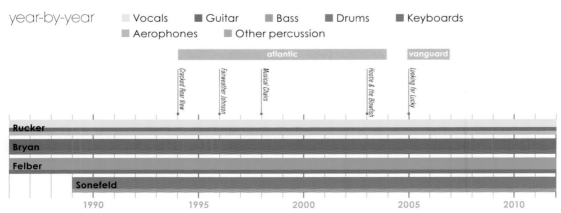

humble pie 1968–2002

Steve Marriott
b. Jan 30, 1947
d. April 20, 1991

Peter Frampton
b. April 22, 1950

Greg Ridley
b. Oct 23, 1947
d. November 19, 2003

Jerry Shirley
b. February 4, 1952

Clem Clempson
b. September 5, 1949

Anthony "Sooty" Jones
b. Aug 24, 1953
d. Sept 21, 1999

Bobby Tench
b. September 21, 1944

Formed at the end of 1968 in Essex, England, the "supergroup" Humble Pie combined the talents of Small Faces front-man **Steve Marriott**, The Herd's **Peter Frampton**, and Spooky Tooth bass player **Greg Ridley**. Their hard-edged blues-rock sound featured three lead vocalists, two of whom were also highly accomplished guitarists. Signed to the Immediate label, Humble Pie quickly found themselves in the U.K. Top Five with their 1969 debut, "Natural Born Bugie." This was followed by an eclectic but successful mix of blues-rock and acoustic whimsy, *As Safe as Yesterday*.

Before the year was out, a sophomore effort had appeared. *Town and Country* reduced the rock quotient, introducing a gentler folk-inspired sound. The timing was unfortunate: with Immediate filing for bankruptcy, the album emerged with no promotion and went largely unnoticed.

New management encouraged Marriott to direct Humble Pie toward the lucrative heavy rock market, and his raw, bluesy vocals began to dominate the band's albums. By 1971, Humble Pie were in greater demand from U.S. rock audiences than they were in their homeland, cementing their growing success with 1971's live *Performance—Rockin' The Fillmore*, which took the band into the *Billboard* Top Twenty for the first time. Frampton, however, was unhappy at the band's musical direction and decided to go it alone.

With Marriott in sole control, the group grew even heavier. "He was one of my heroes," said Kiss's Paul Stanley. "I saw Marriott perform live with Humble Pie and it was like being at a church revival." *Smokin'* (1972) proved to be the band's commercial peak—later albums declined in quality and sales. Marriott's personal habits had become problematic and, with their finances in chaos, Humble Pie disbanded in 1975. Marriott reformed them in the eighties with little success: he died in a house fire in 1991. Bassist Ridley, drummer **Jerry Shirley**, and guitarist **Bobby Tench** reunited for 2002's *Back on Track,* featuring former Bad Company man Dave "Bucket" Colwell.

Having left Humble Pie in 1972, Frampton embarked on what looked to be a low-key solo career. Albums like *Wind of Change* and *Frampton's Camel* made little headway, but persistent touring in the U.S. paid off with his breakthrough—1975's *Frampton,* an album of appealing pop/rock that highlighted his growing confidence as a songwriter.

Songs from *Frampton* would reappear a year later on *Frampton Comes Alive!,* a slow burner that debuted at No. 191 on the *Billboard* chart. Few could have predicted that this live recording would turn him into a star and become the biggest-selling album of 1976. Frampton would never recapture this level of success, but remained a popular concert draw. **TB**

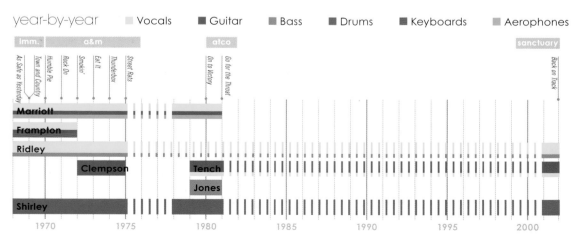

year-by-year ■ Vocals ■ Guitar ■ Bass ■ Drums ■ Keyboards ■ Aerophones

imm. a&m atco sanctuary

As Safe as Yesterday | Town and Country | Humble Pie | Rock On | Smokin' | Eat It | Thunderbox | Street Rats | On to Victory | Go for the Throat | Back on Track

Marriott
Frampton
Ridley
Clempson
Tench
Jones
Shirley

1970 1975 1980 1985 1990 1995 2000

hüsker dü 1979–1987

Bob Mould
b. October 16,
1961

Grant Hart
b. March 18,
1961

Greg Norton
b. March 13,
1959

"It was clear who was taking over the world," sang **Bob Mould** in 2002. "It wasn't going to be me." The man behind two of alternative rock's greatest groups did indeed remain largely on the sidelines while the likes of the Pixies and Nirvana reaped the rewards of his endeavors—but that makes much of his back catalog a treasure chest of mostly unheard classics.

Mould rose to fame (of sorts) with drummer and singer **Grant Hart** and bassist **Greg Norton**. As Minneapolis-based hardcore trio Hüsker Dü, they were first famed more for the speed at which they played than for their music. But bitter competition between Mould and Hart drove each to write ever finer songs. After 1984's Zen Arcade—an extraordinary, albeit incomprehensible, concept album recorded in mostly first takes over forty hours—the pair packed 1985's New Day Rising and Flip Your Wig, 1986's Candy Apple Grey, and 1987's Warehouse: Songs and Stories with an embarrassment of songwriting riches.

Unfortunately, not even the backing of Warner Bros. in their latter years could promote the trio from critical acclaim to mainstream success. "Hüsker Dü are making quite important music now," observed former Led Zeppelin singer Robert Plant, "and people aren't hearing it because it never gets played."

More damage was done to the group by Mould and Hart's rivalry, exacerbated by the latter's drug problem. The suicide of their manager was the final straw, and the band fell apart on tour at the end of 1987. The coruscating live album The Living End (1994)—a de facto best of—proved a fine epitaph.

In the aftermath, Norton moved into the catering business, and Hart pursued a mostly low-key solo career, of which the highlights are 1989's Intolerance and 1991's ambitious Last Days of Pompeii (the latter recorded with the short-lived Nova Mob).

Mould recorded two increasingly gloomy solo albums before uniting with bassist David Barbe and drummer Malcolm Travis as Sugar. With their leader belatedly acknowledged as a "godfather of grunge"—although "grumpy uncle of grunge" is more fitting—Sugar made good on Hüsker Dü's potential. The classic Copper Blue (1992) slammed into the British Top Ten, as did 1993's brutal Beaster and 1994's melodious File Under: Easy Listening. But after four years of touring and recording—compounding Mould's hearing problems—Sugar dissolved.

Mould returned to the sidelines, grumbling "I hate alternative rock" on his self-titled 1996 solo album. After a nominally final foray into poppy hardcore—1998's self-mockingly titled The Last Dog and Pony Show—he pursued an increasingly electronic career, before bringing guitars back to the forefront on 2005's Body of Song. He is increasingly amenable to recognizing his past, with his solo shows often heavy on Hüsker and Sugar classics—2012 even found him playing the whole of Copper Blue. And while a frosty relationship with Hart ensures Hüsker Dü's patchily produced catalog remains un-remastered and often unavailable, Mould seems to have made peace with acts who made his formula their own, guesting on Foo Fighters' Wasting Light (2011) and at their shows. **BM**

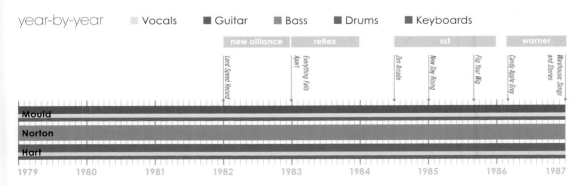

year-by-year   ▪ Vocals   ▪ Guitar   ▪ Bass   ▪ Drums   ▪ Keyboards

new alliance | reflex | sst | warner

Land Speed Record | Everything Falls Apart | Zen Arcade | New Day Rising | Flip Your Wig | Candy Apple Grey | Warehouse: Songs and Stories

Mould
Norton
Hart

1979   1980   1981   1982   1983   1984   1985   1986   1987

inxs 1977–present

Michael Hutchence
b. January 22, 1960
d. November 22, 1997

Andrew Farriss
b. March 27, 1959

Jon Farriss
b. August 10, 1961

Tim Farriss
b. August 16, 1957

Garry "Gary" Beers
b. June 22, 1957

Kirk Pengilly
b. July 4, 1958

"There's no drugs or drinking problems. So I think, 'Phew, I've survived.' I really have." A bold claim from **Michael Hutchence** in 1992, just five years before he took his own life with cocaine, alcohol, and prescription drugs. But then what did the world expect from the lead singer of a band called INXS?

At the time of his death, Hutchence had been touring and promoting the Australian band's tenth album *Elegantly Wasted*—whose title alone, reports said, was further evidence of the singer's hedonistic tendencies. While his partner Paula Yates claimed later that Hutchence had died accidentally trying for the sexual high only possible through "auto-asphyxiation," it was actually—according to the coroner's report—frustration about not having access to his daughter that drove the singer to suicide.

INXS had started out in Sydney in 1977 as The Farriss Brothers. **Andrew**, **Jon**, and **Tim Farriss** were the siblings in question. Looking outside the family, they drafted in **Garry "Gary" Beers**, **Kirk Pengilly** and Andrew's school pal, Hutchence.

Despite non-Farrisses equaling the number of brothers, everyone seemed happy enough with the band tag—until, that is, they met Gary Morris,

manager of fellow Australian act Midnight Oil. Morris offered the "Brothers" a support slot and suggested they changed their name. On September 1, 1979, a "new" band called INXS made their live debut.

Around thirteen months later, a low-budget album of the same name was released on the independent Deluxe label. It did not exactly make headlines—or hits—but was promising enough for Deluxe to invest a little more in its successor. *Underneath the Colours* justified the expense, reaching No. 15 in Australia.

Hearing their songs on jukeboxes, on the radio, and whistled in the street gave INXS the confidence to look further afield. By the time *Shabooh Shoobah* was released in 1982, it was with major-label distribution. As a result, the album charted in the U.S., where it earned a gold award, and the single "The One Thing" cracked the Top Thirty. (Back home, it made No. 5.)

American tours supporting Adam and the Ants, Hall & Oates, and The Go-Go's helped build the kind of audience INXS had down under, while a stint as opener for compatriots Men at Work proved Antipodean roots need not be a barrier to U.S. success. They just needed the right record... Unfortunately, 1984's *The Swing* was not it, making little

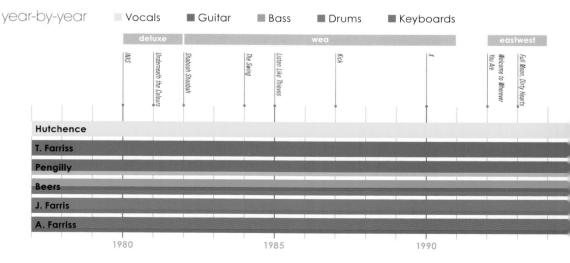

year-by-year   Vocals   Guitar   Bass   Drums   Keyboards

3.3M	9.8M	3.6M	3.2M
Listen Like Thieves (1985)	*Kick* (1987)	*X* (1990)	*Greatest Hits* (1994)

Jon Stevens
b. October 8, 1961

JD Fortune
b. September 1, 1973

Ciaran Gribbin
b. 1976

impression in America and even less in the U.K. It did, however, chart well in France, Argentina, Canada, and elsewhere, and became INXS's first No. 1 in Australia. So, not a flop by any means, but still not a smash in the "major" territories. And then, in 1985, they released *Listen Like Thieves* and everything changed.

While the album's first single, "This Time," sank without trace, its follow-up, "What You Need," gained huge airplay in the States and rocketed into the Top Five. As the rest of the world (bar the U.K.) followed suit, the band thanked their lucky stars that producer Chris Thomas (whose resume included mixing Pink Floyd's *Dark Side of the Moon*) had forced them into a few days' extra work. "We'd already finished the album but Chris told us there was still no 'hit'," Andrew Farriss recalls. "We left the studio that night knowing we had one day left to deliver a 'hit'. Talk about pressure." In desperation, Farriss pulled out all his old demos and, forty-eight hours later, "Funk Song No. 13" had evolved into the powerful "What You Need."

With Britain's *NME* calling INXS "a depressingly definitive example of excruciating, boring, incredibly unimaginative MTV rock," it was always going to take longer to break into the U.K. market. But with

Kick (1987), they managed it. And this time they were not taking any chances with the hits. "We wanted to make an album where all the songs were possible singles," Pengilly explained. With "New Sensation," "Never Tear Us Apart," "Devil Inside," and "Need You Tonight" charting worldwide, they clearly succeeded.

Ten years after the Farrisses had set out, INXS was one of the biggest acts in the world—and with that came new pressures. Hutchence could not move without someone taking his picture. His relationship with fellow Australian pop star Kylie Minogue arguably resulted in an increased public demand for concert tickets and copies of the band's *X* (1990).

However, despite the eclectic gems on *Welcome to Wherever You Are* and cameos by Ray Charles and Chrissie Hynde on *Full Moon, Dirty Hearts*, sales had waned by the time of Hutchence's death. (*Elegantly Wasted* even fell short of the Australian Top Ten.)

New singers **Jon Stevens** (briefly) and **JD Fortune**—the latter hired after he won the *Rock Star: INXS* reality TV show—and albums *Switch* and *Original Sin* failed to lead the band back to former heights. But with the announcement, in September 2011, of fourth frontman **Ciaran Gribbin**, INXS continue to *kick*. **JaH**

■ Aerophones

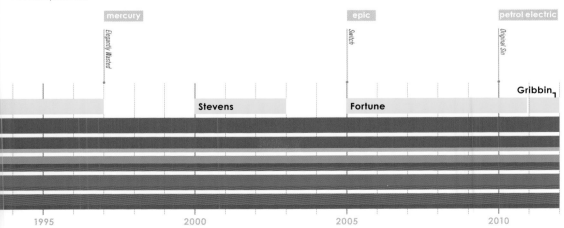

iron butterfly 1966–present

Doug Ingle
b. September
9, 1945

Danny Weis
b. September
28, 1948

Ron Bushy
b. December
23, 1945

Erik Braunn
b. August 11,
1950

Lee Dorman
b. September
15, 1942

**Larry
Reinhardt**
b. July 7, 1948
d. Jan 2, 2012

Mike Pinera
b. September
29, 1948

**Philip Taylor
Kramer**
b. July 12, 1952
d. Feb 12, 1995

Few acts in rock are so closely tied to one song as Iron Butterfly are to "In-A-Gadda-Da-Vida." It is mentioned in every conversation about the San Diego act—usually as the main topic. Often, such conversations lead to heated debates: one side proclaiming "In-A-Gadda-Da-Vida" to be a prime example of sixties psychedelia, the other arguing that it is nothing more than bloated nonsense. (A third party might counter that there is little difference between the two.)

There is, however, no debating that "In-A-Gadda-Da-Vida" is quite a song: a spiraling opus of excess that took up the entire second side of the Butterfly's 1968 album of the same title. It clocked in at over seventeen minutes—nineteen on 1970's *Live*—and featured church organ, one of the stoniest grooves ever recorded, a nonsensical chorus, and a lengthy drum solo. And it was just what the public wanted to hear: "In-A-Gadda-Da-Vida" was a worldwide hit, especially with the emerging album-oriented rock radio format, and earned its parent album the first-ever platinum certification in the U.S.

Vocalist and keyboardist **Doug Ingle**, the song's author, had been prepping for that success for most his life—the Nebraska native got his musical

education from his father, a church organist, prior to his family moving to San Diego. He formed Iron Butterfly in 1966, quickly shuffling through a variety of lineups before striking upon the one—featuring guitarist **Danny Weis**, tambourine player Darryl DeLoach, bassist Jerry Penrod, and drummer **Ron Bushy**—heard on 1968's debut *Heavy*.

It was easy to hear the influence of predecessors Jefferson Airplane and The Doors (both of whom Iron Butterfly had opened for) on that first record, but there was something else going on—a movement from acid rock toward what would later become known as heavy metal. DeLoach, Weis, and Penrod had left the band (DeLoach to become a gourmet chef, Weis and Penrod to form Rhinoceros) by the time *Heavy* began climbing the U.S. chart, on its way to No. 78. Bassist **Lee Dorman** and guitarist **Eric Braunn** came in to complete Iron Butterfly's classic lineup.

That was the cast that went into the studios to record the sophomore set *In-A-Gadda-Da-Vida*. They came up with solid songs to kick off the album—notably "Termination," released as an overseas single—but all of side one seemed a mere prelude to what was waiting for fans once they flipped the

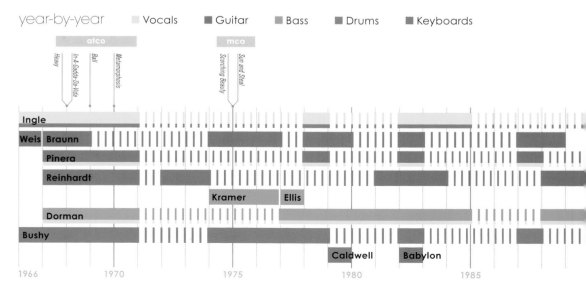

year-by-year   ■ Vocals   ■ Guitar   ■ Bass   ■ Drums   ■ Keyboards

7.3M
In-A-Gadda-Da-Vida
(1968)

1.2M
Ball
(1969)

500,000
Iron Butterfly Live
(1970)

500,000
Metamorphosis
(1970)

Keith Ellis
b. March 19, 1946
d. Dec 12, 1978

Bobby Caldwell
b. unknown

Guy Babylon
b. December 20, 1956
d. Sept 2, 2009

Robert Tepper
b. unknown

Charlie Marinkovich
b. October 7, 1959

Martin Gerschwitz
b. unknown

record over. Ironically, the song that was to become the band's calling card was not supposed to be titled "In-A-Gadda-Da-Vida"—it was written as "In the Garden of Eden." But Ingle slurred the words in the studio and everyone liked the results.

A ridiculously edited version (chopping off more than fourteen minutes) was released as a single in the U.S.—where it climbed into the Top Thirty—but that would not cut it for the devoted fans who eventually pushed the parent album to multi-million sales. *In-A-Gadda-Da-Vida* became the Atlantic label's biggest seller, holding that claim until the fourth album by Led Zeppelin (who had supported and upstaged the Butterfly on the British quartet's first American tour in late 1968 and early 1969).

The band remained intact for 1969's more melodic *Ball*, which hit No. 3 in the U.S. and yielded two Top 100 hits, "Soul Experience" and "In the Time of Our Lives." They were even scheduled to play at the Woodstock festival, and duly despatched a telegram containing a list of directives to the stage manager: "You will send helicopter to LaGuardia. Pick us up, bring us back. We will go immediately onstage, in front of everybody else, and then we will be given

a helicopter and flown back." The stage manager's reply? "Fuck off." They did not play.

Braunn left before 1970's *Metamorphosis*, which hit U.S. No. 16, but a bigger blow came when Ingle split after its release. The group trudged on for another year, before calling it quits in 1971. A revised lineup—with Braunn, Bushy, and keyboardist **Philip Taylor Kramer**—returned with *Scorching Beauty* (1975) and *Sun and Steel* (1976). Unfortunately, both records failed to crack the Top 100.

The group has since gone through more than three dozen lineup changes but remained active in every year except 1986. Iron Butterfly have spent decades living off past success—and have yet to record a follow-up to *Sun and Steel*.

But perhaps they do not need to. "In-A-Gadda-Da-Vida," in all of its notoriously excessive grandeur, continues to fascinate to this day. Slayer covered it for 1987's *Less Than Zero* soundtrack, rapper Nas sampled it on "Hip Hop Is Dead," and it has been used in such films as *Freddy's Dead: The Final Nightmare*. And, in 1995, the band received pop culture's greatest nod of approval when "In-A-Gadda-Da-Vida" was featured in an episode of *The Simpsons*. **JiH**

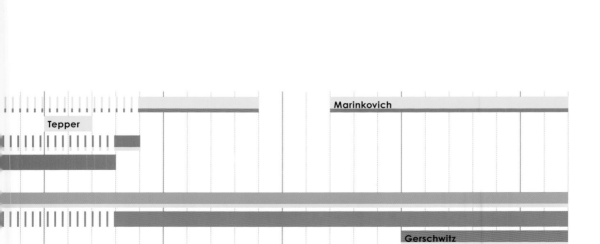

Tepper

Marinkovich

Gerschwitz

1990   1995   2000   2005   2010

iron maiden 1975–present

Steve Harris
b. March 12, 1956

Bruce Dickinson
b. August 7, 1958

Adrian Smith
b. February 27, 1957

Dave Murray
b. December 23, 1956

Janick Gers
b. January 27, 1957

Nicko McBrain
b. June 5, 1952

Paul Day
b. April 19, 1956

Ron "Rebel" Matthews
b. Unknown

Alongside Black Sabbath and Metallica, Iron Maiden are one of the most influential metal bands ever to don spandex. The London group—a six-piece since 1999—have demonstrated for over three decades that what most fans want is a consistent entity with an iconic image, an instantly recognizable sound, and songs about warfare, conquest, and science fiction.

It is a testament to founder member, bassist, and chief songwriter **Steve Harris**'s determination that Maiden existed for over four years before coming close to commercial success. After forming the band in 1975, Harris went through a carousel of guitarists, singers, and drummers before hitting on a relatively stable lineup, comprising singer **Paul Di'Anno**, guitarists **Dave Murray** and **Dennis Stratton**, and drummer **Clive Burr**. The self-released *Soundhouse Tapes* EP from 1979 was snapped up by Maiden's fanbase, a core of devotees who had been attracted by the band's ambitious live show and powerful, melodic tunes.

Maiden's self-titled 1980 debut album hit No. 4 in the U.K. and spearheaded the "New Wave Of British Heavy Metal" (NWOBHM). This new sound took the old demons-and-wizards tropes of traditional, Sabbath-style metal and added the speed and aggression of

punk. Alongside Def Leppard, Saxon, and Diamond Head, Maiden were this new wave's obvious leaders, with fans including future Metallica founder Lars Ulrich: "My heart and soul were in England with Iron Maiden."

Like Leppard, Maiden went on to transcend the NWOBHM genre tag. After *Killers* (1981), for which Stratton was replaced by **Adrian Smith**, the band fired Di'Anno and recruited the operatically throated **Bruce Dickinson** (ex-Samson) for Maiden's first true classic and first U.K. chart-topper, *The Number of the Beast*. Controversy engulfed certain parts of the U.S. owing to the album's splendidly Satanic cover art, which depicted Maiden's horrific mascot Eddie as a devilish puppet-master. However, the music was what counted, and songs such as "The Prisoner," "Children of the Damned," and "Run to the Hills" (the latter a U.K. Top Ten hit) ensured that Maiden made a huge impact on the international rock scene.

As the decade unfolded, the unstoppable group issued a sequence of essential albums. Their live shows (propelled by new drummer **Nicko McBrain**, who took over from Burr in 1982) were as memorable as their music, with high points including 1984–85's World Slavery Tour (leading to 1985's fine in-concert set *Live*

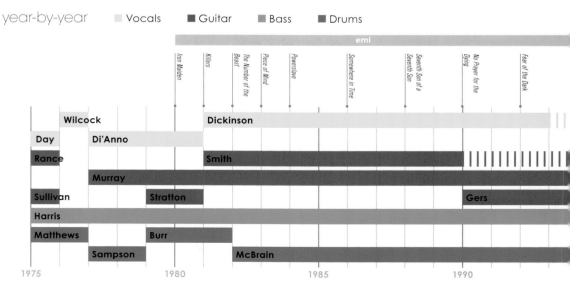

year-by-year ■ Vocals ■ Guitar ■ Bass ■ Drums

emi

Iron Maiden *Killers* *The Number of the Beast* *Piece of Mind* *Powerslave* *Somewhere in Time* *Seventh Son of a Seventh Son* *No Prayer for the Dying* *Fear of the Dark*

Wilcock | Dickinson
Day | Di'Anno
Rance | Smith
Murray
Sullivan | Stratton | Gers
Harris
Matthews | Burr
Sampson | McBrain

1975 · 1980 · 1985 · 1990

5.1M
*The Number of
the Beast*
(1982)

3.9M
Piece of Mind
(1983)

3.9M
*Somewhere in
Time*
(1984)

3.7M
Powerslave
(1986)

Terry Rance
b. Unknown

Dave Sullivan
b. Unknown

**Dennis
Wilcock**
b. Unknown

**Doug
Sampson**
b. June 30, 1957

Paul Di'Anno
b. May 17, 1958

**Dennis
Stratton**
b. Nov 9, 1954

Clive Burr
b. March 8, 1957

Blaze Bayley
b. May 29, 1963

After Death) and a triumphant headline slot at the Donington Monsters of Rock festival in 1988, then the world's most prestigious metal fixture. With that year's semi-progressive, U.K. chart-topping *Seventh Son of a Seventh Son*, Maiden's songwriting hit a new peak.

While they remained enviably successful, the following decade was a period of turmoil. Dickinson, the band's most outspoken and visually important character, had always been a man of many faces—novelist, airline pilot, and world-class fencer among them. But after a third U.K. chart-topper (1992's *Fear of the Dark*) and even a No. 1 single (1990's "Bring Your Daughter... to the Slaughter"), he quit in 1993 to launch a moderately successful solo career.

Smith also departed, obliging Harris to recruit ex-Gillan guitarist **Janick Gers** alongside Wolfsbane singer **Blaze Bayley**. This lineup released *The X Factor* (1995) and *Virtual XI* (1998), neither of which matched up to Maiden's previous work. Fans found it hard to accept Bayley, a competent but unremarkable singer, and many felt that Harris's songwriting lacked the raw excitement of Maiden's eighties albums.

This period in the doldrums came to an end in 1999, when Dickinson and Smith returned to the fold.

Gers remained on board, making Maiden that rare thing, a three-guitar band. Since then, they have plowed an acclaimed furrow as a classic metal act, one of the few to survive the great cull of the nineties, and certainly the only metal band (apart from Metallica) that tours on a truly grandiose scale.

The revived lineup instantly reversed the pattern of waning chart placings with a trio of big-hitters: 2000's solid comeback *Brave New World*, 2003's stirring *Dance of Death*, and 2006's war-dominated *A Matter of Life and Death*. In recent years, however, the focus has been less on albums and more on their live show, which is a spectacle like no other. Between 2008 and 2011, Dickinson actually piloted the band and twelve tons of equipment around the world on a custom-painted Boeing 757 (dubbed "Ed Force One"), as documented in the 2009 documentary *Flight 666*.

The title of 2010's *The Final Frontier* attracted inevitable speculation that it would be the group's last album, but Harris and his troops have made it clear that Eddie will be stalking the Earth for some years yet. Iron Maiden remain one of the world's truly unique acts: a band with their own sound, their own image, and their own mission. Long may they reign. **JM**

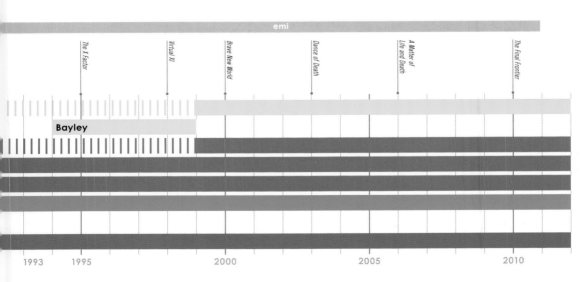

Iron Maiden (1980)

The Number of the Beast (1982)

Piece of Mind (1983)

Steve Harris is flanked by the debut's singer **Paul Di'Anno** and guitarist **Dennis Stratton.**

Harris, Clive Burr, Dave Murray, Adrian Smith, and **Bruce Dickinson.**

Powerslave (1984)

Burr's successor **Nicko McBrain** enjoys the gold and platinum haul.

Somewhere in Time (1986)

Seventh Son of a Seventh Son (1988)

Fear of the Dark (1992)

Murray on the World Piece Tour with the band's mascot, Eddie.

The X Factor (1995)

A Matter of Life and Death (2006)

The Final Frontier (2010)

Dickinson and **Harris,** who often jostled for space centerstage, on the World Slavery Tour.

Dickinson rocks Toronto on the A Matter of Life and Death Tour.

Dickinson with **Janick Gers** on his penultimate tour before quitting the Irons in 1993.

Harris and **Murray** in extremis as the Seventh Tour of a Seventh Tour hits New Jersey in 1988.

Murray and **Harris** (with **Gers** peeking out) marvel at new singer **Blaze Bayley**'s dancing…

Gers celebrates twenty years as the "new boy" at the Sonisphere festival in 2010.

the jam 1972–1982

Paul Weller
b. May 25, 1958

Bruce Foxton
b. September 1, 1955

Rick Buckler
b. December 6, 1955

Steve Brookes
b. Unknown

If **Paul Weller** has a smile, he does not appear to have ever used it professionally. Not when The Jam were enjoying six successful U.K. studio albums, not when The Style Council bestrode the charts—with added U.S. success—and not when his solo career earned him the moniker "The Modfather," and spawned such celebrity champions as Noel Gallagher.

Maybe that permanent scowl could be traced to those early days in Woking, Surrey, England, back in 1972. With him on bass, **Steve Brookes** and **Bruce Foxton** on lead and second guitar, and **Rick Buckler** on drums, The Jam set out to take the pub circuit by storm. It would be a long five years of shows and more shows before the world began to pay attention. But that was the time Weller needed to fall in love with The Who, The Kinks, and their sixties contemporaries, and rebrand his band as Mods. Sharp suits, Small Faces-style hair, and a right-wing stance (adopted more for provocation than political reasons) made them stand out against the backdrop of raggedy U.K. punk.

All they needed now was the music. With Brookes out, Weller switched to guitar, leaving Foxton to pick up bass duties. Musically, the trio were as lean as their appearance suggested. When Polydor signed them in 1977, they proved it to a wider audience. "In the City" and an album of the same name gave them a taste of chart success, followed seven months later by *This Is*

the Modern World (boasting a cover of Wilson Pickett's "In the Midnight Hour"). This production line took its toll on Weller creatively, reflected in the next singles— "News of the World" and "David Watts"—being Foxton and Ray Davies compositions respectively.

With the main man having caught his breath, *All Mod Cons* (1978) was virtually an all-Weller affair, with "Down at the Tube Station at Midnight" and "A Bomb in Wardour Street" standing out. Then *Setting Sons* (1979) was trailed by the magnificent "The Eton Rifles." This gave them their first U.K. Top Ten single and marked a definite switch to "socialist" sentiments. (That early Conservatism, they insisted, had been the record company's idea.) "I can understand how tough it [was] on Rick and Bruce when I presented them with a song like that and virtually told them when to play," Weller later conceded to writer Patrick Humphries. "It must have been especially frustrating for Bruce because he has such a distinctive style. But 'Eton Rifles' was an exception. Most of the time all I had were rough ideas and fragments, and we'd hammer them out together, with everybody contributing ideas."

The new decade saw even greater success. Four U.K. No. 1s began with "Going Underground" (a double A-side with "Dreams of Children"), then the Beatles-inspired "Start!," "Town Called Malice," and "Beat Surrender," the latter from their sixth and final

year-by-year   ■ Vocals   ■ Guitar   ■ Bass   ■ Drums

In the City

	1972	1973	1974	1975	1976	1977
Weller						
Brookes						
Foxton						
Buckler						

album, *The Gift* (1980). "They represent everything that is vitally important…" wrote Pete Townshend in *Time Out.* "No one likes musical categories, but The Jam are a great rock band in the old tradition." (Having impressed another member of the old guard, Weller played on Peter Gabriel's third solo album, in 1980.)

Despite their being more popular than ever, Weller split the band in 1982—much to the disappointment and shock of Foxton and Buckler. His rationale was, he said, his desire to try something new. After a decade honing their sound, he did not want to taint the name of The Jam with—possibly failed—experimentation. However, complained Foxton a decade later, "Paul never discussed what he was feeling with us. And he hasn't done since… Maybe he was right: maybe we couldn't have persevered with the new direction he was moving in. But I always thought Rick and myself were amiable enough chaps to give it a go if he'd asked us. But he never did."

Relations between the three members took a distinctly frosty turn: it would be twenty-eight years before any of them shared a stage, when Foxton guested at a London show by Weller in May 2010 (playing "The Eton Rifles" and "The Butterfly Collector").

Weller's subsequent collaboration with keyboard player Mick Talbot as The Style Council produced four successful albums and a distinctive soulful sound on hits such as "You're the Best Thing" and "Money Go Round (Part 1)." Only "Walls Come Tumbling Down" came close to evoking the sound of his old band.

With 1984's "My Ever Changing Moods," The Style Council achieved something that The Jam never did: a Top Thirty hit in the U.S. But, in 1989, Weller decided to sound the death knell for the band, a decision encouraged by Polydor rejecting their final album *Modernism: A New Decade.* (This departure into deep house music would eventually emerge in 1998.)

A self-titled 1992 album reminded the public that Weller was still around, but it was 1993's *Wild Wood* that proved he was as essential as ever. Then *Stanley Road* (1995)—with artwork by *Sgt. Pepper* sleeve designer Peter Blake—and "The Changingman" became the defining points of his solo career.

Of his eight following albums, 2002's *Illumination* (featuring Noel Gallagher of Oasis and Kelly Jones of the Stereophonics), 2008's *22 Dreams* (featuring Noel Gallagher, Robert Wyatt, and Blur's Graham Coxon), and 2012's *Sonik Kicks* (featuring Gallagher and Coxon on the same song) all topped the U.K. chart, while the rest hit the Top Five. The experimental *22 Dreams* and 2010's *Wake Up the Nation* (which featured a contribution from Bruce Foxton, hence his London cameo that year) even won Weller his first American hits in twenty years. That's entertainment, indeed. **JaH**

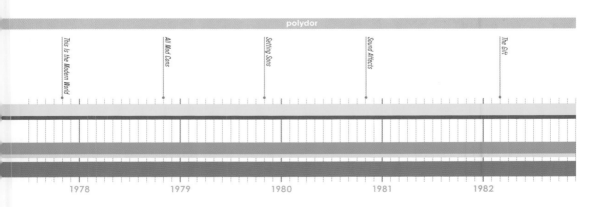

In the City (1977)

This Is the Modern World (1977)

All Mod Cons (1978)

Setting Sons (1979)

Sound Affects (1980)

The Gift (1982)

Paul Weller backstage, one month after the release of *In the City*.

Rick Buckler, **Weller**, and **Bruce Foxton**, around the time of *This Is the Modern World*.

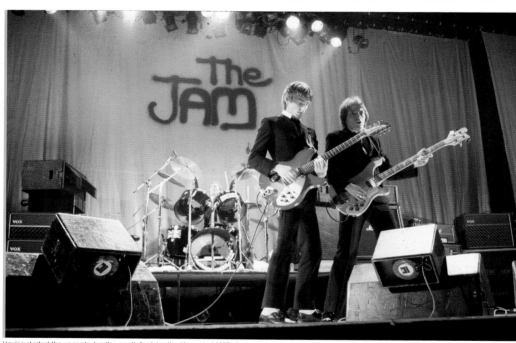

Having started the year playing the capital's clubs, the trio ended 1977 playing at London's prestigious Hammersmith Odeon on December 18.

The Jam hit the United States in March 1978 for their second set of dates in the country.

The Jam at the Palladium in New York, February 1980. "American audiences are more into that rock 'n' roll thing; 'Yeah, let's just rock out,'" observed **Weller**, adding "It's just not my scene."

The sharp suits get a rest in 1980, the year of the trio's first No. 1 hits.

The Jam rock the Rainbow in London, May 1979.

Weller wows the crowd at The Jam's last British TV appearance, on Channel 4's *The Tube*.

jane's addiction 1985–present

Perry Farrell
b. March 29, 1959

Eric Avery
b. April 25, 1965

Stephen Perkins
b. September 13, 1967

Dave Navarro
b. June 7, 1967

Flea
b. October 16, 1962

Martyn LeNoble
b. April 14, 1969

"From a decade that will be remembered musically as the one that gave us new wave and all those hair bands," wrote rocker-turned-raconteur Henry Rollins in 1997, "Jane's was a stand-out whose records still deliver and whose shows are still talked about."

Psi-Com band-mates **Perry Farrell** and **Eric Avery** created Jane's Addiction, named after roommate Jane Bainter ("I didn't like it…" she recalled, "but I didn't think the band would go anywhere"). With guitarist Chris Brinkman and drummer Matt Chaikin, they played a handful of shows in late 1985. Brinkman was replaced, in quick succession, by Rick Parker, Mark Pritchard, and Ed Dobrydino (the last-named appearing on the band's first demo), but the classic lineup was birthed in 1986, with drummer **Stephen Perkins** and guitarist **Dave Navarro**.

Sinewy rhythms, pyrotechnic riffing, and Farrell's shamanistic charisma made the quartet a sensation. The faux live *Jane's Addiction* (1987)—with crowd noise looted from a Los Lobos show—made no chart impact, and *Nothing's Shocking* (1988)—featuring Red Hot Chili Peppers' bassist **Flea** and Fishbone horn players Angelo Moore and Christopher Dowd—stalled at U.S. No. 103. Nonetheless, word-of-mouth about their extraordinary songs and shows, and publicity-

generating controversy surrounding *Nothing's Shocking*'s artwork made them *the* alternative band of the late eighties. "Get bigger than Sonic Youth, but you couldn't get as big as Jane's Addiction," recalled Courtney Love. "Those were the rules."

By 1990, however, drugs (particularly heroin) and financial disagreements were tearing Jane's apart. *Ritual de lo Habitual* (1990)—featuring violinist Charlie Bisharat (of new age act Shadowfax), jazz pianist Geoff Stradling, and string arrangements by Beach Boys collaborator John Philip Shenale—was their last all-new album for thirteen years. After a fractious tour, including the debut of the Farrell-masterminded Lollapalooza festival, Jane's split in 1991.

Farrell and Perkins created Porno for Pyros, whose self-titled 1993 debut album hit the U.S. Top Three. (*Good God's Urge,* featuring three members of Bauhaus, followed in 1996.) Avery and Navarro formed Deconstruction, who made one self-titled and, by their own admission, song-free album in 1993 before the guitarist joined the Chili Peppers later that year. Meanwhile, Perkins launched the side project Banyan, whose three albums from 1997 to 2004 feature Porno for Pyros' Mike Watt, the Beastie Boys' Money Mark, and Flea and his fellow Chili Pepper John Frusciante.

year-by-year ■ Vocals ■ Guitar ■ Bass ■ Drums

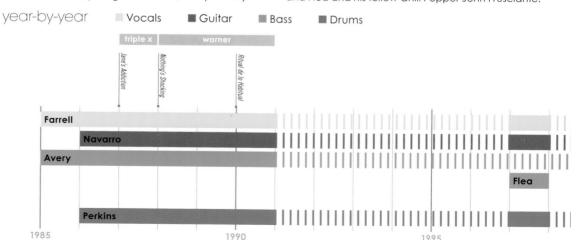

triple x | warner

Jane's Addiction | Nothing's Shocking | Ritual de lo Habitual

Farrell

Navarro

Avery

Flea

Perkins

1985 · 1990 · 1995

Chris Chaney
b. June 14, 1970

Duff McKagan
b. February 5, 1964

In 1997, Farrell, Perkins, Navarro, and Flea regrouped as Jane's Addiction for the "Relapse" tour (documented on 2003's self-indulgent *Three Days* DVD) and *Kettle Whistle* compilation, the latter of which rescued the 1986 classic "Slow Divers" from unreleased obscurity. Thereafter, Flea returned to the Chili Peppers, from whom Navarro was dismissed for his druggy unreliability in 1998. Meanwhile, Farrell pursued a largely ignored solo career, with 1999's fine career retrospective *Rev* and 2001's all-new *Song Yet to Be Sung*. Navarro guested on the latter, as he also did on tracks by Alanis Morissette (on whose 1995 debut "You Oughta Know" he played with Flea), Marilyn Manson (1998's "I Don't Like the Drugs (But the Drugs Like Me)"), Christina Aguilera (2002's "Fighter"), Guns N' Roses (1999's "Oh My God"), Mariah Carey (a 2003 cover of Def Leppard's "Bringin' on the Heartbreak"), and Janet Jackson (1995's "What'll I Do").

The comparatively cleaned-up Jane's Addiction reunited again in 2001, now with Porno for Pyros' bassist **Martin LeNoble**. However, by the time of 2003's *Strays*—produced by Alice Cooper/Pink Floyd veteran Bob Ezrin—**Chris Chaney** (who had toured with Alanis Morissette before being replaced, coincidentally, by Eric Avery) was on bass. The album earned their

highest international chart placings and, with the searing "Just Because," bequeathed their first single to enter the public consciousness since *Ritual de lo Habitual*'s barking "Been Caught Stealing."

However, after another increasingly acrimonious tour, the band splintered in late 2003. With Extreme guitarist Nuno Bettencourt, Farrell created Satellite Party, whose lovely *Ultra Payloaded* (1997) featured New Order's Peter Hook, ex-Pearl Jam/Chili Peppers man Jack Irons, the inevitable Flea and Frusciante, and a vintage vocal by The Doors' Jim Morrison. Meanwhile, Farrell's former bandmates became The Panic Channel, whose sole album achieved the remarkable feat of being worse than *Deconstruction*.

All these efforts were eclipsed when, in 2008, Farrell, Perkins, and Navarro reunited with Avery as Jane's Addiction. After a year of touring, including a co-headliner with Nine Inch Nails, Avery quit, to be replaced by former Guns N' Roses bassist **Duff McKagan**. Musical differences meant this union lasted just six months, before TV on the Radio's Dave Sitek helped them record the slick *The Great Escape Artist* (2011). When the band returned to the road, the long-suffering Chaney was back on bass. "These are," Navarro admitted in 2011, "volatile relationships." **BM**

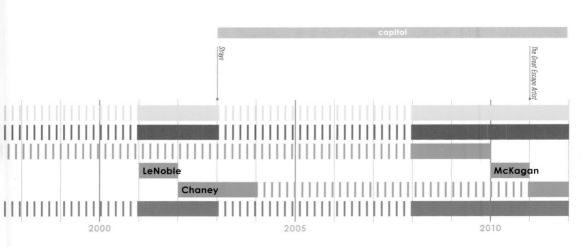

capitol

Strays

The Great Escape Artist

LeNoble

Chaney

McKagan

2000   2005   2010

jefferson airplane / starship 1965–present

Marty Balin
b. January 30, 1942

Paul Kantner
b. March 17, 1942

Jorma Kaukonen
b. December 23, 1940

Jack Casady
b. April 13, 1944

Signe Anderson
b. September 15, 1941

Grace Slick
b. October 30, 1939

Skip Spence
b. April 18, 1946
d. April 16, 1999

Spencer Dryden
b. April 7, 1938
d. Jan 11, 2005

San Franciscan band Jefferson Airplane soared as *the* soundtrack to America's late sixties counterculture, with its psychedelia, pot, and anti-Vietnam War, anti-establishment protest. RCA's biggest act (after Elvis), this musical hybrid of misfits and mavericks managed to keep airborne for eight years, even though the tremulous Airplane parts were always threatening to come unriveted. And then, miraculously, they took off into hyperspace as Jefferson Starship.

Singer **Marty Balin** formed the band to tap into the new electrified folk rock scene in the mid-sixties, and opened a venue called the Matrix with Bill Thompson (later the group's manager) in which to play. He recruited rhythm guitarist and singer **Paul Kantner**, and chose **Signe Anderson** to accompany his tenor on stage and on their debut album. But the voice and look forever linked with the band belongs to **Grace Slick**. She was Kantner's muse after Anderson left owing to family commitments and she stole Balin's limelight—her pretty, preppy face belied

her razor sharp, strident, and expletive ridden vocals (just the thing to peeve the older generation). Grace also brought along a formidable track record as a songwriter, having penned the classic "White Rabbit" and performed "Somebody to Love" in her previous band The Great Society. These songs, now reworked, became the signature tunes and first Top Ten hits featuring Jefferson Airplane's "jet age sound."

That sound—a folk-garage-acid mix—and indeed the band's whole persona were infused with a potent cocktail of marijuana, LSD, cocaine, and amphetamines. "White Rabbit," in fact, was a paean to acid with the immortal lyrics "Remember what the dormouse said—feed your head, feed your head," while the sleeve of 1972's *Long John Silver* converted into a cigar (i.e. stash) box. Being stoned often led the band to create fresh, experimental, and exciting music, underpinned by **Jorma Kaukonen**'s edgy reverb guitar and **Jack Casady**'s deft bass (he also played on Hendrix's *Electric Ladyland*).

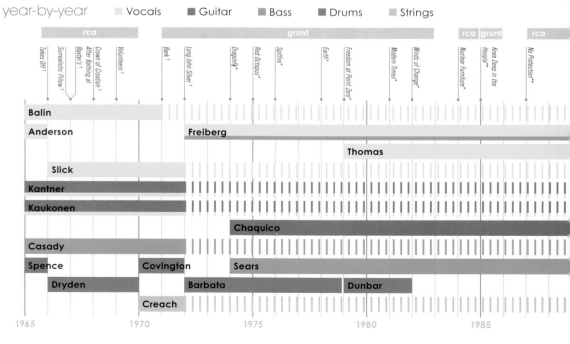

○   ○   ○   ○

4M
Red Octopus
(1975)

1.5M
Spitfire
(1976)

1.5M
Earth
(1978)

1.7M
Knee Deep in the Hoopla
(1985)

Papa John Creach
b. May 28, 1917
d. Feb 22, 1994

John Barbata
b. April 1, 1945

Joey Covington
b. June 27, 1945

Aynsley Dunbar
b. January 10, 1946

David Freiberg
b. August 24, 1938

Craig Chaquico
b. September 26, 1954

Pete Sears
b. May 27, 1948

Mickey Thomas
b. December 3, 1949

The constant haze of joints also made it easier for the band to splinter. However, despite having four singer-songwriters—a tricky set-up in any band—Jefferson Airplane created a string of classic albums from 1967's *Surrealistic Pillow* to 1969's *Volunteers*.

The band fell apart in 1972. Kaukonen and Casady focused on their splinter group Hot Tuna, while Kantner and Slick began to beam down from Jefferson Starship (a name first used for 1970's excellent, sci-fi themed album *Blows Against the Empire*, credited to Paul Kantner & Jefferson Starship, and featuring Jerry Garcia, David Crosby, and Graham Nash).

Balin—the overlooked architect of the Airplane—begrudgingly boarded Jefferson Starship in 1975. But the band were now far more successful in sales and chart terms than the Airplane ever were: *Red Octopus* (1975) hit U.S. No. 1. However, insisted guitarist **Craig Chaquico**, "Everybody was doing music based solely on their artistic, creative inspiration and intuition. Nobody thought for a second about the charts."

When the band's fortunes waned in the early eighties, they streamlined themselves to the critically reviled Starship—minus the "Jefferson" and with Slick the sole remaining original Airplane pilot. Among a trio of U.S. No. 1s was the karaoke classic "We Built This City"—a drum machine-laden homage to those long-gone San Francisco days. Inevitably, as Starship crashed, so the Airplane took flight once again. Balin, Slick, Kantner, Kaukonen, and Casady were joined by journeyman drummer Kenny Aronoff for a self-titled comeback album in 1989, after which the now sixty-year-old Slick bowed out of the music business, arguing that rock music should belong to the young.

Amid ensuing, bewildering changes in lineup and branding, the Airplane were inducted (by the Grateful Dead's Phil Lesh) into the Rock and Roll Hall of Fame in 1996. "We're like a semi-professional baseball team..." remarked Kantner at the time of the relaunched Jefferson Starship's *Jefferson's Tree of Liberty* (2008). "We're not really professional musicians." **JaH**

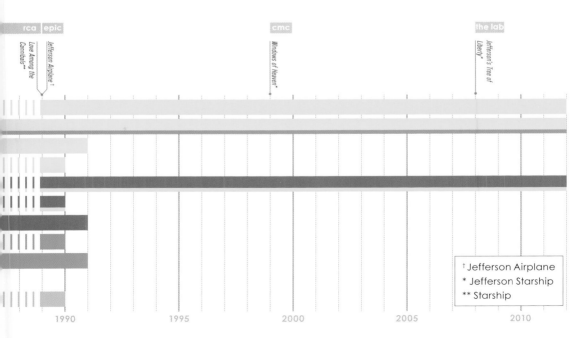

† Jefferson Airplane
* Jefferson Starship
** Starship

jethro tull 1967–present

Ian Anderson
b. August 10 1947

Mick Abrahams
b. April 7, 1943

Clive Bunker
b. December 12, 1946

Glenn Cornick
b. April 23, 1947

Martin Barre
b. November 17, 1946

Jeffrey Hammond-Hammond
b. July 30, 1946

John Evan
b. March 28, 1948

Barriemore Barlow
b. September 10, 1949

Daft but not punk, **Ian Anderson**—who most people think *is* Jethro Tull—has mesmerized fans worldwide for over forty years. Striking one of rock's most iconic and unlikely poses, this dishevelled tramp turned fish-farming businessman is still standing, albeit on one leg (the other leg locked over his knee) as he twirls his flute baton-style, then plays it one-handed, rasping through the mouthpiece. Add a shock of frizzy hair, a shabby, checkered coat, lace-up boots, elegant tights, and a cod piece, and you have the iconic Tull image (albeit one that has not been a reality for decades now). He has played over 2500 concerts, based on over 250 self-penned songs from more than thirty albums (with sales of over sixty million copies). "Less is more" has never flown with Jethro Tull.

The first incarnation of the band—The Blades—came together in 1967: Anderson, guitarist Michael Stephens, bassist **Jeffrey Hammond-Hammond**, and drummer **John Evan** (who would return on keyboards in 1970). By 1968, they were Jethro Tull, named after the eighteenth-century English inventor of the seed drill (or "Jethro Toe," thanks to an error at the pressing plant responsible for their first single, 1968's "Sunshine Day."): Anderson, bassist **Glen Cornick**, drummer **Clive Bunker**, and guitarist **Mick Abrahams**.

This Was (1968) had plenty of Abrahams's bluesy solos, but there were poppier folk and flute elements that were not to his liking; he left to form Blodwyn Pig. **Martin Barre** joined, and the Tull became hit-makers: "Living in the Past," "Sweet Dream," and "Witch's Promise" made the U.K. Top Ten in 1969 and 1970.

Stand Up (1969), boasting a pop-up centerfold sleeve (now much sought after by collectors), topped the British chart and took Tull into the U.S. Top Twenty, while the prog rock-infused *Benefit* (1970) earned their first U.S. gold certification.

With Hammond-Hammond back in the fold, they submerged into hard rock on 1971's *Aqualung*—their all-time best-seller, whose influence can be heard in the likes of Iron Maiden and Tool. Anderson's sartorial oddness, fiendish laugh, and manic stare were all put to good effect as he transformed into the old man on the album's artwork.

In contrast, 1972's *Thick as a Brick*—Tull's first U.S. chart-topper—married evocatively English acoustic folk textures with a sub-Monty Python tale, fleshed out by Anderson's twelve-year-old alter-ego Gerald Bostok over a single, forty-three-minute track. Painstakingly rehearsed and often utilizing first takes, it developed into "the mother of all concept albums"

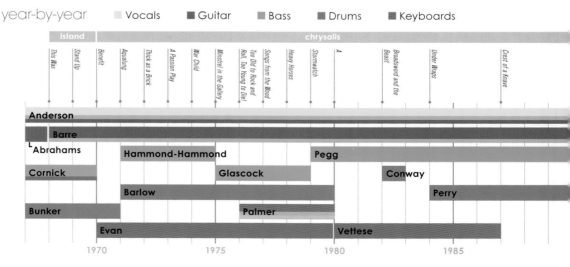

year-by-year   ■ Vocals   ■ Guitar   ■ Bass   ■ Drums   ■ Keyboards

1.6M	7.2M	1.9M	2.5M
Stand Up (1969)	Aqualung (1971)	Thick as a Brick (1972)	M.U.—The Best of Jethro Tull (1976)

Dave Pegg
b. November 2, 1947

John Glascock
b. May 2, 1951
d. Nov 17, 1979

David Palmer
b. July 2, 1937

Gerry Conway
b. September 11, 1947

Peter-John Vettese
b. August 15, 1956

Andrew Giddings
b. July 10, 1963

Doane Perry
b. June 16, 1954

Jonathan Noyce
b. July 15, 1971

(Anderson's own words): "a mindboggler of what was then relatively complex music, lyrically complex and confusing and above all a bit of a spoof." A live rendition from Madison Square Garden, beamed around the world via satellite in 1978 (quite an innovation then), gives a good account of the band in all its bombastic glory as Anderson's Dickensian showmanship delivers a first-rate Fagin.

That Tull had become more popular in the U.S. than back at home grew clear when *A Passion Play* (1973) became their second American No. 1 while being mauled by a U.K. press fed up with prog rock pretensions. It was duly announced that Tull would cease touring forever—a music press "scoop" brokered without the band's knowledge by their manager to get publicity.

War Child (1974)—one of Tull's ambitious rock opera projects, with string arrangements by **David Palmer**—saw a return to shorter, structured songs (including their last U.S. hit "Bungle in the Jungle"). *Minstrel in the Gallery* (1975) trod a somewhat tired troubadour path, but it was nothing compared to the shambolic *Too Old to Rock 'n' Roll: Too Young to Die!* Conceived as a stage musical about an aging rocker who somehow becomes a trendsetter, the album—

steered again by David Palmer, who joined as a keyboard player—was their first in six years to fall short of the U.S. Top Ten and U.K. Top Twenty.

Tull duly retreated to a safer folk-rock setting for 1977's *Songs from the Wood* and 1978's *Heavy Horses*. Anderson's production work for Steeleye Span (1974's *Now We Are Six*) and the addition of Fairport Convention multi-instrumentalist **Dave Pegg** (replacing bassist **John Glascock**, who tragically died after open heart surgery) proved valuable influences.

Eager to explore new directions, Anderson conceived 1980's synthesizer-laden *A* as a solo project (only Martin Barre remained from 1979's *Stormwatch*), but was persuaded to issue it under the Tull name. Business as usual was restored on *The Broadsword and the Beast* (1982) before electronics reared their head once more on *Under Wraps* (1984).

Crest of a Knave (1987) spurred a revival of their fortunes (Tull, controversially, beat Metallica to a "best hard rock" Grammy) and, even when their album output slowed, the band (in which only Barre and drummer **Doane Perry** are constants) continued to play for fans both old and new. Showing no signs of slowing, Anderson hit the road in 2012, playing *Thick as a Brick* and its sequel, credited to him alone. **JaH**

■ Aerophones   ■ Other percussion   ■ Strings

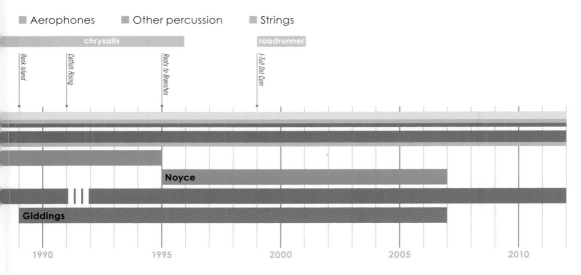

elton john 1962–present

Elton John
b. March 25, 1947

Caleb Quaye
b. October 9, 1948

Roger Pope
b. Unknown

Dee Murray
b. April 3, 1946
d. January 15, 1992

Nigel Olsson
b. February 10, 1949

Davey Johnstone
b. May 6, 1951

Ray Cooper
b. August 19, 1942

Fred Mandel
b. 1956

Sir Elton Hercules John—CBE, Rock and Roll Hall of Famer, multiple Grammy winner, prolific hit-maker, tireless charity fundraiser, art lover, co-writer of music's biggest-selling single—has traveled a long, long way since first tinkling the ivories as three-year-old Reginald Dwight in a London suburb.

At eleven, with his parents' rock 'n' roll records ringing in his ears, "Reggie" won a scholarship to the Royal Academy of Music. From there, via a $20-a-week residency as a hotel pianist, he founded The Corvettes, then Bluesology, the band that provided him with his big break. Bluesology backed visiting American soul artists before coming to the attention of crooner Long John Baldry, who secured their services. Soon disenchanted with this arrangement, Dwight discovered Bernie Taupin, a songwriter from Lincolnshire, after both responded to a Liberty Records talent advertisement in the *New Musical Express*. The pianist's new stage name married the forenames of Bluesology sax player Elton Dean (later to join Soft Machine) and Long John Baldry.

Elton formed his own band, initially ex-Spencer Davis Group bass guitarist **Dee Murray** and drummer **Nigel Olsson**, but soon there was a revolving door of more than twenty guitarists, drummers, percussionists (notably the perennial **Ray Cooper**), keyboard wizards, and backing singers. Although credited on just two singles since their inception in 1970, the Elton John Band have been regular touring and recording companions for their flamboyant front-man, adding muscle to countless John-Taupin classics.

Four decades after his first hit, and with an incredible thirty U.S. and U.K. chart-topping albums and singles to his credit, the biggest-selling pop act of the seventies (and the man who has sold more albums on each side of the Atlantic than any other British male) is still standing, and then some: Elvis and Frank Sinatra are the only solo males that can match or better his transatlantic chart success.

Among the many highlights are four consecutive No. 1 albums on both sides of the Atlantic in 1973 and 1974 (*Don't Shoot Me I'm Only the Piano Player*, *Goodbye Yellow Brick Road*, *Caribou*, and *Greatest Hits*), thirteen U.S. million-selling singles, a U.K. chart-topping reinvention more than three decades into his career courtesy of boy band Blue ("Sorry Seems to Be

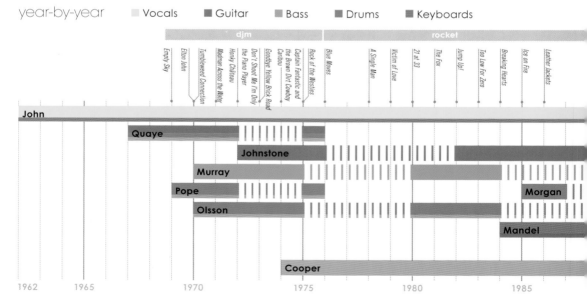

year-by-year ◼ Vocals ◼ Guitar ◼ Bass ◼ Drums ◼ Keyboards

6.8M	5M	26.4M	10M
Goodbye Yellow Brick Road (1973)	Don't Shoot Me I'm Only the Piano Player (1973)	Elton John's Greatest Hits (1974)	Elton John's Greatest Hits Volume II (1977)

Charlie Morgan
b. August 9, 1955

Guy Babylon
b. Dec 20, 1956
d. September 2, 2009

Bob Birch
b. July 14, 1956

John Jorgenson
b. July 6, 1956

John Mahon
b. Unknown

Kim Bullard
b. May 6, 1955

the Hardest Word"), a re-mix of a 1979 chart flop ("Are You Ready for Love") and a hook-up with rapper 2Pac ("Ghetto Gospel"). Elton has sold an estimated 250 million records worldwide... and counting.

In September 1997, following the death of his close friend, Diana, Princess of Wales, Elton and Taupin penned new lyrics to their Marilyn Monroe tribute, 1973's "Candle in the Wind." After an emotional performance to a worldwide TV audience at the princess's funeral and amid an unprecedented outpouring of grief, the George Martin-produced "Candle in the Wind 1997" became the fastest and biggest-selling single since records began in the U.S. (more than eleven million copies sold), the U.K. (nearly five million) and worldwide (thirty-three million).

Away from the charts, Elton has awards and achievements to burn: an Oscar (with Sir Tim Rice) for "Can You Feel the Love Tonight" from the movie *The Lion King*; six Grammys (notably the 1999 "Legend" award); four Brits and eleven Ivor Novello awards; an appearance as the Pinball Wizard in a 1975 film adaptation of The Who's rock opera *Tommy*; inductions into the Songwriters (with Taupin) and Rock

and Roll Halls of Fame in 1992 and 1994, respectively; and a star on the Hollywood Walk of Fame. The flower-loving "Rocket Man," who was the first popular Western singer to perform in what was then the USSR, is also the president—and has twice been chairman—of his beloved Watford Football Club.

But life has not always been so rosy for Elton. By the mid-seventies, following his most successful period in the charts, he was battling alcohol and drug addiction. He has also been a victim of the eating disorder bulimia and has one failed marriage—to German sound engineer Renate Blauel—behind him. Since 2005, however, he has been in a civil partnership with Canadian film director David Furnish.

Elton's ability to bounce back from addiction, illness, and personal turmoil—and his willingness to use his fame and fortune for the benefit of others—is a testament to this much-loved entertainer. In 1992, he established the Elton John AIDS Foundation, which has raised a staggering $200 million for people living with the disease in more than fifty countries worldwide. In recognition of his charity work, Elton was knighted by Queen Elizabeth II on February 24, 1998. **MW**

J

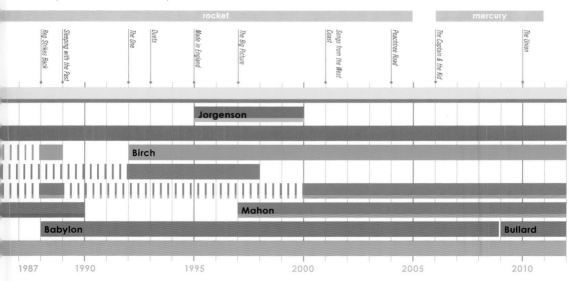

 Aerophones   ■ Other percussion

Elton John (1970)

Honky Chateau
(1972)

**Goodbye Yellow
Brick Road** (1973)

Blue Moves (1976)

Too Low for Zero
(1983)

**Sleeping with the
Past** (1989)

The One (1992)

Made in England
(1995)

**Songs from the
West Coast** (2001)

The Union (2010)

Elton John in 1970, at the start of his prolific recording career as a solo artist.

The newly-arrived superstar at home in Windsor, England, in 1972.

With *Goodbye Yellow Brick Road* having provided a third U.S. and second U.K. No. 1, **Elton** was on a high at London's Hammersmith Odeon in December 1973.

With **Davey Johnstone** on 1976's Louder Than Concorde (But Not Quite As Pretty) tour.

With fellow superstar Rod Stewart at a Liza Minnelli show in 1983.

John during the Victoires de la Musique awards ceremony, France, in 1989.

At the Oakland Coliseum, Los Angeles, on October 30, 1992, on a tour for *The One*.

John plays "Candle in the Wind" at the funeral of Diana, Princess of Wales, in 1997.

At Andre Agassi's Grand Slam for Children fundraiser in Las Vegas, in 2001.

Elton and Leon Russell, with whom he cut *The Union*, on U.S. TV's *Good Morning America*.

journey 1973–present

Neal Schon
b. February 27, 1954

Gregg Rolie
b. June 17, 1947

Ross Vallory
b. February 2, 1949

George Tickner
b. September 8, 1946

Prairie Prince
b. May 7, 1950

Steve Smith
b. August 21, 1954

Aynsley Dunbar
b. January 10, 1946

Robert Fleischman
b. Unknown

Journey are *the* American AOR band, selling millions in the seventies and eighties without many record-buyers having a clue as to the members' individual identities. Appropriately, they began life as a group of sessionmen—the Golden Gate Rhythm Section—playing around the Bay Area of San Francisco.

Keyboardist **Gregg Rolie** and guitarist **Neal Schon** had been mainstays of Santana, while bassist **Ross Vallory** and rhythm guitarist **George Tickner** had played in psychedelic group Frumious Bandersnatch. Drummer **Prairie Prince**, on loan from The Tubes, completed the original quintet. Rechristened Journey, and with Prince replaced by **Aynsley Dunbar** (latterly a Frank Zappa sidekick), they signed to the Columbia label and issued their self-titled debut in early 1975.

On *Journey*—and its successors *Look Into the Future* (1976) and *Next* (1977)—lyrics and vocals were very much secondary to instrumental rock, just as in Santana. But the record label issued an ultimatum: they wanted a front-man. **Robert Fleischman** proved a short-stayed solution in 1977, making way for **Steve Perry** (who joined the band on the road while the Fleischman-fronted incarnation were supporting Emerson Lake & Palmer) to become the final piece of the Journey jigsaw. His anguished falsetto became much-imitated by American singers of the era.

Infinity (1978) redefined their sound and took them to the edge of the pop Top Twenty. It benefited from Perry's presence and also that of U.K. producer Roy Thomas Baker, fresh from making his name with Queen and supervising their "Bohemian Rhapsody" period. While most of the band members were happy with the commercial rewards their new style brought them, Dunbar packed his sticks and quit for Jefferson Starship, leaving drum duties to **Steve Smith**.

Schon admitted the metamorphosis was a learning curve for him. Writing with Perry was a different discipline from anything he had done before. But the reward came in a string of early eighties hits—dubbed the "dirty dozen" by the band—that projected Journey into the pomp-rock stratosphere.

Evolution (1979) gave the band their first *Billboard* Top Twenty hit, "Lovin', Touchin', Squeezin'," while 1980's *Departure* reached No. 8 on the album chart and included the Top Thirty hit "Any Way You Want It."

Rolie left after 1981's live *Captured* (dedicated to recently deceased AC/DC front-man Bon Scott), to be replaced by **Jonathan Cain** from the Babys. Determined to streamline and modernize the band's sound, Cain muscled into the Schon-Perry songwriting team, and replaced organs with synthesizers. Their defining statement was on its way.

year-by-year   ■ Vocals   ■ Guitar   ■ Bass   ■ Drums   ■ Keyboards

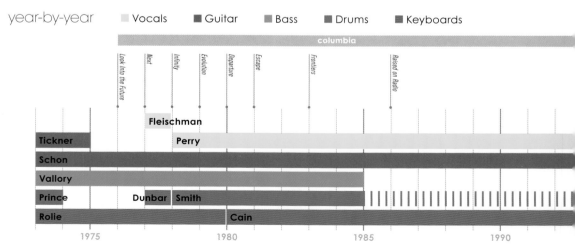

5.8M
Departure
(1980)

12.4M
Escape
(1981)

9.9M
Frontiers
(1983)

19.5M
Greatest Hits
(1988)

Steve Perry
b. January
22,1949

Jonathan Cain
b. February 26,
1950

Steve Augeri
b. January 30,
1959

Jeff Scott Soto
b. November
4, 1965

Arnel Pineda
b. September
5, 1967

Deen Castronovo
b. August 17,
1965

Escape—the band's eighth and biggest-selling original album—topped the U.S. album chart in 1981 and went nine times platinum, thanks to three Top Ten hits: "Who's Cryin' Now," "Don't Stop Believin'," and "Open Arms." Journey also graced the soundtracks for the movies *Heavy Metal* (1981) and *Tron* (1982).

1983's *Frontiers* cemented their status, reaching No. 2 on the U.S. chart (and providing the group's first and last U.K. Top Ten album chart entry). Thanks to four hits—"Separate Ways (Worlds Apart)," "Faithfully," "Send Her My Love," and "After the Fall"—it sold six million copies in their homeland.

Success brought inevitable attempts at solo stardom. In 1984, Schon united with Sammy Hagar, Kenny Aaronson, and another Santana alumnus, Michael Shrieve as HSAS, for *Through the Fire*. But when Perry's *Street Talk* (also 1984) proved he did not need Journey behind him to sell millions of albums, the writing was on the wall. Replacing Smith and Valory with Mike Baird and Randy Jackson, the band managed a final album, *Raised on Radio*, in 1986, then splintered. Their epitaph, 1988's *Greatest Hits*, sold around a million a year for the ensuing decade.

Schon, Perry, Cain, Smith, and Valory reunited for 1996's *Trial by Fire*, scoring a first Grammy nomination in the process. But Perry's health problems cut the comeback short. After a less lengthy wait, the band carried on without him, which both parties have done with varying degrees of success to this day.

Front-men **Steve Augeri** and **Jeff Scott Soto** came and went, but the band played on, benefiting from their faceless image. A 2008 tour with Filipino singer **Arnel Pineda** made Journey one of the year's top-grossing live acts, while a second album with him, *Eclipse*, hit U.S. No. 13 in 2011.

Journey invited critical wrath in their heyday with many now-common practices like selling their images for video games, making commercials for beer, and being filmed for fly-on-the-wall documentaries. "There's nothing wrong with being commercial," Schon instructed *Kerrang!* magazine. "It's just another way of saying you're successful, getting a wider audience." Figures back up his conviction: forty-seven million album sales in the U.S. make them one of the nation's top thirty best-selling bands.

Journey undertook a U.S. tour in 2005 to celebrate the thirtieth anniversary of their first album, playing songs from their entire career. Meanwhile, "Don't Stop Believin'" took on a life of its own: its use in TV shows *The Sopranos*, *Scrubs*, and *Glee* propelled cover versions and the original into international charts. When it comes to arena rock, Journey still rule. **MHe**

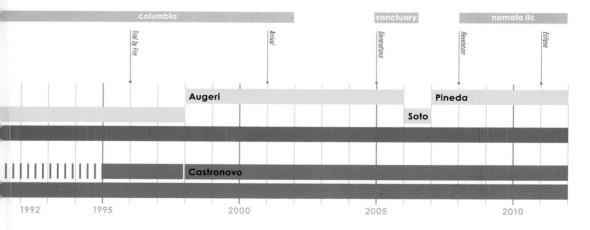

columbia — sanctuary — nomota llc

Trial by Fire — Arrival — Generations — Revelation — Eclipse

Augeri — Pineda

Soto

Castronovo

1992 — 1995 — 2000 — 2005 — 2010

joy division / new order 1978–present

Ian Curtis
b. July 15, 1956
d. May 18, 1980

Bernard Sumner
b. January 4, 1956

Peter Hook
b. February 13, 1956

Stephen Morris
b. October 28, 1957

Gillian Gilbert
b. January 27, 1961

Phil Cunningham
b. December 1974

To spearhead one music genre is the dream of most artists. Not content with being post-punk pioneers, the three-quarters of Joy Division that carried on as New Order also lit the way from industrial wastelands to the dance floor. But their futuristic sounds of the eighties were a long way removed from the rough early edges of the northern English quartet Warsaw: vocalist **Ian Curtis**, guitarist **Bernard Sumner**, bass gunslinger **Peter Hook**, and drummer **Stephen Morris**.

After a change of name to Joy Division came a change of sound in the studio. Much of that was attributable to wayward genius producer Martin Hannett, who realized that space and mood were vital for *Unknown Pleasures* (1979), to complement Curtis's troubled, contemplative lyrics. "The way [Hannett] treated instruments and recorded drums was really revolutionary," said Hook. "The production inflicted this doomy mood over the album."

On the cusp of an American tour and the release of *Closer*—somber, despondent, another cannot-be-denied classic—the band was stopped in its tracks by Curtis's tragic and untimely suicide in May 1980. Distressed to the point of no return by both the disintegration of his marriage and the increasing frequency of his epileptic seizures, he hanged himself at his Macclesfield home.

As New Order, the band tentatively stepped back into circulation, with **Gillian Gilbert** on keyboards and Sumner a reluctant front-man. The latter's vocals could be thin and hesitant, but lent their new aesthetic an appropriate fragility. Success, however, was far from assured: some wondered if the surviving members would go the same way as The Doors post-Morrison. *Movement* (1981) provided inconclusive evidence.

It was a different story with the group's singles, which were often excluded from their albums. "Temptation" in 1982 suggested a band that could not only match but surpass the brilliance of its previous incarnation. Influences had been soaked up in New York's clubs, then given an identity all of their own. Hook's bass often led the melody rather than taking the traditional role as ballast-provider.

Myths had built up around the band since Curtis's death. There was an unknowable quality to the group that a lack of interviews and Peter Saville's high-art, minimum-information sleeves for the Factory label's releases did nothing to dispel. With the opening of a nightclub in Manchester, the Haçienda, New Order seemed to be more a way of life than just a band.

Not that music took a back seat. *Power, Corruption & Lies* (1983) began a four-album sequence that defined the commercial, danceable

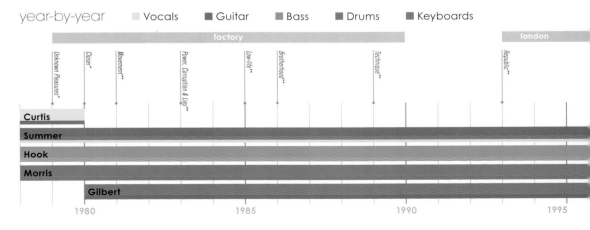

year-by-year ■ Vocals ■ Guitar ■ Bass ■ Drums ■ Keyboards

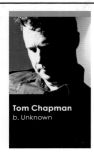

Tom Chapman
b. Unknown

end of U.K. electronic music for the eighties. The sublime, confident *Low-life* (1985) was followed by *Brotherhood* (1986), before *Technique* (1989) ended the decade on a dazzling note. "A rare and ravishing triumph," wrote British music paper *Melody Maker*.

Meanwhile, the behemoth that was "Blue Monday" pulsed in and out of the chart after its initial release in 1983. In six throbbing minutes, the U.K.'s best-selling twelve-inch single of all time reset the controls for what could make a hit—and gave the band an anthem to rival Joy Division's immortal "Love Will Tear Us Apart" from 1980. Little seemed beyond them: 1990's U.K. No. 1 "World in Motion" even instilled credibility into the usually horrific singles that banged the drum before inevitable major-tournament disappointments for the England soccer team.

During their period of greatest triumph, the seeds of discord were sown. This was initially expressed, however, via side projects such as Hook's rocky Revenge, Gilbert and Morris's The Other Two, and Sumner's Electronic union with ex-Smith Johnny Marr (Electronic also featured collaborations with the Pet Shop Boys and Kraftwerk's Karl Bartos).

Republic (1993), the first New Order album in four years, spawned "Regret," which went Top Five in the U.K. and Top Thirty in the U.S. But it was the band's last for eight years, their internal friction being aggravated by their stake in the financially disastrous Haçienda.

They reunited in 1998 for a headlining set at the U.K.'s Reading festival, then—with Gilbert replaced by **Phil Cunningham** of British indie also-rans Marion— set to work on a new album. With Smashing Pumpkin Billy Corgan helping in the studio and on tour, *Get Ready* (2001) began in sparkling fashion: the hit "Crystal" was exactly how fans would have wished to be reacquainted with the band.

However, traveling in different directions, Sumner and Hook were pulling the band apart. The group had often traded on a chill wind blowing through its best work; on *Waiting for the Sirens' Call* (2005) there was now the sense of something stale in the air. Matters descended even further in the following years, with counter-claims of blame often played out in the press. Said Morris: "Bernard and Peter have quite a complicated relationship… It's very Spinal Tap."

Hook pronounced New Order dead in 2007. On announcing the formation of Bad Lieutenant, even Sumner said: "I don't want to make music as part of New Order." However, in 2011, a lineup minus Hook, but with Gilbert—plus Bad Lieutenants Cunningham and bassist **Tom Chapman**—returned to the stage once again, to surprised and delighted reviews. **CB**

■ Other percussion

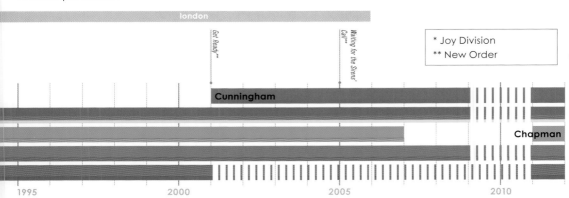

* Joy Division
** New Order

Unknown Pleasures (1979)

Closer (1980)

Movement (1981)

Joy Division—left to right: **Bernard Sumner, Stephen Morris, Ian Curtis,** and **Peter Hook**—perform at Bowdon Vale Youth Club, Altrincham, England, on March 14, 1979.

Power, Corruption and Lies (1983)

Gillian Gilbert, Morris, Sumner, and **Hook** perform for the U.K.'s ITV channel in 1981.

Curtis sings at the Lyceum, London, on February 29, 1980.

Low-life (1985)

Brotherhood (1986)

Technique (1989)

New Order in the eighties (clockwise from top): **Hook, Morris, Gilbert,** and **Sumner.**

Sumner, Stratocaster in hand, takes the mike in 1983.

Republic (1993)

Get Ready (2001)

No

Waiting for the Sirens' Call (2005)

Gilbert, Sumner, Morris, and **Hook** perform on British TV's *The Tube* in 1986.

Artful distortion in 1989 (clockwise from right): **Gilbert, Sumner, Hook,** and **Morris.**

Gilbert plays the Reading festival, England, in 1993.

A New Order BBC TV performance on October 11, 2001; **Phil Cunningham** (left) replaced **Gilbert** earlier that year.

Hook gets down but not necessarily dirty with New Order in 2005.

Cunningham onstage at the Wireless Festival, Hyde Park, London, on June 24, 2005.

judas priest 1970–present

Al Atkins
b. October 11, 1947

K.K. Downing
b. October 27, 1951

Ian Hill
b. January 20, 1951

Rob Halford
b. August 25, 1951

Glenn Tipton
b. October 25, 1947

Richie Faulkner
b. January 1, 1980

Scott Travis
b. September 6, 1961

Les Binks
b. April 5, 1948

There is a persuasive argument in favor of Judas Priest being the world's first heavy metal band. Although fellow Birmingham, England, residents Black Sabbath were tuning their guitars low and singing about Satan four years before Priest released an album, it has been observed—by members of both bands—that Sabbath retained a blues-rock element. Pure heavy metal, if such a thing exists, therefore came later—and Priest are one of a very short list of its possible originators.

Formed in 1969 by singer **Al Atkins**, guitarist Kenneth "**K.K.**" **Downing**, bassist **Ian Hill**, and drummer John Ellis, Priest took their name from Atkins's previous band, who in turn had taken it from Bob Dylan's 1967 song "The Ballad of Frankie Lee and Judas Priest."

Dismayed by the group's dire financial straits, Atkins left in 1973 and **Rob Halford** took his place. The following year, a second guitarist—**Glenn Tipton** from the Flying Hat Band—was added. Tipton and Downing would become one of metal's great guitar duos, while Halford's thrilling vocal range was also a benchmark.

With the classic front four in place, Priest—backed by a series of drummers—set about delivering metal to the masses. Although *Rocka Rolla* (1974) and *Sad Wings of Destiny* (1976) barely registered on charts,

the band's songwriting and performing skills improved with every tour. Their live reputation duly earned them a deal with the CBS label's subsidiary, Columbia.

In 1977, *Sin After Sin*—produced by Deep Purple bassist Roger Glover—featured the great session drummer Simon Phillips and an inspired cover of Joan Baez's "Diamonds and Rust." *Stained Class* (1978) was another high point, with signature songs such as "Exciter" and a cover of American songwriter Gary Wright's "Better By You, Better Than Me." But Priest hit big for the first time in 1980 with their splendidly over-the-top *British Steel*. Hitting No. 4 in the U.K., it contained their biggest-scoring singles to date, "Living After Midnight" and "Breaking the Law"—the latter accompanied by a video in which the band hold up a bank… with guitars. Now *that's* metal.

Priest's domination of the genre—notably in the U.S., where they out-sold even Iron Maiden—seemed unbreakable: *Screaming for Vengeance* (1982) went double platinum. But with 1986's *Turbo*, the band—in a bid to remain contemporary—began to incorporate mainstream elements such as keyboards into its music. While British fans grumbled, the U.S. contingent rewarded them with another platinum album.

year-by-year Vocals Guitar Bass Drums

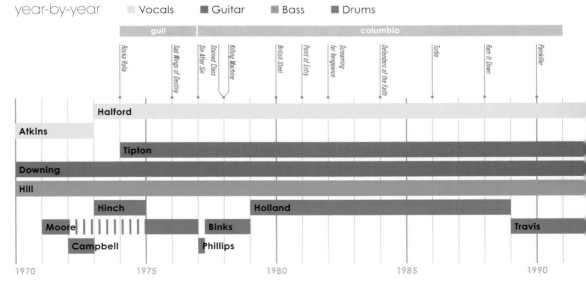

2M	3.5M	2M	3.7M
British Steel (1980)	**Screaming for Vengeance** (1982)	**Defenders of the Faith** (1984)	**Turbo** (1986)

Dave Holland
b. April 5, 1948

Alan Moore
b. 1947

Chris Campbell
b. Unknown

John Hinch
b. July 19, 1947

Simon Phillips
b. February 6, 1957

Tim "Ripper" Owens
b. September 13, 1967

A career-threatening low point came in 1990 when the band were forced to defend themselves in a Nevada court: they were accused of subliminally influencing two youths who shot themselves in 1985 while listening to a Priest album—a tragedy blamed on supposed "backmasking" (inserting a reversed message) in the song "Beyond the Realms of Death." The case was ultimately dismissed, but Halford describes it as a pivotal point in heavy music: had the prosecution won, artistic freedom of speech for musicians might have been irrevocably affected.

Priest returned with a vengeance, unleashing the vicious *Painkiller* in 1990 with new drummer **Scott Travis**, but this proved a brief renaissance: Halford left two years later, citing a desire to work on a side project, Fight. In common with Iron Maiden, who lost Bruce Dickinson for similar reasons, neither band nor singer sold well when apart. Halford formed a gothic duo called 2wo before touring under his own name, with much media attention directed his way in 1998 after he came out as gay during an MTV interview.

Minus Halford, the remaining members recruited **Tim "Ripper" Owens** (ex-Winter's Bane), who had performed in a Priest tribute band. His singing was impressive, but Owens was hampered by expectations that Halford would return. The fortunes of the two studio and two live albums that he recorded with Priest between 1997 and 2003 suffered accordingly.

The inevitable reunion occurred in 2003, prompted by the *Metalogy* box set, on which all the members collaborated. In 2005, they unleashed the old-school metal masterpiece *Angel of Retribution*, making its follow-up, *Nostradamus* (2008), all the more surprising. An operatic, symphonic concept album with few of the usual metal elements, *Nostradamus* left many fans feeling uncertain about their idols' future. Indeed, a farewell tour, titled Epitaph, took place in 2011 after Downing left (he was replaced by the unknown **Richie Faulkner**).

However, their enduring appeal was confirmed by the hits set *The Chosen Few* (2011), on which each song was "chosen" by stars such as Alice Cooper, Ozzy Osbourne, and members of Metallica, Slayer, Whitesnake, the Scorpions, Def Leppard, and Guns N' Roses. "What we'll be looking for in the long term," Downing told *Kerrang!* magazine in 1987, "is to be considered legendary... for being the foremost in what we do: heavy metal." Mission accomplished. **JM**

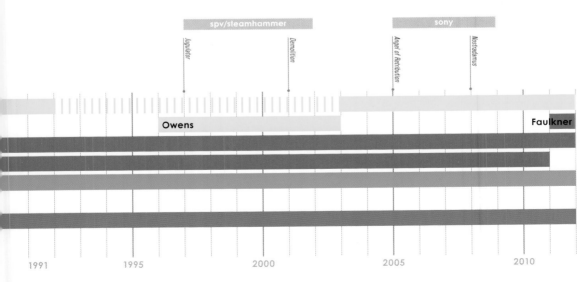

the killers 2001–present

Brandon Flowers
b. June 21, 1981

Dave Keuning
b. March 28, 1976

Dell Neal
b. Unknown

Matt Norcross
b. Unknown

Brian Havens
b. Unknown

Ronnie Vannucci Jr.
b. February 15, 1976

Mark Stoermer
b. June 28, 1977

The Killers' heady brew of pop and rock nods to their acknowledged seventies and eighties influences, from David Bowie and Bruce Springsteen to New Order (whose "Crystal" video bequeathed their name) and the Pet Shop Boys. And they have established a simple formula for success: great songs, and romanticized observations in the grand storytelling tradition.

Brandon Flowers (vocals) and **Dave Keuning** (guitar) founded the group in Las Vegas in 2001, often gigging as a duo, but sometimes joined by **Dell Neal** (bass) and **Matt Norcross** (drums). The following year, **Brian Havens** replaced Norcross before **Ronnie Vannucci Jr.** came in permanently. **Mark Stoermer** (bass) completed the lineup, who were snared by indie label Lizard King in Britain, then Island at home.

Hot Fuss (2004) proved a phenomenon. Its hits "Jenny Was a Friend of Mine," "Mr. Brightside," "Smile Like You Mean It," "Somebody Told Me," and "All These Things That I've Done" grabbed the listener with relentless hooks and never let go. The album duly topped the U.K. chart and sold three million at home.

The Killers also nurtured a huge live following thanks to their exciting concert performances, in which Flowers' showmanship and yearning voice are complemented by Keuning's chiming guitar and the immaculate rhythm section of Stoermer and Vannucci Jr. At 2005's Live8 show, they performed "All These Things That I've Done," lines from which were also sung at the event by Robbie Williams, Coldplay, and U2.

The widescreen visions of *Sam's Town* (2006) at first seemed less catchy than their debut. But, when the dust settled, the album came to be seen as every bit as masterly, thanks to songs such as "When We Were Young," "For Reasons Unknown," "Read My Mind," and the title track. The album duly followed its predecessor to the top in the U.K. and hit No. 2 in the U.S.

After *Sawdust* (2007)—a collection of oddities, covers, and B-sides—*Day & Age* (2008) proved a lighter affair, with a more intimate feel. This is not to say that tracks such as "Human," "Spaceman," "A Dustland Fairytale," and "Losing Touch" skimped on grand gestures—we are talking about The Killers, after all—but there was a more resigned tone, helped by a broader sprinkling of keyboards. The album was consequently not quite so striking, but still made U.S. No. 6 and, yet again, U.K. No. 1.

The group confirmed their live reputation with *Live at the Royal Albert Hall* (2009) and headlined huge shows at London's Hyde Park in 2009 and 2011.

In a sabbatical from group duties, both Stoermer and Vannucci Jr. brought out solo albums. Inevitably, both were eclipsed by Flowers' splendid *Flamingo* (2010), which sounded like a more convincing third Killers album than *Day & Age*. "I do feel like I'm carrying the Killers torch up there," he remarked. "And hopefully I become a better front-man and a better performer. I can apply that to the next Killers record. And we'll just be all the better for it." **MiH**

year-by-year ■ Vocals ■ Guitar ■ Bass ■ Drums ■ Keyboards

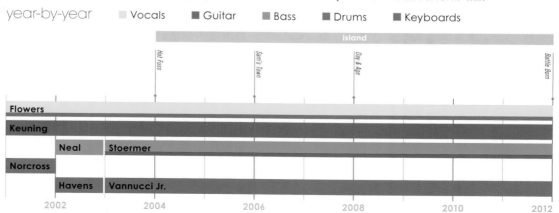

island

Hot Fuss | Sam's Town | Day & Age | Battle Born

Flowers
Keuning
Neal | Stoermer
Norcross
Havens | Vannucci Jr.

2002   2004   2006   2008   2010   2012

king crimson 1969–2009

Robert Fripp
b. May 16, 1946

Ian McDonald
b. June 25, 1946

Michael Giles
b. March 1, 1942

Greg Lake
b. November 10, 1947

Pete Sinfield
b. December 27, 1943

Bill Bruford
b. May 17, 1949

Adrian Belew
b. December 23, 1949

Tony Levin
b. June 6, 1946

The extraordinary King Crimson had at least three distinct phases: the first (and most successful) as pioneers of symphonic rock; the second as outriders on the fringes of progressive and jazz rock; the third as musical explorers of the most advanced kind. In each genre they left their mark.

Robert Fripp (guitar), **Ian McDonald** (woodwind, keyboards), **Greg Lake** (vocals, bass), **Michael Giles** (drums), and **Pete Sinfield** (lyrics) came together as King Crimson in London in 1969. Fripp had previously been in Giles, Giles, & Fripp with Michael and his brother Pete, but it was soon apparent that this new group was in a completely different league. Their debut *In the Court of the Crimson King* (1969), a hit on both sides of the Atlantic, was the quintessential symphonic rock record: the title track and "Epitaph" were drenched in majesty, while "21st Century Schizoid Man" was brutally powerful.

The fallout from a U.S. tour caused quarrels when the group recorded again. Pete Giles replaced Lake on bass, but his brother Michael quit to form a short-lived duo with McDonald. Mel Collins (flute, saxophone) and Gordon Haskell (vocals) also joined. Despite the changes, *In the Wake of Poseidon* (1970) was a wonderful sequel and another hit.

Drummer Andy McCulloch joined for *Lizard* (1970), full of shimmering, glacial surfaces and featuring jazz pianist Keith Tippett and Yes singer Jon Anderson. Boz Burrell (bass, vocals) and Ian Wallace (drums) came in for the alternately serene and frenetic *Islands* (1971), which proved to be the original Crimson's swansong.

The group broke up in 1972, but Fripp was soon back with new players: John Wetton (bass, vocals), former Yes star **Bill Bruford** (drums), David Cross (violin, keyboards), and Jamie Muir (percussion), with Richard Palmer-James, a founding member of Supertramp, providing lyrics. The group recorded the excellent *Larks' Tongues in Aspic* (1973) before Muir departed. Crimson became even tighter, exhibiting their strengths on 1974's *Starless and Bible Black* and *Red*— only for Fripp to disband the group once more.

This time the gap was much longer. When Crimson returned, former Frank Zappa guitarist **Adrian Belew** and Peter Gabriel bassist **Tony Levin** had joined Fripp and Bruford. On *Discipline* (1981), *Beat* (1982), and *Three of a Perfect Pair* (1984), the quartet extended the boundaries of hard rock and jazz-rock—before, again, retreating into the wilderness for ten years.

In 1994, Trey Gunn (guitar, bass) and Pat Mastelotto (drums) joined to make Fripp's "double trio" concept a reality, although Bruford and Levin (temporarily) left four years later. *Thrak* (1995), *The ConstruKction of Light* (2000), and *The Power to Believe* (2003) proved fascinating examples of the group's questing, experimental phase, before another, possibly final, hiatus commenced in 2009. **MiH**

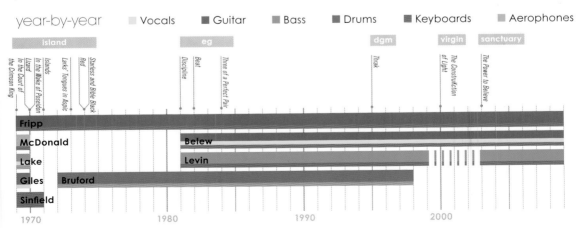

year-by-year ■ Vocals ■ Guitar ■ Bass ■ Drums ■ Keyboards ■ Aerophones

kings of leon 1999–present

Caleb Followill
b. January 14, 1982

Matthew Followill
b. September 10, 1984

Jared Followill
b. November 20, 1986

Nathan Followill
b. June 26, 1979

Few bands have come equipped for instant media coverage as readily as Tennessee's Kings of Leon. Comprising three brothers and a cousin, all with the same surname, the four musicians had spent their youth in religious isolation, traveling the U.S. with their evangelical preacher fathers. For this reason, none of the Kings knew much about the world in general, let alone rock music, before forming their band—one of many reasons why their ascent to fame and fortune has been so remarkable.

Vocalist and guitarist **Caleb Followill** and drummer **Nathan Followill**, first and second sons, moved from their home in Oklahoma to Nashville in 1997, hoping to enter the music business. Between temporary jobs such as house-painting, the duo played bars and cafés under the name The Followills, with their songs a mélange of country and rock.

News of their music came to a New York manager, Ken Levitan, who arranged a deal with RCA. The brothers roped in their younger brother **Jared Followill** to play bass (although, at sixteen years old, he had never played the instrument before) and their cousin **Matthew Followill** to play guitar.

An introductory EP, *Holy Roller Novocaine* (2002), immediately attracted the press. With their beards, painfully cool haircuts, skinny jeans, and endorsement by The Strokes, they were an obvious target for

tastemakers in the U.K., where Levitan first launched them. When the press found out about the Followills' quaint family life and their religious convictions (the four men claimed, truthfully or otherwise, to be virgins), their profile rose still higher.

The years that followed were every young man's rock 'n' roll dream. Although the Kings remained relatively unknown in their home country, Britain embraced them, supermodels flung themselves at them, and publications both high- and low-brow covered them with glory. The four men worked their way through endless female admirers and an equally limitless supply of booze and narcotics, as endless tabloid exposés reveled in the details.

Although their media-enhanced Christian virtue quickly fell away, the Kings' musical talents blossomed, with two quickfire albums—*Youth & Young Manhood* (2003) and *Aha Shake Heartbreak* (2004)—establishing a winning formula of mumbled, hard-to-decipher vocals and barnstorming country-rock. "It's really stripped down…" said Paul Weller of *Aha…*, "but the result is really tough and muscular."

With maturity came commercial success: the Followills topped the U.K. album chart for the first time with 2007's more musically crafted *Because of the Times*, named after a religious conference that the men had attended as youths. Caleb sang in a

year-by-year ■ Vocals ■ Guitar ■ Bass ■ Drums

rca

Youth & Young Manhood

Aha Shake Heartbreak

C. Followill

M. Followill

J. Followill

N. Followill

1999   2000   2001   2002   2003   2004   2005

1M
Aha Shake
Heartbreak
(2004)

1M
Because of the
Times
(2007)

6.2M
Only by the
Night
(2008)

2.3M
Come Around
Sundown
(2010)

more confident, enunciated manner and Matthew's guitar lines were simpler and more memorable. Some older fans were uncertain about this new, mainstream sound, but a new generation of listeners came on board, attracted by the Kings' new music and image (the beards and long hair were also phased out).

The band took a giant step forward in 2008 with their fourth album and second U.K. No. 1. Pearl Jam front-man Eddie Vedder, reported Caleb, "was one of the first people to hear *Only by the Night,* and he said, 'You're about to ride a big wave.'" Vedder was proved right, as "Sex on Fire" and "Use Somebody" conquered the world's charts. "I'm happy for those guys," said Dave Grohl. "When I hear live drums and real guitars and people singing on the radio, it makes me feel that there's still hope for this world."

As Matthew was now using a delayed guitar sound reminiscent of U2, comparisons with that band flew freely, with some listeners attracted by the stadium-sized dynamics of the new songs and others regretful that the Kings had abandoned their roots. Whatever the alleged failings of this stylistic left turn, the public bought into it wholeheartedly and the band were firmly established as arena-fillers (hence the 2009 DVD, *Live at the O2 London, England*).

With Britain conquered, the Kings and their team have spent the subsequent years attempting to break new ground in America, with a certain amount of success. The band surrounded themselves with the accoutrements of rock 'n' roll, launching a fashion line and a record label: Nathan and Caleb also married their long-time girlfriends, perhaps signaling the beginning of an era of domestic respectability. However, some cracks in the intra-band relationships have been evident, with front-man Caleb issuing barbed comments to an unreceptive crowd at Scotland's T in the Park festival in 2009 and smashing his guitar in frustration: newspaper reports also alleged financial disagreements within the group.

The Kings' fifth album, *Come Around Sundown,* appeared to answer these rumors on its release in 2010: a sunny, relaxed piece of work, it was more contemplative than the band's previous albums. Peaking at No. 2 at home, it gave the band their third U.K. chart-topper, and hit No. 1 in Australia, Canada, Ireland, Austria, Belgium, Germany, and Switzerland.

It remains to be seen whether the Kings of Leon will continue along their present path. Immense success greeted the four young men early in life (elder statesmen Nathan and Caleb are only in their early thirties, with Jared and Matthew in their twenties)— and, as the Followills themselves once might have put it, the good Lord alone knows whether this will prove to be a blessing or a burden. **JM**

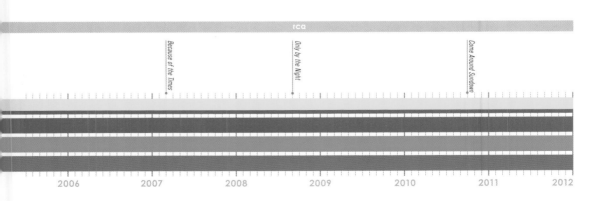

the kinks 1963–1996

Ray Davies
b. June 21, 1945

Dave Davies
b. February 3, 1947

Pete Quaife
b. December 31, 1943
d. June 23, 2010

Mick Avory
b. February 15, 1944

John Dalton
b. May 21, 1943

John Gosling
b. February 6, 1948

Having been given guitars as teenagers by their parents, north London brothers **Ray** and **Dave Davies** started out in the Ray Davies Quartet. With school friend **Pete Quaife** on bass, they turned into The Ravens. Finally, in 1963, with former Rolling Stones drummer **Mick Avory**, the group became The Kinks and signed to the Pye label.

After two failures, the band's third single "You Really Got Me" hit No. 1 in the U.K. and No. 7 in the U.S. Thanks to Dave's earthy guitar riffing, the song became a prototype for heavy metal—and was quickly followed by the equally influential hit "All Day and All of The Night" and a second U.K. chart-topper "Tired of Waiting for You" (later covered by Green Day). Their self-titled debut album—known as *You Really Got Me* in America—was a hit in 1965 on both sides of the Atlantic.

Over the following two years, The Kinks notched up a further seven U.K. hits—including the No. 1 "Sunny Afternoon" and classic "Waterloo Sunset"—all written by elder brother Ray. Meanwhile, *Kinda Kinks* and *The Kinks Kontroversy* (both 1965), *Face to Face* (1966), and *Something Else by The Kinks* (1967) continued their run of domestic success on the album chart. (Thereafter, their albums performed better in

the U.S. than at home.) However, in-fighting between the members—particularly the ever-fractious Davies brothers—and with their management resulted in the group not touring America for four years.

In 1966, bassist Quaife quit for three months, during which he was replaced by **John Dalton**. Ray Davies followed suit in 1967, but was away for less than a week. Just months later, Dave Davies enjoyed a solo U.K. hit with his brother's song "Death of a Clown."

Ensuing years saw the band's albums grow more conceptual, albeit less commercially successful, with 1968's *The Kinks Are the Village Green Preservation Society* (originally featuring the classic "Days," and belatedly acclaimed as their finest work) and 1969's *Arthur (Or the Decline and Fall of the British Empire)* (featuring the minor hit "Victoria," later covered by The Fall). The latter marked Dalton's formal debut, Quaife having quit for good.

Lola Versus Powerman and the Moneygoround Part One (1970) restored The Kinks to the U.S. Top Forty, thanks to the witty hits "Lola"—for which broadcasters insisted a reference to Coca-Cola was replaced by "cherry cola," although the song's cross-dressing theme went unchallenged—and "Apeman" (the latter the band's last British Top Ten hit).

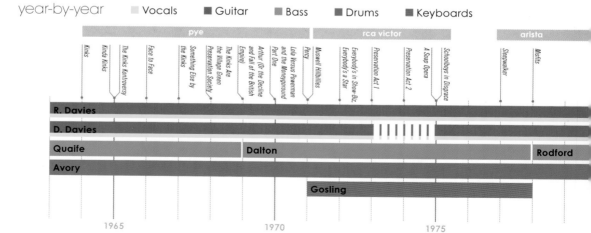

year-by-year   ■ Vocals   ■ Guitar   ■ Bass   ■ Drums   ■ Keyboards

Jim Rodford
b. July 7, 1945

Ian Gibbons
b. Unknown

Bob Henrit
b. May 2, 1944

Mark Haley
b. Unknown

During five years on the RCA label, from 1971, The Kinks notched up just one chart record at home: the Caribbean-influenced "Supersonic Rocket Ship." In the U.S., their albums made only the lower reaches of the chart, despite the flair of Ray Davies's writing. "Celluloid Heroes," from 1972's *Everybody's in Show-Biz, Everybody's a Star,* is one of his finest songs.

A new deal with Arista revived The Kinks' fortunes. In America, *Sleepwalker* (1977), *Misfits* (1978), *Low Budget* (1979), the live *One for the Road* (1980), *Give the People What They Want* (1981), and *State of Confusion* (1983) all made the Top Twenty. The latter even yielded their first major hit in more than a decade, in the whimsical form of "Come Dancing."

Alongside his Kinks duties, Ray—who briefly left the band in 1970 and 1973—pursued solo projects, including acting, producing, and composing. Brother Dave, who quit The Kinks for two years in 1973, released three solo albums. One, *Dave Davies* (1980), hit the U.S. Top Fifty under the title *AFLI-3603.*

After Ray appeared in the 1986 movie *Absolute Beginners*—which also featured David Bowie and Sade—The Kinks signed new deals, with London in the U.K. and MCA in the U.S., but neither *Think Visual* (1986) nor *UK Jive* (1989) met with much success. In

1989, drummer Avory quit, to be replaced by **Bob Henrit**. (Avory reappeared in the touring act The Kast Off Kinks, who have also given a home to **Jim Rodford**, the band's bassist from 1978 to 1996, **Ian Gibbons**, keyboardist from 1979 to 1989 and 1992 to 1996, **John Gosling**, keyboardist from 1971 to 1978, Dalton, Henrit, Quaife, and even, at a handful of shows, Ray Davies).

The group's final studio album, *Phobia* (1993), was notable for the song "Hatred (A Duet)," which provided insight into the Davies' brothers' ongoing relationship. Its chorus: "Hatred is the only thing that keeps us together." However, even "hatred" could not keep The Kinks together and, in 1996, they finally split.

Dave Davies issued a new solo work in 2007, while Ray Davies undertook a series of tours and albums. Lauded as an inspiration by Paul Weller, Noel Gallagher, and Damon Albarn, he added an Ivor Novello Award for an Outstanding Contribution to British Music to his 2004 OBE (Order of the British Empire) medal. And, in 2012, his re-worked classics album *See My Friends* paid ample tribute to The Kinks' impact, its roster including Bruce Springsteen, Metallica, Jackson Browne, Jon Bon Jovi, Pixies' Black Francis, Mumford & Sons, Alex Chilton, Snow Patrol's Gary Lightbody, and The Smashing Pumpkins' Billy Corgan. **BS**

K

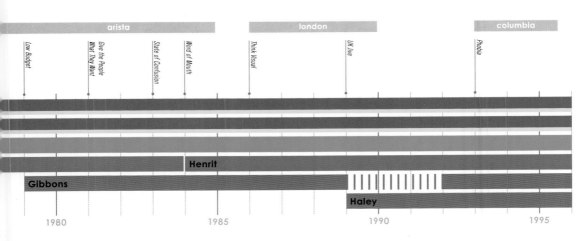

kiss 1972–present

Gene Simmons
b. August 25, 1949

Paul Stanley
b. January 20, 1952

Peter Criss
b. December 20, 1945

Ace Frehley
b. April 27, 1951

Bob Kulick
b. January 16, 1950

Anton Fig
b. August 8, 1952

The power of the Kiss brand—hammered home via merchandise from condoms to coffins—has powered them through years of lineup changes. New Yorkers **Gene Simmons** and **Paul Stanley** had envisaged a power trio in the hit-making mold of Mountain and Grand Funk Railroad, hence their enlisting drummer **Peter Criss** in 1972. But when the format's limitations became apparent they sought a guitarist. Among those to audition was **Bob Kulick**, who re-entered the story later, but the successful applicant was **Ace Frehley**. (Criss and Frehley's views on drink and drugs diverged—to career-crippling effect—from those of Simmons and Stanley, who made up for their abstinence by bedding groupies by the thousand.)

With the lineup settled, Kiss developed their now-trademark makeup. Fans of The Beatles and Alice Cooper, Simmons and Stanley wanted a band where each member had a recognizable identity. They became the Demon and Starchild, Criss the Cat and Frehley the Spaceman. Their heavy rock 'n' roll was honed on 1974's *Kiss* and *Hotter Than Hell*, and 1975's *Dressed to Kill*. But, as they toured the U.S., their blood-spitting, fire-breathing show provoked more comment and sales than their music. "They're a good band,"

Alice Cooper noted drily after seeing Kiss at a record label showcase in 1974. "All they need is a gimmick."

The quartet's big break came with *Alive!* (1975), a touchstone for future stars from Slash of Guns N' Roses to Dimebag Darrell of Pantera. Being a member of the Kiss Army became de rigueur among U.S. teens. This fanbase, married to the Casablanca label's over-the-top promotion, made Kiss seem bigger than they actually were. For three years in the seventies—despite being outsold by the Stones, Led Zeppelin, and Pink Floyd—they were voted America's most popular act.

While critics hated them, fans lapped up *Destroyer* and *Rock and Roll Over* (both 1976), and *Love Gun* and *Alive II* (both 1977). But, by 1978, cracks were showing. Frehley and Criss resented Simmons and Stanley's control, while the founders despaired of their partners' indulgences. (Kulick had deputized for an incapacitated Frehley on studio cuts for *Alive II*.)

After 1978's hits set *Double Platinum*, in a mad mix of publicity stunt and damage limitation, the band issued simultaneous solo albums. Criss's was the worst, Stanley's the best, Simmons's the most star-studded (from Joe Perry and Bob Seger to Donna Summer and Cher), and, surprisingly, Frehley's the most successful.

year-by-year ▪ Vocals ▪ Guitar ▪ Bass ▪ Drums

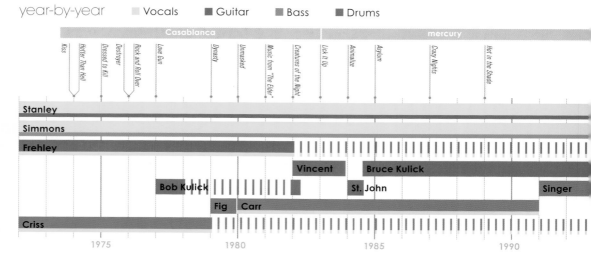

Eric Carr
b. July 12, 1950
d. November 24, 1991

Vinnie Vincent
b. August 6, 1953

Mark St. John
b. February 7, 1956
d. April 5, 2007

Bruce Kulick
b. December 12, 1953

Eric Singer
b. May 12, 1958

Tommy Thayer
b. November 7, 1960

Still together in name if not spirit, they recorded 1979's *Dynasty* before Criss (whose duties on *Dynasty* and 1980's *Unmasked* were filled by **Anton Fig**) was replaced by **Eric Carr**. The band's star had waned at home, but an Australian tour was rapturously received. Nevertheless, a re-think was needed, hence 1981's baffling rock opera *Music from "The Elder"* (the soundtrack to a never-made movie). Exasperated by this shift from hard rock, Frehley quit, although his image graced the sleeves of 1982's compilation *Killers* (on new cuts for which he was again replaced by Kulick) and the skull-crushing *Creatures of the Night*.

Among guitarists on the latter was **Vinnie Vincent**. Enlisted full-time, he was part of the excitement when Kiss shed their makeup to promote 1983's *Lick It Up*. But by 1984 he was out—replaced first by **Mark St. John**, then by **Bruce** "brother of Bob" **Kulick**, both of whom played on 1984's platinum-selling *Animalize*.

Asylum (1985), *Crazy Nights* (1987), *Smashes, Thrashes, & Hits* (1988), and *Hot in the Shade* (1989) kept sales ticking over, but Kiss were eclipsed by acts they had inspired, such as Mötley Crüe. "Forever," written with Bruce Kulick's former employer Michael Bolton, was a hit but, by the nineties, Kiss were again a cult concern. Carr's death from cancer (on the same day as Freddie Mercury) compounded their woes.

They forged ahead with Alice Cooper/Black Sabbath drummer **Eric Singer**, but *Revenge* (1992) and *Alive III* (1993)—despite their heavier feel and U.S. Top Ten placings—were overshadowed by grunge-era acts that they had also inspired. In 1995, Simmons and Stanley bowed to the inevitable: enlisting Criss and Frehley for *MTV Unplugged* (1995), then a blockbusting reunion. *Psycho Circus* (1998) gave them a new U.S. chart high (No. 3), but neither Criss nor Frehley contributed much to it. By 2001, after a so-called "farewell" tour, Singer was filling in for the former.

In February 2003, Kiss returned to the road. For the orchestra-embellished recording of *Kiss Symphony: Alive IV* (2003), Criss was back but Frehley had been replaced by band associate **Tommy Thayer**. On a tour that year with Aerosmith, the lineup settled: Simmons, Stanley, Thayer (in Frehley's makeup), and, yet again, Singer (in Criss's makeup). Confounding skeptics, 2009's rollicking *Sonic Boom*—their first new album in a decade—was kept off the U.S. No. 1 spot only by Michael Bublé. And, in 2012, Kiss threatened another assault on senses and sensibilities with *Monster*. **BM**

K

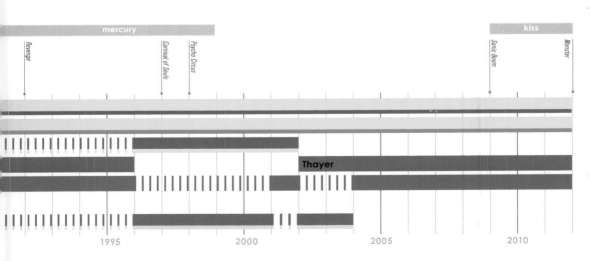

Kiss (1974)

Destroyer (1976)

Love Gun (1977)

Gene Simmons gets into character, backstage in 1974.

Stanley (top), **Peter Criss**, **Ace Frehley**, and **Simmons**, in Westminster, London.

Dynasty (1979)

Paul Stanley lends a hand with preparations, backstage in 1977.

Music from "The Elder" (1981)

Creatures of the Night (1982)

Lick It Up (1983)

Frehley and **Stanley**—the guitarists who powered most of the band's most seminal songs—in a moment of harmony in Chicago in September 1979.

Revenge (1992)

Psycho Circus (1998)

Simmons, **Frehley**, new drummer **Eric Carr**, and **Stanley**—the lineup responsible for 1981's musically excellent but commercially doomed *Music from "The Elder."*

Sonic Boom (2009)

Simmons and new guitarist **Vinnie Vincent**, who debuted on *Creatures of the Night*.

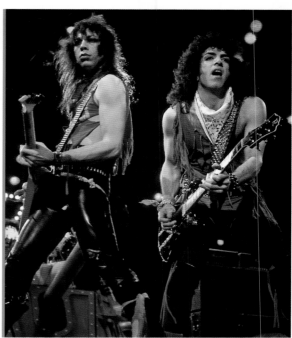

Vincent and **Stanley** in Chicago, on the *Lick It Up* tour—their first without makeup.

Simmons, guitarist **Bruce Kulick**, and **Stanley** exact *Revenge* on London in 1992.

The reunited originals—who would later cut *Psycho Circus*—with rapper **Tupac Shakur**.

With **Eric Singer** in Criss's stage makeup, and new guitarist **Tommy Thayer** in Frehley's, **Stanley** and **Simmons** rock Britain's Download festival the year before the quartet cut *Sonic Boom*.

korn 1993–present

Jonathan Davis
b. January 18, 1971

Reginald Arvizu
b. November 2, 1969

James Shaffer
b. June 6, 1970

David Silveria
b. September 21, 1972

Brian Welch
b. June 19, 1970

Ray Luzier
b. June 14, 1970

Rumors of nü-metal's demise have been greatly exaggerated. True, it is not as "nü"—and arguably not as incendiary—as it was in the nineties, but the genre's pioneers are still going strong after nearly a decade. Led by former mortuary science student **Jonathan Davis**, Korn could have been dead and buried when nü-metal lost its impetus. But with a reputation built on loud and boisterous gigs, straight-talking lyrics relating to taboo subjects such as childhood bullying and sexual abuse, and a string of acclaimed albums, they have achieved consistency and longevity that their peers could only dream of.

With their soul-baring catharsis, Korn have distanced themselves from old-school metal favorites like Iron Maiden and Metallica since their 1993 demo *Neidermeyer's Mind*, produced by Ross Robinson (who also manned the desk for Slipknot). Railing against the suffocation of smalltown America, their nü-metal was raw, energetic, controversial, and eager to give vulnerable, misunderstood teenagers a life-altering image and attitude makeover.

Davis, **Reginald** "Fieldy" **Arvizu**, **James** "Munky" **Shaffer**, **David Silveria**, and **Brian** "Head" **Welch** formed in Bakersfield, California, from the ashes of heavy metal outfit L.A.P.D. Their self-titled debut album, featuring finished versions of three songs from *Neidermeyer's Mind*, struck a chord with metalheads the world over but sickened non-believers with its disturbing cover art—a young girl on a swing at the mercy of a tall, shadowy figure, with her shadow hanging by the neck from the "K" of the group's logo.

They spent most of the year after the album's release on tour. A handful of dates were with nü contemporaries the Deftones, but their ascendancy was secured on more high-profile outings with Danzig (alongside an up-and-coming Marilyn Manson), Megadeth, and Monster Magnet. By the time they were mid-way through a 1996 tour with Ozzy Osbourne, *Korn* had been certified gold in the U.S.

Described by one critic as a "basket-case full of contradictions," the group crashed into the U.S. Top Three with *Life Is Peachy*. As their fanbase swelled and they toured with protégés Limp Bizkit, *Peachy* spawned the singles "No Place to Hide," "Good God," and "A.D.I.D.A.S." ("All Day I Dream About Sex"). They also received an inadvertent promotional boost from student Eric Van Hoven, who arrived at his Michigan school wearing a Korn shirt. Branding the group "indecent," "vulgar," and "obscene," an assistant principal handed the teenager a one-day suspension. When news of Van Hoven's plight filtered through to Bakersfield's finest, they filed a cease

year-by-year ▪ Vocals ▪ Guitar ▪ Bass ▪ Drums ▪ Other percussion

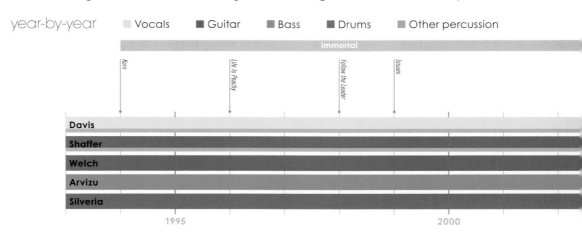

5.1M
Korn
(1994)

4.1M
Life Is Peachy
(1996)

7.3M
Follow the Leader
(1998)

5M
Issues
(1999)

and desist order against the assistant principal and shipped a truckload of Korn shirts to a local radio station, who handed them to students at the school.

Follow the Leader (1998) gave Korn a first U.S. chart-topper, while its standout track, "Freak on a Leash," bagged a Grammy in 2000 for Best Short Form Music Video (it was also nominated for an incredible nine MTV Video Music Awards). Further fueled by "Got the Life," the furious *Follow the Leader* became their worldwide bestseller. Meanwhile, the group launched the Family Values tour with Rammstein, Ice Cube, Orgy, and Limp Bizkit (whose popularity would shortly eclipse that of their benefactors).

Issues (1999) followed *Leader* to the top spot in their homeland, selling 573,000 copies in its first week. In the presence of Puff Daddy and Busta Rhymes, the album was performed in its entirety at Harlem's Apollo Theater—the first rock concert at the historic soul venue since an appearance by Buddy Holly in 1957.

By 2001, nü-metal had reached its commercial zenith, with Limp Bizkit (whose singer Fred Durst had directed the video for the *Issues* hit "Falling Away from Me"), Staind, and Linkin Park all ripping up the charts. Meanwhile, Korn's prolific output continued with 2002's *Untouchables* (whose "Here to Stay" won a Grammy for Best Metal Performance) and

2003's *Take a Look in the Mirror*. The latter, billed as a "reconsideration of their sound," was their last to feature Welch—he found the church, renounced his sins (namely an addiction to methamphetamine), and bailed out of the band. (The guitarist's journey from rock to redemption is described in his 2007 book *Save Me from Myself: How I Found God, Quit Korn, Kicked Drugs, and Lived to Tell My Story*.)

Greatest Hits Vol. I—featuring covers of Cameo's "Word Up!" and Pink Floyd's "Another Brick in the Wall" and "Goodbye Cruel World"—marked the end of Korn's deal with the Immortal label. *See You on the Other Side* (2005), *MTV Unplugged* (2007)—featuring a cover of Radiohead's "Creep" and cameos by The Cure and Evanescence's Amy Lee—and an untitled eighth studio album formed part of a $25 million deal with Virgin. In 2007, drummer **Ray Luzier** signed up as a full-time replacement for Silveria (whose place had been filled on a temporary basis by Frank Zappa sidekick Terry Bozzio, Bad Religion's Brooks Wackerman, and Slipknot's Joey Jordison).

Korn's current deal with the Roadrunner label has spawned *Korn III: Remember Who You Are* (2010) and the dubstep-flavored *The Path of Totality* (2011). Both have added to a global sales total of over thirty-five million. Anything is possible if kids eat their Korn. **MW**

■ Aerophones   ■ Strings

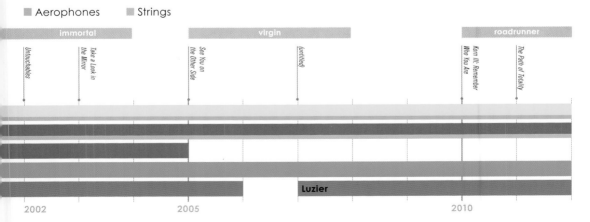

kraftwerk 1970–present

Ralf Hütter
b. August 20, 1946

Florian Schneider
b. April, 7 1947

Wolfgang Flür
b. July 17, 1947

Karl Bartos
b. May 31, 1952

Fritz Hilpert
b. May 31, 1956

Henning Schmitz
b. December 26, 1953

Between 1974 and 1981, Kraftwerk pioneered many of the techniques on which most modern pop music is based. They explored the creative possibilities brought to music by synthesized sound and automated rhythms, and used them to make records that subtly and wittily commented on the ever-changing relationship between humans and machines.

Florian Schneider and **Ralf Hütter** were classical music students in Dusseldorf when they formed an experimental rock group, Organisation. The band's one album, *Tone Float* (1970), was released only in the U.K. and was largely ignored. Schneider and Hütter disbanded Organisation and used the German word for "power station" for a new band. Kraftwerk's innovative instincts were soon evident: *Kraftwerk* (1971) was an album of instrumental music laced with electronic effects and sudden tempo changes.

Various musicians had short stays in early lineups, including **Klaus Dinger** and **Michael Rother**, who would undertake avant-garde adventures as Neu! Hütter left for a few months, but Schneider persuaded him to return for *Kraftwerk 2* (1972), another all-instrumental set which they recorded with a drum machine. *Ralf and Florian* (1973) brought greater

use of synthesizers and, on "Ananas Symphonie," Kraftwerk's first use of electronically treated vocals.

The twenty-two-minute title track of *Autobahn* (1974) was at once both shockingly new and soothing, its steady electronic pulse a precursor of trance music. With swooping synthesized sounds evoking both the momentum and the monotony of motorway journeys, it provided Kraftwerk's breakthrough when an excerpt from the track became an international hit. (The song's repeated "fahren, fahren, fahren"— German for driving—was regularly misinterpreted as an homage to The Beach Boys' hit "Fun, Fun, Fun.")

Radio-Activity (1975) used vocoders and ominous electronic tones on an album themed around radiation and radio broadcasting. It was the first album made by what is regarded as the classic lineup, with Hütter, Schneider, and electronic percussion player **Wolfgang Flür** joined by **Karl Bartos**.

The title track of *Trans-Europe Express* (1977) namechecked David Bowie and Iggy Pop, then residents of Berlin. Bowie returned the compliment with the track "V-2 Schneider" on his *"Heroes"* album. "Hall of Mirrors" was a slow, sinister commentary on image and celebrity, while "Showroom Dummies"

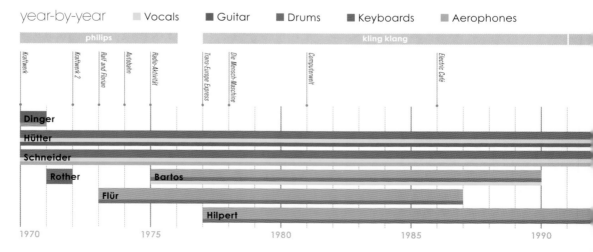

year-by-year   ▪ Vocals   ▪ Guitar   ▪ Drums   ▪ Keyboards   ▪ Aerophones

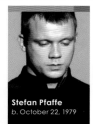

Stefan Pfaffe
b. October 22, 1979

Klaus Dinger
b. March 24, 1946
d. March 21, 2008

Michael Rother
b. September 2, 1950

took a more light-hearted look at artifice, a theme reflected in the sleeve photos of the group imitating mannequins. *Trans-Europe Express* was available in English-language and German-language editions, a policy that Kraftwerk would continue on later albums.

On *The Man-Machine* (1978), Kraftwerk combined sonic science with inspired songwriting to devastating effect—"The Model," with its dry dissection of urban glamor, and the anthemic retro sci-fi of "The Robots" were just two examples of the album's wit and craft. The latter number inspired the construction of actual robots with faces modeled on Kraftwerk's own, which became a highlight of the group's live shows.

Computer World (1981) offered a thoughtful and playful examination of the impact of information technology. "Computer Love," which foretold the rise of online dating, was paired with "The Model" as a double A-sided single and became a UK No. 1.

The next Kraftwerk album was delayed when Hütter was badly injured in a bicycle accident. Ironically, the one product of the sessions that reached the public was a 1983 single celebrating cycling, "Tour de France." After cancellations and revisions, *Electric Café* finally appeared in 1986, and

received a mixed response. The album's working title had been *Techno Pop*, a title that was reinstated when the record was re-released in 2009. By then, it could be seen that Kraftwerk had accurately anticipated many of the developments in dance music since the album's original release.

Flür left Kraftwerk in 1987 and was replaced by **Fritz Hilpert**. Bartos also quit before the band returned to touring in 1991 to promote the remix album *The Mix*, and **Henning Schmitz** took his place. No more new material appeared until the December 1999 release of "Expo 2000." The single reached the U.K. Top Thirty, and Kraftwerk sent their robots to stand in for them on BBC TV's *Top of the Pops*.

Tour de France Soundtracks (2003) celebrated a century of the titular race with a collection of tracks loosely linked to the cycling theme. Kraftwerk toured the world in 2004, and *Minimum Maximum*—a fine live album taken from that tour—followed in 2005. Florian Schneider ended his thirty-eight years as a member of Kraftwerk in 2008, and **Stefan Pfaffe** joined their live line-up. In 2012, New York's Museum of Modern Art hosted an eight-night stint by the band, in which they played an album a night, starting with *Autobahn*. **DJ**

■ Other percussion

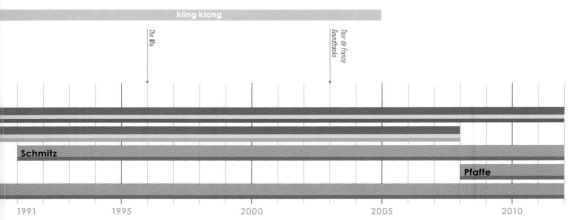

lacuna coil 1996–present

Andrea Ferro
b. August 19, 1973

Marco Coti Zelati
b. August 19, 1975

Raffaele Zagaria
b. unknown

Claudio Leo
b. unknown

Leonardo Forti
b. unknown

Christina Scabbia
b. June 6, 1972

As rare as Kate Bush albums and much less melodious, European metal bands were once at a premium. Aside from mavericks like Switzerland's Celtic Frost, Denmark's Mercyful Fate, and Spain's Baron Mojo, the genre was dominated by Britain and America. But after the advent of black metal, you could hardly hurl an axe without hitting an act from the continent—and, today, the most innovative acts in death, black, industrial, and even quaint old "heavy" metal are often European. Few, however, have scaled the commercial heights of Italy's Lacuna Coil. Their most recent three efforts sailed into the U.S. Top Twenty, and two topped *Billboard*'s independent albums chart..

Singers **Andrea Ferro** and **Christina Scabbia**, bassist and chief composer **Marco Coti Zelati**, guitarists **Claudio Leo** and **Raffaele Zagaria**, and drummer **Leonardo Forti** convened as Ethereal in 1996. Discovering that their name had already been taken, they became Lacuna Coil—an Italian/English blend that translates as "empty spiral."

After recording a self-titled EP in 1997, the band embarked on their first tour, only to splinter amid what they described as "anxiety, stage-fright and intense emotions." Drummer Markus Freiwald (later of Sodom)

replaced Forti, and guitarist Anders Iwers (of Tiamat) covered for Leo and Zagaria, before permanent replacements **Cristiano Mozzati** (drums) and **Cristiano Migliore** (guitar) were enlisted in 1998. The latter was temporarily replaced on tour, owing to injury, by Node guitarist Steve Minelli, while keyboardist Alice Chiarelli also passed through the ranks.

Following the making of their debut album *In a Reverie* (1999), Lacuna Coil's line-up was completed by second guitarist Marco Biazzi. Relentless touring included bottom of the bill appearances at Italy's Gods of Metal festival and the Netherlands' Dynamo Open Air event, both headlined by Metallica.

By 2000, the group had acquired a modest but loyal following across Europe, hence the swift release of that year's *Halflife* EP (which featured an implausible—but, as it turned out, prophetic—cover of "Stars" by poppy British dance act Dubstar).

After the group's first European headlining tour, *Unleashed Memories* (2001) crept into the lower reaches of the German chart. Further live work with the likes of Dimmu Borgir preceded their first American trek, with Portuguese metallers Moonspell. In 2002, the *Comalies* album took them onto metal magazine

year-by-year   ■ Vocals   ■ Guitar   ■ Bass   ■ Drums   ■ Keyboards

century media

In a Reverie

Unleashed Memories

Comalies

Ferro								
Scabbia								
Zagaria	**Migliore**							
Leo		**Biazzi**						
Zelati								
Forti	**Mozzati**							

1996   1997   1998   1999   2000   2001   2002   2003   2004

Cristiano Migliore
b. May 20, 1971

Cristiano Mozzati
b. August 13, 1973

Marco Biazzi
b. April 3, 1977

covers, while its opening song, "Swamped," secured a place in the *Rock Band* computer game and *Resident Evil* movie franchises. Further boosted by the single "Heaven's a Lie," *Comalies* eventually clambered into the Top Ten of *Billboard*'s independent albums chart.

Finally a "name" in metal circles, Lacuna Coil toured with the likes of Tiamat and Opeth, and seemed poised to eclipse veteran headliners like Danzig, Type O Negative, and Anthrax. Accordingly, they won a slot on the 2004 bill of Ozzy Osbourne's U.S.-traveling Ozzfest event, and broadened their palette with occasional acoustic shows.

With the market primed, the superb *Karmacode* (2006)—complete with an attention-grabbing cover of Depeche Mode's hit "Enjoy the Silence"—took Lacuna Coil into the Italian Top Twenty and U.S. Top Thirty. On tour with Rob Zombie and Bullet for My Valentine in the U.S., Zelati added another string to his composer/bassist bow: cooking pasta for the assembled acts and their road crews.

Throughout 2006 and 2007, the group were inescapable, including another Ozzfest slot, heavy rotation on TV rock channels, and the "Hottest Chicks in Metal Tour," on which Christina Scabbia flew the

female flag alongside Within Temptation's Sharon den Adel. The vocalist also graced Megadeth's 2007 re-working of their own "A Tout la Monde," while Lacuna Coil joined that band's "Gigantour" bill in Australia.

After the live *Visual Karma (Body, Mind and Soul)* and the career-spanning compilation *Manifesto of Lacuna Coil*, 2009's *Shallow Life* disappointed only those who expected the band to better *Karmacode*. Their following remained strongest in the U.S., where the album blasted straight into the Top Twenty and "Spellbound" became their biggest single to date.

The virtually unnoticed absence of an injury-plagued Zelati from the start of the *Shallow Life* tour suggested most eyes remained on Scabbia, whose discography had been embellished by cameos on Alter Bridge's re-working of their own "Watch Over You" and Apocalyptica's "S.O.S. (Anything but Love)."

Dark Adrenaline (2012), yet another U.S. smash, confirmed Lacuna Coil as one of modern metal's most unlikely successes. Never afraid of a challenge, they even took on R.E.M.'s classic "Losing My Religion." "We didn't do it to find approval from R.E.M. or their fans," said Scabbia defiantly. "The song sounded like a Lacuna Coil song with R.E.M. lyrics." **BM**

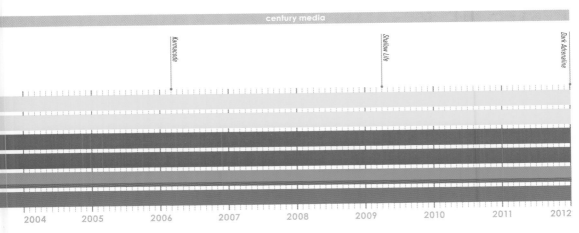

century media

Karmacode

Shallow Life

Dark Adrenaline

2004   2005   2006   2007   2008   2009   2010   2011   2012

led zeppelin 1968–1980

Robert Plant
b. August 20, 1948

Jimmy Page
b. January 9, 1944

John Paul Jones
b. January 3, 1946

John Bonham
b. May 31, 1948
d. September 25, 1980

The numbers are eye-popping. Led Zeppelin's worldwide record sales have been estimated at an astronomical 300 million—more than 115 million units in the United States alone. These insanely impressive totals make Zeppelin the fourth bestselling act in the U.S. (where the British group enjoyed by far their greatest success) and the sixth best-selling act on the planet. One can single out specific album success—such as 1971's *Led Zeppelin IV*, one of the five best-selling records of all time in America—or just consider that eight of the band's nine studio albums have been certified platinum-plus in multiple countries.

Statistics are one thing but the story must also be told with due reverence to all they accomplished musically, including pioneering the album-oriented rock concept and, more dramatically, forging a style that would dominate throughout the seventies.

That's an impressive résumé for a fairly hastily assembled group that owed its existence and its first bookings to another act—The Yardbirds. Guitarist **Jimmy Page** flew with the 'birds from 1966 until the band's 1968 breakup, which occurred immediately prior to concert bookings in Scandinavia. Looking to make good on the obligation, Page recruited vocalist **Robert Plant** and drummer **John Bonham**—both from the Band of Joy—and studio bassist **John Paul Jones**, and christened them the New Yardbirds. The quartet

made their concert debut in Gladsaxe, Denmark, on September 7, 1968. One month later, they changed their name, under the threat of legal action from The Yardbirds' Chris Dreja, and entered Olympic Studios in Barnes, southwest London, to begin recording their self-titled debut.

Led Zeppelin, unleashed in January 1969, was a powerful showcase for Plant's soaring vocals, Page's exquisite electric guitar, and Jones and Bonham's punishing rhythm section. The sound had much in common with Cream and other British blues-rockers of yore, but the whole package felt new and exciting. "I can't put a tag to our music," Page said in a press release. "I wish someone would invent an expression, but the closest I can get is contemporary blues." Someone would invent two expressions that worked well—hard rock and heavy metal—although Zeppelin, particularly Plant, resisted the latter label.

Having reached the Top Ten in the U.S. and U.K. with their debut, the band saw their star rise to even greater heights with the same year's *Led Zeppelin II*, which knocked The Beatles' *Abbey Road* from the U.S. No. 1. "We literally wrote the album on the road," Jones told writer Craig Rosen, "and, whenever there were a couple of hours between shows, we booked a studio and went in and recorded." The result was a must-have blueprint for all aspiring hard rockers.

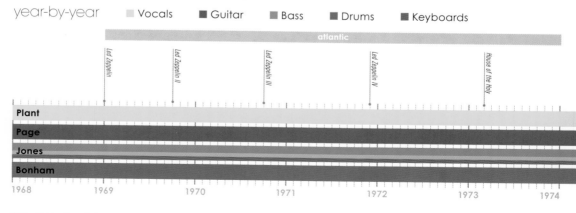

year-by-year   ■ Vocals   ■ Guitar   ■ Bass   ■ Drums   ■ Keyboards

atlantic

Led Zeppelin   Led Zeppelin II   Led Zeppelin III   Led Zeppelin IV   House of the Holy

Plant
Page
Jones
Bonham

1968   1969   1970   1971   1972   1973   1974

The group showed a different side with 1970's *Led Zeppelin III*, composed in a remote Welsh cottage and built as much on folk as blues. But the quartet struck the perfect balance between their two musical sides on 1971's untitled album, commonly known as *Led Zeppelin IV*. It catapulted the band into uncharted territory, eventually selling some twenty-three million copies in the U.S. alone (making it the third best-selling album in that country), and produced the winning hits "Black Dog" and "Rock and Roll." Yet it was a track not officially released as a single—the iconic "Stairway to Heaven"—that became Zep's true calling card and gift to the album-oriented rock format.

Myths surrounding the band during the first half of the seventies were almost as large as their record sales—tales of their hedonistic ways on the road were bountiful. But after 1973's lovely *Houses of the Holy*, 1975's brutal *Physical Graffiti*, and 1976's underrated *Presence,* the darker elements seemed to take over. Page was gripped by drug addiction, and Plant's six-year-old son died of a stomach infection in 1977. The final blow came during rehearsals for a U.S. tour in support of *In Through the Out Door* (1979)—Bonham was found dead of alcohol-related asphyxiation in September 1980. His band-mates, regarding Bonham as irreplaceable, decided to put an end to Zeppelin. A superior outtakes set, *Coda,* appeared in 1982.

Plant's solo career began with *Pictures at Eleven* (1982) and *The Principle of Moments* (1983) going Top Ten and platinum in the U.S. His later albums include 1990's splendid *Manic Nirvana* (featuring Page) and a Grammy "Album of the Year"-winning collaboration with bluegrass star Alison Krauss, 2007's *Raising Sand*.

After a soundtrack for *Death Wish II* and a stint with Bad Company singer Paul Rodgers in The Firm, Page focused on remastering Zeppelin's catalog for archive releases. An album with Whitesnake's David Coverdale (1993's *Coverdale Page*) preceded two with Plant: 1993's *No Quarter* and 1998's *Walking into Clarksdale*. Meanwhile, Jones collaborated with acts including Diamanda Galas, the Butthole Surfers, and R.E.M. before rocking once more with Them Crooked Vultures, alongside Dave Grohl of the Foo Fighters and Josh Homme of Queens of the Stone Age.

After disappointing sets at Live Aid in 1985 and the Atlantic label's fortieth anniversary show in 1988, Zeppelin's reunion concert in December 2007 at London's O2 Arena—featuring Bonham's son Jason on drums—proved an emotional and musical triumph. When Plant declined to make the reunion permanent, Page, Jones, and Bonham rehearsed with Aerosmith's Steven Tyler and Alter Bridge's Myles Kennedy—but ultimately decided to leave alone a legacy that richly deserves all the credit it so often receives. **JiH**

■ Strings

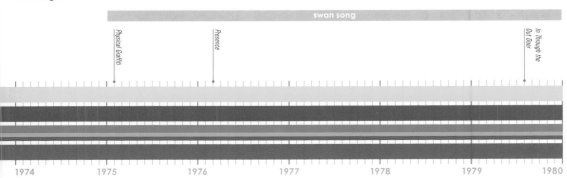

Led Zeppelin
(1969)

Led Zeppelin II
(1969)

Led Zeppelin III
(1970)

Led Zeppelin IV
(1971)

Houses of the Holy
(1973)

Physical Graffiti
(1975)

Presence (1976)

**In Through the Out
Door** (1979)

The band's first public performance together—(left to right) **John Paul Jones, Robert Plant, Jimmy Page,** and **John Bonham** were billed as The New Yardbirds.

Bonham, Plant, and **Jones** sleep between shows on a 1969 tour of the U.S.

Plant with Fairport Convention's Sandy Denny, who provided the only guest vocal in their catalog: 1971's "The Battle of Evermore."

Plant and **Page** hold court at a press conference before a show at the Forum, Los Angeles, on September 4, 1970.

Page (with **Plant** in the background) at Madison Square Garden, New York, July 29, 1973.

Plant and **Page** at Madison Square Garden during Led Zeppelin's 1977 U.S. tour.

Plant, **Page**, and **Bonham** at one of five shows at London's Earls Court in May 1975. Thereafter, the original lineup played only two more concerts in their home country, both in 1979.

Jones, **Plant**, **Page**, and **Bonham** in Rotterdam on June 21, 1980, on their final tour. "Morale was very high," Jones told TheCelebrityCafe.com in 2000. "We were in really good spirits."

legião urbana 1982–1996

Renato Russo
b. March 27, 1960
d. October 11, 1996

Dado Villa-Lobos
b. June 29, 1965

Marcelo Bonfá
b. January 30, 1965

Renato Rocha
b. Unknown

Eduardo Paraná
b. Unknown

Bone disease is rarely a catalyst for rock superstardom. However, following surgery for epiphysiolysis in 1975, fifteen-year-old Brazilian Renato Manfredini Jr. spent six months immobile in bed, doing little but listening to music and fantasizing about becoming a musician.

In his late teens, under the stage name **Renato Russo**—inspired by philosophers Bertrand Russell and Jean-Jacques Rousseau, and painter Henri Rousseau—he formed the punk rock group Aborto Eletrico ("Electric Abortion"). Four years, several arguments, and zero albums later, the group split.

Russo briefly performed as a solo artist before founding Legião Urbana (Portuguese for "Urban Legion") with **Marcelo Bonfá** (drums), **Eduardo Paraná** (guitars), and Paulo Paulista (keyboards) in Brasília in 1982, although Paraná and Paulista were band members for barely five minutes. **Dado Villa-Lobos**, the great-grandnephew of noted composer Heitor Villa-Lobos, replaced Paraná on guitar, and in 1985 **Renato Rocha** completed the quartet on bass.

As frontman and vocalist, Russo quickly found himself as a new voice of eighties youth. Poetry, literature, and politics informed his lyrics and Russo became one of Brazil's most significant songwriters. He sparked a connection with the country's disaffected young generation, exasperated with

recession and debt, poor health, and education, and tales of corrupt politicians.

Russo had been influenced by British rock bands of the late seventies in his Aborto Eletrico days, and he was now likewise moved by downbeat new wave and post-punk acts from across the Atlantic, such as The Smiths, The Cure, and PiL. Joy Division fans must surely have thought "Ainda É Cedo" from Legião Urbana's self-titled 1985 debut album owed more than a nod to the Manchester group's "A Means to an End."

After the modest success of Legião Urbana's debut, the follow-up *Dois* appeared in 1986. Its title, meaning "Two," referred to the band's intended number of discs before their record label, EMI-Odeon, rejected the idea of a double album.

Russo had written most of the songs on their third album *Que País É Este* (1987) almost a decade earlier, performing some solo or as part of Aborto Eletrico. Despite including one track about a nuclear power plant, and a nine-minute epic about a murdered drug trafficker, with 168 lines and no chorus ("Faroeste Caboclo"), the album shifted over 500,000 copies.

As the band's popularity soared, their fans' enthusiasm led to chaotic shows. A crush at a gig in Brasília left one female fan dead. At another concert, a crazed fan chased the band off stage, causing a

year-by-year   ■ Vocals   ■ Guitar   ■ Bass   ■ Drums

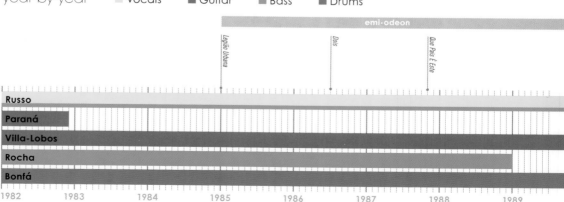

emi·odeon

Legião Urbana | Dois | Que País É Este

	Russo
	Paraná
	Villa-Lobos
	Rocha
	Bonfá

1982   1983   1984   1985   1986   1987   1988   1989

riot that saw dozens of people injured. The violent disturbances heightened Russo's stage fright and subsequently the band played live as little as possible.

Rocha quit before the release of the fourth album, 1989's *As Quatro Estações*, and Russo took over bass duties. Some fans were alienated by songs about love and family, and lyrics hinting at Russo's bisexuality. He came out as gay during an interview the following year and briefly lost some followers, but the album went on to be one of Legião Urbana's most successful.

V (1991) saw a return to bleaker subjects, with tales of drug abuse and reflections on Brazil's economic crisis. By then, Russo had been diagnosed with AIDS, although this was not made public while he was alive, and his increasing dependency on alcohol ensured *V*'s promotional tour in 1992 was short.

Música P/ Acampamentos ("Music for camping," 1992)—a collection of rarities, including a cover of The Rolling Stones' "Gimme Shelter," and a medley of The Righteous Brothers' "You've Lost That Lovin' Feelin'," John Lennon's "Jealous Guy," and The Beatles' "Ticket to Ride"—preceded a sixth studio set, *O Descobrimento do Brasil* ("The discovery of Brazil," 1993). This, Russo explained, was about his drug rehabilitation ("I was almost following Cobain's steps, but I have found people to help me"). Russo then proved himself to be quite the prolific multilinguist, releasing two solo albums: a set of cover versions in English, *The Stonewall Celebration Concert,* which included tracks as diverse as Stephen Sondheim's "Send In The Clowns" and Madonna's "Cherish"; and the Italian-language album *Equilibrio Distantei,* which helped to popularize Italian music in Brazil.

The self-produced *A Tempestade, ou O Livro dos Dias* ("The Tempest, or The Book of Days") was released in September 1996, but Russo died three weeks later, having stopped taking his AIDS medication. His bandmates dissolved Legião Urbana eleven days after his passing, revealing that much of that last album had been recorded "in a lot of pain" because of Russo's illness.

In 1997, unreleased tracks from the *A Tempestade* sessions, completed with additional musicians— including former member Rocha—appeared on the posthumous *Uma Outra Estação*. A collection of songs left off Russo's two solo albums was also released.

Compilations and live albums, including the successful *Acústico MTV*, have kept Legião Urbana in the Brazilian charts in the years since they disbanded. Total sales of around twenty million have helped establish them as one of the biggest bands in the music-loving country's history. **RJ**

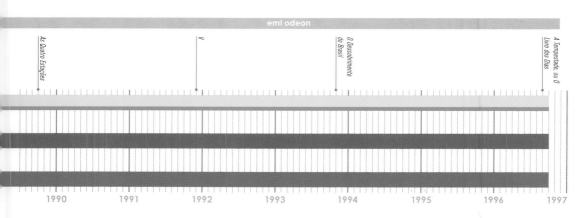

john lennon 1968–1980

John Lennon
b. October 9, 1940
d. December 8, 1980

Yoko Ono
b. February 18, 1933

Klaus Voorman
b. April 29, 1942

Nicky Hopkins
b. February 24, 1944
d. September 6, 1994

Alan White
b. June 14, 1949

Jim Keltner
b. April 27, 1942

"He had just come from being in the biggest group on the planet," Lenny Kravitz told *Rolling Stone* of **John Lennon**'s solo career. "Most people in his position would say, 'How do I keep this up? I don't want to come down off this pedestal.' He didn't care. He got butt naked… with his dick hanging out."

Lennon's solo discography in fact began while he was still a Beatle, with November 1968's *Unfinished Music No.1—Two Virgins*. But it is indeed remembered for its nude picture of the star and his soon-to-be wife, **Yoko Ono**. Neither that album nor 1969's *Unfinished Music No.2—Life with the Lions* and *Wedding Album* made much impression on charts, but the summer's "Give Peace A Chance" hit the U.K. Top Three and U.S. Top Twenty. The single was credited to the Plastic Ono Band, a name used again when Lennon played in Toronto in September with Eric Clapton, bassist **Klaus Voorman** and future Yes drummer **Alan White** (hence the Top Ten album *Live Peace in Toronto 1969*).

Featuring the talents of George Harrison and producer Phil Spector, 1970's "Instant Karma" was a Top Five success on both sides of the Atlantic. At the end of the year, the stark *John Lennon/Plastic Ono*

Band followed it into the charts' upper reaches. "The attitude and emotion of that album are harder than any punk rock I've ever heard," remarked Kravitz.

In August 1971, Lennon left Britain for the last time. *Imagine*—completed before his departure and issued a month later—hit No. 1 around the world. Celebrated for its lovely title track and "Jealous Guy," the album also included the vicious "Crippled Inside" and "How Do You Sleep?"—the latter a barely veiled attack on Paul McCartney, featuring Harrison on slide guitar.

When Lennon and Ono were threatened with deportation from the U.S. (allegedly related to a 1968 cannabis bust), they left "sugar-coated" sounds behind. "Women is the Nigger of the World" was the sole, minor hit from 1972's *Some Time in New York City*, a political/avant garde double album made with Voorman, drummer **Jim Keltner** (who had also played on *Imagine*), New York band Elephant's Memory, and Frank Zappa's Mothers of Invention. It was, inevitably, out-sold by 1973's more song-oriented *Mind Games*.

Lennon's battle to remain in America—which extended to him seeking a pardon from the Queen for the drug offence—ran until October 1975, when

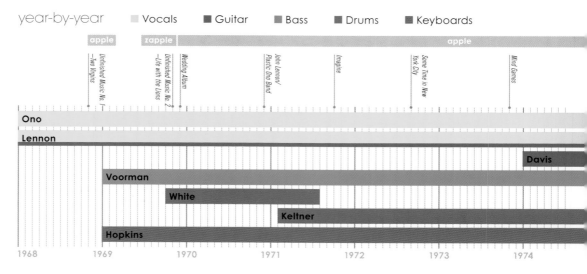

year-by-year   ■ Vocals   ■ Guitar   ■ Bass   ■ Drums   ■ Keyboards

apple   zapple   apple

Unfinished Music No.1 —Two Virgins · *Unfinished Music No. 2 —Life with the Lions* · *Wedding Album* · *John Lennon/ Plastic Ono Band* · *Imagine* · *Some Time in New York City* · *Mind Games*

Ono

Lennon

Davis

Voorman

White

Keltner

Hopkins

1968   1969   1970   1971   1972   1973   1974

Jesse Ed Davis
b. September 21, 1944
d. June 22, 1988

the deportation order was reversed. In the intervening years, he embarked on his infamous "lost weekend," often in the company of singer Harry Nilsson, whose *Pussy Cats* (1974) he produced.

Nilsson, Elton John, and Lennon's eleven-year-old son Julian contributed to *Walls and Bridges* (1974), which returned him to the U.S. No. 1. Elton played on "Whatever Gets You Thru' The Night" and made Lennon promise that he would guest at a live show if the song topped the chart. This it duly did, and a terrified Lennon joined the star onstage at New York's Madison Square Garden in November 1974, to play that song, plus "Lucy in the Sky with Diamonds" and "I Saw Her Standing There." His first live appearance in over two years would also be his last.

Rock 'n' Roll (1975)—a set of fifties and sixties covers—gave Lennon a No. 6 hit on both sides of the Atlantic. Later that year, David Bowie's "Fame"—co-written by Lennon—topped the U.S. chart, and the hits set *Shaved Fish* rounded off this first phase of the former Beatle's solo career. Following the birth of his son Sean in October, Lennon "retired," to focus on fatherhood in his and Ono's New York apartment.

He was finally granted a green card, confirming his U.S. residency, in 1976, and returned to the studio in the summer of 1980, with Ono, to make the album *Double Fantasy*. But in December, a week after its release, Lennon was shot dead by Mark Chapman—who, hours earlier, had collected his autograph on a copy of the new album. *Double Fantasy* promptly topped international charts, as did its "(Just Like) Starting Over." Subsequent hits "Woman" and "Watching the Wheels" shared charts with reissues of 1971's "Imagine" and "Happy Xmas (War is Over)."

Lennon was honored for his Outstanding Contribution to British Music by both the Brit and Ivor Novello awards, while *Double Fantasy* won the 1982 Grammy for Album of the Year. Unreleased songs were compiled on 1984's gold-selling *Milk and Honey*, while an August 1972 show was issued as *Live in New York City* (1986). A host of compilations included the multi-platinum *The John Lennon Collection* (1982) and *Lennon Legend: The Very Best of John Lennon* (1997).

His legacy, for all its inconsistencies, continues to inspire contemporary rock stars, perhaps most notably Kurt Cobain and Oasis's Gallagher brothers. **BS/BM**

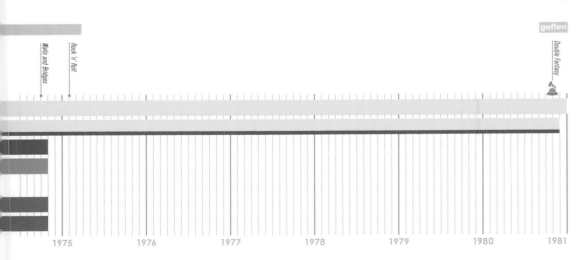

**Unfinished Music
No.1—Two Virgins**
(1968)

**Unfinished Music
No.2—Life with the
Lions** (1969)

Wedding Album
(1969)

**John Lennon/
Plastic Ono Band**
(1970)

Imagine (1971)

**Some Time in New
York City** (1972)

Mind Games
(1973)

Walls and Bridges
(1974)

Rock 'n' Roll (1975)

Double Fantasy
(1980)

John Lennon and **Yoko Ono** in a London studio in 1968.

Lennon sleeps on a hospital floor beside **Ono**. The scene appears on the sleeve of *Unfinished Music No.2—Life with the Lions* (1969).

Lennon and **Ono** perform with the newly formed and experimental Plastic Ono Band in 1969.

During their seven-day protest against war and violence, **Lennon** and **Ono** receive the press in the Presidential Suite of the Hilton Hotel, Amsterdam, on March 27, 1969.

Black Power leader Michael X trades a pair of Muhammad Ali's bloodied boxing shorts for the newly cut hair of **Lennon** and **Ono** on February 19, 1970.

Lennon and **Ono** pose at their home, Tittenhurst Park, Berkshire, England, during the making of *Imagine* in 1971.

On August 30, 1972, **Lennon** and **Ono** perform at New York's Madison Square Garden, to benefit a facility for children with learning difficulties.

Lennon enjoys a night out in Los Angeles with Alice Cooper.

In the last live performance of his career, **Lennon** appears with Elton John at Madison Square Garden, on November 28, 1974.

Left to right: Art Garfunkel, Paul Simon, **Ono**, and **Lennon** at the Grammys on March 1, 1975, at the Uris Theater, New York.

Fans cluster around **Lennon** as he leaves the Hit Factory recording studio in Times Square, New York, after a session for his final album *Double Fantasy* in August 1980.

limp bizkit *1994–present*

Fred Durst
b. August 20, 1970

Sam Rivers
b. September 2, 1977

John Otto
b. March 22, 1977

Wes Borland
b. February 7, 1975

DJ Lethal
b. December 18, 1972

Mike Smith
b. October 11, 1973

Equally lauded and despised, Limp Bizkit succeeded where so many others failed: they took the rap-rock genre and turned it into a commercial juggernaut. They were not first to the party, which had been going on at least since Aerosmith and Run-D.M.C. collaborated on "Walk This Way" in 1986, but they were the band that carried the party to the next level. Limp Bizkit quickly became as popular as any act in rap or rock—and, for a few years, challenged the biggest names in pop for chart supremacy.

None of that impressed most critics, who slammed the group, reserving extra venom for outspoken vocalist **Fred Durst**. But negative reviews could not stop fans—some thirty-three million records were sold.

Durst had worked in a number of Jacksonville area bands before he starting an outfit that would combine both of his musical passions—metal and hip-hop—in 1994. He first joined forces with two cousins, bassist **Sam Rivers** and drummer **John Otto**, then guitarist **Wes Borland** and turntablist **DJ Lethal**, aka Leor Dimant. Limp Bizkit developed a die-hard local following with a high-energy live show, but it was not until Durst met Korn that they got their first big break. Durst played the band some demos and they landed an opening slot on the nü-metal superstars' tour.

Consequently, Flip/Interscope signed them up to record their first full-length album, *Three Dollar Bill, Yall$*.

Released in 1997, the debut generated impressive sales—eventually peaking at U.S. No. 22. Fans were hooked by its powerful hybrid sound and it went on to double-platinum sales. *Significant Other*, released in 1999, debuted at No. 1 in the U.S. and established Limp Bizkit as one of the top new bands in the world.

Chocolate Starfish and the Hot Dog Flavored Water (2000) sold more than a million in its first week and was eventually certified six times platinum. Critics, however, despised it, with *Entertainment Weekly* naming it the year's worst album. All the negative criticism—not just of the band, but of the rap-rock genre as a whole—began to catch up with Limp Bizkit by the time they released 2003's *Results Might Vary* (minus Borland). It went platinum, but the writing was on the wall and—after 2005's *The Unquestionable Truth (Part 1)* (with Borland)—the Bizkit went on hiatus.

While the intervening years have not changed critics' views on Durst, Limp Bizkit acquired a nostalgic appeal. The comeback album *Gold Cobra* (2011) restored them to the U.S. Top Twenty, and their shows have been well-received. A new album, *Stampede of the Disco Elephants,* was threatened for 2012. **JiH**

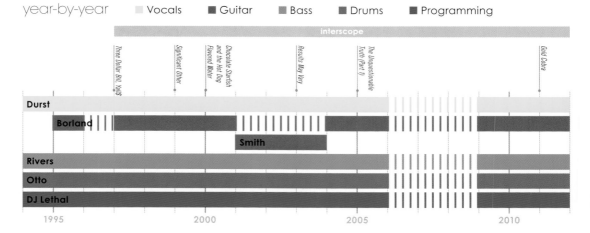

year-by-year ■ Vocals ■ Guitar ■ Bass ■ Drums ■ Programming

interscope

Three Dollar Bill, Yall$
Significant Other
Chocolate Starfish and the Hot Dog Flavored Water
Results May Vary
The Unquestionable Truth (Part 1)
Gold Cobra

Durst
Borland
Smith
Rivers
Otto
DJ Lethal

1995　　　2000　　　2005　　　2010

linkin park 1999–present

Mike Shinoda
b. February 11, 1977

Rob Bourdon
b. January 20, 1979

Brad Delson
b. December 1, 1977

Joe Hahn
b. March 15, 1977

Phoenix Farrell
b. February 8, 1977

Chester Bennington
b. March 20, 1976

"I'm very happy when I hear new stuff like Linkin Park," remarked Rudolf Schenker of the Scorpions in 2001. His enthusiasm was not shared by everyone: the group's overnight success and MTV ubiquity led to suggestions that they were nü-metal's very own Backstreet Boys. Fast forward a decade, however, and Linkin Park have three international chart-topping albums under their belts, can still headline stadium shows, and have left all their nü contemporaries in the commercial dust.

The band began as Xero, a post-high school project for **Mike Shinoda**, **Rob Bourdon**, and **Brad Delson**. With **Joe Hahn**, **Dave "Phoenix" Farrell**, and **Chester Bennington**, Xero became Hybrid Theory, then Linkin Park (a reference to Lincoln Park, Santa Monica, in the band's home state of California).

Dazzling videos, the might of Warner Bros., and songs that effortlessly bridged any remaining gaps between metal and hip hop ensured that Linkin Park were an immediate success. *Hybrid Theory* became the best-selling album of 2000, and spawned a platinum-selling remix set, *Reanimation* (2002). Guests on the latter included Korn's Jonathan Davis, Staind's Aaron Lewis, Deftones' Stef Carpenter, Sneaker Pimps' Kelli Ali, Taproot's Stephen Richards, and rappers Pharaohe Monch and Black Thought.

Relentless touring confirmed their international appeal, and *Meteora* (2003) duly smashed in at the top of charts around the world. Illustrating the twin foundations of their sound, Linkin Park toured with Metallica and united with Jay-Z for 2004's mash-up mini-album *Collision Course*—inevitably, another U.S. No. 1 and million-seller. "The whole group, as far as how professional they were in putting this together, was very impressive," Jay noted. "I'm used to having to carry people and they showed me something else."

After a variety of side projects, the group reconvened, with Midas-touch producer Rick Rubin, for *Minutes to Midnight* (2007). The nü-metal bubble had long since burst, but Linkin Park's ability to storm to No. 1 in every major territory remained unchanged. This massive international popularity was confirmed by stadium shows, including one in Britain immortalized on 2008's *Road to Revolution: Live at Milton Keynes* (featuring a collaboration with Jay-Z).

The double platinum single "New Divide" (from a *Transformers* movie soundtrack) and *A Thousand Suns* (2010), again helmed by Rubin, maintained their defiance of commercial trends. With the launch of a Linkin Park video-creation iPhone app in 2012, their supremacy seems unassailable. **BM**

year-by-year

■ Vocals   ■ Guitar   ■ Bass   ■ Drums   ■ Keyboards   ■ Programming

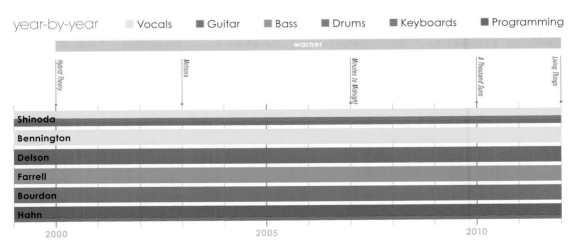

little feat 1969–present

Lowell George
b. April 13, 1945
d. June 29, 1979

Bill Payne
b. March 12, 1949

Richie Hayward
b. February 6, 1946
d. August 12, 2010

Roy Estrada
b. April 17, 1943

Paul Barrere
b. July 3, 1948

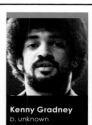

Kenny Gradney
b. unknown

With their intoxicating blend of rock 'n' roll, country, folk, and southern fried boogie, Little Feat were—in their day—one of the most intelligent, innovative, and exciting bands around.

Lowell George (vocals/guitar) started the band with **Bill Payne** (keyboards/vocals) in Los Angeles in 1969. The guitarist had served a short stint in Frank Zappa's Mothers of Invention, after Zappa produced tracks for his earlier band The Factory, a combo that also featured **Richie Hayward** (drums). After Payne unsuccessfully auditioned for Zappa's band, he and George formed Little Feat, with Hayward and former Mothers bassist **Roy Estrada**.

George had already cut a demo of his signature song, "Willin'," with his friend Ry Cooder. This track would serve as both inspiration and direction for the new band's sound, major features of which were George's slide guitar and world-weary, soulful vocals.

With Zappa's help, they signed to Warner Bros. and recorded two critically acclaimed but poorly selling albums, the fumbling *Little Feat* (1971) and the more refined *Sailing Shoes* (1972). Estrada left soon after to join Captain Beefheart's Magic Band, and the group expanded to include **Paul Barrere** (guitar) and former Delaney and Bonnie musicians **Kenny Gradney** (bass) and **Sam Clayton** (congas).

The new lineup added a New Orleans funk swagger to their ever-growing pallet of influences and soon proved to be a spectacular live act. With George as producer, they recorded *Dixie Chicken* (1973)—now considered a landmark release—but it sold no better than its predecessors and, demoralized, the band split. Payne joined The Doobie Brothers' touring band, while the others went into session work.

But, eventually, Warner realized how superb Little Feat really were. With the promise of the label finally putting some serious promotional muscle behind the band, the group reconvened and recorded the successful *Feats Don't Fail Me Now* (1974).

At the start of 1975, the band played two gigs at the Rainbow in London as part of a Warner package tour and impressed everyone with their stunning live sets. Their reputation, particularly in England, as one of rock's most vital and important bands was enhanced

year-by-year   ■ Vocals   ■ Guitar   ■ Bass   ■ Drums   ■ Keyboards

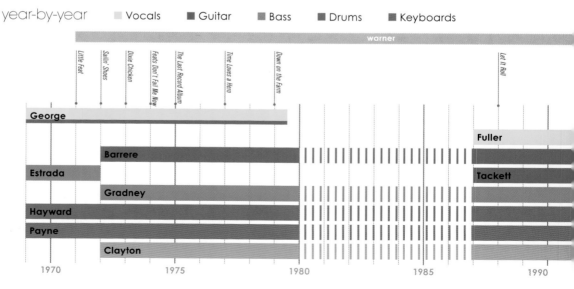

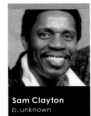

Sam Clayton
b. unknown

Fred Tackett
b. August 30, 1945

Craig Fuller
b. unknown

Shaun Murphy
b. unknown

Gabe Ford
b. June 8, 1973

even further by a legendary bootleg album of a killer live radio broadcast, *Electrif Lycanthrope*.

Little Feat had finally arrived but, on The *Last Record Album* (1975) and *Time Loves a Hero* (1977), with his own songwriting contributions now at a bare minimum, George felt Payne and Barrere had too much influence within the band. He disliked intensely the pair's new progressive jazz-rock leanings, and relations between them degenerated into antagonism and ill-feeling.

The spectacular live double *Waiting for Columbus* was their best-selling album yet. However, George—with both his health and interest in the band declining fast—walked out of the recording sessions for the next album, declaring his intentions to disband Little Feat and then reform the group without Payne and Barrere.

The label had just released *Thanks, I'll Eat It Here*, George's first, and as it turned out only, solo album, put together mostly from covers he had recorded in previous years. In the summer of 1979, he set out on tour in support of its release. But that outing ended abruptly with his untimely death on June 29 from a

drug-induced heart attack, aged just thirty-four. The remaining members completed the recordings for *Down on the Farm* (1979) before disbanding altogether. *Hoy-Hoy!* (1981), a double album of outtakes and archive live material, highlighted their undoubted brilliance but George's death inevitably spelt the end of them as a true creative force.

They re-formed in 1987 with guitarist **Fred Tackett** and vocalist **Craig Fuller**, recording the commercially successful *Let It Roll* (1988). But Warner, unhappy with the jazz-rock elements of the follow-up, *Representing the Mambo* (1990), dropped the band.

After one more album, Fuller left in 1993 to be replaced by female vocalist **Shaun Murphy**. This new lineup lasted sixteen years, releasing live albums and occasional studio efforts on various small labels.

As a hugely popular fixture on the live jam band circuit, Little Feat have continued to this day. Murphy, after five albums and over 1,400 live appearances, departed in 2009. And, sadly, Hayward succumbed to cancer in August 2010; he was replaced by **Gabe Ford**, the band's drum technician. **MD**

■ Other percussion

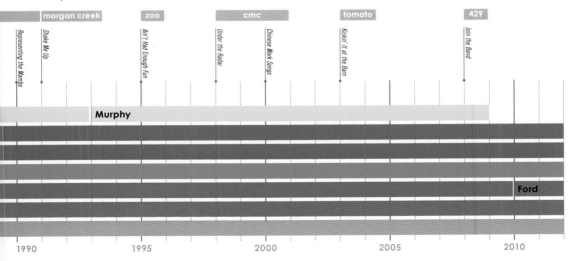

loudness 1981–present

Minoru Niihara
b. March 12, 1960

Akira Takasaki
b. February 22, 1961

Masayoshi Yamashita
b. November 29, 1961

Munetaka Higuchi
b. Dec 24, 1958
d. November 30, 2008

Masayuki Suzuki
b. 1973

Many believed that Loudness would be the Japanese hard rock act to finally conquer America. The band, who became a hit in their homeland within months of forming in Osaki in 1981, had all the elements—incredible players (especially shredder-supreme **Akira Takasaki**), a powerful vocalist (**Minoru Niihara**), a metal sound that echoed the popular flavor of the day, solid songs, and a glam metal wardrobe (which could have been lifted straight out of Ratt's closet).

Loudness would get their shot in 1985, when they became the first Japanese hard rock act to sign an international deal with a major U.S. label—Atco Records. It turned out to be a modest victory, with two Loudness albums charting in the U.S. Top 100, but what was at risk of being lost was equally significant. Loudness's fascination with America, which led to the band replacing Niihara with Yankee vocalist Michael Vescera, did not go over well with fans in the Land of the Rising Sun. In fact, Loudness would eventually give up on America, a few years after the country gave up on the band, and return to courting its longtime fan base. The group, with some two-dozen full-length studio efforts under their belt, are now considered one of the all time great Japanese metal acts.

Given the band's mighty work ethic, it is ironic that Loudness emerged from a group dubbed Lazy. Guitarist Takasaki and drummer **Munetaka Higuchi** toiled away in that mainstream pop-rock outfit from 1977 to 1981, before bolting to join the rising tide of Japanese metal artists like Bow Wow. They hooked up

with Niihara and bassist **Masayoshi Yamashita** and Loudness were born, quickly landing a record deal and dropping the Japanese-language debut *The Birthday Eve* (1981). The band released three albums over the next three years, a pace they have kept for much of their career. The fifth album, 1985's *Thunder in the East*, was a thoroughly Western affair—recorded in Los Angeles with producer Max Norman and sung entirely in English. Thanks to "Crazy Nights" (Loudness's biggest American hit), *Thunder in the East* became the first offering from a Japanese act to chart in the *Billboard* 200, peaking at No. 74. The following year's *Lightning Strikes* did even better—No. 64—but U.S. listeners were clearly losing interest by 1987's *Hurricane Eyes*, which stalled at *Billboard* No. 190.

Former Obsession front man Michael Vescera replaced Niihara at the microphone in 1988, but the clear ploy to entice more U.S. listeners was ineffective, and EZO front-man Masaki Yamada took the mic for much of the nineties. Although some fans were dismayed by the band's new direction—which embraced radio-friendly pop-metal—Loudness continued to sell well in their homeland.

Niihara returned to the fold for *Spiritual Canoe* (2001), but Higuchi died in 2008 after a lengthy battle with liver cancer. In 2011, the band released its twenty-fourth studio album, *Eve to Dawn*. However, the best introductions to their discography remain the storming first two of their eight live albums, 1983's *Live-Loud-Alive: Loudness in Tokyo* and 1987's *8186 Live*. **JiH**

year-by-year ▪ Vocals ▪ Guitar ▪ Bass ▪ Drums

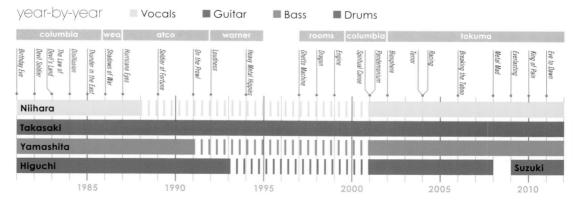

love 1965–2005

Arthur Lee
b. March 7, 1945
d. August 3,
2006

**Johnny
Echols**
b. February 21,
1947

**Bryan
MacLean**
b. Sept 25, 1946
d. December
25, 1998

Kenny Forssi
b. March 30,
1943
d. January 10,
1998

**Alban
"Snoopy"
Pfisterer**
b. September
27, 1946

**Michael
Stuart**
b. July 29, 1944

Tjay Cantrelli
b. unknown
d. unknown

Love are best remembered for acid rock masterpiece *Forever Changes*, ranked fortieth on *Rolling Stone's* 500 Greatest Albums of All Time and inducted, eventually, into the Grammy Hall of Fame in 2008.

Performing as The Grass Roots in 1965 and with a lineup of **Arthur Lee**, **Johnny Echols**, Don Conka, **Bryan MacLean**, and John Fleckenstein, they competed with another Los Angeles band with the same name until Lee's outfit eventually called themselves Love. In November 1965, Fleckenstein was replaced by **Kenny Forssi**, then drummer Conka left to be replaced by **Alban "Snoopy" Pfisterer**. With the lineup now stabilized, Love released their self-titled folk-rock debut album in March 1966.

By August, with Pfisterer switching from drums to keyboards and with new drummer **Michael Stuart** and woodwind player **Tjay Cantrelli**, the band had concocted a John Coltrane-influenced sound that resulted in the release of *Da Capo*. The music was described as a free form blending of jazz and rock before the term "fusion" was familiar. Although the album spawned Love's biggest U.S. single, "7&7 Is," in January 1967, Pfisterer and Cantrelli were fired: the material Lee and MacLean were writing for the next album demanded an orchestral sound, played by a five-man group with strings and horns. Orchestral pop

was the dazzling hallmark of Love's acclaimed third album, *Forever Changes*. The title was a prophetic one because, in August 1968, the band fractured and Lee put together a new blues-rock lineup, adding Frank Fayad, Jay Donnellan, and George Suranovich. That fall, Suranovich was briefly out of the band after a disagreement with Lee over money, and was temporarily replaced by Drachen Theaker. With Theaker on board, the band cut tracks that surfaced on their next two albums, *Four Sail* and *Out Here*.

With Gary Rowles added and Suranovich returning, the band delivered *False Start* (1970), notable for a guest appearance by Jimi Hendrix. After recording the lackluster *Love Lost* in 1971, the band broke up. Lacking much of his earlier inventiveness, Lee nevertheless created a new soul and R&B-oriented Love featuring Robert Rozelle, Melvan Whittington, and Joe Blocker and set about recording *Black Beauty* (released, after Lee's death, in 2011).

In 1974, the band released *Reel to Real*, before yet another break-up in 1975. Not until the early nineties did Lee resurrect the Love brand, when Rozelle, Whittington, Gary Stern, and Tony Mikesell got together to make the final album, *Arthur Lee and Love*. Their ever-popular live appearances continued until a year before Lee's death in 2006. **BC**

year-by-year   ◻ Vocals   ◼ Guitar   ◼ Bass   ◼ Drums   ◼ Keyboards

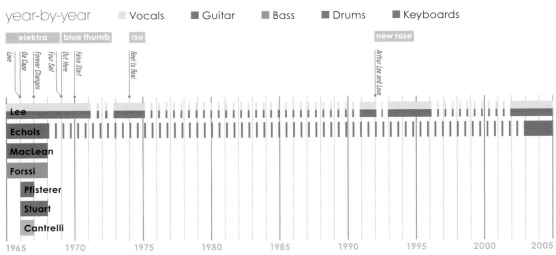

lynyrd skynyrd 1964–present

Gary Rossington
b. December 4, 1951

Ronnie Van Zant
b. Jan 15, 1948
d. October 20, 1977

Allen Collins
b. July 19, 1952
d. January 23, 1990

Bob Burns
b. November 24, 1950

Larry Junstrom
b. June 22, 1949

Rickey Medlocke
b. February 17, 1950

Ed King
b. September 14, 1949

Artimus Pyle
b. July 15, 1948

It was a good thing Lynyrd Skynyrd immediately taught fans how to say their unusual name—the title of 1973's debut record was (Pronounced 'leh-'nérd 'skin-'nérd)—because listeners would repeat it often from that point forward. The band practically burst out of the gate as the definitive Southern rock act, arguably flying past the Allman Brothers on the back of the almighty cut "Free Bird"—and their stranglehold on the genre would tighten over the next four years. There is really no telling how high Lynyrd Skynyrd could have eventually soared had a 1977 air crash not claimed the lives of three band members and shattered the worlds of those left behind.

How it began, however, can be traced back to 1964, when a trio of childhood pals—charismatic vocalist **Ronnie Van Zant**, guitarist **Gary Rossington**, and **Allen Collins**—formed the Noble Five in Jacksonville, Florida. One year later, the troupe, which by then included drummer **Bob Burns** and bassist **Larry Junstrom**, was going by the moniker My Backyard. Then, in 1970, the group began calling itself "Leonard Skinnerd"—a backhanded compliment to the musicians' former gym teacher, Leonard Skinner, at

Robert E. Lee High School—and the name eventually morphed into the current one.

Touring through the South into the early seventies, Skynyrd were distinguished by a hard-hitting, guitar-drenched sound heavily influenced by British rockers like Cream, The Rolling Stones, and The Yardbirds. Unlike the Allmans' jazz-influenced improvisational workouts, which at times seemed built to thrill the tie-dyed masses at Bill Graham's Fillmore clubs, this was real Deep South boogie, drawing inspiration from backwoods blues and real-deal country.

Having cut demos in 1971 in Alabama's Muscle Shoals studio, the group snared Al Kooper, who would produce Skynyrd's first three albums. The Blood, Sweat & Tears founder encountered them during a week-long residency at an Atlanta club. "Each night I'd hear another great original song…" he told Rolling Stone, "and knew I'd found the band I was searching for."

(Pronounced 'leh-'nérd 'skin-'nérd) (1973) was nothing less than one of the greatest debut records of the era. The album, which rose to No. 27 in the U.S., produced four of the group's signature songs—the mournful "Tuesday's Gone," the reflective "Simple

year-by-year

◻ Vocals ◼ Guitar ◼ Bass ◼ Drums ◼ Keyboards

mca

(Pronounced 'leh-'nérd 'skin-'nérd)
Second Helping
Nuthin' Fancy
Gimme Back My Bullets
Street Survivors

R. Van Zant

J. Van Zant

Rossington

Collins

Medlocke

King

Gaines

Junstrom

Wilkeson

Burns

Pyle

Powell

1965   1970   1975   1980   1985

Steve Gaines
b. September 14, 1949
d. October 20, 1977

Leon Wilkeson
b. April 2, 1952
d. July 27, 2001

Billy Powell
b. June 3, 1952
d. January 28, 2009

Johnny Van Zant
b. February 27, 1960

Michael Cartellone
b. June 7, 1962

Peter Keys
b. May 30, 1965

Hughie Thomasson
b. Aug 13, 1952
d. September 9, 2007

Ean Evans
b. September 16, 1960
d. May 6, 2009

Man," the ruckus-raising "Gimme Three Steps," and the anthemic "Free Bird." The latter has long stood as one of rock's most famous songs—its status cemented, for better or worse, by fans who yell "Freeeee Biiiiiiird!" at concerts, no matter who is on stage. Ironically, the song, perhaps best known for its epic three-guitar showdown, would not become a Top Twenty hit until 1975—one year after the band's sophomore effort, the appropriately named *Second Helping*, hit shelves. By that point, Lynyrd Skynyrd was already a star act, thanks in no small part to the irresistible "Sweet Home Alabama," which gave the band its first Top Ten hit.

The good times kept right on rolling, as 1975's *Nuthin' Fancy* finally admitted the band into the U.S. album chart Top Ten. A fourth album, *Gimme Back My Bullets*, stalled at No. 20, but Skynyrd reached their chart peak with 1977's *Street Survivors*, which hit No. 5. However, three days after its release, disaster struck.

On October 20, 1977, the band's tour plane—nicknamed, of course, "Free Bird"—crashed in Mississippi, killing founding member Van Zant, guitarist **Steve Gaines**, and backup vocalist **Cassie Gaines**. The loss—especially of Van Zant, widely considered the heart and soul of the band—was too much to take, and Lynyrd Skynyrd would call it quits. *Gold & Platinum*, released in 1979 and eventually certified triple-platinum in the U.S., served as an excellent summation of all the band had accomplished in the span of five studio albums. And that appeared to be it for the Lynyrd Skynyrd saga, until the surviving members came together on the tenth anniversary of the crash and embarked on a major tour. Decades later, Lynyrd Skynyrd—fronted by Ronnie's brother, **Johnny Van Zant**, on vocals—is still trucking right along and delighting fans in concert. Among the members is former Blackfoot leader **Rickey Medlocke**, who had briefly sung and drummed for Skynyrd in 1970.

That the ever-rotating cast of players would find work on the road is really no surprise in the nostalgia-driven classic rock world. More of a shock is that the group has maintained such a healthy recording career. Lynyrd Skynyrd have released six studio albums since reforming in 1987, and these have done well on the charts. Indeed, the group's twelfth studio album, 2009's *God & Guns*, was Skynyrd's first Top Twenty offering since *Street Survivors*. **JiH**

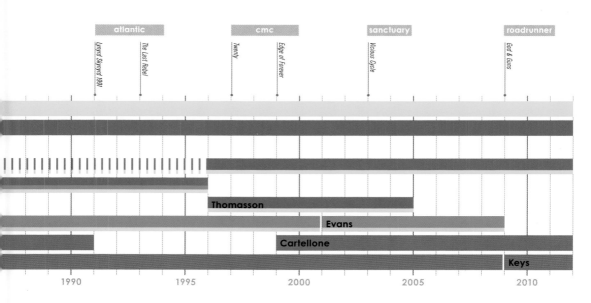

magma 1969–present

Christian Vander
b. February 21, 1948

Klaus Basquiz
b. Unknown

Francis Moze
b. Unknown

Stella Vander
b. December 12, 1950

Jannick Top
b. Unknown

Benoit Wideman
b. Unknown

For centuries, the possibility of extraplanetary travel has provided inspiration to all manner of artists. So it should not be too surprising to discover an early seventies concept album by a French progressive rock group telling the story of a group of people fleeing a doomed Earth to settle on a new planet. Things start to get weird when you realize that the lyrics are sung in the planet's native tongue—Kobaïan—and that the band's subsequent albums continued this mythology, using the same language. Welcome to the world of **Christian Vander** and Magma, with a concept whose sheer scale is unparalleled in rock history.

Magma were formed in Paris in 1969, the brainchild of classically trained percussionist Christian Vander. He was also an adept pianist who created complex compositions, his influences including Carl Orff, Béla Bartók, and John Coltrane.

The impetus for Magma purportedly came from a vision of the Earth's spiritual and ecological decline so disturbing that Vander felt compelled to pursue it as a musical theme. The band's initial lineup featured Vander, vocalist **Klaus Basquiz**, fusion bassist **Francis Moze** (later of Gong), and other young classical and jazz musicians working in Paris at that time.

Emerging in 1970, Magma's eighty-two-minute, self-titled debut laid the groundwork for Vander's emerging vision. There were two striking aspects to *Magma*. Although the sound fell broadly into Soft Machine's jazz-fusion territory, it combined Coltrane-inspired rock with classical influences. More curious, though, was the polarizing use of an invented language, which made the group too "difficult" for some listeners. Vander invented Kobaïan—a mix of Slavic-Germanic elements and jazz-inspired scat-yodeling—because "French just wasn't expressive enough." The Kobaïan lyrics were never directly translated on any of Magma's albums but, over the years, Vander provided meanings for certain words.

1001° Centigrades (1971) could be described as a transitional album. The story continued with the Kobaïan people returning to Earth in a bid to save the planet. While still nominally jazz rock, the album's first side—taken up with a twenty-two-minute Vander composition, "Rïah Sahïltaahk"—pointed in a new direction. Its multiple phases were packed with abruptly changing time signatures, tempos, and intensities, and a continually shifting dominance of brass, woodwind, and keyboards.

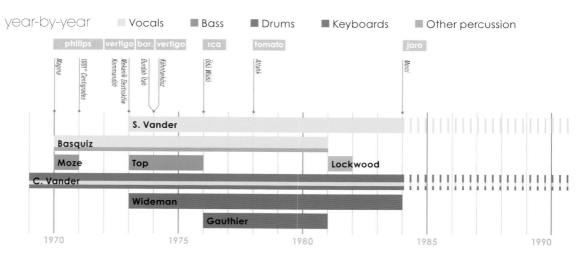

year-by-year ▇ Vocals ▇ Bass ▇ Drums ▇ Keyboards ▇ Other percussion

Patrick Gauthier
b. Unknown

Didier Lockwood
b. February 11, 1956

The following two years saw Magma hitting a masterful creative peak. By 1973's *Mekanïk Destructïw Kommandoh*, the former jazz leanings had softened, with a new emphasis on the human voice—Orff's *Carmina Burana* was a clear influence. The album showcased singer Basquiz's extraordinary vocal range, and featured a large number of choral singers, among them Vander's wife **Stella**, who would participate in all of Magma's subsequent recordings. *Mekanïk Destructïw Kommandoh* also saw the debut of **Jannick Top**, whose heavy bass would inspire in Vander a new rhythmic style.

The transition to what Vander described as "zeuhl"—the Kobaïan word for "celestial music"—was completed by 1974's more minimalist *Kohntarkosz*. The album continued the devotional themes begun on its predecessor, telling the story of a Kobaïan archaeologist who undergoes a spiritual vision while uncovering an ancient Egyptian tomb—a tale that unfolded over several subsequent Magma albums.

Following 1975's triumphant concert recording *Live/Hhaï*, Magma entered a period of commercial decline. *Üdü Wüdü* in 1976 saw the introduction of synthesizers and cheesy rhythm boxes, while Vander scaled down his compositional role. *Attahk* (1978) indicated a loss of direction, the band's sound now incorporating elements of funk, gospel, and even pop, and was followed by Magma entering hibernation until the disappointing *Merci* in 1984.

Having performed sporadically as Magma, in the mid-nineties Vander formed a new version of the band to perform and record two new albums. *KA (Kohntarkosz Anteria)* in 2004 and *Ëmëhntëhtt-Ré* in 2009 completed this musical adventure.

Although Magma are still operational, it is their early output that has had the greatest impact, emerging at a time when it was possible for a "concept band," creating complex music, to amass a large following. They failed to trouble the best-seller charts but were influential on a small body of like-minded musicians. Vander's description of Magma's music as "zeuhl" would later became a recognized music genre, comprising French and Belgian bands such as Zao, Art Zoyd, and Univers Zero. Curiously, most contemporary zeuhl artists hail from Japan, where the likes of Ruins and Koenji Hyakkei occupy a similar musical territory to "classic" Magma—and, of course, sing in their own made-up languages. **TB**

 Strings

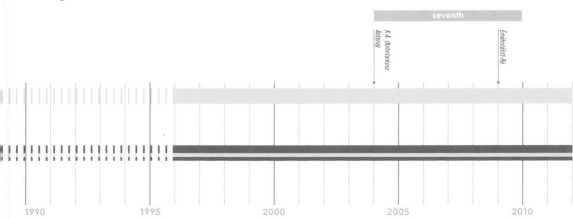

yngwie malmsteen 1983–present

Yngwie Malmsteen
b. June 30, 1963

Ron Keel
b. 1961

Graham Bonnet
b. December 23, 1947

Jeff Scott Soto
b. November 4, 1965

Jens Johansson
b. November 2, 1963

Barriemore Barlow
b. September 10, 1949

Marcel Jacob
b. January 30, 1964
d. July 21, 2009

Mark Boals
b. December 5, 1958

Even though virtuoso rock guitar could hardly have been described as the height of fashion during the early eighties, that decade was to see the sudden emergence of a new type of musician: one who played rock and metal with a degree of technical accomplishment more usually found in jazz and classical circles. Prominent names such as Steve Vai, Joe Satriani, Eddie Van Halen, and **Yngwie Malmsteen** upped the ante for every aspiring young rock player and were a seminal influence on the "shredding" generation that followed.

Yngwie (pronounced "Ing-vay") Malmsteen was born in 1963 in Stockholm, Sweden. As a troubled seven-year-old, he was inspired to take up the guitar after seeing TV footage of Jimi Hendrix setting his guitar aflame at the Monterey Pop festival. By the age of ten he had mastered the Hendrix songbook, and developed an admiration for Ritchie Blackmore's classically inspired lead playing in Deep Purple.

Under the influence of his elder sister, Malmsteen developed an interest in classical composition, which included an obsession with nineteenth-century violin virtuoso Niccolò Paganini (1782–1840). Malmsteen found himself attracted both to Paganini's musical mastery and his flamboyant "wild man" image. By his mid-teens, the prodigy had all but given up on his schooling and was instead practicing the guitar

obsessively, formulating a neo-classical style that was centered on an impressive ability to play arpeggiated solos at a scarcely believable speed.

Malmsteen soon became frustrated with the somewhat limited possibilities and opportunities offered in his native Sweden. In 1982 he contacted Mike Varney of U.S. metal label Shrapnel Records, who—impressed by his playing and technical ability—flew him to the U.S. to record with Nashville quartet Steeler (fronted by **Ron Keel**). But Malmsteen quickly came to the attention of more prominent rockers, and left Steeler to join Alcatrazz, featuring former Rainbow frontman **Graham Bonnet** (the band also very briefly featured Clive Burr of Iron Maiden). Malmsteen played on the band's first two albums, which were moderate commercial successes. (His replacement in Alcatrazz was the equally spectacular Steve Vai.)

Malmsteen's 1984 debut album featured **Jeff Scott Soto** on vocals and Jethro Tull's **Barriemore Barlow** on drums. *Rising Force*—its name reminiscent of Ritchie Blackmore's classic *Rainbow Rising*—featured guitar heroics of such startling speed and complexity that it created a new benchmark in rock. Eddie Van Halen, warned David Lee Roth, was "gonna have to learn how to pronounce 'Yngwie.'" The album hit No. 60 in the U.S. and was nominated for a Grammy; in 2009, *Guitar World* rated it No. 1 in a list of shred classics.

year-by-year ▦ Vocals ▪ Guitar ▪ Bass ▪ Drums ▪ Keyboards

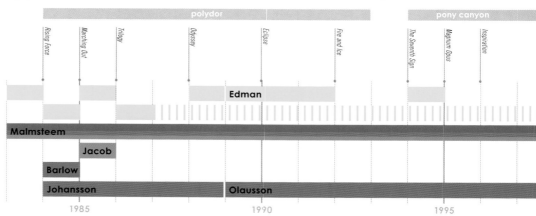

Joe Lynn Turner
b. August 2, 1951

Göran Edman
b. April 28, 1956

Mats Olausson
b. 1961

Michael Vescera
b. June 13, 1962

Mats Leven
b. September 11, 1964

Cozy Powell
b. December 29, 1947
d. April 5, 1998

Doogie White
b. March 7, 1960

Tim "Ripper" Owens
b. September 13, 1967

Malmsteen followed up with more of the same with *Marching Out* (1985), whose lyrical quotient indicated a considerably less sophisticated way with words than music. *Trilogy* (1986) gave Malmsteen a third *Billboard* album hit at No. 44, and cemented his reputation as the prime purveyor of symphonic metal.

In 1987, his band—now credited as "Yngwie J. Malmsteen's Rising Force"—was joined by another former Rainbow vocalist, **Joe Lynn Turner**. ("A match made in heaven!" declared Ritchie Blackmore, tongue firmly in cheek.) However, the band's progress was brought to a dramatic halt when Malmsteen drove his E-Type Jaguar into a tree. "I had, like, a brain hemorrhage…" he told *Rock Scene*. "It resulted in my right hand not being able to move properly… I had to practice so much more in order to play somewhat the same. But once it healed, I reached another plateau because I had all that practice behind me."

It would be a further year before the new lineup was able to record. With lyrical duties handed to Turner, *Odyssey* was a more radio-friendly rock album. Malmsteen's playing was notably more restrained, lacking the pyrotechnic aggression of his earlier work. The album included the heavily aired single "Heaven Tonight," which introduced Malmsteen to a wider, less guitar-centered audience. In spite of the indifference of rock critics, by now on the lookout for another

prodigy, *Odyssey* sneaked into the *Billboard* Top Forty, and remains his most commercially successful album.

In 1989, Rising Force embarked on a tour that—unusually for its time—took in the Soviet Union, and was documented on *Live in Leningrad*. The star then returned to Sweden, where he formed a new outfit for *Eclipse* (1990). By this time, he was experiencing a critical and commercial decline. Such was his influence on a generation of players that techniques that had once baffled and astonished were now increasingly standard fare. Malmsteen's status in other parts of the globe was still in its ascendancy, however, and 1992's *Fire and Ice* debuted at No. 1 in Japan.

In 1997, Malmsteen produced what he considers his most important work, *Concerto Suite for Electric Guitar and Orchestra in Eb Minor, Op. 1*, a classical composition with electric guitar as the solo instrument. (Four years later he was able to perform this work live in Tokyo with the New Japan Philharmonic Orchestra.)

Malmsteen's output over the past decade has featured former Judas Priest front-man **Tim "Ripper" Owens** and, inevitably, another Rainbow veteran, **Doogie White**. There was even a welcome glimpse of humor: after the belated distribution of a recording of a 1988 incident—in which he berated a stewardess with the immortal "You've released the fucking fury"—Malmsteen titled his 2005 album *Unleash the Fury*. **TB**

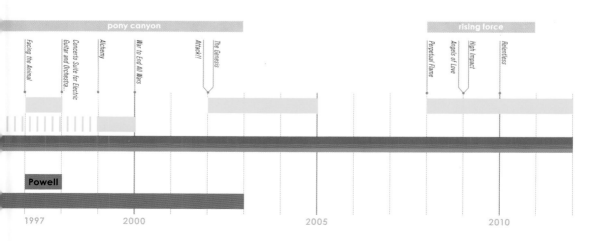

manic street preachers 1986–present

James Dean Bradfield
b. February 21, 1969

Nicky Wire
b. January 20, 1969

Sean Moore
b. July 30, 1968

Richey Edwards
b. December 22, 1967
d. February 1, 1995

Manic Street Preachers had No. 1 singles about the Spanish Civil War ("If You Tolerate This Your Children Will Be Next"); No. 1 albums named after speeches made by long-dead politicians (*This Is My Truth Tell Me Yours*); and audiences with Cuban leader Fidel Castro (in 2001). If its members had remained faithful to their manifesto, the group would have imploded after just one huge hit album. But then we would have been denied one of the U.K. music scene's most intriguing, contrary, politicized, and polarizing careers. Oh, and a load of great, incendiary, and intelligent music.

After a false start in the mid-eighties with a lineup that included Miles Woodward, known as "Flicker," on bass, the us-against-the-world quartet from south Wales was settled—**James Dean Bradfield** (guitar/vocals), **Nicky Wire** (bass), **Richey Edwards** (rhythm guitar), and **Sean Moore** (drums). Early singles such as "Motown Junk" (1991) and "You Love Us" (1992) seemed to verge on punk pastiche, with heavy debts to The Clash. With its metal guitars, their debut album *Generation Terrorists* (1992) swam against the tide of indie shoegazing, but did so successfully enough to reach U.K. No. 13. In a career that was to be characterized by confounding expectations, the album ultimately proved to be a calling card rather than a signing-off. "At least we broke our own rules," remarked Bradfield in 2004.

Two 1992 singles edged the Manics toward the mainstream: "Motorcycle Emptiness," whose yearning guitar was a clear nod to their heroes Guns N' Roses' "Sweet Child o' Mine," and a U.K. Top Ten cover of the theme from the TV show *M*A*S*H*, "Suicide is Painless."

Gold Against the Soul (1993) is not greatly loved by the band, but it became their first Top Ten album entry in the U.K. Said Chemical Brother Ed Simons of "La Tristesse Durera (Scream to a Sigh)"—one of four Top Forty singles from it—"What it really has, like all great dance records, is that integral sense of transcendent melancholy."

Success and *Gold Against the Soul*'s smoother sound could not disguise the worsening personal problems experienced by Richey Edwards. These had been most publicly demonstrated in an act of self-mutilation during an interview with then-NME writer Steve Lamacq: to show that deeds were as important to the band as words, he carved "4 REAL" into his arm. Lamacq, complained Edwards, "couldn't conceive that people can be so frustrated and pissed off that they're prepared to hurt themselves."

The Holy Bible came out in the U.K. in early 1994, but was overshadowed later the same year by two albums that came to define the era—*Definitely Maybe* by Oasis and Blur's *Parklife*. Where those sold millions, the only place *The Holy Bible* reached No. 1

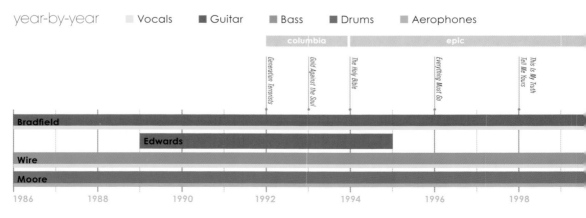

year-by-year   ■ Vocals   ■ Guitar   ■ Bass   ■ Drums   ■ Aerophones

was on *NME*'s Fifty Darkest Albums Ever. Nicky Wire described the album as "full of disgust with humanity."

A destructive gig in London at the end of 1994 was Edwards's last stage appearance. Just weeks later, he was missing, presumed dead.Even by Manics standards, the future was bleak. "We are haunted by ghosts," reflected Wire. Out of this, though, appeared the almost total triumph of *Everything Must Go* (1996). Although Edwards received credits on a handful of tracks, the lyrical focus fell on Wire. "I'm not pretending to be the same kind of lyricist as Richey," he admitted. "I don't reach the depths of madness and self-hatred that he did." However, an arresting opening line—"Libraries gave us power"—allied to "a bit of R.E.M., a bit of Ennio Morricone" from Bradfield made "A Design for Life" an instant anthem.

This Is My Truth Tell Me Yours (1998) completed their transformation from a purely U.K. chart concern— albeit triple platinum-selling one—to a band with a strong international profile. For the Manics, a purity of purpose always co-exists with a need for popularity. "I couldn't survive on critical acclaim alone," said Wire. After the success of *This Is My Truth...* the pendulum swung the other way for 2001's back-to-basics *Know Your Enemy* (featuring a cameo by My Bloody Valentine's Kevin Shields). However, the non-album single "The Masses Against the Classes" gave them a second U.K. chart-topper (after 1998's "If You Tolerate This Your Children Will Be Next").

Lifeblood (2004) did not live up to its title, its polite posturing marking a band whose life force seemed to be ebbing away—more the Middle-Aged than Manic Steet Preachers. *Send Away the Tigers* (2007) was a partial return to form, notably in its hit duet with the Cardigans' Nina Persson, "Your Love Alone is Not Enough." But in more typical Manics fashion, it took the lyrics of a dead man (at his parents' instigation, Edwards was legally declared deceased in November 2008) to revive a spirit that was at best dormant and, concluded many, gone for good. Thirteen years separated Edwards bequeathing a folder of lyrics and the band using its contents as the basis for the best— read most uncompromising—Manics album in years, *Journal for Plague Lovers*, released in 2009.

The exit that was planned for 1992 came to pass—sort of—almost two decades on, with the band announcing a hiatus in the slipstream of the hook-heavy *Postcards from a Young Man* (2010) and the singles collection *National Treasures* (2011). "You're only this hateful and angry once, really," Wire had said in 1991. Like everything the Manics do, this is subject to debate and revision. Thankfully, nothing much has changed. Said Wire in 2011: "There's just so much hate within this band." And we love them for it. **CB**

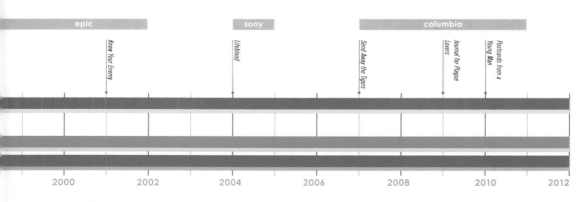

mano negra / manu chao 1987–present

Manu Chao
b. June 21, 1961

Santiago Casariego
b. Unknown

Antoine Chao
b. 1963

Thomas Darnal
b. 1963

Philippe "Garbancito" Teboul
b. Unknown

Olivier Joseph "Jo" Dahan
b. Unknown

Manu Chao is a singer-songwriter and political activist whose multilingual music combines a kaleidoscopic range of styles. Ska, punk rock, French *chanson*, salsa, and reggae are just a few of the ingredients in the heady musical cocktail for which Chao has coined the term "*patchanka*," derived from a Mexican slang expression meaning a wild party. "I don't trust labels," he declared in 2007. "I'm Manu, that's all."

Chao was born in Paris to Spanish parents in 1961. He achieved little success with his first band, Les Hot Pants, but fared far better with his next project. Mano Negra (Black Hand) were conspicuously influenced by The Clash, especially *Sandinista!*. Their core members were Chao, his trumpeter brother **Antoine Chao**, and their drummer cousin **Santiago Casariego**.

The first single, "Mala Vida," became a hit in France in 1987, and the debut album *Patchanka* appeared the following year. It spanned a dizzying variety of styles, centering on ska and punk but incorporating a venture into rap on "Killin' Rats." More musicians were recruited to form a touring band, and Mano Negra was an eight-piece by the time

Puta's Fever was released in 1989. The founding trio were joined on the album by guitarist **Daniel Jamet**, bassist **Olivier "Jo" Dahan**, keyboard player **Thomas Darnal**, percussionist **Philippe "Garbancito" Teboul**, and trombone player **Pierre Gauthé**. The album's title, roughly translating as "Whore's Fever," was an ironic allusion to accusations of selling out that the group faced after signing to Virgin, but the lyrical content showed the band's radical outlook was intact.

Puta's Fever was a hit in Europe, enabling Mano Negra to embark on a world tour in 1990. They were well received in Europe, but a U.S. tour with Iggy Pop was an unhappy experience. They avoided touring in English-speaking nations from then on, but continued to record in English, doing so more than ever on 1991's *King of Bongo*, whose rock orientation disappointed some listeners. Their second album of that year was the pointedly titled *Amerika Perdida* ("Lost America"), a compilation containing no songs in English.

In 1992 Mano Negra toured South America on a cargo ship, frequently performing free concerts. The strains of the lengthy excursion caused friction within

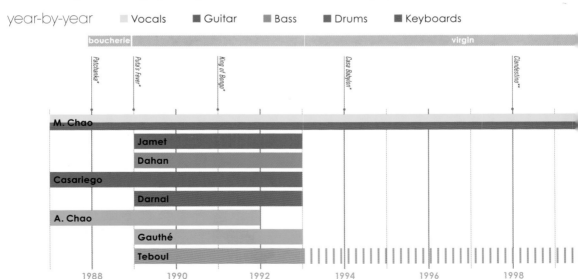

year-by-year   ▪ Vocals   ▪ Guitar   ▪ Bass   ▪ Drums   ▪ Keyboards

Daniel Jamet
b. 1960

Pierre Gauthé
b. Unknown

Madjid Fahem
b. 1973

Jean Michel "Gambeat" Dercourt
b. Unknown

David Bourguignon
b. Unknown

the band, and Antoine Chao left at the tour's end. The remaining members began work on a new studio album, but Mano Negra disintegrated as 1993 went on. Dahan and Jamet quit during the sessions for what would become their final album. The effective end of the band came in late 1993 during another eccentric touring venture: a trip around Colombia by train so stressful that, by its end, Manu Chao and Darnal were the only remaining members. Nonetheless, *Casa Babylon* (1994) was well received, reviewers praising its overtly political lyrics and striking stylistic diversity.

A legal dispute broke out between Manu Chao and some of his former bandmates over the use of the name Mano Negra, resulting in the formal end of the group in 1995. Chao then assembled a new outfit for live performances, which he named Radio Bemba Sound System after the communication network used by rebel forces in the Cuban revolution that brought Fidel Castro to power. Chao spent some time traveling in South America and researching the various forms of street music found there, and those musical styles heavily influenced his first solo album, *Clandestino*

(1998). Most of the album was sung in Spanish and some of the lyrics were his most political to date, but it was a lighthearted English-language track that became Chao's biggest solo hit: the hypnotically catchy reggae/rap hybrid "Bongo Bong."

Chao established a new base in Barcelona and recorded *Proxima Estacion: Esperanza* (2001) in his home studio there. The title roughly translates as "Next Stop: Hope," reflecting the optimistic mood of another restlessly genre-hopping, multilingual album. However, his next studio album was a dramatic departure. Released only in France, 2004's *Sibérie m'était contéee* [sic] was a collection of French-language songs in the *chanson* style.

La Radiolina (2007) returned Chao to more familiar territory, with plenty of polemical lyrics and simple melodies among its twenty-one tracks. Its first single, "Rainin' in Paradize," proved remarkably prescient about the breakdown of Western society. "A lot of people think the problems are always in the third world and they're gonna be safe," he told *Harp*, "but the shit has already hit the fan." **DJ**

M

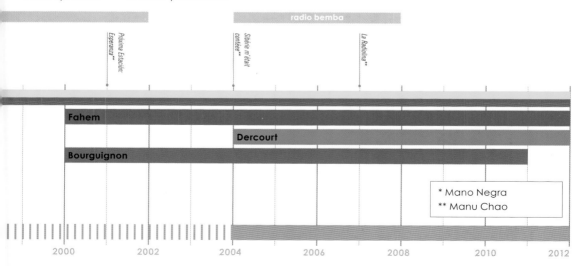

■ Aerophones   ■ Other percussion

radio bemba

Proxima Estacion: Esperanza**

Sibérie m'était contéee**

La Radiolina**

Fahem

Dercourt

Bourguignon

* Mano Negra
** Manu Chao

2000   2002   2004   2006   2008   2010   2012

marillion 1979–present

Steve Rothery
b. November
25, 1959

Mick Pointer
b. July 22, 1956

**Brian
Jelliman**
b. Unknown

Fish
b. April 25, 1958

Diz Minnitt
b. Unknown

Mark Kelly
b. April 9, 1961

**Pete
Trewavas**
b. January 15,
1959

Andy Ward
b. September
28, 1952

Progressive rock means never having to say you are sorry—and, despite the sneers of many a mainstream commentator, British progressive rock band Marillion continue to hold their heads high after three decades at the coalface. Sustained by a loyal coterie of fans and an innovative approach to business modeling, the group are as active now as they were at the time of their commercial heyday in the mid-eighties.

The band began life as Silmarillion, which was formed by drummer **Mick Pointer** and bassist Doug Irving. The name was later changed to Marillion, following the departure of two early members, and it was at that point that guitarist **Steve Rothery** and keyboard player **Brian Jelliman** joined.

In 1981, bassist **Diz Minnitt** replaced Irving and outspoken singer Derek "**Fish**" Dick arrived. Early shows in southeast England's, Buckinghamshire area revealed their love of classic progressive acts such as Genesis and Yes—but, as time passed (and the lineup stabilized when Jelliman was replaced by **Mark Kelly** and Minnitt by **Pete Trewavas**), a more individual style was honed. Fish's lyrics were poetic yet gritty, while the band blended virtuosity with memorable tunes.

A significant fanbase began to accumulate after a session for BBC Radio One in 1982. That same year, Fish stressed to *Kerrang!* magazine their anxiety to avoid "being classed as a second Genesis." Yet that was indeed the first comparison that Marillion's extended songs, unusual time signatures, inventive lyrics and Peter Gabriel-esque vocals conjured up.

Script for a Jester's Tear (1983), *Fugazi* (1984), and the live *Real to Reel* (1984) were U.K. Top Ten hits, and began a run of seven consecutive gold-selling albums— a remarkable achievement in an era dominated by Duran Duran and Wham!. By the summer of 1985—with drummer **Ian Mosley**, who had joined at the end of 1984—they were second only to ZZ Top at Britain's prestigious Monsters of Rock festival (with Bon Jovi and Metallica further down the bill).

The flawless U.K. No. 1 *Misplaced Childhood* (1985) boosted Marillion's appeal into the mainstream, with the hits "Kayleigh" and "Lavender" featuring infectious melodies and choruses. The album even cracked the *Billboard* Top Fifty, while the U.S.-only compilation *Brief Encounter* reached No. 67. (The band's Stateside profile subsequently dipped after a tour supporting Rush, with the Netherlands and Germany proving their most loyal overseas markets.)

The first successful phase of the group's career ended in 1988, after the introspective U.K. No. 2

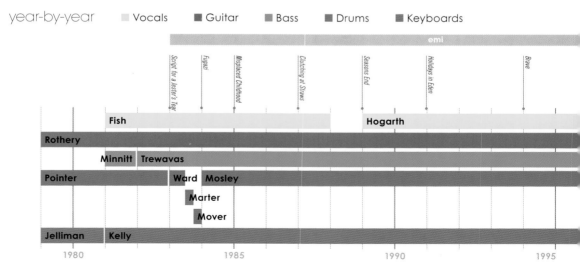

year-by-year   ■ Vocals   ■ Guitar   ■ Bass   ■ Drums   ■ Keyboards

emi

Script for a Jester's Tear
Fugazi
Misplaced Childhood
Clutching at Straws
Seasons End
Holidays in Eden
Brave

Fish   Hogarth

Rothery

Minnitt   Trewavas

Pointer   Ward   Mosley

Marter

Mover

Jelliman   Kelly

1980   1985   1990   1995

John Marter
b. Unknown

Jonathan Mover
b. May 4, 1963

Ian Mosley
b. June 16, 1953

Steve "H" Hogarth
b. May 14, 1959

Clutching at Straws and its tour. Fish left, unhappy with the group's then-manager and the relentless concert schedule. His vision of their next album (not shared by the band)—in which sound effects of a radio being re-tuned would punctuate Marillion playing covers of their favorite songs—belatedly bore fruit with his 1993 solo set *Songs from the Mirror*. (Fish's actual Marillion epitaph was instead 1988's live *The Thieving Magpie*.)

Many predicted the demise of the band, as Fish had been Marillion's focal point. However, a more than capable replacement was found in How We Live singer **Steve "H" Hogarth**, whose vocal style meshed perfectly with the band's music.

The Hogarth-era albums—notably 1994's *Brave*—were conceptually inventive and musically ambitious, and the first three maintained Marillion's U.K. Top Ten streak. But their brand of experimental rock was almost as unfashionable as it was possible to be in the mid-nineties, when grunge and Britpop held sway. With grim inevitability, the band's longtime label EMI declined to renew their contract after *Afraid of Sunlight* (1995) and the live *Made Again* (1996).

However, enforced independence proved to be a blessing in disguise. Signed to a smaller label, Castle, and unable to fund a U.S. tour in 1997, Marillion turned to their American followers, who raised the necessary finance. The connection between band and fans had been fostered by the group's use of the internet in 1996, making it among the first groups to do so: in fact, a 1999 album was titled *Marillion.com*. This genuinely progressive approach was extended by 2001's wryly titled *Anoraknophobia*, which was again funded by fans before any actual recording took place—a now common but then innovative practice.

Since then, Marillion has functioned on a more or less independent basis, issuing studio and live albums through its own Intact label and occasionally (as with the physical release of 2008's *Happiness is the Road*) collaborating with EMI. From their studio in Buckinghamshire, the members control their live schedules, press commitments, recording, and merchandise—making them one of the first examples of a truly independent, twenty-first-century band.

Many observers still criticize Marillion's music for its supposedly archaic, unfashionable nature, but to little noticeable effect. When Britain's most visible TV chat-show host Jonathan Ross said in 2004, "Marillion sing about goblins," Rothery coolly responded, "We recorded *Script for a Jester's Tear* twenty-two years ago. I think that was when Ross had his own hair." **JM**

M

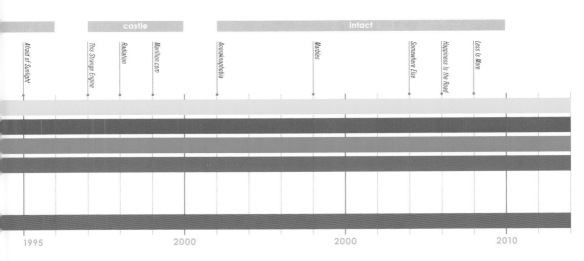

matchbox twenty 1995–present

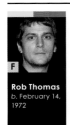

Rob Thomas
b. February 14, 1972

Kyle Cook
b. August 29, 1975

Paul Doucette
b. August 22, 1972

Adam Gaynor
b. November 26, 1963

Brian Yale
b. November 14, 1968

Ryan MacMillan
b. Unknown

"The music biz is pretty fast paced and there are a lot of hypes," observed **Rob Thomas** in 1998, "but there are always people who like quality songs—and, if you're writing and performing quality songs, I think you last longer." His band Matchbox Twenty, with global sales of over forty million, confirm that point.

Thomas, **Paul Doucette**, and **Brian Yale** drifted through various Orlando, Florida-based groups before forming Matchbox 20 with **Kyle Cook** and **Adam Gaynor** in 1995. The photogenic quintet's radio-friendly hooks and mainstream appeal quickly endeared them to an international audience. Their debut album *Yourself or Someone Like You* (1996) earned an astonishing twelve platinum awards in the U.S. alone, thanks to the hits "Push" and "3 AM."

By the time the group—rebranded Matchbox Twenty from the original Matchbox 20—returned in 2000 with *Mad Season*, their charismatic front-man was a Grammy-winning superstar. "Smooth," a million-selling collaboration between co-writer Thomas and rock heavyweight Carlos Santana, spent a staggering twelve weeks in pole position on the *Billboard* Hot 100. Named the second most successful single in U.S. chart history (behind Chubby Checker's "The Twist"), it inspired the video for the group's own first No. 1 single, "Bent." Portrayed as an indestructible man of steel, Thomas is run over, slapped, and kicked by his envious bandmates, but somehow lives to tell the tale.

Real-life tensions thankfully failed to materialize and *More Than You Think You Are* followed in 2002. The set's first single, "Disease," was a co-write between Thomas and Rolling Stone Mick Jagger, but it was "Unwell" that returned Matchbox Twenty to familiar territory—the American Top Five. After being named Favorite Musical Group at the 2004 People's Choice Awards, the four-time Grammy nominees went on hiatus, allowing Thomas to concentrate on writing his first solo album, ...*Something to Be* (2005). When the band re-formed in 2007, they filled the void left by Gaynor with a promotion for drummer-turned-rhythm guitarist Doucette. The appointment of former Push Stars drummer **Ryan MacMillan** restored Matchbox Twenty to their full complement of five members.

The compilation album *Exile on Mainstream* (2007) showcased six new songs, including the smash "How Far We've Come." Nonetheless, the accompanying world tour, which visited Australia, New Zealand, and the U.K., marked the end of another chapter in the history of Matchbox Twenty, and Thomas resumed his solo career with *Cradlesong* (2009).

However, with a new album, *North,* appearing in 2012, the story is yet to end. "I want to be one of those people on the radio that other people are bitching about," said Thomas. "I hope to be like Jagger: still doing this in my sixties, but in an age-appropriate way—not shaking my ass too much." **MW**

year-by-year ▢ Vocals ▪ Guitar ▪ Bass ▪ Drums ▪ Keyboards
▪ Other percussion ▪ Strings

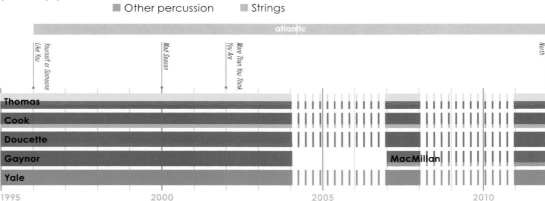

dave matthews band 1991–present

Dave Matthews
b. January 9, 1967

Carter Beauford
b. November 7, 1957

LeRoi Moore
b. September 7, 1961
d. August 19, 2008

Stefan Lessard
b. June 4, 1974

Peter Griesar
b. March 19, 1969

Tim Reynolds
b. December 15, 1957

Boyd Tinsley
b. May 16, 1964

The Dave Matthews Band (DMB) have defied categorization in a career that has now entered a third decade. But while they continue to muddy the waters of rock, pop, jazz, funk, roots, folk, and world music with their distinctively complex loose-limbed jams, they remain, almost exclusively, an American phenomenon. They have sold more than thirty million records in the U.S. since breaking out of Charlottesville, Virginia, with *Under the Table and Dreaming*. Their sales equate to thirty-five RIAA certifications for gold, platinum, and multi-platinum albums—the same number as The Beach Boys, Queen, and The Who. Five of their seven studio albums have debuted consecutively at No. 1; *Everyday* (2001) got there on first-week sales of 755,000.

Founders **Dave Matthews** (vocals/guitar), **Carter Beauford** (drums) and **LeRoi Moore** (saxophone) were, according to South African-born Matthews, "heinously bad" the first time they jammed together. But with **Stefan Lessard** (bass) and **Peter Griesar** (keyboards) adding muscle and **Boyd Tinsley** throwing all manner of stringed instruments into the mix, the group secured a regular slot at a popular Charlottesville nightclub, which in turn led to 1993's independently released, predominantly live *Remember Two Things*.

Having infiltrated the college campus circuit, DMB signed with RCA, scoring instant success with "Ants Marching," "Satellite," and "What Would You Say" from *Under the Table and Dreaming* (1994). With Matthews' "otherworldly and elegantly elastic" voice in heavy rotation on radio, the eclectic *Crash* (1996) soared to No. 2 and spawned five hits, notably the gorgeous "Crash into Me." Their place at rock's top table confirmed, DMB launched a legislation-altering attack on profit-making bootleggers, hammering a final nail into the underground industry's coffin with the wildly successful *Live at Red Rocks 8.15.95* (1997).

Busted Stuff (2002) surfaced from sessions with legendary producer Steve Lillywhite. Before *Stand Up* (2005) emerged, DMB had entertained 100,000 fans at New York's Central Park (raising $2 million for charity in the process) and a global audience of millions at Philadelphia's Live8 concert. Matthews and Tinsley also both had solo projects under their belts. "Gravedigger," from the former's *Some Devil*, won a Grammy for Best Male Rock Vocal Performance.

Big Whiskey & the GrooGrux King (2009) continued DMB's impressive run of opening week numbers with in excess of 400,000 albums sold. A reunion with Steve Lillywhite bodes well for their next album. **MW**

M

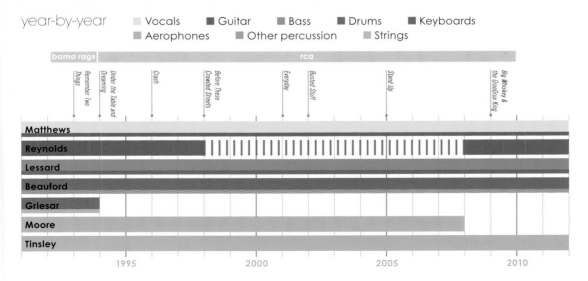

year-by-year — Vocals ■ Guitar ■ Bass ■ Drums ■ Keyboards ■ Aerophones ■ Other percussion ■ Strings

john mayall's bluesbreakers 1963–2008

John Mayall
b. November
29, 1933

John McVie
b. November
26, 1945

Eric Clapton
b. March 30,
1945

Peter Green
b. October 29,
1946

Jack Bruce
b. May 14, 1943

**Mick
Fleetwood**
b. June 24, 1947

Mick Taylor
b. January 17,
1949

**Aynsley
Dunbar**
b. January 10,
1946

A key figure in the story of British blues, **John Mayall** is noted less perhaps for his own musical talents than for his role as a mentor, with some of the biggest names of the sixties' London blues scene passing through the ranks of his band, the Bluesbreakers. Working as a graphic designer by day and playing the blues by night in the clubs of Manchester, John Mayall was thirty years old when Alexis Korner—the "godfather" of British blues—convinced him that he could make a full-time living from music by moving to London.

Mayall made his debut at London's Marquee club in 1963, and quickly became a fixture on the city's live music scene. This period is documented by his debut album, 1964's concert recording *John Mayall Plays John Mayall* (featuring **John McVie** on bass).

Mayall's breakthrough year was 1965, when he was joined by The Yardbirds' twenty-year-old guitar sensation **Eric Clapton**. As Mayall's concerts attracted larger crowds, Clapton's fluid soloing took the limelight, and together they cut *Blues Breakers with Eric Clapton*, which peaked at No. 6 in the U.K. The album had been conceived as another live recording, with bass by **Jack Bruce**. However, the tape's poor quality led it to be replaced by studio sessions with the returning McVie. Clapton's tenure with Mayall would be brief: in 1966, he left to form Cream with Bruce.

On 1967's *A Hard Road*, Clapton was replaced by **Peter Green**, who established a formidable

reputation of his own on instrumental tracks such as "The Supernatural." Like Clapton, Green would only stick around for one album, leaving with two other Bluesbreakers—bassist McVie and drummer **Mick Fleetwood**—to form Fleetwood Mac.

Green's successor was the eighteen-year-old **Mick Taylor**, with whom the Bluesbreakers achieved a third successive UK Top Ten album, *Crusade*, in 1967. Taylor would prove a valuable sideman, also playing on 1968's *Bare Wires*, which gave Mayall his first taste of U.S. chart success. Although the Bluesbreakers were disbanded that year, Taylor continued to work with Mayall until 1969, when he joined The Rolling Stones.

At the end of the sixties, Mayall moved to the U.S. and adopted a "low volume" approach to his work, creating larger bands that eschewed his former "heavy lead guitar and drums" format. His style of blues became less fashionable in the seventies and he became less prominent, but he revived the Bluesbreakers name for touring in the eighties. As a nominally solo star, Mayall enjoyed a renaissance with *A Sense of Place* (1990) and *Wake Up Call* (1993). The guest list for *Along for the Ride* (2001) confirmed Mayall's status: alongside Taylor, Green, Fleetwood, and McVie were the likes of Gary Moore, Jeff Healey, Steve Cropper, Steve Miller, and Billy Gibbons. And even as his ninth decade approaches, Mayall shows little interest in calling time on his solo career. **TB**

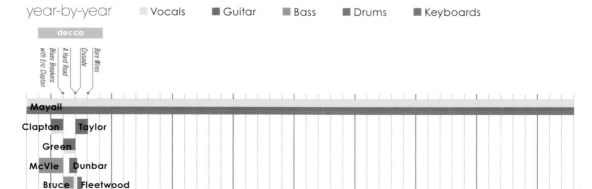

mc5 1963–1972

Rob Tyner
b. December 12, 1944
d. September 17, 1991

Wayne Kramer
b. April 30, 1948

Fred "Sonic" Smith
b. Sept 13, 1949
d. November 4, 1994

Michael Davis
b. June 5, 1943
d. February 17, 2012

Dennis Thompson
b. September 7, 1948

The cultural landscape of 1967 may have been dominated by San Francisco's hippies, but over in Detroit the MC5 were forging a very different agenda, laying the foundations for the eventual emergence of punk rock. Their music was fast, intense, and deafeningly loud—and they had politics to match.

The Motor City Five formed in 1964 with a core of bassist-turned-vocalist **Rob Tyner** and guitarists **Fred "Sonic" Smith** and **Wayne Kramer**, initially as a beat group playing at teenage parties. Within a year, an interest in free jazz led Smith and Kramer to experiment with distorted guitar sound and feedback. With bassist **Michael Davis** and drummer **Dennis Thompson** (replacing Pat Burrows and Bob Gaspar, respectively) the group, now calling themselves the MC5, landed a regular gig at the Grande Ballroom, Detroit, and quickly built up a fanatical following.

They caught the eye of John Sinclair, who was gaining notoriety as leader of the White Panthers, a left-wing political faction with a manifesto of "total assault by any means necessary." With Sinclair as manager, the MC5 became the White Panthers' house band, acting as musical conduits for political rhetoric. In 1968, they performed as part of the "Yippie" protests against the Vietnam war at the 1968 Democratic National Convention in Chicago, which were broken up by riot police. Spotted by an A&R executive, the MC5 were signed to the Elektra label.

The band's reputation is almost entirely down to their proto-punk classic debut album, *Kick Out the Jams*, arguably the most powerfully energetic live album ever made. Controversy broke out surrounding the obscenities in the rallying call of the title track. The influential Hudson's record store chain refused to stock the album, which resulted in Elektra producing an alternative censored version. Sinclair responded by taking out an advert in the underground press captioned: "Kick in the door if the store won't sell you the album… on Elektra Records—Fuck Hudson's!" But with the store now refusing to stock any of the label's artists, the band were quickly dropped.

Meanwhile, U.S. authorities had taken a growing interest in the White Panthers, and John Sinclair was eventually jailed for a narcotics offense. Without their mentor the radical politics vanished, the band signed with Atlantic, and the garage thrash was replaced by stripped-down rock 'n' roll. The ensuing album, 1970's *Back in the USA*, alienated many fans and sold poorly; the 1971 follow-up, *High Time*, failed even to chart and the band were dropped again. With mounting drug problems, the MC5 played one final gig in Detroit on New Year's Eve, 1972, before disbanding.

Frequently cited as important influences, Tyner, Smith, and Kramer all traded on their status as bona fide godfathers of the punk movement. Smith married Patti Smith and Kramer is still playing today. **TB**

M

year-by-year   ■ Vocals   ■ Guitar   ■ Bass   ■ Drums

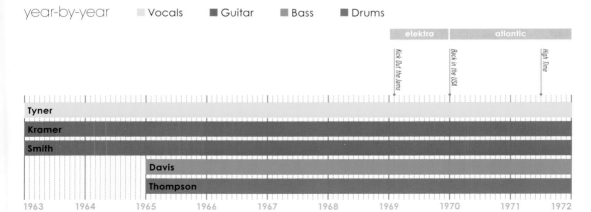

paul mccartney 1970–present

Paul McCartney
b. June 18, 1942

Linda McCartney
b. September 24, 1941
d. April 17, 1998

Denny Laine
b. October 29, 1944

Henry McCullough
b. July 21, 1943

Jimmy McCulloch
b. June 4, 1953
d. September 27, 1979

Ringo Starr
b. July 7, 1940

"Paul quits The Beatles," announced the *Daily Mirror* on April 10, 1970. Actually, the other three Fabs had all variously called it a day in the previous two years, only to rejoin the fold, but McCartney's declaration was the one made public, and saw him pilloried as a prime mover—along with Yoko Ono and Allen Klein—in breaking up pop's best-loved band.

In truth, **Paul McCartney** had worked manfully to keep The Beatles together following the death of their manager, Brian Epstein, in 1967, and fell into a boozy depression when the Fabs were no more. "I seriously thought about giving up music," he admitted in 2004.

His solo debut, *McCartney* (1970), hit U.K. No. 2 and U.S. No. 1, and featured the excellent "Maybe I'm Amazed," though critics—and the other ex-Beatles—panned its rough 'n' ready homeliness. *Ram* (1971), recorded with his wife **Linda McCartney**, elicited a similarly lukewarm reception, but contained a U.S. chart-topper in "Uncle Albert/Admiral Halsey."

Wild Life (1971) marked the birth of Wings—the McCartneys joined by ex-Moody Blue **Denny Laine** and a revolving roster of sidemen. Like its predecessors —and the follow-up, *Red Rose Speedway* (1973)—it was critically slated but commercially triumphant, and McCartney's can-do attitude saw him take the band on the road, turning up unannounced at student campuses in the U.K. "I kind of admire the way he got off his pedestal," John Lennon admitted in 1980.

Regularly dismissed as seventies soft-rockers, Wings actually stirred up controversy with the 1972 single "Give Ireland Back to the Irish"—a response to the Bloody Sunday massacre in Northern Ireland—and "Hi, Hi, Hi." Both were banned by the BBC, the latter because of alleged sexual references.

"My Love" gave Wings their first U.S. chart-topper in 1973, a year that also saw McCartney's all-guns-blazing theme for the Bond movie *Live and Let Die*, and the album that saw him return to form: *Band on the Run*. Strong writing (notably "Jet," "Bluebird," "Let Me Roll It," and the title track) and excellent ensemble playing made it a hit with critics and punters alike. *Venus and Mars* (1975) and *Wings at the Speed of Sound* (1976) were lesser efforts, but the 1975–76 Wings world tour proved a resounding success. Its Stateside leg was celebrated in the triple-set *Wings Over America* (1976)—the band's fifth U.S. chart-topper.

Wings hit the singles chart regularly throughout the seventies: the bagpipe-friendly "Mull of Kintyre" —the band's only U.K. No.1—became the country's best-selling single since his old band's "She Loves You" in 1963. However, following a drug bust in Japan, McCartney folded Wings to go solo again in 1980 with

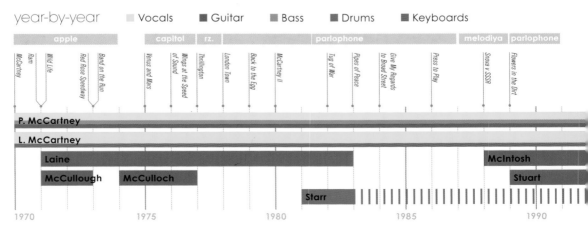

year-by-year   ■ Vocals   ■ Guitar   ■ Bass   ■ Drums   ■ Keyboards

Robbie McIntosh
b. October 25, 1957

Hamish Stuart
b. October 8, 1949

Rusty Anderson
b. January 20, 1959

Abe Laboriel Jr.
b. 1971

James McCartney
b. September 12, 1977

the self-made *McCartney II:* a diverse set including the irrepressibly boppy "Coming Up," which earned Lennon's seal of approval, and the wistful "Waterfalls."

Tug of War (1982) and *Pipes of Peace* showed his pop chops were still in order. The former featured "Ebony and Ivory"—a plea for racial harmony with Stevie Wonder that became one of the year's biggest hits—and "Here Today," his touching nod to Lennon, murdered in December 1980. *Give My Regards to Broad Street* (1984) yielded one of his finest solo songs, "No More Lonely Nights" (graced by Pink Floyd's David Gilmour, who had previously played alongside other guitar heroes on Wings' 1979 set *Back to the Egg*).

However, it was five years before McCartney's critical stock rose again with 1989's *Flowers in the Dirt*, featuring four co-writes with spiky new wave songsmith Elvis Costello. In between, he helped close the 1985 Live Aid concert in London, though a dodgy microphone muted much of his vocal on "Let It Be."

McCartney showed an admirable openness to diversity and collaboration in the nineties, dipping into the classical world with 1991's *Liverpool Oratorio* (composed with, and conducted by, Carl Davis), 1997's *Standing Stone,* and 1999's *Working Classical*. Another new collaboration, this time with Killing Joke bassist-turned-producer Youth, saw the birth

of The Fireman, a pseudonym under which he released leftfield electronica such as *Rushes* (1998) and *Electric Arguments* (2008). Together with Welsh new psychedelicists Super Furry Animals, the two produced *Liverpool Sound Collage* (2000), on which McCartney revisited the sonic experiments that had informed The Beatles' more out-there tracks, such as *Revolver*'s "Tomorrow Never Knows," alongside snippets of studio chat from the Fabs themselves.

Flaming Pie (1997)—its title a nod to Lennon's quip that the name The Beatles had been conjured when "a man came unto us on a flaming pie"—and 1999's cover version set *Run Devil Run* (featuring Gilmour and Deep Purple's Ian Paice) attracted further plaudits.

In the new century, shaken by the 9/11 World Trade Center tragedy—which he'd witnessed—McCartney helped set up the Concert for New York City and released the well-received charity single "Freedom!"

Subsequent years brought the increasingly strong *Driving Rain* (2001), *Chaos and Creation in the Backyard* (2005), and *Memory Almost Full* (2007)—all providing evidence aplenty that Macca's muse is far from dead. Even the vintage collection *Kisses on the Bottom* (2012)—the sort of folly that would once have seen him pilloried—earned respectable reviews and his customary high chart rankings. **RD**

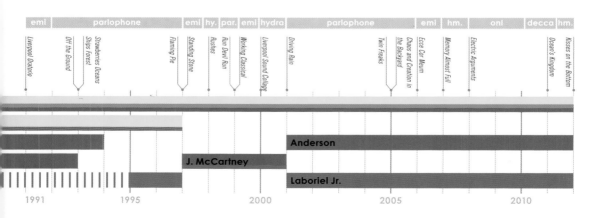

McCartney (1970)

Band on the Run (1973)

Back to the Egg (1979)

McCartney II (1980)

Pipes of Peace (1983)

Flowers in the Dirt (1989)

Flaming Pie (1997)

Run Devil Run (1999)

Driving Rain (2001)

Memory Almost Full (2007)

Linda and **Paul McCartney** in a New York studio in 1970.

In 1973, the year of *Red Rose Speedway* and *Band on the Run*.

Wings' last lineup: (back) **Paul**, Laurence Juber, (front) Steve Holley, **Denny Laine**, **Linda**.

Michael Jackson, Kim Wilde, Pete Townshend, and **Paul** in 1983.

Paul at home in Britain's Sussex, after his deportation from Japan for marijuana possession.

With Pete Townshend at The Concert for New York City.

Back on the road for the first time in a decade, in August 1989.

Promoting The Beatles' *Anthology* retrospective with **Ringo** and George, just after starting work on *Flaming Pie*.

Back at the Cavern club in Liverpool, promoting *Run Devil Run*, with Pink Floyd's David Gilmour, Deep Purple's Ian Paice, and guitarist Mick Green.

Live in London for *Memory Almost Full*'s launch, looking as remarkably youthful as ever...

meat loaf 1967–present

Meat Loaf
b. September 27, 1947

Shaun "Stoney" Murphy
b. Unknown

Steve Buslowe
b. Unknown

Bob Kulick
b. January 16, 1950

Paul Jacobs
b. Unknown

Mark Alexander
b. December 26, 1963

A cursory glance at Michael Lee Aday's vital stats—including that once hefty waistline—confirms that the Texas native is not your average rock star. With a blown fuse (quite literally) here and a near-death experience there, **Meat Loaf**'s rock and roll dreams have come through and made him one of the most admired, yet most ridiculed, icons in rock.

Michael (born Marvin) had music in his veins from the get-go courtesy of a mother who sang in a gospel quartet. In the summer of 1967, after relocating to California as a nineteen-year-old, he formed his first band, Meatloaf Soul. Surviving a fall from a balcony at a house the group used for rehearsals, the "Man of Steel" was destined to rub shoulders with the likes of The Who, Pink Floyd, Janis Joplin, and Alice Cooper as "ringmaster" of The Floating Circus (the third incarnation of Meatloaf Soul), wearing—in the words of bandmate Rick Bozzo—"his soon-to-be signature tuxedo with red cummerbund; barefoot of course."

By 1969, with many of the musicians (in Bozzo's words) "surfing, mentally messed up from drugs," or bagging "cushy jobs working for their dads," Meatloaf was going nowhere fast and turned to theater,

landing a role in a Detroit production of the musical *Hair*. Then, alerted to his vocal prowess, the Motown label signed him up, with fellow cast member **Shaun "Stoney" Murphy**. The pair briefly raided the U.S. chart with the *Stoney and Meatloaf* album cut "What You See Is What You Get." (Murphy would later sing with Eric Clapton before joining Little Feat in 1993.)

Meatloaf returned to the stage with the Broadway cast of *Hair*, but it was the audition for his next acting role (The Public Theater's *More Than You Deserve*) that transformed his life. There, he met Jim Steinman—composer, lyricist, producer, and the man who would be instrumental in shaping Meat's career.

Still a couple of years from his first association with those creatures that hang upside-down in caves, Meatloaf played "ex-delivery boy"-turned-zombie Eddie in *The Rocky Horror Show*, reprising his role for the 1975 movie version. But the larger-than-life star of more than fifty movies and TV shows was now ready to ditch his "Hot Patootie" for a full-blown rock career, initially providing guest vocals on Ted Nugent's Top Forty album *Free-for-All*. However, it was a second slice of Meat Loaf—now two words rather than one—

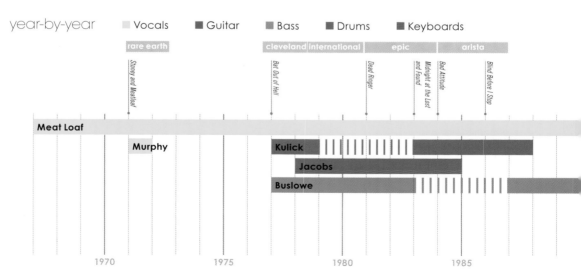

year-by-year ■ Vocals ■ Guitar ■ Bass ■ Drums ■ Keyboards

28.6M
Bat Out of Hell
(1977)

14.8M
Bat Out of Hell II:
Back Into Hell
(1993)

5.2M
Welcome to the
Neighbourhood
(1995)

2.5M
Couldn't Have
Said It Better
(2003)

John Miceli
b. May 29, 1961

Kasim Sulton
b. December 8, 1955

Paul Crook
b. February 12, 1966

Randy Flowers
b. Unknown

Dave Luther
b. Unknown

that spectacularly exposed him to a worldwide audience, when 1977's *Bat Out of Hell* took flight.

Rolling out a few numbers barely does the album justice, but here goes: approaching thirty million copies sold worldwide, including fourteen million in the U.S. alone, and more than *nine* years on the U.K. chart, including 244 weeks in the Top Forty—an achievement unmatched by any other solo artist. No mean feat considering the seven-track album peaked modestly at No. 14 in the U.S. and No. 9 in the U.K.

Despite an epic, million-selling single ("Two Out of Three Ain't Bad") from *Bat Out of Hell*, Meat Loaf's U.S. career was frequently all revved up with no place to go. Incredibly, *Bat*'s title track has failed to chart on three occasions, and early eighties albums *Dead Ringer* (source of the rousing Cher duet, "Dead Ringer for Love"), *Midnight at the Lost and Found*, and *Bad Attitude*—all Top Ten hits in the U.K.—fell short of the Top Forty in his homeland. Meat has spoken candidly about his struggle to be taken seriously as a rock musician, and one might argue that negative publicity toward his theatrical stage antics and "silly" songs blunted his post-*Bat* sales potential.

However, in 1993, armed with some of the longest and daftest titles in rock history—"Life Is a Lemon and I Want My Money Back," "Objects in the Rear View Mirror May Appear Closer Than They Are"—and with Steinman back by his side, Meat scored his first transatlantic No. 1s with the long-awaited *Bat* sequel, *Back Into Hell*, and its Grammy-winning lead single, "I'd Do Anything for Love (But I Won't Do That)."

After two more mega-sellers—1995's *Welcome to the Neighbourhood* and 2003's *Couldn't Have Said It Better*—the final album of the *Bat* trilogy, *The Monster Is Loose*, returned Meat to global Top Tens in 2006. And despite announcing his retirement in 2007, Meat was back in 2010 with the U.K. platinum puller *Hang Cool Teddy Bear* and in 2012 with *Hell in a Handbasket*.

Meat has triumphed over adversity throughout his life. He endured an alcoholic father and a catalog of creative differences with Steinman, was branded a "circus clown," and has survived Wolff-Parkinson-White Syndrome, cocaine, vocal malfunctions, being hit on the head during shot put at high school, and starring in a Spice Girls movie. You could say he has been to hell and back several times over. **MW**

M

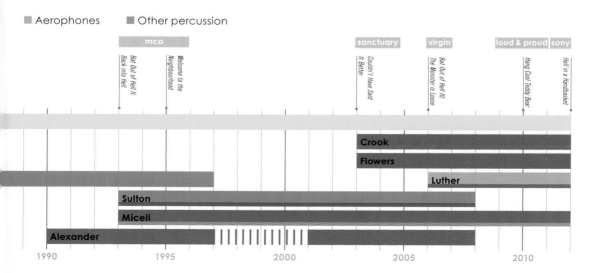

■ Aerophones   ■ Other percussion

mca | sanctuary | virgin | loud & proud | sony

Bat Out of Hell II: Back Into Hell | *Welcome to the Neighbourhood* | *Couldn't Have Said It Better* | *Bat Out of Hell III: The Monster is Loose* | *Hang Cool Teddy Bear* | *Hell In a Handbasket*

Crook
Flowers
Luther
Sulton
Miceli
Alexander

1990 | 1995 | 2000 | 2005 | 2010

megadeth 1984–present

Dave Mustaine
b. September 13, 1961

David Ellefson
b. November 12, 1964

Chris Broderick
b. March 6, 1970

Shawn Drover
b. May 5, 1966

Chris Poland
b. December 1, 1957

Gar Samuelson
b. Feb 18, 1958
d. July 22, 1999

Jeff Young
b. March 31, 1962

Marty Friedman
b. December 8, 1962

Alongside Metallica, Slayer, and Anthrax, Megadeth form a quarter of the so-called Big Four, an elite group that popularized thrash metal in the eighties. Thrash—a faster, more aggressive form of the heavy metal that had influenced all the bands—found a commercial home thanks to its combination of melodic hooks and uncompromising riffage. And no band mastered this trick as ably as Megadeth.

Founded by ex-Metallica guitarist **Dave Mustaine** with bassist **David Ellefson** (nicknamed "Junior" to avoid confusion, to his irritation) in 1984, Megadeth started life with the aim of being faster, heavier, and generally more "metal" than Mustaine's former band, against whom he harbored a very public grudge.

While this was a futile ambition (Metallica went on to become metal's biggest band of all time), the band nonetheless unleashed a sequence of classic albums, fueled by their leader's world-class guitar pyrotechnics and knack for a catchy chorus. After what Mustaine described as a "$4,000 piece of crap first album" (1985's *Killing Is My Business… and Business Is Good*), the group's first major hit was *Peace Sells… but Who's Buying?* (1986). The album was a stormer, despite tensions between the two Daves, guitarist **Chris Poland**, and drummer **Gar Samuelson** that threatened to derail it, exacerbated by all four being drug abusers at the time. A side-effect of Mustaine's habit was that he often derided his contemporaries in public, establishing feuds against a raft of bands including Slayer and Pantera. (In later years, he

claimed—with some justification—that the media encouraged and promoted these disagreements.)

Megadeth stepped up their game with *So Far, So Good… So What?* (1988) and *Rust in Peace* (1990), by their most commercially successful lineup, featuring guitarist **Marty Friedman** and drummer Nick Menza. This platinum-selling period of success peaked with the U.S. Top Five albums *Countdown to Extinction* (1992) and *Youthanasia* (1994), but fashions were changing in metal and Megadeth found it difficult to expand their profile through the rest of the decade.

After a final U.S. Top Ten million-seller—1997's *Cryptic Writings*—they made an ill-advised switch to a softer sound with *Risk* (1999) and *The World Needs a Hero* (2001). Then Mustaine injured his arm, rendering him unable to play guitar, and dissolved the band. A lawsuit from Ellefson seemed to spell the end, but Mustaine returned after a year's physiotherapy with a new lineup and album, *The System Has Failed* (2004).

Since then Megadeth have rebuilt their profile with admirable speed, releasing acclaimed albums that adhere to the technical thrash template that made them famous. Now clean and sober and with the feud with his old band (mostly) resolved, Mustaine has become an elder statesman of thrash, revered once more for his musical and songwriting skills.

Against all expectations, Ellefson rejoined Megadeth in 2010 in time for a Big Four tour series initiated by Metallica, and the two Daves' comeback album, *Th1rt3en*, marks a welcome return to form. **JM**

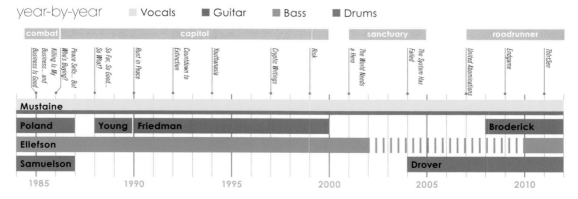

men at work 1979–present

Colin Hay
b. June 29, 1953

Ron Strykert
b. August 18, 1957

Greg Ham
b. September 27, 1953
d. April 19, 2012

Jerry Speiser
b. 1953

John Rees
b. unknown

There are plenty of argumentative bands in this book, but Men at Work hold a special place: the lead guitarist was arrested in 2009 for threatening to kill the lead vocalist. But let us start in happier times.

Colin Hay, born in Scotland, emigrated to Australia with his parents when he was fourteen. He later formed an acoustic duo with **Ron Strykert**, who he had met while working on a stage musical. In 1979, they expanded into a pub band with **Greg Ham** (keyboards), **Jerry Speiser** (drums), and classical violinist **John Rees** (bass). Influenced by The Police and The Cars, they called themselves Men at Work and secured a residency at a hotel in Melbourne. A CBS accountant spotted them there and recommended them to the A&R division. As a result, they made *Business as Usual* with U.S. producer Peter Mclan.

Hay said that he wrote "Who Can It Be Now" "in the middle of the bush with my girlfriend." The song, a study in paranoia, topped the charts in Australia and, after a successful tour supporting Fleetwood Mac, in the U.S. The follow-up, "Down Under," was about Australians who go overseas and want to return, parodying Aussie life with its "fried-out combies" and Vegemite sandwiches. Mclan suggested the reggae rhythm and its promotion was helped by a comic video, heavily rotated on MTV. (When the publishers of a 1934 song, "Kookaburra," sued for plagiarism, the judge ruled that only Ham's flute line was similar and they were awarded five per cent of the royalties.)

Having achieved the rare feat of topping the U.K. and U.S. albums and singles charts simultaneously, the stage was well set for *Cargo* (1983). A bleak album, lacking the distinctiveness of *Business as Usual*, it nonetheless promptly went platinum, thanks to its hits "Overkill" and the anti-war "It's a Mistake."

Rees and Speiser left during the making of 1985's *Two Hearts*. The album was completed with session musicians and synthesizers, and even managed to be certified gold in the U.S., but arguments over management and songwriting royalties left Hay on his own, including a tour of China with a makeshift band. He developed a solo career with *Looking for Jack* (1987), *Wayfaring Sons* (1990), *Peaks and Valleys* (1993), and *Topanga* (1995), appeared in films, and toured in Ringo Starr's All-Starr Band in 2003.

Hay and Ham reformed a version of Men at Work for a South American tour, which led to the live *Brazil* (1996). The lineup has varied ever since. They appeared at the 2000 Summer Olympics in Sydney with actor Paul Hogan of *Crocodile Dundee* fame, but Strykert did not join them because he felt he had been cheated out of royalties. Instead, he worked with the Nudist Funk Orchestra, cut a solo album, *Paradise* (2009), and was arrested when he threatened to kill Hay. The singer assured fans that Strykert did not mean it—but, like the protagonist of "Who Can It Be Now," he may be wary when somebody knocks at his door. **SL**

M

year-by-year   ▪ Vocals   ■ Guitar   ■ Bass   ■ Drums   ■ Keyboards   ▪ Aerophones

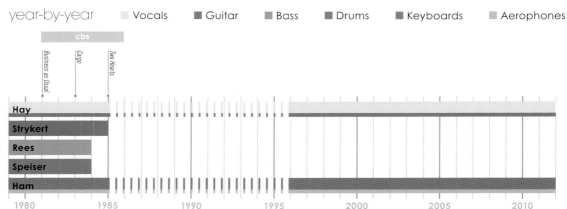

metallica 1981–present

James Hetfield
b. August 3, 1963

Lars Ulrich
b. December 26, 1963

Kirk Hammett
b. November 18, 1962

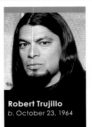

Robert Trujillo
b. October 23, 1964

Dave Mustaine
b. September 13, 1961

Ron McGovney
b. November 2, 1962

San Francisco-based quartet Metallica are metal's biggest-selling band and have been since the mid-nineties, when their expert combination of anthemic songs and dynamic live performances first elevated the band to the top of the international music scene. Some have labeled the group "this generation's Led Zeppelin," with good reason: the number of Metallica albums (five of which topped the U.S. chart) sold over the band's three decades is approaching 100 million, and they continue to play the biggest stadiums with little indication that any members are slowing down.

Those members' every move is scrutinized in the rock media these days, a scenario that could scarcely have been imagined when the first incarnation of Metallica gathered in Los Angeles in late 1981. Guitarist and singer **James Hetfield**, a fan of stadium rock acts such as Aerosmith, had been through a series of high-school bands, but only made headway when he met Danish drummer **Lars Ulrich** through a musicians-wanted ad in a local magazine.

The pair had jammed before and parted ways, but their second meeting was driven by Ulrich's need to form a band: he had offered to provide a song for a compilation, *Metal Massacre*. Adding Hetfield's roommate **Ron McGovney** on bass and recruiting session guitarist Lloyd Grant, the group cut "Hit the Lights."

Metallica replaced Grant with hotshot guitarist **Dave Mustaine** and began to tour the Los Angeles area. Demo recordings appeared, the most widely-distributed of which was 1982's *Power Metal*, but the group made serious progress when McGovney was replaced by San Francisco native **Cliff Burton**. A move north to Burton's home town followed and, in early 1983, the band traveled to New York, where record-store owner Jon Zazula had offered to help them find a deal. After fruitless attempts to raise industry interest, Zazula founded the Megaforce label to release Metallica's debut album, *Kill 'Em All*, recorded after they replaced the erratic Mustaine with Exodus guitarist **Kirk Hammett**. The album's fast, aggressive blend of intensity and melody established the thrash metal sound in America: within a couple of years, Metallica were the leaders of the genre's so-called Big Four, alongside Slayer, Anthrax, and Megadeth (the last of these formed by a very bitter Mustaine).

The Hetfield/Hammett/Burton/Ulrich lineup—Metallica's most critically acclaimed incarnation—unleashed scene-redefining albums in *Ride the Lightning* (1984) and *Master of Puppets* (1986). Their profile exploded on a U.S. tour with Ozzy Osbourne, but a tragic setback occurred in September 1986 when Burton died in a tour-bus accident in Sweden.

M

year-by-year ■ Vocals ■ Guitar ■ Bass ■ Drums

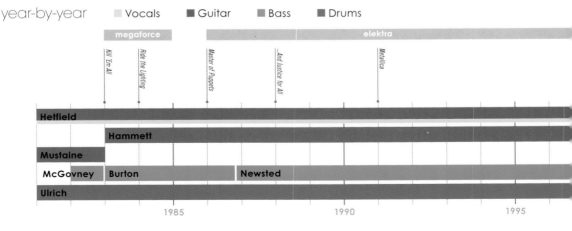

Cliff Burton
b. February 10, 1962
d. September 27, 1986

Jason Newsted
b. March 3, 1963

The originator of many of Metallica's most musically beguiling passages and an authority within the band, Burton had taught Hetfield elements of musical theory that informed 1988's ...And Justice for All. The brutal album—a Top Ten smash on both sides of the Atlantic—featured (albeit barely audibly) their new bassist, former Flotsam and Jetsam man **Jason Newsted** (who had made his Metallica debut with 1987's jolly The $5.98 E.P.—Garage Days Re-Revisited).

In 1991 Metallica took a giant leap toward the mainstream with their fifth, self-titled set, aka "The Black Album." This dispensed with the thrashier elements of their earlier work and, unlike Justice, placed Newsted's bass high in the mix for a rich sound that paid enormous dividends. As the album soared towards fifteen million sales in the U.S. alone, Metallica became a touring machine, embarking on global jaunts that lasted years. (A bad-tempered excursion with Guns N' Roses in 1992 left Metallica the clear winners). Meanwhile, even two albums held in lesser regard by fans—Load (1996) and ReLoad (1997)—topped charts around the world and sold millions.

A covers album, Garage, Inc. (1998), and a live set recorded with the San Francisco Symphony, S&M (1999)—though both enjoyable and multi-million-selling—suggested Metallica's innovatory spirit was waning. When they did pursue a new direction, it was with 2003's deliberately under-produced St. Anger (which went multi-platinum around the world despite being very hard to listen to). The album's self-destructive conception was documented in the gripping movie Some Kind of Monster, which followed the band's experiences with rehab and therapy and the replacement of Newsted by former Suicidal Tendencies and Ozzy Osbourne bassist **Robert Trujillo**.

Metallica returned from the abyss with the above-average Death Magnetic (2008) and toured as part of a Big Four of Thrash package in 2010, also the year of their induction into the Rock and Roll Hall of Fame. A collaboration with Lou Reed—2011's Lulu—met with universal horror, but the group's thirtieth anniversary in December of that year occasioned celebratory shows, whose guests included Dave Mustaine, Ozzy Osbourne, Black Sabbath's Geezer Butler, Alice in Chains' Jerry Cantrell, and Judas Priest's Rob Halford.

Long a constant on the international summer festival circuit, Metallica launched their own event, Orion Music + More, in 2012. As illustrated by 2009's phenomenal DVDs Français pour une nuit (2009) and Orgullo, Pasión Y Gloria: Tres Noches en la Ciudad de México, the band and their classic-packed repertoire remain a force to be reckoned with on stage. **JM**

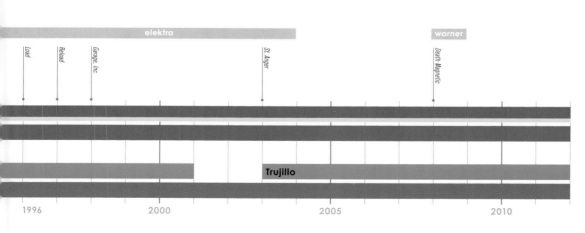

elektra

warner

Load

ReLoad

Garage, Inc.

St. Anger

Death Magnetic

Trujillo

1996   2000   2005   2010

Kill 'Em All (1983)

Ride the Lightning (1984)

Master of Puppets (1986)

...And Justice for All (1988)

Metallica (1991)

Load (1996)

Reload (1997)

Garage, Inc (1998)

St. Anger (2003)

Death Magnetic (2008)

Cliff Burton and **James Hetfield** in 1981, playing the songs that would become *Kill 'em All*.

Burton, **Lars Ulrich**, **Hetfield**, and **Kirk Hammett** ride the lightning.

Burton, whose death in 1986 dealt the band a tragic blow.

With bassist **Jason Newsted** (far left) and mascot "Doris" on the Damaged Justice tour.

Now one of the biggest bands on the planet, Metallica rock Britain's Sheffield Arena in November 1992, on the mammoth Wherever We May Roam tour.

Hetfield and Ulrich in Illinois in June 1996, on the Lollapalooza leg of the Poor Touring Me tour for *Load*.

Hetfield and Ulrich—the band's founders and creative driving forces—rockin' Worcester, Massachusetts, in 1997.

Hammett on the Garage Remains the Same tour in 1999.

Rob Trujillo channeling the spirit of Cliff Burton on the Madly in Anger with the World tour, in Belgium in 2003.

With The Kinks' Ray Davies on a break from *Death Magnetic* duties.

midnight oil 1976–2002

Rob Hirst
b. 1955

Andrew James
b. Unknown

Jim Moginie
b. May 18, 1956

Peter Garrett
b. April 16, 1953

Martin Rotsey
b. February 18, year unknown

Peter Gifford
b. 1955

Bones Hillman
b. 1958

Australian rock band Midnight Oil created music that appealed to both mind and body. Their sound was energetic and danceable, while the lyrics dealt sensitively with nuclear proliferation, the environment, and the plight of Australia's indigenous people.

Based in Sydney, drummer **Rob Hirst**, bassist **Andrew James**, and keyboard player/guitarist **Jim Moginie** were performing under the name Farm when, in 1972, they were joined by law student **Peter Garrett**. Playing a set that drew heavily on English progressive rock, Farm remained a part-time occupation until Garrett completed his degree in 1976, from which time they became known as Midnight Oil. With a new name came a departure in their music, the addition of second guitarist **Martin Rotsey** heralding a shift toward a faster, more aggressive rock style.

Midnight Oil gigged furiously in their early days, playing over 200 shows a year. They quickly built up a solid following on the Sydney bar circuit based on a reputation for loud, high-energy performances. Their 1978 debut, *Midnight Oil*, was less successful in capturing the essence of the band's live work, but their growing cult following nonetheless pushed it into the lower reaches of the Australian chart.

Signed to CBS, the band were expected to reap international rewards with *Place Without a Postcard*. The experience, however, was not a happy one: the dilution of their new wave sound for a more commercial style placed an uncomfortable emphasis on Garrett's vocals. A balance between adventurous modern pop and Garrett's increasingly political lyrics was finally struck on 1982's *10, 9, 8, 7, 6, 5, 4, 3, 2, 1*. This proved to be "The Oils'" breakthough, hitting the Australian Top Three, remaining on the chart for the next four years, and providing an opportunity for the band to broaden their fanbase for the first time.

Peter Garrett was now becoming newsworthy in his own right. Cutting an imposing, shaven-headed figure, he ran a high-profile—if ultimately unsuccessful—campaign as a candidate for the Nuclear Disarmament Party at elections in 1984.

In 1987, Midnight Oil produced their defining album, *Diesel and Dust*. It topped the chart at home, and hit the Top Thirty in Europe and the U.S., thanks to "Beds Are Burning," a global smash that dealt with the return of Australia's desert lands to Aboriginal tribes. The band cemented their international success with heavy touring and similarly styled big-sellers such as *Blue Sky Mine*, *Earth and Sun and Moon*, and *Breathe*.

In 2002, committing himself to Australian politics, Garrett announced he was leaving the band. As a candidate for the Australian Labor Party, he won a seat at the 2004 elections, and three years later was named Minister for the Environment, Heritage, and the Arts. The Midnight Oil name was laid to rest, and is now revived only for one-off benefit concerts. **TB**

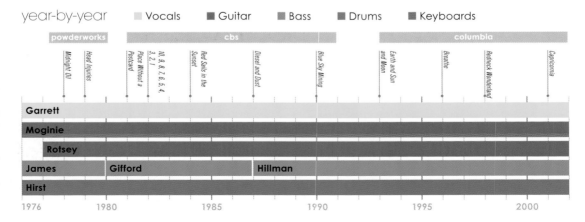

year-by-year ▪ Vocals ▪ Guitar ▪ Bass ▪ Drums ▪ Keyboards

	powderworks	cbs		columbia

Albums: *Midnight Oil*, *Head Injuries*, *Place Without a Postcard*, *10, 9, 8, 7, 6, 5, 4, 3, 2, 1*, *Red Sails in the Sunset*, *Diesel and Dust*, *Blue Sky Mining*, *Earth and Sun and Moon*, *Breathe*, *Redneck Wonderland*, *Capricornia*

	1976	1980	1985	1990	1995	2000
Garrett						
Moginie						
Rotsey						
James → Gifford → Hillman						
Hirst						

steve miller 1966–present

Steve Miller
b. October 5, 1943

Lonnie Turner
b. February 24, 1947

Tim Davis
b. November 29, 1943

Gary Mallaber
b. October 11, 1946

Byron Allred
b. October 27, 1948

David Denny
b. February 5, 1948

Norton Buffalo
b. Sept 28, 1951
d. Oct 30, 2009

Gerald Johnson
b. Unknown

"Enter **Steve Miller**: man without a face" ran the headline on a *Rolling Stone* feature in 1976. It was not a jibe. On all his albums, his visage had been blurred, even masked, and the laid back blues-jazz-rock guitarist himself had said: "I want people to enjoy my music. I don't want to be a personality." So there you have it: one of rock's "A-list," happy to give the limelight to his alter egos—"The joker," "The space cowboy," "The gangster of love," and, er, "Maurice."

Little Steve had a formative upbringing. At five years old, he was given advice and encouragement by guitar legend Les Paul. Bluesman T-Bone Walker played guitar at his house when Miller was nine. At fourteen, Miller backed electric blues pioneer Jimmy Reid in a Dallas bar. This was a boy with pedigree, even before he hustled gigs in Chicago with Muddy Waters, Howlin' Wolf, and The Butterfield Blues Band.

But blues was not a happening scene, whereas San Francisco's psychedelia was. The guitarist played at the Matrix club on the same night Grace Slick joined Jefferson Airplane on stage. This good omen was sealed by a record-breaking $50,000 deal with no artistic strings. Steve headed to London to hang out with The Beatles' engineer Glyn Johns, who gave Miller's albums segued tunes and the best effects that two four-track machines could muster. Jamming with Paul McCartney one night led to two cuts on *Brave New World,* on which Macca is credited as Paul Ramon. (Nearly thirty years later, the two collaborated again on McCartney's *Flaming Pie.*)

The Steve Miller Band went through myriad personnel shifts—college friend Boz Scaggs played guitar on the first two albums—as they charged through albums and tours (supporting Hendrix and the Grateful Dead). It was a blur of rushed deadlines, band tensions, marriage, divorce, a broken neck, hepatitis, and having his guitar overdubbed by Jesse Ed Davis (because Miller had to do a promo tour). At one point he retreated home for eight months, only to re-emerge to self-produce his 1973 *Billboard* No. 2 album *The Joker* and its chart-topping title track.

After another hiatus, Miller emerged with his best songs yet, of which "Rock 'n Me," referencing Free's "All Right Now," gave him another U.S. No. 1. His third, "Abracadabra," came in 1982, but Miller's standout song is *Circle of Love*'s sixteen-minute "Macho City"— which, with its funky feel and trippy effects, made him an unlikely New York disco darling of the eighties.

Tired of playing the songs that comprised his thirteen million-selling *Greatest Hits 1974–78,* Miller took time out again before returning with *Bingo!* (2010) and *Let Your Hair Down* (2011). "Never in my wildest dreams," he admitted, "did I think that I'd be the guy on the radio that you can't move." **JaH**

M

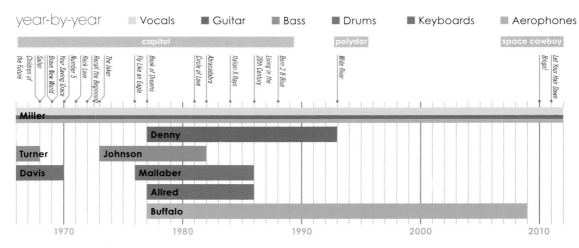

year-by-year ■ Vocals ■ Guitar ■ Bass ■ Drums ■ Keyboards ■ Aerophones

capitol · polydor · space cowboy

Children of the Future / Sailor / Brave New World / Your Saving Grace / Number 5 / Rock Love / Recall the Beginning... / The Joker / Fly Like an Eagle / Book of Dreams / Circle of Love / Abracadabra / Italian X Rays / Living in the 20th Century / Born 2 B Blue / Wide River / Bingo! / Let Your Hair Down

Miller

Denny

Turner

Johnson

Davis

Mallaber

Allred

Buffalo

1970 · 1980 · 1990 · 2000 · 2010

moby grape 1966–present

Skip Spence
b. April 18, 1946
d. April 16, 1999

Jerry Miller
b. July 10, 1943

Peter Lewis
b. July 15, 1945

Bob Mosley
b. December 4, 1942

Don Stevenson
b. October 15, 1942

"What's purple and lives at the bottom of the sea? Moby Grape." Lousy joke. Great band.

They formed in San Francisco in late 1966. Grueling eight-hour-day rehearsals at a converted paddleboat-turned-club, dubbed the Ark—in Sausalito, over the Golden Gate Bridge—morphed them into a tight, high-energy powerhouse. With three gutsy guitarists (**Skip Spence**, formerly drummer for the Jefferson Airplane, **Jerry Miller**, and **Peter Lewis**), plus bassist **Bob Mosley** and drummer **Don Stevenson**, the group were able to produce glorious five-part harmonies. And all five were songwriters.

Soon Moby Grape were the most talked-about band in San Francisco. Swamped by attention from labels, they opted to sign with Columbia and utilize the production skills of David Rubinson. (Thirty years on, Rubinson remembered their music as "the tightest, most musical, high-intensity stuff I'd ever heard.")

The exhilarating *Moby Grape* (1967) was recorded for a meagre $11,000 in three weeks. ("Fantastic!" said Robert Plant, who covered "Naked, If I Want To" and "8.05.") It alternated lovely acoustic offerings ("8:05") and ecstatic rock ("Hey Grandma" and "Fall on You"), run through with stinging solos. Spence's joyous "Omaha" ("It's so out of sight, bein' in love!") was probably their defining moment. Then the hype set in.

An overexcited Columbia released five singles from the album simultaneously, fatally diffusing their impact ("Omaha" made a meager No. 88 on the *Billboard* chart—and it was to be their only charting single). An over-the-top launch party at the Avalon Ballroom in June 1967 smacked queasily of over-commercialization, denting the band's credibility among nascent fans and critics. And it backfired anyway. Over 700 wine bottles were prepared, each bearing a special Moby Grape label—but no-one had thought to supply a single corkscrew. A stunning display of 10,000 purple orchids dropped snowflake-like onto the throng, but the smooth petals made the dancefloor treacherous. It all rather smacked of the circus—right down to an elephant, painted purple, lumbering down Sunset Boulevard.

Not long after, Spence, Miller, and Lewis were caught with marijuana and accused of consorting with underage girls in Marin County. The band appeared at the prestigious Monterey Pop festival, but legal complications saw them dropped from D.A. Pennebaker's documentary film of the event, *Monterey Pop* (1968). The album, however, made No. 24 and stayed on the *Billboard* charts for a more-than-respectable six months. But—incredibly—their momentum was already faltering.

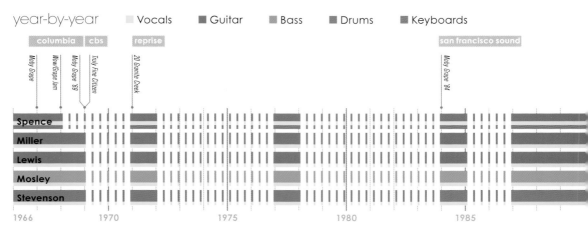

year-by-year   □ Vocals   ■ Guitar   ■ Bass   ■ Drums   ■ Keyboards

Sessions for the follow-up double set *Wow/Grape Jam* (1968, a U.S. No. 20) were highlighted by hard partying and sliding attention spans—though Columbia's Clive Davis had brought the band from Los Angeles to New York to work precisely to curtail such distractions. The tight ensemble playing, concision, and focus of their debut had vanished: "All the strings and horns on that album were there to make up for the lack of having a band," Stevenson admitted nearly thirty years later. Lewis briefly quit; Spence binged on acid. But still they could cut it— witness Spence's biker outing "Motorcycle Irene" and his bizarre thirties throwback "Just Like Gene Autry; A Foxtrot" (set to play at 78 rpm and recorded with extra pops and crackles for "authenticity"), and Miller and Stevenson's funky, tongue-in-cheek "Murder in My Heart for the Judge."

Spence's appetite for LSD, alcohol, heroin, and cocaine led to a gradual unraveling—at one point he was wielding an axe in the studio, and he allegedly kept a pet rat that he had trained to snort lines of cocaine with him. His addictions and subsequent mental illness saw him first detained in New York's Tombs prison, then temporarily committed to New York's Bellevue Hospital. (Afterward, he headed for Nashville to record the fractured but compelling *Oar*, released in 1969.) His contribution to the decent *Moby Grape '69* (1969; U.S. No. 113)—"Seeing," with its chorus of "Save me!"—made for a gripping goodbye.

Even as a Spence-less four-piece, Moby Grape impressed, easily able to cut it live. But their luck was running out. Mosley quit to join the U.S. Marines (briefly, as he was diagnosed with paranoid schizophrenia). Manager Matthew Katz won legal rights to the band's name and put his own fake Grape on the road. Lewis, Miller, and Stevenson recorded their final set, the country-inflected *Truly Fine Citizen* (1969), with session musician Bob Moore on bass; songs were credited to "T. Dell'Ara"—their road manager— to avoid legal hassle from Katz. And then they split.

Thrown together too quickly, burdened with impossible expectations, Moby Grape were stymied from the start. Touchingly, though, regular reunions took place in the subsequent decades (including Spence, before his death from lung cancer in 1999), mostly for live appearances—though the ex-Grapes also released four albums, including an arresting five-song set, *The Melvilles* (1990), issued only on cassette. Those get-togethers were born out of genuine friendship and the knowledge of just how good they had been. And, in July 2006, they finally won back the right to use that name. **RD**

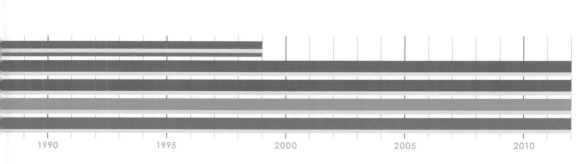

the moody blues 1964–present

Denny Laine
b. October 29, 1944

Ray Thomas
b. December 29, 1942

Graeme Edge
b. March 30, 1942

Mike Pinder
b. December 27, 1941

Clint Warwick
b. June 25, 1940
d. May 15, 2004

John Lodge
b. July 20, 1945

In one of rock's earliest brand sponsorship deals, five musicians from Britain's Midlands adopted the name MB Five in return for two thousand pounds' worth of sponsorship from local brewers Mitchells & Butlers. However, the Birmingham-based group—keyboardist **Mike Pinder**, guitarist **Denny Laine**, flautist and vocalist **Ray Thomas**, drummer **Graeme Edge,** and bassist **Clint Warwick**—soon became The Moody Blues.

At the tail-end of a British tour with Chuck Berry in January 1965, their aching "Go Now"—a cover of an R&B song by Bessie Banks—topped the U.K. chart. It also hit No. 10 in the U.S., although follow-up releases and their debut album, 1965's *The Magnificent Moodies,* failed to make much impact.

The quintet supported The Beatles on their final British tour in December 1965, but the following year saw the exits of Warwick (replaced for a Danish tour by Rod Clarke) and Laine (later to reappear alongside ex-Move man Trevor Burton in the splendidly named Balls, then Paul McCartney's Wings).

The group split in October 1966... only to re-form the following month, with bassist/vocalist **John Lodge** (who had played with Thomas and Pinder in their pre-Moodies band Ed Riot & the Rebels) and guitarist/vocalist **Justin Hayward** (who had asked singer Eric Burdon for a job in a new lineup of The Animals, only

for Burdon to recommend him to Ray Thomas instead). The new band moved to Belgium to avoid punitive U.K. taxes and plotted their evolution from pop into conceptual progressive rock.

The first result, unveiled over a year later, could not have been more jaw-dropping: the sumptuous, transatlantic Top Ten hit "Nights in White Satin." The conceptual *Days of Future Passed* (1967), based on themes of different times of day and night, made No. 3 in the U.S. and No. 27 at home, and heralded a fruitful, decade-long relationship with producer Tony Clarke.

With a modest stealth that made Pink Floyd look like Led Zeppelin, the next ten years saw The Moody Blues become one of Britain's most internationally successful acts. "There was a lot of pressure," Hayward told writer Craig Rosen. "The nature of the business was that every record you made was tremendously important." "Tremendously important" wasn't a view shared by the rock press, who dismissed the band when they paid them any attention at all. "Moody Blues devotees seemed to think they were getting something higher toned than mere rock," sneered *Rolling Stone.* "They were kidding themselves."

Nonetheless, of the seven studio albums the group issued between 1968 and 1978, three topped the U.K. chart (1969's *On the Threshold of a Dream,* 1970's

M

year-by-year ■ Vocals ■ Guitar ■ Bass ■ Drums ■ Keyboards

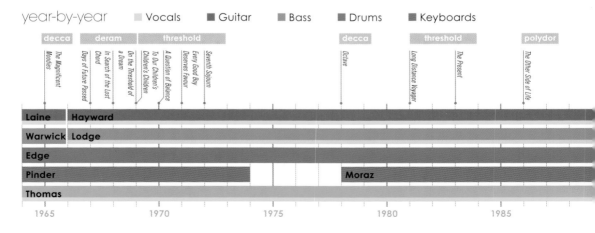

Justin Hayward
b. October 14, 1946

Patrick Moraz
b. June 24, 1948

A Question of Balance, and 1971's *Every Good Boy Deserves Favour*), and one (1972's *Seventh Sojourn*) hit No. 1 in the States. The latter's path to success was smoothed by the belated Stateside success of "Nights in White Satin," which in turn sent *Days of Future Passed* into the U.S. Top Ten, just weeks before *Seventh Sojourn*. The latter bequeathed "I'm Just a Singer (in a Rock 'n' Roll Band)," their first major hit since "Question" from *A Question of Balance*.

After a nine-month world tour, with Mike Pinder exhaused, the Moodies split in early 1974. Hayward and Lodge forged ahead with 1975's *Blue Jays*, another transatlantic success that yielded the U.K. Top Ten hit "Blue Guitar" (eclipsing Pinder's *The Promise*, Ray Thomas's *From Mighty Oaks,* and The Graeme Edge Band's *Kick Off Your Muddy Boots*).

The band re-formed in 1978 but, by the time *Octave* (1978) was released, producer Tony Clarke— effectively "the sixth Moody"—had quit. Nonetheless, the album took them straight back into transatlantic best-seller charts. Meanwhile, Hayward scored a hit with "Forever Autumn" from Jeff Wayne's *War of the Worlds* album. Their profile was maintained by a successful world tour—before which Pinder quit and was replaced by former Yes keyboard player **Patrick Moraz**—and a U.K. hit reissue of "Nights in White Satin."

Long Distance Voyager (1981) produced by Pip Williams (he joined them after a run of success with Status Quo, whose resemblance to the Moodies ended at nationality), took a year of work. The effort was rewarded when the album followed *Seventh Sojourn* to the top of the U.S. and Canadian charts, and went Top Ten at home. "It was like being in a gang again," Hayward told Craig Rosen. "We had that feeling again of all being together."

When the follow-up, 1983's *The Present,* flopped, it seemed the Moodies' time had passed. However, *The Other Side of Life* (1986)—produced by David Bowie sidekick Tony Visconti—restored them to the big league, thanks to the U.S. hit "Your Wildest Dreams."

Subsequent albums traced a gentle commercial decline. After Moraz's acrimonious departure in 1991, Bias Boshell and Paul Bliss were recruited to complete *Keys of the Kingdom* (1991). Neither that nor *Strange Times* (1999) were major successes, but the band remained a reliable draw on the live circuit.

Thomas retired in 2002, leaving Edge, Hayward, and Lodge as the band's nucleus. (Flautist Norda Mullen graced 2003's Christmas-themed *December*). With new keyboard player Alan Hewitt they continue to tour successfully, while live sets and compilations add to their multi-million-selling legacy. **BS/BM**

M

■ Aerophones

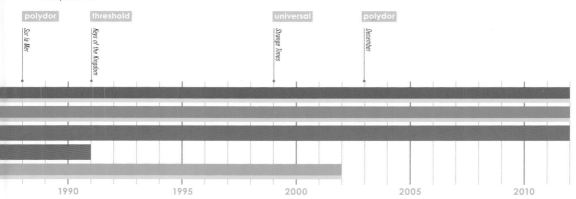

van morrison 1958–present

Van Morrison
b. August 31, 1945

Peter Bardens
b. June 19, 1945
d. January 22, 2002

Jim Armstrong
b. July 24, 1944

Ray Elliot
b. September 13, 1943

Jack Schroer
b. January 12, 1944
d. June 23, 1995

Jef Labes
b. June 26, 1947

John Platania
b. December 31, 1946

David Hayes
b. February 9, 1950

Born in Belfast in 1945, **Van Morrison** is one of rock's most idiosyncratic artists. In a career spanning five decades, he has earned a curmudgeonly reputation but is revered for epochal records and a refusal to compromise. "When I see Van now," wrote J. Geils Band front-man and R&B expert Peter Wolf in *Rolling Stone*, "I still see the same raw power and passion that he displayed more than forty years ago."

Morrison carved a career in music from a young age, settling into a local R&B scene in his early teens and touring internationally with The Monarchs before his eighteenth birthday. His name, however, was made on his return home when he formed Them with members of another Belfast band, The Gamblers.

Them enjoyed immediate success, with "Here Comes the Night" and "Baby Please Don't Go" breaching the U.K. Top Ten in 1965. But within a year of their breakthrough, they split and Morrison headed to New York to work with producer Bert Berns on fashioning a signature solo style.

Blue-eyed soul, R&B—call it what you will—Morrison brought his firebrand persona to established forms, creating an instant classic with "Brown Eyed

Girl" and assembling songs that would make up his solo debut, *Blowin' Your Mind!* (1967). The album's hurried release on Bang Records was against Morrison's wishes and, after Berns' sudden death, he set about wresting control of his career. This pursuit of artistic freedom saw his contract bought by Warner, who gave him space to record a first great statement.

Astral Weeks (1968) marked a dramatic shift from the Berns sessions, with Morrison creating a wild fusion of jazz, soul, and folk, framing lyrical streams of consciousness. He was backed by seasoned jazz players who worked their magic from the loosest instructions while the singer delivered timeless, fiercely evocative tales of "Madame George" and "Cyprus Avenue." The album made little impact at the time, but became a mainstay of all-time classic lists.

Moondance (1970) relied on a more conventional structure but lacked none of its predecessor's soul. "Into the Mystic" and "And It Stoned Me" are wide-eyed epiphanies, while "Moondance" is a romantic swing. These more approachable songs drove *Moondance* into the *Billboard* Top Thirty. Astonishingly prolific, Morrison released another album in 1970, *His*

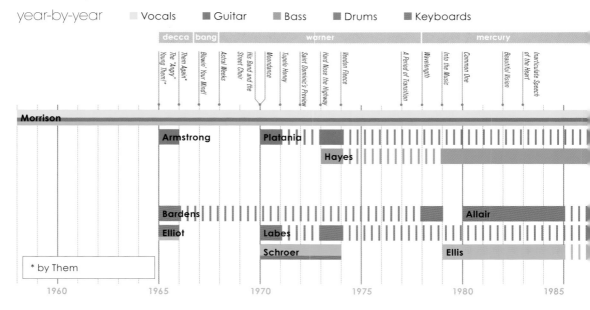

year-by-year   ▫ Vocals   ◼ Guitar   ◼ Bass   ◼ Drums   ◼ Keyboards

Pee Wee Ellis
b. April 21, 1941

John Allair
b. Unknown

Georgie Fame
b. June 26, 1943

Nicky Scott
b. Unknown

Liam Bradley
b. Unknown

Matthew Holland
b. Unknown

Geraint Watkins
b. February 5, 1951

Band and the Street Choir, which featured the U.S. Top Ten hit "Domino." The mood was sustained on 1971's *Tupelo Honey*, initially conceived as a country album and recorded live with minimal studio fuss. Morrison would stretch himself again on *Saint Dominic's Preview* (1972) with its lengthy, semi-improvised epics "Listen to the Lion" and "Independence Day" nuzzling up against the straight, joyous pop hit "Jackie Wilson Said (I'm in Heaven When You Smile)."

Although 1973's *Hard Nose the Highway* proved underwhelming, Morrison served a timely reminder of his talents with the following year's live *It's Too Late to Stop Now*, a thrilling tour de force recorded with the Caledonia Soul Orchestra and featuring a legendary, extended version of "Cyprus Avenue." Morrison's golden run would come to an end later that year with *Veedon Fleece,* before a three-year hiatus.

Returning in 1977 with *A Period of Transition*, Morrison embarked on another barely broken series of fine albums. *Wavelength*, *Into the Music*, and *Common One* showcased his retreat into spiritualism and his Celtic roots without snubbing commercial possibilities—*Into the Music* even yielded his first

solo U.K. hit single, "Bright Side of the Road." "Van demonstrated his fantastic love for all of this wonderful music," observed Mark Knopfler of Dire Straits, "but he also pushed out the sides of it all the time."

As the eighties wore on, Morrison found a smoother sound and made unexpected in-roads into mainstream radio with *Avalon Sunset* (1989), thanks to its gorgeous ballad "Have I Told You Lately" and a surprising duet with British pop mainstay Cliff Richard, "Whenever God Shines His Light." His new-found reach bled into *Enlightenment* (1990) and its "Real Real Gone," but mainly into *The Best of Van Morrison* (also 1990) which spent more than a year on the U.K. chart.

Typically, Morrison shrank from the mainstream, principally into the blues where he spent much of the next twenty years, often alongside **Georgie Fame**, but also in association with blues legends John Lee Hooker and B.B. King. Critical praise thinned out, but there was still much to enjoy on 1999's robust *Back on Top*, 2002's picking over of past glories on *Down the Road*, and 2005's *Billboard* Top Thirty hit *Magic Time*. Five decades down the line, Morrison's place in the rock pantheon remains unthreatened. **MaH**

M

■ Aerophones

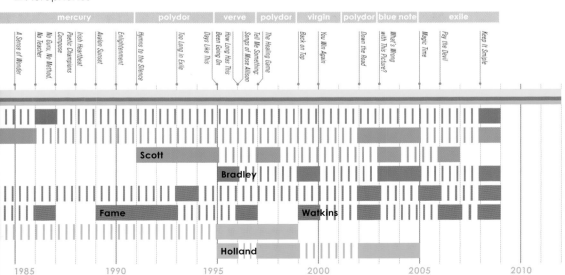

mötley crüe 1981–present

Vince Neil
b. February 8, 1961

Mick Mars
b. May 4, 1951

Nikki Sixx
b. December 11, 1958

Tommy Lee
b. October 3, 1962

John Corabi
b. April 26, 1959

Randy Castillo
b. December 18, 1950
d. March 26, 2002

Glam rock, hair metal, poodlecore—whatever you choose to name the uniquely Californian variant of hard rock that emerged from Los Angeles in the early eighties, the music owes a debt to Mötley Crüe, the band who first added hairspray to heavy metal. While rockers wearing makeup were nothing new—thanks to Kiss, Alice Cooper, and the New York Dolls—Mötley refined the recipe and met with enormous success.

The group were the invention of bassist **Nikki Sixx** (born Frank Feranna, Jr., he legally adopted his stage name in later years). Having played the L.A. club scene in the band London—which he founded in 1978 and which, after his departure, included future members of Guns N' Roses, W.A.S.P., and Cinderella—Sixx sought a group with better prospects. He encountered drummer **Tommy Lee** (Thomas Bass), who recruited high-school friend and singer **Vince Neil** (Vincent Wharton). Guitarist **Mick Mars** (Robert Deal) joined after placing an advertisement in a music newspaper. Mötley Crüe were born.

The band's early years were chaotic, if only a small percentage of their autobiography *The Dirt* is to be believed. Between writing and playing, the quartet worked their way through bewildering amounts of groupies and drugs in an apparently endless parade

of debauchery that would have killed lesser—or less lucky—men. But this did not stop them creating classic albums that stand the test of time three decades later, beginning with 1981's *Too Fast for Love* (issued on Mötley's own Leathür label, then remixed by Queen producer Roy Thomas Baker and issued on Elektra).

Controversy was never far away: *Shout at the Devil* (1983) caused an uproar for its supposedly satanic connotations. The furor was helped along by tales of supernatural occurrences that had allegedly taken place in the studio during its recording.

As the decade passed, the Crüe honed their image and writing. *Girls, Girls, Girls* (1987) and its hit title track (accompanied by a video heavy on Harleys, bourbon, and strippers) established them as the poster boys for heavy metal hedonism.

But the party could not last and the four took time out to clean up: Sixx and Neil quit heroin and alcohol respectively (only to both lapse later). In Sixx's case, this was timely: an overdose had left him clinically dead in 1987, although he was revived by paramedics (he immortalized the incident in "Kickstart My Heart"). Unlike many reformed musicians, Mötley Crüe continued to write good music in sobriety, releasing the career-best and U.S. No. 1 *Dr. Feelgood* in 1989.

year-by-year ■ Vocals ■ Guitar ■ Bass ■ Drums

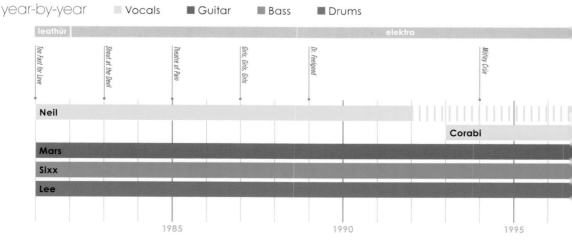

Samantha Maloney
b. December 11, 1975

As with many hair-metal bands, the Crüe suffered from the advent of grunge and alternative rock in the early nineties. Bands such as Warrant, Ratt, and Cinderella—who owed much to Mötley—lost their profile almost entirely, with only Guns N' Roses and Mötley themselves surviving the cull. However, the band barely scraped by, especially after Neil quit for a solo career in 1992. His replacement, ex-Scream singer **John Corabi**, did an assured job on 1994's self-titled comeback album, but fans missed the charismatic Neil and the Crüe faced oblivion.

After a couple of years of bickering with their label and with each other, the Neil-fronted incarnation returned with 1997's gold-selling *Generation Swine*. Having made it through the ensuing tour despite Sixx attempting to throttle the singer, they set out again in 1998 for a *Greatest Hits* excursion. This time it was Lee—who had had plenty of time to ponder his future with Mötley and his own Methods of Mayhem while in jail for tussling with Pamela Anderson—who walked.

The group enlisted ex-Ozzy Osbourne drummer **Randy Castillo** and issued the gloriously self-parodic *New Tattoo* (2000), only for it to sink without a trace. Then cancer forced Castillo (who sadly died in 2002) to cede the drum stool to Hole's **Samantha Maloney**.

While Sixx formed Brides of Destruction with Guns N' Roses founder Tracii Guns, Mötley's commercial fortunes got a shot in the arm with 2001's *The Dirt*, a jaw-droppingly candid autobiography. Inevitably, the classic lineup reunited to capitalize on this good fortune, with the platinum-selling hits set *Red, White, & Crüe*, and a customarily spectacular tour.

In the aftermath, remastered and live albums jostled solo efforts by Sixx (the gripping *Heroin Diaries* book and Sixx:A.M.'s album of the same name, made with future Guns N' Roses guitarist DJ Ashba); Lee (the *Tommyland* book and a second Methods of Mayhem album); and Neil (the droll autobiography *Tattoos & Tequila* and a covers album of the same title).

Saints of Los Angeles (2008) restored them to the U.S. Top Five for the first time in over a decade, and the group embarked on the first of two summer Crüe Fests. Neil suggested a 2012 residency in Las Vegas may be the band's last hurrah, only for them to announce a tour that year with Kiss (thirty years after the Crüe first supported their New York godfathers— an excursion that ended with Sixx and Lee getting intimately acquainted with then Kiss drummer Eric Carr's girlfriend). And, as we've seen, not even death can keep the Crüe down. **JM/BM**

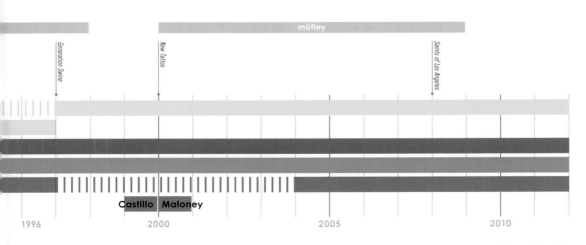

Too Fast for Love
(1981)

Shout at the Devil
(1983)

Theatre of Pain
(1985)

Girls, Girls, Girls
(1987)

Dr. Feelgood
(1989)

Mötley Crüe (1994)

Generation Swine
(1997)

New Tattoo (2000)

**Saints of Los
Angeles** (2008)

Singer **Vince Neil** emulates the *Too Fast for Love* cover pose.

Tommy Lee's kit tilts on the *Theatre of Pain* tour. The album's cover is on his bass drums.

With Ozzy Osbourne, clutching gold awards for *Shout at the Devil*.

Nikki Sixx rocks New York on the *Girls, Girls, Girls* tour.

Mick Mars—the band's "musical heartbeat," says **Vince Neil**—onstage.

Neil's replacement, **John Corabi**, gets into the Motley spirit.

The late **Randy Castillo**, drummer on the under-rated *New Tattoo*.

The reunited **Mars**, **Lee**, **Sixx**, and **Neil** make an impression at the Guitar Center's RockWalk in Hollywood, in 1997.

The inaugural Crüe Fest explodes at the Verizon Wireless Music Center, in Noblesville, Indiana, in 2008.

motörhead 1975–present

Lemmy
b. December 24, 1945

Phil Campbell
b. May 7, 1961

Mikkey Dee
b. October 31, 1963

Larry Wallis
b. 1949

Lucas Fox
b. Unknown

Phil Taylor
b. September 21, 1954

Occupying an uncategorizable space somewhere between heavy metal, biker rock, and rock 'n' roll, Motörhead have been making music that is loud and violent—but still intelligent—since 1975. At the time of writing, the band—led, as ever, by singer and bassist Ian "**Lemmy**" Kilmister—have released no fewer than twenty studio albums and a similar number of live records, compilations, and EPs. Motörhead are an international rock institution—and, when their time is up, as it no doubt will be within the next decade or so, they will be irreplaceable.

Lemmy, as he is universally known, is the band's linchpin and a man whose opinions and image have allowed him to transcend the status of mere musician to become a genuine icon. While the contributions of the many other talents who have passed through Motörhead should not be underestimated, in many ways the story of Lemmy and his band are one and the same. He earned his dues in the mid-sixties, playing in a variety of R&B and psychedelic rock bands and roadieing for none other than Jimi Hendrix, before joining space-rock experimentalists Hawkwind.

Drugs rapidly became a way of life for Lemmy, whose consumption of speed and acid became legendary: however, they also led to his departure from Hawkwind, who fired him in 1975 after a drugs

bust in North America. Irritated, he formed a new group, Motörhead, named after the last song he had written for his old band: the name is biker slang for a speed user (and was a much better choice than his defiant initial idea, Bastard).

It took two years for Motörhead to find their feet. After a brief dalliance with guitarist **Larry Wallis** and drummer **Lucas Fox**, the Motörhead lineup stabilized as Lemmy plus **"Fast" Eddie Clarke** on guitar and **Phil "Philthy Animal" Taylor** on drums. This trio has become regarded as the classic Motörhead, and it is certainly true that most of the band's best-known songs were written by that lineup. By 1982, however, both backing musicians were gone, leading Lemmy to state in one interview: "Did I leave them or did they leave me?" The legacy of the Clarke/Taylor lineup remains impressive all these years later, with albums such as Overkill (1979), Ace of Spades (1980), and the U.K. chart-topping No Sleep 'Til Hammersmith (1981) among the era's most essential rock releases.

Joined by ex-Thin Lizzy guitarist **Brian Robertson** and sometime Saxon drummer **Pete Gill**, Lemmy soldiered on, releasing a sequence of albums in the eighties that contained many a classic song, although they lacked the raw attitude of Motörhead's earlier work. Robertson did not last long: ejected in 1983 after

M

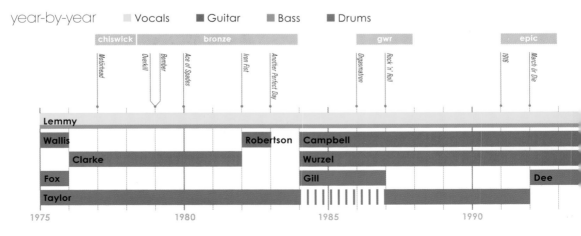

year-by-year ▪ Vocals ▪ Guitar ▪ Bass ▪ Drums

chiswick | bronze | gwr | epic

Motörhead · Overkill · Bomber · Ace of Spades · Iron Fist · Another Perfect Day · Orgasmatron · Rock 'n' Roll · 1916 · March ör Die

Lemmy

Wallis | Robertson | Campbell

Clarke | Wurzel

Fox | Gill | Dee

Taylor

1975 | 1980 | 1985 | 1990

"Fast" Eddie Clarke
b. October 5, 1950

Pete Gill
b. June 9, 1951

Brian Robertson
b. September 12, 1956

Würzel
b. October 23, 1949
d. July 9, 2011

arguments over his stage attire and reluctance to play old material, he was replaced by two six-stringers, **Phil Campbell** (ex-Persian Risk) and Michael **"Würzel"** Burston, the latter a complete unknown who had sent Lemmy an audition cassette. However, plagued by unreliable managers and record companies, the band struggled to find a niche, even when the erratic but frequently brilliant Taylor returned in 1987 (his comeback album, Rock 'n' Roll, also featured a spoken cameo by Monty Python's Michael Palin).

According to Lemmy, who wrote about Motörhead's ever-changing fortunes in his 2002 autobiography White Line Fever, the band would have split had he not moved to live in Los Angeles in the early nineties. With easier access to the rock 'n' roll industry (not to mention bourbon and groupies), he took his group to a new level, attracting deals with labels including Sony and recording a series of above-average albums (powered from 1993's Bastards onward by drummer **Mikkey Dee**).

Since then Motörhead has plowed a profitable furrow, releasing albums every couple of years and benefiting immensely from its leader's presence in the media—he appears in the occasional film and television commercial and was the subject of a self-titled biopic in 2010. Lemmy was even invited to address the Welsh Assembly in 2007 on the evils of heroin, the drug that killed the love of his life, Susan Bennett, back in the seventies.

Since 1995, Motörhead have been a trio: when Wurzel left (sadly, he succumbed to heart disease in 2011), Campbell took over the guitar playing. However, the band's music continues to be critically and commercially applauded. In recent years, their albums have been produced by Cameron Webb, an American console-tweaker who has given the music a polished, but still heavy, sound. Although Motörhead's naysayers claim that their albums tend to sound the same (not true), those who take the time to listen know that Lemmy and his troops are still firing on all cylinders. Axe-man extraordinaire Steve Vai guested on Inferno (2004), while Kiss of Death (2006) boasted cameos by Poison guitarist CC DeVille and Alice in Chains bassist Mike Inez. Incredibly, over thirty years after the band's formation, Motörizer (2008) and The Wörld Is Yours (2010) were their first releases to sneak into the Top 100 of Billboard's album chart.

Now that he is in his mid-sixties, Lemmy's time as a touring musician may end sooner rather than later, but he refuses to relinquish the rock 'n' roll lifestyle and may die on stage, if he dies anywhere—some believe him to be immortal. His best songs certainly are. **JM**

M

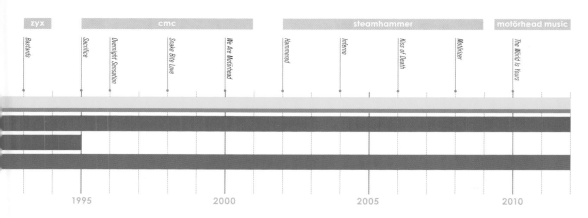

zyx — cmc — steamhammer — motörhead music

Bastards · Sacrifice · Overnight Sensation · Snake Bite Love · We Are Motörhead · Hammered · Inferno · Kiss of Death · Motörizer · The World Is Yours

1995 · 2000 · 2005 · 2010

mott the hoople 1969–2009

Overend Watts
b. May 13, 1947

Dale "Buffin" Griffin
b. October 24, 1948

Mick Ralphs
b. March 31, 1944

Verden Allen
b. May 26, 1944

Ian Hunter
b. June 3, 1939

Morgan Fisher
b. January 1, 1950

M

Mott the Hoople released seven interesting albums and a series of excellent singles between 1972 and 1974, but generally only dented the U.K. charts. However, their influence far outstrips their success.

The group had its origins in Hereford, England. **Overend Watts** (bass) and **Dale "Buffin" Griffin** (drums) were joined in 1968 by **Mick Ralphs** (guitar) and **Verden Allen** (organ) in The Silence after they had played in rival local bands. They were snapped up by producer Guy Stevens, and singer **Ian Hunter** completed the lineup (original vocalist Stan Tippins generously became their road manager). Stevens was determined to manage a group called Mott the Hoople after reading Willard Manus's novel of that title—the band reluctantly adopted the name in 1969.

Their self-titled debut album (1969) was a fascinating mix of hard rock ("Rock and Roll Queen") with Hunter's Dylanesque inflections ("Half Moon Bay") and fine cover versions ("At the Crossroads"). As the group toured, it crept into the lower reaches of the charts in the U.S. and U.K., and was followed by Mad Shadows (1970). The latter's songs were dark

and evocative—Hunter's introspective musings, such as "When My Mind's Gone," were juxtaposed with straightforward rockers like Ralphs's "Thunderbuck Ram." But it was as a live outfit that the group built their reputation, with fanatical followers at every U.K. show. The challenge was to translate that live energy and feeling of excitement onto vinyl.

Wildlife (1971) contained songs that were closer to lush country rock, including "Waterlow" and "Angel of Eighth Avenue," but did not achieve a breakthrough. Brain Capers (also 1971) showed signs of the strains on the group and, despite the live favorite "Sweet Angeline," yielded similarly disappointing sales.

Two things kept the group together when they were on the verge of splitting. The first was the adulation of fans at concerts; the second was the intervention of David Bowie. Fresh from stardom with Ziggy Stardust, Bowie generously gave the group a new song, "All the Young Dudes." It gave Mott a massive hit, which Bowie underlined by producing their album. Also called All the Young Dudes (1972), the record was uneven, but "One of the Boys,"

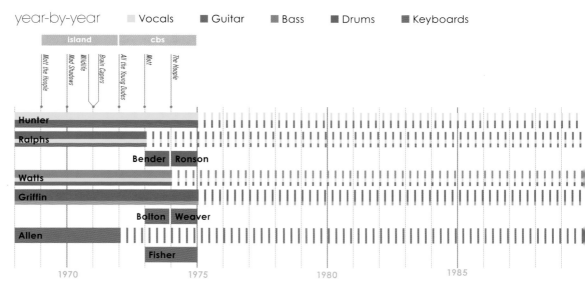

250,000	750,000	750,000	250,000
All the Young Dudes (1972)	**Mott** (1973)	**The Hoople** (1974)	**Mott the Hoople Live** (1974)

Mick Bolton
b. 1948

Ariel Bender
b. December 23, 1946

Mick Ronson
b. May 26, 1946
d. April 29, 1993

Blue Weaver
b. March 11, 1947

Martin Chambers
b. September 4, 1951

"Ready for Love/After Lights" and a version of The Velvet Underground's "Sweet Jane" (Bowie was championing Lou Reed in similar fashion at the time) helped make it their biggest to date.

This triumph boosted the group's confidence, and *Mott* (1973) contained a sharp selection of songs, including "Ballad of Mott the Hoople" (Hunter was always keen on chronicling their adventures, in diaries and on record). Its hits, "Honaloochie Boogie" and "All the Way from Memphis," climbed to No. 12 and No. 10, respectively, in the U.K. Yet the band's bonds were loosened by their transformed fortunes. The disillusioned Verden Allen was replaced by pianist **Morgan Fisher** in time for *Mott,* then Mick Ralphs left to form Bad Company. Spooky Tooth guitarist Luther Grosvenor, calling himself **Ariel Bender** for obscure legal reasons, came in, as did organist **Mick Bolton**.

The group's final studio album, *The Hoople* (1974) revisited their winning formula. The magnificent singles "The Golden Age of Rock 'n' Roll" and "Roll Away the Stone" were its cornerstones, although "Marionette" perhaps told the real story. Bar a live set

later that year, it was their highest-charting U.S. album (No. 28), but the end was close at hand. Bolton and Bender were replaced by former Strawb **Blue Weaver** (keyboards) and Bowie's guitarist, **Mick Ronson**. But after two wonderful yet underperforming singles— "Foxy Foxy" and "Saturday Gigs"—and another U.S. tour, the group decided to split up at the end of 1974.

Fisher, Watts, and Griffin persisted for a while with a version of the group called Mott, recording *Drive On* (1975) and *Shouting and Pointing* (1976), but it was not the same. Hunter and Ronson played together for many years, until the latter's cruelly premature death in 1993. In the meantime, the group's name was kept alive by admirers like Mötley Crüe's Nikki Sixx and Def Leppard's Joe Elliott. But that seemed to be that.

However, in October 2009, the group re-formed for triumphant shows at London's Hammersmith Apollo. Watts, Ralphs, Allen, Hunter, and Griffin (with **Martin Chambers** from the Pretenders assisting with drumming owing to the latter's Alzheimer's disease) earned a rapturous response, captured in the 2011 documentary *The Ballad of Mott the Hoople*. **MiH**

■ Other percussion

M

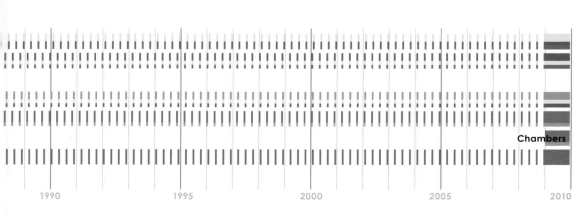

Chambers

1990   1995   2000   2005   2010

mudhoney 1988–present

Mark Arm
b. February 21, 1962

Steve Turner
b. March 28, 1965

Dan Peters
b. August 18, 1967

Matt Lukin
b. August 16, 1964

Guy Maddison
b. March 31, 1965

Perennial bridesmaids Mudhoney were the forefathers of grunge, leading the way on Seattle's Sub Pop label before stablemates Nirvana grabbed the glory. They rose from the ashes of local band Green River (also the alma mater for Jeff Ament and Stone Gossard of Pearl Jam): front-man **Mark Arm** (formerly Mark McLaughlin) and guitarist **Steve Turner** (who had left earlier) hooked up with drummer **Dan Peters** and ex-Melvins bassist **Matt Lukin** to broker the new band.

Taking their name from a Russ Meyer movie, the nascent Mudhoney made a splash with the 1988 EP *Superfuzz Bigmuff*—named, somewhat disappointingly, after Turner's preferred effects pedal—and the short, sharp, shocking "Touch Me I'm Sick." They struck up a rapport with the daddies of U.S. alt. rock, Sonic Youth, covering each other's songs and touring the U.K. together. There, Mudhoney gained a reputation for shows that spun out of control—Arm once memorably invited the entire audience to join the band on stage. In the U.K., *Superfuzz Bigmuff* made its mark on the independent charts before the band's self-titled 1989 debut album cemented their caustic, calculatedly messy sound.

Every Good Boy Deserves Fudge followed in 1991 and gave the band a healthy chart placing (U.K. No. 34) as grunge became rock's one true path (Peters had played on Nirvana's 1990 single "Sliver" before Dave Grohl became their drummer). Mudhoney were broadening their palette, with Arm adding organ to his instrumental mix. The natural next step came with

a break from Sub Pop: the band signed to the Warner imprint Reprise in 1992 and conjured up *Piece of Cake*, another U.K. Top Forty album.

Their next set would come at a crossroads for the grunge scene, following Nirvana front-man Kurt Cobain's suicide in 1994. *My Brother the Cow* (1995) featured a meditation on Cobain, "Into Your Schtick," as disaffected critics began to turn their backs on Mudhoney and their ilk. It would be another three years before *Tomorrow Hit Today* (1998) turned up with a recalibrated, more bluesy style.

The turn of the century saw Lukin leave, to be replaced—after short stints by Wayne Kramer (of the MC5) and Steve Dukich—by bassist **Guy Maddison**. There were more changes afoot, as Mudhoney returned to Sub Pop for 2002's *Since We've Become Translucent*. Confrontational and ambitious in equal measure, this was a return to form, and paved the way for 2006's warmly received *Under a Billion Suns*. (In the interim, Arm deputized for Rob Tyner on an MC5 revival tour in 2004.) After 2008's *The Lucky Ones*, Mudhoney turned full circle, putting out a deluxe *Superfuzz Bigmuff* and playing it in full at New York's All Tomorrow's Parties festival in 2010.

Rolling back the years again, they joined Pearl Jam on the latter's PJ20 anniversary tour in 2011, in the process celebrating their common roots. It was a festival of nostalgia but—more than two decades down the line—Mudhoney's searing, distorted take on punk had lost none of its potency. **MaH**

year-by-year   ■ Vocals   ■ Guitar   ■ Bass   ■ Drums

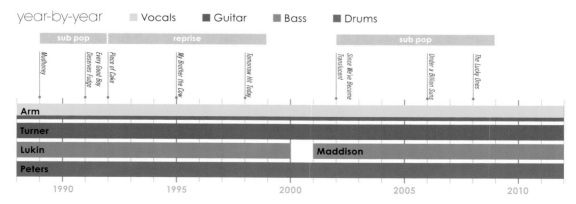

muse 1994–present

Matt Bellamy
b. June 9, 1978

Chris Wolstenholme
b. December 2, 1978

Dominic Howard
b. December 7, 1977

"They're very good boys and extremely talented," declared Brian May of Queen. "And, like us, they have their tongue in cheek a lot of the time." One of contemporary hard rock's most exciting acts, Muse have amassed a vast following through a combination of magnificent live shows and stirring anthems that touch on conspiracy and catastrophe.

Matt Bellamy (guitars, keyboards, vocals), **Chris Wolstenholme** (bass), and **Dominic Howard** (drums) met at school in the seaside town of Teignmouth, Devon, in southwest England. Although they had played together before, the genesis of the group dates to 1994 when, as Rocket Baby Dolls, they won a local "battle of the bands" competition. Deciding to get serious, they settled on the name Muse (because, they claimed, it looked good on posters).

The group spent several years formulating their vision and rehearsing, while playing live and building a fan base. They had released two EPs before their first album, *Showbiz*, emerged in 1999. Crammed with interesting material, such as "Sunburn" and the title track, it established Muse as a group to watch.

Origin of Symmetry (2001)—featuring the gems "Plug in Baby," "Feeling Good," and "New Born"—confirmed their potential and sold well in the U.K. However, their American record label felt Bellamy's histrionic vocal style would harm its prospects, and demanded a re-mix. The group refused, and the album was not released in the U.S. until 2005.

Meanwhile, Muse had broken into the front ranks with *Absolution* (2003). Powerful mini-epics such as

"Time Is Running Out" and "Stockholm Syndrome" were juxtaposed with restrained hymns of brooding splendor like "Sing for Absolution." The group's supersonic onslaught framed Bellamy's alternately yearning and overwrought vocals to immaculate effect. The whole package was wrapped in artwork by Pink Floyd's sleeve designer, Storm Thorgerson.

Muse also established a reputation for delivering huge, imaginative shows. They defied the impossible, using a trio format to soundtrack the apocalypse (later fleshing out their onstage sound with guest keyboard player and percussionist Morgan Nicholls).

Stomping into international Top Tens, *Black Holes and Revelations* (2006) supercharged their blueprint of punchy, dramatic songs into an extravagant space opera. "Supermassive Black Hole," "Starlight," and "Knights of Cydonia" were unsettling yet uplifting standouts. The superb live recording *HAARP* (2008) testifies to their grandeur.

The Resistance (2009), another worldwide smash, solidified their status as one of rock's greatest groups and biggest draws. Songs like "Uprising," "Resistance," and the ambitious "Exogenesis: Symphony" raised their standard to a new level, and shows on the accompanying tour were even more spectacular than before. Amid a welter of awards that the group has won over the past decade, *The Resistance* earned a Grammy for Best Rock Album of 2010. Reported work with rock's orchestrator *du jour* David Campbell suggests there will be no scaling down of their ambitions for *The 2nd Law* (2012). **MiH**

M

year-by-year

■ Vocals ■ Guitar ■ Bass ■ Drums ■ Keyboards

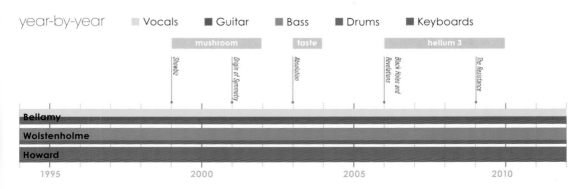

mushroom   taste   helium 3

Showbiz
Origin of Symmetry
Absolution
Black Holes and Revelations
The Resistance

Bellamy
Wolstenholme
Howard

1995   2000   2005   2010

os mutantes 1966–present

Sérgio Dias Baptista
b. December 1st, 1951

Rita Lee
b. December 31st, 1947

Arnaldo Baptista
b. July 6th, 1948

Liminha
b. 1951

Dinho Leme
b. Unknown

Antonio Pedro
b. Unknown

Rui Motta
b. Unknown

Túlio Mourão
b. January 18, 1952

On April 1, 1964, armed forces seized control of Brazil, initiating twenty years of martial law. From this harsh environment arose a late sixties counter-revolution: Tropicália, a cultural movement that encompassed theater, music, and poetry, and from which many artists would emerge—including Caetano Veloso and Gilberto Gil. Central to the movement's manifesto was *antropófago* ("cannibalism") that encouraged cross-genre pollination to create something unique. Arguably the most visible example was Os Mutantes.

Formed in 1966 by brothers **Sérgio Dias** and **Arnaldo Baptista** with vocalist **Rita Lee**, Os Mutantes ("The Mutants") brought a sense of playfulness to the sometimes earnest Tropicália circle. By the time they recorded their 1968 debut album, Os Mutantes had melded American psychedelia with Brazilian samba and bossa nova, a sound both of its time yet unique. The experiment was repeated with greater critical and commercial success on 1969's *Mutantes* and a third period classic, 1970's *A Divina Comédia ou Ando Meio Desligado* ("A Divine Comedy or I Am a Bit Disconnected"). However, while popular among Brazilian teens, Os Mutantes would remain little known to the outside world for another two decades.

In 1972, Lee—the band's focal point—left to pursue a solo career that would encompass rock, disco, and her own TV show. Arnaldo Baptista followed shortly afterward. Os Mutantes began to veer toward progressive rock, although works such as 1974's *Tudo Foi Feito Pelo Sol* ("Everything Is the Sun") remained just as curious to Western ears.

Disbanding in 1978, the group would have stayed a solely Brazilian phenomenon were it not for a cult that evolved over the following decade. Original Brazilian LPs, particularly the first three albums, began filtering into Europe and the U.S. By the early nineties, Os Mutantes were being cited as an influence on artists with no visible South American connections: in 1993 Kurt Cobain wrote to Arnaldo Baptista calling for Os Mutantes to reform; five years later, Beck enjoyed a hit with "Tropicália," his own tribute to the group. Recordings from 1973 and 1970, respectively, were issued as *A e o Z* (1992) and *Tecnicolor* (2000).

Outside interest in Os Mutantes was a surprise to Sérgio Dias. In 2006, he formed a new version of the band, which played to acclaim on the global festival circuit—new vocalist Bia Mendes proving an effective substitute for Rita Lee. *Haih… or Amortecedor,* the first new Os Mutantes album in over thirty years, illustrated that the reappearance of Dias was no exercise in cheap nostalgia but the return of a creative artist who had merely taken an unusually long break. **TB**

year-by-year

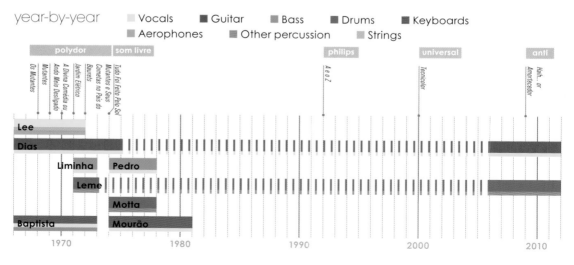

my bloody valentine 1983–present

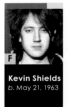

Kevin Shields
b. May 21, 1963

Colm Ó Cíosóig
b. October 31, 1964

Dave Conway
b. Unknown

Debbie Googe
b. October 24, 1962

Bilinda Butcher
b. September 16, 1961

Take Phil Spector's Wall of Sound. Raise it. Add dreamy melodies. Then bury them under exquisitely crafted noise. And you might have My Bloody Valentine.

Drummer **Colm Ó Cíosóig**, New York-born **Kevin Shields**, vocalist **Dave Conway**, and his keyboardist girlfriend Tina Durkin quit Dublin first for Holland, then (inspired partly by The Birthday Party) Berlin. There, they recorded their debut mini-LP *This Is Your Bloody Valentine* (1985), whose dark post-punkery made little impression. The band relocated to London, where Durkin left and bassist **Debbie Googe** joined. But after a series of EPs and another mini-LP (1987's *Ecstasy*), My Bloody Valentine—named for a 1981 slasher movie— were still, as Shields reflected in 1991, merely a "Jesus and Mary Chain rip-off band."

Guitarist/singer **Bilinda Butcher** replaced Conway in 1987. This, coupled with extended studio time, resulted in a breakthrough: the crackling EP *You Made Me Realise*. Building on the momentum, their debut album *Isn't Anything* (1988) boasted waves of fuzzy, reverb-soaked guitar and soft harmonies blanketing Butcher's languorous vocals. These brutal and beautiful soundscapes—couple with their infamously loud shows—saw the Valentines become figureheads for the U.K.'s "shoegazing" scene.

Two years in the making, involving countless engineers in nearly twenty studios, *Loveless* (1991) proved another landmark. Masterminded by Shields— the sole musician on most of the album—it was recorded in mono, for greater punch. Rather than employing hordes of effects, Shields used the tremolo arm of his guitar to shape and twist pitch and timbre.

Q magazine hailed *Loveless* as "a virtual reinvention of the guitar," and Brian Eno declared that its closer, "Soon," "set a new standard for pop." (Accordingly, Coldplay's Eno-produced "Chinese Sleep Chant" is a fine Valentines pastiche.) The supporting tour was provocative—volumes were so loud they hurt, the band hammering on one chord in "You Made Me Realise" for ten minutes at a time.

However, with recording costs estimated at £250,000, *Loveless* nearly sank the Creation label. Then it only made U.K. No. 24, and the Valentines found themselves label-less. They moved to Island and began a third album, but Shields's perfectionism proved too much and the others slipped away. Shields busied himself with home recordings, emerging to play with Dinosaur Jr., Yo La Tengo, and Primal Scream (he appeared on 2000's *Xtrmntr* and toured with them). He also provided music for the 2003 movie *Lost in Translation* and Patti Smith's *The Coral Sea* (2005/6).

In 2008, the Valentines kicked off a worldwide reunion tour with two deafening sets at London's ICA (earplugs were dispensed to the crowd). In 2012—the year Googe joined Primal Scream—long-mooted remastered versions of *Isn't Anything* and *Loveless* appeared alongside a compilation of their early EPs. However, despite Shields' admission that "all that stuff I was doing in 1996 and 1997 was a lot better than I thought," we're still waiting for that third album. **RD**

M

year-by-year   ▢ Vocals   ■ Guitar   ■ Bass   ■ Drums

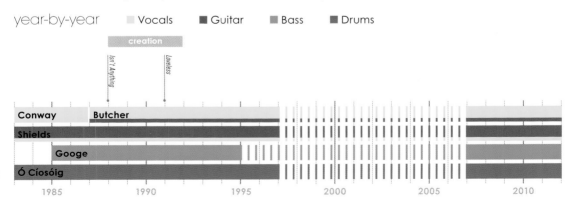

creation

Isn't Anything

Loveless

Conway   Butcher

Shields

Googe

Ó Cíosóig

1985   1990   1995   2000   2005   2010

neu! 1971–1975

Klaus Dinger
b. March 24, 1946
d. March 21, 2008

Michael Rother
b. September 2, 1950

Thomas Dinger
b. October 28, 1952
d. April 9, 2002

Hans Lampe
b. Unknown

Emerging in 1971 from Düsseldorf in Germany, the duo Neu! ("New!") were among the founding fathers of "krautrock," influencing the course of punk and new wave and inspiring artists such as David Bowie and Radiohead. Prior to forming Neu!, **Klaus Dinger** and **Michael Rother** were original members of Kraftwerk— whose importance in modern music is indisputable.

Having left Kraftwerk during abortive sessions for the band's second album, drummer Dinger and guitarist Rother regrouped in Hamburg with German studio legend Conny Plank. Their 1972 debut album, Neu!, is widely regarded as one of the high points of the krautrock genre. The tone was set from the opening track, "Hallogallo," which heralded the first appearance of Dinger's "motorik" beat, a simple, uninterrupted four-four rhythm with few fills or other embellishments that became a defining characteristic of the band's sound. Atop the driving beat sat Rother's spacious, pulsing bass lines and atmospheric guitar soundscapes. A seminal piece of work, even today Neu! still sounds remarkably fresh.

A year later, Neu! 2 followed the same formula, the exhilarating eleven minutes of "Für immer" remaining one of the band's recorded highlights. The album's genesis took a curious turn when Dinger and Rother discovered they had used their entire recording budget with only one side of material completed. Refused a further advance, they came

up with the ingenious solution of filling up side two by mechanically manipulating the tapes of an earlier single. While by no means an easy listen, the result could be considered a prototype "remix"—the post-production of multiple versions of the same track later popular in reggae and dance music.

Having completed Neu! 2, the duo took a two-year hiatus, regrouping for Neu! '75. During this time, however, their musical interests had begun to diverge. What emerged was a split album: side one, recorded as a duo, was gentler than its predecessors, dominated by Rother's fluid guitar and keyboard textures; side two, however, was driven by Dinger's newly acquired interest in rock music. Handing over the drumming duties to his brother **Thomas** and **Hans Lampe**—who were instructed to play simultaneously— Klaus Dinger switched to guitar and vocals. The heavily distorted beat and his sneering voice on the track "Hero" would influence the U.K. punk scene as well as David Bowie. (The latter divided his own Low into distinct halves, reminiscent of Neu! '75.)

Although Neu! performed as a four-piece, the widening chasm between Rother and Dinger made it impossible to continue; shortly after the release of Neu! '75 the band dissolved. Rother went on to enjoy a prolific solo career, also collaborating with Cluster and Brian Eno; the Dinger brothers and Lampe formed the much-touted La Düsseldorf. **TB**

year-by-year ▢ Vocals ▪ Guitar ▪ Bass ▪ Drums

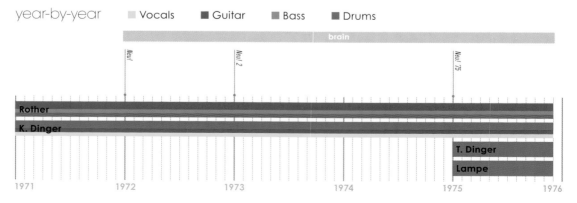

the new york dolls 1971–present

Sylvain Sylvain
b. February 14, 1951

Billy Murcia
b. 1951

Johnny Thunders
b. July 15, 1952
d. April 23, 1991

Arthur "Killer" Kane
b. February 3, 1949
d. July 13, 2004

David Johansen
b. January 9, 1950

Jerry Nolan
b. May 7, 1946
d. January 14, 1992

Straddling glam and punk, the Dolls were commercial non-starters—but as influential as an earthquake.

Sylvain Sylvain, **Billy Murcia**, and **Johnny Thunders** united in 1970, naming themselves Dolls after the New York Dolls' Hospital, a toy repair shop. Thunders and Murcia hooked up in another band with **Arthur "Killer" Kane** in 1971, as did **David Johansen** in October. Sylvain replaced original guitarist Rick Rivets and the New York Dolls were born. By summer 1972, they had a weekly spot at the Mercer Arts Center.

The Dolls played scrappy, livewire rock 'n' roll, Johansen and Thunders an out-there parody of Jagger and Richards. In 1972, they embarked on a U.K. tour, to the delight of fledgling Sex Pistol Steve Jones, whose verdict was "out-of-control kind of stuff that I'd never seen before." In London, however, a comatose Murcia drowned in a bath. The shell-shocked band drafted in new drummer **Jerry Nolan**.

Todd Rundgren took charge of their self-titled debut album. The band hated his production but "Looking for a Kiss," "Trash," and "Personality Crisis" still sound deliriously fresh. "The last rock 'n' roll band," trumpeted the U.K.'s *Melody Maker*, though the album won zero airplay. But their 1973 European tour proved a pivotal inspiration for U.K. punks; anticipating Vicious

and Siouxsie, Thunders even sported a swastika armband. Future Smiths front-man Morrissey adored them, becoming president of their British fan club.

Johansen persuaded Shangri-Las mastermind Shadow Morton to produce *Too Much Too Soon* (1974); applauded today, it was panned at the time. Quarrels ensued, notably between Johansen and Thunders. Throw in Kane's alcoholism and Thunders and Nolan's fondness for heroin, and the end seemed nigh.

Cue Malcolm McLaren, a Dolls devotee who clad them in red leather and gave them a hammer-and-sickle backdrop onstage. In 1975, Thunders quit, going back to New York to form The Heartbreakers with Nolan. The unsteady Kane was summarily fired, and Johansen and Sylvain called it a day in late 1976.

Thunders overdosed in 1991; Nolan followed a year later. But the surviving Dolls enjoyed a reunion, at Morrissey's request, for 2004's Meltdown festival in London—a triumph and a wish come true for Kane, who died of leukemia the next month. Sylvain and Johansen struck on with new Dolls (including Blondie's Frank Infante, Hanoi Rocks' Sami Yaffa, and Bowie guitarist Earl Slick), completing three solid albums, and even playing iconic punk venue CBGBs (for the first time) in 2006. They've earned their happy ending. **RD**

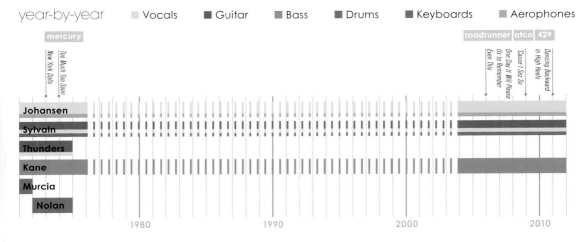

year-by-year   ■ Vocals   ■ Guitar   ■ Bass   ■ Drums   ■ Keyboards   ■ Aerophones

nickelback 1995–present

Chad Kroeger
b. November 15, 1974

Mike Kroeger
b. June 25, 1972

Ryan Peake
b. March 1, 1973

Mitch Guindon
b. March 10, 1970

Ryan Vikedal
b. May 9, 1975

Daniel Adair
b. February 19, 1975

"We all just wanna be big rock stars / And live in hilltop houses, drivin' fifteen cars…" Forty-five million records sold worldwide? Four multi-platinum albums in the United States? More awards than a standard trophy cabinet can hold? Wish granted. Someone find these guys a garage big enough for fifteen automobiles!

Nickelback were, of course, established musicians long before the tongue-in-cheek "Rockstar" and its star-studded video saturated radio and television in 2006. Let us remind ourselves how it happened.

The group broke out of Alberta, Canada, in 1995, consisting of three Kroegers—brothers **Chad** and **Mike**, and their cousin Brandon—and **Ryan Peake**. Mike's job as a cashier at Starbucks handed the group their name on a plate: customer buys coffee, hands over cash, Mike does his stuff, dishes out change: "Here's a nickel back, sir."

A limited-edition seven-track EP, *Hesher* (1996), was the first Nickelback material offered for public consumption. Despite front-man Chad Kroeger's subsequent desire to "bury that album as fast as I can," one copy changed hands for over $400 on eBay in 2001—approximately sixty times its original value.

Nickelback's first full-length album, 1996's *Curb*, found the quartet in an uncompromising mood: distorted guitar riffs, Chad's raw vocals, and a disturbing Nirvana-esque ditty about a boy wanting

to shoot himself to discover if he goes to Heaven or Hell ("Fly"). In the first of the band's Spinal Tap-esque personnel turnovers, *Curb* marked the end of the road for Brandon Kroeger, whose replacement was drummer **Mitch Guindon**. In 1998, Guindon quit for a "real" job and **Ryan Vikedal** climbed on board.

The State, issued at the turn of the century, kicked off a prolific period for the self-managing Nickelback. Over the course of six years and four albums, the boys went from post-grunge also-rans to world-conquering, radio-friendly rock heavyweights—much to the chagrin of a number of short-sighted music critics.

Silver Side Up (2001) featured a trio of airplay monsters: "Never Again," "Too Bad," and their Grammy-nominated signature tune, "How You Remind Me." All three crowned the Mainstream Rock Tracks chart (for a combined nineteen weeks), while "How You Remind Me"—incredibly, the last No. 1 rock record on the *Billboard* Hot 100 until 2007—bothered Top Ten charts across the globe *and* became the most played song on U.S. radio in the 2000s, with 1.2 million spins. On the Silver Side Up tour, the band headlined over Jerry Cantrell, the then solo guitarist from their most obvious musical ancestors, Alice in Chains. "I had the guys come up and play with us on some Alice in Chains tunes…" Cantrell recalled. "We had a real fun time on the tour. It was a good thing."

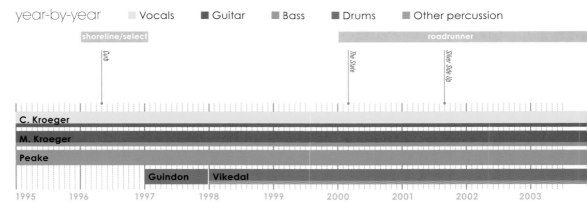

year-by-year ■ Vocals ■ Guitar ■ Bass ■ Drums ■ Other percussion

In 2002, Chad Kroeger temporarily ditched his day job to provide a lead track for the *Spider-Man* movie soundtrack. The resulting "Hero"—essentially a duet with Saliva's Josey Scott but also featuring the talents of Matt Cameron (Pearl Jam/Soundgarden), Tyler Connolly (Theory of a Deadman), and Nickelback's very own Mike Kroeger—was summed up by the *NME:* "commercial grunge + MOR sensibility = Nu-MOR hit." To that we add: winning formula = worldwide smash.

Back in Nickelback's world, *The Long Road* (2003) turned triple platinum in the U.S. within six months of its release, and its lead single, "Someday," gave them a second No. 1 in Canada.

Nickelback's next two albums, 2005's *All the Right Reasons* (their first with 3 Doors Down graduate **Daniel Adair** on drums) and 2008's *Dark Horse*, each spawned an incredible *seven* U.S. singles. Among them were "Gotta Be Somebody" and "If Today Was Your Last Day" from *Dark Horse* and "Photograph," "Far Away," and the aforementioned "Rockstar" from the eight million-selling *Right Reasons*. "Rockstar" has the distinction of being one of only twenty-five singles to accumulate fifty weeks in the U.K. Top Seventy-Five. Its witty video—starring, among others, Gene Simmons of Kiss, Ted Nugent, Kid Rock, ZZ Top's Billy Gibbons, pop star Nelly Furtado, and rapper Lupe Fiasco—undoubtedly helped.

The success of *Right Reasons* led to a World Music Award for the World's Best-Selling Rock Artist of 2006, two American Music Awards, three *Billboard* Music Awards, and two Juno Awards, including a third Group of the Year accolade. In 2006, Nickelback became the first non-British or Irish winner of the U.K.'s coveted Record of the Year Award. They have claimed a huge thirty-one major awards since 2001.

If ever the world needed to feel good again, that time is *Here and Now*. Cutting through the hyperbole of the Roadrunner label's press release that accompanied Nickelback's seventh studio album in 2011, *Here and Now* shifted 226,714 first-week copies in the United States to debut at No. 2, just 419 units shy of Michael Bublé's chart-topping *Christmas*.

Negative headlines have plagued the group for the past decade, but for every "Why Nickelback is the world's most hated band" or "Nickelback named No. 1 musical turnoff" article, there are plenty of fans willing to pay homage to their idols, among them admirers like Coldplay's Chris Martin and rapper/producer Timbaland. One thing is for sure: Nickelback have paid their dues and have nothing to prove.

Just one ambition remains for "Rockstar" Chad Kroeger and his associates: "My own star on Hollywood Boulevard / Somewhere between Cher and James Dean is fine for me." Watch this space. **MW**

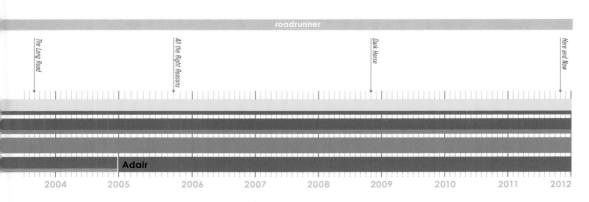

nine inch nails 1988–present

Trent Reznor
b. May 17, 1965

Chris Vrenna
b. February 23, 1967

Richard Patrick
b. May 10, 1968

Jeff Ward
b. Nov 18, 1962
d. March 19, 1993

James Woolley
b. Unknown

Danny Lohner
b. December 13, 1970

Robin Finck
b. November 7, 1971

Charlie Clouser
b. June 28, 1963

"A small lad with a tuba," as David Bowie described him in *Rolling Stone,* Michael **Trent Reznor** grew up to study engineering and fuse influences from Depeche Mode to Public Enemy. The result: Nine Inch Nails, in which Reznor would be the only constant.

A first tour in 1988 found him accompanied by drummer Ron Musarra and keyboardist **Chris Vrenna**. The latter contributed to *Pretty Hate Machine* (1989), which, recalled Bowie, "birthed the first real mainstream breakthrough for industrial rock." In the year of touring that made NIN famous, Vrenna switched to drums (replaced temporarily by **Jeff Ward** for stints on the Lollapalooza festival and with Guns N' Roses), future Filter front-man **Richard Patrick** played guitar, and keyboard duties switched from Nick Rushe to David Haymes, Lee Mars, then **James Woolley**.

Broken (1992)—featuring PiL drummer Martin Atkins—took NIN into the U.S. Top Ten and spawned the remixed *Fixed*. Then came *The Downward Spiral* (1994), NIN's commercial zenith. Guests included Bowie's guitarist Adrian Belew, drummer Andy Kubiszewski (leader of Reznor's pre-NIN band Exotic Birds), and Jane's Addiction sticksman Stephen Perkins. Additional guitar was by **Danny Lohner**—who, alongside **Robin Finck**, bolstered a new live lineup.

The ensuing tour included Reznor, Finck, Lohner, Woolley, and the returning Vrenna's scene-stealing

set at August's Woodstock '94 event. That same month, Reznor's ascendancy to alt-rock godhead was secured by his *Natural Born Killers* soundtrack, which zigzagged brilliantly from Patsy Cline to Dr. Dre.

After Woodstock and the *Further Down the Spiral* re-mix album, *Downward Spiral* programmer **Charlie Clouser** replaced Woolley. The band co-headlined twenty-six dates with—and arguably upstaged—Bowie, promoting his industrial-influenced *1. Outside.*

In 1996, Reznor bequeathed his crown to Marilyn Manson. Having signed Manson to his Nothing label, Reznor co-produced his protégé's *Portrait of an American Family* (1994) and *Smells Like Children* (1995) and took his band on tour. This endorsement, coupled with the gruesome crooner's own fanbase, sent the Reznor co-produced *Antichrist Superstar* (1996) into the U.S. Top Three. (Manson and Bowie featured on Reznor's second soundtrack, 1997's *Lost Highway.* NIN also overhauled Bowie's single "I'm Afraid of Americans," the video for which starred Reznor.)

The Fragile (1999), sequenced by producer Bob Ezrin, boasted new drummer **Jerome Dillon** and NIN's largest supporting cast. Guests included Belew, Bowie's pianist Mike Garson, Helmet's Page Hamilton, Pop Will Eat Itself man turned film soundtracker Clint Mansell, and former Ministry/future R.E.M. drummer Bill Rieflin. The ensuing tour—captured on 2002's *And All*

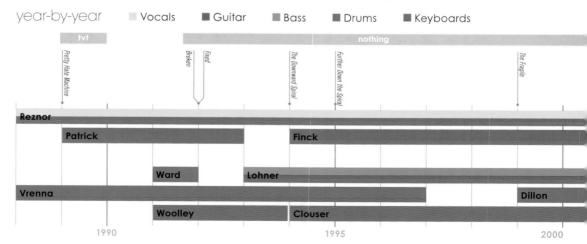

year-by-year ■ Vocals ■ Guitar ■ Bass ■ Drums ■ Keyboards

tvt

nothing

Pretty Hate Machine · *Broken* · *Fixed* · *The Downward Spiral* · *Further Down the Spiral* · *The Fragile*

Reznor

Patrick **Finck**

Ward **Lohner**

Vrenna **Dillon**

Woolley **Clouser**

1990   1995   2000

Jerome Dillon
b. July 16, 1969

Alessandro Cortini
b. May 24, 1976

Aaron North
b. March 22, 1979

Jeordie White
b. June 20, 1971

Josh Freese
b. December 25, 1972

Justin Meldal-Johnsen
b. Mar 26, 1970

Ilan Rubin
b. July 7, 1988

That Could Have Been—featured Clouser, Lohner, and Dillon alongside the returning Finck. The latter had spent 1997–1999 as Slash's replacement in Guns N' Roses, a position to which he returned in 2006/2007.

Thereafter, Reznor tinkered with Tapeworm, a side-project with Lohner and Clouser. Years of on-off work attracted names such as Page Hamilton, Pantera's Phil Anselmo, and Tool's Maynard James Keenan. But, bar two songs performed by Keenan's own side-projects A Perfect Circle and Puscifer, no results emerged. Instead, *With Teeth* (2005) saw Reznor shedding most names from his past, bar drummer Dillon and co-producer Alan Moulder. Dave Grohl drummed on half of its songs, but the key contributor was programmer Atticus Ross, an associate of film composer Barry Adamson (whose music had graced *Natural Born Killers* and *Lost Highway*).

With Teeth followed *The Fragile* to No. 1 in the U.S., and gave Reznor his highest U.K. chart placing, No. 3. A new touring lineup featured punk band The Icarus Line's guitarist **Aaron North**, bassist **Jeordie White** (née Twiggy Ramirez of Marilyn Manson), and keyboardist **Alessandro Cortini** (formerly of The Mayfield Four, the group that spawned Alter Bridge's Myles Kennedy). Six months into the tour, Dillon was replaced on drums by stand-in Alex Carapetis, then **Josh Freese**, latterly of Guns N' Roses and A Perfect Circle.

The North-White-Cortini-Freese lineup toured in support of *Year Zero* (2007), which promoted Atticus Ross to co-producer. Its Public Enemy-esque noise included brass—a NIN first—and hip-hop poet Saul Williams, whose coruscating *The Inevitable Rise and Liberation of NiggyTardust!* (2007) was produced and largely co-written by Reznor. He also sang on its cover of U2's "Sunday Bloody Sunday."

Fulfilling contractual obligations with a *Year Zero* re-mix album, Reznor embraced self-released, download albums. In quick succession came 2008's sprawling *Ghosts I–IV*—featuring Belew and Dresden Dolls' drummer Brian Viglione—and taut *The Slip*. The ensuing tour saw Finck return once more, with Cortini, Freese, and bassist **Justin Meldal-Johnsen**, a long-time associate of Beck. Finck and Meldal-Johnsen remained for a four-man lineup on what Reznor claimed would be NIN's final tour, in 2009, alongside ex-Lostprophets drummer **Ilan Rubin**. Jane's Addiction completed a dream double bill on part of the trek.

In the aftermath, Reznor recorded with his wife Mariqueen Maandig and Atticus Ross, christening the project How to Destroy Angels. Meanwhile, he and Ross won an Academy Award for their soundtrack for *The Social Network* (2010) and scored *The Girl with the Dragon Tattoo* (2011). However, he reassured fans, "Nine Inch Nails is not dead." **BM**

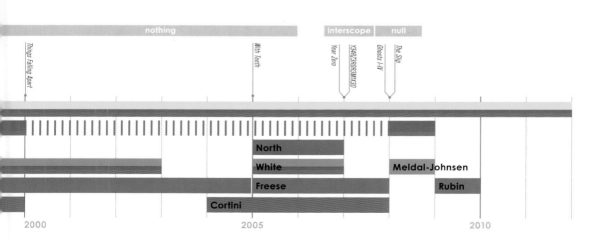

nirvana 1987–1994

Kurt Cobain
b. February 20, 1967
d. April 5, 1994

Krist Novoselic
b. May 16, 1965

Dave Grohl
b. January 14, 1969

Aaron Burckhard
b. November 14, 1963

Dale Crover
b. October 23, 1967

Dave Foster
b. Unknown

There are not many acts in the history of rock 'n' roll that seemed to change everything: what people listened to, what they wore, and even how they acted. Count The Beatles and Elvis among that number, for sure. But the pickings grow mighty slim after that. Nirvana, however, was one of those acts. The pride of Aberdeen, Washington—a city located roughly 100 miles outside of Seattle—made one of the biggest splashes of all time with 1991's *Nevermind*. The ripple touched all corners of pop culture, from fashion (flannel shirts and knitted caps, shockingly, would be seen on Paris runways) to film (the Seattle music scene was the backdrop to 1992's hit *Singles*).

Nevermind represented the coming of age of grunge, the term used to label all the new bands— some worthy, some not so much—that embraced a hardcore sound built on throat-tearing vocals, muddy guitars, contrasting tempos, and, often, a heavy sense of angst. It was the moment that many alt-rockers thought they had been waiting for, when they got to kick aside the "cool kids" and run the party. The rise of Nirvana and other similar acts—notably, Pearl Jam, Alice in Chains, and Soundgarden—caused a drastic

flip in public taste and, for a few years, made Seattle the center of the musical universe. It also cut short the careers of countless pop-metal acts—if not for Nirvana, hairsprayed, spandex-clad acts like Skid Row might still be enjoying commercial success.

Grunge would experience its own backlash, thanks to a deluge of hastily signed inferior acts, and was pretty much passé by the late nineties. However, Nirvana's music—but not, unfortunately, the band itself—was strong enough to outlast the trend and rise above the label. Vocalist **Kurt Cobain** committed suicide on April 5, 1994 at the age of twenty-seven, leaving behind one of rock's truly essential songbooks as well as one eternal question: What could this band have accomplished if they had had more time?

Cobain was an avid music fan growing up in Washington, with tastes ranging from The Beatles and Led Zeppelin to The Stooges and Velvet Underground. He then discovered the act that most influenced his own. "When I heard the Pixies for the first time," he said, "I connected with that band so heavily I should have been *in* that band—or at least in a Pixies cover band." Instead, he toiled briefly in the short-lived punk

year-by-year   ▢ Vocals   ▪ Guitar   ▪ Bass   ▪ Drums   ▢ Strings

sub pop

Bleach

Cobain

Everman

Novoselic

Burckhard

Foster

Crover

Channing

1987   1988   1989   1990

Chad Channing
b. January 31, 1967

Jason Everman
b. August 16, 1967

Dan Peters
b. August 18, 1967

Pat Smear
b. August 5, 1959

Lori Goldston
b. Unknown

act Fecal Matter, before hooking up with bassist **Krist Novoselic** to start Nirvana in 1987. They first enlisted drummer **Aaron Burckhard** (one of a half-dozen men to carry the beat for the band), but had switched to **Chad Channing** and (on three tracks) **Dale Crover** for their full-length debut on the Sub Pop label. Released in 1989, *Bleach* showcased a heavy Black Sabbath influence and did respectable business for an indie release over the next two years.

That was enough to earn the band—by then featuring future Foo Fighter **Dave Grohl** on drums—a contract with David Geffen's new DGC label: a signing that was tantamount to catching lightning in a bottle. Propelled by "Smells Like Teen Spirit"—which quickly became Generation X's definitive anthem—1991's *Nevermind* became a runaway smash, moving some 400,000 copies per week in the U.S. by year-end. The record pushed Michael Jackson's *Dangerous* from No. 1 in America and topped the charts in several other countries, on its way to eventual worldwide sales of almost twenty-five million.

Three more Top Twenty U.S. hits, including the brooding "Come as You Are," established Cobain as a writer of great significance and had commentators referring to him as "the voice of a generation." "That kid," remarked Bob Dylan, "has heart."

Cobain, to put it mildly, was uncomfortable with the attention. He was torn between his roots in the underground and the demands of success, which seemed to play havoc with his already fragile health (including an undiagnosed stomach problem). He sought relief in heroin and a relationship, then marriage, with Hole's Courtney Love (seen by many, fairly or not, as Nirvana's Yoko Ono).

None of that would stop Nirvana from releasing what some see as their crowning achievement. *In Utero*, a ragged, unexpected counterpoint to the polish of *Nevermind*, topped the U.S. charts upon release. It was a work of fragile beauty, untamed will, and unmistakable genius, highlighted by such achingly personal tracks as "All Apologies" and "Pennyroyal Tea." It turned out be the band's swansong, one tragically punctuated when Cobain put a shotgun to his head some six months later. The posthumous *MTV Unplugged in New York* would precisely underscore what was lost on April 5, 1994. **JiH**

N

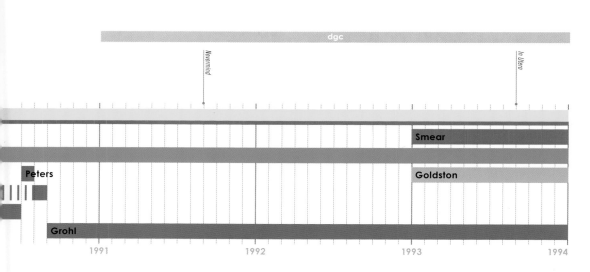

dgc

Nevermind

In Utero

Smear

Peters

Goldston

Grohl

1991   1992   1993   1994

Bleach (1989)

Nevermind (1991)

In Utero (1993)

Kurt Cobain meets his public in Cambridge, Massachusetts, on April 18, 1990.

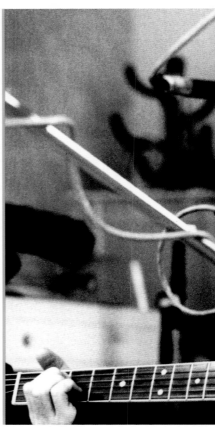

Cobain records at the Hilversum studio, the Netherlands, in 1991.

Cobain is captured seeking sustenance in 1990.

Dave Grohl records with Nirvana in Los Angeles in 1992.

Cobain enjoys backstage hospitality in Belfast, Northern Ireland, in 1992.

Krist Novoselic performs for *MTV Live and Loud* at Pier 28 in Seattle, Washington, in December 1993.

Novoselic, veteran crooner Tony Bennett, Grohl, and touring guitarist Pat Smear at the MTV Awards in 1994.

Cobain takes center stage with cellist Lori Goldston, Novoselic, Grohl, and Smear to record *MTV Unplugged in New York* at Sony Studios on November 18, 1993.

oasis 1991–2009

Noel Gallagher
b. May 29, 1967

Liam Gallagher
b. September 21, 1972

Paul "Bonehead" Arthurs
b. June 23, 1965

Paul "Guigsy" McGuigan
b. May 9, 1971

Tony McCarroll
b. June 27, 1972

Alan White
b. May 26, 1972

The Oasis saga played out in public for so long that the tunes that made the band, for a time, the most exciting on the planet were overshadowed by tabloid headlines. Wind back to the mid-nineties, though, and even the jaundiced were caught up in **Noel Gallagher**'s yearning, soaring songs—equal parts punch to the gut and TLC for the soul.

The Rain were a north-of-England go-nowhere four-piece, with little in their favor apart from a name inspired by The Beatles (a recurring raiding point) and a lead singer with a thuggish attraction. With **Liam Gallagher** were guitarist **Paul "Bonehead" Arthurs**, bassist **Paul "Guigsy" McGuigan** and drummer **Tony McCarroll**. Their transformation into a more substantial proposition was effected by the addition of Gallagher's elder brother, Noel, who became strategist-in-chief for the newly named Oasis.

In contrast to many of the signals sent out by the grunge movement, Gallagher believed life was for embracing rather than enduring or, in the case of Kurt Cobain, exiting early. Thus, "Live Forever" and not "Lithium." Oasis's debut album *Definitely Maybe* (1994) duly distilled the stomp of glam, the guitar power of the Sex Pistols, the melodic appreciation of The Beatles, and the thunder of The Who. "We do feel completely untouchable," declared Noel. "How

could you feel anything other than the greatest band in the world?" Even Thurston Moore of arch-experimentalists Sonic Youth was impressed: "Oasis certainly galvanized this country because of what they represented: Lads making grand pop music."

Not everyone shared such opinions. One *NME* review called them "also-rans." Hole's Courtney Love was less diplomatic: "Oasis must die. Do not buy Oasis records." But the juggernaut had created the U.K.'s fastest-selling debut album. And that was just the start.

Definitely Maybe was still in the chart when, just thirteen months later, *(What's The Story) Morning Glory?* elevated the band to an even higher plane. McCarroll was ousted—"He wouldn't have been able to drum the new songs," said Noel—to be replaced by **Alan White**, brother of Paul Weller regular Steve White. The production lacked the drive that propelled its predecessor, but the songs' strength assured the album of success. While "Wonderwall," "Champagne Supernova," and the majestic "Cast No Shadow" were anthems for the ages that made superstars of the band at home, their abrasive charms also started to work on America, where the album reached No. 4.

Oasis's ascension to rock's top table was confirmed with two huge shows at Britain's Knebworth Park in 1996, following the likes of Led Zeppelin and

year-by-year   ■ Vocals   ■ Guitar   ■ Bass   ■ Drums   ■ Keyboards

creation

Definitely Maybe

(What's the Story) Morning Glory

Be Here Now

L. Gallagher

N. Gallagher

Arthurs | **Archer**

McGuigan | **Bell**

McCarroll | **White**

1992   1994   1996   1998

Gem Archer
b. December 7, 1966

Andy Bell
b. August 11, 1970

Zak Starkey
b. September 13, 1965

Chris Sharrock
b. May 30, 1964

Pink Floyd. The world they had coveted for so long was theirs for the taking: they were even joined on stage by one of their heroes, John Squire of The Stone Roses. (Roses singer Ian Brown, then severely at odds with Squire, promptly dubbed Oasis "piss-poor" cocaine abusers who were "wasting all of our time.")

Be Here Now (1997)—while never quite the bloated beast that an inevitable backlash judged it to be—made the mistake of believing that the way to improve songs was to extend them to the point where even Gallagher's melodies outstayed their welcome. It was still a chart crusher—No. 1 in the U.K., No. 2 in the U.S.—but, from that point, the band had to settle for a position as "just" one of the biggest bands on the planet, rather than the undisputed titleholder.

The Oasis swagger was less evident on *Standing on the Shoulder of Giants*, but the likes of "Gas Panic" indicated greater reflection, with Noel having ditched the cocaine that engulfed *Be Here Now*. This was the departure point for Pauls Arthurs and McGuigan, which made a negligible difference to the band's sound (especially as Liam was showing early, if faltering, signs that big brother did not hold a monopoly on songwriting). Guitarist **Gem Archer** shunted over from indie no-hopers Heavy Stereo while **Andy Bell**, formerly of Ride and Hurricane #1,

swapped lead for bass. This new lineup both strutted and stuttered on 2000's live *Familiar to Millions*.

In the U.K., they remained bulletproof, but U.S. interest was tailing off. It is a defendable standpoint that, from album number four, the band was always playing catch-up with its own history. Both *Heathen Chemistry* (2002)—after which White was replaced by **Zak Starkey**, son of Ringo—and *Don't Believe the Truth* (2005) were sturdy rather than inspired. However, the first half of *Dig Out Your Soul* (2008) was outstanding, laying claim to an update of a sixties sound that was much more than just secondhand psychedelia.

"We'll always have Paris," says Rick to Ilsa in the movie *Casablanca*. Memories are less fond for the Gallaghers, a bust-up in the French capital having turned the fissure between the brothers into a chasm that destroyed the band in 2009. "I simply could not go on working with Liam a day longer," said Noel. For now, Liam has Beady Eye (with Bell, Archer, and ex-Icicle Works drummer Chris Sharrock) while Noel has his High Flying Birds. While fans dearly wish for a reunion, Noel remains refreshingly irreverent. "I don't think two blokes having the same fucking argument for sixteen years over and over is the stuff of opera," he remarked to *Spin*. "*Oasis: The Opera* would be very short. The fat lady would refuse to sing it." **CB**

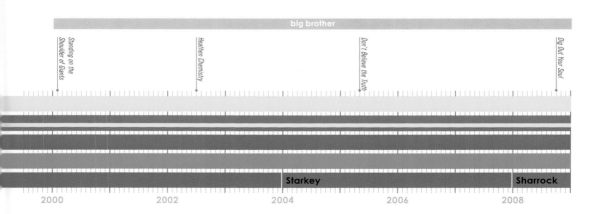

big brother

Standing on the Shoulder of Giants

Heathen Chemistry

Don't Believe the Truth

Dig Out Your Soul

Starkey

Sharrock

2000   2002   2004   2006   2008

Definitely Maybe
(1994)

**(What's the Story)
Morning Glory**
(1995)

Be Here Now
(1997)

**Standing on the
Shoulder of Giants**
(2000)

Heathen Chemisty
(2002)

**Don't Believe the
Truth** (2005)

Dig Out Your Soul
(2008)

Paul "Guigsy" McGuigan, Paul "Bonehead" Arthurs, Tony McCarroll, and **Liam Gallagher** at their first London show, at the Water Rats' Splash club. January 1994.

Liam Gallagher, headlining Britain's Glastonbury festival in 1995.

Brothers grim **Liam** and **Noel Gallagher** on stage at Earls Court in London in 1997.

In the aftermath of *Standing on the Shoulder....*, the band celebrate "ten years of noise and confusion" at London's Shepherd Bush Empire in October 2001.

Gem Archer, **Liam Gallagher**, and **Andy Bell** at the Coachella festival, California, in 2002.

Noel, a.k.a. "The Chief," at Melbourne's Festival Hall in 2005.

On August 28, 2009, six months after this gig in Munich, Germany, **Noel Gallagher** quit the band.

offspring 1984-present

Bryan "Dexter" Holland
b. December 29, 1965

Greg Kriesel
b. January 20, 1965

James Lilja
b. Unknown

Kevin "Noodles" Wasserman
b. February 4, 1963

Ron Welty
b. February 1, 1971

Adam "Atom" Willard
b. August 15, 1973

Never mind the seventies, here are The Offspring.

Anyone who thought punk rock's legendary, foul-mouthed tirade had fizzled out with the Sex Pistols had to think again in the early nineties. That was when the genre received a timely mainstream revival, thanks to Green Day and this bunch of Californian screamers.

Huntington Beach gave birth to The Offspring in 1984 when erstwhile drummer **Bryan "Dexter" Holland** and **Greg K.** (aka **Greg Kriesel**) ran into each other (not literally) on their high-school cross-country team, leading to the formation of Manic Subsidal. **James Lilja** joined when Holland switched to vocals, and Doug Thompson completed the group's inaugural lineup. In 1985, Thompson's friend Jim Benton was Lilja's brief replacement, by which time Thompson himself had been replaced by high-school janitor **Kevin "Noodles" Wasserman**. Crucially, Noodles was older than both Holland and Kriesel and allegedly earned his place in the Manics because he could buy alcohol for his under-age bandmates.

After ditching the Manic Subsidal moniker in 1986, The Offspring issued the seven-inch single "I'll be Waiting"/"Blackball" on their Black Label imprint, named after a brand of beer (spot the emerging theme). In 1987, drummer **Ron Welty**, aged sixteen, signed up when the future Dr. James Lilja, MD, hung

up his sticks to concentrate on a medical degree in gynecological oncology. (He was not the only academic Offspring: Holland earned a master's degree in molecular biology.)

The group's self-titled, vinyl-only 1989 debut, issued on Nemesis Records, was produced by Thom Wilson, whose CV included the likes of the Dead Kennedys and Social Distortion. Wilson remained at the helm for 1991's *Baghdad* EP (on the Plastic Head label), featuring a cover of the rock standard "Hey Joe."

However, The Offspring first made an impact with *Ignition* (1992), on Epitaph, which led to live dates with the likes of No Doubt and the wonderfully named Californian outfit Voodoo Glow Skulls.

The Offspring went mainstream when *Smash* (1994) lived up to its title by soaring to No. 4 in the U.S., spurred on by the hits "Come Out and Play" and "Self Esteem"—on which Holland declared "I may be dumb but I'm not a dweeb / I'm just a sucker with no self esteem." Their second Epitaph release sold twelve million, making it rock's biggest-selling independent label album ever, and enabled the band to quit their day jobs. "I was still the custodian at an elementary school when *Smash* was playing on MTV," Noodles told *Kerrang!* "The six-year olds were all recognizing me from the video while I was cleaning up their piss."

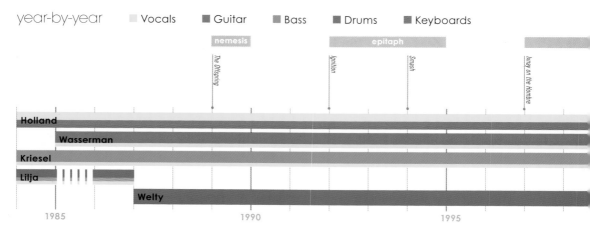

year-by-year ◼ Vocals ◼ Guitar ◼ Bass ◼ Drums ◼ Keyboards

12M	**2M**	**11.6M**	**2.4M**
Smash	Ixnay on the	Americana	Conspiracy
(1994)	Hombre	(1998)	of One
	(1997)		(2000)

Pete Parada
b. July 9, 1974

After contributing a cover of The Damned's "Smash It Up" to 1995's *Batman Forever* soundtrack, The Offspring spent much of 1996 entangled in legal wrangles with Epitaph. But, in 1997, their major-label debut—*Ixnay on the Hombre* (try the internet for an uncensored interpretation of the title)—yielded the hits "All I Want," "Gone Away," and "I Choose."

Still riding a commercial wave, the group rolled out *Americana* (1998), an album notable for a barely recognizable parody of Morris Albert's sentimental ballad "Feelings," the Beatles/Simon and Garfunkel-inspired "Why Don't You Get a Job?," and "Pretty Fly (For a White Guy)," a U.S. flop that crashed into the U.K. singles chart at No. 1 in January 1999. The song is perhaps most fondly remembered for the mock-German nonsense that passed for an intro: "Gunter, glieben, glauchen, globen"—borrowed from Def Leppard's "Rock of Ages"—was a foreign language education (of sorts) for disaffected punks everywhere.

After delivering the Ramones' "I Wanna Be Sedated" in the movie *Idle Hands* and playing at the Woodstock '99 festival, The Offspring returned with *Conspiracy of One*. Its lead single, "Original Prankster," was offered as a free download on the group's website, but only after the Columbia label threatened legal action over their plans to offer the whole album

online. The file-sharing advocates had the last laugh, however, donating a portion of *Conspiracy*'s profits to Napster co-founder Shawn Fanning.

"Prankster" was an appropriate title for The Offspring's run-in with Guns N' Roses front-man Axl Rose. He filed a cease-and-desist order when the Californians announced their new album would be called *Chinese Democrazy (You Snooze, You Lose)*, a reference to Guns N' Roses' long-awaited *Chinese Democracy*. The joke was on Rose when someone pointed out the date of the announcement—April 1.

Chinese Democrazy turned out to be *Splinter*, which featured, ironically enough, Guns N' Roses drummer Josh Freese, following Welty's departure in 2003. Welty's full-time replacement, **Adam "Atom" Willard**, lasted long enough to grace *Greatest Hits* (2005), but left in 2007 to focus on Angels & Airwaves, leaving **Pete Parada** as the group's fifth drummer.

"You're Gonna Go Far, Kid," from *Rise and Fall, Rage and Grace*, spent eleven weeks atop the U.S. Modern Rock Tracks chart on its way to selling 500,000 (the group's first U.S. single to reach that landmark).

Two decades on from *Ignition*, the band prepared *Days Go By* for 2012. "A message of hope," Holland told *Rolling Stone*, "is what I really wanted people to take away from this record." Pretty fly indeed. **MW**

■ Other percussion

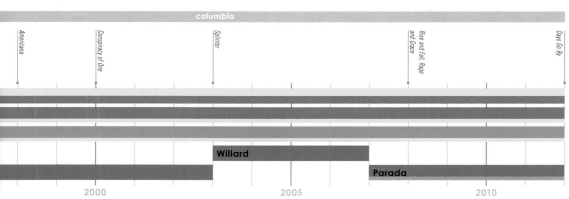

pantera 1981–2003

Darrell Abbott
b. Aug 20, 1966
d. Dec 6, 2004

Vinnie Paul Abbott
b. March 11, 1964

Rex Brown
b. July 27, 1964

Terry Glaze
b. November 29, 1964

Philip Anselmo
b. June 30, 1968

Donnie Hart
b. Unknown

In the nineties, metal's biggest exponents—Metallica and Iron Maiden—struggled with personnel issues and questionable musical choices. While the genre was never likely to die out, for some years it seemed in recession, with one notable exception. Texas quartet Pantera rose from humble (indeed, faintly ridiculous) beginnings to become one of metal's best-loved acts.

Founded by brothers "Diamond" **Darrell Abbott** (guitar) and **Vinnie Paul Abbott** (drums) in Arlington, Texas in 1981, Pantera initially focused on Kiss-inspired glam rock that highlighted Darrell's virtuosity. Joined by bassist **Rex Brown** (dubbed "Rexx Rocker") and a carousel of singers—the longest-standing being **Terry Glaze**—the band released four albums on their own Metal Magic label. Although a local following was soon established, true success came only when Glaze was replaced by **Philip Anselmo** in 1987 and the band switched their style to a harder, more thrash-indebted metal that led to a deal with Atlantic subsidiary Atco.

Cowboys from Hell (1990) showcased a new sound based on synchronized riffs and kick drums, topped by Anselmo's barked vocals. The thrash generation embraced Pantera, who rewarded their followers with the magnificent *Vulgar Display of Power* in 1992. This album, Pantera's best, contained songs that became iconic in modern metal: "Walk," "A New Level," and "Fucking Hostile." As Pantera toured the world, Darrell

(now trading as "Dimebag") was lauded as a guitar hero in the Eddie Van Halen/Randy Rhoads tradition.

Far Beyond Driven (1994) and *The Great Southern Trendkill* (1996) were invigorating—and the former was a surprise U.S. No. 1—but Pantera failed to take the necessary steps toward becoming metal's biggest band. Perhaps this was due to Anselmo's drug issues (he survived a heroin overdose in 1996), or changing fashions in metal, but even the fine *Reinventing the Steel* (2000) could not stop the rot. The events of 9/11 finished Pantera: stuck in an Irish hotel room, unable to fly after the terrorist attacks, the members argued to the point of splitting up. Anselmo severed contact with the Abbotts and a war of words erupted in the media.

The members embarked on new bands (Anselmo with Superjoint Ritual and later Down, in which he was joined by Brown; the Abbotts with Damageplan), expectations of a reunion remained high. Tragically, this was rendered impossible by the murder of Darrell Abbott in December 2004, when a disturbed fan shot him dead on stage. But his work with Pantera ensures his legacy, and the profile of this most mercurial of bands has, if anything, risen higher since his death.

In 2012, Anselmo was cautious when Vinnie Abbott mooted a reunion with Zakk Wylde on guitar. "It would be rough not to see Dimebag on stage to my left," he told loudwire.com. "I would feel naked." **JM**

year-by-year   ■ Vocals   ■ Guitar   ■ Bass   ■ Drums

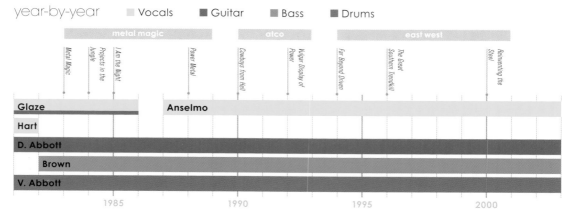

pavement 1989–2010

Stephen Malkmus
b. May 30, 1966

Scott Kannberg
b. August 30, 1966

Gary Young
b. May 3, 1953

Mark Ibold
b. October 17, 1962

Bob Nastanovich
b. August 27, 1967

Steve West
b. December 8, 1966

From shambolic origins in late-eighties California, Pavement became one of alternative rock's most insidiously influential acts in the next decade.

Formed in San Joaquin County by guitarist and singer **Stephen Malkmus** and guitarist **Scott Kannberg** (a.k.a. Spiral Stairs), they began zipping out EPs at a smart rate. The first, 1989's *Slay Tracks (1933–1969)*, was cut at the home studio of producer and original drummer **Gary Young** and—thanks to a blend of underground acclaim and limited pressings—became a collector's item. On the 1990 follow-up *Demolition Plot J-7*, Jason Fawkes took over on drums before internal tensions saw Young back again. The ramshackle lo-fi recipe remained unchanged.

Emerging from the EP cycle after 1991's *Perfect Sound Forever*, Pavement got down to business with **Mark Ibold** on bass and the release of their debut album *Slanted and Enchanted* (1992). Percussionist **Bob Nastanovich** was brought in, too, mainly to counter the unreliability of Young, who tended to disrupt shows with clowning rather than drumming. Matters came to a head on tour: Young was booted out, **Steve West** came in, and Nastanovich remained.

Crooked Rain, Crooked Rain (1994) suggested an intensifying of focus as the band edged away from a heavy debt to The Fall—a debt Fall leader Mark E Smith derided—and flirted with pop on "Cut Your

Hair." Malkmus was also confident enough to take potshots at The Smashing Pumpkins and Stone Temple Pilots on "Range Life." A touch of arrogance was fair: after a breakthrough with a compilation of the EPs, 1993's *Westing (By Musket & Sextant)*, Pavement albums would regularly hit the U.K. charts, although the U.S. market was destined to be largely resistant.

Wowee Zowee (1995) returned to experimentation, but that was no obstacle to progress. Pavement's free-associating lyrics and crisp, angular music were becoming a pervasive influence, most explicit in U.K. band Blur's change of tack on their self-titled 1997 album. That same year, Pavement bounced back to commercial appeal with *Brighten the Corners* and the dry, quirkily anthemic "Stereo," but internal disputes meant there would be just one more album. *Terror Twilight* (1999), produced by Nigel Godrich, arrived riven with tension, epitomized by a show at the Coachella festival where Malkmus barely managed to sing. Pavement would not last much longer.

Such events made it much more gratifying and unexpected when Pavement re-formed for ecstatically received shows in 2010. There were no new records— Malkmus was devoted to his Jicks, Kannberg to Spiral Stairs—just the extensive compilation *Quarantine the Past* (named after a line in 1994's "Gold Soundz") and a satisfying sense of closure. **MaH**

year-by-year　■ Vocals　■ Guitar　■ Bass　■ Drums　■ Other percussion

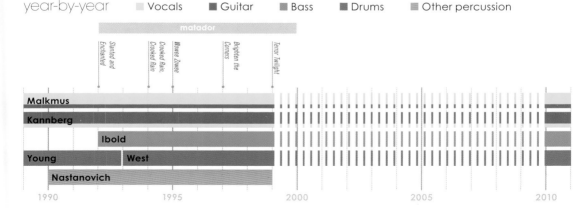

pearl jam 1991–present

Jeff Ament
b. March 10, 1963

Stone Gossard
b. July 20, 1966

Mike McCready
b. April 5, 1966

Eddie Vedder
b. December 23, 1964

Dave Krusen
b. March 10, 1966

Matt Chamberlain
b. April 17, 1967

The missing link between the Grateful Dead and Spinal Tap, Pearl Jam have a loyal following, myriad live albums, and a drummer-crowded family tree.

When Seattle grunge progenitors Green River splintered in 1988, guitarists **Stone Gossard** and Bruce Fairweather, and bassist **Jeff Ament**, recruited singer Andrew Wood and drummer Greg Gilmore to form Mother Love Bone. Wood died before their debut's release, inspiring his roommate, Soundgarden's Chris Cornell, to create a tribute. The resultant *Temple of the Dog* (1991) featured Cornell, Ament, Gossard, Soundgarden drummer **Matt Cameron**, guitarist **Mike McCready** (a friend of Gossard), and **Eddie Vedder**. The latter had entered the picture when Gossard, Ament, and McCready tried to enlist ex-Chili Peppers drummer **Jack Irons** for a new band. Irons declined (leaving drumming on their demos to Cameron and Chris Friel, from McCready's previous group Shadow) but suggested his friend Vedder as a singer.

With drummer **Dave Krusen**, Gossard, Ament, McCready, and Vedder formed Mookie Blaylock. In 1991, they became Pearl Jam—the "jam" in homage to Neil Young's extended songs. Having recorded *Ten*

(featuring Kronos Quartet cellist Walter Gray) and featured in Cameron Crowe's Seattle-set *Singles*, the band dispensed with Krusen, then struggling with alcohol. They auditioned future Rage Against the Machine man Brad Wilk but settled on ex-Edie Brickell drummer **Matt Chamberlain**. However, unwilling to tour, Chamberlain lasted just two months before nominating his own replacement: **Dave Abbruzzese**.

With Nirvana illuminating the Seattle scene, Pearl Jam's star rose. When they joined 1992's Lollapalooza tour, their nearly year-old debut had hit the U.S. Top Ten. (*Ten* eventually outsold *Nevermind* by three million in the U.S.) In its wake, Gossard united with members of another Seattle band, Satchel, to create the group Brad and *Shame* (1993), the first of their four albums.

Pearl Jam set a first-week sales record with 1993's *Vs.* The album was their first with Brendan O'Brien— soon to become one of rock's biggest producers. Uncomfortable with his new, iconic status, Vedder seized control of the group and crafted 1994's jarring (but multi-million-selling) *Vitalogy*. During its recording, drum duties passed from Abbruzzese to an old friend: Jack Irons. Meanwhile, McCready and Ament formed

year-by-year · Vocals · Guitar · Bass · Drums · Keyboards

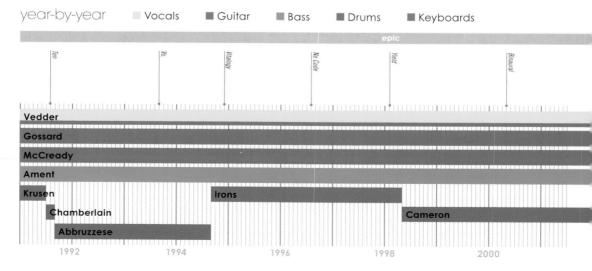

Dave Abbruzzese
b. May 17, 1968

Jack Irons
b. July 18, 1962

Matt Cameron
b. November 28, 1962

Boom Gaspar
b. 1953

the side-projects Mad Season (with Alice in Chains' singer Layne Staley) and Three Fish, respectively.

Mirror Ball (1995) saw the band backing Neil Young, with whom they toured. Contractual red tape, and minimal input by Vedder (then entangled in "a pretty intense stalker problem") meant the album was credited to Young alone. The fractured band's *No Code* (1996) was their last U.S. No.1 for a decade. *Yield* (1998) marked a revival of the band's verve yet proved Irons' swansong. In the wake of Soundgarden's split, Matt Cameron returned in time for *Live on Two Legs* (1998) and a fan club single cover of Wayne Cochran's 1961 flop "Last Kiss." A commercial release of the latter became, in 1999, their biggest hit.

From 2000 to 2001, their discography exploded via McCready's side-project The Rockfords, Gossard's solo *Bayleaf*, and multiple live albums from a tour for the group's rollicking *Binaural*. The latter featured Cameron's wife April on viola, cellist Justine Foy (who had played on Soundgarden's *Superunknown*), Crowded House producer Mitchell Froom on keyboards, and percussion by Prince associate Wendy Melvoin and Elvis Costello's drummer Pete Thomas.

Riot Act (2002) marked the addition of keyboard player **Boom Gaspar**—now a mainstay of Pearl Jam's live incarnation—and the group's estrangement from the mainstream. With their European profile at a ten-year low, Pearl Jam's U.S. fanbase was eroded by their anti-President Bush stance. Unrepentant, they joined the 2004 Vote for Change tour with Bruce Springsteen.

Relief came with 2006's *Pearl Jam*. Its political fire was leavened by humor (not least its meaningless avocado artwork) and refreshingly accessible songs. More bounty came via Vedder's splendid *Into the Wild* soundtrack (2007), which eclipsed Ament's solo *Tone* (2008), featuring King's X front-man Doug Pinnick.

The revival was completed by 2009's *Backspacer*, their first album produced by Brendan O'Brien since *Yield* and first U.S. No.1 since *No Code*. In 2011, Vedder issued *Ukulele Songs* while the band celebrated their anniversary with the Cameron Crowe-directed documentary *PJ20*. Now the only one of Seattle's big-sellers to have survived without splitting or fatalities, Pearl Jam co-headlined the U.K.'s 2012 Isle of Wight festival alongside Springsteen and Tom Petty. "We're still," said Vedder, "wondering where it might go." **BM**

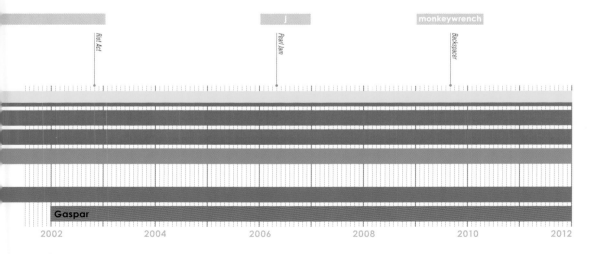

tom petty & the heartbreakers 1976–present

Tom Petty
b. October 20, 1950

Mike Campbell
b. February 1, 1950

Benmont Tench
b. September 7, 1953

Ron Blair
b. September 16, 1948

Stan Lynch
b. May 21, 1955

Howie Epstein
b. July 21, 1955
d. February 23, 2003

Tom Petty and the Heartbreakers have been one of America's most authoritative and entertaining rock groups for over thirty-five years. Magnificent live, they combine musical clout and (usually) restrained power with songs that often champion the underdog.

The group originated in Gainesville, Florida, in 1970, when **Tom Petty** (vocals, guitar) and **Mike Campbell** (lead guitar) were in Mudcrutch, whom **Benmont Tench** (keyboards) joined in 1972. When the band moved to L.A., but split due to a lack of success, these three enlisted **Ron Blair** (bass) and **Stan Lynch** (drums) to form Tom Petty and the Heartbreakers.

Their self-titled 1976 debut album was a slow-burning classic at home, but songs like "American Girl" and "Breakdown" ensured they eventually hit the jackpot. Quicker success arrived in the U.K. where the album went to No. 24 and "Anything That's Rock 'n' Roll" charted on the back of a triumphant tour.

You're Gonna Get It! (1978) rose to U.S. No. 23 and was equally successful musically, with "Listen to Her Heart," "I Need to Know," and the title song all expert distillations of their sound. *Damn the Torpedoes* (1979),

a U.S. No. 2, is the quintessential Heartbreakers record, with every song a gem, from "Refugee" and "Here Comes My Girl," to "Louisiana Rain" and the catchy "Don't Do Me Like That" (their first U.S. Top Ten single). *Hard Promises* (1981) all but repeated the trick, with "The Waiting," "A Thing About You" and "A Woman in Love (It's Not Me)" being particular highlights.

However, the strains of success began to tell: Blair left and was replaced by **Howie Epstein** in time for *Long After Dark* (1982), which showcased excellent songs like "You Got Lucky," "Straight Into Darkness," and "Change of Heart." *Southern Accents* (1985) edged into experimental territory with "Don't Come Around Here No More" and "It Ain't Nothin' to Me" (both co-written with producer Dave Stewart), but *Pack Up the Plantation: Live!* (1985) proved a more straightforward, rousing record of the band's show.

In 1987, *Let Me Up (I've Had Enough)* ended with the title track, a plaintive cry that Petty was shortly to answer. Its "Jammin' Me" was co-written by Petty, Campbell, and Bob Dylan—the group having toured as Dylan's backing band, supporting him and ex-Byrd

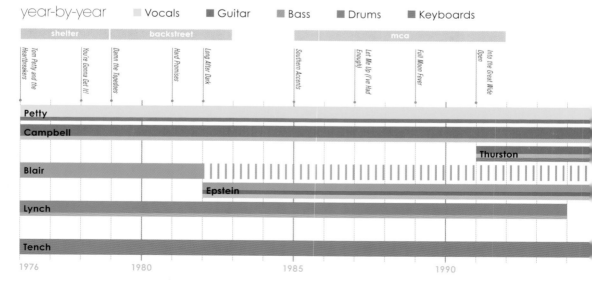

year-by-year ■ Vocals ■ Guitar ■ Bass ■ Drums ■ Keyboards

shelter | backstreet | mca

Tom Petty and the Heartbreakers | You're Gonna Get It! | Damn the Torpedoes | Hard Promises | Long After Dark | Southern Accents | Let Me Up (I've Had Enough) | Full Moon Fever | Into the Great Wide Open

Petty

Campbell

Thurston

Blair

Epstein

Lynch

Tench

1976 | 1980 | 1985 | 1990

Scott Thurston
b. January 10, 1952

Steve Ferrone
b. April 25, 1950

Dave Grohl
b. January 14, 1969

Roger McGuinn as well as playing their own set. Petty teamed up with Dylan, George Harrison, Roy Orbison, and Jeff Lynne to form the Traveling Wilburys, who released two albums in 1988 and 1990. In between, he recorded the solo *Full Moon Fever* (1989), produced by Lynne. Hits like "I Won't Back Down" and the glorious "Free Fallin'" made it the biggest commercial success of Petty's career at that point.

When the group reunited in 1991, they hired **Scott Thurston** (rhythm guitar, keyboards) to flesh out their already full sound. The resulting *Into the Great Wide Open* (1991) was another resounding success, with "King's Highway," "Learning to Fly," and the title track conjuring those vast spaces they traverse so smoothly.

Another fine solo effort by Petty, *Wildflowers* (1994), marked the start of a successful relationship with producer Rick Rubin that would also yield the accomplished soundtrack *She's the One* (1996) and the laid-back *Echo* (1999). Meanwhile, Lynch was sacked and, after a brief stint by Nirvana's **Dave Grohl** (before he started the Foo Fighters), drummer **Steve Ferrone** joined the Heartbreakers at the end of 1994.

In 2002, the Heartbreakers were inducted into the Rock and Roll Hall of Fame. But by the time of the recording of *The Last DJ* later that year, bassist Epstein was on his way out as a result of the heroin addiction that was to contribute to his tragic end in 2003 (Ron Blair returned to replace him). With unfortunate irony, the same year saw the Heartbreakers' 1993 *Greatest Hits* clocking up its ten millionth sale in the U.S.

Petty's third solo album, *Highway Companion*, arrived in 2006, before he, Campbell, and Tench revived the Mudcrutch name for a self-titled, U.S. Top Ten album (2008). Its guitar was by original Mudcrutch member Tom Leadon—brother of the Eagles' Bernie—who had originally shared solos with Campbell.

The superb *Live Anthology* (2009) kept fans busy before *Mojo* (2010), suffused with a bluesier feel than the group's previous work. "I'm very glad it worked out this way," Petty told *Mojo* magazine. "I didn't do it to make money... I thought I was giving up the chance to make money. Musicians who are constantly employed are very few. But I was sure I'd make enough to get by and I'd be happy doing it." **MiH**

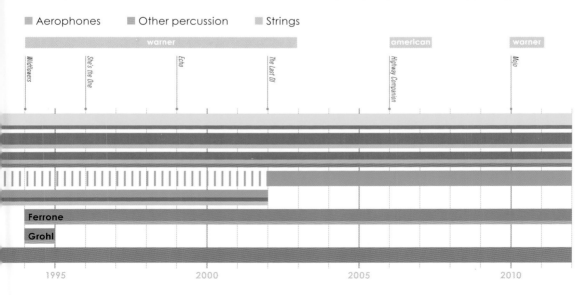

■ Aerophones   ■ Other percussion   ■ Strings

warner   american   warner

Wildflowers | She's the One | Echo | The Last DJ | Highway Companion | Mojo

Ferrone

Grohl

1995   2000   2005   2010

pink floyd 1965–2005

Roger Waters
b. September 6, 1943

Nick Mason
b. January 27, 1944

Rick Wright
b. July 28, 1943
d. September 15, 2008

Syd Barrett
b. June 1, 1946
d. July 7, 2006

Bob Klose
b. 1945

David Gilmour
b. March 6, 1946

"You'd have to be daft as a brush to say you didn't like Pink Floyd," conceded John Lydon in 2010, over three decades after his "I hate Pink Floyd" shirt was etched into Sex Pistols folklore. "They've done great stuff."

"Great stuff" was far from assured when London-based architecture students **Roger Waters**, **Nick Mason**, and **Rick Wright** convened in 1963 to perform R&B covers under names like Sigma 6. In 1964, with guitarist **Bob Klose** and inspirational front-man **Syd Barrett**, they evolved into The Tea Set and recorded their first demo. By 1965, the group had become The Pink Floyd Sound, named after Carolina blues players Pink Anderson and Floyd Council.

Minus Klose and that extraneous "Sound," the Floyd became psychedelic London's house band. With the experimental Barrett at the helm, their repertoire, recalled Mason, was "abstract rhythm and blues, performing rather nasty operations on Chuck Berry material." Barrett's songwriting, however, flourished with 1967's hits "Arnold Layne," "See Emily Play," and The Piper at the Gates of Dawn. The epic "Astronomy Domine" and "Interstellar Overdrive" signposted the Floyd's trajectory into outer space.

Drugs fueled the unreliable Barrett's exit and—after reportedly attempting to enlist Jeff Beck—the Floyd replaced him with **David Gilmour**. Finally blessed

with a superb musician, they continued to experiment with unconventional sounds, exemplified by 1969's half live (good), half studio (mostly bad) Ummagumma, their first album to enter Billboard's Top 100.

With Atom Heart Mother—a U.K. chart-topping flirtation with "classical rock"—the Floyd entered the seventies as cult arena-fillers. They streamlined their music on Meddle (1971) and Obscured by Clouds (1972), with Waters' lyrics preoccupied by the trappings of stardom, futility of war, and injustice of society. These sober themes were leavened by Gilmour and Wright's sumptuous musicianship and—on their first U.S. chart-topper, Dark Side of the Moon (1973)—saxophonist Dick Parry and singer Clare Torry.

Propelled by the hit "Money," Dark Side of the Moon transformed the band into superstars. Only Led Zeppelin rivaled their mystique, yet the Floyd had no Page or Plant-esque icon. So anonymous that they could walk through their own audiences undetected, the band soundtracked their ambivalence to success with 1975's bleak Wish You Were Here and 1977's vicious Animals. A tour for the latter saw the addition of guitarist Snowy White, who combined duties with the Floyd and Thin Lizzy for the ensuing four years.

The group's live show had evolved into a mélange of sight, sound, and inflatables—notably an iconic

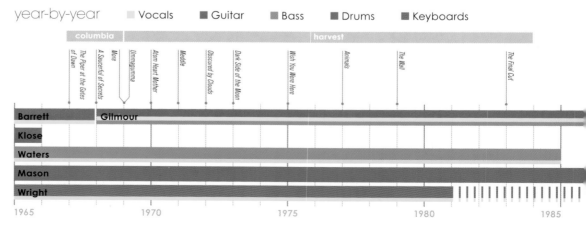

flying pig. Amid these theatrics, Waters fretted that his messages were being overlooked—frustration that fueled the band's most ambitious project: *The Wall* (1979). Gilmour and co-producer Bob Ezrin knocked Waters' demos into shape and session players— including Toto drummer Jeff Porcaro and jazz guitarist Lee Ritenour—bolstered the sound. Its fuse lit by the chart-topping "Another Brick in the Wall," the work consumed the band for four years, spawning a movie in 1982. But after refereeing bitter power struggles between Waters and director Alan Parker, Gilmour's strained relationship with the former finally snapped.

In 1983, *The Final Cut* omitted Wright—fired for apathy in 1979 and allowed onto the *Wall* tours as a contributor only—and relegated Gilmour and Mason to session players on Waters' "requiem for the post-war dream." Disregarding the relative failure of both this and his solo *The Pros and Cons of Hitch Hiking,* Waters left the band in 1985. Gilmour and Mason opted to continue without him; recalling Wright to make them, said the guitarist, "stronger, legally and musically." Litigation duly ensued. "The argument," Waters reflected twenty years later, "was me rather pompously—and, I admit now, erroneously— suggesting that, because I wasn't in the band anymore, that the brand and band name should be retired."

The "brand" proved the winner. Waters' star-studded revival of *The Wall* (1990) and the best-selling of his solo albums (*Amused to Death,* 1992) were no match for the Floyd's record-breaking tours and international successes *A Momentary Lapse of Reason* (1987), *The Division Bell* (1994), and the live *Pulse* (1995).

After the latter, the band effectively ceased to be, yet their legacy lived on in artists as diverse as Marilyn Manson and Radiohead. Floydian output became, said Mason, a "recycling business" of reissues and compilations, most notably 2001's *Echoes.*

A heartwarming coda came four decades after The Pink Floyd Sound's debut. Urged by *Wall* movie star and event organizer Bob Geldof, Waters, Gilmour, Mason, and Wright reunited to headline 2005's Live8. The event was touching and timely—Wright died of cancer just three years later.

Waters professed to be interested in further work, but Gilmour resisted: the two factions appeared separately at a tribute show for Barrett, who died in 2006. The success of Gilmour's *On an Island* (2006) vindicated his resolve, although he guested on a single date on Waters' *The Wall* tour in 2011. With the surviving members nearing seventy, further reunions seem highly unlikely—but then there are those who thought they were doomed without Syd Barrett. **BM**

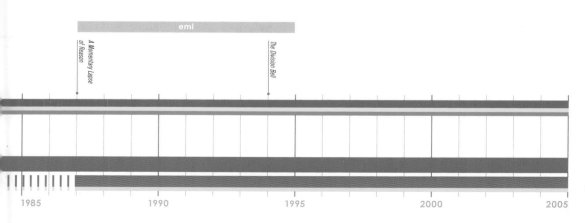

The Piper at the Gates of Dawn (1967)

Ummagumma (1969)

Meddle (1971)

Dark Side of the Moon (1973)

Wish You Were Here (1975)

Animals (1977)

The Wall (1979)

The Final Cut (1983)

A Momentary Lapse of Reason (1987)

The Division Bell (1994)

Nick Mason, **Roger Waters**, **Rick Wright**, and **Syd Barrett** laying down tracks—a far cry from the sophisticated studio scenarios of later years.

Pretty in Pink: **Mason**, **David Gilmour**, **Wright** and **Waters**.

Wright, **Waters**, and **Mason** live in Rotterdam, shortly before beginning to record *Meddle*.

Touring *Dark Side…* with backing singers and, second from right, saxophonist **Dick Parry**.

Waters and **Mason** at Nassau Coliseum, New York, in June 1975.

Touring bassist and guitarist **Snowy White, Mason**, and **Waters** on the In The Flesh tour for the *Animals* album at Wembley Empire Pool in London, in March 1977.

The teacher and the band, including extra drummer Willie Wilson, at a final *Wall* concert.

Bob Geldof in a still from the 1982 *Wall* movie. *The Final Cut* was originally its soundtrack.

The Floyd's iconic pig returns on the extended Momentary Lapse tour, in Belgium in 1989.

Two pigs? Check. Lots of lights? Check. Explosions? Check. The Floyd bring their full artillery for a performance of "One of These Days (I'm Going to Cut You Into Little Pieces)" in 1994.

pixies 1986–present

Black Francis
b. April 6, 1965

Kim Deal
b. June 10, 1961

Joey Santiago
b. June 10, 1965

David Lovering
b. December 6, 1961

It is not entirely fair to liken the Pixies to the Velvet Underground—they did better on the charts than Lou Reed's crew—but it is also not far off the mark. As with the Velvets, the Pixies cannot be properly evaluated by sales. A more appropriate gauge is the impact the band had. With disciples ranging from David Bowie to Radiohead, it is arguable that only R.E.M. exerted more influence on modern rock during that decade.

Unfortunately, the Pixies did not quite stick around long enough—at least on their first go-round—to reap the benefits of all they had sown. Their best albums came out before the general public was really ready, and the group was splintering by the time Nirvana and other attentive students turned their sound into the commercial juggernaut known as alt rock.

Born in Boston—after college chums **Black Francis** (Charles Thompson IV) and **Joey Santiago** enlisted **Kim Deal** and **David Lovering**—the Pixies did not debut as polished musicians. Deal had never even played the bass when she auditioned to be the bassist (lured by an ad that cited Hüsker Dü and folk trio Peter, Paul, and Mary). But they did not need jazz chops to carry out their plan. Borrowing from the Hüskers, and paying attention to fellow New Englanders Throwing Muses, the Pixies minted a signature sound of toothy guitar and pointy pop hooks with their first demo (known as *The Purple Tape*). It was impressive enough to persuade British label 4AD (famed for the Cocteau Twins) to sign the band and release 1987's EP *Come On Pilgrim*, which hit No. 5 on the U.K. indie chart.

The Pixies found greater acclaim with their full-length debut, 1988's Steve Albini-produced *Surfer Rosa*, which spent more than a year on the U.K. indie charts. Success came a bit slower in the U.S., where it took *Surfer Rosa* seventeen years to go gold. However, the album's combination of taboo lyrical content and a start-stop musical dynamic caught the ears of many future stars—including Kurt Cobain, who would call upon Albini to produce Nirvana's *In Utero*.

The stone-cold classic *Doolittle* (1989) provided a road-map for the alt-rock explosion of the nineties and became the band's first U.S. hit. The surf-inspired *Bossanova* (1990) was another winner. However, by this point, band relationships had grown tense, especially between Francis and Deal. Each pursued outside projects, the former working as a solo artist (eventually taking the name Frank Black), the latter leading The Breeders. The group managed one more solid affair, 1991's *Trompe le Monde* (one of Dave Grohl's all-time favorites) before calling it quits in 1993.

The Pixies' legend, however, only grew stronger in their absence. When they reunited in 2004, they found the biggest fan base of their career waiting. And when Radiohead were booked to headline over them at 2004's Coachella festival, Thom Yorke declared: "The Pixies opening for us is like The Beatles opening for us… There's no way we can follow the Pixies!"

Sadly, not even Bono's beseeching can persuade the band to record a new album. "We're afraid," Santiago admitted, "that it might cause friction." **JiH**

year-by-year ▪ Vocals ▪ Guitar ▪ Bass ▪ Drums

the pogues 1982–present

Shane MacGowan
b. December 25, 1957

Spider Stacy
b. Dec 14, 1958

Jem Finer
b. July 20, 1955

James Fearnley
b. October 9, 1954

Andrew Ranken
b. November 13, 1953

Philip Chevron
b. June 17, 1957

Darryl Hunt
b. May 4, 1950

Terry Woods
b. December 4, 1947

The Pogues are celebrated for "Fairytale of New York," a 1987 Christmas hit that has returned to the U.K. Top Twenty every year since 2006. It defines British and Irish festivities as much as Bing Crosby's "White Christmas."

Versed in folk and punk, **Shane MacGowan**, **Spider Stacy**, **Jem Finer**, and **James Fearnley** united in London in 1982. They called themselves Pogue Mahone (really "pòg mo thòin," Gaelic for "kiss my ass," and hence promptly abbreviated), added **Andrew Ranken** and bassist Cait O'Riordan to the lineup, and issued "Dark Streets of London" on their own label. Having supported The Clash on a U.K. tour, they were signed by the Stiff label and recorded *Red Roses for Me*. Its gems included "Waxie's Dargle," on which Stacy supplied percussion by hitting his head with a beer tray. An EP, *Poguetry in Motion*, and an appearance in Alex Cox's surreal western *Straight to Hell* ensued.

Rum, Sodomy & the Lash—featuring MacGowan's astonishing "A Pair of Brown Eyes"—was produced by Elvis Costello, whom O'Riordan married and joined on tour. **Darryl Hunt** replaced her in The Pogues, who united with The Dubliners for the frenzied "The Irish Rover," their first Top Ten hit.

Then came "Fairytale of New York" with Kirsty MacColl, and *If I Should Fall from Grace with God* (1988), produced by Steve Lillywhite (MacColl's husband). The lineup now included **Philip Chevron** and **Terry Woods**, a multi-instrumentalist from Steeleye Span. Lillywhite produced *Peace and Love* (1989) and The Clash's Joe Strummer took over for *Hell's Ditch* (1990), but MacGowan's writing was faltering. In 1991, the band sacked him after one hangover too many. (Quite amicably, as they then went out for something to eat.) Strummer took MacGowan's place for booked dates, then Stacy became lead vocalist.

Waiting for Herb (1993) boasted the hit "Tuesday Morning," but *Pogue Mahone* (1996) spelled the end. MacGowan and his new band, The Popes, recorded *The Snake* (1994) and *The Crock of Gold* (1997), while his abrasive growl cropped up on a cover of the Eurovision winner "What's Another Year" and a version of "What a Wonderful World" with Nick Cave.

The Pogues reunited with MacGowan in 2001 and initiated a tradition of Christmas tours. At their best, the Pogues' hybrid of folk, rock, and punk has a magical *joie de vivre*—and we can all drink to that. **SL**

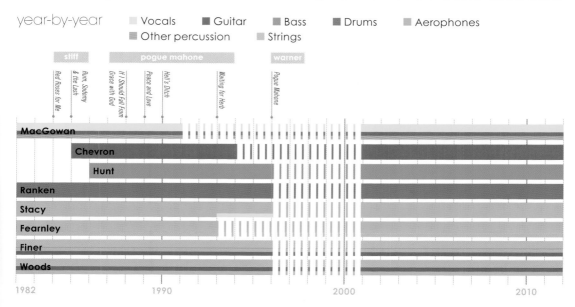

year-by-year   ■ Vocals   ■ Guitar   ■ Bass   ■ Drums   ■ Aerophones
■ Other percussion   ■ Strings

stiff   pogue mahone   warner

Red Roses for Me | Rum, Sodomy & the Lash | If I Should Fall From Grace with God | Peace and Love | Hell's Ditch | Waiting for Herb | Pogue Mahone

MacGowan
Chevron
Hunt
Ranken
Stacy
Fearnley
Finer
Woods

1982   1990   2000   2010

the police 1977–2008

Sting
b. October 2, 1951

Stewart Copeland
b. July 16, 1952

Andy Summers
b. December 31, 1942

Henry Padovani
b. October 13, 1952
d. October 18, 2011

It is easy to forget, but before saving the rain forests, Tantric sex sessions, and questionable acting made him an occasional figure of derision, **Sting**—born Gordon Sumner, but nicknamed after he wore a yellow-and-black striped sweater—was founder of The Police: briefly the biggest band on the planet.

Formerly an English teacher from Newcastle, singer and bass-player Sting set off for London in search of fame and fortune. Having hooked up with American drummer **Stewart Copeland** (latterly of progressive folkies Curved Air) and French guitarist **Henry Padovani**, success seemed tantalizingly close. However, a single released under the band name The Police—"Fall Out"—failed to chart. A side project involving ex-Gong mainstay Mike Howlett saw Sting and Copeland team up with guitarist **Andy Summers** (whose résumé included stints with Soft Machine and Eric Burdon's Animals) as, first, Strontium 90, then The Elevators. But it was as The Police that Sting, Summers, and Copeland would find the recipe for success in 1977—albeit once Padovani had departed.

With Copeland's brother Miles enticed to manage them on the strength of the early song "Roxanne," a deal with A&M was soon forthcoming. Copeland's fascination with Sting's plaintive tale of a prostitute was not, unfortunately, shared by radio stations. Neither did they like the suicidal overtones of "Can't

Stand Losing You," giving their 1978 debut album *Outlandos d'Amour* almost no chance of charting. Embarking on a large-scale charm offensive, the newly peroxided trio set out on tours across Britain and America, whipping up enough positive reaction for A&M to give them another push. On their re-release, "Can't Stand Losing You," "Roxanne," and "So Lonely" were hits on both sides of the pond. The album also reached No. 6 in the U.K. and No. 23 in the U.S.

The Police's mix of white reggae with new wave rock sensibilities was more exaggerated on their second album, *Reggatta de Blanc*, in 1979, with "Walking on the Moon" demonstrating the band's pared-down power. The song reached No. 1 in the U.K., matching the album's poppier first single "Message in a Bottle." Sting, it seemed, knew how to write. (He also made a notable cameo in the 1979 movie adaptation of The Who's *Quadrophenia*.)

The hits "De Do Do Do, De Da Da Da" and "Don't Stand So Close to Me" from *Zenyattà Mondatta* (1980) boosted The Police's profile worldwide. The funky album cut "Voices Inside My Head" became a New York disco favorite, while Summers's instrumental "Behind My Camel"—despite being roundly loathed by Sting and Copeland—snared a Grammy award.

Ghost in the Machine (1981) made an even bigger mark. Recorded partly at George Martin's studio on

year-by-year   ■ Vocals   ■ Guitar   ■ Bass   ■ Drums

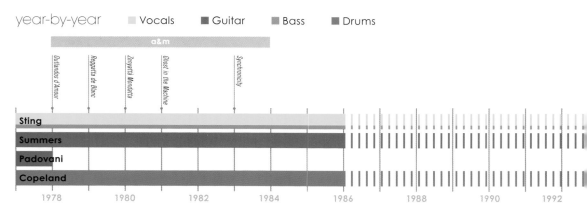

Montserrat, the Caribbean influence oozed into "Every Little Thing She Does Is Magic," which topped the U.S. rock chart. At home, that song and "Invisible Sun" both hit No. 1, despite the latter's controversial theme of the troubles in Northern Ireland.

Not everyone was content, however. It was one thing critics assuming that The Police was "Sting plus two others," but, by *Ghost in the Machine*, Summers suspected the singer might be thinking that, too. Sting would arrive with such high-quality demos that there was little opportunity for the guitarist (or Copeland, who regularly butted heads with Sting) to contribute as they once had. "All the really creative and dynamic stuff was being lost," Summers complained. "We were ending up backing a singer doing his pop songs."

As tensions grew, Copeland and Sting had to be pulled apart during the making of *Synchronicity* (1983). Tellingly, each member recorded in separate rooms. With the band's reggae feel all but gone, and synthesizers dominating songs such as "Wrapped Around Your Finger" and "Synchronicity I," Summers felt that he had entered his worst nightmare.

The rest of the world, however, loved it. The album and its classic "Every Breath You Take" topped charts around the globe, while both won Grammys for Best Rock Performance, with the single also winning Song of the Year. In the U.S.—where The Police sold out

New York's Shea Stadium in a repeat of The Beatles' triumph in 1965—*Synchronicity* spent seventeen weeks at No. 1 and ultimately sold eight million copies.

The world was theirs, but instead Sting played the lead in the flop sci-fi movie *Dune* (1984), recorded his first solo album, *Dream of the Blue Turtles,* and sang on Dire Straits' "Money for Nothing" (both 1985). Following three Police shows for Amnesty International in 1986, there was an abortive attempt at recording new material—the sole result being a rotten remake of "Don't Stand So Close to Me," appended to the hits set *Every Breath You Take,* that became their fifth U.K. chart-topper. But, according to Summers, "It was clear Sting had no real intention of writing for The Police."

Sting had no trouble writing for himself. *Nothing like the Sun* (1987) featured the hits "Fragile," "We'll Be Together," "Englishman in New York," and "Be Still My Beating Heart," while *The Soul Cages* (1991) and *Ten Summoner's Tales* (1993) continued his global success. *Mercury Falling* (1996), *Brand New Day* (1999), and *Sacred Love* (2003) maintained a platinum-coated run so strong that no one saw a year-long, thirtieth anniversary Police reunion tour coming in 2007.

A year—and nearly four million ticket sales—later proved it was back to business as usual. However, Sting warned fans, "There will be no new album, no big new tour… that's it for The Police." **JeH**

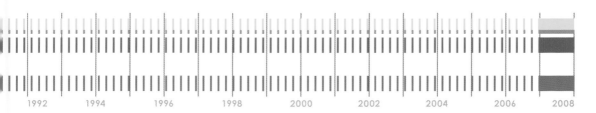

Outlandos
d'Amour (1978)

Reggatta de Blanc
(1979)

Zenyattà
Mondatta (1980)

Ghost in the
Machine (1981)

Synchronicity
(1983)

Left to right: **Andy Summers, Stuart Copeland, and Sting** police one of the passages at Waterloo station on the London Underground in 1978.

Copeland and **Sting** sweating in '78.

In a harbinger of later tension, **Sting** and **Copeland** pretend to push **Summers** into the River Thames during a London photoshoot in 1979.

Summers plays a Telecaster with The Police in 1979.

Copeland, Sting, and Summers during a photoshoot for the sleeve of *Zenyatta Mondatta*.

The Police live on the *Ghost in the Machine* tour in 1982.

Sting and Summers at the Sports Arena, Los Angeles, in January 1981.

Police work continues with a U.S. performance in 1983; more than eight million copies of that year's album, *Synchronicity*, have been sold in the United States.

iggy pop / the stooges 1967–present

Iggy Pop
b. July 21, 1947

Ron Asheton
b. July 17, 1948
d. January 4,
2009

**Scott
Asheton**
b. August 16,
1949

**Dave
Alexander**
b. June 3, 1947
d. February 10,
1975

**James
Williamson**
b. October 29,
1949

**Scott
Thurston**
b. January 10,
1952

**Brian
Glascock**
b. July 17, 1948

Hunt Sales
b. March 2, 1954

One of rock's most mesmeric performers, **Iggy Pop** had (and retains) the wild qualities of an intelligent, hyperactive child following unfettered instincts. Originally he fronted The Stooges, purveyors of sleaze-filled garage rock, before going solo for nearly thirty years. The group recently re-formed but, for both Pop and the Stooges, sales have never approached the heights of their formidable reputation.

First known as the Psychedelic Stooges, vocalist James Osterberg (known as Iggy from one of his earlier groups, the Iguanas), guitarist **Ron Asheton**, drummer **Scott Asheton**, and bassist **Dave Alexander** were all from Detroit. They came together late in 1967, inspired partly by local hard rock gods the MC5, and partly by Chicago blues musicians. Signed when the Elektra label came to seal a deal with headliners the MC5, the group seemed ready for take-off.

It was not to be. *The Stooges* came out in 1969 to mixed critical reaction and relatively few sales. But cuts such as "No Fun" and "I Wanna Be Your

Dog" crystallized their sneering boredom and wild sexuality—punk before its time. *Fun House* was issued in 1970 with much the same lack of effect. Despite more great tracks—"TV Eye" and "Loose"—the album was only later recognized as a seminal masterpiece.

So it was not success that ripped the group apart, but overindulgence. Most of the members were on heroin. By contrast, Alexander was an alcoholic and had to quit in 1970 (he died in 1975), replaced briefly by Thomas "Zeke" Zettner, then Jimmy Recca. Iggy persuaded saxophonist **Steve Mackay**, who had played on *Fun House*, to join their tour, and **James Williamson** came in as a second guitarist, but the brief magic was over and the Stooges split up in 1971.

While Iggy was nursing his own heroin habit, he met **David Bowie**, who persuaded him to come to London to record. They were joined by Williamson and, eventually, the Asheton brothers, with Ron relegated to playing bass. The result was *Raw Power*, whose phenomenal songs were somewhat diluted

year-by-year ☐ Vocals ■ Guitar ■ Bass ■ Drums ■ Keyboards

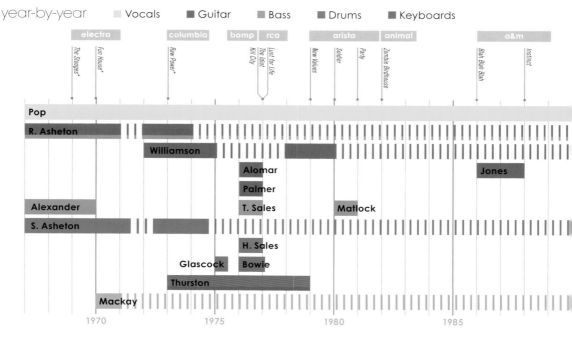

250,000	250,000	1M	500,000
The Stooges (1969)	Raw Power (1973)	Lust for Life (1977)	The Idiot (1977)

Tony Sales
b. June 26, 1951

David Bowie
b. January 8, 1947

Carlos Alomar
b. January 9, 1951

Phil Palmer
b. September 9, 1952

Glen Matlock
b. August 27, 1956

Steve Jones
b. September 3, 1955

Mike Watt
b. December 20, 1957

Steve Mackay
b. September 25, 1949

by Bowie's primitive recording techniques that no amount of re-mixing has ever been able to put right.

Touring for another year was enough to finish off the vulnerable group. Iggy was admitted to rehab in 1974 and kept quiet for a couple of years, despite escaping to record excellent songs with Williamson in 1975 (issued as 1977's *Kill City*). Then Bowie whisked him away to Berlin and they began prospecting.

Iggy's golden year was 1977. Both of his influential collaborations with Bowie, *The Idiot* and *Lust for Life*, were commercially and critically successful. Meanwhile, Iggy toured with a band that included **Hunt Sales** (drums), **Tony Sales** (bass), and **Carlos Alomar** (guitar), plus Bowie playing keyboards.

Williamson was back to produce *New Values* (1979) and *Soldier* (1980), although he was fired for wanting a fuller sound on the latter (featuring ex-Sex Pistol **Glen Matlock**) than Iggy would allow.

For a notorious hellraiser, Iggy turned out a run of consistent albums with guests. Blondie's Chris Stein produced *Zombie Birdhouse* (1982), and another Sex Pistol, **Steve Jones**, underpinned the success of *Blah Blah Blah* (which saw the return of Bowie). Jones can also be heard on *Instinct* (1988). *Brick by Brick* (1990) boasted stars including Slash and Duff of Guns N' Roses and Kate Pierson, and *American Caesar* (1993) expanded on its themes. Among the subsequent albums, *Naughty Little Doggie* (1996) included the gorgeous Johnny Thunders tribute "Look Away," and *Skull Ring* (2003) featured a reformation of the original Stooges with **Mike Watt** on bass, plus contributions from Green Day, Peaches, and Sum 41.

Recent sightings prove that Iggy is still one of the most riveting live performers around. His longevity has been enhanced by the rebirth of the Stooges in 2003 and a series of impressive gigs. (The Stooges entered the Rock and Roll Hall of Fame in 2010.) When Ron Asheton died in 2009, Williamson returned to the fray. Meanwhile, Iggy diverted onto a jazzy path that yielded *Préliminaires* (2009) and *Après* (2012). **MiH**

■ Aerophones

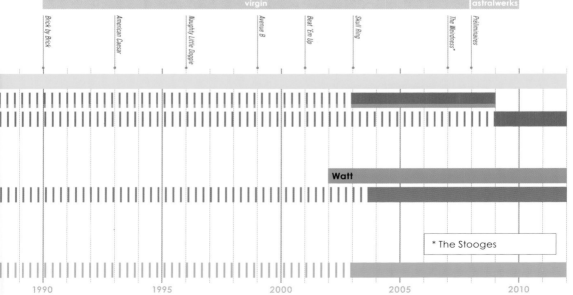

The Stooges (1969)

Fun House (1970)

Raw Power (1973)

The Idiot (1977)

Lust for Life (1977)

Blah Blah Blah (1986)

Brick by Brick (1990)

Skull Ring (2003)

The Wierdness (2007)

Préliminaires (2008)

The Stooges and MC5 pose with friends and executives after both groups signed to the Electra label in 1969.

Clockwise from bottom left **Iggy Pop, Scott Thurston, Ron Asheton, James Williamson,** and **Scott Asheton** on October 30, 1973.

Meeting of minds: **Iggy** and **David Bowie** in Germany in 1977.

Iggy and **Bowie** perform in 1977.

Iggy rides the crowd at Crosley Field, Cincinnati, Ohio, in June 1970.

With **Bowie**, backstage after an Iggy concert at The Ritz, New York, in 1986.

With Guns N' Roses guitarist Slash in 1990.

Iggy and James Hetfield of Metallica during the MTV Video Music Awards at Radio City Music Hall, New York, on August 28, 2003.

Mike Watt, Iggy, Scott Asheton, and **Ron Asheton** perform in New York in 2007.

Iggy takes centerstage at Studio 105, La Maison de la Radio, Paris, on May 28, 2009.

popol vuh 1969–2001

Florian Fricke
b. February 23, 1944
d. Dec 29, 2001

Daniel Fichelscher
b. March 7, 1953

Holger Trulzsch
b. unknown

Frank Fiedler
b. unknown

Conny Veit
b. unknown

Robert Eliscu
b. unknown

Djong Yun
b. unknown

Klaus Wiese
b. January 18, 1942
d. Jan 27, 2009

Popol Vuh was not so much a group in the usual sense as a vehicle for the influential experimentations of **Florian Fricke**. The music is often bundled into the krautrock category, but it is more accurate to think of it as the forerunner of today's new age and electronic music. Like most forerunners, Fricke was the best, but increasingly his music came to be devotional in form and content, harking back to older Christian traditions and utterly separate from the rock explosion. "Popol Vuh is a mass for the heart," he told writer Gerhard Augustin in 1996. "It is music for fove."

Fricke founded Popol Vuh—it means "meeting place" or "gathering under the sign of the sun" in Mayan—in Munich with **Holger Trulzsch** (drums) and **Frank Fiedler** (synthesizers) in 1969. He preferred to work in the studio, so Popol Vuh seldom played live.

It is true that their first two albums, *Affenstunde* (1970) and *In den Gärten Pharaos* (1971), had links to what came to be known as krautrock and, in particular, to the waves of sound associated with Tangerine Dream. For their *Zeit* (1972), remembered band leader Edgar Froese, "We invited Florian Fricke to the sessions. He owned the only big modular Moog

synth in Germany, but we didn't know how to use it that well. So we were forced into learning how the thing worked." (Amon Düül II also borrowed the Moog for their own 1972 album, *Wolf City*).

By *Hosianna Mantra* (1972), Fricke had moved away from such electronic instrumentation and reverted to acoustic sounds, with himself on piano. His meeting with singer **Djong Yun** was partly the reason—he claimed her voice was so perfect for his work that it ended his attempts to imitate vocal sounds with electronics. There were other new musicians: guitarist **Conny Veit**, oboe player **Robert Eliscu**, and tamboura player **Klaus Wiese**.

Shortly afterward, guitarist and drummer **Daniel Fichelscher** (from Amon Düül II) signed up. He proved to be the longest-serving collaborator, starting with the uplifting *Seligpreisung* (1973), on which Fricke sang for the first time, as Yun was not available. The music was pouring out of Fricke at that time, and he followed up with *Einsjäger und Siebenjäger* (1974) and *Das Hohelied Salomos* (1975), with vocals coming from Yun once again and sitar by **Alois Gromer**.

Aguirre (1975) saw a partial return to the heavenly

year-by-year
■ Vocals ■ Guitar ■ Drums ■ Keyboards ■ Aerophones

| liberty | pilz | kosmische | ua. | ohr | ua. | brain | egg | brain | innovative communication | uniton |

Affenstunde | *In den Gärten Pharaos* | *Hosianna Mantra* | *Seligpreisung* | *Das Hohelied Salomos* / *Einsjäger und Siebenjäger* | *Aguirre* | *Letzte Tage—Letzte Nächte* | *Söhne des Lichts—Bruder des Schattens—Herz aus Glas* | *Nosferatu* | *Die Nacht der Seele* | *Sei Still, wisse ICH BIN* | *Agape—Agape*

Yun

Knaup

Fichelscher

Trulzsch | Veit

B. Fricke | Eliscu

F. Fricke

Fiedler

Karrer

Wiese

Gromer

de Jong

1970   1975   1980   1985

P

Renate Knaup
b. unknown

Alois Gromer
b. unknown

Ted de Jong
b. unknown

Chris Karrer
b. unknown

Bernd Wippich
b. unknown

Bettina Fricke
b. unknown

choral effects of the first two albums. But Fricke was not backtracking. Some of the music was more than three years old and had been used, to supreme effect, as the soundtrack to Werner Herzog's *Aguirre, Wrath of God* (1972), a magnificent study of Spanish conquistadors at the end of their tether in South America. It proved to be the start of a very fruitful artistic relationship, with Fricke scoring three further Herzog movies—*Herz aus Glas* (1977), *Nosferatu* (1978), and *Cobra Verde* (1987)—and contributing to *The Enigma of Kaspar Hauser* (1974) and *Fitzcarraldo* (1982). However, Herzog was unusual in that he would often use music already written, rather than asking his composers to write music to suit the action.

Meanwhile, the general trend toward a modern style of sacred music was maintained and Popol Vuh continued to produce albums at a prolific rate. After the slightly rockier *Letzte Tage, Letzte Nachte* (1976) came the more somber *Brüder des Schattens—Söhne des Lichts* (1978) and *Die Nacht der Seele* (1979), both of which had Yun singing on them, with **Renate Knaup**, another refugee from Amon Düül II, joining her. On the latter, Fricke took up singing once again and,

with Amon Düül's **Chris Karrer** on soprano sax and Yun gone, he maintained vocal duties for *Sei Still, wisse ICH BIN* (1981), *Agape—Agape* (1983) and *Spirit of Peace* (1985), albeit supported by Knaup.

The group had produced sixteen albums in as many years. Output now started, almost inevitably, to diminish. *For You and Me* came out in 1991 and was the last album to feature Fichelscher, although he guested on *City Raga* (1995), a suite of songs based on Indian rhythms. These two releases showed the influence of guitarist and keyboard player Guido Hieronymus, as did the final studio album, *Shepherd's Symphony*, in 1997.

The last Popol Vuh release, *Messa di Orfeo* (1998), was, uncharacteristically, a live recording from the Time Zones festival in Molfetta, near Bari, Italy. But no one ever suggested that Fricke did things in a conventional manner. To the end, he remained almost impossible to categorize, conceding only that his songs could be defined as "magic music." His group managed the difficult feat of repeating key themes over many different albums yet always moving ahead. Tragically, he died following a stroke late in 2001. **MiH**

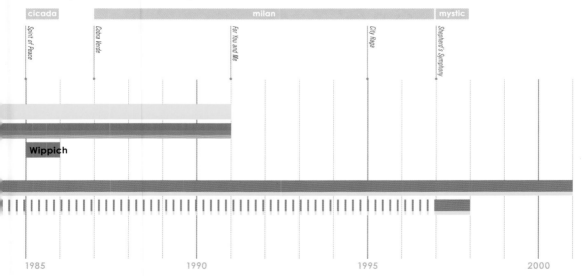

■ Other percussion   ■ Strings

elvis presley 1954–1977

Elvis Presley
b. January 8, 1935
d. August 16, 1977

Scotty Moore
b. December 27, 1931

Bill Black
b. September 17, 1926
d. October 21, 1965

D.J. Fontana
b. March 15, 1931

James Burton
b. August 21, 1939

"This was punk rock…" marveled U2's Bono to *Rolling Stone*. "**Elvis** changed everything—musically, sexually, politically." There had been rhythm and blues before Elvis, and country music, too. But in July 1954, he cut a cover of Arthur Crudup's R&B hit "That's All Right Mama" with guitarist **Scotty Moore** and bassist **Bill Black**—and gave it a country twang. He coupled it with Bill Monroe's bluegrass waltz "Blue Moon of Kentucky"—pepped up with an R&B beat. From that fusion grew rockabilly, and from *that* rose rock 'n' roll. "Before Elvis, everything was in black and white," said Keith Richards. "Then came Elvis. Zoom, glorious Technicolor." For John Lennon, the distinction was even more stark: "Before Elvis, there was nothing."

The joyous adrenalin rush of the five singles Presley cut for Sam Phillips's Sun label between July 1954 and August 1955 (drummer **D.J. Fontana** was hired in late 1954) marked a seismic shift in popular music. In their course, he morphed from an unknown artist with a penchant for crooning into a rising star. By 1956, RCA had snapped him up—a deal masterminded by new manager Colonel Tom Parker. From then until his draft into the U.S. Army in 1958, Presley cut definitive singles, including the reverb-drenched "Heartbreak Hotel" (his first U.S. No. 1 and the top-selling single of 1956), the poppy "All Shook Up," and the staggering "Hound Dog"—which sparked an inspired relationship with

songwriters Jerry Leiber and Mike Stoller. "Hound Dog" also sparked controversy when Presley performed a hip-grinding rendition on *The Milton Berle Show*.

The draft slowed the star's momentum—though the Colonel had stockpiled material to release during Presley's military service in Germany. On his return, the fine *Elvis Is Back!* (1960) demonstrated a broader stylistic range. Initially, the quality of Presley's records—such as the semi-operatic "It's Now or Never" (a worldwide, multi-million-selling No. 1) and the heartfelt "Are You Lonesome Tonight?"—suggested business as usual (with Moore and Fontana returning for studio work). The soundtrack to his film *Blue Hawaii* (1961)—featuring the enduring "Can't Help Falling in Love with You"—was outsold in the sixties only by that for the musical *West Side Story* (1961).

Within a few years, however, the stream of movies that an increasingly out-of-shape Elvis churned out—at the Colonel's insistence—during the sixties lowered his standing considerably. (Only 1964's comic *Viva Las Vegas* came anywhere close to fulfilling the promise of his greatest on-screen role, 1958's *King Creole*.)

Presley's comeback stemmed from his deeply rooted love of gospel music. Originally recorded in 1960, "Crying in the Chapel" gave him a U.S. Top Three hit in 1965. Its success spawned an album in the same vein—*How Great Thou Art*—that earned Presley his

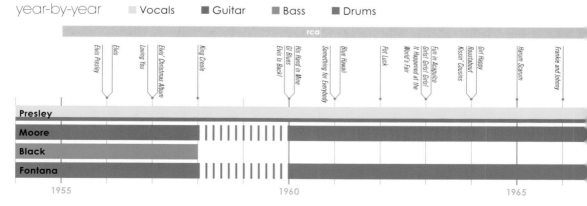

year-by-year   ■ Vocals   ■ Guitar   ■ Bass   ■ Drums

5M
Elvis
(1956)

15M
**Elvis' Christmas
Album**
(1957)

9M
**Elvis' Golden
Records**
(1958)

5M
Blue Hawaii
(1961)

first Grammy (for Best Sacred Performance). It led to a TV show—subsequently known as "the comeback special"—in 1968 in which the leather-clad, slimmed-down star injected his early hits with a new vibrancy. He closed with "If I Can Dream," a plea for universal brotherhood sung with throat-shredding intensity. Afterward, he told the show's producer that he would never again record a song he did not believe in.

He did, of course. But the late sixties and early seventies marked a genuine second coming. The superb *From Elvis in Memphis* (1969) featured the sobering "In the Ghetto," while the same sessions produced his final U.S. No. 1, "Suspicious Minds." Booked for shows at the Las Vegas Hilton, he set new attendance records. Backed by the TCB ("Taking Care of Business") band, led by guitarist **James Burton**, he delivered high-energy, funky sets—witness the exhilarating "Polk Salad Annie" on 1970's *On Stage*.

The hits continued apace. In 1972, "Burning Love" even saw a return to rock 'n' roll, and the epic concert staple "American Trilogy"—melodramatic overkill in other hands—succeeded because of Presley's disarming sincerity. Increasingly, however, he turned to reflective, bittersweet ballads such as "Always on My Mind" (1972)—perhaps to broaden his audience, but also informed by the disintegration of his marriage (he had wed Priscilla Ann Wagner in 1967).

Presley packed out New York's Madison Square Gardens for four shows in 1972, while *Aloha from Hawaii* (1973) saw a show broadcast to an estimated 1.5 billion people. An album of the latter provided his first U.S. No. 1 since *Roustabout* was knocked off the top by The Beatles in 1965, but he was now a troubled man. Relentless touring, Vegas residencies, an addiction to prescription drugs, and a burgeoning weight problem saw him become a parody by mid-decade, often given to rambling on-stage monologues. Miraculously, he could still cut it sometimes: his take on "Unchained Melody," from *Moody Blue* (1977) was brave, and the funky "Way Down" gave him a U.K. No. 1—posthumously. Elvis Presley's tired body finally gave out on August 16, 1977.

Re-releases, tourism to his Graceland home, shows such as the *Cirque du Soleil Viva Elvis* extravaganza, and the revitalization of the 1968 soundtrack off-cut "A Little Less Conversation" have made Elvis more commercially successful than ever. He is currently the second-richest dead celebrity, according to Forbes, with profits of $55 million in the year to October 2011.

Rock critic Lester Bangs, for one, knew that—despite his long, sad decline—Presley's impact would be imperishable: "I can guarantee you one thing," he wrote in his obituary for *Village Voice*, "We will never agree on anything as we agreed on Elvis." **RD**

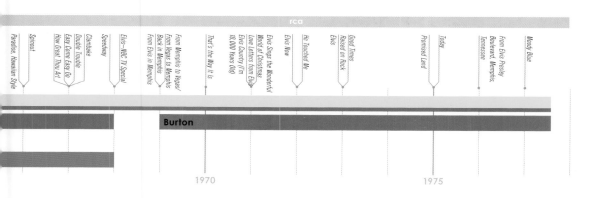

Elvis Presley (1956)

King Creole (1958)

Elvis Is Back!
(1960)

Blue Hawaii (1961)

**Elvis—NBC TV
Special** (1968)

**From Elvis in
Memphis** (1969)

That's the Way It Is
(1970)

He Touched Me
(1972)

Today (1975)

Moody Blue (1977)

The King's Cadillac gets a parking ticket on January 29, 1956.

Working on the soundtrack to *King Creole,* on January 15, 1958.

Frank Sinatra welcomes back a hero from military service on May 12, 1960.

Strolling with Joan Blackman in the 1961 movie *Blue Hawaii.*

The black biker's jacket is dusted off for the comeback special on June 27, 1968.

Presley chats with his father, Vernon, following a Las Vegas performance in August 1969.

Backstage with Sammy Davis, Jr. on August 10, 1970—the opening night of his third season at the Showroom International Hotel, Las Vegas.

Enduring yet another press conference at the New York Hilton on June 6, 1972.

Presley in concert at the Nassau Coliseum, Uniondale, New York, on July 19, 1975.

Sporting his "Arabian" jumpsuit in Austin, Texas, on March 28, 1977.

pretenders 1978–present

Chrissie Hynde
b. September 7, 1951

James Honeyman-Scott
b. Nov 4, 1956
d. June 16, 1982

Pete Farndon
b. June 12, 1952
d. April 14, 1983

Martin Chambers
b. September 4, 1951

Robbie McIntosh
b. October 25, 1957

Malcolm Foster
b. January 13, 1956

Adam Seymour
b. Unknown

Andy Hobson
b. Unknown

Chrissie Hynde worked for Malcolm McLaren, hung out with The Damned and Paul Simonon of The Clash, and, as legend has it, once proposed marriage to Sid Vicious. In other words, she was about as entrenched in the U.K. punk scene as a young lady from Akron, Ohio, could possibly be at the end of the seventies.

She would emerge from that tutelage in 1978 and quickly chart her own direction with the Pretenders, a group that was more punk in attitude than in sound. From the start—or, at least, by 1980's self-titled debut album—the group were borrowing equally from Kinks-style Britpop, fifties rock 'n' roll, vintage American soul, and contemporary new wave (adding a punk snarl for good measure).

Hynde seemed born to be one of rock's all-time great female stars, and it did not take her long to join that elite club after the public got an earful of that first record. Her larger-than-life public persona overshadowed all others who would contribute to the Pretenders' legacy—and there would be many—but it also helped the group survive tough moments, such as the drug-related deaths of two founding members.

Arriving in London in 1973, Hynde was a band leader without a band until, five years later, she united with guitarist **James Honeyman-Scott**, bassist **Pete Farndon**, and drummer **Martin Chambers** to form the Pretenders' classic lineup. That quartet's finest hour would be its first: *Pretenders* was one of the era's best

debuts. An international blockbuster, it topped the U.K. chart, hit No. 9 in the U.S., and thrust the band into the forefront of the so-called Second British Invasion.

The foursome managed one more album, 1981's *Pretenders II*, before disintegrating in tragic rock 'n' roll fashion. Farndon's drug use got him kicked out of the band in 1982, just two days before Honeyman-Scott was found dead of cocaine-related heart failure on June 16. On April 14 of the following year, Farndon drowned in his bathtub after overdosing on heroin.

Thus began the era—which continues to this day—in which fans would need a scorecard to keep track of all the band's many different lineups (which fleetingly included Smiths guitarist Johnny Marr and Parliament-Funkadelic keyboardist Bernie Worrell).

Yet, from an ever-shuffling deck, Hynde kept right on dealing aces: 1984's *Learning to Crawl* and 1986's *Get Close* both rank as career highlights. Hynde was in peak form, both as a singer and a songwriter, during this period, crafting punchy and poignant pop gems (1983's "Middle of the Road," 1986's "Don't Get Me Wrong") that would stand the test of time.

After time off to raise her children, she returned in the next decade to lead various versions of the Pretenders on pugnacious efforts like 1994's *Last of the Independents*. And Hynde could still conjure up that old magic on 2008's *Break Up the Concrete*—the Pretenders' first U.S. Top Forty hit since *Get Close*. **JiH**

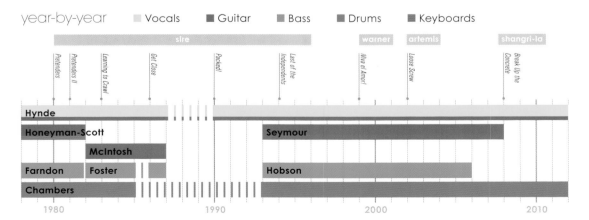

year-by-year ■ Vocals ■ Guitar ■ Bass ■ Drums ■ Keyboards

prime circle 2001-present

Ross Learmonth
b. July 5, 1981

Gerhard Venter
b. Unknown

Marco Gomes
b. March 21, 1976

Dirk Bisschoff
b. November 13, 1972

Neil Breytenbach
b. March 27, 1975

Dale Schnettler
b. November 10, 1982

Prime Circle formed in late 2000 in Witbank, South Africa, when members of two bands that split on the same night came together. **Marco Gomes** (bass), **Dirk Bisschoff** (lead guitar), and **Gerhard Venter** (drums) drafted in vocalist **Ross Learmonth**, who had been "looking for a job."

The four-piece signed to independent label The David Gresham Record Company and started work on their debut album, *Hello Crazy World*. Released in 2002, the first single "Hello" became an airplay staple, reaching No. 1 in their home country. It was even adopted by South Africa's national cricket team as its official song, despite the lyrics having nothing to do with sport. "Let Me Go" was another chart-topper and was followed into the Top Five by "My Inspiration." With platinum sales of more than 45,000, *Hello Crazy World* became South Africa's biggest-selling rock album.

Its success saw the band move in bigger circles, supporting U.S. rockers Live on their South African tour in 2003. Two years later, they performed alongside Queen and Annie Lennox at the second Nelson Mandela 46664 benefit concert for HIV/AIDS and humanitarian projects in George, South Africa. Later in 2005, the sophomore set *Live This Life* hit stores, en route to earning gold status within a year.

Hailed for their live shows, the band issued *Living in a Crazy World,* a DVD captured at The Function Room in Johannesburg, then a greatest hits in 2007.

Now with **Neil Breytenbach** on keyboards and **Dale Schnettler** replacing Venter on drums, the band took their time producing a third album. They recorded thirty tracks, selected the final tracklist, and only then approached record labels. Freshly signed to EMI, Prime Circle released *All or Nothing* in 2008, followed by a live DVD of the same name.

The group promoted the album with live dates in Europe and a sold-out first tour of India, where "Consider Me" was a surprise No. 1 the week after the final concert. They returned to South Africa to find the same song at the top of their own chart.

For *Jekyll & Hyde* (2010), the band made clear their bid for international stardom by hiring Aerosmith producer Kevin Shirley and Guns N' Roses mastering engineer George Marino. Having earned a reputation for ballads, Prime Circle now had a grittier, heavier sound. The shift in style did no harm. "Breathing" rocketed to No. 1 on regional stations within days of airing and the album went gold in nine days. *Jekyll & Hyde* earned the band a record six South African Music Award nominations in 2011—although they took home only one trophy, for Best Rock Album—and secured their rank as the country's biggest rock band.

On their ten-year anniversary as a group, Prime Circle were more popular than ever, despite domestic challengers such as The Parlotones. They remain in better shape than most to fulfill global ambitions. **RJ**

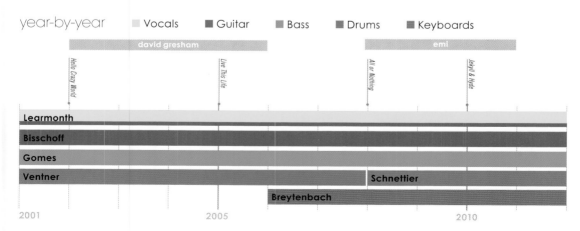

prince 1978–present

Prince
b. June 7, 1958

Lisa Coleman
b. August 17, 1960

Doctor Fink
b. 1957

Dez Dickerson
b. 1955

Bobby Z
b. 1956

Brown Mark
b. 1962

Wendy Melvoin
b. January 26, 1964

Susannah Melvoin
b. January 26, 1964

A one-man phenomenon, Prince Rogers Nelson won enormous success in the eighties and early nineties before becoming a cult icon—albeit one who scored four U.S. Top Three albums between 2004 and 2009. **Prince**, as he has been known throughout his career (despite a period during which he renamed himself an unpronounceable symbol), has an eye for talent-spotting fine musicians: **Sheila E.** and **Candy Dulfer** are among those who have lined up beside him. While drawing on predecessors such as Jimi Hendrix, Sly Stone, and Parliament-Funkadelic, Prince has created an extraordinary legacy of his own.

In 1977, Prince scored a deal with Warner Bros. as a solo artist—writing, performing, arranging, and producing his music himself. Debuting in 1978 with *For You*, the prodigy increasingly fused guitar-based funk with salacious lyrics in a stripped-down, establishment-baiting style. As Prince's ambitions grew, his combination of funk, rock, and soul—in which horns were replaced by synths—became known as "the Minneapolis Sound," an approach taken up by fellow

musicians in his Minnesota hometown. Among them were The Time, who were involved in the movie version of *Purple Rain* (1984). Marking the grand coming-out of Prince's band The Revolution (who had made a low-key debut on the preceding *1999*), this boasted classics such as "When Doves Cry," "Let's Go Crazy," and the epic title track. The accompanying movie was an awe-inspiringly egotistical vehicle for the diminutive genius's fictionalized autobiography.

Setting his forays into the film world to one side, Prince could do no wrong in the eighties. A sequence of dazzling albums issued from his Paisley Park studio in Minneapolis: *Around the World in a Day* (1985), *Parade* (1986), *Sign 'o' the Times* (1987), and *Lovesexy* (1988). This inspired output explored funk, rock, psychedelia, and haunting electronica. As for singles, Prince unleashed gem after gem—"Raspberry Beret," "Kiss," "Sign 'o' The Times," and "Alphabet St." among them. He maintained an air of mystique throughout this period, giving infrequent interviews and making opaque statements shrouded in spiritual references.

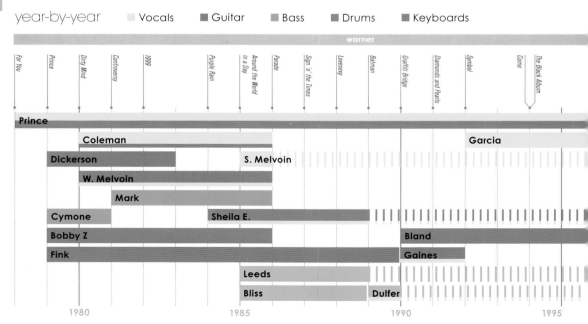

year-by-year ◼ Vocals ◼ Guitar ◼ Bass ◼ Drums ◼ Keyboards

warner

For You | Prince | Dirty Mind | Controversy | 1999 | Purple Rain | Around the World in a Day | Parade | Sign 'o' the Times | Lovesexy | Batman | Graffiti Bridge | Diamonds and Pearls | Symbol | Come | The Black Album

Prince

Coleman — Garcia

Dickerson — S. Melvoin

W. Melvoin

Mark

Cymone — Sheila E.

Bobby Z — Bland

Fink — Gaines

Leeds

Bliss — Dulfer

1980 · 1985 · 1990 · 1995

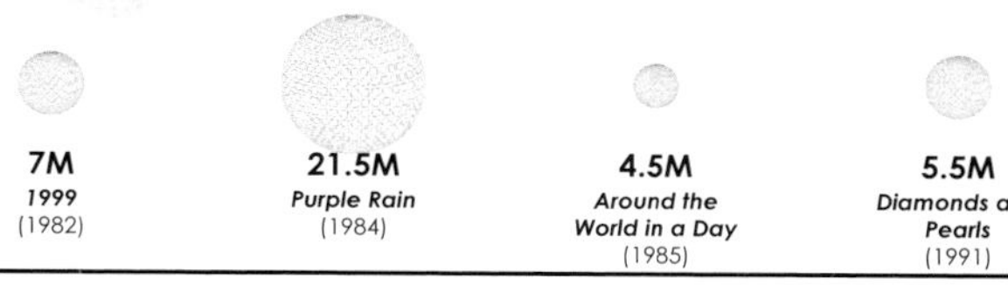
7M
1999
(1982)
21.5M
Purple Rain
(1984)
4.5M
Around the World in a Day
(1985)
5.5M
Diamonds and Pearls
(1991)

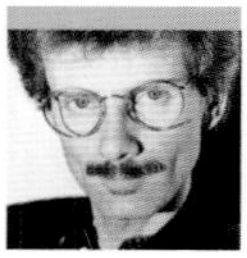

Eric Leeds
b. January 19, 1952

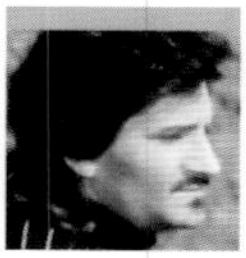

Atlanta Bliss
b. Unknown

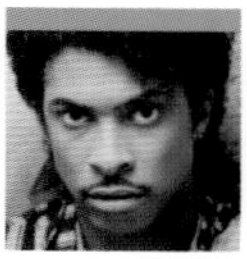

André Cymone
b. June 27, 1958

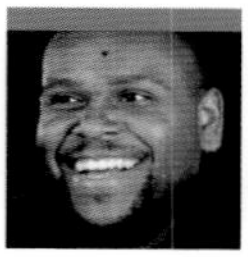

Michael Bland
b. March 14, 1969

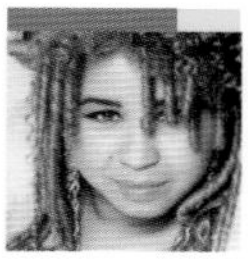

Rosie Gaines
b. June 26, year unknown

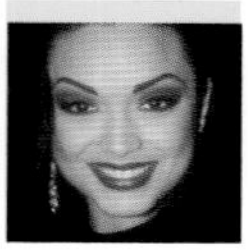

Mayte Garcia
b. November 12, 1973

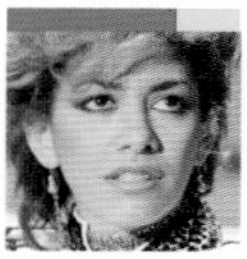

Sheila E.
b. December 12, 1957

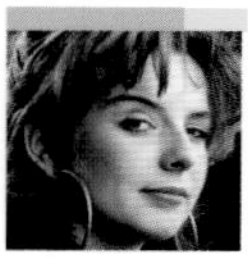

Candy Dulfer
b. September 19, 1969

In the nineties, with The Revolution's successors the New Power Generation, Prince refused to temper his enigma even as his success waned. *Diamonds and Pearls* (1991) and *Symbol* (1992) proved his last multi-million-sellers for over a decade. (1993's now largely forgotten *Come* and 1995's return-to-form *The Gold Experience* "merely" went gold on both sides of the Atlantic, while his best album of the period—1996's soundtrack to Spike Lee's *Girl 6*—sold only to fanatics.)

To the wider public, Prince's music took a back seat to his eccentricities in the nineties. Despite including his first U.K. No. 1 single—1993's exquisite "The Most Beautiful Girl in the World"—the period in which he renamed himself was laughed off as a rich man's folly. Meanwhile, an extended battle with Warner Bros. received an unsympathetic response, especially when he appeared in public with "Slave" written on his cheek. (The contract-terminating *The Black Album,* recorded in 1987 but withheld until 1994, and *Chaos and Disorder,* which limped out in 1996, barely troubled chart compilers.)

However, after seemingly final flings with major labels (EMI and Arista) for 1996's flawed but frequently fantastic *Emancipation* and 1999's inexplicably gold-selling *Rave Un2 the Joy Fantastic,* Prince became one of the first internationally famous musicians to embrace the internet as a distribution tool. By the new millennium, he was selling albums on his own label as downloads—a slow process in the pre-broadband era but one that presaged equivalents such as iTunes. Take-up of these albums enabled Prince to continue his operations in the relatively lean years.

Few expected him to return to the commercial forefront. But *Musicology* (2004) marked a return to major label distribution, and was followed into the U.S. Top Three by *3121* (2006), *Planet Earth* (2007), and *LOtUSFLOW3R* (2009). With his tours once again doing blockbusting business, Prince was quick to capitalize on the trend for fans spending more on concerts than on downloads, and staged a headline-snaring twenty-one dates at London's O2 Arena in 2007. He remains among the planet's greatest showmen. **JM**

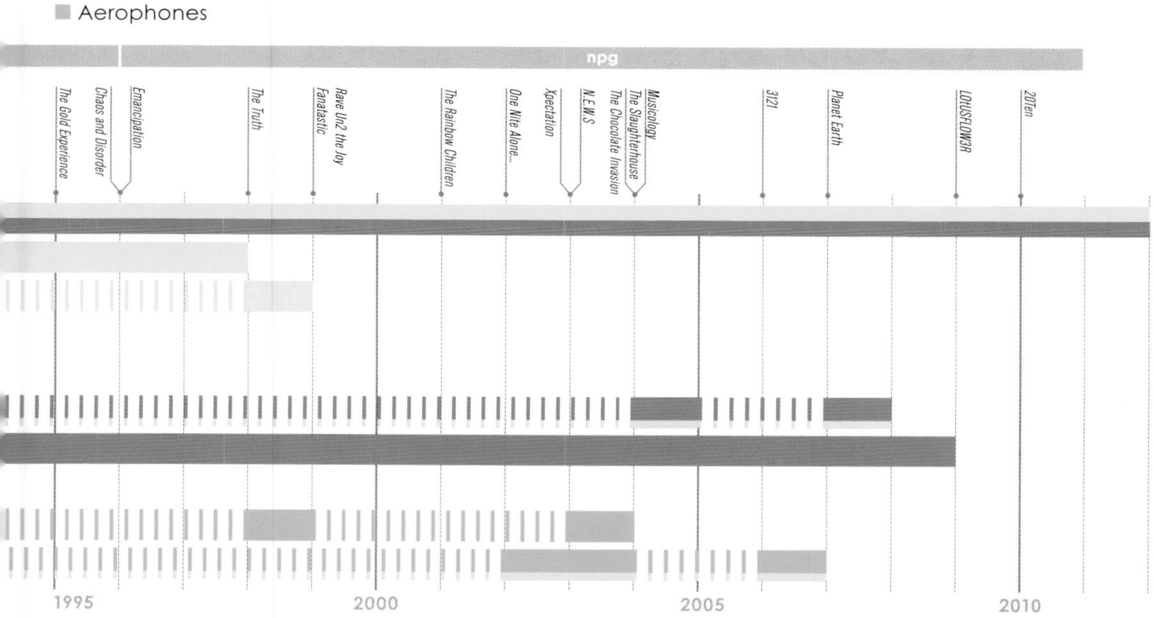
Aerophones
npg
The Gold Experience
Chaos and Disorder
Emancipation
The Truth
Rave Un2 the Joy Fanatastic
The Rainbow Children
One Nite Alone...
Xpectation
N.E.W.S
The Chocolate Invasion
The Slaughterhouse
Musicology
3121
Planet Earth
LOtUSFLOW3R
20Ten
1995
2000
2005
2010

Dirty Mind (1980)

1999 (1982)

Purple Rain (1984)

Around the World in a Day (1985)

Parade (1986)

Sign 'o' the Times (1987)

Diamonds and Pearls (1991)

The Gold Experience (1995)

Musicology (2004)

20Ten (2010)

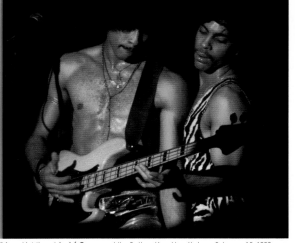

Prince (right) and André Cymone at the Bottom Line, New York, on Feburary 15, 1980.

With guitarist Dez Dickerson—who would sing on 1999's title track—at the Palladium, New York, on December 2, 1981.

The Revolution—Brown Mark, Doctor Fink, Bobby Z, Prince, Lisa Coleman, and Wendy Melvoin—at the Forum in Inglewood, California, on February 19, 1985.

Intense guitar from the regal one in 1985.

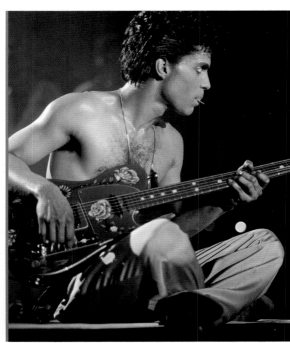

Prince focuses on some knob work at Wembley Arena, London, in 1986.

A high-energy performance in Rotterdam, Netherlands, in 1987.

On 1991's Nude tour, when he took to playing "Nothing Compares 2 U" for the first time.

"Love Symbol" with then-wife **Mayte Garcia** at Wembley Arena, London, in 1995.

Beyoncé and **Prince** perform his hits at the 2004 Grammy Awards show in Los Angeles.

His stage outfit adorned with the *20Ten* album artwork, **Prince** performs at the fortieth Roskilde Festival, in Denmark, on July 4, 2010.

the prodigy 1990–present

Liam Howlett
b. August 21, 1971

Keith Flint
b. September 13, 1969

Maxim Reality
b. March 21, 1967

Leeroy Thornhill
b. October 8, 1968

Dance music that ruled the airwaves in the nineties is, if you believe the press, dead and gone. But the genre's most successful exponents, The Prodigy, continue to headline festivals and release big-selling albums. That is testament to bandleader **Liam Howlett**'s talent for writing stadium-sized songs, the charismatic presence of vocalists **Keith Flint** and Keith "**Maxim Reality**" Palmer, and the public's appetite for aggressive music, either from a computer or a guitar.

In the early nineties, Howlett—from the town of Braintree in Essex, England—began to make frantic music based on drums, bass, and comedy samples from sources such as vintage television commercials. Like many other young musicians, he was contributing to the rise of rave and techno music, designed to accompany the consumption of ecstasy, the drug that had fueled the dance scene since the late eighties. Approached by clubbers Flint, Palmer, and **Leeroy Thornhill**, who suggested turning his music into a live act, Howlett formed a quartet based on his keyboard sounds and the often astounding dance moves of the other three (initially joined by female MC Sharky). "All we wanted to do," he recalled, "was play the clubs we were going to as ravers."

With the band signed to the XL label, *Experience* was issued in 1992. Its introductory hit, "Charly," added samples from a seventies road-safety film to a siren-like electronic riff. Club-goers responded with alacrity, and a host of singles in the same lightweight vein followed from other acts. *Experience* also yielded the enduring classic "Out of Space" (with samples from Max Romeo and the Ultramagnetic MCs), but little of the rest suggested the group's longevity was assured.

However, touring—coupled with hip-hop fan Howlett being anxious to distance the band from the rave scene that his band had been accused of ruining—saw The Prodigy toughen up. (Their evolution is documented in 1995's frequently deranged—and sadly unavailable on DVD—video *Electronic Punks*.)

In 1994, The Prodigy proved their staying power with the extraordinary *Music for the Jilted Generation*, which crashed into the U.K. album chart at No. 1. With only "One Love" (initially issued as a 1993 single under the name Earthbound to wrong-foot critics) and "No Good (Start the Dance)" betraying their rave roots, the album was a head-spinning blend of intimidating electronica and pounding percussion.

With extra weight added by British indie rockers Pop Will Eat Itself (on "Their Law") and a sample from Nirvana's "Very Ape" (on "Voodoo People"), *Jilted Generation* made The Prodigy the dance band that rock fans could like. "They just came blazing out of the corner," enthused former Led Zeppelin front-man Robert Plant, "and it's brilliant."

year-by-year ▢ Vocals ▪ Keyboards ▪ Programming

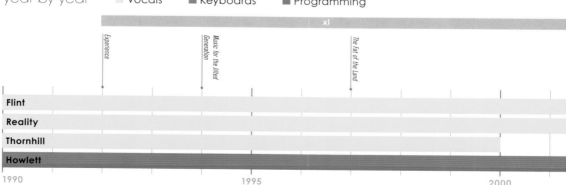

Howlett explained that the change in direction had been inspired by a visit to the U.S., where he witnessed the newly-formed Rage Against The Machine and was inspired by their fusion of metal and hip-hop. Had he not solidified the band's sound, it is likely The Prodigy would have ended up like so many early-nineties dance acts—on the scrapheap.

Further touring honed Maxim and Flint's demonic stage personae, which came to fruition on the U.K. No. 1s "Firestarter" and "Breathe." The former saw the band's profile explode worldwide, while the latter was voted "single of the year" in metal magazine *Kerrang!*, confirming The Prodigy's victorious entry into the rock arena. Accordingly, *The Fat of the Land* (1997)—which eschewed the techno of its predecessor in favor of rock and hip-hop—topped charts around the world.

With guitarist "Gizz" Butt (later replaced by Rob Holliday, who also played with Marilyn Manson), The Prodigy conquered the world (including an Australian trek with the Foo Fighters). Meanwhile, the hit "Smack My Bitch Up" courted controversy with its ambiguous lyric and sex, drugs, 'n' vomit-splattered video. The Beastie Boys even asked them not to play the song when the two bands shared a festival bill in 1998—a request that an incredulous Howlett pointedly refused.

In the post-*Fat* hiatus, Howlett cut the excellent *Dirtchamber Sessions Volume One* (1999), Thornhill

quit the music business, and Maxim issued the solo *Hell's Kitchen* (2000). Flint took the lead on the band's 2002 single "Baby's Got a Temper," but a deteriorating relationship with Howlett meant he was nowhere to be heard on *Always Outnumbered, Never Outgunned* (2004). The album did, however, find room for Noel and Liam Gallagher of Oasis, and "The Way It Is," a spectacular reinvention of Michael Jackson's "Thriller."

Although *Always Outnumbered...* provided the third of the band's five U.K. No. 1 albums, it ultimately sold the least well. Normal service was restored by 2005's *Their Law: The Singles 1990–2005* and 2009's *Invaders Must Die*. The latter boasted Dave Grohl drumming on two cuts, but otherwise marked a move back to The Prodigy's dance roots. Nonetheless, the band—with Howlett and Flint reconciled—had so successfully blurred the boundaries (to the benefit of upstarts like Pendulum and Chase & Status) that few eyebrows were raised when they headlined the second stage at U.K. metal festival Download in 1999.

By 2012, with huge shows at Britain's Milton Keynes Bowl (captured on the *World on Fire* DVD) behind them, The Prodigy had graduated to Download's main stage, alongside Metallica and Black Sabbath. Howlett duly promised the music paper *NME* that the band's next album—provisionally titled *How to Steal a Jet Fighter*—would be "heavier, darker." **JM/BM**

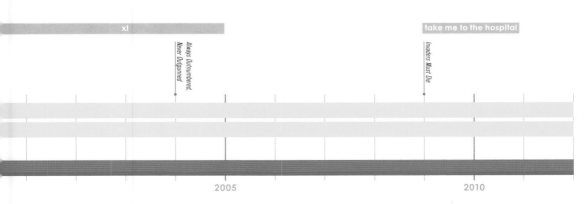

Experience (1992)

Music for the Jilted Generation (1994)

The Fat of the Land (1997)

Always Outnumbered, Never Outgunned (2004)

Invaders Must Die (2009)

Liam Howlett (left) and Leeroy Thornhill in an atmospheric 1992 photo.

Howlett, Keith Flint, Thornhill, and Maxim Reality on the "Voodoo People" video shoot.

The band collect the first of four MTV "Best Dance" awards they won from 1994 to 1998

Maxim and Flint unveil their demonic personae at 1996's Phoenix festival.

Maxim at the Brixton Academy, London, in December 2004.

Flint's lunatic persona helped to sweep The Prodigy onto the world stage.

Nearly twenty years after their formation, The Prodigy perform at Britain's Download festival in 2009.

public image ltd 1978–present

John Lydon
b. January 31, 1956

Lu Edmonds
b. September 24, 1957

Bruce Smith
b. Unknown

Scott Firth
b. Unknown

Keith Levene
b. July 18, 1957

Jah Wobble
b. August 11, 1958

Jim Walker
b. Unknown

Martin Atkins
b. August 3, 1959

The Sex Pistols may have triggered moral panic in the U.K., but Public Image Ltd (a.k.a. PiL) were, for their first few years, much more musically terrifying. If *Never Mind the Bollocks* set off an acid reflux, PiL's classic *Metal Box* strode straight into heart-attack territory.

It was in mid-January 1978 that Johnny Rotten—soon to revert to **John Lydon**—vocalized what his body language had been saying for some time: "I am sick of working with the Sex Pistols." Guitarist **Keith Levene** was equally unhappy with the direction taken during his stint with a pre-fame incarnation of the Pistols' rivals, The Clash. When the two met, Levene said, "There was a hatred, a cynicism, a kind of darkness."

There were more likeminded attitudes when Lydon recruited a friend, **Jah Wobble**, on bass, while drummer **Jim Walker** was the only option Lydon entertained from extensive auditions: "He sounds like Can's drummer." The band name was inspired by a Muriel Spark novel exploring "what can happen to you if you don't control your public image."

Their throbbing debut single, "Public Image," was an incendiary statement of intent that broached the U.K. Top Ten, but was misleading. *Public Image—First Issue* (1978) was a different beast that repelled more than it reached. That situation has turned about face

over time, but "Theme"—nearly ten minutes of twisted brilliance—is a more representative introduction than the single, and there can be no more withering attack, on both musical and lyrical levels, than "Religion."

In early 1979, the drum stool barely had time to get cold as sticksmen came and went, including Vibrator Eddie Edwards. Richard Dudanski left a telling imprint on the next project, but it was the combustible nucleus of Lydon/Levene/Wobble that dominated the spaces and shards of sound on *Metal Box*. It was not only the metal-canister packaging (not available in the U.S.) that set it apart. "There was," observed Massive Attack's 3D, "nothing even close to it."

Wobble departed in August 1979 (for a career first as a train driver, then as an ambassador for multi-cultural music), leaving PiL with no bassist. No problem. That left room on *Flowers of Romance* for the tribal thunder of **Martin Atkins**, later to drum with Killing Joke and Ministry (Levene also took a turn behind the kit). Yet again, the band put daylight between themselves and post-punk pretenders.

In the early eighties, while Levene was increasingly lost to drugs, Lydon was also struggling for direction. After the longest gap between albums, *This Is What You Want... This Is What You Get* (1984) proved hardly

year-by-year
■ Vocals ■ Guitar ■ Bass ■ Drums ■ Keyboards

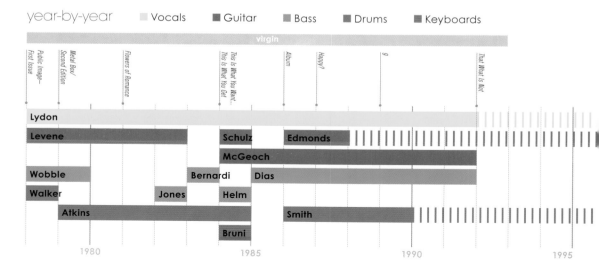

Pete Jones
b. September 22, 1957

Louis Bernardi
b. Unknown

Bret Helm
b. circa 1959

Mark Schulz
b. Unknown

Jebin Bruni
b. Unknown

John McGeoch
b. Aug 25, 1955
d. March 4, 2004

Allan Dias
b. Unknown

worth the wait. Levene's departing shot was to take the master tapes and issue them as *Commercial Zone* earlier the same year. *This Is What You Want… This Is What You Get* included a version of "This Is Not a Love Song," a U.K. No. 5 hit in 1983, but, without the customary studio conflict, the band's cutting edge was dulled. A 1983 tour featured musicians Lydon had picked up in New Jersey, including guitarist Joseph Guida and bassist **Louis Bernardi**.

This best-overlooked period was banished by *Album*, whose marketing (other formats were titled *Cassette* and *Compact Disc*) matched the sharpness of the music. A touring band that included **Jebin Bruni** (guitars/keyboards) and guitarist **Mark Schulz** showed promise, but all that remains of their contributions are a few co-writing credits. The roll call of replacements was awesome: Cream's Ginger Baker, Yellow Magic Orchestra founder Ryuichi Sakamoto, and former Frank Zappa stunt guitarist Steve Vai. The sound was closer to conventional rock, even stepping into metal territory on "F.F.F.," but it worked. The theme of its hit "Rise" ("South African interrogation techniques," said Lydon) did not stop the single reaching U.K. No. 11.

Guitarist **John McGeoch** (formerly of Siouxsie & the Banshees and Magazine) joined **Lu Edmonds**

(once of The Damned), drummer **Bruce Smith** (The Slits, The Pop Group), and bassist **Allan Dias** in stability (of sorts). *Happy?* (1987) and 9 (1989) fell short of past glories, but yielded enough gems—notably "Seattle" and "Disappointed"—to ensure the solidity of 1990's *The Greatest Hits, So Far*. A fresh hit, "Don't Tell Me," tackled environmental issues long before other acts began paying lip service to being green.

Before *That What Is Not* (1992), Dias quit to deal with drug problems that left him "completely burned out," and the band itself was mothballed later in the year. Thereafter, Lydon crashed back into the charts with 1993's Leftfield collaboration "Open Up," revived the Pistols, and transformed from terror to national treasure. But, as the shock of the Pistols' resurrection wore off, there was talk of PiL. "We were," he said in 2008, "like a symphony orchestra with machine guns. It would be great to revisit."

Accordingly, 2009 saw Lydon, Lu Edmonds (whose tinnitus had forced him to leave the band in 1988), Bruce Smith, and **Scott Firth** (bass/keyboards) play shows that were much better examples of on-form PiL than two anaemic live albums (*Paris au Printemps* in 1980 and *Live in Tokyo* from 1983). "Sex Pistols were too rigid," said Lydon. "PiL explains me better." **CB**

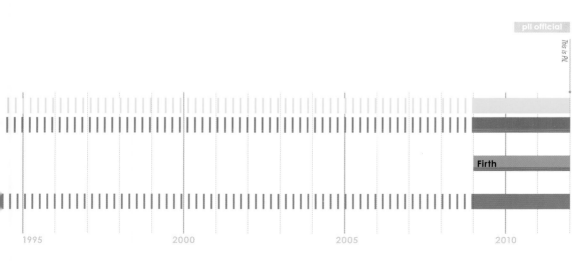

1995 2000 2005 2010

queen 1971–present

Freddie Mercury
b. September 5, 1946
d. November 24, 1991

Brian May
b. July 19, 1947

Roger Taylor
b. July 26, 1949

John Deacon
b. August 19, 1951

Paul Rodgers
b. December 17, 1949

For a band lauded as one of the most highly educated in rock—three degrees, a diploma, and a PhD for "Dr. Bri"—you would expect Queen to be able to count. Yet when they celebrated their official fortieth anniversary in 2011, there was no mention of the fact that **Freddie Mercury** (born Farrokh Bulsara in Zanzibar), **Brian May**, and **Roger Taylor** had been performing under the banner "Queen" since the summer of 1970. And not a peep, either, about the fact that Mike Grose, Barry Mitchell, and Doug Bogie were all trialed as bass players before **John Deacon** eventually got the gig permanently in February 1971.

As far as the record-buying public is concerned, the Queen story really began, albeit falteringly, in 1973, with the release of their self-titled debut album, then again more emphatically the following year with its successor, *Queen II*. The latter yielded their first U.K. hit, Mercury's "Seven Seas of Rhye." With multi-tracked vocals (from all but Deacon), six-string landscapes courtesy of Brian's homemade guitar, and bombastic anthems sitting alongside heartstring-tugging ballads, *Queen II* introduced the unmistakeable "Queen sound" and raised the bar for generations to come ("You can see why we nearly called it *Over the Top!*" Taylor later admitted). Guns N' Roses' Axl Rose was just one of the fans to fall under Queen's spell, enthusing that they "taught me about all forms of music."

On stage, Queen were just as dramatic (once stardom hit, they were dressed in theatrical black or white by designer Zandra Rhodes). "At a time when bands wore the same as the audience, we wanted to stand out," May said. Thanks to Mercury, who had run a clothes stall in London's Kensington Market and was rarely seen in anything so conventional as a pair of jeans, they certainly did that.

A homegrown following was one thing but Queen needed international success. A U.S. tour supporting Mott the Hoople opened doors, which they kicked in with the first single from 1974's *Sheer Heart Attack*. Mercury's "Killer Queen" charted around the world, even reaching No. 12 in the U.S.—despite it being, according to the singer, about "a high-class call girl." The versatile album also featured the vicious "Stone Cold Crazy," later covered by Metallica.

Now they had the world's attention, Queen got really inventive on *A Night at the Opera* (1975). On an album containing Japanese folk, twenties whimsy, and a guitar-only version of "God Save the Queen," it would take something special to stand out. But "Bohemian Rhapsody" was very special indeed. With its blend of ballad, rock, and even opera—and an accompanying video credited with pioneering the genre—it held No. 1 status in the U.K. for nine weeks and became the band's signature tune.

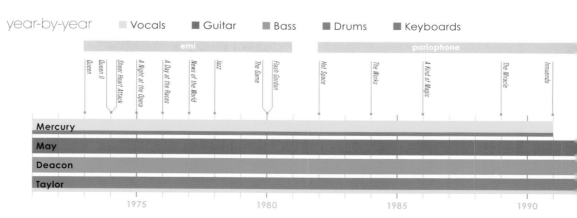

year-by-year · Vocals · Guitar · Bass · Drums · Keyboards

7.7M	**6.6M**	**21.4M**	**5.3M**
News of the World	*The Game*	*Greatest Hits*	*Greatest Hits II*
(1977)	(1980)	(1981)	(1991)

A foray into gospel on "Somebody to Love" from *A Day at the Races* (1976) saw another international hit, and "Teo Torriatte," sung in Japanese, was a thank-you to a territory that had adopted the band early on. "We encountered something like Beatlemania there," Roger revealed. Back home, Queen headlined a show at London's Hyde Park in front of 150,000 fans.

Issued at the tail-end of punk, *News of the World* (1977) tempered Queen's customary grandiosity with pared-back cuts. The two extremes were represented by May's brutal "We Will Rock You" and Mercury's showy "We are the Champions." Twinned as a single, the pair crashed Top Tens around the world.

With *Jazz* (1978)—"Not one of our finest hours," admitted Taylor—boasting a very European feel and the splendid *Live Killers* (1979) sourced from concerts on the continent, the band's profile dipped slightly in the States. But any thoughts that Queen had blown it in America were dispelled by "Crazy Little Thing Called Love" in 1979. A rockabilly number composed by Mercury in a Munich hotel room's bubble bath, it gave Queen their first of two U.S. No. 1s from *The Game*—the second only coming after nagging from a superfan. "Michael Jackson persuaded us to release 'Another One Bites the Dust' as a single," Taylor recalled. "I admit we were reluctant." *The Game* itself gave the band their only U.S. chart-topping album.

Ironically, an attempt to repeat that success with 1982's "funkier" *Hot Space* failed and Queen's days at the top in America were numbered. But not in Europe, where 1984's *The Works*—and its hits "Radio Ga Ga" and "I Want to Break Free"—restored them to the top of most charts. A triumphant performance at Live Aid in 1985 saw Queen rightly celebrated as superstars, laying the foundations for a stadium tour in 1986 to promote *A Kind of Magic*. After Mercury's final concert with the band—a vast spectacular at Britain's Knebworth—it was three years before they returned with *The Miracle* and a further two before *Innuendo*. Tellingly, there were no tours accompanying either—but plenty of rumors. On November 23, 1991, the truth came out: Mercury announced that he had contracted the AIDS virus. He died the following day.

Made in Heaven, using unreleased performances by the singer, was released in 1995, and a tribute to him, "No One But You (Only the Good Die Young)," marked Deacon's last act before his retirement. Yet two decades after Mercury's death, the Queen name thrives in the hands of May and Taylor. Two tours and an album (2008's *The Cosmos Rocks*) with **Paul Rodgers**, a globe-spanning stage show (*We Will Rock You*), a forthcoming Hollywood bio-pic, and shows with *American Idol* star Adam Lambert have added further chapters to a history still being written. **JeH**

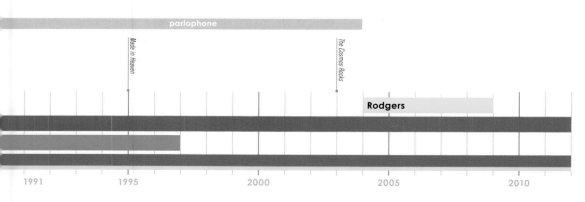

parlophone

Made in Heaven

The Cosmos Rocks

Rodgers

1991   1995   2000   2005   2010

Queen (1973)

Sheer Heart Attack (1974)

Left to right: Ian Hunter, **Freddie Mercury**, Overend Watts, Morgan Fisher, and **Roger Taylor** at a 1973 party with Mott the Hoople.

A Night at the Opera (1975)

Brian May, Mercury, Taylor, and **John Deacon** appear on BBC TV's *Top of the Pops* in November 1974.

A Day at the Races (1976)

Taylor and **Mercury** at a free concert in Hyde Park, London, on September 18, 1976.

News of the World (1977)

The Game (1980)

Deacon's bass underpins **Mercury** in a 1975 performance.

The Works (1984)

A Kind of Magic (1986)

The Miracle (1989)

The Cosmos Rocks (2008)

Mercury bestrides the world like a pop colossus in 1977.

Mercury sings in his memorable harlequin garb in 1977.

Mercury in fabulous pants at Wembley Arena, London, in 1984.

Queen onstage at Leiden, Netherlands, on November 27, 1980.

Mercury and **May** etch themselves into legend at Live Aid in 1985.

May records with Black Sabbath's Tony Iommi in July 1989.

Mercury at London's Wembley Stadium—the venue for 1985's Live Aid and a 1992 tribute show for him—in 1986.

Paul Rodgers sings at the 46664 Concert in Celebration of Nelson Mandela's Life in London on June 27, 2008.

queens of the stone age 1997–present

Josh Homme
b. May 17, 1973

Troy van Leeuwen
b. January 5, 1968

Michael Shuman
b. August 20, 1985

Dean Fertita
b. September 6, 1970

Joey Castillo
b. March 30, 1966

Nick Oliveri
b. October 21, 1971

Dave Grohl
b. January 14, 1969

Mark Lanegan
b. November 25, 1964

Formed by guitarist and singer **Josh Homme**, Queens of the Stone Age were initially that rare thing: an act that was genuinely ahead of its time yet still reaped commercial rewards. For their first eight years, QOTSA sounded like the future of rock music, with hyperbolic media plaudits such as "the coolest man in the world" laid at Homme's feet. After that acclaimed period, the rest of the music world appeared to catch up and QOTSA are now "merely" a very highly respected facet of Homme's sprawling output.

Some of the band's success can be attributed to Homme's experience as a member of Kyuss, the Californian band who pioneered the so-called desert rock sound. Like its contemporary, grunge, desert rock combined heavy guitar riffs with catchy choruses and melodies, a hybrid approach that Homme brought to QOTSA's first, self-titled album in 1998. Charting creditably for a debut (U.S. No. 122, U.K. No. 48), Queens of the Stone Age was a lighter, more digestible work than Kyuss's fully-leaded material.

Following the enlistment of bassist **Nick Oliveri**—also a Kyuss alumnus—audiences responded in huge numbers to Rated R and Songs for the Deaf (2000 and 2002 respectively). Between them, these contained several unforgettable singles: the controversial, drug-themed "Feel Good Hit of the Summer," "The Lost Art of Keeping a Secret," "No One Knows," and "First It Giveth." Of the two albums, which represent QOTSA's

best and most successful work to date, the latter is the more accessible, perhaps because Homme and Oliveri were joined by Foo Fighter **Dave Grohl** and Screaming Trees frontman **Mark Lanegan**.

As the years passed, QOTSA became surrounded by a colorful cult of personality. Tales of backstage debauchery, whether accurate or not, abounded, and the combination of the intellectual Homme, the punk Oliveri (who sometimes stripped naked on stage) and the superstar Grohl made the band iconic.

However, Homme fired Oliveri after Songs for the Deaf (for reasons that vary according to who you ask), and replaced Grohl and Lanegan with a fluid cast of musicians when they returned (amicably) to their own bands. Subsequent QOTSA albums have been interesting and respectable, but somehow the essential danger that stemmed from his lyrical cleverness and melodic songwriting has diminished.

Nonetheless, there are gems aplenty on Lullabies to Paralyze, which stormed to No. 5 in the U.S. in 2005 and Era Vulgaris (2007). Far from being a spent force, Homme continues to seek new challenges, recording an ongoing series of albums under the collective name Desert Sessions, forming the supergroup Them Crooked Vultures with Grohl and Led Zeppelin bassist John Paul Jones, and producing the Arctic Monkeys. QOTSA are also likely to resurface, in what Homme describes as a "trancey, broken" form. **JM**

year-by-year   ■ Vocals   ■ Guitar   ■ Bass   ■ Drums   ■ Keyboards

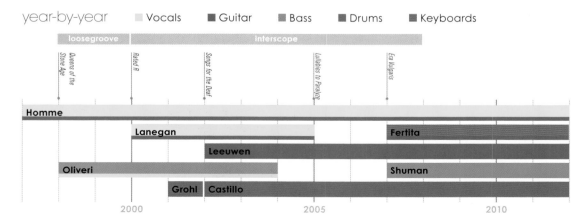

queensrÿche 1981–present

Geoff Tate
b. January 14, 1959

Michael Wilton
b. February 23, 1962

Scott Rockenfield
b. June 15, 1963

Eddie Jackson
b. January 29, 1961

Chris DeGarmo
b. June 14, 1963

Kelly Gray
b. Unknown

Mike Stone
b. November 30, 1969

Parker Lundgren
b. Unknown

There is little about Queensrÿche's early days to suggest that they would someday be considered as one of progressive metal's greatest acts. Listen to their self-titled debut EP, recorded in 1982 in Redmond, Washington, and you will hear players who wore their mainstream metal influences proudly. They initially seemed intent on following in the paw prints of Def Leppard, not finding themselves mentioned in the same breath as The Who and Pink Floyd.

In retrospect, however, it is clear that any band boasting vocalist **Geoff Tate**—a Washington State transplant from (then) West Germany, who would one day become a noted wine enthusiast—was never going to be just a run-of-the-mill metal act. "Our approach is a melodic, dynamic one," guitarist **Chris DeGarmo** informed *Kerrang!* magazine. "We're trying to capture the intensity of heavy metal rather than just thrashing out the same old riffs."

The saga began in the early eighties. DeGarmo, drummer **Scott Rockenfield**, bassist **Eddie Jackson**, and guitarist **Michael Wilton** united in the hard rock cover band Cross+Fire, which changed its name to The Mob. They needed a singer and tried to enlist Tate, who played hard to get for months and only joined on a part-time basis before finally signing on once record labels came calling. Newly christened Queensrÿche, the group signed with EMI in 1983.

The first release was essentially a re-release of the 1982 EP but generated positive reviews and reached No. 81 in the U.S. *The Warning* (1984) and 1986's *Rage for Order* (1986) brought steady sales—and exhibited artistic growth—but their career fully bloomed in both respects with *Operation: Mindcrime* (1988). This gripping, ambitious concept album never rose higher than No. 50 in the U.S., yet remained on the chart for a year, earning a gold certification.

That set the scene for the band's commercial zenith: *Empire* (1990) went triple-platinum in the U.S. on the strength of their only Top Ten hit, the gorgeous power-ballad "Silent Lucidity" (boasting orchestration by Pink Floyd and Bowie collaborator Michael Kamen).

Thanks to dedicated fans, the band weathered the advent of grunge and alt-rock better than most of their contemporaries: 1994's *Promised Land* rose to No. 3 and platinum sales in the U.S. That was the group's last big seller, but far from their final worthy effort. Queensrÿche kept on delivering interesting prog-metal, even returning with gusto to the concept album format for 2006's long-awaited *Operation: Mindcrime II* and 2009's *American Soldier*.

In 2012, Wilton, Jackson, Rockenfield, and Parker Lundgren (the band's latest guitarist after DeGarmo quit in 1997) recruited singer Todd La Torre to form Rising West, putting Queensrÿche's future in doubt. **JiH**

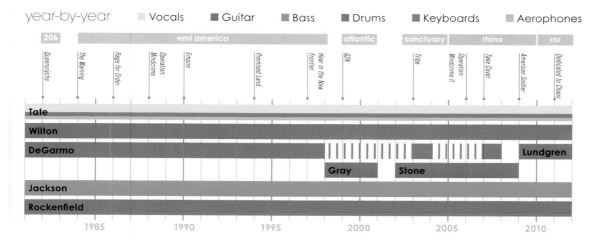

year-by-year   ■ Vocals   ■ Guitar   ■ Bass   ■ Drums   ■ Keyboards   ■ Aerophones

radiohead 1991–present

Thom Yorke
b. October 7, 1968

Jonny Greenwood
b. November 5, 1971

Colin Greenwood
b. June 26, 1969

Ed O'Brien
b. April 15, 1968

Phil Selway
b. May 23, 1967

Panic, alienation, disgust, despair—just because the personnel in Radiohead has been settled for more than two decades does not indicate an absence of darker, more destructive emotions. For most of that time, the band has enjoyed unbroken success, yet there has been as much conflict as in much more volatile lineups. The difference here? It is intertwined with personal consciences, internal battles that have bled into the work of one of music's game-changers.

Before Radiohead, first came Oxfordshire five-piece On a Friday. Different name, same faces: singer (and occasional guitarist and keyboard player) **Thom Yorke**, guitarist **Jonny Greenwood**, his older brother and bassist **Colin**, second guitarist **Ed O'Brien**, and drummer **Phil Selway**. A switch to a moniker inspired by a Talking Heads song was followed by their debut, *Pablo Honey* (1993). Some bands burst out fully formed; it was not so here, with an album that owed too much to grunge influences, and which sold more than it deserved to after "Creep," with Greenwood Jr's crunching guitar, picked up airplay in America. (There, the song forged a link between grunge and emo—a micro-genre known, thanks to a quote about Radiohead in the movie *Clueless*, as "mope rock.")

"Creep" reached the U.K. Top Ten, but the tag of one-hit wonders did not dangle around the band's

necks for too long: *The Bends* (1995) was rapturously received. *Rolling Stone* praised its "exploded emotional palette," and the notoriously self-critical Yorke conceded that his lyrics for "Fake Plastic Trees"—one of five U.K. hits from the album—were the first with which he was almost content. Radiohead, said Michael Stipe of R.E.M. (with whom they toured in 1995), were "so good they scare me."

Having scarred audiences by playing new songs while supporting Alanis Morissette in 1996, Radiohead lurched into the leftfield the following year. Disdain for politicians, dislocation from technology, and dismay at what the group saw as the easy musical options exercised by the Britpop movement all informed *OK Computer*. It was immediately hailed as the band's masterpiece, despite Yorke previewing it as "sort of skiffle-Pink Floyd that sounds like Queen." (Floyd's Roger Waters said that he "really liked" the album, while their unsurprisingly different-minded David Gilmour expressed a preference for *The Bends*.)

Given that the pre-teen Yorke's first song was called "Mushroom Cloud," his grim themes came as little surprise, but the album tapped into fears about the approaching new millennium. It is debatable whether the U.K. Top Three has, before or since, been home to anything as weird as "Paranoid Android."

year-by-year   ▪ Vocals   ▪ Guitar   ▪ Bass   ▪ Drums   ▪ Keyboards

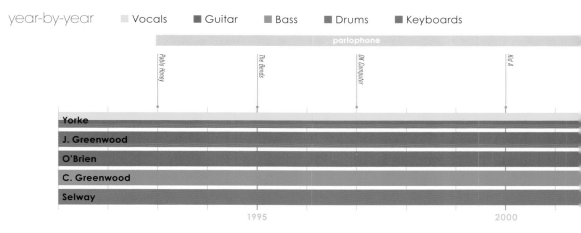

Still the internal doubts remained, even after a headline slot at Britain's Glastonbury festival in 1997 that is regarded as one of the event's greatest-ever performances. "We thought we'd blown it in the biggest possible way," said Colin Greenwood.

Having documented their unease on 1998's video *Meeting People Is Easy,* the band determined to veer even further away from rock orthodoxy. *Kid A* (2000) and its companion piece *Amnesiac* (2001) came at no small cost to the band's internal dynamics. "There was a lot of turning up and hanging around and wondering what to do next and not doing anything, and then going home," said Greenwood Sr. "Every day. For weeks and weeks. It's very soul sapping."

But the stranger they became, the more the world loved them. *Kid A* took the U.S. No. 1 slot to kick off a run of Top Three albums. Yorke's battle to open *Kid A* with "Everything in its Right Place" was an ideal way of signposting its cold love for electronica, but influences across the two albums even included jazz from British trumpeter Humphrey Lyttelton. Yorke's keening voice was one of the band's unique selling points, so it was a characteristically contrary next step to play it down. Underpinning everything was the imperative to shed what Yorke saw as the straitjacket of "it's not a song unless it's got a guitar in it, or whatever nonsense."

Ironically, *Hail to the Thief* (2003) returned the band to a more conventional approach, but charges of water-treading did not come only from outside the band. Of the band's fourth U.K. chart-topper, Yorke said: "What we were doing was becoming routine. It felt like we were doing it because we didn't really know what else to do." The frontman stepped outside the band for the gorgeous *The Eraser* (2006) while Jonny Greenwood redefined film soundtracks with 2007's *There Will Be Blood.*

Like its predecessor, 2007's beautiful *In Rainbows* did not rip up the rule book, but saved its innovation for its system of pay-what-you-want downloads. And after 2009's heartbreaking "Harry Patch (In Memory Of)," there was no consideration for slipping into comfortable and unchallenging middle age with *The King of Limbs* (2011). On a record dominated by skittering and unsettling rhythms, Phil Selway sounded on some cuts as if he were aiming to personify the title of his band's most opinion-dividing album.

The restless search for bars to raise and boundaries to push continues. "We always have a feeling that we can do better. There's always acres and acres of room for improvement," said Jonny Greenwood. "Maybe that's what keeps us going. Imagine being satisfied with something." **CB**

R

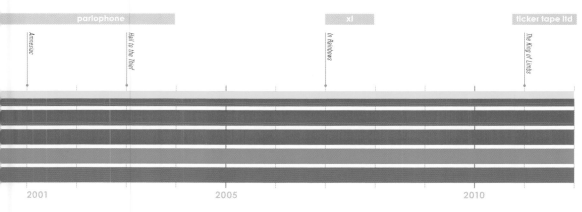

parlophone   xl   ticker tape ltd

Amnesiac   *Hail to the Thief*   *In Rainbows*   *The King of Limbs*

2001   2005   2010

Pablo Honey
(1993)

The Bends (1995)

OK Computer
(1997)

Kid A (2000)

Amnesiac (2001)

Hail to the Thief
(2003)

In Rainbows (2007)

The King of Limbs
(2011)

Ed O'Brien, **Thom Yorke**, **Phil Selway**, **Jonny Greenwood** and **Colin Greenwood** in 1993.

Yorke backstage in Cambridge, England, in November 1995.

Jonny Greenwood, his arm in a brace, on stage in 1997.

Yorke, the driving force behind *Kid A*'s unconventional sound, in the Netherlands in 2000.

By now regarded as one of rock's finest live bands, Radiohead hit Florida's Cruzan Amphitheatre on the *In Rainbows* tour, in May 2008.

Jonny Greenwood, Yorke, Selway, Colin Greenwood, and Ed O'Brien in London, in a shoot to promote *Kid A*'s "sequel," *Amnesiac*—the third of five consecutive U.K. No. 1 albums.

After a sensational set at Britain's Glastonbury festival in 1997, Yorke and O'Brien feature in Radiohead's second headlining slot, in 2003.

Yorke at New York's Roseland Ballroom in 2011—one of a series of shows that preceded a world tour for *The King of Limbs* in 2012.

rage against the machine 1990–present

Zack de la Rocha
b. January 12, 1970

Tom Morello
b. May 30, 1964

Tim Commerford
b. February 26, 1968

Brad Wilk
b. September 5, 1968

Los Angeles quartet Rage Against the Machine are rather political in the same way that the surface of the sun is rather warm. Their intense drive has sustained them for their twenty years as a band, and provided them with endless targets for lyrical inspiration. Although critics have sneered at the group's willingness to sign with a major label for its resolutely anti-corporate albums, RATM continue to plough a furrow that places message resolutely over medium.

Formed by guitarist **Tom Morello** in 1991, Rage Against the Machine also features rapper **Zack de la Rocha**, whose politically active parents had given him a high-octane zeal; bassist **Tim Commerford**, a school friend of de la Rocha; and drummer **Brad Wilk**, who had auditioned for Morello's previous band, Lock Up. In that earlier group, the guitarist had honed an unusual, hard-hitting guitar style based on inventive effects and razor-sharp riffs. This approach became the core of RATM's music, committed to demo tape after club gigs and submitted to the Epic label. The subsequent deal did not represent an ideological clash, said Morello, because it allowed the musicians complete control over their music.

The band's self-titled debut, issued in 1992, was a breathtaking piece of work. Its stern, uncompromising view of the modern world as a media-controlled hell, populated by zombies and governed by a callous military-industrial complex, spoke to the slacker generation just as much as Rage's contemporaries like Nirvana. The band's most striking songs—"Killing in the Name," "Bullet in the Head," "Know Your Enemy" and "Wake Up"—became regulars on MTV and radio, a remarkable achievement given their raw anger and frequently graphic language.

Although Rage recorded two more albums (*Evil Empire* and *The Battle of Los Angeles*) and a covers collection (*Renegades*) before calling it a day in 2000, they never really equaled that stunning first record. Latterday singles such as "Bulls on Parade" and "People of the Sun" had power, certainly, but after the rise of nü-metal—in many ways, the logical extension of RATM's signature sound—fans had other, heavier bands to follow, each with its own lyrical fury.

In the hiatus before their much-publicized reunion in 2007, Morello, Wilk and Commerford united with Soundgarden singer Chris Cornell for three U.S. Top Ten albums as Audioslave. But there was a palpable sense of expectation for the original band to reform and, when they did so, crowds surged to their shows.

A splendid dose of publicity came at the end of 2009 when "Killing in the Name" became a Christmas No. 1 in the U.K. after a Facebook campaign was set up in protest against the usual chart domination by a reality TV winner. RATM repaid the compliment by playing a free concert in London the following summer. As modern-day protests go, this one had all the right elements: a modern, technological platform for the people; a corporate adversary; and an anthem for a generation. Somehow it seemed to sum up the band's entire career in one stroke. **JM**

year-by-year ■ Vocals ■ Guitar ■ Bass ■ Drums

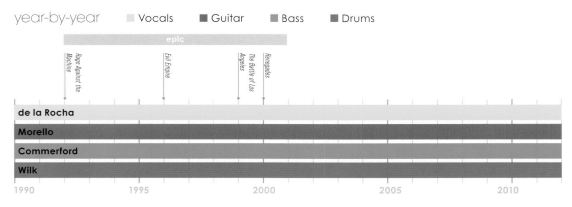

rainbow 1975–1997

**Ritchie
Blackmore**
b. April 14, 1945

**Ronnie
James Dio**
b. July 10, 1942
d. May 16, 2010

**Graham
Bonnet**
b. December
23, 1947

Cozy Powell
b. December
29, 1947
d. April 5, 1998

Roger Glover
b. November
30, 1945

**Joe Lynn
Turner**
b. August 2,
1951

**Bobby
Rondinelli**
b. July 27, 1955

Doogie White
b. March 7, 1960

Ritchie Blackmore is one of classic rock's most accomplished guitarists, and a man who resolutely treads his own path. So when his band Deep Purple changed its sound in 1974 and that change was not to his liking, he left to form Rainbow. Purple were among the planet's biggest bands at the time, touring in a private jet and playing to stadiums. Simply walking away to found a new band took serious conviction.

But Blackmore's gamble paid off. Enlisting Elf singer **Ronnie James Dio** and Dio's bandmates Craig Gruber (bass), Gary Driscoll (drums), and Micky Lee Soule (keyboards) and cutting *Ritchie Blackmore's Rainbow*, the guitarist established the band as a credible project. He also quickly gained a reputation as a man not to be trifled with, firing the entire band bar Dio for the follow-up. The classic *Rainbow Rising* (1976) featured Jimmy Bain (bass), Tony Carey (keyboards) and **Cozy Powell** (drums). Musicians came and went over the next few years, notably former Purple bassist **Roger Glover**. Dio decamped for Black Sabbath when Blackmore made it clear that he wanted Rainbow to drop its sword-and-sorcery focus and move into commercial rock territory.

Ex-Marbles singer **Graham Bonnet** came aboard for the new era, which—as Blackmore predicted—saw Rainbow meet with significant success, thanks to a new sound. The group will always be remembered for "Since You Been Gone," a 1979 radio-rock anthem.

Subsequent albums with Bonnet's successor **Joe Lynn Turner** maintained Rainbow's transatlantic commercial superiority over rival post-Purple projects Whitesnake and Gillan. However, the re-formation of the classic Mark II lineup of Deep Purple put Rainbow on ice in 1984.

When Purple fractured once again a decade later, Blackmore reconvened Rainbow, with Scottish singer **Doogie White** and session musicians. *Stranger in Us All* (1995) was a decent slab of modern rock, albeit one unlikely to compete with *Rainbow Rising*. While the new band enjoyed a three-year run, Blackmore became fixated on performing Renaissance music, and called time on Rainbow in 1997 to do exactly that. His new band, Blackmore's Night, has toured ever since to a rather unusual niche market of audiences wearing leather jerkins and other medieval garments.

Despite the absence of Blackmore from the rock scene and exhortations from fans for reunions of Rainbow (and indeed a Blackmore-led Purple), his band's songs have only grown in popularity. A touring tribute band called Over the Rainbow is led by Blackmore's son Jürgen, and several of the group's best-known songs were performed live by groups such as Dio and the Hughes-Turner Project. Many fans petitioned for a reunion of Blackmore with Ronnie James Dio but, sadly, the vocalist's death to stomach cancer in 2010 rendered such a dream impossible. **JM**

year-by-year   ■ Vocals   ■ Guitar   ■ Bass   ■ Drums

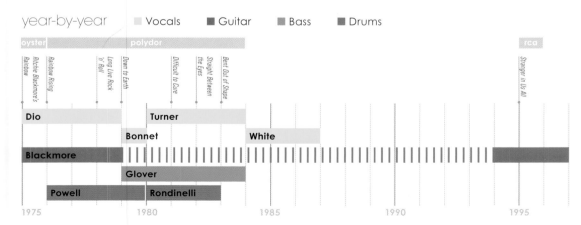

rammstein 1993–present

Till Lindermann
b. January 4, 1963

Paul H. Landers
b. December 9, 1964

Christian "Flake" Lorentz
b. November 16, 1966

Richard Z. Kruspe
b. June 24, 1967

Oliver Riedel
b. April 11, 1971

Christoph "Doom" Schneider
b. May 11, 1966

Rammstein were among the progenitors of what in 1995 was dubbed by the music press in Europe as "Neue Deutsche Härte"—"New German Hardness." It describes a crossover style combining groove metal with elements of techno and industrial electronica. In Rammstein's case, that meant a brutally intense form of hard rock with lyrics sung in German in a deep, domineering male voice, with visual presentations that skirt pornography, homoeroticism, and military chic. Oh, and lots of explosions.

Formed in 1993, Rammstein's roots were in the East Berlin punk band Feeling B. Active for a decade, the band had featured guitarist **Paul H. Landers** and keyboard player **Christian "Flake" Lorentz**. They were joined briefly in the early nineties by Leipzig-born drummer **Till Lindermann**, a former swimmer once in contention for a place in the East German Olympic team. The trio formed Rammstein: with Lindermann as lead singer, they entered and won a competition to make a professional demo. Provocative from the beginning, the band took their name from a 1988 German air show disaster at the Ramstein USAF air base in which seventy spectators were killed and many more injured: aptly, given the band's sound, the word also describes a medieval stone battering ram.

Expanding to a six-piece lineup, with lead guitarist **Richard Z. Kruspe**, bassist **Oliver Riedel** and drummer **Christoph "Doom" Schneider**, Rammstein quickly established a reputation for powerful and theatrical live performances.

After the band's first single, "Du riechst so gut," their debut album *Herzeleid* ("Heartbreak") appeared in September 1995, its powerful electro-metal striking an immediate chord with German youth. The ingredients of the characteristic Rammstein sound—stomping drums, rolling bass, cascades of feedback, clipped electronic beats, and over-enunciated vocals (seemingly presented without a flicker of irony)—were in place from the very beginning, and the album effortlessly sailed into the German Top Ten. Some critics may have been uncomfortable with song titles such as "Der Meister" ("The Master") and "Weißes Fleisch" ("White Flesh"), sleeve artwork showing the musclebound band posing bare-chested and stern-faced, and a video that included excerpts from the 1936 Berlin Olympics by Hitler's filmmaker of choice, Leni Riefenstahl—but Rammstein would always be firm in their denial of fascist tendencies.

German bands—especially those singing in their native tongue—have rarely made a lasting impression

year-by-year

□ Vocals ■ Guitar ■ Bass ■ Drums ■ Keyboards

motor

Herzeleid *Sehnsucht* *Mutter*

Lindermann

Landers

Kruspe

Riedel

Schneider

Lorentz

1994   1996   1998   2000   2002

on the international music scene. By the beginning of 1996, Rammstein were already setting themselves up as an exception by performing in London as part of MTV's *Hanging Out* series. Their exposure was further broadened when Nine Inch Nails' Trent Reznor selected two songs from *Herzeleid* in his capacity as music director for David Lynch's movie *Lost Highway*.

In November 1996, Rammstein decamped to the Mediterranean island of Malta to record their critical second album. Two singles released in the first half of 1997—"Engel" ("Angel") and "Du Hast" ("You Have")—went gold and hit the German Top Five.

When *Sehnsucht* ("Longing") emerged in the summer of 1997, it entered Germany's chart at No. 1 while, in a frenzy of exposure, two earlier singles surged back into the Top Twenty. *Sehnsucht* featured six different front covers, each depicting a member of the band wearing bizarre facial equipment constructed from kitchen utensils. As the band toured the U.S. with Ice Cube, Korn, and Limp Bizkit, the album gave Rammstein their first *Billboard* chart success, reaching No. 45 and earning the band a Grammy nomination. It remains the only album sung entirely in German to be certified platinum in the U.S. (later Rammstein albums incorporated some English lyrics).

After 1999's concert album *Live aus Berlin*, Rammstein retreated to the south of France to record *Mutter* (2001)—their third album to top the German charts. By now, they were a huge international live draw, their shows increasingly outlandish spectacles. Indeed, vocalist Lindemann became a licensed pyrotechnician, his signature trick being to perform entire songs while engulfed head to toe in flames. Kruspe describes their often misinterpreted shows as "a combination of humor, theater, and our East German culture," acknowledging that "ninety-nine per cent of the people don't understand the lyrics, so you have to come up with something to keep the drama in the show."

With the success of 2004's *Reise, Reise* ("Journey, Journey") and 2005's *Rosenrot* ("Rose Red"), Rammstein were acknowledged by *Billboard* as the biggest-selling German-language band of all time. This position was cemented in 2009 with the band's crowning achievement, *Liebe ist für alle da* ("Love Is There for Everyone") which topped charts throughout continental Europe and reached the Top Twenty for the first time in both the U.K. and U.S. The 2011 "greatest hits" collection *Made in Germany 1995–2011* summed up their extraordinary career so far. **TB**

R

■ Programming

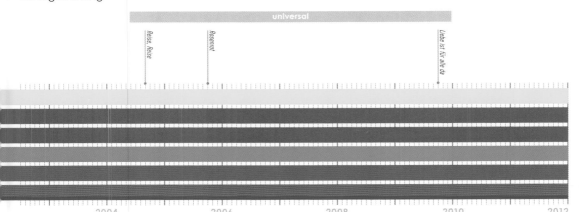

ramones 1974–1996

Joey Ramone
b. May 19, 1951
d. April 15, 2001

Dee Dee Ramone
b. September 18, 1952
d. June 5, 2002

Johnny Ramone
b. October 8, 1951
d. September 15, 2004

Tommy Ramone
b. January 29, 1952

Marky Ramone
b. July 15, 1956

Richie Ramone
b. August 11, 1957

U2? Metallica? Red Hot Chili Peppers? Green Day? To get just one of those four acts to appear on a tribute album would be a coup. To get all of them—plus, on 2003's *We're a Happy Family*, Kiss, The Pretenders, Marilyn Manson, Pearl Jam's Eddie Vedder, and Tom Waits—takes a special kind of band. A band like the Ramones, who turned musical limitations into strengths and influenced everyone from the Sex Pistols (who attended their first British tour in 1976) to Springsteen (who wrote "Hungry Heart" for them before keeping it for himself). They could not play too well, but they were fast, they were loud, and they were so cool that, even with all three of the founding members sadly dead, their names still adorn t-shirts around the world.

In the Forest Hills suburb of New York, the band convened in 1974: John Cummings (guitar), Doug Colvin (bass), and Jeffry Hyman (drums). Yet Colvin, already using heroin, found he could not sing *and* play bass, so Hyman became the vocalist and Tamás Erdélyi, a sound engineer, played drums.

Colvin renamed himself **Dee Dee Ramone**—a nod to Paul Ramon, a pseudonym Paul McCartney used on a Steve Miller album. Hyman became **Joey Ramone**, Cummings **Johnny Ramone**, and Erdélyi **Tommy Ramone**. Every song started with Dee Dee's soon-to-be trademark "One-two-three-four!"

The Ramones became effectively the house band of Manhattan's punk club CBGB in Manhattan. "Our first show was just the bartender and his dog," Joey recalled, "but then we got the Warhol, arty crowd." At CBGB, they honed their appearance into an iconic image of shaggy hair, black leather jackets, and long legs astride. This unity masked internal clashes born from Joey's liberalism and Johnny's right-wing views.

In 1976, they cut their self-titled debut album for Sire, transforming it from an underground label to a haven for influential alternative music (the Dead Boys, Talking Heads, and The Cure would follow). *Ramones* cost $6,000—and you might wonder why it cost even that much. Most songs were written by Dee Dee from personal experience, including "Blitzkrieg Bop" (with its cry of "Hey ho, let's go"), "Now I Wanna Sniff Some Glue," and "Judy Is a Punk."

They appeared at London's Roundhouse with the Flamin' Groovies and the Stranglers on July 4, 1976. "You don't have to be good," Johnny Rotten told them, "Just get out there and play."

Leave Home (1977) included "Pinhead," which immortalized the band's "gabba, gabba, hey!" catchphrase. (A prompt reissue of the album replaced "Carbona Not Glue" with "Babysitter" after the household cleansing manufacturer Carbona

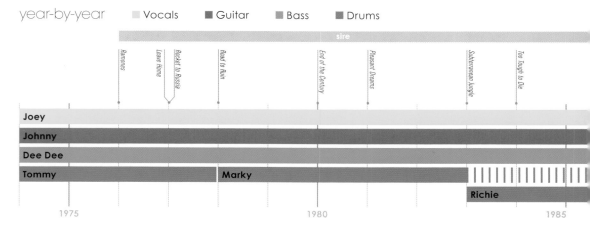

C.J. Ramone
b. October 8, 1965

took legal action). *Rocket to Russia* (1977) boasted "Teenage Lobotomy," "Rockaway Beach" (their biggest U.S. hit), and the Beach Boys-esque "Sheena is a Punk Rocker," which made the U.K. Top Thirty.

In 1978, Tommy tired of touring but remained their producer. His successor, **Marky Ramone** (Marc Steven Bell), debuted on 1978's fine *Road to Ruin*, featuring "I Wanna Be Sedated." In 1979 came their live gem *It's Alive* and an appearance in the movie *Rock 'n' Roll High School,* produced by quickie merchant Roger Corman (amusingly, "Teenage Lobotomy" is subtitled).

One wall of sound met another when they united with producer Phil Spector for 1980's *End of the Century,* which defied punk convention by paying tribute to the fifties and sixties on "Do You Remember Rock 'n' Roll Radio." The album included outside musicians—of the Ramones, only Joey remained on Spector's "Baby I Love You," which hit the U.K. Top Ten, charting higher than the Ronettes' original. Joey liked the album, but Johnny scorned the overdubbing and called it "watered-down Ramones." (Further slick production characterized 1981's *Pleasant Dreams,* this time courtesy of 10cc's Graham Gouldman.)

Marky was dismissed for alcohol-related issues in 1983 and **Richie Ramone** (Richard Reinhardt) joined. In 1985, with Tommy producing, they returned to the fast lane for *Too Tough to Die.* Richie left after *Animal Boy* (1986) amid a dispute about merchandising profits. Blondie's Clem Burke filled in for two shows as Elvis Ramone before Marky—now cleaned up—returned for *Halfway to Sanity* (1987). The following year's hits set, *Ramones Mania,* would be band's only album to go gold in their home country.

Dee Dee left during *Brain Drain* (1989) to go solo, but continued to write for the group. His replacement, Chris Ward, became **C.J. Ramone**—who broke his arm when he rode a Harley-Davidson on stage in Germany. As a lyric in *Mondo Bizarro* goes, "Touring, touring, it's never boring." When the Ramones were featured as cartoons in *The Simpsons,* some might have wondered if there was any difference.

After a covers album, *Acid Eaters* (1994), they announced their "retirement" with *¡Adios Amigos!* Their final dates were on the Lollapalooza festival—the last, in August 1996, being issued as *We're Outta Here!* Dee Dee returned and guests included Motörhead's Lemmy, with whom they performed his "R.A.M.O.N.E.S." Posthumous honors piled up: a Rock and Roll Hall of Fame induction and a Lifetime Achievement award at the Grammys. "I'd like to congratulate myself," said Dee at the first, "and thank myself and give myself a big pat on the back." **SL**

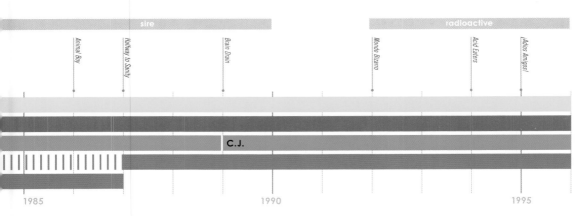

red hot chili peppers 1983–present

Anthony Kiedis b. November 1, 1962	**Josh Klinghoffer** b. October 3, 1979	**Flea** b. October 16, 1962	**Chad Smith** b. October 25, 1961

John Frusciante b. March 5, 1970

Hillel Slovak b. April 13, 1962 d. June 25, 1988

Jack Irons b. July 18, 1962

Dave Navarro b. June 7, 1967

The enormous success and longevity of the Red Hot Chili Peppers could never have been predicted. When they formed in 1983, punk bands played small clubs, funk was a niche musical genre, and slapping bass guitars was almost criminally unfashionable. That this Los Angeles foursome combined those elements and met with worldwide acclaim is one of rock's most unusual outcomes—even more so given that their progress has been hindered by addiction and death.

It all began when L.A. high school students **Anthony Kiedis** (vocals) and Australian-born Michael "**Flea**" Balzary (nicknamed for his energetic stage moves) began playing songs together, united by a love of hardcore punk and seventies funk bands such as Sly & the Family Stone and Parliament-Funkadelic. "Funk," Flea assured *Kerrang!* magazine, "is as heavy as shit." The pair recruited drummer **Hillel Slovak** (guitar) and **Jack Irons** (drums), although the latter duo were also in a band called What Is This? This dual commitment was the first contributor to a constantly shifting lineup through much of their career. In fact, after the band, which began life as Tony Flow & The Miraculously Majestic Masters of Mayhem, renamed themselves the Red Hot Chili Peppers and scored a deal with EMI America, Slovak and Irons did not play on their self-titled debut album in 1984. Instead, **Jack**

Sherman and **Cliff Martinez** played guitar and drums respectively. Slovak returned for 1985's *Freaky Styley* (produced by funk godfather George Clinton) and Irons in 1987 for *The Uplift Mofo Party Plan*.

These early albums established the Chili Peppers' idiosyncratic funk-punk, propeled by Kiedis's semi-rapped, semi-sung vocals and Flea's expert slap bass. The group's profile rose impressively, thanks to the 1987 hit "Fight Like a Brave" and the Beatles-spoofing "socks on cocks" cover of 1988's *The Abbey Road E.P.*

However, tragedy struck when Slovak succumbed to a heroin overdose in 1988. Grieving, Irons left the band (he later joined Pearl Jam), and—after a period of uncertainty in which P-Funk guitarist **DeWayne McKnight** and Dead Kennedys drummer **D. H. Peligro** filled in—permanent replacements **John Frusciante** and **Chad Smith** were added. The former was a Slovak disciple who claimed to have learned everything he knew about funk guitar from his late idol, and the latter brought a strong rock style that gave the Chilis a much-needed commercial edge. *Mother's Milk* (1989) was the new lineup's first release, and became the band's most notable success yet, largely thanks to a hit cover of Stevie Wonder's "Higher Ground."

Greater exposure came in 1991, however, when production guru Rick Rubin agreed to tweak the

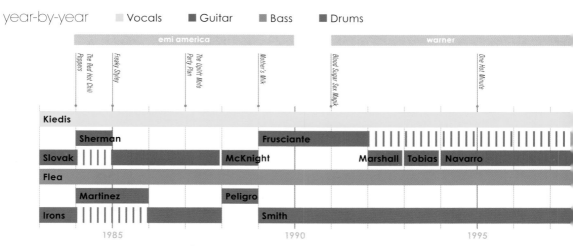

year-by-year ▪ Vocals ▪ Guitar ▪ Bass ▪ Drums

14.5M	5M	14.9M	9.2M
Blood Sugar Sex Magik (1991)	**One Hot Minute** (1995)	**Californication** (1999)	**By the Way** (2002)

Cliff Martinez
b. February 5, 1954

D.H. Peligro
b. Date July 9, 1959

Arik Marshall
b. February 13, 1967

Jack Sherman
b. January 18, 1956

DeWayne McKnight
b. April 17, 1954

Jesse Tobias
b. April 1, 1972

faders on the Chilis' *Blood Sugar Sex Magik*. Along with Nirvana's *Nevermind* and Metallica's *Metallica*, both released mere months beforehand, *Blood Sugar* became one of the alternative rock generation's must-have albums, leading to hits such as "Give It Away" and the ballad "Under the Bridge."

But while on tour to promote the album, Frusciante began to buckle under the stresses of fame and developed a crippling heroin addiction, just as his predecessor had done before him. In May 1992, he quit, to be replaced first by Zander Schloss, then **Arik Marshall** (who lasted for the band's headlining slot on the Lollapalooza tour and *Simpsons* cameo in 1993), then **Jesse Tobias** (who would subsequently resurface alongside Alanis Morissette and, later, Morrissey).

Kiedis, Flea and Smith returned in 1994 with a new guitarist, **Dave Navarro** of Jane's Addiction. However, the resultant *One Hot Minute*—despite containing fine songs and going double platinum in the U.S.—failed to match the impact of *Blood Sugar Sex Magik*. As the funk-rock that the Chilis had pioneered was evolving into the heavier nü-metal sound, it seemed that the band might fade. Navarro was ousted after rumors of more drug addiction—but, just as all hope seemed gone, Frusciante returned to the fold, now cleaned up after a life-threatening few years of addiction.

Once again Rick Rubin enabled a rebirth for the Chili Peppers: one of equally giant proportions to their breakthrough almost a decade earlier. The intermittently pretty *Californication* (1999) and utterly gorgeous *By the Way* (2002) established the band as a stadium-sized force to be reckoned with, especially in the U.K. and Europe, where the Chilis topped charts and headlined at arenas and festivals—*Live in Hyde Park* gave the band their second U.K. No. 1 in 2004. Perhaps the new sound lacked the raw danger of the eighties albums and the stripped-down emotion of the *Blood Sugar Sex Magik* era, but the Chilis' smoother sound was welcomed by a new audience—combined worldwide sales of *Californication* and *By the Way* approach twenty-five million.

Greatest Hits (2003) helped fill the gap before 2006's *Stadium Arcadium*, a bloated set that earned middling reviews yet yielded the platinum-selling U.S. hit "Snow (Hey Oh)." Wisely, the group embarked on a long hiatus, during which Smith joined Van Halen's Sammy Hagar and Michael Anthony in Chickenfoot, Flea played with Radiohead's Thom Yorke and Blur's Damon Albarn, and Frusciante departed once more.

I'm with You (2011) was cut with new guitarist Josh Klinghoffer and contained the sort of radio-friendly rock that ensures the band are set for the future. **JM**

R

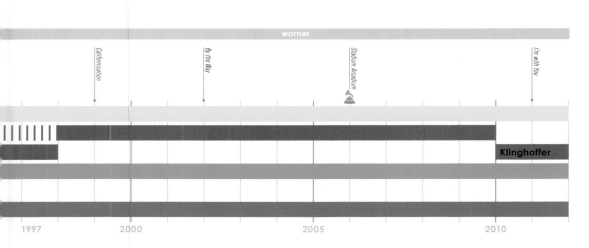

warner

Californication

By the Way

Stadium Arcadium

I'm with You

Klinghoffer

1997   2000   2005   2010

The Red Hot Chilli Peppers (1984)

Freaky Styley (1985)

The Uplift Mofo Party Plan (1987)

Mother's Milk (1989)

Blood Sugar Sex Magik (1991)

One Hot Minute (1995)

Californication (1999)

By the Way (2002)

Stadium Arcadium (2006)

I'm with You (2006)

Left to right: **Flea**, **Cliff Martinez**, and **Anthony Kiedis** perform at The Roxy, Hollywood, on September 9, 1984.

Martinez, Flea, Kiedis, and **Hillel Slovak** ham it up for the camera in 1985.

Flea, Slovak, and **Kiedis** pose with **Jack Irons** in Minneapolis, in January 1987.

Kiedis with new guitarist **John Frusciante** (right).

Flaming headgear distinguishes a Peppers performance in Stanhope, New Jersey, in August 1991.

Kiedis and **Navarro** at the Cow Palace, San Francisco, on April 6, 1996.

Brilliant lightbulb costumes conceal **Dave Navarro** (left) and **Kiedis** at the Woodstock festival, August 14, 1994.

Chad Smith (drums) and **Kiedis** at the Shoreline Amphitheater in Mountain View, California, on June 18, 1999.

Flea and **Frusciante** perform in Belgium in 2002.

A laid-back **Flea, Kiedis,** and **Frusciante** entertain at the Grammy Awards, Los Angeles, on February 8, 2006.

Flea with **Josh Klinghoffer** in Sunrise, Florida, on April 2, 2012.

r.e.m. 1980–2011

Michael Stipe
b. January 4, 1960

Peter Buck
b. December 6, 1956

Mike Mills
b. December 17, 1958

Bill Berry
b. July 31, 1958

In the early eighties, when overpowering ballads, "hair metal," and bombastic production values dominated the charts, R.E.M. provided a much-needed antidote: mystery. From the eerie shot of kudzu vines on their debut album cover to **Michael Stipe**'s blurred vocal delivery, this band intrigued.

Formed in Athens, Georgia, R.E.M. evolved an idiosyncratic, ringing sound built on **Peter Buck**'s Rickenbacker guitar—he favored subtle arpeggios over power chords—and Stipe's rootsy vocals. **Mike Mills** supplied melodic bass and backing vocals, with **Bill Berry** on drums and vocals. The band cut their debut single, "Radio Free Europe," for indie label Hib-Tone in mid-1981. A sizzling slice of post punk, it attracted critical plaudits and record company interest. The *Chronic Town* E.P. followed, marking their debut for the I.R.S. label. A re-recorded "Radio Free Europe" kicked off the debut album *Murmur* (1983), but other pleasures abounded—notably the brooding "Talk About the Passion," the carefree "Shaking Through," and the quietly sublime "Perfect Circle." *Rolling Stone* made it their album of the year (over Michael Jackson's *Thriller*).

Reckoning (1984), an assured follow-up, boasted the wistful wonders "So. Central Rain (I'm Sorry)," "Camera," and "Time After Time (AnnElise)," and a hit-that-never-was in "(Don't Go Back To) Rockville."

Fables of the Reconstruction (1985) was cut in London with Fairport Convention/Nick Drake producer Joe Boyd. Ill at ease in an unfamiliar country, the group were in low spirits, hence the album's subdued sound (exceptions being the funked-up "Can't Get There from Here" and "Driver 8"). The mythology of the South pervades the album, notably on "Old Man Kensey" and the plaintive, banjo-led "Wendell Gee."

Lifes Rich Pageant (1986) was bigger and bolder—witness the clarion-call "Begin the Begin," the euphoric "These Days," and an uplifting take on The Clique's "Superman," sung by Mills. (The group peppered their live sets and B-sides with cover songs; *Document* boasts a fine version of Wire's "Strange.") Subtler delights included the richly melodic "Fall on Me" and the touching Civil War memento "Swan Swan H." The result was their first U.S. gold album.

As R.E.M. grew in confidence and stature—aided by intensive touring and college-radio support—their songs graduated from reflections on personal relationships to the wider world, with Stipe's lyrics becoming less impressionistic, more direct. *Document* (1987), their first platinum album, addressed a dark period of past U.S. politics—with implications for the Reagan era—on "Exhuming McCarthy." "The One I Love"—a twisted rejection note—gave the band a first genuine hit (U.S. No. 9), while another standout

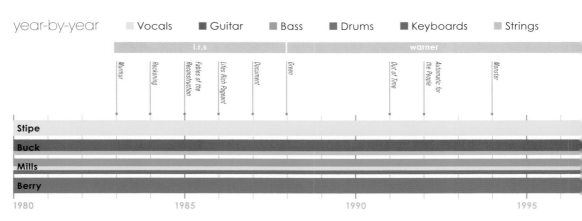

year-by-year ▪ Vocals ▪ Guitar ▪ Bass ▪ Drums ▪ Keyboards ▪ Strings

i.r.s — warner

Murmur | *Reckoning* | *Fables of the Reconstruction* | *Lifes Rich Pageant* | *Document* | *Green* | *Out of Time* | *Automatic for the People* | *Monster*

Stipe
Buck
Mills
Berry

1980 — 1985 — 1990 — 1995

was "It's the End of the World as We Know It (And I Feel Fine)," whose helter-skelter imagery recalled Bob Dylan's "Subterranean Homesick Blues."

Green (1988) marked the band's debut for Warner, and saw them shake up proceedings by regularly switching instruments. (It is also the first to feature Buck playing mandolin, on the spine-tingling trio "Hairshirt," "The Wrong Child," and "You Are the Everything.")

Despite the rap-friendly opener "Radio Song" (featuring KRS-One), *Out of Time* (1991) was a country-tinged affair. Boosted by the worldwide smash "Losing My Religion," and featuring Kate Pierson of The B-52's on three cuts (including "Shiny Happy People"), it proved a career high and sold over sixteen million copies, providing the band with their first U.S./U.K. No. 1 and bagging three Grammys in the process.

Another multi-platinum smash, *Automatic for the People* (1992), confirmed R.E.M. as superstars, despite their failure to tour and the album's downbeat atmosphere—prompting (unfounded) rumors about Stipe's health. From the sobering "Drive"—which references David Essex's 1973 hit "Rock On"—to the Andy Kaufman tribute "Man on the Moon," and the inspiring "Everybody Hurts," quality abounded.

Having decided to return to the road for the first time since the end of the *Green* tour, the group created 1994's crunchy *Monster*. In complete contrast to the subdued palette of *Out of Time* and *Automatic For the People*, this transatlantic No. 1 nodded to grunge, rocking out engagingly on "Star 69," and paying tribute to Stipe's late friend Kurt Cobain on "Let Me In." Now stadium-fillers, R.E.M. renewed their Warner contract in a deal said to be worth $80 million. However, the gamely experimental *New Adventures in Hi-Fi* (1996), a U.S. No. 2 and U.K. No. 1, sold "only" five million copies. More damagingly, Berry—weary of the rock-star treadmill—announced his departure. (The *Monster* tour had seen him collapse on stage from a brain aneurysm, while Mills and Stipe were hospitalized with less serious ailments.)

Subsequent albums charted well without enjoying the acclaim heaped on earlier efforts. However, *Up* (1998) and *Around the Sun* (2004)—while frustratingly inconsistent—included some of their most affecting songs (including the former's "At My Most Beautiful" and the latter's "I Wanted to Be Wrong"). The jingly-jangly *Reveal* (1999) played it straighter, while the feisty *Accelerate* (2008) provided their seventh U.K. chart-topper, and restored them to the U.S. Top Three.

After 2011's *Collapse into Now* sank faster than any of its predecessors (despite featuring Peaches, Eddie Vedder, and Patti Smith), R.E.M. split on September 21 that year. Their heyday may have been long gone, but during that heyday they were untouchable. **RD**

R

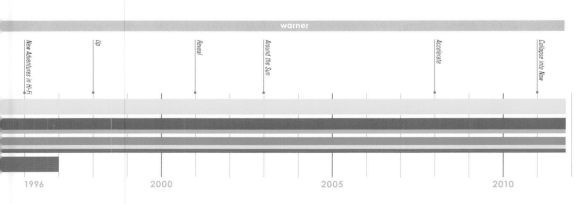

Murmur (1983)

Lifes Rich Pageant (1986)

Green (1988)

Out of Time (1991)

Automatic for the People (1992)

Monster (1994)

Up (1998)

Reveal (2001)

Around the Sun (2004)

Accelerate (2008)

Michael Stipe and **Peter Buck** opening for The Police at New York's Shea Stadium in 1983.

Stipe on the *Green* tour, at the Netherlands' Pinkpop festival, in 198

Buck, Mike Mills, Bill Berry, and **Stipe** around the time of *Lifes Rich Pageant*.

Stipe and **Buck** film a Dutch TV appearance on the day *Out of Time* is released.

R.E.M. play songs from the then forthcoming *Reveal* at 2001's Rock

Mills and **Stipe** with 1992's "Best International Group" BRIT award.

Clutching belated MTV Video Music awards for "Everybody Hurts" in the year of *Monster*.

Stipe at a Tibet Freedom show where they debuted songs from *Up*.

Rockin' with Bruce Springsteen on 2004's Vote for Change tour.

Recording a U.S. TV appearance in New York, in 2008.

the rolling stones 1962–present

F

Mick Jagger
b. July 26, 1943

F

Keith Richards
b. December 18, 1943

F

Brian Jones
b. February 28, 1942
d. June 3, 1969

F

Bill Wyman
b. October 24, 1936

Charlie Watts
b. June 2, 1941

F

Ian Stewart
b. July 18, 1938
d. December 12, 1985

Dick Taylor
b. January 28, 1943

Mick Taylor
b. January 17, 1948

"The Stones are a different kind of group," observed **Mick Taylor**. "I realized that when I joined them. It's not really so much their musical ability, it's just they have a certain kind of style and attitude which is unique."

Mick Jagger, **Keith Richards**, and **Brian Jones** formed The Rolling Stones in 1962 with bassist **Dick Taylor** and pianist **Ian Stewart**. By 1963 Taylor had gone (to resurface fronting The Pretty Things) and the rhythm section consisted of bassist **Bill Wyman** and drummer **Charlie Watts**. (The latter succeeded future Kinks sticksman Mick Avory, who rehearsed with the band, and Tony Chapman, with whom the Stones played their first show, in London, on July 12, 1962.)

Their name taken from the Muddy Waters song "Rollin' Stone," the group were regulars at London clubs before they signed to the Decca label—minus Stewart, who was relegated to become chief roadie and a studio-only musician. Three hits—"Come On" (the first of several Chuck Berry covers), "I Wanna Be Your Man" (written for them by Paul McCartney and John Lennon), and "Not Fade Away" (by Buddy Holly)—preceded their self-titled debut album, which topped the British chart. In America it was re-titled *England's Newest Hit Makers* and peaked at No. 11.

By the end of 1966, the group had racked up six U.K. No. 1s. "(I Can't Get No) Satisfaction" also topped the U.S. chart, while *Out of Our Heads* became their first *Billboard* album chart No. 1 in 1965. The Stones stumbled only with 1967's *Their Satanic Majesties Request,* an attempt to board *Sgt. Pepper's* psychedelic bandwagon (though it bequeathed the fine "2,000 Light Years from Home" and "2000 Man").

A more productive reinvention yielded 1968's hard-rockin' "Jumpin' Jack Flash" and bluesy *Beggars Banquet,* paving the way for 1969's hard-rockin', bluesy, and brilliantly nasty *Let It Bleed.* The latter proved the swansong for Brian Jones, who drowned in 1969. Mick Taylor, of John Mayall's Bluesbreakers, replaced him and hence graced the 1970 live album *Get Yer Ya-Yas Out!* (drawn from a 1969 tour that effectively invented arena rock as we know it now).

As the band became superstar tax exiles, their golden era continued, thanks to 1971's cocaine-infused *Sticky Fingers*—the first of eight consecutive U.S. No. 1 studio albums. *Exile on Main St* (1972) hit a standard they could only hope to match, never exceed. *Goats Head Soup* (1973) and *It's Only Rock 'n Roll* (1974) are less celebrated, although each has their

R

year-by-year ■ Vocals   ■ Guitar   ■ Bass   ■ Drums   ■ Keyboards

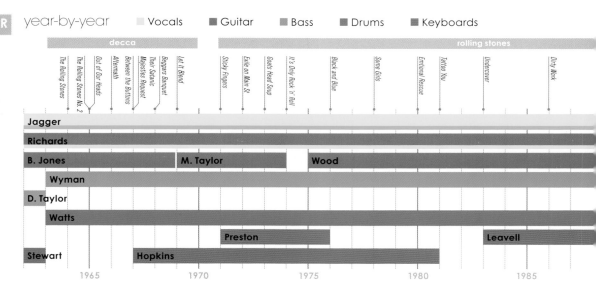

Ronnie Wood
b. June 1, 1947

Billy Preston
b. September 2, 1946
d. June 6, 2006

Nicky Hopkins
b. Feb 24, 1944
d. Sept 6, 1994

Chuck Leavell
b. April 28, 1952

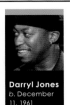

Darryl Jones
b. December 11, 1961

share of classics (the former's "Angie" and "Coming Down Again" and the latter's title track and "Time Waits for No One"). However, with heroin having made life with the band increasingly less fun, Taylor quit in 1975. Harvey Mandel and Wayne Perkins, who applied for his job, wound up on 1976's underrated *Black and Blue,* although its artwork featured the man who got the job: ex-Faces guitarist **Ronnie Wood.**

The Stones survived Richards' career-threatening drug bust in 1977 to score the biggest-selling album of their career: *Some Girls* (1978), boosted by the U.S. chart-topping "Miss You." *Emotional Rescue* (1980) continued their success into the new decade, but was eclipsed by *Tattoo You* (1981) and an ensuing stadium tour that set a visual and commercial yardstick for all that followed. (Throughout much of their career, and especially post-1980, the Stones' success has been based more on sales of tickets than of albums.)

After the live *Still Life* (1982), the Stones floundered. With even Watts dabbling in heroin, Jagger grew impatient with the band, and plotted a solo career that yielded 1985's million-selling *She's the Boss.* The Stones eked out 1983's platinum *Undercover* but, by *Dirty Work* (1986), the singer and Richards were at

each other's throats. In the ensuing hiatus, the guitarist made the excellent *Talk Is Cheap* (1988), before the Stones regrouped for *Steel Wheels* (1989). The tour that followed—the band's first in seven years—again raised the bar for everyone else. (The Stones broke their own money-making records in 1994 and 2005.)

Jagger and Richards—the "Glimmer Twins"—were jointly inducted into the American Songwriters Hall of Fame in 1993. That same year, Bill Wyman quit, to be replaced by **Darryl Jones**, only for *Voodoo Lounge* (1994) to return the Stones to the top of the U.K. chart for the first time in fourteen years.

Bridges to Babylon (1997), the best-of *Forty Licks* (2002, the year that saw Jagger knighted for services to music), and *A Bigger Bang* (2005) each prompted huge sales and tours. And, after years of hit-and-miss live albums and videos, the Stones got the memorial they deserved in the form of Martin Scorsese's movie *Shine a Light* in 2008. Two years later, a reworked version of *Exile on Main St* topped the U.K. chart and hit U.S. No. 2, a full thirty-eight years after the original had headed both lists. And with further rumblings in 2012—the year of the group's fiftieth anniversary—the tale may yet not be over. **BS/BM**

R

■ Aerophones

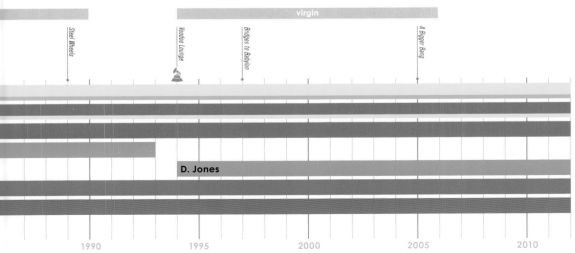

The Rolling Stones
(1964)

Aftermath (1966)

Performing "Not Fade Away" on U.K. TV's *Ready Steady Go!*, 1964.

Jones and **Mick Jagger** recording the brilliant *Beggars Banquet* in London, June 1968.

Beggars Banquet
(1968)

Let It Bleed (1969)

Brian Jones's sitar was key to the *Aftermath* classic "Paint It Black."

Sticky Fingers
(1971)

Exile on Main St
(1972)

Guitarist **Mick Taylor**, who took over from Jones on *Let It Bleed*.

Some Girls (1978)

Tattoo You (1981)

Voodoo Lounge
(1994)

Jagger poses with the Andy Warhol-designed *Sticky Fingers* sleeve.

A Bigger Bang
(2005)

Jagger, **Richards**, and eternal "new boy" **Ronnie Wood** on the *Tattoo You* tour in 1982.

Taylor and **Jagger** at New York's Madison Square Garden in 1972.

Wood backstage at a show in New York with Paul McCartney.

Jagger and **Richards** on a stage set designed by Japanese artist Kazuhide Yamazaki.

Jagger on the spectacular *Voodoo Lounge* stage set in 1994.

Wood, **Jagger**, and **Richards** at the prestigious Super Bowl half-time show at Ford Field in Detroit, in 2006.

roxy music 1970–present

Bryan Ferry
b. September 26, 1945

Bryan Eno
b. May 15, 1948

Andy Mackay
b. July 23, 1946

Roger Bunn
b. July 19, 1942
d. July 28, 2005

Phil Manzanera
b. January 31, 1951

Paul Thompson
b. May 13, 1951

Graham Simpson
b. October 13, 1943

David Bowie's knowingly camp performance of "Starman" on BBC institution *Top of the Pops* in July 1972 is renowned as one of *those* moments in pop TV. Less so Roxy Music's debut a month later, though it was similarly pivotal: guitarist **Phil Manzanera** sporting bug-eye shades; oboe player **Andy Mackay** in a high-collared sci-fi cape; and sneering black-haired singer **Bryan Ferry**, remembered by Siouxsie Sioux in 1997 as "an evil Elvis." The song they played—"Virginia Plain" (U.K. No. 4)—sounded vibrantly new, Ferry's arch lyrics delivered in a quivering vibrato over Manzanera's raucous guitar and **Brian Eno**'s moaning synth.

Early Roxy Music blended fifties decadence and glamor with avant-garde angularity, with Ferry and Eno's art school background a driving force. (**Graham Simpson**, the first in a comically long line of bassists, was succeeded by Rik Kenton, Roger Bunn, John Porter, future Ian Gillan associate John Gustafson, former King Crimson member John Wetton, Alan Spenner, and future Adam Ant sidekick Gary Tibbs.)

Their self-titled debut album (U.K. No. 10), in 1972, was a diverse and dazzling set that launched the Roxy motif of a glamorous model on each album cover. *For Your Pleasure* (1973; U.K. No. 4) maintained the standard, setting driving, witty offerings such as "Do the Strand" and "Editions of You" against bleaker fare.

Eno's urge to experiment, and ego bumps with Ferry, prompted his departure (replaced by Eddie Jobson), after which he has followed a successful and willfully diverse career as solo artist and producer.

Now led by Ferry, the band created *Stranded* (1973; U.K. No. 1), boasting the fizzing hit "Street Life" and transfixing longer pieces "A Song for Europe" and "Mother of Pearl." Roxy finally cracked the U.S. Top Forty with *Country Life* (1974), notable for "The Thrill of It All" and the resounding "All I Want Is You."

By 1975, Roxy were a more conventional rock act, albeit one capable of producing the catchy hit "Love Is the Drug." They folded in 1976, but reconvened for *Manifesto* in 1978, a radio-friendly set featuring the hits "Angel Eyes" and "Dance Away." *Flesh + Blood* (1980) and *Avalon* (1982) continued the run of hits, while a tribute cover of John Lennon's "Jealous Guy" provided their only U.K. No. 1 single in 1981.

Roxy split again in 1983 (the live *Heart Still Beating* providing a belated epitaph), but 2001 brought the first of several reunion tours (minus Eno). Tantalizingly, a 2006 get-together saw Eno return but, despite work in the studio, no album resulted. In truth, their defining statements had long since been made. As Andy Mackay noted with delight in 2011, "The songs from the first two Roxy albums still sound really weird…" **RD**

year-by-year

Vocals ■ Guitar ■ Bass ■ Drums ■ Keyboards ■ Aerophones

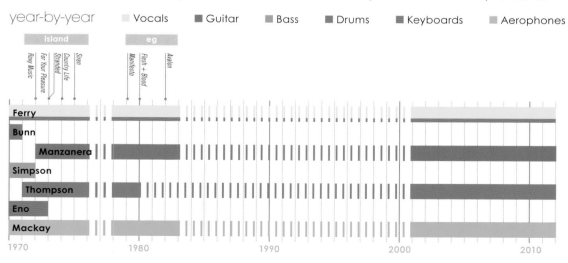

todd rundgren *1970–present*

Todd Rundgren
b. June 22, 1948

Mark "Moogy" Klingman
b. Sept 7, 1950
d. Nov 15, 2011

John Siegler
b. unknown

Ralph Schuckett
b. March 2, 1948

Willie Wilcox
b. unknown

Roger Powell
b. March 14, 1949

Kasim Sulton
b. December 8, 1955

Asked why the New York Dolls had returned to Todd Rundgren in 2009, thirty-six years after he produced their classic debut, front-man David Johansen said simply, "Todd's fucking great." The songwriter, multi-instrumentalist, and producer first revealed his skills as part of Philadelphia's Anglophile band The Nazz in the late sixties. He went on to issue two albums of sophisticated pop, then hit his stride with *Something/Anything?* (1972), most of which saw him writing, singing, playing, and producing everything. The album yielded a transatlantic hit: "I Saw the Light."

Meanwhile, Rundgren's work on albums by the likes of Badfinger and Sparks earned him a reputation as a brilliant producer—a skill shown to full effect on the dazzling and inventive *A Wizard, a True Star* (1973) and *Todd* (1974). Toward the end of the year he assembled Utopia, initially a progressive outfit, whose output was to run parallel to his own for the next decade.

Initiation (1975) also had progressive leanings and cosmic themes, but Rundgren returned to more down-to-earth classic pop/rock for *Faithful* (1976) and *Hermit of Mink Hollow* (1978). In 1977 Meat Loaf's multi-million selling *Bat Out of Hell* confirmed his Midas touch as a producer, while Utopia—with an eye on the emerging New Wave—were pared down to a democratic power pop quartet (which they stayed until splitting in 1986).

The eighties saw a splintering of his styles that was to test the patience of all but the most ardent fans. *Healing* (1981) was a keyboard-driven concept album, *The Ever Popular Tortured Artist Effect* (1983) returned to his pop roots, and *A Cappella* (1985) was made without instruments, using just multi-tracked vocals.

After a four-year gap, during which he produced XTC's classic *Skylarking* (1986), Rundgren returned to form with *Nearly Human* (1989). However, subsequent albums on smaller labels, such as 1993's *No World Order,* were notable more for their perplexing genre-hopping experimentation than for their songwriting.

In 2001 Rundgren teamed up with Alan Parsons and John Entwistle for tours on which they performed The Beatles' *Abbey Road*, and in 2005 he joined the reformed Cars for an extensive outing. Meanwhile, his own albums—including two returns to form, *Liars* (2004) and *Arena* (2008)—went largely ignored.

But then, in 2009, he assembled a band to perform *A Wizard, a True Star* at a handful of shows. As his once sublime vocals got knocked back into shape, new fans discovered his impressive legacy and old fans celebrated his return. *Todd* and *Healing* have also been revived live and, at the start of 2011, he convened a version of the progressive Utopia lineup to play their material to appreciative audiences. **MD**

R

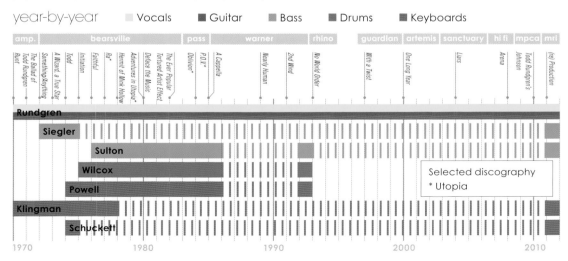

year-by-year ▫ Vocals ▪ Guitar ▪ Bass ▪ Drums ▪ Keyboards

Selected discography
* Utopia

rush 1968–present

Alex Lifeson
b. August 27, 1953

John Rutsey
b. May 14, 1953
d. May 11, 2008

Geddy Lee
b. July 29, 1953

Neil Peart
b. Septmember 12, 1952

"I always like to consider us the world's most popular cult band," commented bassist, singer, and keyboard player Gary "**Geddy**" Lee of the act that made him famous. Founded in Toronto, Canada, by fifteen-year-old guitarist **Alex Lifeson**, Rush was conceived in 1968 as a "power trio" in the style of Cream and the Jimi Hendrix Experience. Within two weeks, bassist and vocalist Jeff Jones was out (later to play with gospel rockers Ocean and Tom Cochrane's Red Rider), and Lifeson's helium-voiced classmate Lee was in. Drummer **John Rutsey** completed the trio, and Rush spent five years honing their skills on the bar circuit, interspersing original material with blues-rock covers.

With little interest from record labels, they made and released 1974's *Rush* themselves. When "Working Man" earned local airplay, Rush were picked up by the Mercury label and the album had a U.S. reissue.

"When we heard that first Rush record," recalled Gene Simmons of Kiss, "we were like, 'What is this? This is like Canadian Zeppelin.'" Kiss took them on tour, by which time Rutsey had left. His replacement, **Neil Peart**, had a dramatic impact on Rush: in Lifeson's words, he "pounded the crap out of those drums." But Peart was also an intriguing lyricist with a penchant for science-fiction. This was evident on *Fly by Night* (1975), which boasted the epic "By-Tor and the Snow Dog." Although Peart told *Kerrang!*, "'Intellectual' is an ugly word, let's face it, unless you're a dried-up stick of a person," Lee dubbed the drummer "the professor."

Ensuing albums saw Rush evolving from their hard rock origins to take in the progressive influences of British bands such as Yes. This was most evident on "The Fountain of Lamneth" and "2112," which took up entire sides of *Caress of Steel* (1975) and *2112* (1976), respectively, and saw Peart's social comment-laden sci-fi yarns underpinned by increasingly complex music. (This had the unfortunate result that, as Rush fan and Foo Fighters drummer Taylor Hawkins rued, "Chicks don't really dig it." Not at all offended, Lee and Lifeson joined Hawkins onstage at a Foos show in 2008 to perform their instrumental "YYZ.")

Beginning with *2112*, which topped their home country's chart, every Rush album for the next two decades would earn at least gold certification in the U.S. and Canada, an achievement that ranks them behind only The Beatles and The Rolling Stones.

Lifeson, Lee, and Peart also acquired an indelible reputation as a powerful live act—and, despite the sophistication of their songs, were able to remain a three-piece. "The level of musicianship," marveled Billy Corgan of The Smashing Pumpkins, "was just insane." This virtuoso economy can be heard on Rush's U.S. Top Forty debut: 1976's *All the World's a Stage*, the first of a succession of popular live releases, to be followed by *Exit... Stage Left* (1981), *A Show of Hands* (1989), *Different Stages* (1998), *Rush in Rio* (2003), *Snakes & Arrows Live* (2008), and *Time Machine 2011: Live in Cleveland* (2011).

year-by-year   ▪ Vocals   ▪ Guitar   ▪ Bass   ▪ Drums   ▪ Keyboards

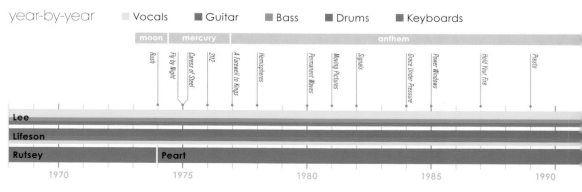

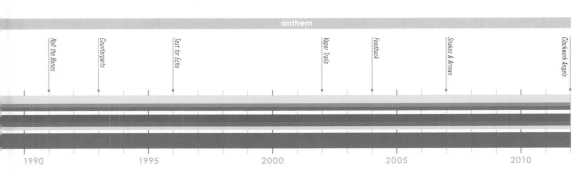

5.3M	3M	2.2M	6.8M
2112	*A Farewell to Kings*	*Permanent Waves*	*Moving Pictures*
(1976)	(1977)	(1980)	(1981)

The band's newfound success was cemented by *A Farewell to Kings* (1977) and *Hemispheres* (1978), which broke them into the U.K. chart. The former yielded the classic "Closer to the Heart," while the latter included the unusually concise perennial "The Trees."

A new decade witnessed a radical departure: on *Permanent Waves* (1980), the progressive epics began to give way to a more accessible, radio-friendly style (influenced, they readily conceded, by The Police). The album also gave Rush an unexpected hit, with the effervescent "The Spirit of Radio." This was followed in 1981 by the fans' favorite, *Moving Pictures*, featuring Rush's signature song, "Tom Sawyer." With its sparse sound, rhythmic complexity, synth drones, and pyrotechnic drumming, it was another unlikely hit.

As the eighties progressed, their sound became oriented toward keyboards. Through *Signals* (1982), *Grace Under Pressure* (1984), *Power Windows* (1985), and *Hold Your Fire* (1987), Lifeson's guitar increasingly gave way to electronics, to his growing discomfort. Nonetheless, the era yielded its share of hits, including "New World Man" (1982), "Distant Early Warning" (1984), "The Big Money" (1985), and "Time Stand Still" (1987), the latter a duet with Aimee Mann.

Hold Your Fire's failure to go platinum confirmed that their bid to be the Pink Floyd of the eighties had been taken as far as it could. *Presto* (1989) began a return to their hard rock roots, completed by the platinum-selling *Roll the Bones* (1991) and fantastic,

frequently brutal *Counterparts* (1993). Such stylistic shifts had little impact on the band's fanbase: by the mid-nineties, Rush had spent over a decade as one of the most successful U.S. and Canadian bands.

After the tour that followed *Test for Echo* (1996), a five-year hiatus ensued when Peart was derailed by personal tragedy: his daughter was killed in a car accident in 1997 and, less than a year later, his wife succumbed to cancer. At the latter's funeral, the drummer told his bandmates, "Consider me retired."

But Rush returned triumphant with *Vapor Trails* (2002) and another rapturously received tour. Having shed their somewhat dour image of old, the usually forward-looking trio plunged into their past with 2004's pummeling covers set *Feedback,* which included songs by The Who, Neil Young, and The Yardbirds.

Snakes & Arrows (2007) earned their customary high chart placings in Canada and the U.S., and restored them to the British Top Twenty for the first time since *Counterparts,* fourteen years earlier.

Then, in 2010, in Sam Dunn and Scot McFadyen's frequently laugh-out-loud biopic *Beyond the Lighted Stage,* a star-studded lineup of admirers, from Trent Reznor to Jack Black, testified to the band's enduring influence and appeal. But the greatest summation of this modest trio's epic ambition came in the chorus of "Caravan," the astounding, age-belying first single from 2012's *Clockwork Angels:* "In a world where I feel so small, I can't stop thinking big." **TB/BM**

the saints 1974–present

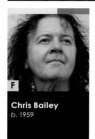

Chris Bailey
b. 1959

Ed Kuepper
b. December 20, 1955

Ivor Hay
b. not known

Kym Bradshaw
b. May 21, 1954

Algy Ward
b. July 7, 1959

Barry Francis
b. not known

The Saints stake a claim to be among the founding fathers of punk, their influence far exceeding their sales. **Chris Bailey** (vocals), **Ed Kuepper** (guitar), and **Ivor Hay** (drums)—schoolmates in Brisbane, Australia —founded the group in 1974 and brought in Jeffrey Wegener (drums). Hay switched to bass until **Kym Bradshaw** joined, after a cameo by Doug Balmanno.

In 1976, their superb debut single, "(I'm) Stranded," earned rave reviews in the U.K. and prompted EMI to sign them. Reminiscent of the Stooges and New York Dolls, they epitomized doomed punk alienation without slavishly following the fashions that pervaded the English scene. Their first album, *(I'm) Stranded* (1977)—also containing the single "Erotic Neurotic"— is a fine, rough example of the genre. They moved to London soon afterward, where **Algy Ward** (later to join The Damned) replaced Bradshaw on bass.

"This Perfect Day," a minor U.K. hit, featured on the excellent *Eternally Yours* (1978), which had a slightly smoother sound. The horn-embellished "Know Your Product" and haunting "Memories Are Made of This" pointed the way for the same year's more soulful, jazzier *Prehistoric Sounds*. "The whole punk rock thing was going on," marveled Nick Cave to

writer Barney Hoskyns, "and they did things with brass sections." Confounding their fans' expectations of a straightforward punk approach, it was not a success, despite critical acclaim. Dropped by their label, the original version of The Saints split in 1979. Hay and Kuepper (who has enjoyed a thriving solo career with a series of other bands) returned to Australia.

Re-forming the group almost immediately, Bailey recruited new disciples **Janine Hall** (bass), **Mark Birmingham** (drums), Bruce Callaway (guitar) and **Barry Francis** (guitar). Bailey brought back the prodigal Hay on drums and keyboards for *The Monkey Puzzle* (1981), while Iain Shedden (drums) came in for 1982's *I Thought This Was Love, But This Ain't Casablanca* (known outside Australia as *Out in the Jungle… Where Things Ain't So Pleasant*). Brian James of The Damned guested on guitar. Both albums had relatively commercial aims that remained mostly unrealized. Meanwhile, guitarists Chris Burnham and Laurie Cuffe had joined, the Saints apparently having a revolving door policy for personnel. (Iain Shedden was to have five separate spells with the group.)

By the time of *A Little Madness to Be Free* (1984), Bailey had released 1983's solo *Casablanca* and

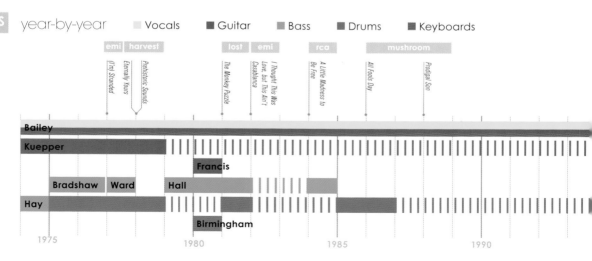

year-by-year ■ Vocals ■ Guitar ■ Bass ■ Drums ■ Keyboards

emi | harvest   lost | emi   rca   mushroom

(I'm) Stranded / *Eternally Yours* / *Prehistoric Sounds* / *The Monkey Puzzle* / *I Thought This Was Love, but This Ain't Casablanca* / *A Little Madness to Be Free* / *All Fools Day* / *Prodigal Son*

Bailey
Kuepper
Francis
Bradshaw | **Ward** | **Hall**
Hay
Birmingham

1975   1980   1985   1990

Janine Hall
b. not known

Mark Birmingham
b. not known

moved back to Australia, where Bradshaw and (yet again) Hay rejoined. A 1984 tour also saw cameos by Kuepper and The Birthday Party's Tracy Pew.

After short stints by Louise Elliott (saxophone) and Richard Burgman (guitar), bassist Arturo LaRizza joined for the first of four spells. Sales of *All Fools Day* (1986) were boosted by the strong single "Just Like Fire Would," which belatedly won The Saints recognition in the U.S. Joe Chiofalo came in on keyboards, Hay left again, and Shedden rejoined before their next recording. *Prodigal Son* (1988)—including the singles "Grain of Sand" and "Music Goes Round My Head," an old Easybeats number—bolstered their newfound popularity. However, never ones to follow a straightforward path, the Saints made no attempt to follow it up. More changes of personnel in 1991 saw Chiofalo joined by Dror Erez on keyboards, Tony Faehse (guitar), and Peter Jones (drums). After these lineup switches, they went into abeyance once more while Bailey concentrated on further solo projects.

In 1994, he moved to Sweden and assembled a new lineup, with drummer Andreas Jornvill, bassist Joakim Tack, and guitarists Mans Wieslander and Ian Walsh. Neither *Howling* (1996), after which the lineup

changed again, nor *Everybody Knows the Monkey* (1998) generated the original excitement, although both had stripped-back production and contained characteristically thought-provoking songs. A new incarnation—with drummer Martin Bjerregaard, bassist Michael Bayliss, and guitarist Andy Faulkner—became a fairly stable unit, by Saints standards.

By the time of *Spit the Blues Out* (2002)—its title a fair summary of its more blues-based content—the group, with Pete Wilkinson (drums) replacing Bjerregaard and alternating with Shedden, had moved to Amsterdam in the Netherlands. They stayed there for the resolutely punkish *Nothing Is Straight in My House* (2005), the players now consisting of Bailey, guitarist Marty Willson-Piper (formerly of The Church and All About Eve), bassist Caspar Wijnberg (latterly succeeded by Jane Mack), and drummer Wilkinson.

Thirty years after their debut, *Imperious Delirium* (2006)—on which Bailey played all the guitars after Willson-Piper departed—proved the fire was still burning. Not the least remarkable aspect of the Saints' long career is how consistent their output has been despite all the changes—a tribute to Bailey's enduring vision. **MiH**

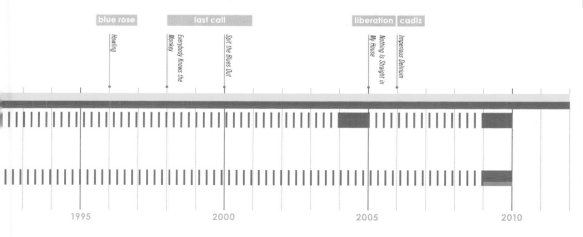

blue rose · *last call* · *liberation* · *cadiz*

Howling · *Everybody Knows the Monkey* · *Spit the Blues Out* · *Nothing Is Straight in My House* · *Imperious Delirium*

1995 · 2000 · 2005 · 2010

santana 1966–present

Carlos Santana
b. July 20, 1947

Gregg Rolie
b. June 17, 1947

David Brown
b. February 15, 1947

Michael Shrieve
b. July 6, 1949

José "Chepito" Areas
b. July 25, 1946

Michael Carabello
b. November 18, 1947

Bob Livingston
b. November 26, 1948

Neal Schon
b. February 27, 1954

Smooth by name, smooth by nature, **Carlos Santana** enjoyed his biggest hit ever with "Smooth," which reached No. 1 in October 1999—exactly thirty years after his powerhouse percussive Afro-Latin rock band had a first entry in the U.S. Top 100 with "Jingo." Sung by Matchbox Twenty's Rob Thomas, "Smooth" stayed at the top for twelve weeks, going on to win Grammys for Song of the Year, and Best Pop Collaboration with Vocals. (Its parent album, *Supernatural,* bagged Album of the Year). From the first bars, you know it can only be Carlos on guitar: the timbre and style of his effortlessly smooth and rounded samba-blues is instantly recognizable. Other Santana trademarks include long, even sustains, alongside occasional psychedelic wails and high-speed jazz licks.

"Smooth" was the first of two smashes from *Supernatural* ("Maria Maria" hit No. 1 for ten weeks), which has sold fifteen million copies in the U.S. alone. It earned so many Grammy nominations that, when Sheryl Crow won Best Female Rock Vocal in 2000, she thanked Carlos for not being in that category.

It was all a long way from the guitarist's humble Mexican beginnings, when—with his mariachi musician father—he played in Tijuana brothels and saloons. His mother took the family to San Francisco, where Carlos formed the Santana Bluesband in 1966.

In the best of its ever-changing incarnations, the band showcased **Gregg Rolie**'s rich organ sound, **David Brown** on bass, **Michael Shrieve** on drums, and **José "Chepito" Areas** on percussion. Concert promoter/producer Bill Graham was an early fan, hence their early shows at San Francisco's Fillmore West and Carlos's first live recording (from the same venue), as part of 1968's *The Live Adventures of Mike Bloomfield and Al Kooper.*

At Graham's insistence, Santana—newly signed to the Columbia label—were enlisted for the Woodstock festival in August 1969. The most significant concert of its generation brought the group to international attention. Millions saw the movie of the event—in which their "Soul Sacrifice" accompanied the audience's mud-soaked antics—and heard the soundtrack triple album. "All of a sudden we went from the streets of San Francisco to arenas," Santana told *Billboard* book author Craig Rosen. "It was kind of like riding the rapids with everything going by so fast."

A self-titled debut album was a straightforward Latin-blues-rock calling card, but *Abraxas* (1970)

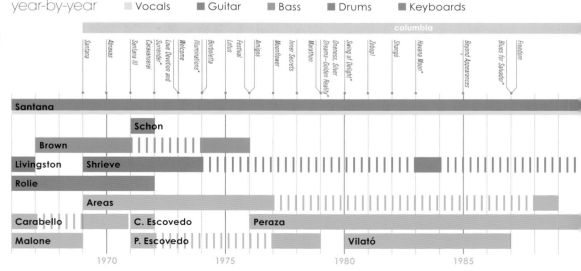

year-by-year ■ Vocals ■ Guitar ■ Bass ■ Drums ■ Keyboards

Coke Escovedo
b. Apr 30, 1941
d. Apr 30, 1985

Pete Escovedo
b. October 13, 1935

Armando Peraza
b. May 30, 1924

Marcus Malone
b. Unknown

Orestes Vilató
b. May 4, 1944

established the Santana sound, with songs such as Fleetwood Mac's blues-drenched "Black Magic Woman," Tito Puente's salsa "Oye Como Va," and the self-penned instrumental "Samba Pa Ti." The album soared into the U.K. Top Ten and to No. 1 in the U.S.

Neal Schon was added on guitar and vocals and **Coke Escovedo** on percussion for 1971's *Santana* (known as *Santana III*, to distinguish it from the band's identically-titled debut). This also made No. 1 in the U.S., despite tensions that had arisen between the band members. "We would fight like cats and dogs to create that chemistry," Santana told Craig Rosen. "You could hear us cussing at each other between takes." Rolie and Schon quit after the album's release, to later find fame and fortune with Journey.

Caravanserai (1972) saw Santana move toward jazz fusion, as Shrieve's influence grew—he and Carlos shared a passion for players like Miles Davis, John Coltrane, and Herbie Hancock. A 1972 version of "In a Silent Way" was a tribute to Davis, and Carlos later guested on fusion stars Weather Report's *This Is This* (1986). The latter was one of more than fifty collaborations that Carlos has undertaken, from 1972's *Carlos Santana and Buddy Miles, Live!* and 1973's

Love Devotion Surrender (with jazz-fusion guitarist John McLaughlin), to 1989's "The Healer," from John Lee Hooker's comeback of the same name. Carlos collected a Grammy for *Blues for Salvador* (1987), a solo album featuring Willie Nelson, Booker T. Jones, and The Fabulous Thunderbirds. He also wrote the score for 1986's Ritchie Havens biopic *La Bamba*, which brought Latin pop to a new generation.

After the career-revitalizing *Supernatural*—which featured Eric Clapton and Dave Matthews, alongside Rob Thomas—the all-star formula was re-applied on *Shaman* (2002). The album (boasting Nickelback's Chad Kroeger, among others) gave Santana a fourth U.S. No.1 and saw the return of Shrieve.

Over eighty side-men have come and gone but Carlos's smooth guitar sound remains. This influential guitarist (not least on Prince) also dared to put his stamp on a clutch of hard rock standards on 2010's *Guitar Heaven*. Amid star turns by Joe Cocker, Rob Thomas, Chris Cornell of Soundgarden, Scott Weiland of Stone Temple Pilots—on songs by the likes of Led Zeppelin and the Stones—the implausible highlight was an audacious and typically idiosyncratic take on AC/DC's "Back in Black," featuring rapper Nas. **JaH**

■ Other percussion

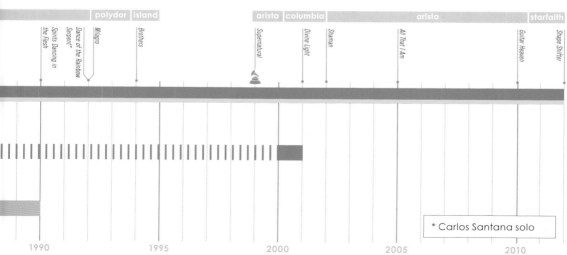

* Carlos Santana solo

scorpions 1965–present

Klaus Meine
b. May 25, 1948

Rudolf Schenker
b. August 31, 1948

Matthias Jabs
b. October 25, 1955

James Kottak
b. December 26, 1962

Pawel Maciwoda
b. February 20, 1967

Francis Buchholz
b. February 19, 1954

Herman Rarebell
b. November 18, 1949

Michael Schenker
b. January 10, 1955

German hard rock has rarely been harder or more rocking than in the hands of the Scorpions, the Hanover quintet that has straddled stages for an astounding forty-seven years and counting. Although in 2010 the group announced plans to retire after a final tour, it would be unwise to write them off.

Guitarist **Rudolf Schenker** formed the band in 1965, with an initial lineup that had mostly dissipated by the release of their debut album, *Lonesome Crow*, seven years later. Musicians passing through the ranks since then have included guitarists extraordinaire **Uli Jon Roth** and Schenker's younger brother **Michael**. But the most commercially successful lineup featured Rudolf Schenker, singer **Klaus Meine**, guitarist **Matthias Jabs**, bassist **Francis Buchholz**, and drummer **Herman Rarebell**. This quintet was responsible for many of the Scorpions' biggest hits in a golden era stretching from the late seventies to the early nineties.

The band first impacted on the public outside Germany thanks to their controversial album artwork. *Virgin Killer* depicted a naked ten-year-old girl, *Lovedrive* boasted a female breast, and *Animal Magnetism* featured a woman sitting faithfully to attention alongside a dog. Once these follies were discarded, however, the Scorpions were revealed as a powerful group of serious musicians. On guitar, they boasted two successive stars: Michael Schenker, then, when he was poached by British rockers UFO, Uli Jon Roth (known at the time as Ulrich Roth). The latter debuted on *Fly to the Rainbow* (1974), but made his mark on *In Trance* (1975), the best of their early albums (not least because he suggested its cover, on which a model with an exposed breast holds his Stratocaster).

However, by the time of 1977's *Taken by Force*, reported new drummer Rarebell, "The band was divided between Ulrich Roth and the others. To me, the band really started to work as a unit after he left."

Having secured a loyal following at home and in Japan (hence 1978's live *Tokyo Tapes*, Roth's swansong), the Scorpions' popularity exploded when they ditched the last lingering acid rock elements of their formative years in favor of big-chorused arena anthems. *Lovedrive* (1979)—the debut of Matthias Jabs (although Michael Schenker, who had fled UFO, guested on three cuts)—charted internationally, winning fans including the young Metallica and Billy Corgan of The Smashing Pumpkins. (The latter would later guest on 2007's *Humanity: Hour 1*.)

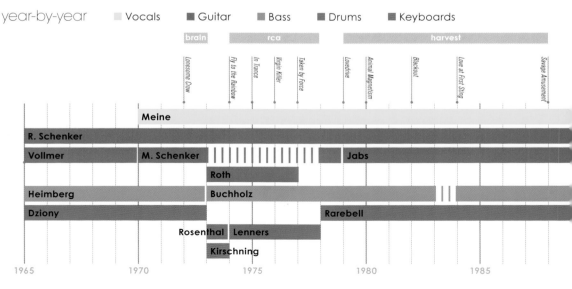

year-by-year   ■ Vocals   ■ Guitar   ■ Bass   ■ Drums   ■ Keyboards

brain   rca   harvest

Lonesome Crow | Fly to the Rainbow | In Trance | Virgin Killer | Taken by Force | Lovedrive | Animal Magnetism | Blackout | Love at First Sting | Savage Amusement

Meine

R. Schenker

Vollmer   M. Schenker   Jabs

Roth

Heimberg   Buchholz

Dziony   Rarebell

Rosenthal   Lenners

Kirschning

1965   1970   1975   1980   1985

S

Lothar Heimberg
b. Unknown

Wolfgang Dziony
b. 1949

Karl-Heinz Vollmer
b. Unknown

Uli Jon Roth
b. December 18, 1954

Jürgen Rosenthal
b. July 29, 1948

Achim Kirschning
b. Unknown

Rudy Lenners
b. Unknown

Ralph Rieckermann
b. August 8, 1962

The group's escalating fortunes saw a run of multi-platinum albums, beginning with *Animal Magnetism* (1980) and *Blackout* (1982). They hit a peak with 1984's *Love at First Sting,* which yielded the hits "Rock You Like a Hurricane" (which even found its way into the formative Green Day's repertoire), "Still Loving You," and "Big City Nights." The charms of the Scorpions' live show (the visual highlight of which came when the members formed a human pyramid) was brilliantly captured on 1985's gonzoid *World Wide Live*. "We give the people all our energy every night," Meine told *Kerrang!*. "We'll go onstage and rock our ass off."

Inevitably, such momentum could last only for so long, and 1988's *Savage Amusement*—home to the hit "Rhythm of Love"—seemed to bookend the band's time in the big league. However, an unexpected leap into the mainstream came three years later, courtesy of Meine's ballad "Wind of Change." The song, heralded by the singer's whistled melody, had been inspired by the group's trip to Russia in 1988, where they played to 150,000 people in Leningrad. "We had never experienced anything like it…" Meine reported. "Soldiers cried when we played [the *Lovedrive* ballad] 'Holiday'." The song was recorded in the summer

of 1990—when the Scorpions participated in Roger Waters's epic re-staging of Pink Floyd's *The Wall* in Berlin, and returned to Russia as conquering heroes for a show alongside Bon Jovi, Ozzy Osbourne, and Mötley Crüe—and appeared on that winter's *Crazy World*. The following year, "Wind of Change" became a sort of unofficial anthem for the fall of the Soviet Union and German reunification. With global sales running into millions, it became the best-selling single of all-time by a German act. This success also ensured the band's survival at a point when grunge was poised to eradicate many traditional rockers.

Thereafter, the Scorpions occupied a respected position as a classic rock band, despite an unsettling foray into pop territory (1999's *Eye II Eye*), an orchestral folly (2000's *Moment of Glory*), and an unplugged live album (2001's *Acoustica*). *Sting in the Tail* (2010) even restored them to the U.S. Top Thirty after a seventeen-year absence. A 2012 album of re-recorded classics, *Comeblack*, is alleged to be their last—but, after so many years, it seems the Scorpions as a concept is bigger than any individual or group of musicians. After all, as Meine remarked, "We are not in this for the fashion or the fame or any of that shit." **JM/BM**

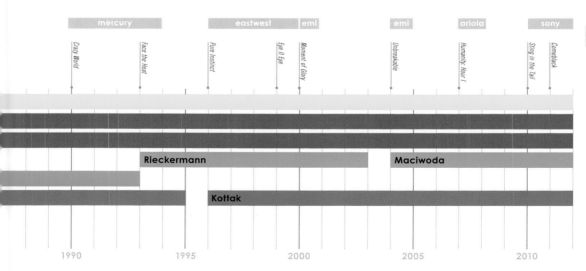

Taken by Force (1977)

Lovedrive (1979)

Animal Magnetism (1980)

Love at First Sting (1984)

Savage Amusement (1988)

Crazy World (1990)

Eye II Eye (1999)

Unbreakable (2004)

Humanity Hour 1 (2007)

Comeblack (2011)

Vintage Scorpions: guitarist **Uli Jon Roth**, bassist **Francis Buchholz**, guitarist **Rudy Schenker**, singer **Klaus Meine**, and drummer **Herman Rarebell**.

New guitarist **Matthias Jabs** rocks Britain's Reading festival in 1979.

Schenker, **Meine**, and **Jabs**: no one ever accused them of being subtle.

Buchholz, **Schenker**, **Meine**, and **Jabs** with the world at their feet.

Rarebell, Meine, Buchholz, Schenker, and Jabs in the hair metal era in which *Savage Amusement* was released.

With Roger Waters at his 1990 performance of *The Wall* in Berlin.

Schenker stings at the Universal Amphitheatre in Los Angeles, in November 2004.

Schenker rocks Le Zenith in Paris on the Eye II Eye tour.

Schenker and Jabs at France's Vieilles Charrues Festival in 2011.

Pawel Maciwoda proves he's the man for the job as the *Unbreakable* tour hits London.

Meine at the Bercy in Paris, in 2011, on what the Scorpions claim is their final tour.

bob seger 1968–present

Bob Seger
b. May 6, 1945

Chris Campbell
b. Unknown

Drew Abbott
b. January 13, 1947

Charlie Allen Martin
b. June 6, 1952

Alto Reed
b. Unknown

Robyn Robbins
b. 1951

"Bob Seger is the voice of the working man," enthused Kid Rock, "and living proof of the American dream."

Michigan native Seger was a nomadic veteran of Detroit's music scene by the time he formed The Silver Bullet Band in 1974. Blessed with a timeless voice that would strike a chord with the "heartland" rock movement, the singer-songwriter began his journey as a sixteen-year-old with The Decibels (a key influence on another Detroit star, Iggy Pop). After a decade-long apprenticeship with a handful of hopefuls, The Bob Seger System infiltrated the U.S. Top Twenty with "Ramblin' Gamblin' Man" (from a 1969 album of the same name)—but it was six years before Seger returned to the singles chart, riddled with Silver Bullets.

The original Bullets—guitarist **Drew Abbott**, bassist **Chris Campbell**, keyboard player Rick Manasa (replaced by **Robyn Robbins** in 1975), drummer **Charlie Allen Martin** (replaced by **David Teegarden** in 1977), and saxophonist **Alto Reed**—appeared, uncredited, on Seger's Seven (1974) and Beautiful Loser (1975). As the celebrated Silver Bullet Band, they were first officially billed on 1976's blockbusting Live Bullet. Like Kiss's Alive!, it was recorded at Detroit's Cobo Hall

and—again like Alive!—it broke into the big time an act more famous for their shows than their records.

Night Moves (1976) took the band into the U.S. Top Ten—although four of its nine tracks were recorded with Seger's "other" group, the Muscle Shoals Rhythm Section (the R&B collective who had backed stars like Aretha Franklin and Wilson Pickett). The album's title song rose into the U.S. and Canadian Top Fives, and gave Seger a first, albeit minor, hit in the U.K.

In 1978, Stranger in Town added more classics to his repertoire: "Still the Same," "Hollywood Nights," "We've Got Tonite," and "Old Time Rock and Roll." (The latter's iconic status was secured when Tom Cruise mimed to it in the 1983 movie Risky Business.)

The group reached a commercial peak in 1980 with the two-time Grammy winner Against the Wind, featuring Eagles stars Glenn Frey, Don Henley, and Timothy B. Schmidt on the hit "Fire Lake." (Seger had written the chorus for, and sung backing vocals on, the Eagles' 1979 hit "Heartache Tonight.") Despite scathing reviews, Against the Wind ended Pink Floyd's fifteen-week run at No. 1 with The Wall on the way to six chart-topping weeks of its own.

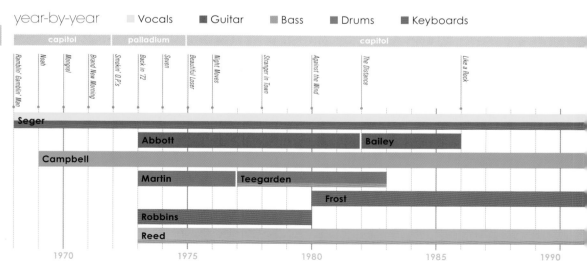

year-by-year ■ Vocals ■ Guitar ■ Bass ■ Drums ■ Keyboards

David Teegarden
b. Unknown

Craig Frost
b. April 20, 1948

Dawayne Bailey
b. Unknown

Seger's charges returned to the Top Ten with each of their next four releases: 1981's live *Nine Tonight*, 1982's *The Distance* (including the hit "Shame on the Moon," featuring Glenn Frey), 1986's *Like a Rock* (featuring Don Henley and Timothy B. Schmidt), and 1991's *The Fire Inside* (featuring Bruce Hornsby and members of Was Not Was, Tom Petty's Heartbreakers, the Eagles, and Bruce Springsteen's E Street Band).

In 1983, Kenny Rogers and Sheena Easton took "We've Got Tonite" to No. 1 on the U.S. and Canadian country charts. Meanwhile, Prince found himself on a U.S. jaunt at the same time as the Silver Bullet Band were touring *The Distance*. Intrigued by Seger's country-tinged anthems, Prince wrote his own: "Purple Rain." In 1987, a solo Seger squeezed in his first (and, to date, only) U.S. chart-topping single, "Shakedown," from the Eddie Murphy movie *Beverly Hills Cop II*.

In 1994 came *Greatest Hits*, featuring a previously unreleased Chuck Berry song ("C'est la Vie") and iconic cover art showing Seger—guitar in hand—standing on a Californian railroad. In 2009, *Billboard* named it the biggest-selling catalog album of the decade, ahead of The Beatles and Michael Jackson.

Among *Greatest Hits'* gems is the *Live Bullet* version of "Turn the Page" (originally from 1973's *Back in '72*), a song that became a 1998 hit in the heavy hands of Metallica. (It had previously been covered by country star Waylon Jennings in 1985. Jennings also tackled "Against the Wind" that year, with Willie Nelson, Kris Kristofferson, and Johnny Cash.) Other rockers to tackle Seger songs include Thin Lizzy (*Back in '72*'s "Rosalie" on their *Fighting*, 1975), Status Quo (*Seven*'s "Get Out of Denver" on 1996's *Don't Stop* and "Old Time Rock and Roll" on 2000's *Famous in the Last Century*), and Rod Stewart ("Still the Same" on his 2006 U.S. chart-topping album of the same name). "I try to write about what I know, maybe with a little content," the modest Seger told *Q* magazine. "Songwriting is miniature work; you don't have a lot of time with your material, so you have to pinpoint it."

Seger was inducted into the Rock & Roll Hall of Fame in 2004, while *Face the Promise*, the Silver Bullet Band's first studio album since 1995, returned them to familiar Top Ten territory in 2006. A new hits set, *Rock & Roll Never Forgets* (2011), is testament to one of the most underrated groups in rock 'n' roll history. **MW/BM**

■ Aerophones   ■ Other percussion

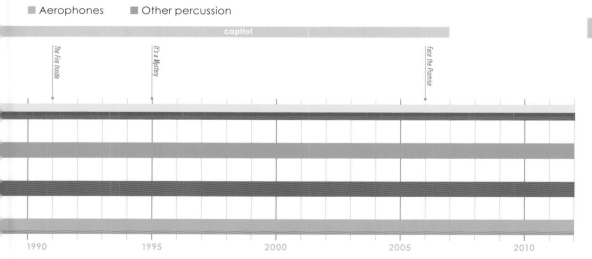

capitol

The Fire Inside

It's a Mystery

Face the Promise

1990   1995   2000   2005   2010

sepultura 1984–present

Max Cavalera
b. August 4, 1969

Igor Cavalera
b. September 4, 1970

Paulo Jr.
b. April 30, 1968

Wagner Lamounier
b. Unknown

Jairo Guedz
b. Nov 25, 1968

Andreas Kisser
b. August 24, 1968

Back in 1985, with Brazil emerging from the grip of a twenty-year military dictatorship, the country's most celebrated metal exponents (congratulations if you can name any of the less celebrated ones) adopted "scary" names and stepped out of the shadows.

Rocked by the death of their diplomat father and influenced by Led Zeppelin, Black Sabbath, and Deep Purple, school drop-outs **Max "Possessed" Cavalera** (lead vocals) and **Igor "Skullcrusher" Cavalera** (drums) channeled their grief into music making. The brothers from Belo Horizonte hired **Jairo "Tormentor" Guedz** (lead guitar) and **Paulo "Destructor" Jr.** (bass) and called themselves Sepultura, Portuguese for "grave." Apparently, Max opted for the name while translating Motörhead's "Dancing on Your Grave" into Portuguese—"Dançando em sua sepultura."

The four-piece first put their fearsome attitude and indecipherable lyrics on record with the self-produced "Bestial Devastation" EP. Recorded in just two days, the release featured "Antichrist," written by founding member and original vocalist **Wagner "Antichrist" Lamounier**, who left Sepultura in 1985 to form the long-running extreme metal outfit Sarcófago (and, later, to become a professor of economics).

Sepultura's first full-length release, *Morbid Visions*, followed in 1986. With the band as yet unable to write in English, the album was shaped by the Satanic verses of influential British metallers Venom. "After we got acquainted with Venom, we stopped listening to Iron Maiden and all that lighter stuff," confirmed Igor.

The group relocated to São Paulo, and Guedz was replaced by **Andreas Kisser**. They forged ahead with *Schizophrenia* (1987) and *Beneath the Remains* (1989). "Total fuckin' hate!" enthused *Kerrang!* magazine in a coveted 'five K' review of the latter, a thrash classic.

By the time they got to Phoenix, Arizona—the host of an early date on 1990's U.S. and European *Beneath the Remains* tour—Brazil's finest were making all the right noises (albeit severely loud ones). "If it's heavier," Max Cavalera told *Kerrang!*, "we're happier."

Homeward bound in early 1991, they entertained 100,000 headbangers at the Rock in Rio festival before unleashing *Arise*, whose title track was shunned by MTV America owing to its apocalyptic religious imagery. The socially adept *Chaos A.D.* (1993), infused with industrial and hardcore punk, gave Sepultura their first Top Forty hit in America and, bizarrely, a Top Ten single ("Territory") in Ireland.

year-by-year

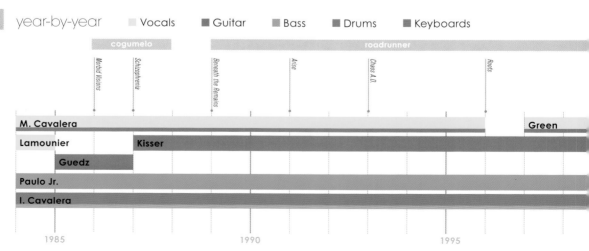

■ Vocals　■ Guitar　■ Bass　■ Drums　■ Keyboards

cogumelo　　roadrunner

Morbid Visions　Schizophrenia　Beneath the Remains　Arise　Chaos A.D.　Roots

M. Cavalera — Green

Lamounier　Kisser

Guedz

Paulo Jr.

I. Cavalera

1985　　1990　　1995

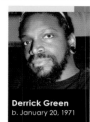

Derrick Green
b. January 20, 1971

Jean Dolabella
b. May 14, 1978

Eloy Casagrande
b. January 29, 1991

The group hit a creative pinnacle with *Roots* (1996), which introduced native Brazilian percussion and influences to their ferocious musical styling. Peaking at No. 4 in the U.K. and smashing into Top Tens across Europe, *Roots*'s defining moments were the singles "Roots Bloody Roots," which narrowly missed the top spot in the heavy metal haven of Finland, and the throbbing, tribal "Ratamahatta," complete with the best music video you have probably never seen.

"Ratamahatta" also marked the departure of Soulfly-bound frontman Max Cavalera, sparked by the death of his stepson with Gloria Bujnowski—his wife and the group's manager—in an automobile accident. Weeks after the tragedy, when the rest of the group confronted the singer about replacing her with a new manager, the still traumatized Max quit in disgust. His replacement was the incendiary Cleveland, Ohio-born vocalist **Derrick Green**.

In the midst of an apparently terminal sales decline, Green slowly won over the skeptics—and no doubt a fair few Max Cavalera fans—with passionate, powerhouse vocals on *Against* (1998), *Nation* (2001), *Roorback* (2003), and *Dante XXI* (2006), the latter the final Sepultura album to feature Igor Cavalera. When Igor reunited with brother Max to form the Cavalera Conspiracy, drumming duties were handled by **Jean Dolabella**, who, in turn, made way for twenty-year-old **Eloy Casagrande** in November 2011.

Post-Cavaleras Sepultura still had a few tricks up their sleeves. In 2008, in a departure from their heavy/death/thrash roots, they starred in a Brazilian TV commercial for Volkswagen, performing a bossa nova track. Toward the end of the same year, they appeared at the Latin Grammy Awards to promote their concept album *A-Lex* (2009). Green, Paulo Jr., Kisser, and Dolabella kicked off 2010 in São Paulo sharing the stage with Metallica in front of 100,000 people, while their album *Kairos* (2011) features a compelling version of The Prodigy's "Firestarter."

Sepultura have sold millions of albums worldwide, impressive given that their lyrics and "machine-gun-tempo mayhem," as the *Phoenix New Times* put it, are impenetrable to the average human ear. MTV even described Sepultura as "perhaps the most important heavy metal band of the nineties," which speaks volumes given that the odds were stacked against them from the start in terms of nationality, language, and the extreme nature of their music. **MW**

■ Other percussion

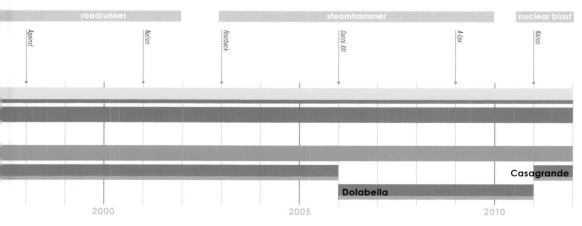

roadrunner   steamhammer   nuclear blast

Against   *Nation*   *Roorback*   *Dante XXI*   *A-Lex*   *Kairos*

Casagrande

Dolabella

2000   2005   2010

sex pistols 1975–present

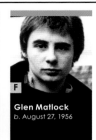

Johnny Rotten
b. January 31, 1956

Sid Vicious
b. May 10, 1957
d. February 2, 1979

Steve Jones
b. September 3, 1955

Paul Cook
b. July 20, 1956

Glen Matlock
b. August 27, 1956

Britain of the mid-seventies seemed a country drained of color. Gray and grainy it may have been, but many people still had an attachment to the status quo, which explains the impact of the band that came to be seen as the public face of punk. "I hate hippies," said **Johnny Rotten** in April 1976. "I hate long hair. I hate pub bands." What he thought of another staple of the day—progressive rock—was earlier made clear when, still known as John Lydon, he walked into the shop owned by entrepreneur Malcolm McLaren and designer Vivienne Westwood wearing a Pink Floyd t-shirt self-amended with "I hate."

That was around the point when youthful alienation started to coalesce into something more. However, **Steve Jones**, in his days as a frontman, and drummer **Paul Cook** had been messing around since the beginning of the decade. Bassist **Glen Matlock** entered the frame in 1974, the same year that trendspotter *par excellence* McLaren was sensing something in the air. A short stint as manager of the New York Dolls whetted his appetite.

It was clear that Jones was better suited to a prominent supporting role, so he shunted across to guitar. That left a vacancy to front a band—by now known as QT Jones & His Sex Pistols—that Richard Hell and Dolls rhythm guitarist Sylvain Sylvain turned down.

Instead, Rotten, as he was soon to be known, became a home-grown legend more celebrated than either.

Controversy was to follow the band everywhere. Whether this was the grand design of McLaren or events that, with hindsight, he credited himself with manipulating, depends on your view of him. With 1976's "Anarchy in the UK" laid down as a marker, the group was passed around like a bomb about to go off: within six months, EMI and A&M signed, paid, then dropped them (both labels were namechecked in "EMI," issued by Virgin.) Then Matlock was dismissed—allegedly for liking Abba and The Beatles—and Rotten's friend John "**Sid Vicious**" Ritchie was brought in. All image and attitude, the latter proved better at making headlines than making music. (Motörhead's Lemmy, who tried to tutor Vicious, told Q magazine: "He had no aptitude for the bass whatsoever… He didn't play it, he hit it. He might as well have been playing air guitar with a broom." Steve Jones played bass on much of the Pistols' post-Matlock output.)

Most of the population had little understanding of the band's method of communication. But opponents deciphered enough of the language used during an early-evening TV appearance—and then brandished on the cover of *Never Mind the Bollocks Here's the Sex Pistols*—to recoil in horror and even take their hysteria

year-by-year ■ Vocals ■ Guitar ■ Bass ■ Drums

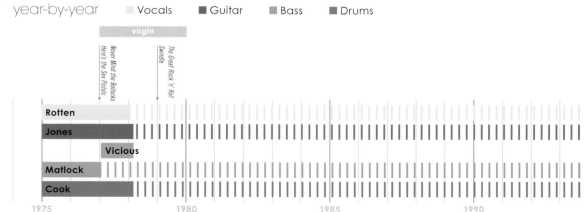

into courtrooms. With all this free publicity, how could the album not assume the U.K. No. 1 slot? *Rolling Stone* saw the changing of the guard: "The rock wars of the 1970s have begun." When *Never Mind...* topped the long-player charts, justice was served after Rod Stewart's "I Don't Want to Talk About It" had denied the Pistols the same spot in the singles rundown for 1977's "God Save the Queen." (Jones later admitted that a Stewart album was the first record he bought.)

Tours were announced and canceled; members were beaten up—in Rotten's case, by aggrieved royalists. As Jones later recalled, without Matlock's melodies, "We were just slung in the deep end and didn't have the time to breathe, much less think about writing songs." With the band in bad shape, shows on Christmas Day 1977 in Britain's Yorkshire (one, oddly, in front of an audience mainly of children) preceded a U.S. tour that was never likely to pass without incident. In midwest and southern states especially, the atmosphere was more hostile than harmonious.

Six months earlier, Rotten had said, "As soon as it gets really boring is when I'm going to fucking stop." Come the last day of the U.S. tour, Vicious was in drug disintegration and, recalled Jones, "I was hating it." From the Winterland Ballroom stage in San Francisco, a version of the Stooges' "No Fun" was a fitting finale.

Staring at the audience, Rotten hammered the point home: "Ever get the feeling you've been cheated?"

The band was dead in the water, but even a corpse can be squeezed for cash. *The Great Rock 'n' Roll Swindle* of early 1979, directed by Julien Temple, took a motley crew of characters (including on-the-run Great Train Robber Ronnie Biggs), an even motlier collection of covers (which made for bizarrely successful singles, such as Vicious's version of "My Way"), and a few fabulous ideas for a double album that preceded McLaren's self-mythologizing film of the same name. It was time that everyone went off and did their own thing: Rotten reverted to Lydon and formed PiL; Cook and Jones became The Professionals. Vicious's sudden death surprised no one.

Just shy of twenty years since the unleashing of "Anarchy in the UK," Lydon, Jones, Cook, and Matlock reunited for a tour. Its third date—in the singer's home territory, London's Finsbury Park—was recorded for 1996's surprisingly fiery *Filthy Lucre Live*.

The group has since belched back into life for further comebacks. And while they may claim otherwise, the expiry of their outsider status was confirmed by a 2006 induction into the Rock and Roll Hall of Fame. "Sex Pistols is a business," admitted Jones, "and we have to keep the ball rolling." **CB**

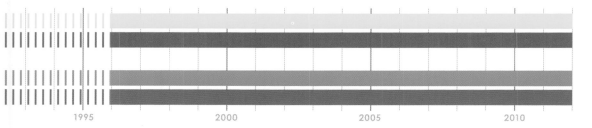

simple minds 1978–present

Jim Kerr
b. July 9, 1959

Charlie Burchill
b. November 27, 1959

Mick MacNeil
b. July 20, 1958

Derek Forbes
b. June 22, 1956

Brian McGee
b. March 8, 1959

Kenny Hyslop
b. February 14, 1951

Mike Ogletree
b. Unknown

Mel Gaynor
b. May 29, 1960

Simple Minds, with their heady mix of art rock and straightforward punch, had enormous success in the eighties. The group formed in Glasgow in 1978, rising from the ashes of short-lived punk band Johnny and the Self-Abusers. **Jim Kerr** (vocals), **Charlie Burchill** (guitar), **Mick MacNeil** (keyboards), **Derek Forbes** (bass) and **Brian McGee** (drums) at first took on the mantle of post-punk observers.

The group's debut album, *Life in a Day* (1979), whose title track was a minor U.K. hit, exhibited their pop sensibilities. However, by the time of *Real to Real Cacophony* (also 1979), Simple Minds had metamorphosed into an experimental New Wave outfit. *Cacophony* did not sell so well, but they started to acquire a strong underground following.

This cult status was enhanced by *Empires and Dance* (1980), on which the group transformed again into commentators on the modern condition, strongly influenced by the glacial soundscapes of European bands such as Kraftwerk. Unfashionably fond of progressive rock ("We must have been the only band," recalled Kerr, "who said, yeah, I like Pink Floyd"), Simple Minds enlisted Gong guitarist Steve Hillage as producer. The result was the twin albums, *Sons and Fascination* and *Sister Feelings Call* (1981)—the former

more cohesive, the latter boasting standout tracks like "The American." Both extended their appeal, while the group were also a growing live attraction.

McGee decided he had had enough of touring and was replaced, in rapid succession, by drummers **Kenny Hyslop**, **Mike Ogletree**, and **Mel Gaynor**. All contributed to *New Gold Dream (81/82/83/84)* (1982), the group's U.K. breakthrough (No. 3), thanks to the hits "Promised You a Miracle" and "Glittering Prize." The group had found a way of writing commercial songs in tune with their futuristic aesthetic.

This happy conjunction persisted for the U.K. No. 1 *Sparkle in the Rain* (1984), featuring "Waterfront," "Speed Your Love to Me," "Up on the Catwalk," and a version of Lou Reed's "Street Hassle." Produced by Steve Lillywhite (who had also assisted U2's ascent), its heavier rock sound was tailor-made for arenas in North America. The group's chances were boosted by their first U.S. No. 1 single, "Don't You Forget About Me," from the movie *The Breakfast Club*. They duly delivered with *Once Upon a Time* (1985), another U.K. No. 1 that also broached the U.S. Top Ten. The hits "Alive and Kicking," "Sanctify Yourself," "All the Things She Said," and "Ghost Dancing" kept it on the British chart for well over a year.

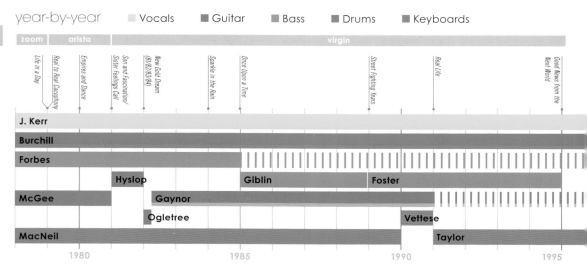

year-by-year

■ Vocals ■ Guitar ■ Bass ■ Drums ■ Keyboards

zoom | arista | virgin

Life in a Day | *Real to Real Cacophony* | *Empires and Dance* | *Son and Fascination/Sister Feelings Call* | *New Gold Dream (81/82/83/84)* | *Sparkle in the Rain* | *Once Upon a Time* | *Street Fighting Years* | *Real Life* | *Good News from the Next World*

J. Kerr
Burchill
Forbes
Hyslop | Giblin | Foster
McGee
Gaynor
Ogletree | Vettese
MacNeil | Taylor

1980 · 1985 · 1990 · 1995

John Giblin
b. February 26, 1952

Eddy Duffy
b. December 30, 1968

Andy Gillespie
b. Unknown

Ged Grimes
b. March 28, 1962

Malcolm Foster
b. January 13, 1956

Peter-John Vettese
b. August 15, 1956

Mark Taylor
b. Unknown

Mark Kerr
b. Unknown

A self-confessed victim of the pressures of life on the road, Forbes left the group in the midst of these triumphs, to be replaced by bassist **John Giblin** (whose CV included stints with Peter Gabriel and Phil Collins). Forbes was not the only one affected by the strains of constant playing, although others held on longer. Nevertheless, the group released a souvenir of their grandest tour—*Live in the City of Light* (1987), another U.K. No. 1—and recorded "Mandela Day" to coincide with their headlining appearance at a Wembley Stadium show in honor of the then-jailed South African activist. Roger Waters even spoke of them as a possible "new Pink Floyd."

Street Fighting Years (1989) was the band's fourth successive U.K. No. 1 album, and the haunting "Belfast Child" their first U.K. chart-topping single. However, American glory was now receding. More disruptions were in the air: bassist **Malcolm Foster** replaced Giblin (who decamped to Propaganda) and, more crucially, MacNeil quit in 1990, to be succeeded first by **Peter-John Vettese**, then **Mark Taylor**. (Giblin and MacNeil's swansong was 1989's *The Amsterdam EP*, featuring a cover of Prince's "Sign 'o' the Times.")

Perhaps as a result, *Real Life* (1991)—source of the hits "Let There Be Love" and "Stand By Love"—had a

more confessional air. The album reached U.K. No. 2, as did 1995's *Good News from the Next World*, which yielded "She's a River" and "Hypnotised." Neither album, however, sold well in the United States.

Neapolis (1998) did not even achieve a U.S. release, although it made the lower reaches of the U.K. Top Twenty, as did its hit, "Glitterball." Owing to record company shenanigans, *Our Secrets Are the Same*, recorded in 2000, was not released anywhere. (It eventually came out as part of 2004's *Silver Box* set.)

Amid these struggles, Foster left and Forbes briefly returned before **Eddy Duffy** joined on bass. (**Ged Grimes** replaced Duffy in 2010.) Gaynor was replaced on drums by Jim's brother **Mark Kerr**. Disillusioned, the group sank beneath the radar, barely troubling charts with 2001's covers album *Neon Lights* and 2002's *Cry*.

A more concerted revival saw the group welcome back Gaynor and bring in **Andy Gillespie** on keyboards. *Black & White 050505* (2005) hinted at a return to their great days, reaching U.K. No. 37. Confusingly, Gillespie quit for two years, and Mark Taylor came back, before the former returned.

Graffiti Soul (2009) gave Simple Minds their first U.K. Top Ten placing for fourteen years. As Jim Kerr remarked in 2012, "It's really not such a bad life." **MiC**

■ Other percussion

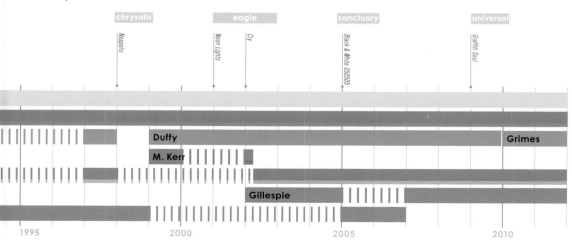

siouxsie and the banshees 1976–2002

Siouxsie Sioux
b. May 27, 1957

Steve Severin
b. September 25, 1955

Kenny Morris
b. February 1, 1957

Peter "P.T." Fenton
b. unknown

John McKay
b. unknown

Budgie
b. August 21, 1957

"I don't embrace the 'legacy' thing," **Siouxsie Sioux** declared in 2007, punk to the last. "I just want to do what I do, and leave me the fuck alone." Fellow stars begged to differ. Her band's songs have been covered by LCD Soundsystem ("Slowdive"), The Mars Volta ("Pull to Bits"), Simple Minds ("Christine"), and Tricky ("Tattoo"), and their influence can be detected in acts from the Cocteau Twins and U2 to Radiohead and Florence and the Machine.

But back in 1976, Sue Dallion and Steven Bailey were just disaffected youths, living outside London and obsessed by the nascent punk movement, led by the Sex Pistols. When they heard that a band had dropped out of a showcase at London's 100 Club, they stepped in. Dallion adopted the name Siouxsie Sioux, with a group inspired by the witch-hunting movie *The Cry of the Banshee* (1970), starring Vincent Price. Bailey picked up a bass for the first time and, with Marco Pirroni (guitar) and Sid Vicious (drums), they jammed a version of The Lord's Prayer (incorporating "Twist and Shout" and "Knockin' on Heaven's Door") for twenty minutes.

Having met an enthusiastic response, Bailey became **Steve Severin** (a reference to the hero of the book *Venus im Pelz,* as namechecked in The Velvet Underground's "Venus in Furs") and the Banshees installed guitarist **John McKay** (after the short-stayed **Pete Fenton**) and drummer **Kenny Morris**. As their following increased, record labels showed interest but balked at the group demanding control of their work.

Eventually Polydor granted their wishes, with the extraordinary *The Scream* being unleashed in 1978. Siouxsie's powerhouse wailing was well suited to The Beatles' "Helter Skelter" and the band hit the U.K. Top Ten with the stand-alone single "Hong Kong Garden." Siouxsie dressed provocatively and exploded the boundaries for female singers. Her ice-queen image and the bleak songs of *Join Hands* (1979) helped create a template for Goths. Meanwhile, **McKay** and **Morris** walked out on the band just after the start of a 1979 tour. **Robert Smith**, from support band The Cure, deputized on guitar, while **Budgie** joined on drums.

With new guitarist **John McGeoch**, formerly of Magazine, the Banshees took flight. "I could say, 'I want this to sound like a horse falling off a cliff,' and he would know exactly what I meant," enthused Siouxsie. The results were 1980's experimental *Kaleidoscope,* 1981's voodoo-inspired *Ju Ju,* and 1982's orchestral

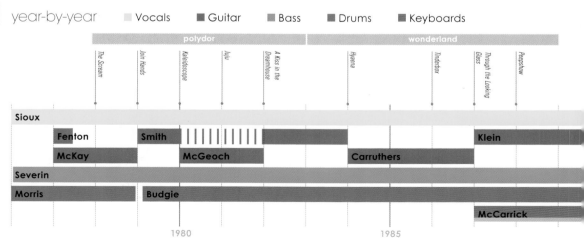

year-by-year ▪ Vocals ▪ Guitar ▪ Bass ▪ Drums ▪ Keyboards

250,000	250,000	250,000	250,000
The Scream (1978)	**Kaleidoscope** (1980)	**Juju** (1981)	**Once Upon a Time: The Singles** (1981)

Robert Smith
b. April 21, 1959

John McGeoch
b. August 25, 1955
d. March 4, 2004

John Carruthers
b. 1958

Jon Klein
b. unknown

Martin McCarrick
b. July 29, 1962

Knox Chandler
b. unknown

and more romantic (by Siouxsie's standards) *A Kiss in the Dreamhouse.* A hits collection, *Once Upon a Time* (1981), became their biggest seller in Britain.

Meanwhile, Siouxsie and Budgie formed the percussion-dominated duo, The Creatures. Debuting with the *Wild Things* EP in 1981, they scored a U.K. hit with a mock big band take on Mel Tormé's "Right Now" in 1983, and produced *Feast* (1983), *Boomerang* (1989), *Anima Animus* (1999), and *Hai!* (2003).

When McGeoch quit in 1982 (later to join Public Image Ltd), Smith returned to the Banshees, doing double time with The Cure (plus a one-off, drug-crazed collaboration with Severin, called The Glove, making 1983's *Blue Sunshine*). With Smith, they cut the live *Nocturne* (1983), *Hyæna* (1984), and a U.K. Top Ten-charting cover of The Beatles' "Dear Prudence."

Smith fled back to The Cure (much to Siouxsie's irritation) and guitarist **John Carruthers** joined in time for the Banshees' U.S. Top 100 debut, *Tinderbox* (1986). The new lineup paid tribute to their inspirations with the covers collection *Through the Looking Glass* (1987), featuring a hit version of "This Wheel's on Fire."

The success continued with 1988's *Peepshow*, featuring multi-instrumentalist **Martin McCarrick** (who

had played on The Glove's album) and new guitarist **Jon Klein** (formerly of Specimen). *Superstition* (1991) yielded their sole U.S. Top Forty single ("Kiss Them for Me"), while the Banshees secured high billing on the first Lollapalooza tour in 1991. They also provided the lead single for the 1992 movie *Batman Returns:* "Face to Face," co-written with Danny Elfman.

After Siouxsie's 1994 duet with Morrissey on a cover of Yma Sumac's "Interlude," the band bowed out with 1995's *The Rapture,* co-produced by the Velvets' John Cale. Disheartened by a lack of record company support, the Banshees disbanded in 1996.

In 2002, Siouxsie, Budgie, and Severin—with former Psychedelic Fur **Knox Chandler**, who had replaced Klein for their last outing, in 1995—reformed for a tour that coincided with *The Very Best of Siouxsie and the Banshees* and led to the live *Seven Year Itch* (2003).

In 2007, Siouxsie released her splendid solo debut, *Mantaray.* With seemingly little chance of another reunion, the box set *At the BBC* (2009) was left to prove just how versatile this influential band were. "We were genuinely miffed when we didn't change the face of pop music," Budgie admitted to *Record Collector,* "but maybe we added another facet to it." **SL**

 Strings

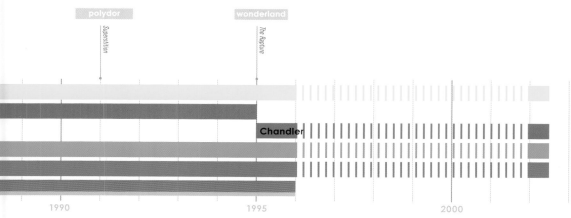

the sisters of mercy 1980–present

Andrew Eldritch
b. May 15, 1959

Gary Marx
b. Unknown

Craig Adams
b. April 4, 1962

Ben Gunn
b. Unknown

Wayne Hussey
b. May 26, 1958

Patricia Morrison
b. January 14, 1962

Andreas Bruhn
b. November 5, 1967

Tony James
b. April 12, 1953

The Sisters of Mercy released only three studio albums, all in their first ten years, but their influence far exceeds their output. The group, largely a vehicle for the lyrical obsessions of **Andrew Eldritch**, embodied the Gothic rock foundations of sex, death, and annihilation, weaving them into a seductive tapestry.

Eldritch formed The Sisters of Mercy in 1980 in Leeds with guitarist **Gary Marx**, a fan of Leonard Cohen (one of whose songs bequeathed their name). A drum machine that Eldritch programmed and christened Doktor Avalanche completed the original lineup. The enlistment of bassist **Craig Adams** in 1981, then guitarist **Ben Gunn**, made the group a viable, albeit sometimes shambolic, live proposition.

Early on, the group concentrated on promoting singles and EPs through their own label, Merciful Release. Cuts like "Alice," "Floorshow," "Temple of Love," and a slow, sinister version of The Rolling Stones' "Gimme Shelter" helped to build their following. Their live shows—and Eldritch's deep voice—grew in confidence until they became swirling miasmas of expressionist atmospherics. The replacement of Gunn by **Wayne Hussey** helped accelerate their progress.

First and Last and Always (1985) should have secured their position as Gothic gods, yet it became their headstone. "Walk Away," "Amphetamine Logic," "No Time to Cry," and the title track were fine slices of gloom, but the group proved disastrously unstable. Marx left to form Ghost Dance, then Adams and

Hussey quit to form The Sisterhood. Eldritch promptly recorded an album, *Gift,* under that name, obliging his ex-cohorts to rename themselves The Mission.

Relaunching the Sisters, Eldritch recruited bassist and Gothic goddess **Patricia Morrison** from The Gun Club, and Meat Loaf collaborator Jim Steinman. The result: 1987's epic *Floodland,* source of the hits "This Corrosion," "Lucretia My Reflection," and "Dominion."

During another hiatus, Eldritch eased out Morrison (who later joined The Damned and married their singer, Dave Vanian). **Tony James**, from Generation X and Sigue Sigue Sputnik, joined for *Vision Thing* (1990), a powerful attack on George Bush. "More" ramped up the ante while "Detonation Boulevard" and the title track thundered the message home. (These and other new hits were rounded up on 1993's *A Slight Case of Overbombing,* the sequel to 1992's equally nifty set of early cuts, *Some Girls Wander by Mistake.*)

The Sisters toured for the first time in five years, but Eldritch felt they were not given enough support. The ensuing spat with his record label meant he refused to record any more material, bar a 1997 effort credited to The SSV Project (Screw Shareholder Value—Not So Much A Band As Another Opportunity To Waste Money On Drugs And Ammunition Courtesy Of The Idiots At Time Warner) that, unsurprisingly, Warner declined to release. The group—effectively Eldritch and whoever he has not fallen out with—still tours sporadically, usually to a rapturous response. **MiH**

year-by-year

■ Vocals   ■ Guitar   ■ Bass   ■ Keyboards   ■ Programming

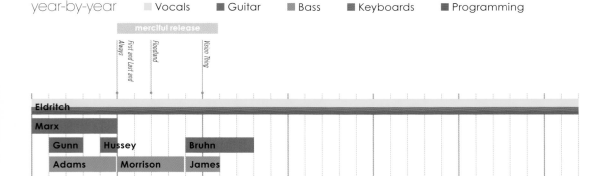

merciful release

First and Last and Always
Floodland
Vision Thing

Eldritch
Marx
Gunn   Hussey   Bruhn
Adams   Morrison   James

1980   1985   1990   1995   2000   2005   2010

skid row 1986–present

Dave "The Snake" Sabo
b. September 16, 1964

Rachel Bolan
b. February 9, 1966

Matt Fallon
b. September 30, 1965

Scotti Hill
b. May 31, 1964

Rob Affuso
b. March 1, 1963

Sebastian Bach
b. April 3, 1968

Johnny Solinger
b. August 3, 1966

For a so-called "hair metal" band, Skid Row certainly possessed talent—especially in the twin-guitar attack of founders **Dave "The Snake" Sabo** and **Scotti Hill** and the huge charisma of vocalist **Sebastian Bach**. They knew how to fashion pop-metal hits that worked well in Chevy Camaros and, as later records proved, had ambitions well beyond most of their heavily hair-sprayed contemporaries. But Nirvana and their flannel-clad buddies hit the scene right as Skid Row hit their commercial prime, pushing the band out of the limelight seemingly well before it was time to go.

However, Sabo had experience of untimely exits. "The Snake" was an early part of Jon Bon Jovi's band, before being shown the door in favor of Richie Sambora. He rebounded nicely in 1986, forming the New Jersey-based Skid Row with bassist **Rachel Bolan** and others who barely stuck around long enough for a cup of coffee. Things began to gel in 1987 when Sabo and Bolan joined forces with Hill, drummer **Rob Affuso**, and **Bach** (the latter replacing Matt Fallon, who also briefly sang in Anthrax). Now recognized as the band's classic lineup, the quintet remained intact into 1996. Meanwhile, Jon Bon Jovi, repaying whatever debt he felt he owed Sabo, used his influence to help the band ink a deal with the Atlantic label in 1988.

Skid Row's self-titled 1989 debut proved a smash, yielding two U.S. Top Ten hits: "18 and Life" and "I Remember You." The album sold more than five million copies in the U.S. and did healthy business elsewhere, including the U.K., where it was certified gold. One album into the game, Skid Row had vaulted to the top of the hair-metal heap, and would cement that position with 1991's heavier *Slave to the Grind*. It debuted at U.S. No. 1, en route to double platinum sales, and drew positive reviews, critics noting the artistic growth between albums.

By then, however, the clock was ready to strike twelve on Skid Row and the entire hair-metal genre. Grunge captured the public's imagination, leading many musicians to trade in their spandex for flannel. Skid Row's classic lineup managed one more album, the sadly overlooked *Subhuman Race*, before Bach bolted in 1996, eventually starting his own solo career (of which the highlight was 2007's *Angel Down*) and acting on Broadway in the title role of *Jekyll & Hyde*.

Skid Row, however, refused to throw in the towel. With **Johnny Solinger** on vocals since 1996, and a succession of drummers after Affuso quit in 1998, they released two post-Bach albums and continued to wave the hair-metal flag proudly in concert. And in 2012, the long-estranged Bach revealed that he would be open to a reunion of the classic lineup. "Four out of five want to do it," he Tweeted. "Believe it or not, I am one of the four who would do it." **JiH**

year-by-year   ■ Vocals   ■ Guitar   ■ Bass   ■ Drums

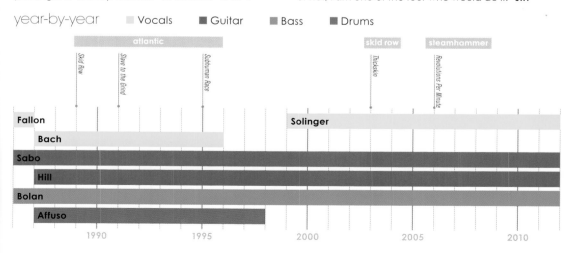

slade 1969–present

Noddy Holder
b. June 15, 1946

Dave Hill
b. April 4, 1946

Jim Lea
b. June 14, 1949

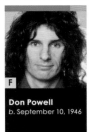

Don Powell
b. September 10, 1946

"It's Chriiistmaaas!" Yuletide festivities in the U.K. begin with these words, belted out by **Noddy Holder** on Slade's million-selling No. 1, "Merry Xmas Everybody." First released in December 1973—although recorded in New York during that year's sweltering summer—the song has revisited the British chart fifteen times. (Cowriter Holder refers to it as "my pension.")

That song aside, think of Slade and most picture boggle-eyed, blond-haired Holder and buck-toothed, top-hatted guitarist **Dave Hill**. For most, they were the face of Slade. But the sound was the domain of Holder and bassist **Jim Lea**. On their way to becoming the U.K.'s best-selling singles act of the seventies, Holder and Lea penned six No. 1's—three of which entered at the top of the chart, a first for any act.

Their genesis began with members of The Vendors (Hill and drummer **Don Powell**) and The Mavericks (Holder) joining forces in the early sixties with Lea. As The 'N Betweens—replete with a skinhead image—they achieved no chart success but attracted the eye of Jimi Hendrix's manager, Chas Chandler. Under his guidance, they became Ambrose Slade (abbreviated after a flop debut album, *Beginnings*), then grew their hair and hitched their wagon to the glam rock train.

A cover of Bobby Marchan's "Get Down and Get With It" did okay, but the smashes came when Lea and Holder joined creative forces. "Coz I Luv You"

topped charts across Europe, setting the scene for "Look Wot You Dun" (No. 4) and "Take Me Back 'ome" (another No. 1). The latter even broke the *Billboard* Top 100, while "Mama Weer All Crazee Now" again took Slade to the top spot in their home country.

In early 1973, "Cum On Feel the Noize" (revived by Oasis in 1996) entered the U.K. chart at No. 1, a feat only The Beatles had previously managed. "Skeeze Me, Pleeze Me" followed. The bar had been set.

The band ended 1973 with their Christmas classic, before *Old New Borrowed and Blue* grabbed the New Year by its throat. By 1975, Slade were bent on breaking America. It was not to be. Despite successful tours, the American influences of *Nobody's Fools* still only charted back home. (However, the group proved a pivotal influence on Kiss.)

After a revitalizing gig at the Reading Festival in 1980, their profile was raised by Quiet Riot's U.S. hit covers of "Cum On Feel the Noize" and "Mama Weer All Crazee Now." "My Oh My" and "Run Runaway" (both 1983) restored Slade to the Top Ten at home and gave them their first notable U.S. successes.

When follow-ups flopped, a weary Holder quit in 1992, with Lea close behind. Powell and Hill ploughed on, issuing *Keep on Rockin!* (1994) as Slade II, and have since returned to the group name for live work with singers Steve Whalley and Mal McNulty. **JeH**

year-by-year

Vocals ■ Guitar ■ Bass ■ Drums
■ Keyboards ■ Other percussion

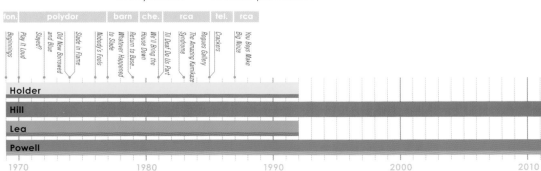

slayer 1981–present

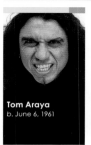

Tom Araya
b. June 6, 1961

Jeff Hanneman
b. January 31, 1964

Kerry King
b. June 3, 1964

Dave Lombardo
b. February 16, 1965

Paul Bostaph
b. March 4, 1964

Mix in Slayer's catalog with the titles of B-grade horror flicks and the result is seamless. Their albums, such as *Hell Awaits* and *Reign in Blood*, read like celluloid nightmares, and share similar themes. Slayer's world, as disturbing as it is enticing, is filled with serial killers, war criminals, torture, terrorism, descents into hell and *Seasons in the Abyss*. Yet few horror films are handled with the intelligence, precision, and power that can be found, to an astonishing extent, on Slayer albums. For they, perhaps more than any other metal act, have remained true to a mission statement: play it hard, play it fast, and take no prisoners. Slayer have earned a position among history's Big Four thrash metal acts, alongside Metallica, Anthrax, and Megadeth. And many would argue that that position is at the very top.

Some people invest their money in stocks and shares, others hide it in mattresses. Singer-bassist **Tom Araya**, a former respiratory therapist, put his savings toward financing Slayer's debut album. It proved a wise investment. Araya's Southern California group—begun by guitarists **Kerry King** and **Jeff Hanneman**, and featuring drummer **Dave Lombardo**—had spent a couple of years playing Iron Maiden covers but were headed in the right direction by the time they made 1983's *Show No Mercy*. While hardly polished, it showcased the band's aggressive brand of shredding

guitar and lightning-fast drums. The lyrics caught up with the music on 1985's *Hell Awaits*: devilish yarns that helped fuel the death metal movement.

Those efforts brought Slayer to the attention of Rick Rubin, who signed the band to his Def Jam label, initiating one of hard rock's greatest producer-artist relationships. Their first collaboration was truly one for the ages: 1986's *Reign in Blood*, a commercial breakthrough and one of metal's greatest albums. The next three each took Slayer higher up the charts, peaking in the U.S. when 1994's *Divine Intervention* crashed the Top Ten—all while Slayer took criticism for lyrics that touched on Satanism and Nazism.

Much of that uproar would die down with the dawn of the twenty-first century, as thrash metal became an accepted part of popular culture and religious zealots focused on hip-hop. "I think the church and the (religious) right now have a lot more to be worried about than Slayer," remarked King in 2001.

Even Grammy voters gave the band their blessing, awarding Slayer Best Metal Performance trophies in 2006 ("Eyes of the Insane," from the U.S. No. 5 *Christ Illusion*) and 2007 ("Final Six"). None of that, thankfully, can be taken as a sign of a kinder, gentler Slayer—who, despite their newfound acceptance, have kept right on releasing terrifyingly good records. **JiH**

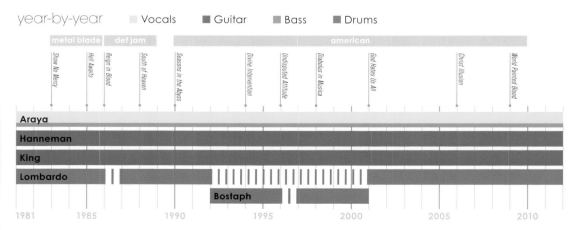

slipknot 1995–present

Anders Colsefni
b. April 15, 1972

Josh Brainard
b. August 6, 1974

Shawn Crahan
b. September 24, 1969

Paul Gray
b. April 8, 1972
d. May 24, 2010

Joey Jordison
b. April 26, 1975

Donnie Steele
b. October 6, 1971

When this metal collective emerged from Des Moines, Iowa, in 1995—their faces covered by horrifying masks and individual members identified only by single-digit numbers—some believed it was a short-lived gimmick to sell their chaotic, uncompromising music.

But nearly two decades on, charts have been conquered, sales have run into millions, and maggots (as their fans are affectionately known) have bred far and wide. (There are 9.8 million on Facebook alone.)

Slipknot's original lineup consisted of percussionist **Shawn Crahan** (nicknamed "Clown," or #6), bassist **Paul Gray** (#2), guitarist **Josh Brainard** (#4), drummer and de facto bandleader **Joey Jordison** (#1), vocalist **Anders Colsefni**, and similarly numberless guitarist **Donnie Steele**. They made their live debut as Meld in December 1995 but took their now familiar name from what became the opening track on a self-released collection of demos, Mate. Feed. Kill. Repeat. (1996).

Steele's exit in 1996 resulted in the appointment of **Craig Jones** (#5), but he was destined for the sampling desk. The guitar vacancy was filled by

Mick Thomson (#7). Front-man Colsefni—demoted to backing vocalist/percussionist when **Corey Taylor** (#8) joined in 1997—also packed his bags, leading to possibly the fastest turnover of percussionists in rock history: Greg Welts, Brandon Darner, and **Chris Fehn** were all #3s but only Fehn survived the reshuffle.

Although the group recorded new demos, their live incarnation secured the services of Korn producer Ross Robinson. "It was our connection as people and also seeing them destroy in Iowa," he told Metal Hammer. "I really instantly fell in love with each of them. It's such a great feeling to connect so deeply with similar hearts." Turntablist **Sid Wilson** (#0) signed up in 1998 and, midway through making their self-titled "official" debut, Brainard was replaced by new #4 **James Root**. Having swelled to a nine-piece, the group unleashed Slipknot (1999), featuring classics like "Surfacing," "Wait and Bleed," and "Spit it Out."

Slipknot's incendiary live shows—including the first of three stints on Ozzy Osbourne's Ozzfest tour—were a breeding ground for maggots (not to mention

year-by-year ▪ Vocals ▪ Guitar ▪ Bass ▪ Drums ▪ Keyboards

ismist

roadrunner

Mate. Feed. Kill. Repeat.

Slipknot

Iowa

Colsefni	Taylor			
Brainard		Root		
Steele	Thomson			
Gray				
Jordison				
Crahan				
		Fehn		
	Jones			
	Wilson			

1996   1998   2000   2002

Craig Jones
b. February 11, 1972

Mick Thomson
b. November 3, 1973

Corey Taylor
b. December 8, 1973

Chris Fehn
b. February 24, 1972

Sid Wilson
b. January 20, 1978

James Root
b. October 2, 1971

group members grappling, stage diving, and, in the early days, setting each other on fire). Their rabid fans propelled the unrelentingly brutal *Iowa* (2001) to the top of the U.K. album chart, ahead of The Strokes' much-hyped debut. At home, it made the Top Three.

A punishing tour yielded the *Disasterpieces* DVD, but also exacerbated tensions that precipitated a hiatus. Corey Taylor and Jim Root revived their pre-Slipknot band Stone Sour, whose self-titled 2002 debut album went gold in the U.S. Joey Jordison founded Murderdolls, featuring singer Wednesday 13, while Shawn Crahan created To My Surprise (whose self-titled 2003 album was unrecognizable as an offshoot of Slipknot), and Sid Wilson initiated an alternative career as drum 'n' bass exponent DJ Starscream.

In 2003, Slipknot reunited in body if not spirit for the ambitious *Vol. 3: (The Subliminal Verses)* with producer Rick Rubin. The fractious band typically disagreed on Rubin's merits, with Taylor particularly critical of the album's vocal sound. Nonetheless, "Before I Forget" won them a Grammy—at the sixth time of asking—for Best Metal Performance. An accompanying video was the first to feature the group unmasked.

In 2005, after the release of *9.0: Live,* Slipknot took another break. Stone Sour returned with the U.S. Top Five hit *Come What(ever) May* (2006), while Jordison played drums for Ministry in 2006 and Korn in 2007. Crahan formed another expectation-defying side-project, Dirty Little Rabbits, for 2007's *Breeding*.

Slipknot returned in 2008 with the U.S. No. 1 *All Hope Is Gone*—but, in May 2010, they were rocked by the death of founding bassist and songwriter Gray from an accidental drugs overdose. In the aftermath, Stone Sour issued *Audio Secrecy* (2010), Jordison joined Rob Zombie's band, and Chris Fehn was enlisted by metallers Will Haven. Occasional live outings by Slipknot, with founding member Donnie Steele covering for Gray, raised fans' hopes that the still-shaken group may make another album. As chief Slipknot visionary Shawn Crahan bluntly noted: "When you're fighting a war, there's gonna be casualties. How far can I go? I'll rip off my arm." **MW**

■ Other percussion   ■ Programming

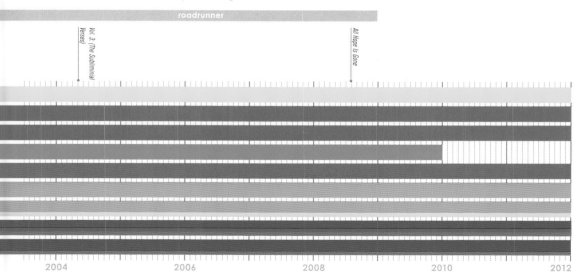

Mate. Feed. Kill. Repeat. (1996)

Slipknot (1999)

Iowa (2001)

Vol 3: (The Subliminal Verses) (2004)

All Hope is Gone (2008)

Anders Colsefni—the band's frontman in the *Mate. Feed. Kill. Repeat.* era.

Shawn Crahan entertains at Ozzfest, Vancouver, in 1999.

"The Nine" in Grand Rapids, Michigan, in 1999.

Slipknot hit Ozzfest at the Shoreline Amphitheater, Mountain View, California, on June 29, 2001.

Corey Taylor in frightening form during Slipknot's Pledge of Allegiance tour in 2001.

Bassist and founder member **Paul Gray** performs in 2004; he died in 2010.

Percussionist **Chris Fehn** at the Astoria, London, in May 2004.

Guitarist **Jim Root** onstage at the Hammersmith Apollo, London, on December 8, 2008.

Joey Jordison on drums as Slipknot headline the Rockstar Energy Mayhem Festival at the Verizon Wireless Amphitheater, San Antonio, Texas, on July 26, 2008.

the small faces / the faces 1965–present

Ronnie Lane
b. April 1, 1945
d. June 4, 1997

Kenney Jones
b. September 16, 1948

Jimmy Winston
b. April 20, 1945

Steve Marriott
b. January 30,
1947
d. April 20, 1991

Ian McLagan
b. May 12, 1945

Rick Wills
b. December 5, 1947

When **Ronnie Lane**, **Kenney Jones**, **Steve Marriott**, and **Jimmy Winston** formed The Small Faces, they could never have imagined that their "Mod" group would eventually turn into the ultimate good time rock 'n' roll band and launch a singer's forty-year solo career.

Even as the four young Londoners celebrated their first hit, "Whatcha Gonna Do About It," in 1965, their lineup changed with keyboard player **Ian McLagan** replacing Winston. With a second hit, "Sha La La La Lee," under their belts, The Small Faces spent more than six months in the U.K. album chart with their self-titled debut, peaking at No. 3.

With the Mod movement thriving, The Small Faces topped the U.K. chart with "All or Nothing" in 1966. In complete contrast to that rabble-rouser was 1967's psychedelic "Itchycoo Park" in 1967, which took the four-piece into the U.S. chart for the first time. "I lifted it from a hymn, 'God Be In My Head'" Lane confessed to *Record Collector*, "and I also got the theme to the words in a hotel in Bath or Bristol. There was a magazine in the room with a rambling account of some place in the country and it was about 'dreaming spires' and a 'bridge of sighs'."

The U.K. chart-topping concept album *Ogden's Nut Gone Flake* (1968) included the group's final Top Ten hit, "Lazy Sunday." In January 1969, Marriott left to form Humble Pie, leaving the remaining three members to recruit The Jeff Beck Group's singer **Rod Stewart** and guitarist **Ronnie Wood**. "We got together with Rod and Ron at the Stones' rehearsal studio one afternoon and played a bit," McLagan told *Circus*, "then we just saw more and more of each other. So the five of us decided to stay together. As soon as Steve left, it was a breath of fresh air." Re-christened The Faces, they signed to Warner, while Stewart pursued a solo career on the Mercury label.

The Faces' debut *Long Player* charted in both the U.K. and the U.S., and for the next six years they and the singer enjoyed parallel careers. However, as Stewart topped charts in Britain and America with "Maggie May," the group came to be billed as Rod Stewart & The Faces, which caused some rancor.

The 1971 Top Ten album *A Nod's as Good as a Wink… to a Blind Horse* featured the hit "Stay with Me." It was quickly followed by the U.K. No. 1 *Ooh La La*, but with Stewart apparently more focused on his solo

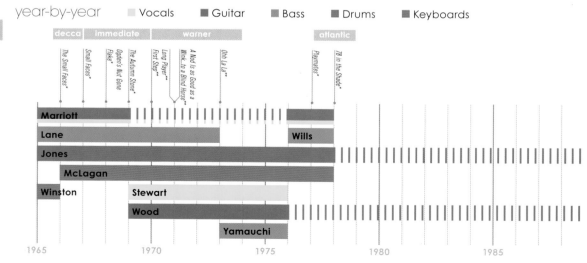

year-by-year   ▪ Vocals   ▪ Guitar   ▪ Bass   ▪ Drums   ▪ Keyboards

500,000	750,000	1.3M	500,000
Small Faces*	Ogden's Nut	A Nod Is as Good	Ooh La La
(1966)	Gone Flake*	as a Wink...**	(1973)
	(1968)	(1979)	

Rod Stewart
b. January 10, 1945

Ronnie Wood
b. June 1, 1947

Tetsu Yamauchi
b. October 21, 1946

Mick Hucknall
b. June 8, 1960

Glen Matlock
b. August 27, 1956

career—his *Never A Dull Moment* reached No. 1 in the U.K. and No. 2 in the U.S.—Lane left The Faces, to be replaced by former Free bassist **Tetsu Yamauchi.**

In 1974 came the live *Coast to Coast Overtures and Beginners*—credited to Rod Stewart & The Faces—and the band's final hit, "You Can Make Me Dance or Anything." Although members of the band supported Stewart on a solo U.S. tour to promote his smash *Atlantic Crossing* (U.S. No. 9 and U.K. No. 1), The Faces finally came to an end in December 1975, by which time Wood had begun working with The Rolling Stones.

In 1976—as the re-released "Itchycoo Park" and "Lazy Sunday" hit the U.K. chart—Jones, McLagan, and Marriott reformed The Small Faces (with former David Gilmour/Peter Frampton associate **Rick Wills** on bass). However, after two failed singles, the band split for the final time. Jones replaced Keith Moon in The Who, McLagan joined The Rolling Stones' touring band, Wills joined Foreigner, and Marriott returned to the U.K. pub circuit until his death in a fire in 1991.

When Stewart bagged a Lifetime Achievement Award at the U.K. Brit Awards in 1993, The Faces reunited for a one-off appearance at the show. The Rolling Stones' bassist Bill Wyman deputized for Lane, who had developed multiple sclerosis (he eventually died from the disease in 1997).

Stewart had continued to hit new heights as a solo star: *A Night on the Town* (1976), *Foot Loose and Fancy Free* (1977), and *Blondes Have More Fun* (1978) made the Top Three in the U.K. and U.S. In 1993, he reunited with Wood for MTV's *Unplugged,* which became a multi-platinum album featuring The Faces' "Stay with Me." The following year, he was inducted into the Rock and Roll Hall of Fame (as were The Faces in 2012.)

In the new millennium, Stewart's career received a major boost when he moved to RCA's J label and began his series of *American Songbook* albums. All five were Top Ten hits on both sides of the Atlantic, with *Volume III* and the *Still The Same... Great Rock Classics of Our Time* collection hitting No. 1 in the U.S.

In 2010 and 2011, a new Faces lineup—minus Stewart—hit the road. Originals Jones, McLagan, and Wood were joined by Simply Red singer **Mick Hucknall** and former Sex Pistols bassist **Glen Matlock.** "They were my all-time favourite band," Matlock told *The Telegraph,* "so to be in them for a bit is great." **BS**

* The Small Faces
** The Faces

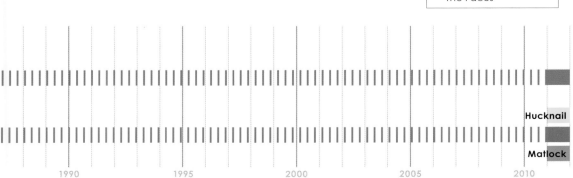

Hucknall

Matlock

1990   1995   2000   2005   2010

The Small Faces
(1966)

Small Faces (1967)

Ogden's Nut Gone Flake (1968)

First Step (1970)

Long Player (1971)

A Nod Is as Good as a Wink... to a Blind Horse (1971)

Ooh La La (1973)

Playmates (1977)

78 in the Shade (1978)

Left to right: **Ronnie Lane, Kenney Jones, Steve Marriott,** and **Ian McLagan** in 1966.

McLagan, Marriott, Lane, and **Jones** with P.P. Arnold (center).

The Small Faces on camera: a color-coordinated portrait of **Marriott, Lane, Jones,** and **McLagan** in 1968.

Group huddle: The Faces conceal theirs in Copenhagen in 1970.

The Faces play the Weeley Festival, England, on August 29, 1971.

Faces **Ronnie Wood** and **Rod Stewart** perform in 1972.

Left to right: **McLagan, Marriott, Rick Wills,** and **Jones** in 1977.

Left to right: **McLagan, Wood, Stewart, Lane,** and **Jones** perform as The Faces on BBC TV's *Top of the Pops* in February 1973.

Clockwise from bottom left: **Marriott, Jones, Wills, McLagan,** and Jimmy McCulloch on tour in 1978.

the smashing pumpkins 1988–present

Billy Corgan
b. March 17, 1967

James Iha
b. March 26, 1968

D'arcy Wretsky
b. May 1, 1968

Jimmy Chamberlin
b. June 10, 1964

Melissa Auf der Maur
b. March 17, 1972

Jeff Schroeder
b. February 4, 1974

"The guitars are every bit as loud as anything you'd want," observed Kiss mainman Gene Simmons of The Smashing Pumpkins, "and on top of that there are pop melodies with all sorts of interesting subject matters." Mighty riffs, potentially chart-busting tunes, and lyrical poetry have indeed dominated the Pumpkins discography—as has a penchant for female bassists.

Guitarists **Billy Corgan** and **James Iha** created the band in Chicago in 1988. After a first show with just a drum machine, they enlisted bassist **D'arcy Wretzky**— with whom Iha had a short-lived romance—then drummer **Jimmy Chamberlin**. In 1990, they began playing outside Chicago and recording their debut album with future Nirvana producer Butch Vig. *Gish* (1991) proved a slow-burner while the Pumpkins toured relentlessly. However, a stint with Pearl Jam and the Red Hot Chili Peppers—plus speculation about Corgan's relationship with a pre-Kurt Cobain Courtney Love—boosted their profile. (Corgan and Love's two decades of recriminations and reconciliations would see him contributing to, then disowning, *Celebrity Skin* and *Nobody's Daughter* by her group Hole.)

The Pumpkins became famously dysfunctional: Chamberlin developed a drug problem, and the megalomaniacal Corgan replaced parts recorded by Wretzky and Iha for *Siamese Dream* (1993). But the turmoil was rewarded when the album—featuring piano by Mike Mills of R.E.M. and violin by David Ragsdale of Kansas—smashed into the U.S. Top Ten.

Pisces Iscariot (1994), a compilation of offcuts and radio sessions, hit No. 4 before the Pumpkins shot to the top with *Mellon Collie and the Infinite Sadness* (1995). This ambitious double set sold five million in its first three months, a figure boosted by the hit "Tonight, Tonight," featuring the Chicago Symphony Orchestra. Keyboardist Jonathan Melvoin, who had worked with Prince alongside his sisters Wendy and Susannah, augmented the Pumpkins' touring lineup. However, when Melvoin fatally overdosed in July 1996, Chamberlin—with whom he had been using heroin—was fired. Just over a month later, the tour resumed, with former Filter drummer Matt Walker and keyboardist Dennis Flemion of The Frogs. (The former also played on Iha's 1998 album, *Let It Come Down*.)

The appropriately downbeat *Adore* (1998) featured guest drummers including Soundgarden's Matt Cameron and Beck's Lenny Waronker. It turned platinum in a month, but the Pumpkins reverted—to Corgan's frustration—to being a cult band, albeit an arena-filling one. On tour, it took three people to fill Chamberlin's place: John Mellencamp's drummer Kenny Aronoff and two percussionists.

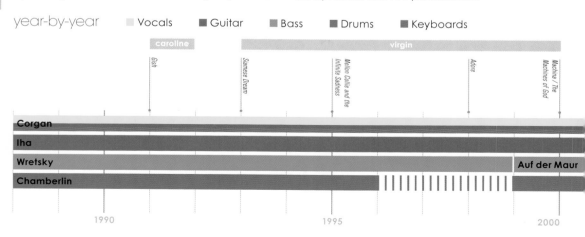

year-by-year   ■ Vocals   ■ Guitar   ■ Bass   ■ Drums   ■ Keyboards

caroline | virgin

Gish | *Siamese Dream* | *Mellon Collie and the Infinite Sadness* | *Adore* | *Machina / The Machines of God*

Corgan
Iha
Wretsky
Chamberlin

Auf der Maur

1990   1995   2000

Ginger Reyes
b. April 22, 1980

Lisa Harriton
b. November 18, 1980

Mike Byrne
b. February 6, 1990

Nicole Fiorentino
b. April 8, 1979

Chamberlin rejoined in early 1999, only for Wretzky to quit later that year. Corgan forged ahead with 2000's gorgeous *Machina / The Machines of God*, featuring David Bowie's keyboardist Mike Garson, but its underwhelming sales prompted the band's label, Virgin, to stymie plans for a sequel. Corgan duly disseminated *Machina II / The Friends & Enemies of Modern Music* via fans and the internet, and announced that the Pumpkins' next tour would be their last. Garson, keyboardist Chris Holmes, and former Hole bassist **Melissa Auf der Maur** completed the lineup that disbanded in December 2000.

After a stint as New Order's tour guitarist, Corgan formed Zwan in 2002 with Chamberlin, indie cult heroes Matt Sweeney and David Pajo, and another female bassist, A Perfect Circle's Paz Lenchantin. (Iha joined A Perfect Circle the following year.) Zwan's gloriously colorful *Mary, Star of the Sea* (2003) hit U.S. No. 3 but the band imploded on tour.

In interviews promoting his largely electronic 2005 solo album *The Future Embrace*—featuring The Cure's Robert Smith duetting on a cover of the Bee Gees' "To Love Somebody"—Corgan blamed Iha for the Pumpkins' demise and denounced Wretzky as a drug casualty, yet announced plans to revive the group. Unsurprisingly, he and Chamberlin proved the

sole survivors of the original lineup: the duo are the only musicians credited on 2007's lumpen *Zeitgeist*, the tour for which featured guitarist **Jeff Schroeder**, keyboardist **Lisa Harriton**, and bassist **Ginger Reyes**. The live lineup was augmented in 2008 by No Doubt brass players Stephen Bradley and Gabrial McNair, Reyes' husband Kristopher Pooley on accordion and keyboards, and violinist Gingger Shankar.

With *Zeitgeist* stalling and fans' patience eroded by a self-indulgent twentieth anniversary tour, Corgan announced in 2009 that he had fired Chamberlin and would issue the conceptual *Teargarden by Kaleidyscope* one song at a time. He also dallied with a psychedelic side project, Spirits in the Sky, featuring Jane's Addiction guitarist Dave Navarro, Catherine drummer (and Wretzky's ex-husband) Kerry Brown, and Electric Prunes bassist Mark Tulin. (The latter replaced Reyes at Pumpkins shows in 2010.)

By the end of 2011, the self-defeating nature of this nuttiness appeared to have dawned on Corgan. With new bassist **Nicole Fiorentino** (formerly of Veruca Salt and Brody Dalle's Spinnerette) and drummer **Mike Byrne**, he laid the groundwork for *Oceania* (2012). "I want my work placed where it belongs…" he instructed *Rolling Stone*. "I want my just desserts. I don't want to be on the outside looking in." **BM**

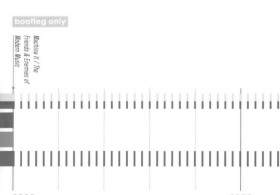

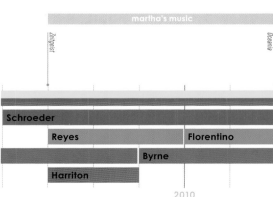

bootleg only

Machina II / The Friends & Enemies of Modern Music

Zeitgeist

martha's music

Oceania

Schroeder

Reyes

Florentino

Byrne

Harriton

2000

2005

2010

patti smith 1974–present

Patti Smith
b. December 30, 1946

Lenny Kaye
b. December 27, 1946

Richard Sohl
b. May 26, 1953
d. June 3, 1990

Ivan Kral
b. 1948

Jay Dee Daugherty
b. March 22, 1952

Bruce Brody
b. Unknown

Patti Smith broke the mold in two ways: she proved that an accomplished poet could forge a successful career in rock music, and that a young woman, a noted style icon, could front a major group without trading on her looks. The Patti Smith Group was an excellent hard rock/new wave band that managed to be both experimental and traditional.

The group began in New York City in 1971 when Smith (vocals) united with **Lenny Kaye** (guitar) to play (mainly poetry) gigs. With **Richard Sohl** (keyboards), they cut a 1974 single coupling a cover of "Hey Joe" with Smith's "Piss Factory." (Smith also wrote songs for boyfriend Allen Lanier's Blue Öyster Cult). With guitarist/bassist **Ivan Kral** and drummer **Jay Dee Daugherty**, the Patti Smith Group came into existence.

Their first album, *Horses* (1975), was a sensation and remains a classic. Smith was on the poetic cutting edge of New York's punk movement and the songs were superb: "Land," "Gloria," "Redondo Beach," and the marathon "Birdland" (Smith would often write one long track for each album). "The most exciting rock album of the year…" enthused the then seventeen-year-old Morrissey in a letter to *Sounds*. "Patti is intriguing without being boring." *Horses* hit U.S. No. 47.

The follow-up, *Radio Ethiopia* (1976), was greatly underrated. Smith said the songs were influenced by Detroit hard rockers the MC5 (whose guitarist **Fred "Sonic" Smith** she was to marry), and Aerosmith's producer Jack Douglas was brought in to beef up the group's muscle. "Ask the Angels" and "Pumping (My Heart)" in particular delivered the goods. However, the album was less commercially successful.

The group built a reputation for exciting shows, with Smith's unpredictability a particular draw. Sometimes she could be a little too unpredictable: in a Florida concert in January 1977, supporting Bob Seger, she fell offstage and broke her neck. During her recuperation, she had time to reassess her career.

Easter (1978) was her resurrection, taking her into the U.S. and U.K. Top Twenty. Its success was boosted by the exhilarating hit "Because the Night," cowritten with Bruce Springsteen. The rollicking "Till Victory," heartfelt "Privilege (Set Me Free)," and provocative "Rock N Roll Nigger" also rode the line between commercial appeal and artistic edge. **Bruce Brody** played keyboards on most of the record—produced by Jimmy Iovine—although Sohl and Allen Lanier also contributed (as did Television's Tom Verlaine).

year-by-year   ■ Vocals   ■ Guitar   ■ Bass   ■ Drums   ■ Keyboards

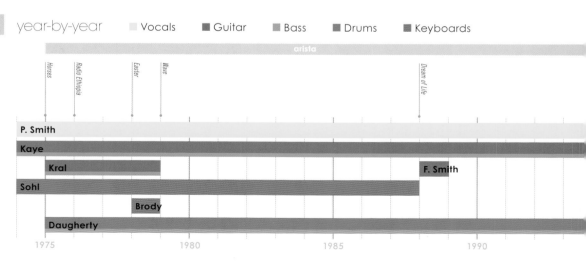

Fred "Sonic" Smith
b. September 13, 1949
d. November 4, 1994

Tony Shanahan
b. Unknown

Oliver Ray
b. Unknown

Jackson Smith
b. 1982

There was another critical reaction against *Wave* (1979), which now seems unjustified. The joyful opener "Frederick" (a paean to the man Smith was to marry), the euphoric "Dancing Barefoot" (later covered by U2) and the stirring "Broken Flag" set up the spoken title track, which seemed to announce her retirement. The album again reached the U.S. Top Twenty.

Nevertheless, the group played their last show in 1979 and Smith committed herself to marriage and motherhood, giving birth to son Jackson and daughter Jesse. Shortly after the latter was born, she made an unexpected return with *Dream of Life* (1988), another underrated album that included "People Have the Power" and "Where Duty Calls." The group reformed without Kaye and Kral; Fred Smith played guitar and shared production duties with Iovine. And then silence once more, as Smith received a series of shattering blows. Great friend and photographer Robert Mapplethorpe, whose label Mer had first released "Piss Factory," died in 1989, followed by keyboard player Sohl in 1990. Worse yet, her husband Fred and brother Todd died in 1994.

After intermittent live appearances in 1995, Bob Dylan invited her on tour at the end of the year.

Gone Again (1996) came to terms with her grief, in the title song, "Dead to the World," and "About a Boy," a tribute to the late Kurt Cobain. **Tony Shanahan** (bass) and **Oliver Ray** (guitar) joined founding stalwart Kaye.

The same personnel recorded *Peace and Noise* (1997), which also boasted a cameo by Michael Stipe (with whom she had sung on R.E.M.'s 1996 hit "E-bow the Letter"). After another tour with Dylan in 1998 came *Gung Ho* (2000), whose title track was an attack on militarism. The group was still together for the excellent *Trampin'* (2004) with its epic songs "Gandhi" and "Radio Baghdad," as well as "Mother Rose" and "Peaceable Kingdom," both hymns to Patti's mother, who had recently died. Guitarist Ray departed in 2006, to be replaced by **Jackson Smith**, Patti's son.

In 2007, the Patti Smith Group were inducted into the Rock and Roll Hall of Fame. Appropriately, *Twelve* (2007) saw Smith covering her favorite rock songs, from Neil Young to Nirvana. Two poetry and music performances with My Bloody Valentine's Kevin Shields were issued as *The Coral Sea* in 2008, a year that also saw the star-studded documentary *Patti Smith—Dream of Life*. An eleventh studio album, *Banga* (2012), confirms that her fire still burns. **MiH**

■ Other percussion

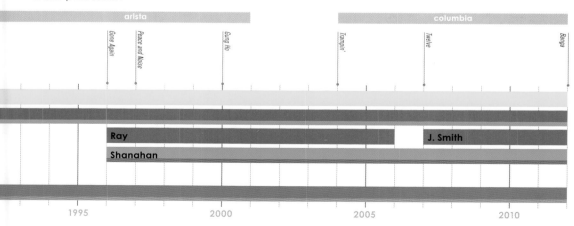

the smiths 1982–1987

Morrissey
b. May 22, 1959

Johnny Marr
b. October 31, 1963

Andy Rourke
b. January 17, 1964

Mike Joyce
b. June 1, 1963

Craig Gannon
b. July 30, 1966

Noel Gallagher of Oasis once observed that The Beatles, The Smiths, and the Sex Pistols said everything about British music that anyone ever needed to know. He was right: each group brought a unique world view that touched a nerve within millions of listeners. Perhaps unexpectedly in The Smiths' case, a large American fanbase was able to connect with their haunting lyrics, based on life in working-class England.

So the music is bleak? Make no mistake, **Stephen Morrissey**'s songs were often exactly that. Heartfelt, bittersweet, depressing, impotent, suicidal, self-indulgent—all these adjectives were liberally applied by both Morrissey's supporters and detractors during and after his group's relatively brief career. But far from being a mere miserablist, he injected his songs with a powerful, knowing sense of humor (in particular about matters sexual and cultural), often adding a dose of anger when it came to subjects that he felt strongly about, including vegetarianism and warfare.

His foil, musically and personally, was guitarist **Johnny Marr** (born John Maher), whose unearthly, textural playing made him a guitar hero and progenitor of the modern indie sound. Backed by bassist **Andy Rourke** (recruited after Dale Hibbert was briefly considered) and drummer **Mike Joyce** (who followed a fleeting stint by future Fall sticksman

Simon Wolstencroft)—Morrissey and Marr set about redefining pop, not from a cultural epicenter such as London but from depressed, rundown Manchester.

The Smiths, who chose their mundane name to contrast with ostentatious contemporary band names such as Spandau Ballet, began by writing songs about the agonies of teenage life. "Hand in Glove," "What Difference Does It Make?," and "Heaven Knows I'm Miserable Now" all addressed the troubles of the particular time and place in which they were written.

Although critics scoffed at Morrissey's unusual, intoned vocals, none could deny the plangent beauty of Marr's guitar playing nor the professionalism of the arrangements on *The Smiths*, their No. 2 debut on the U.K. chart in 1984. Controversy flared over the song "Suffer Little Children," which addressed the Moors Murders in the mid-sixties, in which five children were abducted, murdered, and buried near Manchester, a recent memory for many in the area. However, Morrissey weathered the storm and his band moved rapidly toward British domination.

Entering the chart at No. 1, *Meat Is Murder* (1985) was more assured, with Morrissey targeting both meat-eaters and brutal headmasters. A single, "That Joke Isn't Funny Anymore," fell outside the Top Forty, but has gone on to epitomize the band's career: even

year-by-year ■ Vocals ■ Guitar ■ Bass ■ Drums

rough trade

The Smiths

Morrissey

Marr

Rourke

Joyce

1982 1983 1984 1985

without a repeated riff or chorus to hang radio play on, or indeed a topic that would appeal to anyone other than the most miserable, lovelorn youth, "That Joke..." is now regarded as a classic. That could well be said about The Smiths themselves, as a group at least a decade ahead of its time, doomed to be more read about than listened to during its active career, and only fully appreciated several years after the members went their separate ways. (Although Robert Smith, of the equally morbid The Cure, remained unswayed, telling The Face in 1989: "I hate The Smiths and everything they've ever done... Morrissey is precious, effete, glib, out-of-touch and a million other vile things that I can't be bothered to list.")

Regret, a longing for security, and a wistfulness for times long gone pervaded The Queen is Dead (1986). "Frankly, Mr. Shankly" and "Some Girls Are Bigger Than Others" evoked a view of vintage kitchen-sink England; "There Is a Light That Never Goes Out" reached directly into the hormonal instability of every suffering listener who heard it; and "The Boy with the Thorn in His Side" revealed better than ever the trials of life at this stage of English history.

Although Strangeways, Here We Come (1987) was The Smiths' last studio album, there were no signs that inspiration had started to wane. Immortal songs such as "Girlfriend in a Coma" and "I Started Something I Couldn't Finish" still had the power to captivate the listener. But Morrissey and Marr—the Lennon and McCartney of the eighties—had begun to tire of each other, and a split came later the same year. The live Rank (1988) provided a strong epitaph, but no fewer than ten compilations gleaned from the four original albums, live tracks, and single B-sides have appeared in the quarter-century since then. However, Hatful of Hollow (1984) remains perhaps their strongest collection (including the epic "How Soon is Now?").

Morrissey's solo debut, Viva Hate, was the first of his three U.K. chart-topping albums, to be followed by Vauxhall and I (1994) and Ringleader of the Tormentors (2006). Marr's post-Smiths career tended to be more collaborative, with roles in a succession of new bands—The The, Electronic, Modest Mouse, The Cribs, and his own Johnny Marr and The Healers.

Few bands have carried the weight of a reunion expectation as constantly as The Smiths. The yearning among disciples for them to reunite is ongoing, but the freedom Morrissey and Marr have secured in solo projects means that this wish is likely to remain unfulfilled. "I would rather eat my own testicles than reform The Smiths," the singer told Uncut in 2006, "and that's saying something for a vegetarian." **JM**

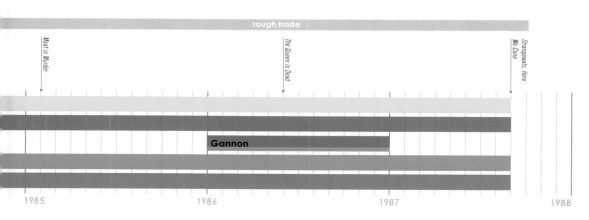

soda stereo 1982–2007

Gustavo Cerati
b. August 11, 1959

Zeta Bosio
b. October 1, 1959

Charly Alberti
b. March 27, 1963

One of the most popular Argentine rock acts of all time? It is an accurate assessment—underscored by the fact that this band broke concert attendance records, set by such international heavyweights as The Rolling Stones, in their homeland. Yet it is also one that ignores what the group accomplished on a much broader geographic plane.

A more appropriate verdict is to cite Soda Stereo as one of the most important acts in Latin rock. Few, if any, did more to break down the musical barriers that existed in Mexico, Central America, and South America, and unite listeners under one *rock en español* flag. Soda Stereo led the charge, freeing the ears of millions to enjoy a much wider spectrum of music. The band probably never intended to mount a crusade—they were never, lyrically speaking, an overtly political group—but nonetheless helped change things for the better. Just ask all the Latin rock acts that later emerged to take advantage of what is now one of the world's major music markets.

In comparison to most South American countries, Argentina had an impressive Latin rock résumé by the time vocalist-guitarist **Gustavo Cerati**, bassist **Zeta Bosio**, and drummer **Charly Alberti** formed Soda Stereo in 1982. The trio, however, could not have timed their emergence any better, hitting the scene just as the country was breaking free from seven years of military rule. A new democracy needed a new soundtrack, one in tune with the youth, and

Soda Stereo were happy to oblige. They leaped to the forefront of the Argentine rock renaissance with 1984's self-titled debut, a Police-like offering with elements of ska, New Wave, and post-punk rock. Yet Soda Stereo were not just selling a sound. The group upped the ante for all South American acts in terms of videos and other visual elements, which helped them seem larger than life to their fans.

The self-produced *Nada personal* (Spanish for "nothing personal") cemented the band's popularity in Argentina in 1985, but they had started looking beyond national borders to extend their fan base. That probably seemed like a pipedream in the mid-eighties, when South American groups rarely toured internationally and Latin rock was only popular in a handful of countries. In 1986, however, Soda Stereo embarked on a first major Latin American tour, which brought the band notice from Chile to Costa Rica.

It was 1986's *Signos* ("signs")—the first Argentine rock album issued on CD—that truly made Soda Stereo an international sensation. The album easily reached platinum status in Argentina but did just as well—or better—in such countries as Chile and Peru. The *Signos* tour—a blockbuster success that took Soda Stereo to Mexico for the first time—yielded 1987's live *Ruido Blanco* ("white noise").

In 1988 the band visited the U.S. to work with producer (and longtime David Bowie guitarist) Carlos Alomar on *Doble Vida* ("double life") in New

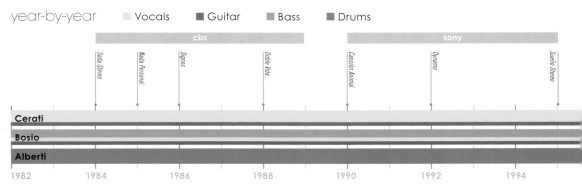

York. In doing so, they reportedly became the first Argentine rock act to record an album entirely in the U.S. Alomar contributed guitar (and even a rap), and embellished Soda Stereo's sound with brass by trumpeter Chris Botti and Tower of Power saxophonist Lenny Pickett. The tour that followed was a massive hit throughout Latin America—notably thirty shows attended by some 270,000 fans in Argentina.

After the 1989 EP *Languis* (three remixes from *Doble Vida*, and a new song, again produced by Alomar), the band returned to the U.S., this time to Miami, to record its fifth studio album, 1990's *Canción Animal* ("animal song"), which many hold to be their finest effort. The work featured a harder, guitar-oriented *rock en español* sound and produced many of the trio's best-known songs, including the hits "De música ligera" ("Of Light Music") and "Un millón de años luz" ("A Million Light Years").

Even MTV Europe was paying attention: an entire program devoted to Soda Stereo tied into the band's first tour of Spain in 1992. That was the year that brought Soda Stereo's sole misstep, *Dynamo*, which marked a turn toward electronic music and British indie styles; it sold comparatively poorly, although some fans regard it as the band's best.

Exhausted after a decade of sweating their way to stardom, the group took time out. Zeta Bosio produced new acts including Dangerous Summer and Aguirre, while Charly Alberti formed the band Plum with Deborah Corral. Meanwhile, Cerati's solo career, which had begun with *Colores Santos,* a 1992 collaboration with Daniel Melero, continued with 1993's *Amor Amarillo*—later to be followed by 1999's *Bocanada;* 2001's collection of group and solo songs *11 Episodios Sinfónicos;* the same year's ambient *+Bien;* 2002's *Siempre es Hoy;* 2006's *Ahí Vamos;* and 2009's *Fuerza Natural.*

The trio bounced back with 1995's *Sueño Stereo* ("stereo dream"), a prog-rock-inspired concept album that went platinum in Argentina within fifteen days. But this proved to be Soda Stereo's last studio offering (although 1996's *MTV Unplugged: Comfort y Música Para Volar* included four studio outtakes). In 1997 the group announced that "different personal and musical misunderstandings" had spurred them to call it quits—an announcement that made front-page news in Argentina. A final show, at the 74,000-capacity River Plate Stadium in Buenos Aires, was captured in *El Último Concierto* (1997).

However, Soda Stereo's popularity only grew in their absence. In 2007, to coincide with the hits set *Gira Me Verás Volver,* they reunited for a triumphant comeback, selling out the River Plate Stadium for an astounding six nights. "The time that has passed since the break-up of Soda Stereo is similar to when you split up with a girlfriend..." Cerati told *The Morning News.* "After several years, you reach a point where you might find her attractive again." **JiH**

soft machine 1966–1984

Robert Wyatt
b. January 28, 1945

Mike Ratledge
b. April 1943

Kevin Ayers
b. August 16, 1944

Daevid Allen
b. January 13, 1938

Andy Summers
b. December 31, 1942

Hugh Hopper
b. April 29, 1945
d. June 7, 2009

Phil Howard
b. Unknown

Elton Dean
b. October 28, 1945
d. February 8, 2006

When progressive rock was at its peak in the early seventies, bands such as Yes, Genesis, and Emerson, Lake & Palmer were among the biggest-selling album artists. Paving the way for the progressive era, the "Canterbury Scene" comprised an intermingling group of musicians whose work melded complex jazz-style improvisation with psychedelic rock, catchy pop melodies, and whimsical lyrics celebrating prosaic aspects of English life—drinking tea, for example. None of the bands enjoyed enormous commercial success, but surely influenced the cultural mood.

This particular tale began in 1964 with The Wilde Flowers, a teenage pop group from the city of Canterbury, southeast England. Variously featured were **Kevin Ayers** (vocals), **Robert Wyatt** (drums, vocals), **Daevid Allen** (guitar), **Hugh Hopper** (bass), Richard Sinclair (guitar, vocals), and Pye Hastings (guitar, vocals). The Wilde Flowers enjoyed no success in the conventional sense, and none of their music appeared on record at the time. And yet its members would go on to form the axes of The Soft Machine and Caravan, two of the most vital forces in English rock in the early seventies; Allen would found Anglo-French experimentalists Gong; and both Ayers and Wyatt would enjoy cult solo careers.

Formed during 1966 by Wyatt, Ayers, Allen, and **Mike Ratledge**—a young jazz pianist with a fondness for the avant-garde tinkling of Cecil Taylor—the band named themselves after a William Burroughs novel, *The Soft Machine*. Ratledge had earlier left Canterbury to study at Oxford University, and so had not joined his friends in The Wilde Flowers.

Playing what was essentially psychedelic rock, The Soft Machine made a mark on the same London underground circuit as the Syd Barrett-era Pink Floyd, at the UFO and Middle Earth clubs. (Wyatt, Hopper, and Ratledge graced Barrett's 1970 solo album *The Madcap Laughs*.) Ratledge's instrumental skill during unusually complex extended improvised sequences set "the Softs" apart from other bands of the time. After an appearance at the French *Nuits Psychédéliques* in the summer of 1967, this unusually cerebral bunch became darlings of the Parisian Left Bank. On their return, however, Australian passport holder Allen was refused entry to Britain. He remained in France (where he formed Gong), and was briefly replaced by future Police-man **Andy Summers**.

The Soft Machine were fortunate in sharing the same management as The Jimi Hendrix Experience, whom they supported on their first major U.S. tour

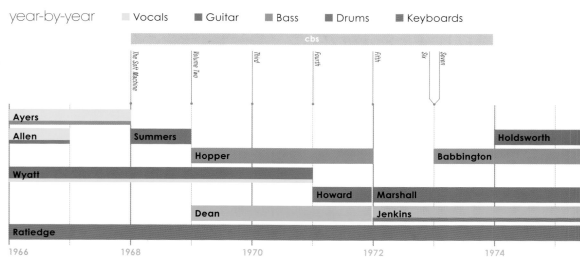

year-by-year   ■ Vocals   ■ Guitar   ■ Bass   ■ Drums   ■ Keyboards

John Marshall
b. August 28, 1941

Karl Jenkins
b. February 17, 1944

Roy Babbington
b. July 8, 1940

Allan Holdsworth
b. August 6, 1946

John Etheridge
b. January 12, 1948

Ric Sanders
b. December 8, 1952

Percy Jones
b. 1947

Steve Cook
b. Unknown

in 1968. While in New York, they recorded their eponymous debut album, a classic of its type that took psychedelic rock into uncharted complexity, at the same time ushering in progressive rock. The U.S. experience was turbulent for the band, however; after their final U.S. date, at the Hollywood Bowl, both Ayers and Wyatt left and The Soft Machine folded.

At the start of 1969, to fulfill a contractual obligation, Ratledge, Wyatt, and composer/bassist Hugh Hopper regrouped to record a second album. Inspired in part by Frank Zappa's *Absolutely Free*, the acclaimed *Volume Two* was very different to the band's debut, heralding a transition to entirely instrumental music. (Softs fan Bryan Ferry would later concede that "They were short of a melody or two.") This was even more marked on *Third* (1970), which appeared in the wake of Miles Davis's crossover milestone *Bitches Brew*. By now, Soft Machine (having lost the definite article) had augmented the core lineup with saxophone player **Elton Dean**, who can be heard to outstanding effect on *Third*'s centerpiece, the eighteen-minute suite "Slightly All the Time."

Following 1971's similarly styled *Fourth*, Wyatt was fired, possibly because of his poppier leanings. "We're English, so we never talked about it," he told

the *Daily Telegraph*. Wyatt formed Matching Mole, who enjoyed two years of critical acclaim before, at a party in June 1973, the drummer fell from an upstairs window. Paralyzed from the waist down and wheelchair-bound, Wyatt terminated Matching Mole and began a solo career of extraordinary breadth and distinction. He remains a much-loved cult icon.

Soft Machine albums became increasingly jazz-oriented. On *Six* (1973), Dean was replaced by reeds/keyboard player **Karl Jenkins**. On *Bundles* (1975), with Ratledge now the only remaining original member, the Soft Machine sound took a dramatic turn with the introduction of high-speed guitar wizard **Allan Holdsworth**. That was Ratledge's final appearance in the band; in the following decade he would concentrate on composition. Yet Soft Machine continued recording and performing until 1984, centered on Karl Jenkins, with other members drawn from the cream of the young U.K. jazz/fusion scene. Their final studio album, 1981's *Land of Cockayne*, featured six-string wizard Allan Holdworth alongside veteran Cream bassist Jack Bruce.

Because the band generally performed at its best in the concert environment, many live recordings have been issued since the group's demise. **TB**

■ Aerophones ■ Strings

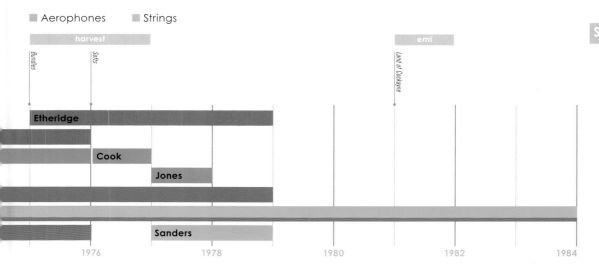

sonic youth 1981–present

Thurston Moore
b. July 25, 1958

Kim Gordon
b. April 28, 1953

Lee Ranaldo
b. February 3, 1956

Richard Edson
b. January 1, 1954

Anne DeMarinis
b. December 11, 1955

Jim Sclavunos
b. Unknown

Punk survivors, sound collagists, art rockers—whatever their form, Sonic Youth endure. "They have a dissonant gift," enthused unlikely fan Nancy Sinatra, "which is not unlike George Gershwin's." The group coalesced gradually through New York's No Wave scene of the late seventies as punk splintered into subgenres (or subgenres filtered into punk) and landed a mentor in ex-Theoretical Girls founder Glenn Branca. Singer and guitarist **Thurston Moore** arrived in New York in 1976 and met Branca's sidekick **Lee Ranaldo** on the circuit, but first formed a band with artist **Kim Gordon**.

After seeing Ranaldo playing guitar with Branca, Moore suggested he come on board. "I don't think Glenn was as interested in how great the Sex Pistols were as songwriters as I was," Moore recalled to *Garageland*. Nonetheless, Branca signed the fledgling band—completed by drummer **Richard Edson**—to his Neutral label and let them cut their teeth on an unofficial debut: *Sonic Youth*, recorded at New York's Radio City Music Hall at the end of 1981.

Initial releases saw a game of musical chairs as Edson departed (later to resurface as a parking garage attendant in the movie *Ferris Bueller's Day Off*). His replacement, drummer **Bob Bert**, was himself eased out in favor of **Jim Sclavunos**. Future Bad Seed Sclavunos remained in the seat for 1983's *Confusion*

Is Sex—a brutal onslaught that did not endear the band to a wider public but nailed the Sonic Youth template—before leaving and allowing Bert to return. This lineup remained secure for only one album, *Bad Moon Rising* (1985), but the set was notable for fully formed songs—notably "Death Valley '69," with fellow No Waver Lydia Lunch—and marked their first, tentative step into the global market.

Yet another switch of drummer saw the arrival of **Steve Shelley**, creating a lineup that would stay unchanged for fifteen years. This team tackled *EVOL* (1986) with a new enthusiasm for melody and structure and appeared to have found focus. But typically—with fIREHOSE's Mike Watt—Sonic Youth chose this moment to diversify, calling themselves Ciccone Youth and throwing themselves into filleting Madonna songs. The project even produced *The Whitey Album* (1988) but Sonic Youth had lost none of their momentum. In fact, with *Sister* (1987) and *Daydream Nation* (1988), they found themselves on a classic run.

The double album *Daydream Nation* gave them an opportunity to flex their creative muscles. It is no coincidence that the group were promptly snapped up by major label Geffen, who assigned them to their DGC imprint in time for 1990's *Goo*. Here Gordon took a more defined leading role and set about using it to

year-by-year ▢ Vocals ▪ Guitar ▪ Bass ▪ Drums ▪ Keyboards

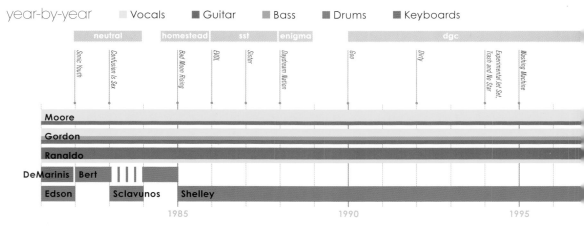

Bob Bert
b. Unknown

Steve Shelley
b. June 23, 1962

Jim O'Rourke
b. January 18, 1969

Mark Ibold
b. October 17, 1962

eulogize Karen Carpenter on "Tunic" and spar with Public Enemy's Chuck D on "Kool Thing," the latter even threatening to be some kind of pop hit.

Now regarded as godfathers of alternative rock, Moore encouraged Geffen to sign Nirvana, Gordon co-produced Hole's debut album, *Pretty on the Inside* (1991), and Sonic Youth toured with Neil Young. With the band's profile raised by association, *Dirty* (1992) and *Experimental Jet Set, Trash and No Star* (1994) were British Top Ten hits, and the latter secured their first Top Forty entry at home.

Live work was put on hold as Thurston and Moore, married in 1984, awaited the birth of their daughter. However, they were soon back, headlining 1995's Lollapalooza tour. ("All Sonic Youth-approved," noted Courtney Love of the supporting bill.) The band also appeared in the *Simpsons* episode "Homerpalooza," for which they performed the show's closing theme.

Thereafter, Sonic Youth complemented *Washing Machine* (1995), *A Thousand Leaves* (1998), and *NYC Ghosts & Flowers* (2000) with EP releases on their own SYR label. *SYR1, SYR2,* and so on gave free rein to their more outré urges while the regular albums—if not exactly accessible—offered less of a difficult ride.

At the turn of the century, producer and avant-garde soloist in his own right **Jim O'Rourke** became a permanent member of the band—taking up bass duties to allow Gordon to concentrate on vocals and bringing extra fizz to the setup with his synthesizers and exploratory sensibilities. The first fruits of the new dynamic were *Murray Street* (2002), which found a critical favor largely denied their late nineties albums. But after 2004's *Sonic Nurse,* O'Rourke left to pursue production duties and issue his own quixotic releases.

O'Rourke was succeeded on bass by **Mark Ibold**, formerly of Pavement. With Sonic Youth's more challenging efforts still being poured into their SYR imprint, *Rather Ripped* (2006) turned out to be concise and direct. "We've done so much stuff with noise music..." said Moore, "that it has become more experimental to *not* do that."

After the compilations *The Destroyed Room* (2006) and *Hits are for Squares* (2008), the band announced the end of their association with Geffen in late 2008. *The Eternal* (2009), issued on Matador, provided their best ever U.S. chart position, No. 18. Then, in 2011, Moore and Gordon revealed they had separated after twenty-seven years. "I just wish the best for Thurston and for Kim..." Ranaldo told gothamist.com. "The band is kind of secondary to that at the moment. [But] there will be Sonic Youth activity of one sort or another down the pike in one way or another." **MaH**

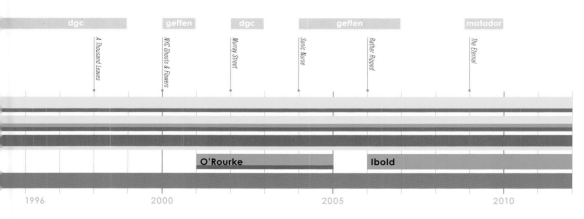

soulfly 1997–present

**Max
Cavalera**
b. August 4,
1969

**Jackson
Bandeira**
b. Unknown

**Marcelo
"Cello" Dias**
b. May 29, 1969

Roy Mayorga
b. April 6, 1970

Joe Nunez
b. June 18, 1975

Marc Rizzo
b. August 2,
1977

**Tony
Campos**
b. March 8, 1973

**David
Kinkade**
b. August 25,
1983

"The older I get, the more psycho I get," confirms **Max Cavalera** on soulfly.com. Cavalera was the heartbeat of Brazilian metal legend Sepultura for more than a decade, and one-half of thrash duo Nailbomb. He now juggles Soulfly with the Cavalera Conspiracy.

Cavalera was in a grim place in 1997. Still haunted by the death of his stepson Dana Wells, a tragedy that precipitated his departure from Sepultura, he sought healing in the thrash sound of Soulfly, with **Jackson Bandeira**, **Marcelo "Cello" Dias**, and **Roy Mayorga**.

Based in Phoenix, Arizona, the men embraced spirituality in their music—until the hatred and anger kicked in. Soulfly's self-titled debut of 1998 was loaded with unpronounceable titles and featured a handful of Cavalera's rock mates, notably Limp Bizkit's Fred Durst and DJ Lethal on the single "Bleed." Eight albums into their career, it remains their best-seller and only Top Twenty success on both sides of the Atlantic, hitting No. 16 in the U.K.

Primitive (2000) was described by U.K. music magazine *Melody Maker* as "an incendiary blend of nü metal reggae and Brazilian rhythms." It dined out on more guests, including co-producer and "Son Song" co-writer Sean Lennon. Following this was *3* (2002), which featured a silent track titled "9-11-01," a tribute to the victims of the attacks on the World Trade Center on that date. Nestled among the uncompromising ferocity, the track spoke volumes.

When *Prophecy* surfaced in 2004, Soulfly was much altered. Guitarist Mikey Doling had made way for **Marc Rizzo**, bass man Bobby Burns had replaced Dias, and **Joe Nunez** had usurped Mayorga on drums. Cavalera ("vocals, four-strings, soul, sitar, lyrical terrorism") was still primary songwriter and producer.

With much of the group's trademark spirituality now removed, the refreshingly experimental *Dark Ages* (2005) came complete with didgeridoo, Jamaican thumb piano, and other influences from the well-traveled Cavalera. Amid its aggressive lyrics, tributes were paid to the frontman's eight-month-old grandson, Moses, and slain buddy Darrell "Dimebag" Abbott, of Pantera and Damageplan fame. *Dark Ages* paved the way for *Conquer* (2008), with its "hardcore beatings, extreme thrash speeds, and many implements of weird sounds that have nothing to do with metal," according to metal-invader.com.

With Cavalera now a two-pronged heavy presence (*Conquer* surfaced just weeks after the Cavalera Conspiracy's debut set *Inflikted*), Soulfly buzzed on with *Omen* (2010). "Murder is this record's state of mind," asserted Cavalera, and the evidence lay like body parts: "Bloodbath & Beyond," "Off with Their Heads," and "Jeffrey Dahmer."

With new members **Tony Campos** and **David Kinkade**, Soulfly marked fifteen years at the top of their game with *Enslaved* (2012). **MW**

year-by-year　■ Vocals　■ Guitar　■ Bass　■ Drums　■ Other percussion

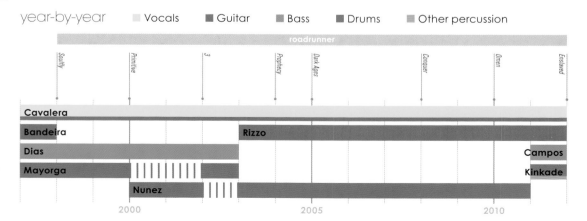

soundgarden 1984–present

Chris Cornell
b. July 20, 1964

Kim Thayil
b. September 4, 1960

Hiro Yamamoto
b. April 13, 1961

Scott Sundquist
b. Unknown

Matt Cameron
b. November 28, 1962

Jason Everman
b. August 16, 1967

Ben Shepherd
b. September 20, 1968

Soundgarden's seminal Seattle sound came to the fore in the nineties, but its foundations were laid back in 1984 when **Chris Cornell**, **Kim Thayil**, and **Hiro Yamamoto** named themselves after *A Sound Garden*, a metal pipe sculpture in the city's Sand Point Park that made "unearthly howling noises in the wind."

Three twenty-somethings became four after Soundgarden's debut gig, when **Scott Sundquist** was hired to allow vocalist and drummer Cornell to concentrate on front-man duties. Their first recordings, in 1986, appeared on a CZ Records compilation alongside **Matt Cameron**'s Skin Yard—and when Sundquist left, it was not long before Cornell, Thayil, and Yamamoto lured Cameron into the 'garden.

The group recorded two EPs—*Screaming Life* (1987) and *Fopp* (1988)—for the Sub Pop label (Nirvana's first home), before issuing their full-length debut, the Grammy-nominated *Ultramega OK* (1988) on another independent label, SST. But that year, Soundgarden signed with A&M, becoming the first grunge act to commit to a major label.

Louder than Love (1989) crept into the lower reaches of the U.S. chart and inspired Metallica's Kirk Hammett to write "Enter Sandman." But a supporting tour was thrown into turmoil when bassist Yamamoto returned to college, leading to the appointment of **Jason Everman** (ex-Nirvana), then **Ben Shepherd**, with whom Soundgarden recorded *Badmotorfinger* (1991).

Curiously described by A&M as "the work of a potent and remarkably versatile ensemble," *Badmotorfinger* was unfortunately released only two weeks after *Nevermind*. But the group were adopted by a mainstream metal audience, thanks in part to a tour with Guns N' Roses, who dubbed them "Frowngarden." The album promptly turned gold.

With their audience primed, the astounding *Superunknown* (1994) crashed into the U.S. chart at No. 1 and yielded the Grammy-winning singles "Black Hole Sun" and "Spoonman." Soundgarden had, noted Q magazine, "transformed themselves into as close as matters to great." But nonstop touring either side of *Down on the Upside* (1996)—including a second main-stage appearance at Lollapalooza in 1996—took its toll on the band and on Cornell's vocal cords. Soundgarden, the group declared, were "eaten up by the business" and disbanded "amicably" in 1997.

In 2010—after a twelve-year hiatus that enveloped Cornell's supergroup Audioslave, three solo albums, and a fabulous *James Bond* theme ("You Know My Name"), not to mention Cameron's tenure in Pearl Jam—Soundgarden were reunited at a secret homecoming gig in Seattle and that year's Lollapalooza. The archive-derived *Telephantasm* (2010) and *Live on I-5* (2011) whetted appetites for a much-delayed sixth studio album in late 2012, trailed by *The Avengers* movie theme, "Live to Rise." **MW**

S

year-by-year ▪ Vocals ▪ Guitar ▪ Bass ▪ Drums

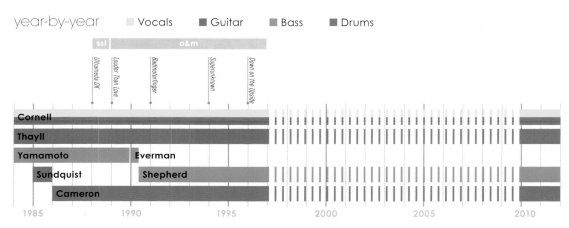

bruce springsteen 1971–present

Bruce Springsteen
b. September 23, 1949

Garry Tallent
b. October 27, 1949

Clarence Clemons
b. January 11, 1942
d. June 18, 2011

Danny Federici
b. January 23, 1950
d. April 17, 2008

Vini Lopez
b. January 22, 1949

David Sancious
b. November 30, 1953

Roy Bittan
b. July 2, 1949

Suki Lahav
b. 1951

"I saw rock and roll's future—and its name is **Bruce Springsteen**." Jon Landau made that remark in a 1974 concert review, but U.S. rock fans would not really catch on until the following year. *Born to Run*, released in 1975, made Springsteen a star. Yet despite its being an impeccable display of heartland rock, Springsteen was just getting started with *Born to Run*, embarking down a road that would one day lead to him being ranked with Bob Dylan and Elvis Presley as among the most important American rockers.

The man they now call "The Boss" was born in New Jersey, the son of a bus driver and a legal secretary. His first guitar, given to him by his mother at age thirteen, reportedly cost eighteen dollars. His working-class upbringing influenced much of the music he went on to make, as did the perceptions and culture of New Jersey. Indeed, no one would represent a single state to a greater extent, or provide its residents with more pride of state, than Springsteen. Even the title of his first album, *Greetings from Asbury Park, N.J.*, was a reference to the Jersey Shore nightlife capital.

That debut record, issued in 1973, failed to crack the U.S. Top 200 but earned stellar reviews. An exuberant piece of poetic bar-band rock, it featured Springsteen's believable vocals and thoughtful lyrics as well as killer musicianship—courtesy of saxophonist **Clarence Clemons** and other members of the as yet-unnamed E Street Band. One listen to the record and it was clear why Springsteen had caught the attention of the Columbia label after years spent honing his act.

While *Greetings* and its quickly released follow-up, *The Wild, the Innocent & the E Street Shuffle* (1973), failed to sell significant numbers initially, Springsteen won converts by touring, routinely staging three-hour-plus shows. His energetic on-stage prowess finally translated to the studio on 1975's *Born to Run*, which produced the anthemic title track and other future FM radio staples. Peaking at No. 3 in the United States, it kickstarted nearly two decades of incredible prosperity, when almost everything Springsteen touched went platinum in multiple countries. His next seven records all hit the Top Five in the U.S. charts, a

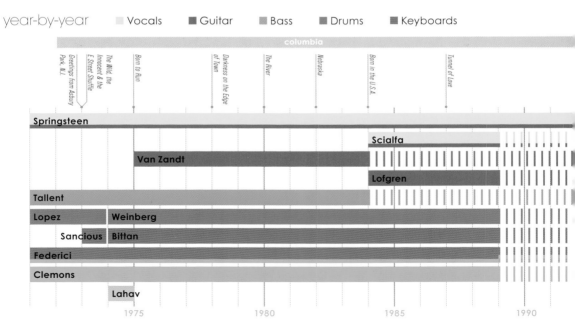

year-by-year   ■ Vocals   ■ Guitar   ■ Bass   ■ Drums   ■ Keyboards

10.8M
Born to Run
(1975)

27.2M
Born in the U.S.A
(1984)

6M
Tunnel of Love
(1987)

10.1M
Greatest Hits
(1995)

Max Weinberg
b. April 13, 1951

Steven Van Zandt
b. November 22, 1950

Nils Lofgren
b. June 21, 1951

Patti Scialfa
b. July 29, 1953

Soozie Tyrell
b. May 5,1957

Charles Giordano
b. 1954

streak interrupted by the remarkable *The Ghost of Tom Joad* (1995), which stopped just outside the Top Ten.

Springsteen mania even swept his first two albums to double-platinum sales in the United States. But his commercial peak was *Born in the U.S.A.* (1984), which ranks alongside Michael Jackson's *Thriller* and Prince's *Purple Rain* as one of the decade's signature albums. By then, Springsteen and the E Street Band were arguably the biggest band in the world. (Ironically, guitarist **Steven Van Zandt** chose this moment to jump ship, and was replaced by **Nils Lofgren**.)

But what is most impressive about Springsteen's peak period is not sales figures (fifteen million and counting for *Born in the U.S.A.* in the U.S. alone) but the ambitious nature of the music. He followed a restless muse, going from 1978's weighty *Darkness on the Edge of Town*, to the pop-rock of 1980's *The River*, to the somber acoustic feel of 1982's *Nebraska*, before finally emerging as the ultimate stadium-rock icon.

Similar diversity has colored Springsteen's recent work, which has ranged from the gorgeous, acoustic-based *Devils & Dust* (2005) to the uproarious roots and folk-rock of *We Shall Overcome: The Seeger Sessions* (2006) and *Live in Dublin* (2007).

Springsteen has also proven capable of adding more classics to his canon, such as 1994's "Streets of Philadelphia." ("It's all downhill from here," he quipped when collecting an Academy Award for the song.) And, in 2002, *The Rising*—a rousing yet thoughtful response to the tragedies of September 11, 2001—did much more than just hit No. 1 on the U.S. chart. It provided a degree of comfort to a nation that had gone through one of its darkest moments.

Springsteen's passionate following took *Devils & Dust* (2005), *Magic* (2007), *Working on a Dream* (2009), and *Wrecking Ball* (2012) to No. 1 on both sides of the Atlantic. All have yielded fresh classics, and he and the E Street Band remain a formidable live act (as illustrated by 2010's splendid *London Calling: Live in Hyde Park* DVD). Despite the deaths of Clemons and keyboard player **Danny Federici**, they returned to the road in 2012 as thrilling a proposition as ever. **JiH**

■ Aerophones   ■ Strings

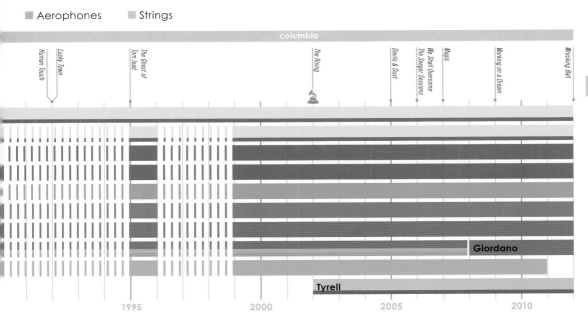

Greetings from Asbury Park, N.J. (1973)

Born to Run (1975)

Darkness on the Edge of Town (1978)

The River (1980)

Born in the U.S.A (1984)

Tunnel of Love (1987)

The Ghost of Tom Joad (1995)

The Rising (2002)

Devils & Dust (2005)

Wrecking Ball (2012)

Bruce Springsteen poses in New Jersey in 1973.

Springsteen with vocalist Ronnie Spector at the Bottom Line Club, New York, in 1975.

Clarence "The Big Man" **Clemons** with Springsteen in San Francisco, in 1978.

Springsteen and future *Friends* star Courteney Cox filming the video for "Dancing in the Dark" in June 1984.

Clemons, Springsteen, bassist **Garry Tallent,** and guitarist **Steven Van Zandt** ham it up at The Spectrum, Philadelphia, on December 8, 1980.

...nes Roy Orbison as an inductee to the Rock and Roll Hall of Fame, in New York, in 1987.

Springsteen's "Streets of Philadelphia" won four Grammys in 1995, including Song of the Year and Best Rock Song.

Performing with wife **Patti Scialfa** in the Netherlands in 2002.

With U2's Bono at the annual Rock and Roll Hall of Fame induction ceremony in 2005.

Springsteen and **Van Zandt** perform with the E Street Band at Madison Square Garden, New York, on April 9, 2012.

status quo 1967–present

Francis Rossi
b. May 29, 1949

Rick Parfitt
b. October 12, 1948

John Coghlan
b. September 19, 1946

Alan Lancaster
b. February 7, 1949

Roy Lynes
b. October 25, 1943

Pete Kircher
b. January 21, 1945

Francis Rossi and **Rick Parfitt** first united as front-men in the mid-sixties, little knowing that they would still be rocking nearly five decades later. Ironically, they were regarded as one-hit wonders after they found it hard to recapture the magic of their 1968 U.K. chart debut "Pictures of Matchstick Men," a classic piece of pop psychedelia (and their sole U.S. success). Instead, they adopted a twelve-bar blues formula, bending it to their skills as guitarists and songwriters. The result was a denim-clad brand of heads-down, no-nonsense boogie not dissimilar to that of America's Grand Funk Railroad. This was a working man's band.

The roots of Quo were in south London, where they came together in 1962 as the Spectres. Guitarist/singer Rossi was initially abetted by bassist **Alan Lancaster** and drummer **John Coghlan**. Parfitt was added in 1965 when his cabaret band the Highlights shared a stage with them at a holiday camp in Somerset. Until the summer of 1970, when he quit en route to a gig in Glasgow, organist **Roy Lynes** made up the numbers. Another crucial figure was road manager Bob Young, who has played harmonica onstage with the band and written many hits with Rossi.

After recording as the Spectres and Traffic Jam, the band adopted their Latin name. The chirpy "Ice in the Sun," made No. 8, one place below "Matchstick

Men," but extensive work in continental Europe saw Quo choose the rock road. The band made major steps toward stardom when they traded their frilly shirts for denim and the Pye label for Vertigo in 1972. Scruffy jeans and dirty trainers somehow projected a "men of the people" image that broke down the barrier between performers and their audience. And Vertigo—the launchpad for Black Sabbath, among others—had its finger on the pulse of seventies rock in a way that Pye (home of Petula Clark) clearly did not.

Quo based their success on a hard-rocking live act and shrewd pop sensibilities. Their singles sold as well as their albums—unusual for the time. A street-level image won them a sponsorship deal with Levi's jeans, and their sound became more sophisticated in the later seventies, when they started working with outside producers. Three U.K. chart-topping albums, Hello (1973), On the Level (1975), and Blue for You (1976), were impressive—Quo were happy to vary the formula just enough to attract outsiders while keeping hard-core fans satisfied. Punk made little impact.

"Down Down" became their one and only U.K. chart-topping single in 1975, but many more graced the Top Twenty. Highlights from the seventies included "Paper Plane" (1972), "Caroline" (1973), "Rain" (1976), and "Whatever You Want" (1979). "Rockin' All Over

year-by-year

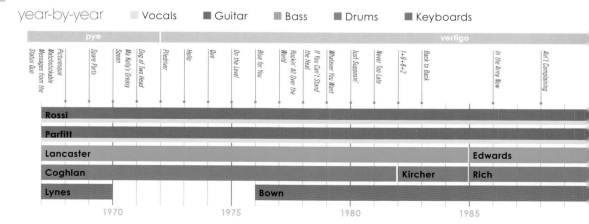

Vocals ■ Guitar ■ Bass ■ Drums ■ Keyboards

Jeff Rich
b. June 8, 1953

Andy Bown
b. March 27, 1946

Matt Letley
b. March 29, 1961

John "Rhino" Edwards
b. May 9, 1953

the World," a cover of a John Fogerty song released as a Quo single in 1977, was the opening number in 1985's Live Aid global jukebox when Quo kicked off proceedings at London's Wembley Stadium.

Keyboardist **Andy Bown** joined in 1976 (having appeared as a session player since 1973), splitting his time between Quo and Pink Floyd in 1980 and 1981. Otherwise, the lineup stayed solid until the eighties, when—in time for the U.K. chart-topping *1+9+8+2*— drum duties passed from Coghlan to **Pete Kircher**, then in 1985 to **Jeff Rich**. Bassist **John "Rhino" Edwards** joined in 1986 when the group reunited after a two-year break. Lancaster launched a legal action from his new home in Australia; it was settled out of court, and Rossi and Parfitt were able to carry on as Quo.

While their shows remained unremittingly boogie-based, the band endeavored to vary their sound in the eighties. "In the Army Now," an atypical ballad, reached U.K. No. 2 in 1986, and an album of the same name maintained an extraordinary run of seventeen U.K. gold records that stretched from 1973's *Hello* to 1988's *Ain't Complaining* (including 1977's thunderous *Live!* and 1980's hit-packed *12 Gold Bars*).

The nineties saw the band struggle, with them recording two whole albums of cover versions and taking on BBC Radio 1 in a battle to have their singles played (Quo were seen as passé by the broadcasting establishment). But 1996's *Don't Stop* narrowly missed the No. 1 slot, and 2002's *Heavy Traffic* was another strong seller. By 2009, when they played the Glastonbury festival, they were established as grand old men of British rock and a national institution. Indeed, a plaque was erected at the site of their first gig in Eltham, south London, back in 1967.

Parfitt has survived health scares that included quadruple bypass surgery and suspected throat cancer. With Rossi, he was awarded the Order of the British Empire in 2010 for services to music.

It is fitting that Quo's twenty-ninth studio album, *Quid Pro Quo* (2011), was first sold as an exclusive edition through a leading U.K. supermarket—the band remain as quintessentially British as fish and chips. To fans' delight, Lancaster and Coghlan reunited with Rossi and Parfitt in 2012 for the filming of a fiftieth anniversary documentary, *Hello Quo*.

"Quo is never going to be the biggest band in the world," Parfitt conceded to *Classic Rock* in 1999, "but the level of success we've had is enough to fulfil everything that I could have wanted. I don't think we were cut out to be a U2 or a Rolling Stones. We're Quo. We are what we are. We've had success everywhere in the world. What more can you want?" **MHe**

S

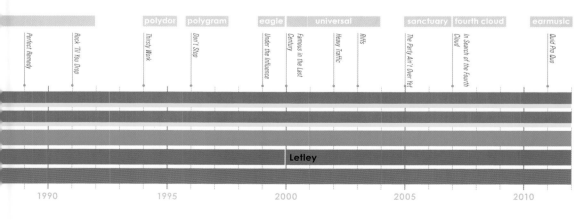

polydor | polygram | eagle | universal | sanctuary | fourth cloud | earmusic

Perfect Remedy | *Rock 'Til You Drop* | *Thirsty Work* | *Don't Stop* | *Under the Influence* | *Famous in the Last Century* | *Heavy Traffic* | *Riffs* | *The Party Ain't Over Yet* | *In Search of the Fourth Cloud* | *Quid Pro Quo*

Letley

1990　　1995　　2000　　2005　　2010

steely dan 1972–present

Donald Fagen
b. January 10, 1948

Walter Becker
b. February 20, 1950

Denny Dias
b. December 1, 1946

David Palmer
b. Unknown

Jeff "Skunk" Baxter
b. December 13, 1948

Jim Hodder
b. December 17, 1947
d. June 6, 1990

Peerless pimps of the coolest studio band of the early seventies, **Donald Fagen** and **Walter Becker** were always happiest writing their sophisticated songs, scoring their jazz-fusiony rhythm charts, and twiddling their production knobs for sonic perfection. If the band could not quite lay down the sound they were looking for, the duo simply hired sessionmen to do it.

School friends from Bard, upstate New York, the young songwriters knocked on New York's Brill Building door, wrote a song for Barbra Streisand, and also one for a movie soundtrack (*You Gotta Walk It Like You Talk It...*), recorded with later Dan member **Denny Dias** on guitar. It was produced by Kenny Vance, who got them a few gigs backing his harmony vocal group Jay and The Americans. Through Vance they met producer Gary Katz, who brought them to ABC/Dunhill Records in Los Angeles to write.

Tucked away in a side office, they rehearsed their own new songs for a debut album with Dias, **Jeff "Skunk" Baxter** (guitar), and **Jim Hodder** (drums). Although Fagen could sing, he preferred to bring in

"Daltreyesque" vocalist **David Palmer** to add a pop veneer to some of the songs. Session guitarist Elliot Randall was also hired to deliver the blistering guitar intro and solo for the upbeat pop of "Reelin' in the Years" (which Jimmy Page once said was his favorite). They had the songs, now they needed a band name; they chose that of a squirting dildo from William Burroughs' junkie novel *Naked Lunch*.

Can't Buy a Thrill yielded two surprise hits: the seductive, Latin-tinged vibe "Do It Again" (U.S. No.6) and "Reelin' in the Years" (U.S. No.11), so the record label pushed the band out on the road to promote it, and into the studio for 1973's *Countdown to Ecstasy*. Fagen took the lead on all the vocals (Palmer quit) and the band performed an assured set of songs including "Show Biz Kids," enhanced by powerful slide guitar from Rick Derringer. This song also demonstrated the duo's tireless pursuit of studio sound perfection: having decided that Hodder's percussive pulse was not sufficiently metronomic, they ran thirty feet of tape loop via recording equipment to outside

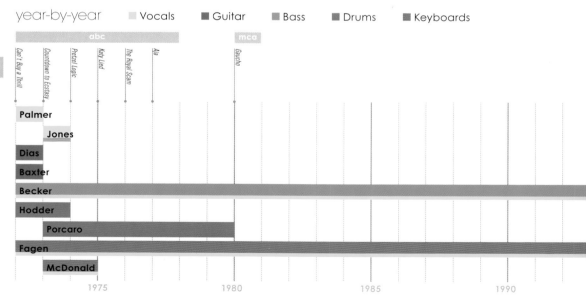

year-by-year   ■ Vocals   ■ Guitar   ■ Bass   ■ Drums   ■ Keyboards

Jeff Porcaro
b. April 1, 1954
d. August 5, 1992

Michael McDonald
b. February 12, 1952

Royce Jones
b. December 15, 1954

the control room and back to achieve the hypnotic effect that drives the song so superbly.

A single from 1974's *Pretzel Logic,* "Rikki Don't Lose That Number," was their biggest chart success—U.S. No. 4. The band's jazz influences were now out in the open: the song's riff was very reminiscent of a Horace Silver piano number, while other tunes included a quirky like-for-like rendition of Duke Ellington's "East St. Louis Toodle-oo," with Becker mimicking a growling trumpet on his wah-wah guitar.

By *Katy Lied* (1975), Becker and Fagen, whose live lineup was augmented by **Jeff Porcaro** on drums and **Michael McDonald** on backing vocals and keyboards, were tired of touring. When they opted to become a purely studio-based unit, Baxter and Hodder quit, followed later by McDonald (to The Doobie Brothers).

The Royal Scam (1976) was the definitive Steely Dan guitar album, driven by Larry Carlton's fluid jazz-blues playing. It was also the only one on which the duo shared songwriting credits—thanks to Paul Griffin's organ work on "The Fez." But it was *Aja* (1977)

that confirmed Steely Dan's shimmering production credentials. It became a definitive laid-back FM-jazz fusion crossover, with Joe Sample, Wayne Shorter, and Tom Scott adding a cool L.A. vibe.

Gaucho (1980) acquired a *Spinal Tap* quality, what with contractual difficulties, Becker being hit by a car, and a version of "The Second Arrangement" being accidentally wiped. It was a recording nightmare, epitomized by fifty-five takes to sign off the mix for a fifty-second fade out on "Babylon Sisters."

Such perfectionism could not be sustained, and the duo split in 1981 to concentrate on solo projects, of which the best-loved is Fagen's *The Nightfly* (1982). When Becker produced his partner's *Kamakiriad* (1993), a transatlantic Top Ten success, fans clamored for a Dan reunion. After a well-received return to the road (hence 1995's *Alive in America*), the pair revived the group name for *Two Against Nature* (2000) with a new backing band. It won four Grammies including Album of the Year, and set the scene for an ongoing series of successful world tours. **JaH**

■ Other percussion

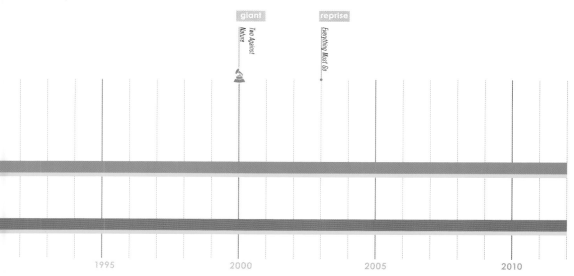

giant

Two Against Nature

reprise

Everything Must Go

1995   2000   2005   2010

steppenwolf 1967–present

John Kay
b. April 12, 1944

Michael Monarch
b. July 5, 1950

Rushton Moreve
b. November 6, 1948
d. July 1, 1981

Goldy McJohn
b. May 2, 1945

Jerry Edmonton
b. Oct 24, 1946
d. November 28, 1993

Nick St. Nicholas
b. September 28, 1943

Larry Byrom
b. December 27, 1948

George Biondo
b. September 3, 1945

The Canadian-American Steppenwolf enjoyed huge success in the late sixties, partly because two great songs from their first album—"The Pusher" and "Born to be Wild"—graced the road movie *Easy Rider* (1969).

John Kay (vocals), **Goldy McJohn** (keyboards), and **Jerry Edmonton** (drums)—then in a Toronto-based group, called Sparrow, on the cusp of breaking through—recruited **Michael Monarch** (guitar) when they moved to California. The group split but reconstituted itself as Steppenwolf—the title of Herman Hesse's novel allegedly suggested by producer Gabriel Mekler—with the addition of **Rushton Moreve** in 1967. Success came instantly.

Steppenwolf (1968) soared to U.S. No. 8, on the back of the bikers' anthem "Born to Be Wild" (written by Edmonton's brother, Dennis), which accelerated to No. 2. *The Second* (also 1968) rose to No. 3 on the *Billboard* chart and contained another smash, "Magic Carpet Ride." Steppenwolf were flying high.

However, internal frictions were tearing the group apart. Moreve left (he later died in a 1981 bike accident) and was replaced by Rob Black, briefly, then **Nick St. Nicholas**, another ex-Sparrow. **Larry Byrom** (guitar) replaced Monarch.

Meanwhile, *At Your Birthday Party* (1969) went Top Ten, and the ambitiously political *Monster* (1969) and *Steppenwolf 7* (1970) kept them in the Top Twenty. The latter was indeed their seventh album, their discography being bolstered by two live albums, 1968's *Early Steppenwolf* and 1970's *Steppenwolf Live.*

By 1971, bassist **George Biondo** and guitarist Kent Henry had joined the group, but the next offering, *For Ladies Only*, fell short of their customary sales. One compilation album later, Steppenwolf broke up in 1972, only to re-form in 1974, now with Bobby Cochran, Eddie's nephew, on guitar. McJohn also quit; Andy Chapin, then Wayne Cook, took over keyboard duties. They rapidly recorded three albums: *Slow Flux* (1974), *Hour of the Wolf* (1975), and *Skullduggery* (1976), before splintering in 1976. Various members, each purporting to represent the real Steppenwolf, toured concurrently in different lineups until 1980.

Negotiations determined Kay's right to the name, leading to *Wolftracks* (1982), *Paradox* (1984), *Rock & Roll Rebels/Feed the Fire* (1987/1996), and *Rise & Shine* (1990). Kay tours with Michael Wilk (keyboards), Gary Link (bass), Danny Johnson (guitar), and Ron Hurst (drums) in a still compelling live act. **MiH**

year-by-year ■ Vocals ■ Guitar ■ Bass ■ Drums ■ Keyboards ■ Aerophones

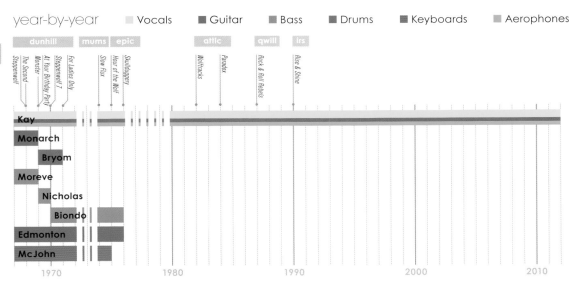

stereophonics 1992–present

Kelly Jones
b. June 3, 1974

Adam Zindani
b. March 5, 1972

Richard Jones
b. May 23, 1974

Javier Weyler
b. July 3, 1975

Stuart Cable
b. May 19, 1970
d. June 7, 2010

Emerging on the heels of Britpop but with a more rock-oriented approach, power trio Stereophonics became Wales's most successful act since the Manic Street Preachers. Like the Manics, **Kelly Jones** (vocals, guitar), **Richard Jones** (no relation; bass), and **Stuart Cable** (drums) created songs that gripped listeners with their tales of the joys and anguish of modern life. Solid riffs and Kelly Jones's hoarse, Rod Stewart-indebted vocals distinguished their delivery.

Word Gets Around (1997), and their first U.K. chart-topper, Performance and Cocktails (1999), established them as a force to be reckoned with, thanks to their defiantly anthemic choruses and infectious melodies. The hits—"Local Boy in the Photograph," "A Thousand Trees," "The Bartender and the Thief," and "Pick a Part That's New" among them—pulsated with energy and a full-sized, polished production that made fans and media all the more curious about the group's roots in the tiny valley village of Cwmaman. With groups such as Catatonia emerging at the same time, the new Welsh rock scene became a talking point and Stereophonics benefited from huge press exposure.

By Just Enough Education to Perform (2001), the group had diversified its approach to an extent, incorporating balladry and acoustic instrumentation and scoring a major hit with a cover of Mike D'Abo's "Handbags and Gladrags." As with so many groups, however, the initial impetus became a little diffused, and fans reacted uncertainly to the sacking of Cable in 2003 for spending too much time away from the group in his other role as a media personality. But after Black Crowes drummer Steve Gorman filled in, Cable's permanent replacement, **Javier Weyler**, gave renewed energy to the band. Stereophonics scored a U.K. No. 1 with "Dakota" from 2005's Language. Sex. Violence. Other? (the song also gave them a second moderate U.S. hit, after 2001's "Have a Nice Day"). Guitarist **Adam Zindani** was recruited in 2008 to enhance the group's live sound.

Although the hysteria that once surrounded them has receded, Jones and company have reached a comfortable commercial plateau. After 2006's Live from Dakota, 2007's Pull the Pin gave them a fifth U.K. No. 1 album, and 2008's Decade in the Sun: The Best of Stereophonics (2008) went double platinum. Fans' grief at Cable's alcohol-related death in 2010 was both genuine and widespread.

The band now have two decades of experience behind them and, while their career has waxed and waned over that time, they still command a considerable live following. Keep Calm and Carry On (2009) kept their sales at a gold-selling level, while an ambitious concept album and accompanying movie were mooted for late 2012. "The complication at the minute," Kelly Jones told WalesOnline, "is a way of releasing all this music in bite-size chunks so people understand it, appreciate it, so it's not too far apart and not too close together." In the meantime, the band were chosen to represent Wales at a London show to mark the start of the 2012 Olympics. **JM**

S

year-by-year ■ Vocals ■ Guitar ■ Bass ■ Drums

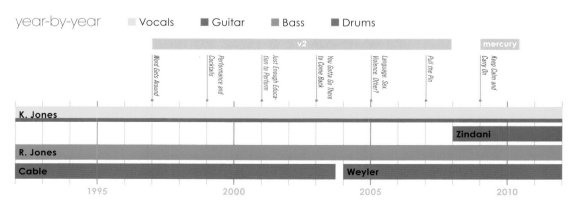

the stone roses 1983–present

Ian Brown
b. February 20, 1963

John Squire
b. November 24, 1962

Pete Garner
b. Unknown

Simon Wolstencroft
b. Unknown

Reni
b. April 10, 1964

Mani
b. November 16, 1962

With only two albums to their name, The Stone Roses enjoy a near mythic reputation for their transcendent flowering and huge impact on groups such as Oasis.

Ian Brown (vocals), **John Squire** (guitar), Andy Couzens (rhythm guitar), **Pete Garner** (bass), and **Simon Wolstencroft** (drums) formally became The Stone Roses in the Manchester area in 1983, although they had played together around Altrincham (a town in Cheshire, near Manchester) since 1980.

The Stone Roses always took their time, and their path to success was checkered. Wolstencroft departed in 1984, to be replaced by Alan "**Reni**" Wren on drums. Couzens quit in 1986 and was not replaced. When Garner left in 1987, Rob Hampson, then Gary "**Mani**" Mounfield, took over on bass. They recorded but shelved an album they were unhappy with, making the singles "Sally Cinnamon" (1987) and "Elephant Stone" (1988) their first real calling cards.

The group's debut album, *The Stone Roses*, came out in 1989 to immediate U.K. critical acclaim. From the magnificent chutzpah of opener "I Wanna Be Adored," to the closing "I Am the Resurrection" (Brown and Squire were big on Messianic imagery), it was a statement of intent. The fragile beauty of the singles "She Bangs the Drums," "Made of Stone," and "Waterfall" showed what the group could achieve.

With the Happy Mondays bringing up the rear, the Roses spearheaded the "Madchester" movement, and the success of the single "Fools Gold" meant they entered 1990 with a seemingly bright future. But the group became locked in legal wrangles over a change of record company, then took an unconscionable time to record their second album. "One Love," a 1990 single, was the last anyone heard for four years. Their triumphant live shows ceased.

Second Coming finally emerged in 1994, but was not what fans were expecting. Years of seclusion had made their sound rougher and more guitar-heavy. "Love Spreads," "Ten Storey Love Song," and "Begging You" were all U.K. hits, but their moment had passed.

When their shows flopped, a round of changes ensued. Reni left and Robbie Maddix deputized on drums, while Nigel Ipinson-Fleming (keyboards) varied the sound. When Squire left to form The Seahorses, the writing was on the wall. Although Aziz Ibrahim joined on guitar, the group split in late 1996. Brown's solo career proved successful and Mani joined Primal Scream, while The Seahorses broke up in 1999.

In 2011, oft-mooted rumors and long-held dreams bore fruit: the classic lineup of Brown, Squire, Reni, and Mani reunited for instantly sold-out stadium shows and a slew of headline slots at festivals in 2012. **MiH**

year-by-year   ▪ Vocals   ▪ Guitar   ▪ Bass   ▪ Drums

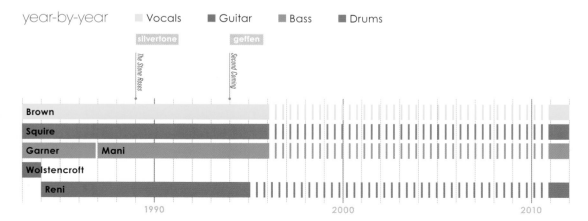

stone temple pilots 1986–present

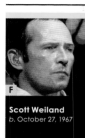

Scott Weiland
b. October 27, 1967

Dean DeLeo
b. August 23, 1961

Robert DeLeo
b. February 2, 1966

Eric Kretz
b. June 7, 1966

Stone Temple Pilots were viewed as bandwagon-jumpers when they threw their weight behind the Seattle sound's mainstream success in 1992. Yet the group—hailing from San Diego, some 1,255 miles down the coast from grunge's heartland—predated Nirvana and Pearl Jam, and their diverse songs set them apart from their angst-ridden peers.

The Pilots took off in 1986 when singer **Scott Weiland** and bassist **Robert DeLeo** met at a Long Beach concert by hardcore punks Black Flag. When the conversation turned to women, they discovered they were dating the same one—but, rather than fighting over her affections, they dumped the Texas-bound beauty, moved into her San Diego apartment, hired drummer **Eric Kretz** and Robert's guitar-playing older brother **Dean**, and started jamming.

Their 1992 debut, *Core*, afforded them a U.S. No. 3 hit, a Grammy for Best Hard Rock Performance ("Plush"), and simultaneous nods for Best and Worst New Band from *Rolling Stone*'s readers and critics, respectively. The only Pilots album Weiland wrote sober (according to a *Rolling Stone* interview in 2007), *Core* was certified eight times platinum in 2001.

The group dodged the sophomore slump with *Purple* (1994). "Interstate Love Song" and "Vaseline" followed "Plush" to No. 1 on the U.S. Mainstream Rock Tracks listing, and the album enjoyed three chart-topping weeks en route to an eventual six million sales.

In 1995, however, Weiland pushed the self-destruct button with heroin and crack cocaine, resulting in numerous convictions, probation violations, stints in rehab, and ultimately jail. Despite this, he contributed to *Tiny Music… Songs from the Vatican Gift Shop* (1996), a sixties-influenced set that preserved their platinum sales. However, most of an accompanying tour was canceled due to Weiland's problems.

When disbandment inevitably occurred in 1997, Kretz and the DeLeo brothers formed Talk Show, while Weiland, against all the odds, released a solo album, *12 Bar Blues*. When both bombed, the Pilots reformed, returning to their hard rock roots on *No. 4* (1999).

With tensions simmering, the bossa nova-infused *Shangri-La Dee Da* (2001) marked the beginning of the end. In 2003 Weiland joined three-fifths of Guns N' Roses in Velvet Revolver, making the U.S. No. 1 *Contraband* (2004) and *Libertad* (2007). Meanwhile, the DeLeos formed Army of Anyone; Kretz, probably wisely, kept a low profile in his L.A. recording studio.

In 2008, a new chapter began. Mellowed by fatherhood and with all four founders still upright, they embarked on a North American tour as a prelude to their self-titled sixth studio album. Legal wrangles with Atlantic aside, the Pilots were flying high again and celebrating the twentieth anniversary of *Core* in 2012. As the biography on their website observes, "Everything happens for a reason." **MW**

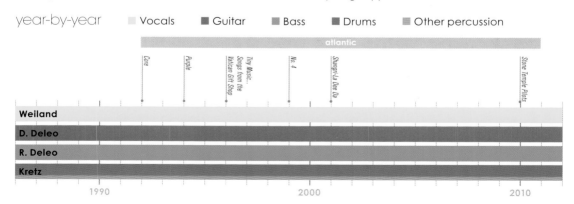

year-by-year   Vocals   ■ Guitar   ■ Bass   ■ Drums   ■ Other percussion

atlantic

Core *Purple* *Tiny Music… Songs from the Vatican Gift Shop* *No. 4* *Shangri-La Dee Da* *Stone Temple Pilots*

Weiland
D. Deleo
R. Deleo
Kretz

1990   2000   2010

the stranglers 1974–present

Jean-Jacques Burnel
b. February 21, 1952

Jet Black
b. August 26, 1938

Dave Greenfield
b. March 29, 1949

Baz Warne
b. March 25, 1964

Hugh Cornwell
b. August 28, 1949

Hans Wärmling
b. July 22, 1943
d. October 12,1995

Even if they did drive to early shows in an ice-cream van, there was a definite fear factor at work where The Stranglers were concerned. Punk, the movement with which they were closely associated, prized youth above most other qualities, but three of the quartet—singer/guitarist **Hugh Cornwell**, keyboardist **Dave Greenfield**, and drummer **Jet Black**—were already too old to be "bad boys" in 1977 (Black was three years older than even Charlie Watts). "Mad men" was closer to the mark. Combative bassist **Jean-Jacques Burnel**—an accomplished martial artist—completed a lineup that often had journalists ducking for cover: kidnap, abandonment in the desert, and, on one occasion, being taped to the Eiffel Tower were regarded as amusing distractions. "We're clean wholesome boys…" said Burnel. "Just like the boys next door—if you happen to live next door to a morgue."

Were they punk or not? Their background as The Guildford Stranglers suggests not. Churning out soft rock covers on the club circuit was not the coolest of credentials, and it left them with few friends on either side of the music spectrum. "We missed that pub rock thing—we were too young and not good enough to be a part of it," said Cornwell. "When the punk thing happened, we were too good and too old… We were a class of one. But it didn't stop our success."

When that success came, it was considerable: three albums in just fourteen months lodged in the U.K. Top Five. The band avoided many of the obligatory names—New York Dolls, MC5, The Stooges—dropped by punk groups with whom they were misleadingly grouped. On *Rattus Norvegicus* and *No More Heroes* (both 1977), and *Black and White* (1978), Greenfield's keyboards (replacing the guitar of the departed **Hans Wärmling**) made The Doors a more obvious musical touchstone. The requisite garage aesthetic came from Black, who sounded to one critic as though "he was hammering the roof on a garden shed."

The songs were often dark vignettes from society's underbelly. The likes of "London Lady," "Hanging Around," and "I Feel Like a Wog," featured lyrics that, contrarily, combined acute intelligence with attitudes (especially toward women) that might have embarrassed a bad hair-metal outfit. The Stranglers were a hit-singles machine, too. The loping "Peaches," the driving "Something Better Change," and the vicious "No More Heroes" all crashed the U.K. Top Ten, with "Five Minutes" and "Nice 'n' Sleazy" close behind. One of the covers that survived from the cull after the group's days as The Guildford Stranglers became an extraordinary reading of Bacharach and David's "Walk on By" that just missed the Top Twenty.

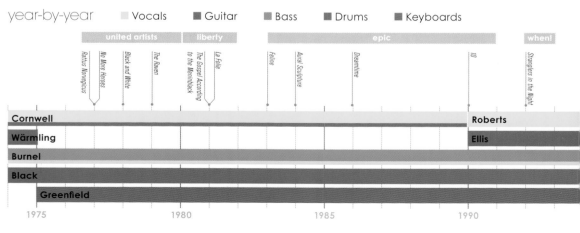

Paul Roberts
b. December 31, 1959

John Ellis
b. June 1, 1952

A group that relished baiting pretty much everyone at every available opportunity could hardly avoid controversy. There were the strippers hired to appear at a 1978 show in south London, Cornwell's three-month jail term for drugs possession in 1980, and a group arrest after a show in Nice, France, later that year (for allegedly inciting a riot). In the studio, the band were moving further away from punk. The change that was noticeable on a fourth smash, *The Raven* (1979), was unmistakeable by the time of *The Gospel According to the Meninblack* (1981), a concept album. The latter, however, won few friends. "Unanimous slagging," recalled Burnel to *Select* magazine. "Even the fans said it was fucking horrible."

Their renaissance had unlikely origins. "I've listened to everything," said Cornwell. "When I was fifteen, I was really getting off on Mose Allison." "Golden Brown," from *La Folie* (1981), duly betrayed jazz influences. Tongue firmly in cheek, Cornwell introduced the band's biggest hit (U.K. No. 2) at the Reading festival as a "heavy metal classic." In reality, it was a hazy, waltz-like paean to heroin.

The Stranglers always sounded less abrasive than most contemporaries. After *Feline* (1983), those edges were smoothed away further on *Aural Sculpture* (1984) and *Dreamtime* (1986), with funk flirtations and bursts of brass. However, although those albums yielded the sublime hits "Skin Deep" and "Always the Sun," it took a couple of sixties covers to revive real interest: "All Day and All of the Night," originally by The Kinks, and "96 Tears," by ? and the Mysterians.

The latter featured on *10* (1990), which proved a swansong for Cornwell, who departed after a gig in August 1990. The rest of the group moved quickly to fill a huge gap left by their first major lineup change in a decade and a half. Duties were split, with **John Ellis**—formerly of The Vibrators and a touring presence with The Stranglers dating back to Cornwell's stint in prison—taking on the guitar and **Paul Roberts** on vocals. As a five-piece, the band recorded four albums, with *Stranglers in the Night* (1993), *About Time* (1995), *Written in Red* (1997), and *Coup de Grace* (1998) all seeming to confirm Cornwell's parting shot that "no chances were being taken any more."

That was accurate until a confounding return to form on the band's thirtieth anniversary with *Norfolk Coast* (2004). More chopping and changing had taken place, with former Toy Doll **Baz Warne** replacing Ellis. And with *Suite XVI* (2006) and *Giants* (2012)— despite being down to a lean four-piece again (Roberts had departed)—The Stranglers showed that not all the life had been squeezed out of them yet. **CB**

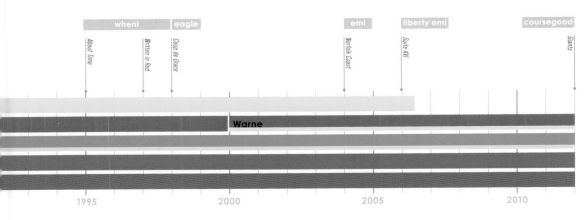

the strokes 1999–present

Julian Casablancas
b. August 23, 1978

Nick Valensi
b. January 16, 1981

Albert Hammond, Jr.
b. April 9, 1980

Nikolai Fraiture
b. November 13, 1978

Fabrizio Moretti
b. June 2, 1980

Singer-songwriter **Julian Casablancas**, guitarist **Nick Valensi**, and drummer **Fabrizio Moretti** met at the exclusive Dwight School in Manhattan. At the age of thirteen, Casablancas had been sent to the L'Institut le Rosey, a boarding school in Switzerland, where he met guitarist **Albert Hammond, Jr.** Bassist **Nikolai Fraiture** completed the lineup. Named The Strokes in 1999, the group spent most of their first year writing material and rehearsing before developing a word-of-mouth reputation as an incendiary live act.

In January 2001, London's Rough Trade label put out their three-song demo as *The Modern Age EP.* In March, The Strokes moved to Manhattan's East Village to cut their first album with producer Gordon Raphael. Released that summer, *Is This It* received tumultuous press acclaim and peaked at No. 33 in the U.S. (To the glee of metal fans, they were denied a widely predicted U.K. No. 1 by Slipknot's 2001 set *Iowa*.)

Is This It inspired, as *Rolling Stone* put it, a "ragged revolt" against DJs and electronic dance music as teenagers once again donned skinny jeans and formed noisy guitar bands. In the wake of The Strokes, acts such as The Hives, The Libertines, Arctic Monkeys, Kings of Leon, and The Vines hit the charts. (Alt-rock troubadour Ryan Adams recorded a sadly unreleased version of the entire album on banjo and pump organ while, he told *Q*, "fucked up on painkillers.")

The Strokes spent much of the following year touring, enjoying enormous festival successes in Europe and opening for The Rolling Stones on two dates of the latter's *Licks* world tour in 2002.

In March 2003, The Strokes were ready to face the tricky task of recording a worthy follow-up. After a false start with Radiohead producer Nigel Godrich, they returned to Raphael and emerged three months later with *Room on Fire*. Without radically altering a winning formula, the album—which hit Top Tens around the world—showed a slightly more refined late-seventies new-wave sound, typified by the hit "12:51," built around Valensi's synth-like guitar riff.

At the end of 2005, The Strokes returned to the studio to take a slightly different direction on *First Impressions of Earth*. More polished and overtly commercial, it received mixed reviews but became the group's first album to top the U.K. chart. A lengthy world tour preceded a protracted hiatus, during which each member worked on solo projects.

When they regrouped in 2009, recording proved a struggle—it would take two years before *Angles* was ready for release. Casablancas deliberately stepped back from the creative process—which he had previously dominated—and recorded his vocals remotely. Experimenting with sampling and multilayered guitars, the album was no less successful than its predecessors, hitting U.S. No. 4 and U.K. No. 3 in 2011. However, Valensi voiced his dissatisfaction, ominously remarking, "I won't do the next album if we make it like this. No way. It was awful." **TB**

year-by-year ■ Vocals ■ Guitar ■ Bass ■ Drums

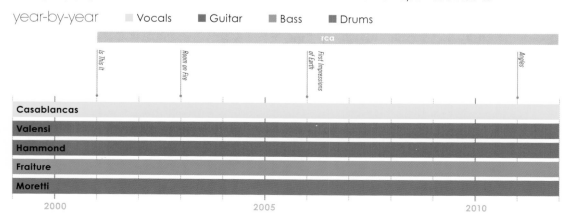

styx 1970–present

Chuck Panozzo
b. September 20, 1947

John Panozzo
b. September 20, 1947
d. July 16, 1996

Dennis DeYoung
b. February 18, 1947

John Curulewski
b. October 3, 1950
d. Feb. 13, 1988

James "J.Y." Young
b. November 14, 1949

Tommy Shaw
b. September 11, 1953

Todd Sucherman
b. May 2, 1969

So critically reviled that they make Journey seem like Radiohead, Styx can afford to ignore such slings and arrows, with four multiplatinum albums to their name, not to mention name-checks from Homer Simpson.

Chicago-born **Chuck** and **John Panozzo** recruited pianist **Dennis DeYoung** and guitarists **John Curulewski** and **James "J.Y. " Young** for their sixties band, The Tradewinds. On signing to the Wooden Nickel label in 1972, the quintet rechristened themselves Styx and developed their pomp-rocking sound (sort of a rockier Yes with fewer complex time signatures). Undeterred by negligible sales of their first four albums, the group built a fan-base by touring beyond Chicago. Meanwhile, DeYoung's ballad "Lady" became a slow-burning success: by May 1975, it had crashed the U.S. Top Ten, while its two-year-old parent album, *Styx II*, earned the first of the band's abundant gold awards.

Thanks to an upgrade to major label A&M and the replacement of Curulewski with golden boy **Tommy Shaw**, Styx cruised into the big time. Both *The Grand Illusion* (1977) and *Pieces of Eight* (1978) hit U.S. No. 6 and went platinum, while "Come Sail Away" provided a singles chart smash. "Babe," another DeYoung-penned weepie, topped the U.S. chart in 1979.

Untouched by the new wave, Styx swept into the eighties. *Cornerstone* (1979) provided their U.K. chart debut and *Paradise Theater* (1981) proved that concept albums could still be viable, going Top Ten on both sides of the Atlantic. But another huge-selling

conceptual affair, *Kilroy Was Here* (1983), proved their undoing. After a preposterously theatrical tour, and infecting even those resistant to Styx's charm with "Mr Roboto," the band were rent by musical and personal differences. With Shaw's exit, the band split, leaving 1984's live *Caught in the Act* as their epitaph.

An inevitable reunion occurred in 1990. With Shaw otherwise employed in Damn Yankees (with Jack Blades of Night Ranger and Ted Nugent), Styx enlisted *Beatlemania* veteran Glen Burtnick on guitar. *Edge of the Century* (1990) was a modest success, while another DeYoung-penned smash, "Show Me the Way," returned them to the U.S. Top Three. By 1995, Shaw was back and **Todd Sucherman** had replaced John Panozzo. The live *Return to Paradise* (1997) was another gold-seller, but *Brave New World* (1999) was eclipsed by platinum awards for *Greatest Hits* (1995).

A resumption of long-standing squabbles between Shaw and DeYoung saw the latter replaced by Lawrence Gowan. Burtnick returned (on bass this time) to back up the ailing Chuck Panozzo, before former Bad English bassist Ricky Phillips filled the position full-time in 2003. Shaw, Young, Sucherman, Gowan, and Phillips now enjoy a prosperous career on the AOR nostalgia circuit with the likes of Foreigner and REO Speedwagon, and even returned to the U.S. Top Fifty for the first time in over a decade with a covers collection, *Big Bang Theory* (2005). "There is," observed Shaw, "a lot to be said for experience." **BM**

year-by-year ▪ Vocals ▪ Guitar ▪ Bass ▪ Drums ▪ Keyboards

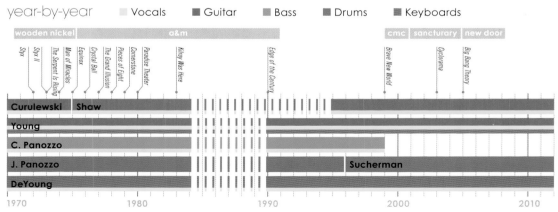

supertramp 1970–present

Rick Davies
b. July 22, 1944

Roger Hodgson
b. March 21, 1950

Dave Winthrop
b. November 27, 1948

Bob Millar
b. February 2, 1950

Richard Palmer-James
b. June 11, 1947

Kevin Currie
b. Unknown

Supertramp began as a progressive group but came to prominence only after they softened their heavy rock with easy-listening elements. They were formed in London, England, when Dutch millionaire Sam Miesgaes wearied of The Joint, a group he had bankrolled, and decided instead to back the new band of one of its members, **Rick Davies**. The new enterprise started life with the name Daddy, featuring Davies on keyboards and vocals and **Roger Hodgson** on bass; with the additions of saxophonist **Dave Winthrop**, drummer **Bob Millar**, and guitarist **Richard Palmer-James** the group became Supertramp.

The failure of their self-titled debut album led to the replacement of Millar by drummer **Kevin Currie** and the addition of bassist **Frank Farrell** (Hodgson having switched to guitar). But Supertramp again made little impression with *Indelibly Stamped* (1971).

When all the recent recruits left, Miesgaes teamed Davies and Hodgson with former Alan Bown Set players **Dougie Thomson** (bass) and **John Helliwell** (saxophone), plus American **Bob Siebenberg** (drums), and gave them a year to get their act together. The group duly tempered their more outré progressive

elements with poppier melodies and irresistible hooks. The result was worth the wait and the investment: after a slow start, *Crime of the Century* (1974) climbed to U.K. No. 4 and yielded the lilting hit "Dreamer."

Hodgson's distinctive falsetto and electric piano gave a trademark sound to his delivery of lyrics that, in a decidedly post-*Dark Side of the Moon* spirit, touched on madness and melancholy. Supertramp had the Floyd beat on one front, though: the album's indignant opener, "School," predated "Another Brick in the Wall" by five years. The gruffer Davies sang the album's second hit, the wry "Bloody Well Right."

Although the group themselves did not rate it, *Crisis? What Crisis?* (1975), with fan favorite "Ain't Nobody But Me," maintained their success. The far better *Even in the Quietest Moments…* (1977), opening with Hodgson's gorgeous "Give a Little Bit," broke Supertramp into the U.S. Top Twenty and secured their first U.S. gold award. (The revitalized *Crime of the Century* finally earned gold status two months later.)

Having relocated to the United States, the band took their time preparing a new album. "Supertramp at that time was a very easy band to be in," Davies

year-by-year   ■ Vocals   ■ Guitar   ■ Bass   ■ Drums   ■ Keyboards

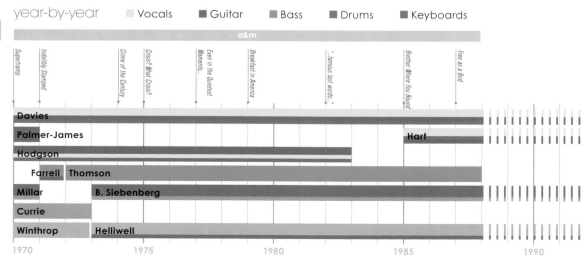

a&m

Supertramp | Indelibly Stamped | Crime of the Century | Crisis? What Crisis? | Even in the Quietest Moments… | Breakfast in America | "...famous last words…" | Brother Where You Bound | Free as a Bird

Davies
Palmer-James — Hart
Hodgson
Farrell | **Thomson**
Millar | B. Siebenberg
Currie
Winthrop | Helliwell

1970   1975   1980   1985   1990

Dougie Thomson
b. March 24, 1951

John Helliwell
b. February 15, 1945

Bob Siebenberg
b. October 31, 1949

Mark Hart
b. July 2, 1953

Jesse Siebenberg
b. February 1977

Frank Farrell
b. March 31, 1947
d. July 19, 1997

told *Billboard* writer Craig Rosen. "We still weren't that big saleswise to start causing the usual friction when the songwriter gets more money than the drummer." The result was *Breakfast in America* (1979), which topped the U.S. chart within two months of its release. Four singles—"The Logical Song," the title track, "Goodbye Stranger," and "Take the Long Way Home"—propelled the album to multi-million sales. This immense popularity drowned the voices of cynics who bemoaned Supertramp's lack of character.

However, differences between Davies and Hodgson became a rift during the demanding world tour that ensued. (The resulting live album—1980's *Paris*—bequeathed a version of "Dreamer" that became a U.S. Top Twenty hit.) The tension between Davies's blues preferences and Hodgson's poppier approach was clearly audible on 1982's "...*famous last words*..."—the source of the band's last major hit, "It's Raining Again"—and there was little surprise when Hodgson left to go solo soon after its release.

After a moderately successful solo album, *In the Eye of the Storm* (1984), Davies revived the band for the well-received *Brother Where You Bound* (1985),

whose epic title track boasted guitar work by Thin Lizzy's Scott Gorham and Pink Floyd's David Gilmour. But as he experimented with synthesized sound, *Free as a Bird* (1987) fell short of the U.S. Top 100—despite "I'm Beggin' You," somewhat implausibly, topping *Billboard*'s Hot Dance Club Play chart—and fared little better at home. Supertramp duly fragmented.

Eight years later, Davies re-formed the group with Helliwell, Siebenberg (whose percussionist son **Jesse** later joined the band too), bassist Cliff Hugo, guitarist Carl Verheyen, brass player Lee Thornburg, and, on keyboards and guitar, former Crowded House associate **Mark Hart**. The resultant *Some Things Never Change* (1997) was a belated return to their most successful style. "We've had entire pop movements come and go between our albums," Davies noted, "and we haven't even noticed."

After another tour in 2002, the band again lapsed into silence. Hopes that a 2010 tour—celebrating the fortieth anniversary of their first album—would feature Hodgson proved in vain. "You need harmony, both musically and personally," said Davies. "Unfortunately, that doesn't exist between us anymore." **GL**

■ Aerophones　　■ Other percussion

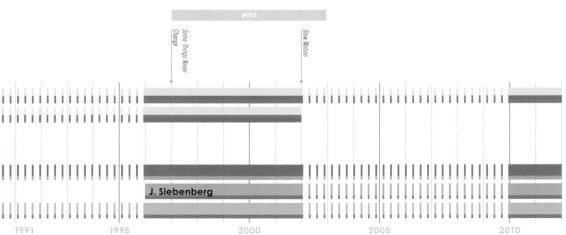

system of a down 1994–present

Serj Tankian
b. August 21, 1967

Daron Malakian
b. July 18, 1975

Shavo Odadjian
b. April 22, 1974

Ontronik "Andy" Khachaturian
b. January 25, 1975

John Dolmayan
b. July 15, 1972

System of a Down made rock 'n' roll feel dangerous once again. That was no small achievement in the 2000s, a decade known for cookie-cutter American Idols, bland pop tarts, and Creed. In comparison, System sounded like a soundtrack to a revolution.

Vocalist **Serj Tankian** and his cohorts—guitarist **Daron Malakian**, bassist **Shavo Odadjian** and drummer **John Dolmayan**—certainly were not afraid to talk politics, explore taboo topics, and challenge the status quo. More often than not, the Armenian-American alt-metal act came out victorious, claiming equal amounts of critical acclaim and commercial success during a career dating back to 1994. All five of their studio albums were million-plus sellers, with three topping the charts in multiple countries, and the group also earned a Best Hard Rock Performance Grammy for the memorable smash "B.Y.O.B." in 2006.

That they achieved all that, and much more, was nearly enough to restore one's faith in public taste. For, without a doubt, System of a Down were never an easy listen. Although inspired by the likes of Ozzy Osbourne and Slayer, they simply did not sound like anybody else out there when they released their 1998 debut. The lyrics were dense and convoluted, often sold with something resembling a Dadaist approach, and usually examined multiple sides of their subjects—a true rock 'n' roll rarity—while the music

was an experimental, though fluid, mix of thrash metal and Middle Eastern rhythms. It was a hearty blend, realized to the fullest on 2001's masterpiece *Toxicity*, and it has continued to age very well.

System of a Down's sound was a product of the members' backgrounds. Tankian was born in Lebanon and Odadjian in Armenia, and both moved to Los Angeles at an early age. They attended Rose and Alex Pilibos Armenian School, with fellow Armenian-American Malakian (who was born in L.A.). As cultures clashed in their real lives, so too would they in the band's compositions, which thrived on the tension.

The three actually met in 1992, while working on different projects at the same studio, which led directly to the formation of the short-lived Soil. It is odd that Soil never took off, given that it included three-fourths of what would become System's original lineup. That first group disbanded in 1994, quickly replaced by System of a Down, first with **Andy Khachaturian** (later of the Apex Theory), then Dolmayan, on drums. The band quickly cultivated a small but passionate international following by releasing a series of demo tapes, which helped them land a deal with Rick Rubin's American label. (Rubin himself would coproduce every System album.)

Released in 1998, the band's self-titled debut yielded two U.S. Top Forty alt-rock hits, "Sugar" and

year-by-year ■ Vocals ■ Guitar ■ Bass ■ Drums ■ Keyboards

american

System of a Down

Toxicity

Steal This Album!

Tankian

Malakian

Odadjian

Khachaturian **Dolmayan**

1994 1996 1998 2000 2002

2.6M
*System
of a Down*
(1998)

5.6M
Toxicity
(2001)

2.4M
Steal This Album!
(2002)

3.2M
Mesmerize
(2005)

"Spiders," but stalled outside of the Top 100 in both the U.S. and the U.K. album charts. Helped by System's slot on Ozzy Osbourne's 1998 Ozzfest tour, it ended up being a word-of-mouth success story, eventually going platinum in the U.S. two years after its release.

The buzz first built by *System of a Down* reached a deafening level with the follow-up, 2001's *Toxicity*. Boasting three hits—the title track, the rock chart No. 1 "Aerials," and the gold-selling "Chop Suey!"— *Toxicity* topped the U.S. and Canadian charts and peaked at No. 13 in the U.K. Most critics were in full agreement with fans—*Spin* even named *Toxicity* the No. 1 album of the year—and the Grammy folks would nominate "Chop Suey!" and "Aerials" for Best Hard Rock Performance in 2002 and 2003, respectively.

After that impressive dance with success, System was perhaps due for its first misstep—and the band certainly stumbled with *Steal This Album!* The title, though hardly original, was a clever reference to the record's origin: unfinished tracks had been leaked to the Internet in 2002, so System decided to quickly finish the tunes and release them as a third album. The result clearly was not great, coming across to many listeners as nothing more than a collection of outtakes and B-sides. Accordingly, by the new *Toxicity* standards, it performed unimpressively on the charts, failing to crack the Top Ten in any major market.

System bounced back in superb fashion in 2005, releasing two chart-topping albums—*Mesmerize* and *Hypnotize*—in a six-month period. *Mesmerize*—the first to hit, in May of that year—proved that both fans and critics were definitely still in the band's corner. It debuted atop the U.S. chart, selling more than 800,000 copies in its first week, and its signature single, "B.Y.O.B.," earned the group their sole Grammy award. In November, *Hypnotize* also debuted at No. 1, and yielded a gold-selling, chart-topping title track.

Then, at the height of their popularity, the group announced in 2006 that they were taking a hiatus, which lasted until 2011. In the interim, Tankian scored a Top Five hit with 2007's *Elect the Dead* (followed by 2010's *Imperfect Harmonies* and live *Elect the Dead Symphony*, and 2012's *Harakiri*), while Malakian and Dolmayan formed Scars on Broadway (a band name Malakian first used for a one-off collaboration with Amen's Casey Chaos in 2003). Their self-titled debut album made the U.S. Top Twenty in 2008.

While fans delighted at the group's return to duty in 2011 (and a tour with the Deftones in 2012), they were warned not to expect a new album anytime soon. "Instead of resting on our laurels," Dolmayan told *Multishow*, "we wanna throw them away and create something new and specific for this generation that they can say is *their* System of a Down." **JiH**

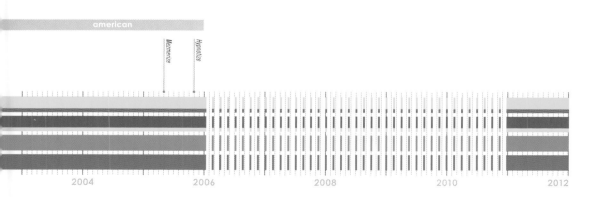

talking heads 1975–1991

David Byrne
b. May 14, 1952

Chris Frantz
b. May 8, 1951

Tina Weymouth
b. November 22, 1950

Jerry Harrison
b. February 21, 1949

One of the most influential bands of the new wave era, Talking Heads actually came together several years before punk's heyday. Founder members **David Byrne**, **Chris Frantz**, and **Tina Weymouth** had been friends at the Rhode Island School of Design (Byrne and Frantz were briefly in a band called The Artistics; Frantz's girlfriend Weymouth would cart the band around) and moved to Manhattan together in 1974.

Byrne and Frantz decided to supplement their fresh New York lifestyle with a fresh New York sound. Weymouth was persuaded to join on bass and the name Talking Heads followed almost as swiftly as their debut gig, a dream slot supporting the Ramones at New York's punk mecca CBGB. That show in June 1975—launching their alien, clean, clipped style—attracted the attention of Seymour Stein, who signed them to his Sire label. (During their CBGB days, Weymouth later recalled, "Lou Reed would take us aside and give us some hilarious tips… Then he'd say, 'Smart move getting a chick in the band—wonder where you got that idea.'") The Heads' debut single, "Love > Building on Fire," was released in February 1977, shortly before they fully realized their sound with the recruitment of **Jerry Harrison** (ex-Jonathan Richman and the Modern Lovers) on keyboards.

With the fiery ostentation of punk around them, Talking Heads' "straight" image stood out. Their debut album, *Talking Heads: 77,* was happy to deal with distinctly un-rock 'n' roll subject matter: out went high-living, nihilism, sex, and drugs; in came songs about, well, buildings and food. Weymouth and Frantz's taut funk rhythm section provided the perfect vessel for the panicky austerity of Byrne's jerky vocal tics, and the debut struck a chord. It and the single "Psycho Killer" were modest U.S. and U.K. hits, but crucially they caught the attention of Brian Eno, ex-Roxy Music, now producer of intriguing sonic adventures.

On tour with the Ramones in spring 1977, Talking Heads met Eno in London and hit it off. Eno recorded a song called "King's Lead Hat" (an anagram of Talking Heads, no less) for his *Before and After Science* (1977) and moved on to produce the Heads' second album, *More Songs About Buildings and Food* (1978). The Eno effect further tightened the band's sound on what is otherwise an unabashedly pop album, even culminating in an enthusiastic take on Al Green's "Take Me to the River." But if Talking Heads were flirting around the edges of the mainstream, their next collaboration with Eno would shy away while paradoxically providing their biggest hit yet.

Fear of Music emerged in 1979, wild and paranoid as ever—that title's no fluke. It almost reached the *Billboard* Top Twenty, as record buyers' appetite for sickly noise and mental breakdown spread.

year-by-year   ■ Vocals   ■ Guitar   ■ Bass   ■ Drums   ■ Keyboards

sire

Talking Heads: 77

More Songs About Buildings and Food

Fear of Music

Remain in Light

Byrne

Weymouth

Frantz

Harrison

1976   1978   1980   1982

But beyond the studio trickery, and in spite of all the crazed innovation, *Fear of Music* piled on the tunes.

Even more of a studio product was *Remain in Light* (1980). "Ambient music and strong lyrics and incredibly inventive percussion and bass parts," enthused Dave Sitek, fêted producer and leader of TV on the Radio, to *Rolling Stone.* "I was a kid, but I still thought, 'I should have been involved in that record!' It was amazing." The last of Eno's production jobs, the album was a fascinating document of intra-band tension. Basic tracks were enlivened by layer after layer as Byrne jammed his way from bare bones to full songs, resulting in odd classics like "Once in a Lifetime."

But these working methods only shed light on the band's fractious state. Byrne and Eno had become their own little club, with Frantz and Weymouth on the other side and Harrison somewhere in between. There were tangible benefits to this, of course: the Byrne/Eno love-in also produced their loop-led masterpiece *My Life in the Bush of Ghosts*, while Frantz and Weymouth formed the Tom Tom Club, blending hip-hop, soul, and funk—plus substantially more sunshine than the day-job—to glorious effect on songs like "Genius of Love."

Still at loggerheads, the band regrouped for 1983's *Speaking in Tongues.* Even as internal relations deteriorated, they bagged their biggest U.S. hit, "Burning Down the House," which peaked at No. 9.

Revitalized if not quite reconciled, they followed this in 1984 with *Stop Making Sense*, a double whammy of live film—directed by Jonathan Demme, later an Oscar winner for *The Silence of the Lambs*—and soundtrack album, featuring (on record) choice cuts from the previous decade and (on celluloid) David Byrne's unfeasibly wide suit.

Talking Heads were now, commercially, at a high watermark and capitalized with their most accessible effort yet, 1985's *Little Creatures,* including the U.K. hit "Road to Nowhere." This found a sleek Talking Heads comfortably tucked into the MTV era, with similar fare to follow on the following year's *True Stories*, a quasi-soundtrack to the movie of the same name. (A song on the latter album bequeathed a new name to an Oxford quintet then known as On a Friday, later to conquer the world as Radiohead.)

They would manage one more album together, taking a different tack on *Naked* (1988) and embracing world music rather the crisp video-age sound that had fattened their wallets. It was a U.K. Top Three and U.S. Top Twenty hit, but their coming asunder was made permanent in 1991. Although they regrouped for a performance when their questing funk received a richly deserved induction into the Rock 'n' Roll Hall of Fame in 2002, there is, sadly, scant likelihood that we will see them again. **MaH**

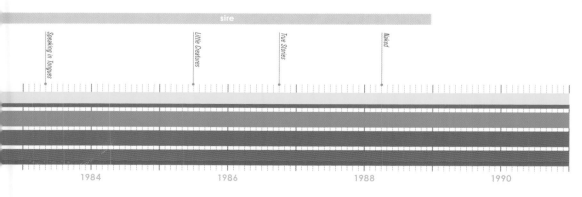

tangerine dream 1967–present

Edgar Froese
b. June 6, 1944

Klaus Schulze
b. August 4,
1947

**Conrad
Schnitzler**
b. 1937
d. August 4,
2011

**Peter
Baumann**
b. January 29,
1953

Chris Franke
b. April 6, 1953

Klaus Krieger
b. Unknown

Steve Jolliffe
b. April 28, 1949

**Johannes
Schmölling**
b. November
9, 1950

Compiling a definitive list of Tangerine Dream's albums is not a task for the weak-willed: since 1970, almost one hundred studio albums have been released under their moniker—*not* including over thirty soundtracks and forty compilations. But among them are gems that are still proving influential today.

The experimental music scene in sixties Germany produced pioneering bands who championed electronic sound, and owed more to the postwar European classical tradition than American blues or rock 'n' roll. The British music press came up with a description for these new bands: for better or for worse, "krautrock" entered the musical lexicon.

Tangerine Dream emerged from West Berlin's Zodiak Free Arts Lab. There, art student **Edgar Froese** and experimental musicians, including **Klaus Schulze** and **Conrad Schnitzler**, staged multimedia events, mixing music, literature, and visual arts.

Released in 1970, Tangerine Dream's debut, *Electronic Meditation,* featured tape collages and drones. The following year, Froese unveiled a very different version of Tangerine Dream. Schulze and Schnitzler were out (to Ash Ra Tempel and Cluster, respectively), and **Chris Franke** and Steve Schroyder were in. Bearing almost no resemblance to its predecessor, 1971's *Alpha Centauri* was reliant on atmospheric organ, swirling electronic sounds, and flute. The first step toward what Froese described as

"kosmische (cosmic) musik," it sold a respectable 20,000 copies to a core audience of German stoners. ("Fly and Collision of Comas Sola" proved a favorite of future Sisters of Mercy main-man Andrew Eldritch, who indulged his Tangerine Dream leanings on the unreleased 1997 album *Feel No Pain*.)

With Schroyder relegated to "guest" status and **Peter Baumann** added, 1972's ambitious double set *Zeit* ("time" in German) comprised four LP side-long songs. The sound was more overtly electronic, with heavy use of the VCS3 synthesizer (best known for The Who's "Won't Get Fooled Again" and Pink Floyd's "On the Run"). Florian Fricke of Popul Vuh guested on his Moog synth, and, with no clear melodies and rhythms, the music seemed out of this world.

The following year's *Atem* ("Breath" in German) was just as experimental, introducing the Mellotron, an electronic keyboard that played pitched tape loops of recorded instruments—in effect, an analog precursor to today's digital samplers. Airplay on BBC DJ John Peel's show introduced Tangerine Dream to a British audience. "We started getting requests for all these German records by people we'd never heard of," Simon Draper, who ran the chain of Virgin record stores with Richard Branson, told *Mojo*. "Of all of them, Tangerine Dream were far and away the most interesting—and the level of interest in them was huge." The Tangs were duly signed to the Virgin label.

year-by-year ■ Vocals ■ Guitar ■ Bass ■ Drums ■ Keyboards

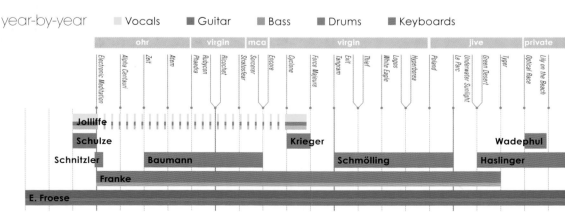

Paul Haslinger
b. Demember 11, 1962

Ralph Wadephul
b. 1958

Jerome Froese
b. November 24, 1970

Linda Spa
b. September 4, 1968

Thorsten Quaeschning
b. Unknown

The investment was rewarded when *Phaedra* (1974) hit the U.K. Top Twenty. (Young fans included not only future progressive rockers like Marillion, but also members of other Virgin acts like The Human League and OMD.) A benchmark in electronic music, *Phaedra* made extensive use of sequencers creating repeating patterns of synthesizer notes. It all but gave birth to the "Berlin School"—a group of artists whose sequenced, synthesized soundscapes typically fitted entire sides of LPs. Among those paying attention was producer Giorgio Moroder, who told *NME*: "I used to know these guys very well, and loved their *Phaedra* album very much." The band's influence is obvious in Moroder's early, often epic work with Donna Summer.

Tangerine Dream hit a commercial peak with 1975's *Rubycon*. Continuing in the "Berlin" style, it followed *Phaedra* into the U.K. Top Twenty. The band toured throughout Europe, improvising loosely in the manner of their studio albums, and their sound evolved to incorporate multilayered sequencer patterns and a greater use of percussion and electric guitar, documented effectively on 1975's live *Ricochet*.

Toward the end of the seventies, the band experimented with more melodic compositions and, on occasion, vocals. After an abortive attempt to make an album with Pink Floyd drummer Nick Mason, they reworked the material as 1976's *Stratosfear*. Then 1977's live *Encore* proved Baumann's swansong

(he later founded the New Age label Private Music). Singer **Steve Jolliffe** and drummer **Klaus Krieger** brought a stronger rock influence to 1978's *Cyclone*, but by 1979's *Force Majeure* the pair had been dropped and the "Berlin" sound had been restored.

Cinema and TV had long provided a fertile setting for Tangerine Dream; 1977's *Sorcerer* became better known for its soundtrack than for the film itself. The band scored more than twenty-five movies in the eighties—memorably, 1981's *Thief* opens with their accompaniment to James Caan's safe-cracking, and 1983's *Risky Business* became as indelibly linked with them as with Bob Seger's "Old Time Rock and Roll."

Thereafter, mainstream popularity waned. But touring throughout Europe and America, and an uninterrupted release schedule ensured that the band remained unchallenged in their field well into the nineties—at which point their influence once again became clear, thanks to latterday ambient acts such as The Orb. Froese promptly created his own TDI label, to issue a bewildering series of original and remix sets. Many feature his son **Jerome**, who joined in 1990.

Froeses's sidekicks now include saxophonist **Linda Spa** (more of a presence at shows than on albums) and keyboardist **Thorsten Quaeschning**, whose work recalls classic-period Tangerine Dream (the band's recorded output is largely down to him and Froese). There are no signs of the phenomenon ending. **TB/BM**

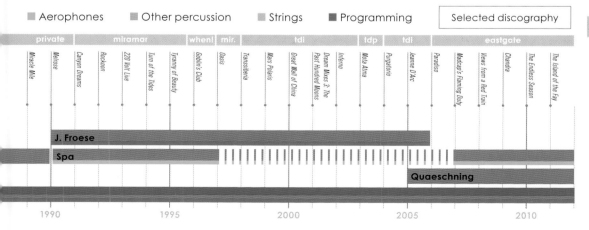

■ Aerophones ■ Other percussion ■ Strings ■ Programming Selected discography

téléphone 1976–1986

Jean-Louis Aubert
b. April 12, 1955

Louis Bertignac
b. February 23, 1954

Corine Marienneau
b. March 7, 1952

Richard Kolinka
b. July 7, 1953

Fronted by Parisian singer/guitarist **Jean-Louis Aubert**, Téléphone successfully fused the swagger of classic rock 'n' roll with the hard edge of punk to become the most popular French band of their time, even making a small impression away from home soil, too.

As a band, Téléphone came together rather by accident. In November 1976, Aubert and drummer **Richard Kolinka** put together a band to fulfill a one-off engagement at a club in Paris. Recruiting guitarist **Louis Bertignac** and bassist **Corine Marienneau**, they performed a chaotic set that mixed Aubert's first songwriting efforts with rock standards. They were loud and aggressive and gelled as a band immediately. Téléphone followed the classic seventies rock model, combining a charismatic frontman with a unique voice, raw, exhilarating guitar heroics, and a solid, powerful rhythm section.

During 1977, Téléphone established themselves locally by supporting visiting punk and New Wave bands from the Britain and America. They soon attracted attention to their own high-energy sets, and that summer released a debut single, the live recording "Hygiaphone." A slab of powerful twelve-bar pub-rock, it earned them a major deal with Pathé-Marconi (EMI). The band's self-titled debut LP was issued that same November.

By 1978, Téléphone had headlined their first national tour. It was *Crache ton venin* (1979) that brought the band stardom in their native land. Selling more than 500,000 copies—a huge volume for the French-speaking market—its success was driven by a hit single, the Bowie-influenced "La bombe humaine," which became Téléphone's signature song.

Téléphone went on brief tours of Italy, Spain, and North America. While in New York, the band recorded their third album, *Au cœur de la nuit* (1981): it also yielded a hugely popular single, "Argent trop cher."

Having conquered the French market, Téléphone now began to take a wider view of their career, signing a lucrative new deal with Virgin. Owner Richard Branson brought in filmmaker Julien Temple (famed for the Sex Pistols movie *The Great Rock And Roll Swindle*) to produce a video for the single "Ça (c'est vraiment toi)." Yet in spite of regular releases and heavy support from Virgin, Téléphone would only ever achieve modest success outside of France.

In June 1982, Téléphone reached a career peak: playing to a crowd of 80,000 in Paris as support to The Rolling Stones. But by the time of *Un autre monde* (1984), a new generation of younger electronic bands had begun to emerge, and Téléphone suddenly no longer appeared to be at the cutting edge of the French music scene. With creative disagreements rife within the band, all four members immersed themselves in solo projects until, in April 1986, Aubert announced that the band had been dissolved. **TB**

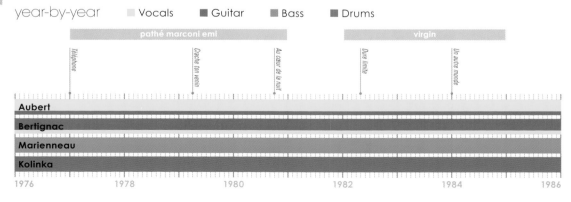

year-by-year   ■ Vocals   ■ Guitar   ■ Bass   ■ Drums

pathé marconi emi | virgin

Téléphone | Crache ton venin | Au cœur de la nuit | Dure limite | Un autre monde

Aubert
Bertignac
Marienneau
Kolinka

1976   1978   1980   1982   1984   1986

television 1974–present

Tom Verlaine
b. December 13, 1949

Richard Hell
b. October 2, 1949

Billy Ficca
b. February 15, 1950

Richard Lloyd
b. October 25, 1951

Fred Smith
b. April 10, 1948

Jimmy Rip
b. Unknown

Seminal figures on the U.S. underground scene in the mid-seventies, Television illustrated the manifest distinction between what was "new wave" on either side of the Atlantic. London was all about visceral energy and attitude; songs were short and sharp; musical chops counted for little, and nothing was more passé than a guitar solo. New York's Television contained two guitar soloists of rare talent and taste. Their first hit, "Marquee Moon" of 1977, featured more than two minutes of interlocking solo play, and, at nine minutes, fifty-eight seconds, it was so long that it had to be split over both sides of the vinyl pressing.

Formed in 1972 and originally known as the Neon Boys, Television comprised **Tom Verlaine** on guitar and vocals, **Richard Hell** on bass and vocals, and **Billy Ficca** on drums. **Richard Lloyd** was added on second guitar in 1974 when they played their first gigs as Television. They quickly became an integral part of the scene centered on Manhattan's CBGB club.

Songwriting duties were split between Hell and Verlaine, but frictions emerged as Hell's punky onstage presence and limited playing ability began to sit at odds with the band's growing musical sophistication. In 1975 he was replaced by **Fred Smith**. Hell continued to play a part on the CBGB scene, cofounding the Heartbreakers with Johnny Thunders and later, Richard Hell and the Voidoids. Malcolm

McLaren later credited Hell's appearance—spiky hair and torn clothes held together with safety pins—as an inspiration for his presentation of the Sex Pistols.

Having recorded an independent single, "Little Johnny Jewell," in 1975, Television signed to Elektra, who issued their 1977 debut, Marquee Moon. Like other legendary New York groups of the period, Television made little impact in the United States. In Europe, however, Marquee Moon was hailed as an immediate classic, reaching the U.K. Top Thirty.

Although Verlaine was a unique vocalist and clever songwriter, the band's sound centered around the interplay between the two skillfully interlocking guitars and the bassline, as can be heard to startling effect during the verse segments of "Marquee Moon."

Although the follow-up album Adventure (1978) charted similar territory, it was generally viewed—unfairly in retrospect—as a grave disappointment. With internal conflict mounting, Television disbanded later that year. Verlaine went on to enjoy a critically lauded solo career, releasing a succession of fine albums throughout the eighties. Owing to his popularity and acceptance by U.K. music fans, he even moved there briefly at this time.

Television reformed in 1992, releasing a self-titled and largely overlooked album. They have remained a sporadic presence ever since. **TB**

year-by-year   Vocals   Guitar   Bass   Drums

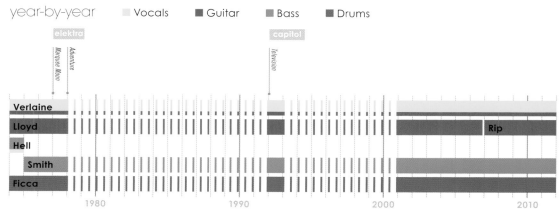

thin lizzy 1969–present

Phil Lynott
b. Aug 20, 1951
d. January 4,
1986

**Brian
Downey**
b. January 27,
1951

Eric Bell
b. September
3, 1947

Gary Moore
b. April 4, 1952
d. February 6,
2011

**Brian
Robertson**
b. September
12, 1956

**Scott
Gorham**
b. March 17,
1951

Snowy White
b. March 3, 1948

John Sykes
b. July 29, 1959

Phil Lynott and **Brian Downey** were at school together in Dublin before joining local bands The Black Eagles and Skid Row. In 1969, they recruited Belfast-born guitarist **Eric Bell** to form Thin Lizzy—named, legend has it, after either a character in the comic *Beano* or an early Ford Model-T car known as the Tin Lizzie.

After *Thin Lizzy* (1971) and *Shades of a Blue Orphanage* (1972) made no impact, the band finally hit with "Whiskey in the Jar" in 1973. But when that year's *Vagabonds of the Western World* failed to chart, Bell left and was replaced first by **Gary Moore** (another Skid Row veteran), then full-time by Scotsman **Brian Robertson** and American **Scott Gorham**.

The new Thin Lizzy switched to the Vertigo label for 1974's *Nightlife,* and finally hit their commercial and musical stride with 1975's *Fighting*. Festival dates and major tours cemented the band's live reputation and, in 1976, they broached the U.K. Top Ten with *Jailbreak*. The album also provided their breakthrough in America, thanks to the immortal transatlantic smash "The Boys are Back in Town."

Sadly, they failed to capitalize on this international success, owing in part to the last-minute cancelation of a U.S. tour in December 1976, after Robertson was

injured in a fight. Infuriated, Lynott fired the guitarist and enlisted Gary Moore for a tour with Queen. Amid this turmoil, 1976's *Johnny the Fox* (recorded with Robertson) and 1977's *Bad Reputation* (with guitars by Gorham, after Moore declined to stay) maintained their musical might, thanks to classics like "Don't Believe a Word" and "Dancin' in the Moonlight."

Having guested on two cuts on *Bad Reputation*, Robertson was reinstated in time for Lizzy's finest hour: 1978's *Live and Dangerous*. However, he was out (again) and Moore was in (again) for 1979's *Black Rose: A Rock Legend,* featuring "Waiting for an Alibi."

Always agreeably rowdy, the atmosphere in the Lizzy camp darkened as Lynott and Gorham took up heroin. "People soon became concerned, especially about Phil," Gorham recalled. "Our management would sneak into our hotel rooms and flush the drugs down the toilet. Phil didn't want to die. He loved life. He just went way over the top in the way he lived it."

When a disgusted Moore quit during a U.S. tour, Lynott enlisted ex-Slik and Rich Kids guitarist Midge Ure (later to front Ultravox) and Manfred Mann Earth Band's Dave Flett to complete the dates. Then, in late 1979, **Snowy White** (a member of Pink Floyd's touring

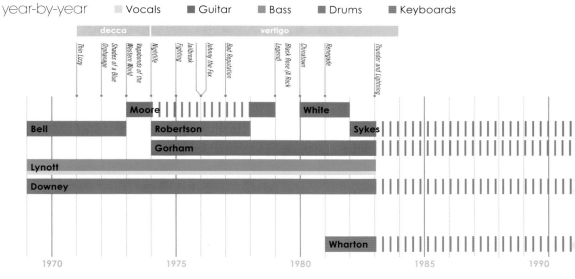

year-by-year ▪ Vocals ▪ Guitar ▪ Bass ▪ Drums ▪ Keyboards

Darren Wharton
b. December 24, 1962

Marco Mendoza
b. May 3, 1963

Ricky Warwick
b. July 11, 1966

Damon Johnson
b. July 13, 1964

Tommy Aldridge
b. August 15, 1950

Michael Lee
b. Nov 19, 1969
d. November 24, 2008

band) became Lizzy's permanent guitarist. Lynott made his solo debut in 1980 with *Solo in Soho* and the single "Yellow Pearl" (cowritten by Ure and a hit after it was adopted as the theme for BBC TV's *Top of the Pops*). The band's *Chinatown* (1980) provided their fourth U.K. Top Ten album, but the hit-free *Renegade* (1981) stalled in the lower reaches of the Top Forty.

A year later, a sixth name was added to the list of Lizzy guitarists when, after the disastrous *Renegade*, White was replaced by ex-Tygers of Pan Tang player **John Sykes**. "I've come along and given them a boot up the arse," he told *Kerrang!* "It sounds good now." *Thunder and Lightning* (1983) was indeed a triumph, from the storming title track to the brooding "The Sun Goes Down." (Sykes later provided a similar turbo boost to Whitesnake's self-titled 1987 comeback.)

However, although the album reversed the band's downward spiral in Europe, the restless Lynott—who had issued his second solo set, *The Phil Lynott Album*, in 1982—decided to split the band. Lizzy played a last date in Nuremberg, Germany, in September 1983. *Life:Live*—recorded at dates both that year and, with White on guitar, in 1981—provided their epitaph a month later. Lynott and Downey formed Grand Slam,

only to find that record companies (and most fans) were interested only in Thin Lizzy. The bassist last tasted chart success with Gary Moore, on the 1985 U.K. hit "Out in the Fields." But even as he resigned himself to having to reform Lizzy, Lynott died of heart failure and pneumonia, aged thirty-five, in 1986.

After a one-off tribute concert in Dublin—with Bob Geldof on vocals—*Dedication: The Very Best of Thin Lizzy* shot into the U.K. Top Ten in 1991. In 1996, Downey, Gorham, Sykes, **Darren Wharton** (keyboard player on the band's final three albums), and **Marco Mendoza** (bassist with Sykes' post-Whitesnake outfit Blue Murder) went back on the road as Thin Lizzy. But Downey quit before 2000's live *One Night Only* (featuring former Whitesnake drummer **Tommy Aldridge**), then Wharton left and the band slid back into inactivity.

Boosted by 2004's U.K. Top Three success *Greatest Hits*, Gorham revived the Lizzy name. Downey, Def Leppard's Vivian Campbell, Guns N' Roses' Richard Fortus, and drummer **Michael Lee** were among those who toured. Since 2010, the lineup has been more settled, with Downey, Gorham, and Mendoza being joined by Wharton, The Almighty's **Ricky Warwick**, and former Alice Cooper guitarist **Damon Johnson. BS/BM**

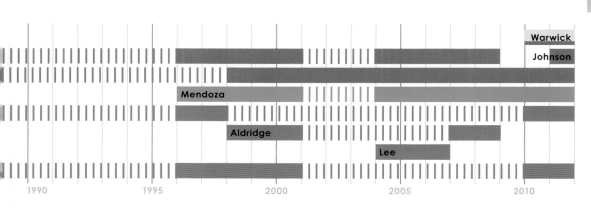

Warwick

Johnson

Mendoza

Aldridge

Lee

1990　　　1995　　　2000　　　2005　　　2010

traffic 1967–1994

Steve Winwood
b. May 12, 1948

Dave Mason
b. May 10, 1946

Chris Wood
b. June 24, 1944
d. July 12, 1983

Jim Capaldi
b. August 2, 1944
d. January 28, 2005

Ric Grech
b. November 1, 1946
d. March 17, 1990

Jim Gordon
b. July 14, 1945

Rebop Kwaku Baah
b. February 13, 1944
d. Jan 12, 1983

Roger Hawkins
b. October 16, 1945

The preposterously young **Steve Winwood** was almost a rock veteran when he formed Traffic in 1967. Having tasted chart joy fronting the Spencer Davis Group at the age of fifteen, it was always likely that he would wrest control of his own destiny—and word had it that he had been plotting to leave Spencer Davis for some time. With a clutch of U.K. No. 1 singles under his belt and a stellar reputation as an R&B singer of character and force, Winwood was hot property. He would fulfill his promise many times over during half a century at the leading edge of British blues-rock.

After the Spencer Davis Group's driving pop-soul, Traffic was a markedly different proposition. Groove-led R&B was still a part of the mix, but Winwood aimed to explore psychedelia and the tougher variations of late-sixties rock. He, drummer **Jim Capaldi**, guitarist **Dave Mason**, and woodwind and keys player **Chris Wood** knew each other from the Birmingham music scene and had played together before Winwood secured his freedom, so the shift to a working quartet was smooth. They decided to "get it together in the country"—sloping off to Oxfordshire to shape their music in bucolic surroundings—and the relaxed ambience suffused their first two singles, "Paper Sun," led by Mason's dreamy sitar, and the psychedelic

"Hole in My Shoe," both released in 1967. Signed to Island, they matched their hit singles with a warmly received debut album *Mr. Fantasy* (also 1967), which went to No. 8 in the United Kingdom.

Despite Winwood's easy transition, not everything went so silkily for Traffic. Mason had left the band before *Mr. Fantasy*'s release but edged back to guest on *Traffic* (1968), in the end a more focused record than its predecessor. *Last Exit* (1969), with Mason gone again, was less robust, with the remaining, overstretched trio recording half the album live to rush it along. The itchy Winwood felt it was time to move on and quickly turned jam sessions with Eric Clapton into full-blown supergroup Blind Faith, with Ginger Baker and **Ric Grech** joining for an instant U.K. No. 1 album. But Winwood showed little appetite to continue and, after Blind Faith's swift split, he and Grech joined Ginger Baker's Air Force. However, even this venture lasted only a handful of shows before Winwood made a start on a solo record, drafting in Wood and Capaldi to help out until the three inexorably became Traffic again. After all the coming and going, the comeback album *John Barleycorn Must Die* (1970) cropped up little more than a year after *Last Exit*. To complete the circle, Grech joined Traffic a few months later.

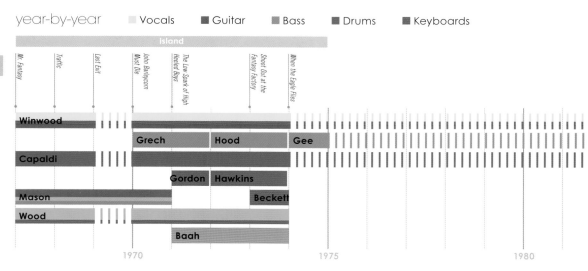

year-by-year   ■ Vocals   ■ Guitar   ■ Bass   ■ Drums   ■ Keyboards

David Hood
b. September 21, 1943

Barry Beckett
b. February 4, 1943
d. June 10, 2009

Rosko Gee
b. Unknown

Randall Bramblett
b. Unknown

Michael McEvoy
b. January 25, 1956

Walfredo Reyes Jr
b. December 18, 1955

As their U.K. profile began to fade, Traffic made inroads into the United States with the acclaimed *The Low Spark of High Heeled Boys* (1971), which followed *John Barleycorn Must Die* into the Top Ten even as it failed to chart back home. *Shoot Out at the Fantasy Factory* (1973) and *When the Eagle Flies* (1974) were also *Billboard* Top Ten entries, but critical reception had cooled and Winwood—suffering from peritonitis—was becoming disaffected. When he walked out, leaving Traffic in disarray, he stepped back into session work for George Harrison, John Martyn, and others, shrinking from the spotlight.

Finally, in 1977, Winwood produced a solo album. His self-titled effort arrived as a huge relief to the Island label, who feared their investment had been in vain. It featured his Traffic bandmate Capaldi as a cowriter, but did not set the charts alight.

However, success was to come with *Arc of a Diver* (1981). This time writing with Will Jennings and George Fleming, Winwood produced and performed the entire record himself, creating a buffed soul sound that took the album into the *Billboard* Top Three, with the single "While You See a Chance" breaking the Top Ten. A brief dip with *Talking Back to the Night* (1982) gave little warning of the commercial bite of its follow-up, *Back in the High Life* (1986). The most refined of Winwood's solo albums, it featured backing vocals from Chaka Khan, James Ingram, and James Taylor, and contributions from R&B legends Nile Rodgers and Arif Mardin. It also included the *Billboard* No. 1 and Grammy-winning single "Higher Love," and justified all the great expectations. The success of *Back in the High Life* and his new status as a U.S. soul player meant Winwood could name his price in a big-bucks move to the Virgin label for *Roll with It* (1988).

Whatever the terms of the deal, *Refugees of the Heart* (1990) was a less effective record but saw Capaldi help out again, which indirectly led to a renewed Traffic. With an otherwise new lineup they toured with the Grateful Dead in 1994, in the same year releasing their eighth studio album, *Far from Home*, a U.K. Top Thirty hit. But there would be no more; Capaldi's death in 2005 ended the band.

With the Traffic reunion behind him, Winwood returned to solo albums, releasing the disappointing *Junction 7* (1997) and the relaxed *About Time* (2003). *Nine Lives* (2008) was more encouraging and Winwood now took the opportunity to kick back, jam with old pal Clapton on tour, and enjoy the proceeds of the career retrospective *Revolutions* (2010). **MaH**

■ Aerophones   ■ Other percussion   ■ Strings

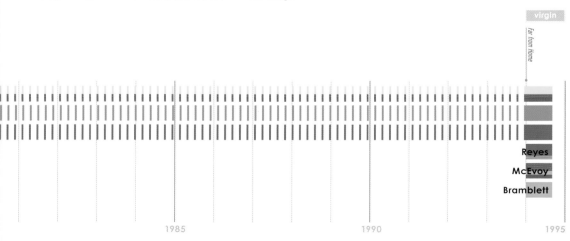

the traveling wilburys 1988–1991

Bob Dylan
b. May 24, 1941

George Harrison
b. February 25, 1943
d. November 29, 2001

Jeff Lynne
b. December 30, 1947

Tom Petty
b. October 20, 1950

Roy Orbison
b. April 23, 1936
d. December 6, 1988

Jim Keltner
b. April 27, 1942

Supergroups were all the rage in the sixties and seventies—Blind Faith, Crosby, Stills and Nash (and Young), and Emerson, Lake and Palmer all managed to contain monstrous egos for a while. But none was as super as The Traveling Wilburys in the eighties.

A starry lineup of **Bob Dylan**, **Roy Orbison**, **George Harrison**, **Tom Petty** and **Jeff Lynne** was scarcely believable, yet the chemistry worked and they even squeezed out a couple of albums at the tail end of the decade. (Harrison was no stranger to supergroups, having played—as L'Angelo Misterioso—with Eric Clapton and Leon Russell in Delaney and Bonnie Bramlett's revue-style act in 1969; and with Clapton, Russell, Ringo Starr, Billy Preston, and Badfinger's Pete Ham at his own Concert for Bangladesh in 1971.)

As folklore would have it, the band came together almost by accident. Lynne had produced Harrison's 1987 comeback album *Cloud Nine* and Warner Bros. wanted a B-side for the 1988 summer single "This Is Love." Harrison and Lynne discussed a team-up at Orbison's house, then decamped to Dylan's studio to make it happen. Petty joined up later, but when the hastily convened band created "Handle with Care," it was deemed too strong for a B-side. The ex-Beatle, Petty told *Mojo*, "listened to it and said, 'This isn't a George Harrison record; let's form a band.'"

The next step was simple. They had enjoyed the experience so much that they planned to make an album of it, taking their name from Harrison and Lynne's studio in-joke about mistakes "we'll bury" in the mix and even coming up with pseudonyms for each member—Harrison was Nelson Wilbury, Lynne was Otis, Orbison was Lefty, Petty was Charlie T., and Dylan came up Lucky. (Dylan "was very good in the Wilburys," enthused Petty. "When somebody had a line, he could make it a lot better in big ways.")

The nicknames were for their own amusement, of course; everyone knew full well who each legend was. And this was no collection of has-beens: Harrison and Lynne had just conjured up the former's most successful work in years; Dylan was enjoying a creative renaissance of his own; and Petty was one of the biggest U.S. rock stars of the decade. Only Orbison was plucked from the doldrums, but the endeavor would provide a springboard for his posthumous solo revival with 1989's *Mystery Girl*. Together, they swapped vocals and dueled with guitars as each rock behemoth gave up his skills with generosity.

The Traveling Wilburys strode into the spotlight in fall 1988 with "Handle with Care" as their debut single. It was an accomplished, chugging number, led by Harrison, buoyed—mainly—by Orbison's

year-by-year   ■ Vocals   ■ Guitar   ■ Bass   ■ Drums   ■ Keyboards

warner bros

Traveling Wilburys Vol. 1

Dylan

Harrison

Lynne

Petty

Orbison

1988   1989

impressively intact high-pitched croon, and driven by the unmistakable production work of Lynne; it made suitable inroads into charts worldwide. The ensuing album, *Traveling Wilburys Vol.1* (1988), was solid too, but slack enough here and there to betray its side-project status. No matter, it could always be shrugged off as a "bit of fun"—there was certainly some of that in the good old boys trading innuendo on "Dirty World." Whatever the intentions, it was a Top Three *Billboard* hit and picked up the Grammy for Best Rock Performance. Another good-time number, "End of the Line," provided a second hit single in 1989.

Orbison sadly passed away during the promotion of the debut—his "You Got It" single hit the Top Three in the U.K. soon after—but the rest of the band were sufficiently pleased with their labors to carry on in "Lefty"'s memory. Sure enough, they re-emerged with the drolly titled second album, *Traveling Wilburys Vol.3* (1990), taking on a new set of names as a reconstituted outfit. This time Harrison was Spike Wilbury, Lynne was Clayton, Petty was Muddy, and Dylan was Boo. Just out of the spotlight, Harrison's long-time drummer **Jim Keltner** kept his own name but would be tagged Buster Sidebury on the 2007 reissues.

Between the two Wilburys albums, Petty's star had risen higher with 1989's global smash *Full Moon Fever*, but there was still appetite among the four surviving "brothers" for their out-of-hand hobby. Vocals were shared liberally once again—although some essential brightness had been lost with Orbison's death—and more larks were had with the single "Wilbury Twist" and sprinkled references to "Twist and Shout" on "Inside Out." *Vol. 3* was not the high-charting triumph its predecessor had been but performed respectably, making the Top Twenty on both sides of the Atlantic.

These deft professionals left it there. They had formed a supergroup unusual for its easy mix of talents, but their epitaph for Orbison sufficed for the band, too. Dylan would continue his latterday upward trajectory, while Lynne and Petty settled into their niches. Although hopes for a reunion lingered for a while, they were eventually dashed by de facto leader Harrison's death in 2001.

There would, however, be an unexpected coda: Harrison's deal with Warner Bros. had expired in the mid-nineties, leaving ownership of the Wilbury albums in his hands. In 2007, the surviving members—with Harrison's son Dhani (credited as Ayrton Wilbury)—repackaged the two albums with bonus tracks for *The Traveling Wilburys Collection* on Wilbury Records. It went straight to No. 1 in the U.K. and Top Ten in the U.S. Clearly, the Wilburys prompted fond memories. **MaH**

■ Aerophones

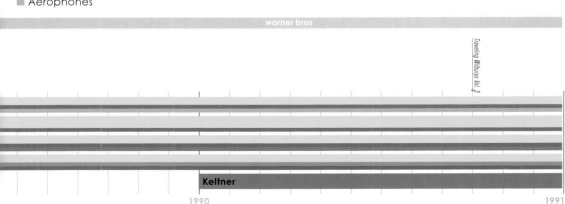

warner bros

Traveling Wilburys Vol.3

Keltner

1990   1991

t. rex 1970–1977

Marc Bolan
b. Sept 30, 1947
d. September
16, 1977

Mickey Finn
b. June 3 1947
d. January 11,
2003

Steve Currie
b. May 20, 1947
d. April 28, 1981

Bill Legend
b. May 8, 1944

Davey Lutton
b. 1946

Gloria Jones
b. September
19, 1947

"I've always dug Marc Bolan and he knows it," said Pete Townshend at the height of glam rock. "And he also knows that I'd let him get away with murder because of what he's doing for rock 'n' roll."

Years spent in Susie & the Hula Hoops and John's Children, and as solo singer Toby Tyler, failed to bring fame and fortune to **Marc Bolan** (né Feld). Hitching a ride on the Pink Floyd-powered psychedelic bandwagon in 1967, he sought new collaborators. He and percussionist Steve Peregrin Took (formerly Stephen Porter) became Tyrannosaurus Rex, teamed up with producer Tony Visconti, and signed to Regal Zonophone. Their debut single, "Debora," hit the U.K. Top Forty ahead of the album *My People Were Fair and Had Sky in Their Hair… But Now They're Content to Wear Stars on Their Brow,* which reached No. 15 in the U.K. in July 1968. It was followed within three months by *Prophets, Seers and Sages, The Angels of the Ages* and, just seven months later, *Unicorn* (U.K. No. 12).

In 1969, Took was replaced by **Mickey Finn**. At Visconti's behest, the band became T. Rex and evolved from acoustic whimsy to electric pop with the hit "Ride a White Swan." With guitarist **Steve Currie** and drummer **Bill Legend**, T. Rex exploded in 1971, topping the U.K. charts with the glam-rocking "Hot Love" and *Electric Warrior* (U.S. No. 32). With his friend and rival David Bowie yet to make a commercial impact, Bolan and his band were the undisputed kings of glam.

"Get It On" topped the U.K. charts in 1971 and, retitled "Bang A Gong (Get it On)," hit the U.S. Top Ten the following year. "Telegram Sam" and "Metal Guru" completed a hat-trick of British chart-toppers. Capitalizing on this wave of success, the hits set *Bolan Boogie* topped the U.K. chart, as did a reissue coupling the first two Tyrannosaurus Rex albums. *The Slider* (1972) missed the top at home but became their greatest U.S. success, hitting No. 17 and U.K. No. 4.

In 1973, new recruits included American singer and writer **Gloria Jones**, who became his girlfriend and the mother of his son Rolan. As Marc Bolan & T. Rex, they hit the charts with "Teenage Dream," a single from *Zinc Alloy and the Hidden Riders of Tomorrow* (1974). But a split from Visconti—working with the now established Bowie—and the departure of Finn in 1975 marked the beginning of the end.

After two years in the doldrums, 1977's *Dandy in the Underworld* was a partial return to commercial form, hitting the U.K. Top Thirty. Bolan's endorsement of punk ("The Pistols," he said, "are a bloody good mirror") and a reconciliation with Bowie also seemed to augur well. But in September that year, aged just twenty-nine, he died in a car accident.

A series of compilations followed—including the Top Five U.K. hit *Best of the 20th Century Boy.* Took and Currie both died within three years of Bolan's death. However, the boppin' elf's legend lives on. **BS**

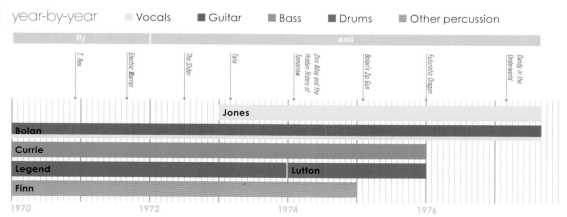

year-by-year   Vocals   Guitar   Bass   Drums   Other percussion

the triffids 1978–1989

David McComb
b. Feb 17, 1962
d. Feb 2, 1999

Phil Kakulas
b. Unknown

Byron Sinclair
b. Unknown

Alsy McDonald
b. August 14, 1961

Robert McComb
b. Unknown

Will Akers
b. Unknown

Jill Birt
b. Unknown

Martyn P. Casey
b. July 10, 1960

By the time they hit London's post-punk circuit in 1984, The Triffids had clocked up six largely uncelebrated years in their Australian homeland. They discovered, however, that their powerful sound dovetailed neatly with prevailing fashions in the U.K. independent scene.

The Triffids evolved from Perth-born **David McComb**'s high-school band, Dalsy. McComb's influences were rock poets: Dylan, Leonard Cohen, Lou Reed, and Patti Smith. The band's first three years were spent in the isolation of Perth, a small city on the country's west coast, more than 2,000 miles (3,200 km) from the twin cultural hubs of Melbourne and Sydney.

In 1983, The Triffids relocated to Sydney and signed to the independent Hot label. But *Treeless Plain*, the band's debut, was largely ignored until it was picked up by London's influential Rough Trade label. Having won rave reviews in the U.K., The Triffids exhausted their savings relocating to London in 1984 and became an immediate hit on the university circuit.

Wider success seemed assured when the *NME* put the band on its cover, a headline declaring 1985 "The Year of The Triffids." A cult following took *Born Sandy Devotional* (1986) and its "Wide Open Road" into the lower reaches of the U.K. charts. McComb's crowning achievement as a songwriter, the album brilliantly articulated the vast expanse of his homeland.

Winning a major deal with Island, The Triffids recorded *Calenture* (1987), which added production sheen to McComb's uplifting songs. The lead single, "Bury Me Deep in Love," failed to hit but, two years later, would be heard by millions in a wedding episode of the Australian soap opera *Neighbours*.

Drawing from a more diverse set of influences, 1989's *The Black Swan* reinforced the growing suspicion that, for The Triffids, commercial success would never match critical acclaim. Well received as ever, the album sold poorly. Dispirited, the band called it a day, fulfilling their contractual obligation with a 1990 live album recorded in Sweden.

McComb remained in London but solo success eluded him. In 1993 he returned to Australia, enrolled in university, and continued a low-key recording career. His health had increasingly been hampered by alcohol and heroin abuse and, in 1996, he had to undergo a life-saving heart transplant. He died three years later while recovering from a car accident.

One of Australia's most literate bands, The Triffids—alongside the Go-Betweens and Nick Cave—altered attitudes to Antipodean rock in the eighties. McComb, posthumously inducted into the Australian music industry's Hall of Fame in 2006, is remembered as one of the nation's finest songwriters. **TB**

year-by-year   ■ Vocals   ■ Guitar   ■ Bass   ■ Drums   ■ Keyboards   ■ Strings

hot   white hot

Treeless Plain · *Born Sandy Devotional* · *In the Pines* · *Calenture* · *The Black Swan*

D. McComb	
Kakulas	
Sinclair	Casey
Akers	
McDonald	
	Birt
R. McComb	

1978   1980   1982   1984   1986   1988

u2 1978–present

Bono
b. May 10, 1960

The Edge
b. August 8, 1961

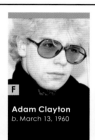

Adam Clayton
b. March 13, 1960

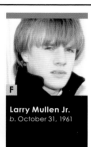

Larry Mullen Jr.
b. October 31, 1961

"They may be the only good anthemic rock band ever," Coldplay frontman Chris Martin enthused to *Rolling Stone*, "...and they are the only band that's been around for more than thirty years with no member changes and no big splits."

Drummer **Larry Mullen Jr.**, then fourteen, recruited singer Paul "**Bono**" Hewson, guitarist David "**The Edge**" Evans, and bassist **Adam Clayton** at a Dublin school in 1976. The initial lineup also featured Edge's brother Dik Evans, Ivan McCormick, and Peter Martin. By the time Feedback, as they were known, landed their first pub gig, McCormick and Martin were out. Dik Evans survived as they evolved into The Hype, but was eased out when they became U2 in 1978.

The quartet made their international debuts with 1980's "11 O'Clock Tick Tock," produced by Joy Division guru Martin Hannett, and *Boy*, helmed by Steve Lillywhite. Meanwhile, relentless touring won influential fans. "I went with Pete Townshend—always one to catch the first whiff of those about to unseat us—to a club in London," Bruce Springsteen told the Rock and Roll Hall of Fame (his highly amusing induction is well worth looking up online). "There they were: a young Bono, single-handedly pioneering the Irish mullet. The Edge—what kind of name was that?—Adam and Larry. I was listening to the last band of whom I would be able to name all of its members."

After the water-treading *October* (1981), dogged touring, notably in the U.S., and *War* (1983) catapulted the band into the big league. The album expanded their palette with brass, backing vocals by Kid Creole's Coconuts, and—on "Sunday Bloody Sunday"—electric violin by Steve Wickham of The Waterboys.

The live *Under a Blood Red Sky* (1983) and accompanying *Live at Red Rocks* video confirmed U2's ascent to flag-waving stardom. To broaden their sonic horizons, Brian Eno and his production partner Daniel Lanois were enlisted for 1984's *The Unforgettable Fire*. (String arrangements were by Noel Kelehan, conductor on Irish entries for the Eurovision Song Contest). The Eno-influenced "Bad" proved a highlight of 1985's live *Wide Awake in America* and U2's set at Live Aid, before the classic *The Joshua Tree* (1987)—its running order compiled by Lillywhite's wife, singer Kirsty MacColl—topped charts worldwide.

Now among rock's biggest bands, U2 issued the po-faced movie *Rattle and Hum* (1988), the superior soundtrack of which featured Bob Dylan, soul label Stax stars The Memphis Horns, blues giant BB King, Tom Petty's keyboardist Benmont Tench, and—on its highlight, "All I Want Is You"—Beach Boys cohort Van Dyke Parks. Completing their homage to newfound muses, U2 covered The Beatles' "Helter Skelter" and coopted Hendrix's "The Star-Spangled Banner."

year-by-year ■ Vocals ■ Guitar ■ Bass ■ Drums ■ Keyboards

U

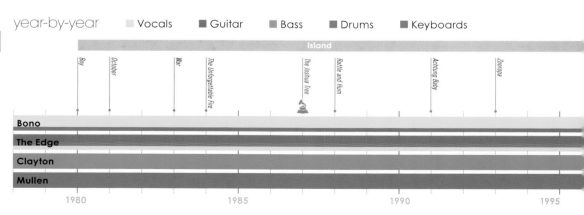

island

Boy | October | War | The Unforgettable Fire | The Joshua Tree | Rattle and Hum | Achtung Baby | Zooropa

Bono
The Edge
Clayton
Mullen

1980　　　　1985　　　　1990　　　　1995

25.3M
The Joshua Tree
(1987)

17.6M
Achtung Baby
(1991)

15M
*The Best of
1980-1990*
(1998)

12.1M
*All That You Can't
Leave Behind*
(2000)

Seemingly boxed into a Simple Minds-shaped corner, the band conceived rock's greatest makeover since *Sgt. Pepper:* out went ersatz blues, in came *Achtung Baby* (1991), engineered by Flood (who coproduced Nine Inch Nails and Depeche Mode after working on *The Joshua Tree*). The kaleidoscopic *Zooropa* (1993) completed the transformation: its fine songs were laced with loops and samples, and Johnny Cash sang on the throbbing "The Wanderer."

Giddy with musical freedom, U2 put Eno in charge, called themselves Passengers, and dropped the bafflingly woozy *Original Soundtracks 1* (1995). Among its contributors were electronic maestros Craig Armstrong and Marius de Vries, who achieved far superior results with Madonna. On the sole highlights were vocal cameos by Clayton (on "Your Blue Room," the bassist's first vocal since a 1983 B-side) and opera singer Luciano Pavarotti (on the hit "Miss Sarajevo").

Struggling for relevance, and with Mullen sidelined by back problems, U2 recruited dance-oriented fellow Passenger Howie B to supply beats. Flood, De Vries, and Happy Mondays producer Steve Osborne added keyboards. The resulting *Pop* (1997) quadrupled Passengers' tally of good songs, but often sounded unfinished. The Popmart tour proved spectacular, but suggested U2 had lost sight of why people liked them: emotionally resonant songs and performances.

After *The Best of 1980–1990* (1998) and Bono's indulgent movie and soundtrack *The Million Dollar Hotel* (2000), a stripped-down U2 emerged with *All That You Can't Leave Behind* (2000), its producers including Spice Girls architect Richard Stannard. Huge sales, an international No. 1 ("Beautiful Day"), seven Grammys, and a sell-out tour—commemorated by 2003's heartwarming *U2 Go Home* DVD—ensued.

The Best of 1990–2000 (2002) preceded *How to Dismantle an Atomic Bomb* (2004), another smash. The roster of producers was joined by Snow Patrol's knob-twiddler Jacknife Lee and *Dark Side of the Moon*'s Chris Thomas, while "One Step Closer" carried an "inspired by" credit for Noel Gallagher of Oasis (who had supported U2 on the Popmart tour).

From an abortive union with producer Rick Rubin, a cover of the Skids' "The Saints Are Coming" with Green Day, and "Window in the Skies"—both included on 2006's *U218 Singles*—outshone everything on *No Line on the Horizon* (2009), helmed by Eno, Lanois, and Lillywhite. However, the ensuing 360° Tour became the highest grossing in rock history.

Plans for multiple follow-ups, involving hit-makers from Black Eyed Peas and Gnarls Barkley, were shelved when *No Line*… sold a "mere" five million copies. "The next thing that people need to hear from U2," admitted Bono, "is not an art project." **BM**

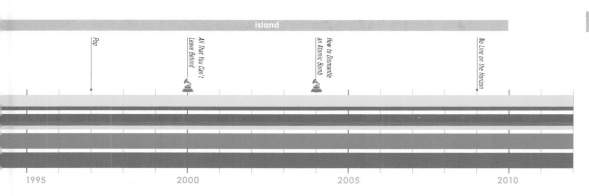

island

Pop

All That You Can't
Leave Behind

How to Dismantle
an Atomic Bomb

No Line on the Horizon

1995   2000   2005   2010

Boy (1980)

War (1983)

The Unforgettable Fire (1984)

The Joshua Tree (1987)

Achtung Baby (1991)

Zooropa (1993)

Pop (1997)

All That You Can't Leave Behind (2000)

How to Dismantle an Atomic Bomb (2004)

No Line on the Horizon (2009)

Left to right: **The Edge, Larry Mullen Jr., Bono,** and **Adam Clayton** perform in Belgium on October 18, 1980, during their *Boy* tour.

Clayton and **Bono** at the 1984 Band Aid recording session.

Bob Dylan joins U2 onstage in L.A. on the Joshua Tree tour in 1987.

Bono and **The Edge** on British TV's *The Tube* in 1983.

Bono—in the character of MacPhisto that he used for songs such as "Lemon"—performs in Paris, France, in June 1993, during U2's Zooropa tour.

Bono as The Fly: the first and most enduring of the alter-egos that he adopted for U2's reinvention on *Achtung Baby*.

The visually extraordinary Popmart tour reaches the Netherlands in the summer of 1997.

Larry Mullen Jr. performs in San Diego on March 28, 2005, at the start of U2's Vertigo tour of that year.

Bono and **The Edge** in one of their Elevation tour set pieces, 2001.

The band perform under New York's Brooklyn Bridge in late 2004.

The record-breaking 360° Tour reaches New Jersey's New Meadowlands Stadium in 2011.

univers zéro 1974–present

Daniel Denis
b. 1953

Roger Trigaux
b. Unknown

Michel Berckmans
b. September 1, 1955

Christian Genet
b. Unknown

Martin Leuwers
b. Unknown

Kurt Budé
b. Unknown

Pierre Chevallier
b. Unknown

Dimitri Evers
b. Unknown

In 1978, British avant-garde rock band Henry Cow initiated a London concert featuring similar-minded artists from continental Europe—among them, Univers Zéro from Belgium. The show's slogan was simple: "The bands the record companies don't want you to hear." Its name, Rock in Opposition (RIO), became that of a genre—less of related musical styles than of a progressive, politically minded attitude.

Having worked with French progressive rockers Magma, Belgian drummer and composer **Daniel Denis** formed Univers Zéro in 1974. Initially influenced by avant-garde classical music and electronic jazz, the band's sound had evolved by the time of their 1977 debut. *Univers Zéro* was a mix of progressive rock and free jazz, but presented by a chamber ensemble with largely acoustic instrumentation: bassoon, viola, violin, harmonium, spinet. The compositions, by Denis or guitarist **Roger Trigaux**, were often dark in tone and showed the influence of Béla Bartók; Denis also championed Albert Huybrechts, a little-known Belgian composer active in the twenties. The sound is encapsulated in the fifteen-minute "Ronde": tightly structured chamber music with asymmetrical rhythms and elements of post-bop jazz. (The album was remixed and reissued in the eighties as *1313*.)

Univers Zéro continued in this vein with 1979's *Heresie*. Denis and Trigaux's songs mined darker depths, with a bleak, dissonant sound that showcased the oboe and bassoon of **Michel Berckmans**.

1981's *Ceux du dehors* ("Those from the outside") witnessed a change in tone following the departure of Trigaux, who left to form his own progressive group, Present. (The album was issued internationally on the Recommended label, itself an influential base for RIO artists, founded in the late seventies by Henry Cow's drummer, Chris Cutler.) With a lighter, less brooding sound than previous works, the album saw the introduction of electronics into the band's music.

Having toured throughout Europe, Univers Zéro resurfaced on record with 1984's *Uzed*, which showed a significant stylistic departure. Synthesizers took an increasingly prominent role, as did the cello textures of new member André Mergen. Denis's compositions had also taken on an increasingly Middle Eastern flavor, most evidently on the opener "Présage."

Working outside the conventional music industry offered Univers Zéro artistic freedom, but there was a commercial corollary: with little in the way of business management, finances were a persistent struggle and, in 1986, Denis decided to fold the band. He made two solo albums before relaunching Univers Zéro in 1999 with Berckmans. Subsequent work has seen the band moving away from their early sound toward more traditional progressive rock territory. **TB**

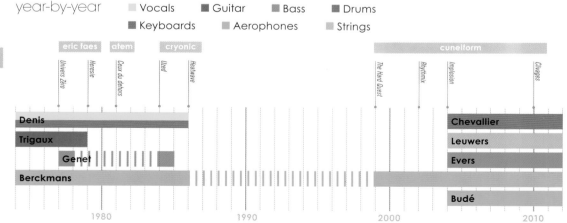

year-by-year ■ Vocals ■ Guitar ■ Bass ■ Drums ■ Keyboards ■ Aerophones ■ Strings

uriah heep 1969–present

Mick Box
b. June 9, 1947

Ken Hensley
b. August 24, 1945

David Byron
b. Jan 29, 1947
d. February 28, 1985

Paul Newton
b. February 21, 1948

Alex Napier
b. Unknown

Gary Thain
b. May 15, 1948
d. December 8, 1975

Trevor Bolder
b. June 9, 1950

Lee Kerslake
b. April 16, 1947

You can't stop the Heep. The British act have endured myriad lineup changes and bad reviews. (Famously, *Rolling Stone*'s Melissa Mills wrote, "If this group makes it, I'll have to commit suicide.") Along the way, they've issued more than fifty studio, live, and compilation albums. In their 1971–1975 heyday, Heep were among the most popular hard rock acts in the U.S. and U.K. When those countries stopped buying their records, the band focused on other nations—notably, Norway and Germany—until their renaissance with *Abominog* in 1982. Today, though they rarely trouble charts, they still tour and put out albums that add to their legacy.

Uriah Heep's roots stretch back to the Stalkers, a group that rocked pubs in England's Essex in the mid-sixties. When the Stalkers split, guitarist **Mick Box** and vocalist **David Byron** enlisted keyboardist-guitarist **Ken Hensley** and bassist **Paul Newton** in a new band, Spice, which became Uriah Heep (after a character in Charles Dickens' *David Copperfield*). Starting with Alex Napier, the band would go through drummers at a Spinal Tap-style rate, utilizing at least four different players in its first six years. (Others to feature in the ranks include **Lee Kerslake**, who also drummed in the first incarnation of Ozzy Osbourne's Blizzard of Ozz, **Trevor Bolder**, former bassist in David Bowie's Spiders from Mars, and Bernie Shaw, Heep's singer since 1986.)

Heep made little noise on the charts with 1970's debut *Very 'Eavy... Very 'Umble* (issued as a self-titled affair in the U.S.), but the response from critics was deafening. "From the first note," critiqued Mills, "you know you don't want to hear any more." But Heep didn't make that an option. The band charged ahead at an astounding pace, releasing a dozen studio albums in its first nine years. They were never shy about showing their grand ambitions on such cuts as the title track to 1971's *Salisbury*, which ran to sixteen minutes and featured a twenty-four-piece orchestra.

The band broke out with *Look at Yourself* (1971), a mostly prog-free rocker that cracked the Top 100 in the U.S. (where fans included future Metallica man Lars Ulrich). The next three albums all went gold in the U.S. Then, just as their popularity waned in America, Heep finally conquered Britain, landing in the Top Ten for the first time with 1975's *Return to Fantasy*. And, as their domestic following faded, the group began to experience great success elsewhere—in Germany, 1977's *Innocent Victim* was a million-seller.

Heep have continued to cultivate new fan bases as old ones slip away: in 1987, they became the first Western band to perform in Soviet Russia. More than forty years into their career, Heep—with Box the sole remaining original member—remain unbowed. **JiH**

year-by-year   ☐ Vocals ■ Guitar ■ Bass ■ Drums ■ Keyboards

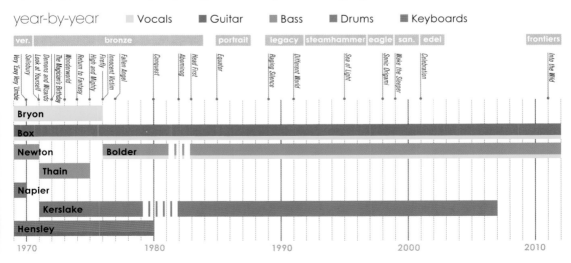

van halen 1974–present

Eddie Van Halen
b. January 26, 1955

Alex Van Halen
b. May 8, 1953

Wolfgang Van Halen
b. March 16, 1991

David Lee Roth
b. October 10, 1954

Sammy Hagar
b. October 13, 1947

Michael Anthony
b. June 20, 1954

Few rock bands have ever landed on the international music scene with such an impact as Van Halen, the Pasadena four-piece that set new standards for both showmanship and musicianship in the late seventies.

The first time most music fans became aware of the band—whose classic lineup was **David Lee Roth** (vocals), **Eddie Van Halen** (guitar), **Michael Anthony** (bass), and **Alex Van Halen** (drums)—was in 1978, when the young upstarts supported metal veterans Black Sabbath. According to popular legend, they blew the ailing Sabbath off their own stage. This was no ordinary rock band; this was nothing less than the end of an era, and the start of a whole new one.

Van Halen had not one but two aces in their pack. The first was Roth, whose electrifying performances—including huge, acrobatic leaps and extravagant audience interaction—had gig-goers spellbound. The second was Eddie, a musician whose unearthly skills made him a game-changer in his field. (Roth alleges that Gene Simmons—credited with "discovering" the band—tried to poach the guitarist for Kiss.) Eddie's neoclassical scales were not new—Ritchie Blackmore of Deep Purple had pioneered the classical/rock crossover in the previous decade—but his high-speed

fretboard tapping was. (Blackmore conceded that Van Halen was "very impressive.") Coupled with howling overdrive, the flurries of notes that he emitted in his solos—initially with his back to the audience in order to avoid being copied by other guitarists—were a highlight of every show. His showcase, "Eruption," even had a place on the band's 1978 debut album.

From that self-titled debut, which eventually sold over ten million albums in the U.S. alone to attain diamond status, Van Halen were unstoppable. Classic album followed classic album, each attempting to be more over-the-top than the last. The songs got slicker as the years passed, with high-charting covers of "Pretty Woman" and "Dancing in the Street" pulling in audiences to arena shows that got bigger and more lavishly produced as the eighties unfolded.

However, the internal friction that fueled the band and made them so entertaining was becoming unbearable. Despite scoring a smash with 1984's keyboard-driven "Jump" (the group's only U.S. No. 1 single), Roth jumped ship and launched a relatively successful solo career. In a move clearly designed to show he didn't need Eddie, the singer enlisted guitar hero du jour Steve Vai for 1986's *Eat 'Em and Smile*.

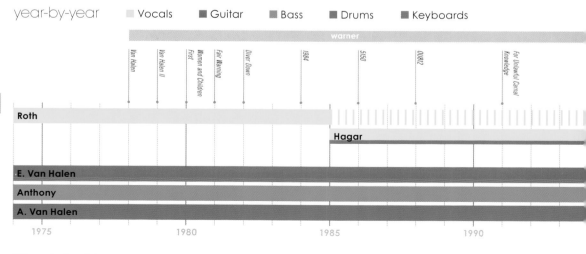

year-by-year   ■ Vocals   ■ Guitar   ■ Bass   ■ Drums   ■ Keyboards

warner

Van Halen
Van Halen II
Women and Children First
Fair Warning
Diver Down
1984
5150
OU812
For Unlawful Carnal Knowledge

Roth

Hagar

E. Van Halen

Anthony

A. Van Halen

1975   1980   1985   1990

Gary Cherone
b. July 26, 1961

The remaining trio recruited ex-Montrose singer **Sammy Hagar** and surprised everyone by heightening their profile, thanks to continued tours and four consecutive U.S. No. 1 albums. In 1988, their Monsters of Rock tour epitomized this golden era: a time of ample record-label budgets and tour revenue that is unlikely to come again. In a way, Van Halen epitomized this period—an unashamedly extrovert group of musicians, delivering an explosive brand of music to an audience with the money to pay for it.

The times that followed were harder. While all the members of Van Halen were wealthy men by the early nineties, audiences were looking elsewhere: shred guitar was far from fashionable in the grunge era. *Balance* (1995) was largely deemed unsatisfactory and Hagar left the band soon after.

Bereft of a front-man for a second time, the Van Halen brothers took the unusual step of recruiting Extreme singer **Gary Cherone**. In hindsight, it is obvious that Cherone, despite being a fine singer, could not hope to compete with either Hagar or Roth in terms of commanding a stage. Fans missed his more charismatic predecessors, *Van Halen III* (1998) was hardly a stellar success, and Cherone quit in 1999.

A near four-year hiatus ensued, during which Eddie underwent a battle with cancer, a divorce, and a hip replacement. When the band regrouped in 2004 with Hagar again at the helm, the sessions were unproductive: the status of founder member Anthony was unclear, and songwriting progressed only sporadically. A bad-tempered tour in 2004 grossed an enormous $55 million, but Anthony was being edged out. His place was taken two years later by Eddie's son Wolfgang, then a mere fifteen years old.

The inevitable reunion with Roth occurred in 2007 amid much public mud-slinging and stints in rehab for Eddie, with a second mega-tour taking place in 2008.

In recent years, comings and goings in the Van Halen camp have sometimes attained farcical proportions, with past and present bandmates throwing in soundbites from all sides (although Anthony and Hagar—now ensconced in a new group, Chickenfoot, with Red Hot Chili Peppers drummer Chad Smith—have usually taken the high road when invited to comment on their old band). However, a re-reunion with Roth produced A *Different Kind of Truth* (2012) and a tour on which this most mercurial of groups proved its mettle once more. **JM**

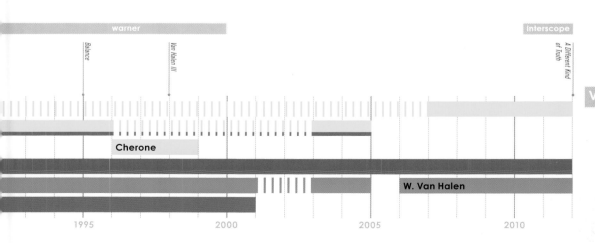

Van Halen (1978)

Van Halen II (1979)

Women and Children First (1980)

Fair Warning (1981)

1984 (1984)

5150 (1986)

For Unlawful Carnal Knowledge (1991)

Balance (1995)

Van Halen III (1998)

A Different Kind of Truth (2012)

Michael Anthony, Alex Van Halen, David Lee Roth, and **Eddie Van Halen** in London, 1978.

Roth limbers up for another scene-stealing performance in 1981.

Roth—arguably *the* rock star of his time—at the Palladium, New York, in May 1979.

Eddie with Michael Jackson, on whose "Beat It" he soloed, in 1984.

Eddie performs at the Dutch Pinkpop Festival in May 1980.

Alex Van Halen with fellow drumming legends Carmine Appice (left) and Ginger Baker (ce...

With new singer **Sammy Hagar** (second from left) at **Eddie**'s house in Los Angeles.

Hagar and **Eddie** perform at Mountain View, California, on October 14, 1995.

Roth at a warm-up show for his second reunion tour with Van Halen, at The Forum in Inglewood, California, in February 2012.

Anthony, new singer (and former Extreme front-man) **Gary Cherone**, and **Eddie** live in California in 1998.

the velvet underground / lou reed

Lou Reed
b. March 2, 1942

John Cale
b. March 9, 1942

Sterling Morrison
b. August 28, 1942
d. August 30, 1995

Angus MacLise
b. March 4, 1938
d. June 21, 1979

Moe Tucker
b. August 26, 1944

Nico
b. October 16, 1938
d. July 18, 1988

Drawing on avant-gardisms, Brill Building-style pop, and primal rock 'n' roll, The Velvet Underground are a keystone of rock. Their sonic world is frequently dark, but occasionally pretty—and always engrossing.

Lou Reed united with the classically trained **John Cale** in The Primitives, later adding guitarist **Sterling Morrison**, who had known Reed at Syracuse University. Inspired by a paperback about S&M found in the street, they renamed themselves The Velvet Underground. Drummer Maureen "**Moe**" **Tucker**—whose monolithic thumping became central to their sound—joined when original percussionist **Angus MacLise** dropped out prior to a gig.

After seeing them at New York's Cafe Bizarre in late 1965, artist Andy Warhol became their patron, drafting in chanteuse **Nico** for a touch of European cool. Warhol also financed their debut LP—and designed its iconic "banana" sleeve. It sold zilch (U.S. No. 171—the highest position of any of their studio sets), but became one of rock's Rosetta stones. No one sang about drugs ("Heroin," "Waiting for the Man," "Run, Run, Run") with such arresting nonchalance, or made sado-masochism ("Venus in Furs") so mesmerizing. The churning "All Tomorrow's Parties" became Warhol's favorite Velvets song.

The follow-up *White Light, White Heat* (1968) was lo-fi, distorted—deliberately so: the band recorded at maximum volume, in the red. "The kind of record you have to be in the mood for," mused The Strokes' Julian Casablancas to *Rolling Stone*. "You have to be in a shitty bar, in a really shitty mood." The title track was a chugalong paean to amphetamine, "The Gift" a twisted love story with a shock ending, narrated in John Cale's melodious Welsh tones. The remorseless, seventeen-minute "Sister Ray" was a jam with odd lyrics, many of them muffled—like "Louie Louie."

Tensions within the band saw Cale depart in 1968—to be replaced by **Doug Yule**—and *The Velvet Underground* (1969) lacked the avant-garde edge he would have supplied. In its place was a renewed emphasis on melody and harmony. "I'm Set Free" and "Beginning to See the Light" were jubilant confessionals, "What Goes On" a joyous jam, and the beautiful "Pale Blue Eyes" simply transfixing.

By *Loaded* (1970)—minus Tucker, then pregnant—a disillusioned Reed was set to quit. As a parting gift, he said, "I gave them an album loaded with hits." Wistful reflections ("New Age," "Oh! Sweet Nothin'") sat alongside rockers like "Sweet Jane" and "Rock 'n' Roll"—both of which Reed would incorporate into his

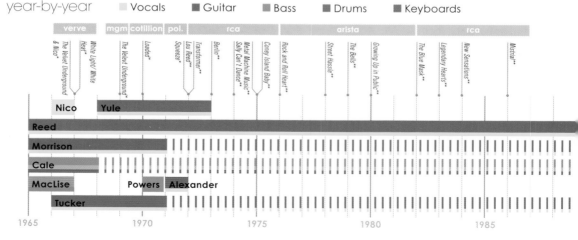

year-by-year   ▢ Vocals   ■ Guitar   ■ Bass   ■ Drums   ■ Keyboards

V

1.1M	500,000	1M	1.1M
Transformer (1972)	*Berlin* (1973)	*Rock 'n' Roll Animal* (1974)	*New York* (1989)

Doug Yule
b. February 25, 1947

Walter Powers
b. Unknown
d. Unknown

Willie Alexander
b. January 13, 1943

solo act. Sterling Morrison left in 1971 to study English literature. In his wake, the Doug Yule-helmed Velvets had little to offer, but endured until 1973.

Reed's first solo album revisited unreleased Velvets tunes and was largely overlooked. His second, *Transformer* (1972), co-helmed by long-term admirer David Bowie and his sidekick Mick Ronson, was a resounding success, alternately strident ("Vicious," "I'm So Free"), quirky ("Andy's Chest," "New York Telephone Conversation"), and plainly enchanting ("Perfect Day"). "Walk on the Wild Side" gave Reed his first and biggest hit, receiving generous airplay despite its near-the-knuckle lyrics.

He followed it with the memorable but harrowing *Berlin* (1973), a concept album about a doomed relationship, taking in "The Bed" (captivating, but mighty bleak) and ending with the oddly uplifting "Sad Song." *Sally Can't Dance* and the live *Rock 'n' Roll Animal* (both 1974) maintained Reed's profile, which he destroyed with *Metal Machine Music* (1975), a double album of shrill feedback that fans returned in their droves. The mellow, melodic *Coney Island Baby* (1975) redressed the balance, while *Street Hassle* (1978) carried a harder edge, reflecting the rise of punk—of which the Velvets were seen as godfathers.

Reed's career stalled somewhat in the eighties, although *The Blue Mask* (1982) and *New York* (1989) were well received. The death of friend and former mentor Andy Warhol in 1987, however, prompted a reunion with his ex-Velvet bandmate John Cale on the moving *Songs for Drella* (1990)—its title a nickname for Warhol ("Dracula" meets "Cinderella").

In 1990, the original four-piece Velvets reunited for a one-off benefit gig, and by 1992 they were once again a gigging concern—hence *LIVE MXMXCIII* (1993). The group played in Europe to acclaim, though arguments between Reed and Cale ruined plans for a U.S. tour. After Morrison passed away in 1995, Cale, Reed, and Tucker performed "Last Night I Said Goodbye to My Friend" at their Rock and Roll Hall of Fame induction in 1996, drawing the story of The Velvet Underground to a respectful close.

The Velvets' vast legacy can be heard in the chugging rhythms of Jonathan Richman's Modern Lovers and Arcade Fire, the art rock of Roxy Music and David Bowie, the dark energy of Joy Division, and the sparseness of Prince's "The Cross." They fed The Jesus and Mary Chain's white noise, Sonic Youth's aural avalanche, and The Strokes' deadpan drawl. "Influential" doesn't begin to cover it. **RD**

 Other percussion   Strings

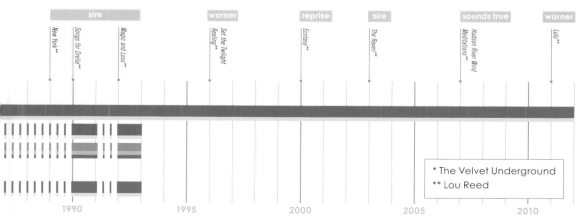

* The Velvet Underground
** Lou Reed

sire | warner | reprise | sire | sounds true | warner

New York** | Songs for Drella** | Magic and Loss** | Set the Twilight Reeling** | Ecstasy** | The Raven** | Hudson River Wind Meditations** | Lulu**

1990 | 1995 | 2000 | 2005 | 2010

the verve 1989–2009

Richard Ashcroft
b. September 11, 1971

Simon Jones
b. May 29, 1972

Nick McCabe
b. July 14, 1971

Peter Salisbury
b. September 24, 1971

Simon Tong
b. July 9, 1972

The Greater Manchester town of Wigan and the words "hotbed of musical creativity" have been uneasy bedfellows since the birth of rock 'n' roll in the fifties, but the ripple of excitement caused by Kajagoogoo/ Limahl in the mid-eighties turned into a tidal wave a decade on when **The Verve** arrived on the scene with their bittersweet symphonies.

In truth, only fifty percent of the group's original lineup—"lips and cheekbones" frontman **Richard Ashcroft** and bass guitarist **Simon Jones**—were actually born in the town. But the Wigan Casino (once dubbed the "best disco in the world" by *Billboard* magazine), rugby league, and the pier made famous by writer George Orwell were all shifted down the search engine pecking order from the moment the psychedelic shoegazers established a foothold in the charts and minds of the record-buying public. They first locked horns in 1989 as students at Wigan's Winstanley College, and made their live debut in 1990.

Ashcroft, Jones, guitarist **Nick McCabe**, and drummer **Peter Salisbury** were signed to Hut Records (a subsidiary of Virgin) as Verve in 1991, and among their first recordings was the single "She's a Superstar." With *A Storm in Heaven* (1993) brewing, Verve called on producer John Leckie—who masterminded The Stone Roses' self-titled debut—and embraced

psychedelic rock. However, their first album failed to ignite at retail despite favorable publicity for their Glastonbury appearance in 1993 and shows with Manchester band Oasis.

In 1994, after a legal tussle with Verve Records, the group gained the definite article but lost their heads at the nomadic Lollapalooza festival in the United States. In a drink- and drug-induced haze, The Verve returned home to begin work on their second album, *A Northern Soul* (1995). Described by one critic as "a traumatic realization of the hopelessness of human existence, a document of fractured mentalities, the sound of four young men old before their time," *A Northern Soul* was released to mixed reviews. Nonetheless, it continued their upward trajectory, peaking at No. 13 in the U.K.

Ashcroft dissolved The Verve, riddled by internal conflict, at Britpop's zenith in the summer of 1995. But he swiftly revived them—initially with **Simon Tong** as McCabe's replacement and then with McCabe and Tong strumming in harmony—ahead of their career-defining third studio album, *Urban Hymns* (1997).

In the summer of 1997, "Bitter Sweet Symphony" ended America's futile resistance to the lads' northern charm with a Top Twenty berth on the *Billboard* Hot 100. The song's Walter Stern-directed video presented

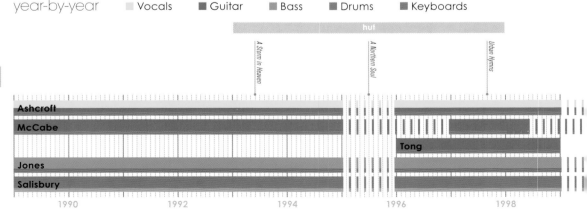

year-by-year   ▨ Vocals   ■ Guitar   ■ Bass   ■ Drums   ■ Keyboards

hut

A Storm in Heaven

A Northern Soul

Urban Hymns

V

Ashcroft

McCabe

Tong

Jones

Salisbury

1990   1992   1994   1996   1998

Ashcroft, loaded with attitude, barging his way along London's Hoxton Street in homage to Massive Attack's "Unfinished Sympathy." Ashcroft labeled "Bitter Sweet Symphony" "the best song Jagger and Richards have written in twenty years"—a reference to a prominent sample of the Andrew Oldham Orchestra's rendition of the Stones' "The Last Time." Accused of plagiarism, The Verve reluctantly surrendered their writing credits, plus 100 percent of the royalties, to the wrinkly duo. "It's a bitter sweet symphony, this life / Try to make ends meet / You're a slave to money then you die…"

Urban Hymns' one-two punch was completed by "The Drugs Don't Work," a title clearly at odds with the fuzzy, room-trashing experimentation of their formative years, or perhaps one tinged with regret and a sign of their growing maturity. The poignant yet depressing ballad (writer Ashcroft compared growing old to "a cat in a bag waiting to drown") debuted at No. 1 in the U.K. on September 7, 1997, and captured the somber mood of the nation following the death of Diana, Princess of Wales, exactly one week earlier.

The Verve were nominated for four Brit Awards in 1998 (winning Best British Group and Best British Album) and *Urban Hymns* was a no-brainer for the Mercury Prize shortlist in the year their homecoming gig attracted 33,000 fans to the Haigh Fest in Greater Manchester. In 2010, *Hymns* was nominated for the Brits' Best British Album of the Last Thirty Years, but the prize went to *(What's the Story) Morning Glory?* The irony was not lost on Noel Gallagher, who years earlier had dedicated *Morning Glory*'s "Cast No Shadow" to "the brilliance of Richard Ashcroft."

The Verve disbanded for a second time in 1999, scattering members far and wide. McCabe had already quit in 1998, to be replaced by pedal steel veteran B.J. Cole. Ashcroft launched a successful solo career, scoring three consecutive U.K. Top Three albums (including the No. 1 *Alone with Everybody* in 2000). Jones and Tong formed The Shining with John Squire prior to Tong replacing Graham Coxon in Blur and playing alongside Damon Albarn in The Good, The Bad & The Queen. Salisbury drummed with Black Rebel Motorcycle Club, and McCabe jammed with John Martyn and The Music. But in 2007 the original lineup buried their differences to mastermind comeback gigs that sold out in twenty minutes, along with an arena tour, headline festival appearances, and, in 2008, another British chart-topper (*Forth*).

Wigan's warriors were terminated for a third time in August 2009, but do not rule out a chapter four. Perhaps, to quote "The Drugs Don't Work," Ashcroft will offer to "sing in your ear again." **MW**

■ Other percussion

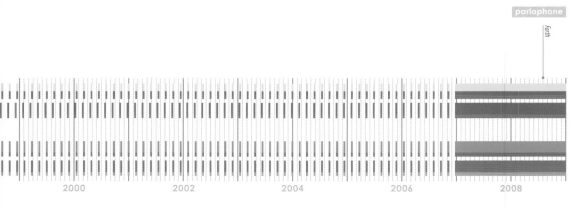

whitesnake 1978–present

David Coverdale
b. September 22, 1951

Doug Aldrich
b. February 19, 1962

Reb Beach
b. August 31, 1963

Micky Moody
b. August 30, 1950

Bernie Marsden
b. May 7, 1951

Neil Murray
b. August 27, 1950

Jon Lord
b. June 9, 1941

Ian Paice
b. June 29, 1948

David Coverdale—singer in the mighty Deep Purple from 1973 until their dissolution in 1976—has proved a wily judge of commercial trends. At the genesis of their lengthy evolution, his band Whitesnake were earthy blues-rockers with obvious Purple influences. In mid-career, they were reinvented as Hollywood-style glam-rockers. Today, after over three decades, they exist as a reliably entertaining synthesis of the two.

In the wake of Purple's messy demise, Coverdale—contractually barred from working in the U.K.—cut vocals for 1977's solo *White Snake* over backing tracks recorded in Britain by musicians including guitarist **Micky Moody** and Purple bassist Roger Glover.

Moody remained for a second solo album, 1978's *Northwinds*, and the formation of a touring band, David Coverdale's Whitesnake. After the *Snakebite* EP (featuring a cover of Bobby Bland's "Ain't No Love in the Heart of the City," thereafter a staple of Whitesnake's live set), Purple's **Jon Lord** became the band's third keyboard player in a year.

By *Trouble* (1978), the lineup had settled: Lord, guitarists Moody and **Bernie Marsden**, bassist **Neil Murray**, and drummer Dave Dowle. But the band that we know today—heavy on guitar riffs and salacious lyrics—emerged with 1979's *Lovehunter*, whose cover featured a naked woman astride a giant python. By the album's release, Dowle (who drummed on both it

and the Japan-only *Live at Hammersmith*) had been replaced by another Purple graduate, **Ian Paice**.

The 1980 album *Ready an' Willing* bequeathed the band's first U.K. Top Twenty hit, "Fool for Your Loving," before *Live… in the Heart of the City* (which included *Live at Hammersmith* as its second half) earned the band their first platinum award. *Come an' Get It* (1981) just missed the U.K. No. 1, and Whitesnake headlined the U.K.'s Monsters of Rock metal festival, only to splinter after a fractious tour of Germany.

Coverdale rebuilt the band in 1982, with Moody, Lord, former Rainbow drummer **Cozy Powell**, guitarist **Mel Galley**, and bassist **Colin Hodgkinson**. Recordings from the end of the previous lineup were dressed up to create *Saints & Sinners* (1982), which buried the classic "Here I Go Again" and "Crying in the Rain" in a morass of mundanity. The lineup lasted for more than a year—including another Monsters of Rock headliner in 1983—but crumbled later that year. Coverdale was exhausted and frustrated by Whitesnake's failure to crack the U.S. market, while Moody—disenchanted with the band's heavier direction—resolved to leave.

Slide It In (1984), the lineup's last gasp, was a substantial improvement on *Saints & Sinners*. However, its flat production prompted Whitesnake's new U.S. label, Geffen, to insist on a remix. Guitarist **John Sykes**, late of Thin Lizzy, and the returning Neil Murray,

year-by-year ▪ Vocals ▪ Guitar ▪ Bass ▪ Drums ▪ Keyboards

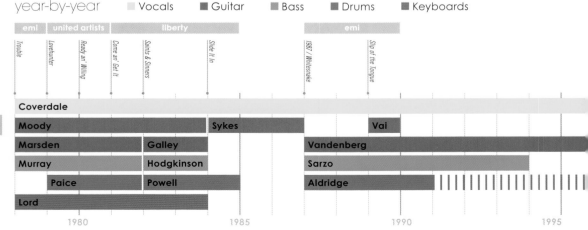

	emi	united artists		liberty				emi	
	Trouble	*Lovehunter*	*Ready an' Willing*	*Come an' Get It*	*Saints & Sinners*	*Slide It In*	*1987 / Whitesnake*	*Slip of the Tongue*	
Coverdale									
Moody						**Sykes**		**Vai**	
Marsden			**Galley**				**Vandenberg**		
Murray			**Hodgkinson**				**Sarzo**		
	Paice		**Powell**				**Aldridge**		
Lord									

| 1980 | 1985 | 1990 | 1995 |

Mel Galley
b. March 8, 1948
d. July 1, 2008

Colin Hodgkinson
b. October 14, 1945

Cozy Powell
b. December 29, 1947
d. April 5, 1998

John Sykes
b. July 29, 1959

Adrian Vandenberg
b. January 31, 1954

Rudy Sarzo
b. November 18, 1950

Tommy Aldridge
b. August 15, 1950

Steve Vai
b. June 6, 1960

replaced Moody and Hodgkinson's parts, and the powerful result hit the U.S. Top Forty (by which time Jon Lord had quit to join the reunited Deep Purple).

Minus Powell (who reappeared in a reconfigured ELP), Coverdale, Sykes, and Murray began work with drummer Aynsley Dunbar. After a lengthy break owing to Coverdale's health problems, the album was completed with guests including guitarist **Adrian Vandenberg** and keyboard player Don Airey.

Vandenberg, ex-Dio guitarist Vivian Campbell, and Ozzy Osbourne's former rhythm section—bassist **Rudy Sarzo** and drummer **Tommy Aldridge**—formed the lineup that conquered the world. *1987*—titled *Whitesnake* in the U.S., and featuring fine reworkings of "Here I Go Again" and "Crying in the Rain" alongside the mighty new classic "Still of the Night"— was a multi-platinum triumph. In the U.S., "Here I Go Again" and "Is This Love" were Top Ten hits, and the album sold five million copies in less than a year. Much of this success was down to an MTV-friendly sound and image, the latter enhanced by Coverdale's future wife Tawny Kitaen's presence in the band's videos.

With Campbell out (later to resurface with Def Leppard), and former Frank Zappa/Public Image Ltd guitar hero **Steve Vai** in, the new formula was inflated to ludicrous (albeit platinum-selling) proportions on *Slip of the Tongue* (1989). Vai was utterly unsuited to

Whitesnake's sound and by the end of 1990—after a third Monsters of Rock headliner (above even Aerosmith)—Coverdale had put the band on ice.

To the incredulity of Led Zeppelin's Robert Plant— who had taken (with some justification) to accusing Coverdale of ripping him off—the singer reappeared on record with Zep guitarist Jimmy Page. The excellent *Coverdale Page* (1993) was a transatlantic Top Five hit, but the union lasted only for one Japanese tour.

When 1994's *Greatest Hits* returned Whitesnake to the charts, Coverdale reconvened the band with Vandenberg, Sarzo, ex-Ratt guitarist Warren DiMartini, and *Coverdale Page* drummer Denny Carmassi. After another hiatus, Whitesnake returned with *Restless Heart* (1997) and a lineup in which Vandenberg was the only constant. But by the end of the year, the band were over again, and Coverdale undertook his first solo album in two decades: 2000's *Into the Light*.

Inevitably, Whitesnake slithered back in 2002, to capitalize on a burgeoning international live market for classic rock. With guitarists **Doug Aldrich** (ex-Dio) and **Reb Beach** (of Winger) heading a customarily unstable lineup, Coverdale scored his highest chart positions in nearly a decade with 2008's *Good to Be Bad*. The resurrection continued with *Forevermore* (2011), and only wear and tear on Coverdale's vocal cords looks likely to threaten the band's future. **JM/BM**

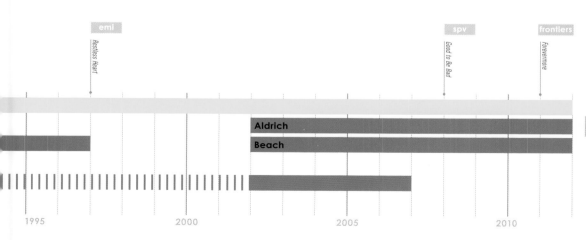

Trouble (1978)

Lovehunter (1979)

Ready an' Willing (1980)

Saints & Sinners (1982)

Slide It In (1984)

Whitesnake (1987)

Slip of the Tongue (1989)

Restless Heart (1997)

Good to Be Bad (2008)

Forevermore (2011)

Neil Murray, Bernie Marsden, David Coverdale, Micky Moody, David Dowle, and **Jon Lord** in August 1978.

Marsden, who sang lead on *Lovehunter*'s standout track "Outlaw."

Coverdale at the Reading Festival, England, in 1980.

Cozy Powell arrived in time to promote, but not play on, *Saints & Sinners.*

Powell, Murray, John Sykes, and **Coverdale** in Rio.

'Snake video star Tawny Kitaen with boyfriend **Coverdale** in 1987.

Tommy Aldridge, Rudy Sarzo, Coverdale, and Adrian Vandenberg make Steve Vai (far right) blush at a Minnesota date on the *Slip of the Tongue* tour, in 1990.

Coverdale onstage with Whitesnake to promote *Restless Heart*.

Drummer Brian Tichy, **Coverdale**, and **Doug Aldrich** in Bournemouth, England, on June 18, 2011.

A customarily rampant peformance from **Coverdale** as the *Good to Be Bad* tour hits the Enmore Theater in Sydney, Australia, on March 28, 2008.

the who 1962–present

Pete Townshend
b. May 19, 1945

Roger Daltrey
b. March 1, 1945

John Entwistle
b. October 9, 1946
d. June 27, 2002

Doug Sandom
b. 1936

Keith Moon
b. August 23, 1947
d. September 7, 1978

Kenney Jones
b. September 16, 1948

In 1962, a surly bunch of young musicians got together in Shepherd's Bush, west London, and created one of rock's greatest and most influential groups. "They smashed through the door of rock 'n' roll," Pearl Jam's Eddie Vedder told *Rolling Stone,* "leaving rubble and not much else for the rest of us to lay claim to."

Pete Townshend (guitar), **Roger Daltrey** (vocals), **John Entwistle** (bass), and **Doug Sandom** (drums) were The Detours—but, in April 1964, everything changed. Out went the older Sandom and in came the younger and wilder **Keith Moon**. After an ignored single as The High Numbers, they reverted to The Who (as they had been known for a few weeks before Sandom's exit).

The quartet forged a reputation for explosive live shows, culminating in the smashing of equipment by the volatile Townshend (whose destruction began as an accident) and Moon (whose destruction was invariably meticulously plotted). The band's first two hits—1965's "I Can't Explain" and "My Generation"—had no less of an earth-shaking impact.

The Who's debut, *My Generation* (issued in the U.S. as *The Who Sings My Generation*) hit the U.K. Top Five. But their reputation was founded more on singles, including 1965's "Anyway, Anyhow, Anywhere," 1966's "Substitute," and 1967's "Pictures of Lily."

Neither of their albums of the time made the same impact, but both are key components of The Who's legacy. *A Quick One* (1966, issued in the U.S. as *Happy Jack* in 1967) contained what Townshend called a mini-opera, "A Quick One While He's Away," and the favorites "Boris the Spider" and "So Sad About Us." *The Who Sell Out* (1967) boasted another mini-opera, "Rael," plus "Armenia, City in the Sky," "Mary Anne with the Shaky Hand," and the soaring, transatlantic Top Ten hit "I Can See for Miles."

In 1967, The Who took their game-changing rock template to the U.S. In June, they stormed the Monterey International Pop Festival in California, upstaging everyone bar Jimi Hendrix. Three months later, on TV's *The Smothers Brothers Comedy Hour,* Moon detonated his drumkit, leaving fellow guest Bette Davis aghast and Townshend with tinnitus.

The Who hit their stride with 1969's ambitious *Tommy* (1969). In this double concept album, the young protagonist—born deaf, dumb, and blind—is dragged through a series of picaresque adventures, including becoming revered as a "Pinball Wizard." The album soared into the U.S. and U.K. Top Five, but its iconic status was secured by The Who's epochal performance at that year's Woodstock festival. The

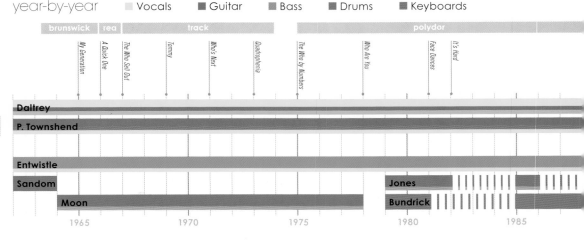

year-by-year ◻ Vocals ■ Guitar ■ Bass ■ Drums ■ Keyboards

| brunswick | rea | track | | polydor | |

My Generation · *A Quick One* · *The Who Sell Out* · *Tommy* · *Who's Next* · *Quadrophenia* · *The Who by Numbers* · *Who Are You* · *Face Dances* · *It's Hard*

Daltrey
P. Townshend

Entwistle
Sandom / Jones
Moon / Bundrick

1965 1970 1975 1980 1985

John "Rabbit" Bundrick
b. November 21, 1948

Zak Starkey
b. September 13, 1965

Simon Townshend
b. October 10, 1960

Pino Palladino
b. October 17, 1957

Simon Phillips
b. February 6, 1957

awesome power of the band's onstage attack can be heard in their legendary *Live at Leeds* (1970)—after which they were regularly and justifiably billed as the world's greatest live rock and roll band.

From the remnants of an abandoned conceptual piece called *Lifehouse* came *Who's Next* (1971), their sole U.K. No. 1 album. From the fluttering introduction of "Baba O'Riley" to the crashing chords of the epic "Won't Get Fooled Again," it was the quintessential rock album. It also, unfortunately, set a standard that chief composer and conceptualist Townshend would find impossible to top. Emerging amid stage and film versions of *Tommy,* 1973's equally ambitious *Quadrophenia* (1973)—the quasi-spiritual story of a young Mod—boasted gems like "5.15" and "Love Reign O'er Me," but, on stage, it often proved incomprehensible and technologically disastrous. (Nonetheless, it inspired a much-loved *Quadrophenia* movie in 1979, and was a clear influence on Green Day's contemporary rock opera *American Idiot.*)

The Who by Numbers (1975) was the exhausted Townshend's self-mocking title for their seventh studio album—a less grand affair, exemplified by the perky "Squeeze Box." By the end of a 1976 tour, The Who had entered the record books as the world's loudest band,

only for Townshend to fret that they had nothing left to say. Amid the advent of punk (including ardent Who fans like The Jam's Paul Weller), the band stayed off the road. They returned in 1978 with *Who Are You,* but then Moon died from an overdose of prescription drugs that he was taking for his alcoholism.

With **Kenney Jones** of The Faces, The Who returned to stadiums, and cut *Face Dances* (1981) and *It's Hard* (1982). But Townshend was finding it harder to write material for Daltrey's voice, and called time in 1982. Bar one-off reunions in 1985 and 1988, that was it until 1989, when a much-expanded lineup undertook the biggest-grossing tour of their career. Within the ranks were keyboard player **John "Rabbit" Bundrick**, Pete's brother **Simon Townshend** on rhythm guitar, and, on drums, the phenomenal **Simon Phillips**.

Subsequent outings—with Ringo Starr's son **Zak Starkey** on drums—kept the flame alive until, on the eve of a 2002 U.S. tour, Entwistle was found dead. Townshend and Daltrey soldiered on with bassist **Pino Palladino** and, in 2006, issued their first new album for twenty-four years, *Endless Wire.* It proved no disgrace, but The Who's latter-day legacy is best exemplified by show-stealing performances at 2001's The Concert for New York City and 2010's Super Bowl. **MiH/BM**

■ Aerophones   ■ Other percussion

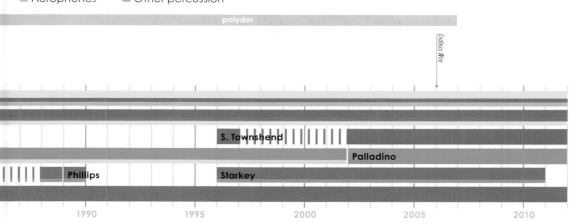

My Generation
(1965)

The Who Sell Out
(1967)

Tommy (1969)

Who's Next (1971)

Quadrophenia
(1973)

**The Who by
Numbers** (1975)

Who Are You
(1978)

Face Dances
(1981)

Endless Wire (2006)

Pete Townshend strikes an iconic pose on the 1966 tour that followed *My Generation*.

Roger Daltrey caught pneumonia from this *…Sell Out* cover shoot.

Daltrey in his *Tommy*-era glory, in Britain's Redcar, in February 1969.

John Entwistle, Steve Winwood, **Daltrey**, Billy Idol, Patti Labelle, Elton John, Phil Collins, and **Townshend** at a 1989 performance of 1969's *Tommy* at the Royal Albert Hall, London.

Townshend and **Keith Moon** help to write the rulebook for arena rock in the 1970s.

Daltrey, Townshend, Moon and John Entwistle in Surrey, England, promoting Who's Next.

The Who with Moon's replacement, former Faces drummer Kenney Jones (second left).

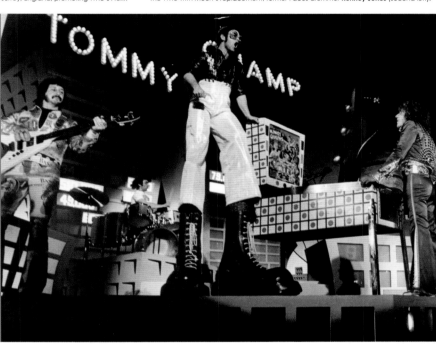

Elton John with Entwistle and Daltrey in the Tommy movie, issued in 1975, the same year as The Who by Numbers.

Townshend and Moon in August 1978; Moon died a month later.

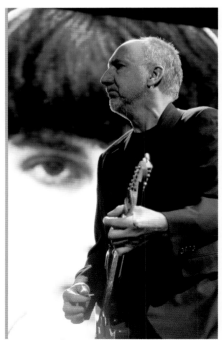

Townshend, in the shadow of Moon, in California in 2006.

x japan 1982–present

"Yoshiki"
(Yoshiki
Hayashi)
b. Nov 20, 1965

"Toshi"
(Toshimitsu
Deyama)
b. Oct 10, 1965

"Taiji"
(Taiji
Sawada)
b. July 12, 1966
d. July 17, 2011

"Pata"
(Tomoaki
Ishizuka)
b. Nov 4, 1965

"Hide"
(Hideto
Matsumoto)
b. Dec 13, 1964
d. May 2, 1998

"Heath"
(Hiroshi
Morie)
b. Jan 22, 1968

"Sugizo"
(Yasuhiro
Sugihara)
b. July 8, 1969

In terms of sales, X Japan's tally, around thirty million, trails well behind several fellow Japanese acts, such as the B'z (eighty million) and Mr. Children (fifty-five million). However, the group is certainly well ahead when it comes to Japanese rock history. X Japan is their nation's answer to both Britain's Queen and the U.S. band Kiss, and the group's career has been characterized by a rare degree of artistic ambition.

X Japan vocalist **"Toshi" Deyama** and songwriter-drummer-pianist **"Yoshiki" Hayashi** have been making music together since they were preteens. They spent their school years leading the band Dynamite (later Noise), before immediately forming a new project in 1982. Not knowing what to call themselves, they used plain "X" as a placeholder, and it stuck.

Fans would get to know the main players by their stage names only. The group's upward career path was set in 1987 when Toshi and Yoshiki were joined by bassist **"Taiji" Sawada** and guitarists **"Pata" Ishizuka** and **"Hide" Matsumoto**—the group's classic lineup. The quintet released their debut *Vanishing Vision*, initially categorized as speed metal, on Yoshiki's own Extasy Records label in 1988.

Later that year, the group signed with Sony and began working on *Blue Blood*. The record, released in 1989, was a commercial chart success, rising to No. 6 in Japan. More significantly, it showed that the group were striving to get out of the speed-metal ghetto. The sound leaned toward symphonic metal, even

borrowing from Johann Sebastian Bach, which was a far better fit for Toshi's operatic voice (reminiscent of Freddie Mercury) and Yoshiki's epic compositions. It also worked well with the group's "visual kei" look, which fully embraced glam rock-style outfits and makeup, and helped turn the band into Japan's ultimate stadium rock act.

The group's music continued along similar tried-and-tested lines with *Jealousy* (1991), which debuted at No. 1 in Japan. Longing for international recognition, however, the band changed its name in 1992 from X to X Japan to avoid confusion with the identically named (but quite different) U.S. punk act.

The international marketplace did not much like X Japan's next offering, *Art of Life* (1993), which consisted solely of a twenty-nine-minute title track, but it topped the charts back in Japan. The group were clearly on a roll (at least in its homeland) when they released their fifth album, *Dahila* (1996)—another No. 1 in Japan—so the group's breakup the following year seemed premature. The farewell gig, held on New Year's Eve, 1997, at the Tokyo Dome, marked a record-breaking eighteenth time the band had sold out Japan's biggest venue. There was talk of a reunion a year later but fans were aghast when the tragic news came through of Hide's apparent suicide. Almost a decade passed before X Japan delighted their fanbase by announcing a long-awaited 2007 comeback, which led to their first U.S. tour in 2010. **JiH**

year-by-year ■ Vocals ■ Guitar ■ Bass ■ Drums ■ Keyboards ■ Strings

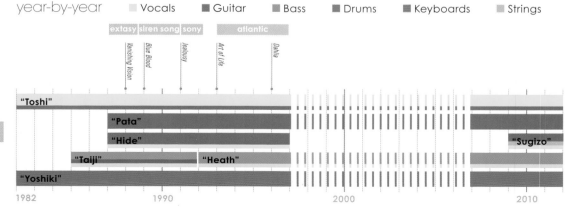

the yardbirds 1963–1968

Keith Relf
b. March 22, 1943
d. May 14, 1976

Paul Samwell-Smith
b. May 8, 1943

Chris Dreja
b. November 11, 1945

Jim McCarty
b. July 25, 1943

Anthony Topham
b. July 3, 1947

Eric Clapton
b. March 30, 1945

Jeff Beck
b. June 24, 1944

Jimmy Page
b. January 9, 1944

While most bands are lucky to boast even one guitar legend, The Yardbirds can lay claim to three: **Jeff Beck**, **Eric Clapton**, and **Jimmy Page**.

In September 1963, when The Rolling Stones went on tour with Bo Diddley, The Yardbirds took over their regular spot as house band at the famed Crawdaddy blues club in Richmond, Surrey. The following month, eighteen-year-old Eric Clapton joined the band, his prodigious ability quickly gaining plaudits.

A record deal with Columbia resulted in a minor 1964 hit with the blues standard "Good Morning Little Schoolgirl," after which The Yardbirds' sound began to go in a more overtly poppy direction. Following "For Your Love"—their breakthrough hit in May 1965 on both sides of the Atlantic—blues purist Clapton walked out to join John Mayall's Bluesbreakers.

Jeff Beck, Clapton's extravagantly talented replacement, played with The Yardbirds at their most commercially successful and creatively fertile time. A string of experimental, hard-edged psychedelic pop classics included "Heart Full of Soul," "Shapes of Things," and "Evil-hearted." The band's most satisfying album, *Yardbirds,* appeared in 1966 (the U.S. title was *Over Under Sideways Down*). Beck's experiments with distortion would influence Dave Gilmour and Slash.

After a reshuffling of personnel, Jimmy Page, one of Britain's busiest session players, joined The Yardbirds. The mouthwatering prospect of a lineup spearheaded by two of Britain's leading guitar talents seemed too good to be true. But live performances often degenerated into a cutting contest between two giant egos and, after an unsuccessful U.S. tour at the end of 1966, Beck was sacked. The Beck–Page Yardbirds recorded just one single: the gloriously unsettling "Happenings Ten Years Time Ago."

The Yardbirds limped on, finally disintegrating in July 1968. Page agreed to fulfill contracted Scandinavian dates with his own four-piece band, billed as The New Yardbirds. Following the tour, this was the group that became Led Zeppelin.

Beck, meanwhile, began a new phase with the most unlikely of hits, the singalong classic "Hi Ho Silver Lining" (1967). But its flip side, the influential guitar instrumental "Beck's Bolero," gave a better indication of where he was headed. With the Jeff Beck Group he recorded two albums, including the proto-heavy rock classic *Truth* (1968), before the group disbanded.

Beck's career thereafter would be eclectic, to say the least, highlighting the guitarist's mastery of multiple genres, be it the Memphis soul of *Rough and Ready* (1972), the jazz-rock of *Blow by Blow* (1975), or the fifties' rockabilly of *Crazy Legs* (1993). "The guitarist's guitarist" was inducted into the Rock and Roll Hall of Fame as a solo artist in 2009. **TB**

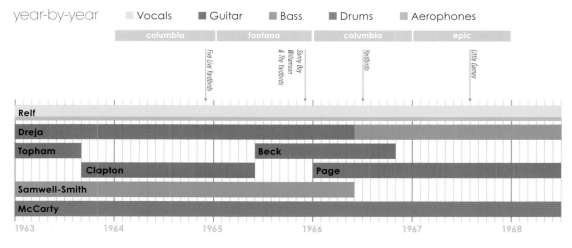

year-by-year   ▨ Vocals   ▪ Guitar   ▪ Bass   ▪ Drums   ▨ Aerophones

	columbia	fontana	columbia	epic
	Five Live Yardbirds	*Sonny Boy Williamson & The Yardbirds*	*Yardbirds*	*Little Games*

Relf
Dreja
Topham   Beck
Clapton   Page
Samwell-Smith
McCarty

1963   1964   1965   1966   1967   1968

yes 1968–present

Jon Anderson
b. October 25, 1944

Chris Squire
b. March 4, 1948

Peter Banks
b. July 15, 1947

Tony Kaye
b. January 11, 1946

Bill Bruford
b. May 17, 1949

Steve Howe
b. April 8, 1947

Rick Wakeman
b. May 18, 1949

Patrick Moraz
b. June 24, 1948

In 1968, a chance meeting of bassist **Chris Squire** and singer **Jon Anderson** in London led to the latter joining the former's band, Mabel Greer's Toyshop, alongside guitarist **Peter Banks**. With keyboard player **Tony Kaye** and drummer **Bill Bruford**, they became Yes. An innovative mix of harmonies, intricate arrangements, original material, and extended covers made them pioneers of what was soon known as progressive rock.

Issued on the Atlantic label, *Yes* (1969) and *Time and a Word* (1970) were critically acclaimed but sold poorly. Realizing that the next album would be their last chance with Atlantic, the group replaced Banks with hot-shot guitarist **Steve Howe**, formerly of Tomorrow, and the classic Yes sound was born.

The Yes Album (1971) sold well and the quintet wowed American audiences. But Kaye, unwilling to embrace emerging synthesizer technology, was next to be shown the door, to be replaced by keyboard wizard **Rick Wakeman** (who had played with David Bowie and The Strawbs). *Fragile* (1971) built on their success and spawned the U.S. hit "Roundabout."

With its side-long title track and only two tracks on side two, *Close to the Edge* (1972) was their most ambitious and best work to date. But as soon as the recording was completed, Bruford was lured away to King Crimson and replaced by Plastic Ono Band drummer **Alan White**. (Recordings featuring both drummers appear on 1973's live triple set *Yessongs*.)

Tales from Topographic Oceans (1973) gave the band their first chart-topper at home, but its sprawling pretentiousness divided both the fans and the group. Uncomfortable with music that he did not understand, Wakeman quit after the ensuing tour. Swiss keyboard player **Patrick Moraz** joined for the uncompromising *Relayer* (1974), which maintained their gold-selling, U.S. Top Ten streak. But after a triumphant tour in 1976, Moraz was fired to make way for Wakeman's return.

With him, the excellent *Going for the One* (1977) returned to a more tuneful approach—hence the U.K. hit "Wondrous Stories." But *Tormato* (1978) proved an unsatisfying—albeit platinum-selling—follow-up, and Anderson and Wakeman left. To widespread surprise,

year-by-year ▣ Vocals ■ Guitar ■ Bass ■ Drums ■ Keyboards

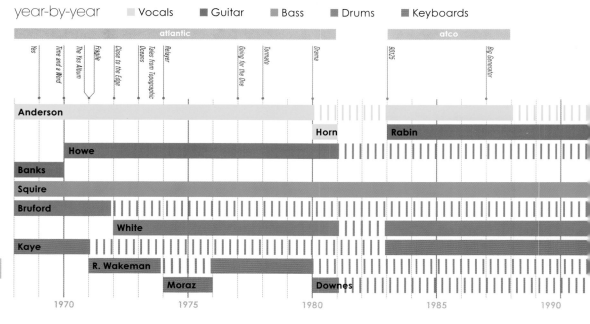

Trevor Horn
b. July 15, 1949

Geoff Downes
b. August 25, 1952

Trevor Rabin
b. January 13, 1954

Igor Khoroshev
b. July 14, 1965

Billy Sherwood
b. March 14, 1965

Oliver Wakeman
b. February 26, 1972

Benoît David
b. April 19, 1966

Alan White
b. June 14, 1949

Trevor Horn and **Geoff Downes** of pop duo Buggles were drafted in. The resultant *Drama* (1980) was better than *Tormato*, and the new lineup sold out three nights at New York's Madison Square Garden, but neither fans nor Horn himself were convinced of the merits of Yes without Anderson, and the group folded.

Howe and Downes formed Asia with John Wetton and Carl Palmer. Squire and White cut demos with Jimmy Page as XYZ ("Ex Yes and Zeppelin"), then formed Cinema with songwriter/guitarist **Trevor Rabin** and Yes veteran Tony Kaye. With their recordings almost complete, Anderson was approached to add vocals and rewrite lyrics. The resultant *90125* (1983), helmed by Horn and issued under the Yes name, went platinum, thanks to the U.S. No. 1 "Owner of a Lonely Heart." *Big Generator* (1987) was another million-seller, but Anderson was unhappy with the band's poppier direction and Horn and Kaye proved incompatible.

While Squire, Rabin, and Kaye endeavored to forge ahead as Yes (with **Billy Sherwood**), their ex-bandmates toured and recorded as Anderson Bruford Wakeman Howe. The two factions then united for a fan-pleasing tour and 1991's *Union*, before Anderson joined a Yes led by Rabin—*Talk* (1994) was mostly the guitarist's work.

Kaye and Rabin left after the *Talk* tour, making way for Howe and Wakeman's return. With them, live and studio work yielded the two *Keys to Ascension* albums. Then Wakeman quit again, leaving keyboard duties to Sherwood and **Igor Khoroshev** on *Open Your Eyes* (1997). Both featured on *The Ladder* (1999), but were gone by *Magnification* (2001), on which orchestral arrangements replaced keyboards.

Wakeman returned in 2002, before health issues obliged both him and Anderson to cease touring. In 2008, Squire, Howe, and White reconvened as Yes with **Benoît David**, vocalist of a Canadian Yes tribute act, and Wakeman's son **Oliver Wakeman**. The former made it onto 2011's *Fly from Here*, produced by Horn, but the latter was replaced by the returning Geoff Downes. The album proved their biggest success since *Talk*, but that did not stop inevitable upheaval: on a 2012 tour, David was replaced by Jon Davison. **MD/BM**

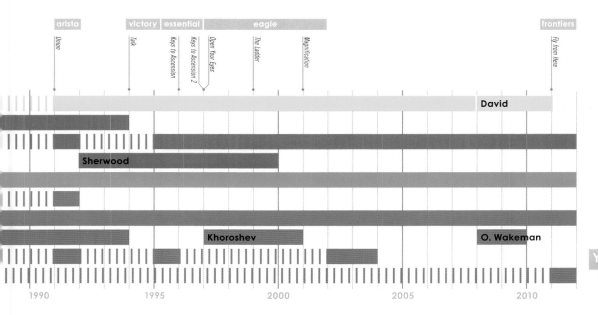

Yes (1969)

Fragile (1971)

Close to the Edge (1972)

Relayer (1974)

Going for the One (1977)

Drama (1980)

90125 (1983)

Union (1991)

Magnification (2001)

Fly from Here (2011)

The formative Yes: **Peter Banks**, **Tony Kaye**, **Chris Squire**, **Bill Bruford**, and **Jon Anderson**

With new drummer **Alan White** at London's Crystal Palace in 1972.

Bruford, Squire, **Steve Howe**, Anderson, and keyboard wizard **Rick Wakeman** creating *Fragile* at London's Advision Studios in August 1971.

Howe, White (top), **Anderson**, **Squire**, and Wakeman's doomed successor **Patrick Moraz**.

Anderson live in Rotterdam on the *Going for the One* tour.

White, **Geoff Downes**, Squire, **Trevor Horn**, and Howe in 1980.

South African songwriter and guitarist **Trevor Rabin**—the key to the band's renaissance and survival—on the successful 9012Live tour.

Wakeman, **Squire**, **Bruford**, **Anderson**, and **White**: five-eighths of the *Union* incarnation.

Yes live in Britain, on the Symphonic tour that followed the release of *Magnification*.

Benoît David—the man with the unenviable task of replacing Jon Anderson—in 2011.

neil young 1968–present

Neil Young
b. November 12, 1945

Billy Talbot
b. October 23, 1943

Ralph Molina
b. June 22, 1943

Danny Whitten
b. May 8, 1943
d. November 18, 1972

Ben Keith
b. March 6, 1937
d. July 26, 2010

Jack Nitzsche
b. April 22, 1937
d. August 25, 2000

Tim Drummond
b. April 20, 1941

Kenny Buttrey
b. April 1, 1945
d. December 9, 2004

Most rock stars build on success and reach a peak. Not **Neil Young**. His assured confidence means he does whatever he wants. Genres as varied as grunge, R&B, rockabilly, and country, and creatively assembled support bands (Stray Gators, Shocking Pinks, Bluenotes, International Harvesters, Crazy Horse) have all contributed to decades of solo music that began when he left Buffalo Springfield in 1967.

His self-titled 1968 debut showed promise but had a restrained, "Made in Laurel Canyon" air. Future Crazy Horse band members **Danny Whitten**, **Ralph Molina**, and **Billy Talbot** helped energize *Everybody Knows This Is Nowhere* (1969), distinguished by chugging guitar riffs, like those on "Cinnamon Girl." But Young's emerging solo career was interrupted when former Springfield co-star **Stephen Stills** came calling in 1969, to add him to Crosby, Stills & Nash.

CSN&Y's *Déjà Vu* became the biggest-selling U.S. album in 1970, but Young's plaintive vocals and vivid songwriting needed more exposure than just the two tracks on that album. With *After the Goldrush*

(1970) and *Harvest* (1972), Young began to eclipse his CS&N peers. Mainstream success arrived courtesy of *Harvest*'s "Heart of Gold"—a hit that, Young reflected, "put me in the middle of the road. Traveling there soon became a bore so I headed for the ditch. A rougher ride but I saw more interesting people there."

Young returned to CSN&Y for a groundbreaking stadium tour in 1974, but his appearance on the cover of *Tonight's the Night* (1975)—black beard and shades—epitomized his dark mood. The album provided a heart-wrenching insight into the drug-related deaths of two friends: Danny Whitten and roadie Bruce Berry. Young reunited with Stills to record *Long May You Run* (1976) and toured with his old adversary and guitar sparring partner. But tiring of the idea mid-tour, he bid Stills goodbye with the telegram, "Dear Stephen. Funny how some things that start spontaneously end that way. Eat a peach, Neil."

The partly live *Rust Never Sleeps* (1979) proved that at least one of rock's old guard was paying attention to punk. On the opening and closing tracks, "My My,

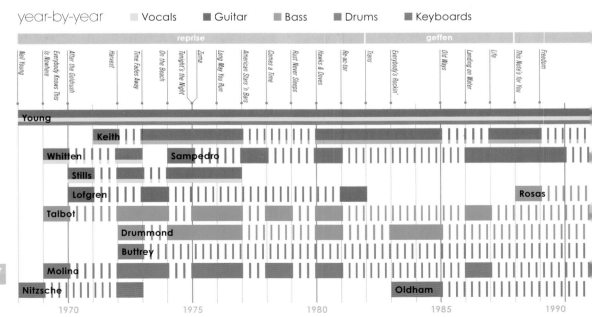

year-by-year ◼ Vocals ◼ Guitar ◼ Bass ◼ Drums ◼ Keyboards

4.6M	9.2M	2.7M	4M
After the Goldrush (1970)	Harvest (1972)	Rust Never Sleeps (1979)	Harvest Moon (1992)

Frank "Poncho" Sampedro
b. Feb 25, 1949

Stephen Stills
b. January 3, 1945

Nils Lofgren
b. June 21, 1951

Spooner Oldham
b. June 14, 1943

Rick Rosas
b. February 15, 1955

Hey Hey (Out of the Blue)" and "Hey Hey, My My (Into the Black)," Young name-checked Johnny Rotten. Years later, Kurt Cobain's suicide note quoted a line from the first song: "It's better to burn out, than to fade away." The album led to a film of the same name and the superb in-concert album *Live Rust* (both 1979).

Disguising his voice with a Vocoder, Young cut *Trans* (1982), dabbled in rockabilly on *Everybody's Rockin'* (1983), and revisited his country roots on *Old Ways* (1985). These were odd but noteworthy albums during a patchy period that ended with the release of several that met with approval from his diehard fans *and* won a new generation's attention. Inventor of grunge? The evidence is plainly there on *Freedom* (1989) and the raw, splintering guitar feedback of *Ragged Glory* (1990) and the live *Weld* (1991).

For his next trick he gave Old Black, his faithful electric guitar, a rest and got back to the country. *Harvest Moon* (1992) was an acoustic throwback to 1970. It returned Young to the multi-million selling mainstream (consolidated by 1993's gorgeous

Unplugged), but his rock credibility and legendary status were confirmed in the nineties by tours with Sonic Youth and Pearl Jam and the well-received *Sleeps with Angels* (1994) and *Mirror Ball* (1995).

A new decade led to a return to that ditch by the side of the road, with *Greendale* (2003). Creatively chaotic, Young's soap opera about a fictitious town was soundtracked by Chuck Berry-esque rock 'n' roll.

The whispered intimacy and reflective nature of *Prairie Wind* (2005) were born when Young suffered a brain aneurysm. But there was no reduction in his output: in a reprise of his bashing of President Nixon on CSN&Y's "Ohio" in 1970, Young turned his attentions to Bush and the U.S. involvement in Iraq. Armed with the powerful *Living with War* (2006), he recalled his own troops and hit the road for a controversial, energetic, and emotional U.S. tour with CSN&Y.

Remaining intrigued by that ditch, Young is still going strong in 2012, hence his film *Neil Young Journeys*, his memoir *Waging Heavy Peace*, and a Crazy Horse album of folk standards, *Americana*. **DR**

■ Aerophones

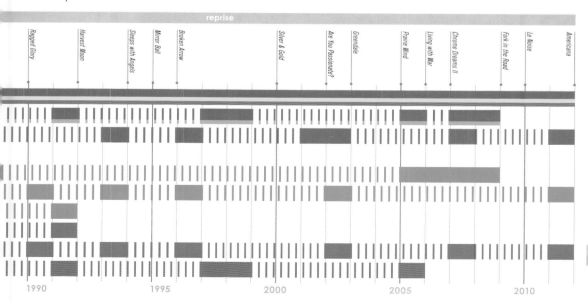

Everybody Knows This Is Nowhere (1969)

Harvest (1972)

Tonight's the Night (1975)

Rust Never Sleeps (1979)

Trans (1982)

Ragged Glory (1990)

Mirror Ball (1995)

Greendale (2003)

Living with War (2006)

Americana (2012)

Neil Young (right) with CSN&Y harmonizers Graham Nash and David Crosby at the ill-fated Altamont Speedway Free Festival, California, on December 6, 1969.

Young at his California ranch during the recording of *Harvest*.

With Bob Dylan and The Band at the SNACK (Students Need Athletics, Culture, and Kicks) benefit show at San Francisco's Golden Gate Park, on March 23, 1975.

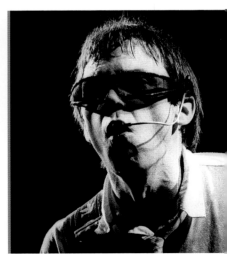

With singer Nicolette Larson at the premiere for his *Rust Never Sleeps* movie in 1979.

The "Transformer Man" on stage in Rotterdam in 1982.

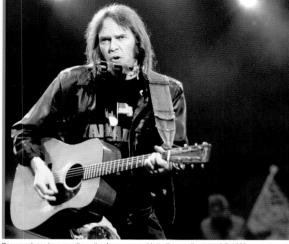

Young returns to acoustic guitar for a concert in Indianapolis on April 7, 1990.

With Aerosmith's Steven Tyler at the Rock and Roll Hall of Fame induction ceremony, New York, in 2003—the year of *Greendale*.

With young disciple Eddie Vedder, whose group Pearl Jam would back him on *Mirror Ball*.

For the 2006 CSN&Y Freedom of Speech tour, **Young** reunites with, from left, **Stills**, Nash, and Crosby, here in Concord, California.

Young inducts Paul McCartney onto the Hollywood Walk of Fame in 2012, the year that also saw the star looking back on the Crazy Horse album *Americana*.

frank zappa 1965–1993

Frank Zappa
b. December 21, 1940
d. December 4, 1993

Ray Collins
b. November 19, 1936

Roy Estrada
b. April 17, 1943

Jimmy Carl Black
b. February 1, 1938
d. Nov. 1, 2008

Don Preston
b. September 21, 1932

Aynsley Dunbar
b. January 10, 1946

Mark "Flo" Volman
b. April 19, 1947

Howard "Eddie" Kaylan
b. June 22, 1947

Frank Zappa was a musical genius of the rarest kind. Over a thirty-year career as a songwriter, guitarist, composer, innovator, producer, and sardonic observer of the human condition, he never stopped creating brilliant and often challenging music.

In the early sixties, Zappa created soundtracks for B-movies. But things really began to happen when he took over R&B band The Soul Giants and transformed them into The Mothers of Invention. The group's debut album, *Freak Out!* (1966)—with its ambitious palette of rock, doo-wop, R&B, jazz, classical, avant-garde, and biting social commentary—was ten steps ahead of anything else issued that year. *Absolutely Free* (1967) was equally innovative, characterized by extended yet tight performances, abrupt time changes, and brilliant lyrics. (Zappa never bought into the counter-culture and satirized it as mercilessly as he did the establishment.) Live performances mixed theatrical improvised sections with cutting-edge playing.

By the time he split the Mothers of Invention in late 1969, he had put out ten albums, both with the band and—beginning with 1967's *Lumpy Gravy*— solo. (Relationships between Zappa and his former

bandmates would rarely be cordial, but drummer **Jimmy Carl Black** would guest at subsequent shows and reappear on 1981's vicious *You Are What You Is*. The latter also included the Mothers of Invention's madcap saxophonist Jim "Motorhead" Sherwood.)

A new lineup—now called simply The Mothers— debuted in 1970, with vocalists **Mark "Flo" Volman** and **Howard "Eddie" Kaylan** from pop band The Turtles, and brilliant new players **George Duke** and **Aynsley Dunbar**. This more theatrical lineup, renowned for outrageous epics about life on the road, lasted until the end of 1971, when an audience member pushed Zappa off a stage in London, causing serious injuries.

He had recovered by 1973, and assembled a new band. **Ruth Underwood** (percussion), drummer Chester Thompson (later of Genesis), and **Napoleon Murphy Brock** (saxophone/vocals) featured in a lineup— continuing as the Mothers until their disbandment in 1974—of breathtaking virtuosity and warmth. Zappa hit new heights on 1973's *Over-Nite Sensation*, 1974's *Apostrophe (')*—featuring Cream's Jack Bruce—and 1975's *One Size Fits All* and *Bongo Fury* (the latter a collaboration with his old friend Captain Beefheart.)

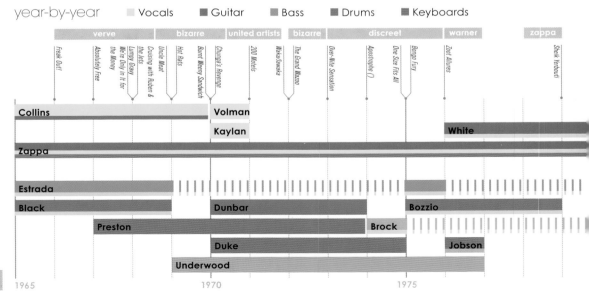

year-by-year   ■ Vocals   ■ Guitar   ■ Bass   ■ Drums   ■ Keyboards

verve   bizarre   united artists   bizarre   discreet   warner   zappa

Freak Out! · *Absolutely Free* · *We're Only in It for the Money* · *Lumpy Gravy* · *Cruising with Ruben & the Jets* · *Uncle Meat* · *Hot Rats* · *Burnt Weeny Sandwich* · *Chunga's Revenge* · *200 Motels* · *Waka/Jawaka* · *The Grand Wazoo* · *Over-Nite Sensation* · *Apostrophe (')* · *One Size Fits All* · *Bongo Fury* · *Zoot Allures* · *Sheik Yerbouti*

Collins
Volman
Kaylan
White
Zappa
Estrada
Black
Dunbar
Bozzio
Preston
Brock
Duke
Jobson
Underwood

1965   1970   1975

Z

George Duke
b. January 12, 1946

Ruth Underwood
b. May 23, 1946

Napoleon Murphy Brock
b. April 23, 1943

Terry Bozzio
b. December 27, 1950

Eddie Jobson
b. April 25, 1955

Ike Willis
b. November 14, 1951

Ray White
b. July 11, 1945

Steve Vai
b. June 6, 1960

After the rock-oriented *Zoot Allures* (1976), Zappa mooted a four-album set entitled *Läther*. The Warner label refused to indulge this expensive folly, hence the separate releases of the live *Zappa in New York* and *Studio Tan* in 1978 and *Sleep Dirt* and *Orchestral Favorites* in 1979. Zappa duly set up his own label and scored his highest-charting album in five years with *Sheik Yerbouti* (1979). That paved the way for the rock opera *Joe's Garage*, issued in two installments in 1979.

Star musicians graduating from his group included guitarists Adrian Belew (later to join Talking Heads, Bowie, and King Crimson), Warren Cuccurullo (who founded Missing Persons with Zappa drummer **Terry Bozzio**, then joined Duran Duran), and **Steve Vai** (who would play with Public Image Ltd, David Lee Roth, and Whitesnake). Bozzio joined the progressive band U.K. alongside King Crimson's John Wetton and former Roxy Music keyboard player **Eddie Jobson**, who had played with him in Zappa's touring band back in 1976. As a musician, however, Zappa was equal to the best of them, as *Shut Up 'n Play Yer Guitar* (1981) testifies.

Zappa's eclectic projects continued up to his untimely death from prostate cancer in 1993. After

"rock" albums such as *Ship Arriving Too Late to Save a Drowning Witch* (1982)—the source of his biggest hit, "Valley Girl," featuring his daughter Moon on vocals—and *The Man from Utopia* (1983) came the dazzling electronic experimentation of *Jazz from Hell* (1986). Thereafter, his discography exploded with live albums, including *Broadway the Hard Way* (1988), featuring Sting; orchestral pieces, such as *The Yellow Shark* (1993); and archive releases, including the six-volume series *You Can't Do That on Stage Anymore* (1988–1992) and the *Beat the Boots* series (1991–2009).

Zappa was posthumously inducted into the Rock and Roll Hall of Fame by Lou Reed in 1995 and given a Grammy Lifetime Achievement Award. His estate has nearly doubled his outsized discography with further archive releases. His son, guitarist Dweezil, keeps his father's music alive with Zappa Plays Zappa, a touring band that debuted in 2006 and occasionally features guests from his father's original lineups.

"Zappa gave me the faith that anything in music was possible," enthused Phish's Trey Anastasio. For Matt Groening, creator of *The Simpsons*, it was even more straightforward: "Frank Zappa was my Elvis." **MD**

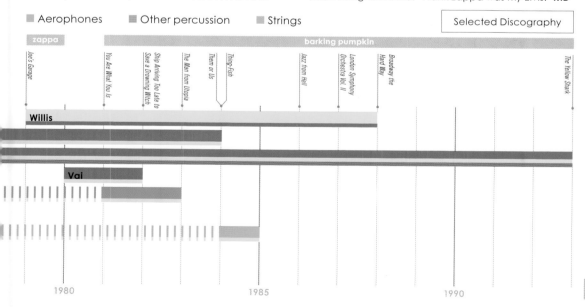

■ Aerophones ■ Other percussion ■ Strings

Selected Discography

zappa | barking pumpkin

Joe's Garage · You Are What You Is · Ship Arriving Too Late to Save a Drowning Witch · The Man from Utopia · Them or Us · Thing-Fish · Jazz from Hell · London Symphony Orchestra Vol. II · Broadway the Hard Way · The Yellow Shark

Willis

Vai

1980 · 1985 · 1990

Freak Out! (1966)

We're Only in It for the Money (1968)

Hot Rats (1969)

Waka/Jawaka (1972)

Apostrophe (') (1974)

Zoot Allures (1976)

Joe's Garage, Act I (1979)

Ship Arriving Too Late to Save a Drowning Witch (1982)

Them or Us (1984)

Broadway the Hard Way (1988)

Frank Zappa circa *Freak Out!*, whose sleevenotes advised fans to "Drop out of school before your mind rots."

Zappa at the Newport Jazz Festival in 1969 —the year of his first solo album, *Hot Rats*.

Zappa with his second wife Gail, at the Oval cricket ground in London, in 1972.

Top: Bunk Gardner, James "Motorhead" Sherwood, **Roy Estrada**, **Jimmy Carl Black**, and Art Tripp. Bottom: Ian Underwood, **Zappa**, and **Don Preston**.

Zappa in Rotterdam on the extensive tour that followed the triumphant *Apostrophe (')*.

On *Saturday Night Live*, shortly after the release of *Zoot Allures*.

In March 1979, the month he began recording *Joe's Garage*.

With daughter Moon Unit, who sang on *Drowning Witch*'s "Valley Girl," and son Dweezil.

Backstage during the 1984 tour to promote *Them or Us*.

Zappa's 1988 tour reaches Rotterdam (Financial losses and inter-band conflicts meant he never toured again).

zz top 1969–present

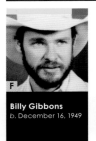

Billy Gibbons
b. December 16, 1949

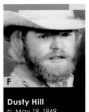

Dusty Hill
b. May 19, 1949

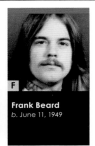

Frank Beard
b. June 11, 1949

"The heartbeat of the whole country," according to Keith Richards, this blues rock trio formed in Houston, Texas. **Billy Gibbons** (vocals and guitar), Joseph "**Dusty**" **Hill** (vocals, bass, and keyboards), and **Frank Beard** (drums) created one of the longest-running stable lineups in rock. Until September 2006, they even kept the same manager, Bill Ham.

The men of the magnificent ZZ Top had played in other Texas-based groups—Gibbons in Moving Sidewalks and Hill and Beard in American Blues (once known as The Warlocks). By 1969, both of these groups had disbanded, and Gibbons invited Beard to join his new enterprise. Beard suggested that Hill join them, and thus the ZZ lineup was finalized.

Their name was speculated to be a combination of two popular brands of rolling papers, Zig Zag and TOP. However, the mischievous Gibbons has also described it as a tribute to bluesmen B.B. King and Z.Z. Hill, and even to the Z-shaped beams in a hay loft.

Having hooked up with Ham and issued their first single, "Salt Lick," on the Scat label, ZZ Top played their first show in February 1970. Incessant touring—centered on Texas, Louisiana, and Mississippi—made them an arena-filling sensation in the American South long before the rest of the U.S. even knew their name.

Issued on London Records, neither ZZ Top's First Album (1971) nor Rio Grande Mud (1972) made much of an impression outside Texas, although the latter's "Francine" became their first U.S. Top 100 hit.

In January 1973, ZZ Top opened for three Rolling Stones shows in Hawaii. "I remember walking out on stage in our standard attire of cowboy boots and a cowboy hat…," Gibbons told Classic Rock, "and someone in the front row shouted out, 'Oh my God, they're a country band!'" With the band's profile duly raised, Tres Hombres (1973) climbed into the U.S. Top Ten and eventually went gold. Its classic "La Grange" was written about the Chicken Ranch, a famous bordello at La Grange, Texas. (The same establishment became the subject of Burt Reynolds and Dolly Parton's 1982 movie The Best Little Whorehouse in Texas.) The album's "Waitin' for the Bus" and "Jesus Just Left Chicago," joined "La Grange" as fan favorites and rock-radio staples.

Fandango! (1975) contained a mixture of live and studio recordings. One of the new studio cuts, "Tush," became ZZ Top's first Top Forty single, while the album again went Top Ten. Tejas (1976)—its title an earlier spelling of the Texas state name—continued their gold-selling streak, and prompted The Worldwide Texas Tour, on which the band performed amid sand, cacti, and even examples of Texan wildlife.

That excursion complete, the road-weary band opted to take a break. During the two-year vacation, Gibbons and Hill grew their trademark chest-length beards. "I thought, 'I hope these guys are not on the run,'" remembered Keith Richards, "'cause that disguise is not gonna work." (In 1984, the Gillette razor

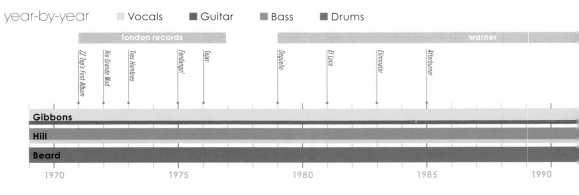

year-by-year   ■ Vocals   ■ Guitar   ■ Bass   ■ Drums

company reportedly offered the trio a million dollars each to shave their beards for a TV commercial. They declined, Gibbons declaring, "We're too ugly.")

The beards were not the only visual marker. The trio almost always appear wearing sunglasses, with Gibbons and Hill also sporting similar black clothing (usually motorcycle leathers) and stetsons or baseball caps. Their eyewear inspired "Cheap Sunglasses," the best-known track from their first album for Warner Bros, *Degüello* (1979). But the biggest U.S. hit from the album was a cover of Sam & Dave's "I Thank You." *El Loco* (1981) sustained the group's success with risqué party anthems like "Pearl Necklace."

However, *Eliminator* (1983) represents ZZ Top's commercial and critical peak. The trio flavored their old-school boogie with sequenced beats, a formula that spawned the hits "Gimme All Your Lovin'," "Legs," "Sharp Dressed Man," and "TV Dinners." *Eliminator*—their first international success (it went quadruple platinum in Britain)—also made them MTV favorites, thanks to videos featuring the customized 1933 Ford coupe that appeared on its cover. In the clips, this gleaming retro-styled vehicle was driven by a trio of glamorous young women (Danièle Arnaud and *Playboy* models Jeana Tomasino and Kymberly Herrin) who appeared as muses to help various troubled people. The band members took a background role as unsuccessful hitchhikers and observers of a running narrative featuring a wide-eyed young gas attendant.

The only blip in their fortunes came in 1984, when Hill accidentally shot himself in the abdomen while removing his boot. "I was in France," Gibbons told *Creem* magazine, "and the operator said, 'Your partner Dusty has been shot.' I said, 'How is he?' and she said, 'I'm sorry monsieur, I don't speak English.'"

Afterburner (1985) and *Recycler* (1990) both sold strongly, although some critics complained that the group were indeed simply recycling the elements that had made *Eliminator* so successful. A cover of Elvis's "Viva Las Vegas," from 1992's *Greatest Hits*, was an international success and, after signing to RCA, they scored another million-seller with *Antenna* (1994).

ZZ Top's commercial fortunes gracefully declined with *Rhythmeen* (1996), *XXX* (1999), and *Mescalero* (2003), although the latter earned critical praise for its adventurousness; alongside the group's familiar gritty boogie were forays into country and Tex-Mex music. (The title refers to Apache Native Americans who depended on the mescal agave as a food source.)

Inducted by Keith Richards into the Rock and Roll Hall of Fame in 2004, the band plotted a new album with producer Rick Rubin. Meanwhile, Gibbons kept himself busy with cameos on work by Queens of the Stone Age, Ministry, Kid Rock, Nickelback, and Everlast. As for what has held the band together for so long, Hill told *Classic Rock*, "It's down to the three of us genuinely enjoying playing together. We still love it, and we still get a kick out of being on stage." **DJ**

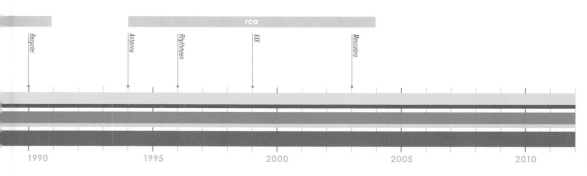

grammy award winners

(L)   Live album
(ST)   Soundtrack album
(*)   Winner of both the Album of the Year and the Best Rock Album Grammy categories

ALBUM OF THE YEAR

Awarded to rock acts featured in *Rock Chronicles*.

1968	*Sgt. Pepper's Lonely Hearts Club Band—*	**1982**	*Double Fantasy—John Lennon*
	The Beatles		*& Yoko Ono*
1970	*Blood, Sweat & Tears—Blood, Sweat & Tears*	**1988**	*The Joshua Tree—U2*
1973	*The Concert for Bangla Desh* (L)—	**1998**	*Time Out of Mind—Bob Dylan*
	George Harrison and Friends	**2000**	*Supernatural* (*)—Santana
1978	*Rumours—Fleetwood Mac*	**2001**	*Two Against Nature—Steely Dan*
1979	*Saturday Night Fever* (ST)—	**2006**	*How to Dismantle an Atomic Bomb—U2*
	Bee Gees and Various Artists	**2011**	*The Suburbs—Arcade Fire*

BEST ROCK ALBUM

This Grammy award was first presented in 1995. Entries that appear in *Rock Chronicles* are indicated in **bold**

1995	*Voodoo Lounge—***The Rolling Stones**	**2004**	*One by One—***Foo Fighters**
1996	*Jagged Little Pill—Alanis Morissette*	**2005**	*American Idiot—***Green Day**
1997	*Sheryl Crow—Sheryl Crow*	**2006**	*How to Dismantle an Atomic Bomb—***U2**
1998	*Blue Moon Swamp—John Fogerty*	**2007**	*Stadium Arcadium—***Red Hot Chili Peppers**
1999	*The Globe Sessions—Sheryl Crow*	**2008**	*Echoes, Silence, Patience & Grace—*
2000	*Supernatural* (*)—**Santana**		**Foo Fighters**
2001	*There Is Nothing Left to Lose—*	**2009**	*Viva La Vida or Death and All His Friends—*
	Foo Fighters		**Coldplay**
2002	*All That You Can't Leave Behind—*	**2010**	*21st Century Breakdown—***Green Day**
	U2	**2011**	*The Resistance—***Muse**
2003	*The Rising—***Bruce Springsteen**	**2012**	*Wasting Light—***Foo Fighters**

BEST ROCK SONG

This Grammy award was first presented in 1992. Entries that appear in *Rock Chronicles* are indicated in **bold**

1992	"The Soul Cages"—Sting	**2003**	"The Rising"—**Bruce Springsteen**
1993	"Layla" (Unplugged)—**Eric Clapton**	**2004**	"Seven Nation Army"—The White Stripes
1994	"Runaway Train"—Soul Asylum	**2005**	"Vertigo"—**U2**
1995	"Streets of Philadelphia"—**Bruce Springsteen**	**2006**	"City of Blinding Lights"—**U2**
1996	"You Oughta Know"—Alanis Morissette	**2007**	"Dani California"—**Red Hot Chili Peppers**
1997	"Give Me One Reason"—Tracy Chapman	**2008**	"Radio Nowhere"—**Bruce Springsteen**
1998	"One Headlight"—The Wallflowers	**2009**	"Girls in Their Summer Clothes"—
1999	"Uninvited"—Alanis Morissette		**Bruce Springsteen**
2000	"Scar Tissue"—**Red Hot Chili Peppers**	**2010**	"Use Somebody"—**Kings of Leon**
2001	"With Arms Wide Open"—Creed	**2011**	"Angry World"—**Neil Young**
2002	"Drops of Jupiter (Tell Me)"—Train	**2012**	"Walk"—**Foo Fighters**

rock and roll hall of fame inductees

Inductees in the performer category of the Rock and Roll Hall of Fame, Cleveland, Ohio
Entries that appear in *Rock Chronicles* are indicated in **bold**

1986
Chuck Berry
James Brown
Ray Charles
Sam Cooke
Fats Domino
The Everly Brothers
Buddy Holly
Jerry Lee Lewis
Little Richard
Elvis Presley

1987
The Coasters
Eddie Cochran
Bo Diddley
Aretha Franklin
Marvin Gaye
Bill Haley
B.B. King
Clyde McPhatter
Ricky Nelson
Roy Orbison
Carl Perkins
Smokey Robinson
Big Joe Turner
Muddy Waters
Jackie Wilson

1988
The Beach Boys
The Beatles
The Drifters
Bob Dylan
The Supremes

1989
Dion
Otis Redding
The Rolling Stones
The Temptations
Stevie Wonder

1990
Hank Ballard
Bobby Darin
The Four Seasons
The Four Tops
The Kinks
The Platters
Simon & Garfunkel
The Who

1991
LaVern Baker
The Byrds
John Lee Hooker
The Impressions
Wilson Pickett
Jimmy Reed
Ike & Tina Turner

1992
Bobby Blue Bland
Booker T. & The M.G.'s
Johnny Cash
The Isley Brothers
The Jimi Hendrix Experience
Sam & Dave
The Yardbirds

1993
Ruth Brown
Cream
Creedence Clearwater Revival
The Doors
Frankie Lymon & The Teenagers
Etta James
Van Morrison
Sly & The Family Stone

1994
The Animals
The Band
Duane Eddy
Grateful Dead
Elton John
John Lennon
Bob Marley
Rod Stewart

1995
The Allman Brothers Band
Al Green
Janis Joplin
Led Zeppelin
Martha and The Vandellas
Neil Young
Frank Zappa

1996
David Bowie
Gladys Knight & The Pips
Jefferson Airplane
Little Willie John
Pink Floyd
The Shirelles
The Velvet Underground

1997
The Bee Gees
Buffalo Springfield
Crosby, Stills & Nash
The Jackson 5
Joni Mitchell
Parliament/Funkadelic
The Rascals

1998
Eagles
Fleetwood Mac
The Mamas & The Papas
Lloyd Price
Santana
Gene Vincent

1999
Billy Joel
Curtis Mayfield
Paul McCartney
Del Shannon
Dusty Springfield
Bruce Springsteen
The Staple Singers

2000
Eric Clapton
Earth, Wind & Fire
The Lovin' Spoonful
The Moonglows
Bonnie Raitt
James Taylor

2001
Aerosmith
Solomon Burke
The Flamingos
Michael Jackson
Queen
Paul Simon
Steely Dan
Ritchie Valens

2002
Isaac Hayes
Brenda Lee
Tom Petty & The Heartbreakers
Gene Pitney
Ramones
Talking Heads

2003
AC/DC
The Clash
Elvis Costello & The Attractions
The Police
The Righteous Brothers

2004
Jackson Browne
The Dells
George Harrison
Prince
Bob Seger
Traffic
ZZ Top

2005
Buddy Guy
The O'Jays
Pretenders
Percy Sledge
U2

2006
Black Sabbath
Blondie
Miles Davis
Lynyrd Skynyrd
Sex Pistols

2007
Grandmaster Flash and The Furious Five
R.E.M.
The Ronettes
Patti Smith
Van Halen

2008
The Dave Clark Five
Leonard Cohen
Madonna
John Mellencamp
The Ventures

2009
Jeff Beck
Little Anthony and The Imperials
Metallica
Run-D.M.C.
Bobby Womack

2010
ABBA
Genesis
Jimmy Cliff
The Hollies
The Stooges

2011
Alice Cooper
Neil Diamond
Dr. John
Darlene Love
Tom Waits

2012
The Beastie Boys
The Blue Caps
The Comets
The Crickets
Donovan
The Famous Flames
Guns N' Roses
The Midnighters
The Miracles
Laura Nyro
Red Hot Chili Peppers
Small Faces/The Faces

bibliography

Dimery, Robert (ed.)
1001 Albums You Must Hear Before You Die
(Universe Publishing/Cassell Illustrated, 2005)

Dimery, Robert (ed.)
1001 Songs You Must Hear Before You Die
(Universe Publishing/Cassell Illustrated, 2010)

Du Noyer, Paul (ed.)
The Story of Rock 'n' Roll (Virgin, 1995)

Frame, Pete
The Complete Rock Family Trees (Omnibus, 1993)

Goddard, Simon
*Mozipedia—The Encyclopedia of Morrissey and
The Smiths* (Ebury Press, 2009)

Harris, John
Hail! Hail! Rock 'n' Roll (Sphere, 2009)

Heatley, Michael (ed.)
Rock & Pop—The Complete Story (Flame Tree, 2006)

Heatley, Michael; Lester, Paul; Roberts, Chris
The Encyclopedia of Albums (Dempsey Parr., 1998)

Hillmore, Peter
Live Aid—The Concert (Sidgwick & Jackson, 1985)

Hoskyns, Barney
Hotel California (John Wiley & Sons, 2007)

Hounsome, Terry
Rock Record 6 (Record Researcher Publications,
1994)

Jeffries, Neil (ed.)
The Kerrang! Direktory of Heavy Metal (Virgin, 1993)

Larkin, Colin (ed.)
The Guinness Encyclopedia of Popular Music
(Guinness, 1992)

MacDonald, Bruno
Rock Connections (Collins Design/Omnibus
Illustrated, 2010)

Makower, Joel
Woodstock: The Oral History (Doubleday, 1989)

Maycock, Stephen
Rock & Pop Memorabilia (Miller's Publications,
1994)

Miller, Jim (ed.)
The Rolling Stone Illustrated History of Rock & Roll
(Plexus, 1992)

Palmer, Tony
All You Need Is Love (Futura, 1976)

Rees, Dafydd; Crampton, Luke
Q Rock Stars Encyclopedia (Dorling Kindersley,
1999)

Roberts, David (ed.)
The Guinness Book of British Hit Singles & Albums
(Guinness, 2006)

Roberts, David
Rock Atlas (Clarksdale, 2011)

Roberts, David (ed.)
Rockopedia (Guinness, 1998)

Rosen, Craig
The Billboard Book of Number One Albums
(Billboard, 1996)

Smith, Steve
Rock Day-By-Day (Guinness, 1987)

Strong, Martin C.
The Great Rock Discography (Canongate, 2004)

Southall, Brian
*Brits 25—The Official Story of Britain's Biggest Music
Show* (British Phonographic Industry Ltd, 2004)

Wenner, Jann S. (ed.)
The 100 Greatest Artists of All Time (Rolling Stone,
2011)

Whitburn, Joel
The Billboard Book of Top 40 Albums
(Billboard, 1995)

Whitburn, Joel
The Billboard Book of Top Pop Singles
(Billboard, 1993)

websites

www.allmusic.com

www.archive.classicrockmagazine.com

www.billboard.com

www.bpi.co.uk

www.britishmusicexperience.com

www.contactmusic.com

www.discogs.com

www.grammy.com

www.ifpi.org

www.members.ozemail.com.au/~cruekiss

www.mojo4music.com

www.rockhall.com

www.rockonthenet.com

www.rocksbackpages.com

www.rollingstone.com

www.thejamuk.org

www.theofficialcharts.com

www.riaa.com

label abbreviations

amp	Ampex
asy	Asylum
at	Atlantic
bar	Barclay
bb	Bureau B
bro	Bronze
bru	Brunswick
c	Caroline
che	Cheapskate
cor	Coral
de	Destiny
eas	Eastworld
fli	Flicknife
fo&d	Fuck Off & Di
fon	Fontana
fp	Flipside
gd	Grateful Dead
gf	Geffen
hm	Hear Music
hy	Hydra
imm	Immediate
itm	Inedit Music
ja	Janus
kkp	Kirin Kid Productions
la	Liberty Artists
lib	Liberty
mf	Music Factory
mir	Miramar
onl	One Little Indian
par	Parlophone
pmk	Potamak
pol	Polydor
ps	Private Stock
rea	Reaction
rnr	Roadrunner
rrp	Reprise
rt	Rough Trade
rz	Regal Zonophone
san	Sanctuary
ta	Takoma
tel	Telstar
ua	United Artists
uni	Universal
v	Virgin
ver	Vertigo
we	WEA
wtr	Water
zap	Zapple
zip	Zippo
zk	Zick Zack

contributors

Chris Bryans (CB) has written about television, sport, and music for twenty years, with his work sneaking into *Radio Times, The Observer, Boxing Monthly, Record Collector,* and *Time Out* (Singapore). He was a contributing editor on *1001 Albums You Must Hear Before You Die* and a contributor on *1001 Songs You Must Hear Before You Die.* As he gets older and his mind turns to such things, he has decided he would like Mogwai played at his funeral.

Terry Burrows (TB) is a university lecturer who has written books on guitar (including 2011's *Guitar Family Trees: The History of the World's Most Iconic Guitars*) and musical instruction. As a musician, he has recorded more than forty albums in a variety of styles and under numerous pseudonyms. He has also taught music and technology courses at university level.

Bruno Ceriotti (BC) is a rock historian who writes artist biographies for music magazines and websites. He also worked as music consultant to a Hollywood film company and for a couple of record labels. In 2011 he published *My Little Red Book*, an annotated day-by-day chronology of the U.S. West Coast band Love.

Mick Dillingham (MD) Music writer, graphic artist, you name it and he hasn't done any of it except for the two mentioned above. Truly, if there ever were a renaissance man for the twenty-first century, then he would be the guy five places behind him in the line for fries.

Robert Dimery (RD) is a freelance writer and the general editor of *1001 Albums You Must Hear Before You Die* and *1001 Songs You Must Hear Before You Die*. He has contributed to *Time Out* (London) and *Guinness World Records,* will admit if pressed to copy-editing *Spice Girls: Live Spice!,* and is currently studying composing music for television and film. Robert lives in London with his lovely wife and a small collection of ukuleles.

Jim Harrington (JiH) is the longtime music critic for the *Oakland Tribune, San Jose Mercury News,* and the Bay Area Newspapers Group, and

was a contributor to *1001 Songs You Must Hear Before You Die.* He spends way too much time listening to Roxy Music and watching the Chicago Blackhawks. His world is filled with Grace—which happens to be the name of his daughter.

James Harrison (JaH) is a writer on popular culture who has contributed to *1001 Songs You Must Hear Before You Die, 1001 Paintings You Must See Before You Die, 1001 Books... 1001 Historic Sites...* (you get the drift). In the seventies he would spin twelve-inch disco singles in awe of Studio 54. He currently listens to Jonquil, Chad Valley, and Bronz—none of whom were selected for the current edition of this book, but who knows what the future might bring?

Drew Heatley (DH) is a journalist whose writings cover music, sport, and technology. He assisted on the *Times'* best-selling title, *Michael Jackson: Life of a Legend* and is the co-author of *Kings of Leon: Sex on Fire,* as well as a range of sporting titles, including *European Football Stadiums* and *Lost League Football Grounds.*

Michael Heatley (MHe) is the author of more than one hundred music-based biographies, as well as factual books on music, sport, and television. His biography of the late DJ John Peel sold more than 100,000 copies, while *Michael Jackson: Life of a Legend* topped the *Times'* best-seller list and has been widely translated.

Mike Hobbs (MiH) is a freelance journalist from London. He has contributed to many music magazines, starting with *Zigzag* in the seventies while still at school (his subject was Genesis). He has had more than twenty books published, ranging from music biographies through ghostwritten "autobiographies" to works of history.

Matthew Horton (MaH) is a freelance music journalist. He is a regular contributor and nostalgic list guru at www.nme.com, occasional columnist for the *Guardian Guide,* and an album reviewer for the BBC and Virgin Media. Matthew contributed to *1001 Songs You Must Hear Before You Die* and blogs at jukeboxjunior.com.

Jeff Hudson (JeH) has written or ghostwritten more than twenty books and has interviewed some of the greatest names in the music industry. He is the proud owner of the Freddie Mercury inflatable that escaped from Queen's concert at Wembley Stadium on July 12, 1986.

Dave Jennings (DJ) worked for the British music paper *Melody Maker* for more than a decade, and has now almost fully recovered. His music-related writing has also appeared in the *Los Angeles Times*, *The Guardian*, and *NME*, and on the feminist music website thegirlsare.com. He lives in Bradford in northern England.

Rob Jones (RJ) is a journalist, editor, and content strategist, based in London. He has written and reported on subjects as diverse as music, sport, construction, energy, and the public sector. He once held the Guinness World Record for eating a Terry's Chocolate Orange in the fastest time.

Spencer Leigh (SL) broadcasts a weekly show on BBC Radio Merseyside. He contributes to magazines and authored *The Beatles in Hamburg*. He writes obituaries for U.K. newspaper *The Independent* and says, "Quite often I have interviewed someone for radio, then written a magazine feature, and finally used the interview when they've died for the obituary."

George Lewis (GL) is a global rock disciple who has seen and written about it all, from the last gigs of Hendrix and The Doors at the Isle of Wight festival, through Mark Knopfler's debut with Brewers Droop at the Nags Head in High Wycombe, to John Fogerty's latest Creedence incarnation, live in Tatarstan.

Bruno MacDonald (BM) co-edited *1001 Songs You Must Hear Before You Die* and *1001 Albums You Must Hear Before You Die*. He edited *Air Guitar: A User's Guide*, *Pink Floyd: Through the Eyes of the Band, Its Fans, Friends, and Foes*, and *Rock Connections*, co-wrote *Rock and Roll Heaven*, and contributed to *The Rough Guide to Rock* and *Guinness Hit Singles*. He lives in Hertfordshire, with high maintenance cats and a very patient wife.

Joel McIver (JM) has authored twenty books on rock music, including *Metallica: Justice for All*, *Machine Head: Inside the Machine*, *Glenn Hughes: The Autobiography*, and *To Live is to Die: The Life and Death of Metallica's Cliff Burton*. His forthcoming titles include the autobiography of Max Cavalera. He contributes to several magazines, is the editor of *Bass Guitar Magazine*, and regularly appears on radio and television.

Olivia McLearon (OM) is a freelance writer and sub-editor from London. Her early musical obsessions were Madonna and Kylie, but discovering Britpop in her teens led to a lifelong love of Blur. Among her claims to fame is that she came face-to-face with Damon Albarn in a club, but was too shy to talk to him. She contributed to *1001 Songs You Must Hear Before You Die* and *Rock Connections*, and has worked on magazines ranging from *Doctor Who Adventures* to *Grazia*.

David Roberts (DR) worked as editor on twenty music book projects at Guinness World Records, including *British Hit Singles* and *Rockopedia*. In 2006 he was appointed consultant, writer, and filmmaker to the British Music Experience visitor attraction at London's O2 venue. Recently he created *Rock Atlas*, a guidebook to the music locations of the United Kingdom and Ireland.

Brian Southall (BS) was a journalist with *Melody Maker* and *Disc* before joining A&M. He moved to EMI and served as a consultant to Warner and HMV. His books include *Abbey Road: The Story of the World's Most Famous Recording Studios*, *Northern Songs: The True Story of The Beatles' Publishing Empire*, *If You Don't Know Me by Now: The Official Story of Simply Red*, *Treasures of the Bee Gees*, and *The Rise and Fall of EMI Records*.

Matthew White (MW) is the world's biggest Chris de Burgh fan, and a freelance writer, editor, proofreader, and researcher whose credits include Guinness World Records' *British Hit Singles & Albums*, *The Virgin Book of British Hit Singles*, and projects for the Official Charts Company. "Matt the Music Man" is the newly appointed music consultant for Guinness World Records.

performer directory

Page numbers in **bold** refer to illustrations.

Def Leppard 152–55, **153, 154, 155**
Collins, Allen
Lynyrd Skynyrd 298–99, **298**
Collins, Phil **530**
Genesis 202–5, **203, 204, 205**
Collins, Ray
Frank Zappa 542–45, **542**
Colomby, Bobby
Blood, Sweat & Tears 74, **74**
Colsefni, Anders
Slipknot 454–57, **454, 456**
Colt, Johnny
The Black Crowes 64–65, **64**
Colwell, Dave "Bucket"
Bad Company 42–43, **43**
Comita, Pete
Cheap Trick 104, **104**
Commerford, Tim
Rage Against the Machine 410, **410**
Constanten, Tom
Grateful Dead 208–9, **209**
Conway, Dave
My Bloody Valentine 345, **345**
Conway, Gerry
Fairport Convention 180–81, **181**
Jethro Tull 252–53, **253**
Cooder, Ry
Captain Beefheart and the Magic Band 96–97, **96**
Cook, Frank
Canned Heat 95, **95**
Cook, Jamie
Arctic Monkeys 36, **36**
Cook, Kyle
Matchbox Twenty 310, **310**
Cook, Paul
Sex Pistols 444–45, **444**
Cook, Steve
Soft Machine 470–71, **471**
Cook, Stu
Creedence Clearwater Revival 132–33, **132**
Cool, Tré
Green Day 210–13, **210, 212, 213**
Cooper, Alice 116–17, **116, 118, 119, 291**
Cooper, Jason
The Cure 142–45, **143**
Cooper, Ray
Elton John 254–57, **254**
Cope, Julian
The Teardrop Explodes 120–21, **120**
Copeland, Stewart
The Police 374–77, **374, 376, 377**
Corabi, John
Mötley Crüe 334–37, **334, 336**
Corgan, Billy
The Smashing Pumpkins 462–63, **462**
Cornell, Chris
Soundgarden 475, **475**
Cornick, Glenn
Jethro Tull 252–53, **252**
Cornwell, Hugh
The Stranglers 488–89, **488**
Cortini, Alessandro
Nine Inch Nails 350–51, **351**
Cosmo, Anthony
Boston 82–83, **83**
Cosmo, Fran

Boston 82–83, **83**
Costa, Gal
Gilberto Gil 206–7, **206**
Costello, Elvis 122–25, **122, 124, 125**
Cotton, Jeff
Captain Beefheart and the Magic Band 96–97, **96**
Coverdale, David
Deep Purple 148–51, **149, 151**
Whitesnake 524–57, **524, 526, 527**
Covington, Joey
Jefferson Airplane/Starship 250–51, **251**
Cox, Billy
Jimi Hendrix 224–27, **224**
Coxon, Graham
Blur 76–77, **76**
Coyne, Wayne
The Flaming Lips 188–89, **188**
Crahan, Shawn
Slipknot 454–57, **454, 456**
Creach, Papa John
Jefferson Airplane/Starship 250–51, **251**
Crespo, Jimmy
Aerosmith 22–25, **23**
Criss, Peter
Kiss 272–75, **272, 274**
Crook, Paul
Anthrax 32–33, **33**
Meat Loaf 318–19, **319**
Crosby, David
The Byrds 92–93, **92**
Crosby, Stills, Nash & Young 134–37, **134, 136, 137**
Neil Young 538–41, **540, 541**
Crover, Dale
Nirvana 352–55, **352**
Cruise, Julee
B-52s 39, **39**
Cullen, Paul
Bad Company 42–43, **43**
Cunningham, Phil
Joy Division/New Order 260–63, **260, 263**
Currie, Kevin
Supertramp 492–93, **492**
Currie, Steve
T. Rex 508, **508**
Curry, Mickey
Bryan Adams 20–21, **20**
Curtis, Ian
Joy Division/New Order 260–63, **260, 262**
Curtis, Sonny
Buddy Holly & The Crickets 232, **232**
Curulewski, John
Styx 491, **491**
Cymone, André
Prince 390–93, **391, 392**
Czukay, Holger
Can 94, **94**

D

Dahan, Olivier Joseph "Jo"
Mano Negra/Manu Chao 306–7, **306**
Dahme, Kimberley
Boston 82–83, **83**
Dailey, Shawn
Hole 230–31, **231**
Dalton, John

The Kinks 270–71, **270**
Daltrey, Roger
The Who 528–31, **528, 530, 531**
D'Angelo, Greg
Anthrax 32–33, **32**
Danko, Rick
The Band 44–45, **44**
Bob Dylan 162–65, **163, 165**
Darnal, Thomas
Mano Negra/Manu Chao 306–7, **306**
Daugherty, Jay Dee
Patti Smith 464–65, **464**
Davey, Alan
Hawkwind 222–23, **223**
David, Benoît
Yes 534–37, **535, 537**
Davies, Dave
The Kinks 270–71, **270**
Davies, Garth
Buzzcocks 90–91, **90**
Davies, Michael "Dik Mik"
Hawkwind 222–23, **222**
Davies, Ray **325**
The Kinks 270–71, **270**
Davies, Rick
Supertramp 492–93, **492**
Davis, Jesse Ed
John Lennon 288–91, **289**
Davis, Jonathan
Korn 276–77, **276**
Davis, Michael
MC5 313, **313**
Davis, Tim
Steve Miller 327, **327**
Day, Paul
Iron Maiden 240–43, **240**
De Albuquerque, Mike
Electric Light Orchestra 172–73, **172**
De Jong, Ted
Popol Vuh 382–83, **383**
De la Parra, Fito
Canned Heat 95, **95**
De la Rocha, Zack
Rage Against the Machine 410, **410**
Deacon, John
Queen 400–3, **400, 402**
Deal, Kim
Pixies 372, **372**
Dean, Elton
Soft Machine 470–71, **470**
DeCarlo, Tommy
Boston 82–83, **83**
Dechert, Gregg
Bad Company 42–43, **42**
Dee, Mikkey
Motörhead 338–39, **338**
DeGarmo, Chris
Queensrÿche 405, **405**
DeLeo, Dean
Stone Temple Pilots 487, **487**
DeLeo, Robert
Stone Temple Pilots 487, **487**
DeLonge, Tom
Blink-182 72, **72**
Delp, Brad
Boston 82–83, **82**
Delson, Brad
Linkin Park 293, **293**
DeMarinis, Anne
Sonic Youth 472–73, **472**
Dempsey, Michael

The Cure 142–45, **142**
Denis, Daniel
Univers Zéro 514, **514**
Denny, David
Steve Miller 327, **327**
Denny, Sandy **284**
Fairport Convention 180–81, **181**
Densmore, John
The Doors 160–61, **160**
Dercourt, Jean Michel
"Gambeat"
Mano Negra/Manu Chao 306–7, **307**
Destri, Jimmy
Blondie 73, **73**
Dettmar, Del
Hawkwind 222–23, **222**
Devoto, Howard
Buzzcocks 90–91, **90**
Deyama, Toshimitsu see "Toshi"
DeYoung, Dennis
Styx 491, **491**
Dharma, Buck
Blue Öyster Cult 75, **75**
Di'Anno, Paul
Iron Maiden 240–43, **241**
Dias, Allan
Public Image Ltd 398–99, **399**
Dias, Denny
Steely Dan 482–83, **482**
Dias, Marcelo "Cello"
Soulfly 474, **474**
Dick, Magic
J. Geils Band 201, **201**
Dickerson, Dez
Prince 390–93, **390, 392**
Dickinson, Bruce
Iron Maiden 240–43, **240, 242, 243**
Dickinson, Luther
The Black Crowes 64–65, **65**
Diermaier, Werner "Zappi"
Faust 187, **187**
Diggle, Steve
Buzzcocks 90–91, **90**
Dillon, Jerome
Nine Inch Nails 350–51, **351**
Ding, Wu
Black Panther 67, **67**
Dinger, Klaus
Kraftwerk 278–79, **279**
Neu! 346, **346**
Dinger, Thomas
Neu! 346, **346**
Dio, Ronnie James
Black Sabbath 68–71, **68, 71**
Rainbow 411, **411**
Dirnt, Mike
Green Day 210–13, **210, 212, 213**
Dixon, Willie
Chuck Berry 62–63, **62**
Djong, Yun
Popol Vuh 382–83, **382**
Dobrow, Bill
The Black Crowes 64–65, **65**
Dolabella, Jean
Sepultura 442–43, **443**
Dolmayan, John
System of a Down 494–95, **494**
Donahue, Jerry
Fairport Convention 180–81, **181**

picture credits

Every effort has been made to credit the copyright holders of the images used in this book. We apologize for any unintentional omissions or errors and would be pleased to insert the appropriate acknowledgement to any companies or individuals in any subsequent editions of the work.

KEY
Band member images: numbered, left to right (1), (2), (3), (4), (5), (6), (7), (8)
Image-only pages: top = t / bottom = b / left = l / right = r / center = c / top left = tl / top center = tc / top right = tr / center top = ct / center bottom = cb / center left = cl / center right = cr / center left top = clt / center left bottom = clb / center right top = crt / center right bottom = crb / bottom left = bl / bottom center = bc / bottom right = br

2 Annamaria DiSanto/WireImage 6–7 Rob Verhorst/Redferns 9 Michael Putland/Getty Images 14–15 Donald Miralle/Getty Images 16 (1) Chris Walter/WireImage (2) Fin Costello/Redferns (3) Stefan M. Prager/Redferns (4) © Jazzbacks at en.wikipedia (5) Anthony Reginato/Newspix/Rex Features (6) Michael Ochs Archives/Getty Images 17 (1) Fin Costello/Redferns (2) Bob King/Redferns (3) Denis O'Regan/Getty Images (4) Michael Ochs Archives/Getty Images (5) Mick Hutson/Redferns (6) Bob King/Redferns 18 tl Michael Ochs Archives/Getty Images tr Michael Ochs Archives/Getty Images cl Bob King/Redferns cr Richard McCaffrey/Getty Images b © Martyn Goddard/Corbis 19 t Fin Costello/Redferns cl © Martyn Goddard/Corbis crt Bob King/Redferns crb Bob King/Redferns bl Michael Putland/Getty Images br Mick Hutson/Redferns 20 (1) Time Life Pictures/DMI/Time Life Pictures/Getty Images (2) © Jim Vallance (3) Dan Miller/Rex Features (4) © Bob Leafe (5) Mick Hutson/Redferns (6) Graham Wiltshire/Redferns 21 (1) Michel Linssen/Redferns (2) © Nicola Wright 22 (1) Paul Bergen/Redferns (2) Mick Hutson/Redferns (3) Marcel Thomas/FilmMagic (4) Jordi Vidal/Redferns (5) Fin Costello/Redferns (6) Michael Putland/Getty Images 23 (1) Richard E. Aaron f Redferns (2) Bob Berg/Getty Images 24 tl Richard McCaffrey/Getty Images tr Richard E. Aaron/Redferns c Gems/Redferns bl Fin Costello/Redferns br Richard E. Aaron/Redferns 25 tl Ellen Poppinga - K & K/Redferns tr Jim Steinfeldt/Michael Ochs Archives/Getty Images cl Jeff Kravitz/FilmMagic cr KMazur/WireImage b Kmazur/WireImage 26 (1) Stuart Mostyn/Redferns (2) Martin Bernetti/AFP/Getty Images (3) Mick Hutson/Redferns 27 (1) Classic Rock Magazine/Getty Images (2) Eddie Malluk/WireImage (3) Jeff Kravitz/FilmMagic (4) Eddie Malluk/WireImage (5) Christie Goodwin/Getty Images (6) Bernd Mueller/Redferns 28 (1) Michael Ochs Archives/Getty Images (2) Scott Gries/Getty Images (3) Gems/Redferns (4) Michael Ochs Archives/Getty Images (5) C Flanigan/FilmMagic (6) C Flanigan/FilmMagic (7) Boston Globe/Boston Globe via Getty Images (8) © Neal Preston/CORBIS 29 (1) Larry Hulst/Getty Images (2) © Carl Lender (3) Steve Eichner/WireImage (4) Angela Weiss/Getty Images (5) Charles Eshelman/FilmMagic (6) Rick Diamond/Getty Images (7) Larry Hulst/Getty Images 30 (1) Michael Ochs Archives/Getty Images (2) Popperfoto/Popperfoto/Getty Images (3) Gijsbert Hanekroot/Redferns (4) Hulton Archive/Getty Images (5) Sylvia Pitcher/Redferns (6) Petra Niemeier - K & K/Redferns 31 (1) Dick Barnatt/Redferns (2) Val Wilmer/Redferns 32 (1) Ethan Miller/Getty Images (2) © David Tyler (3) Michael Ochs Archives/Getty Images (4) © Neilturbin.com (6) Paul Hawthorne/Getty Images (7) Mick Hutson/Redferns (8) Metal Hammer Magazine/Future Publishing 33 (1) Paul Hawthorne/Getty Images (2) © Paul Crook (3) Kevin Winter/Getty Images (4) Larry Marano/Getty Images (5) Mick Hutson/Redferns 34 (1) Mick Hutson/Redferns (2) Mick Hutson/Redferns (3) © Myles Broscoe (4) © Greg Hefner (5) John Shearer/WireImage (6) Mick Hutson/Redferns 35 (1) Maury Phillips/WireImage (2) © Laura Vanags/Banff Indie Band Residencey, courtesy the Banff Centre (3) Mick Hutson/Redferns (4) Mick Hutson/Redferns (5) Mick Hutson/Redferns (6) Tiffany Rose/WireImage 36 (1) Dave M. Benett/Getty Images (2) Dave M. Benett/Getty Images (3) Dave Hogan/Getty Images (3) Dave M. Benett/Getty Images (3) Dave Hogan/Getty Images 37 (1) Michael Putland/Getty Images (2) Michael Putland/Getty Images (3) Michael Putland/Getty Images (4) Donna Santisi/Redferns (5) Robert Knight Archive/Redferns (6) Keystone/Getty Images (8) Robert Knight Archive/Redferns 38 (1) b-2 (2) b-2 (5) b-2 (6) b-2 (7) b-2 (8) b-2 39 (1) Lynn Goldsmith/Corbis (2) Larry Hulst/Getty Images (3) Peter Noble/Redferns (3) Peter Noble/Redferns (3) Peter Noble/Redferns (6) Rex Features (9) Chris McKay/WireImage 40 (1) Jorgen Angel/Redferns (2) Michael Ochs Archives/Getty Images (3) Jorgen Angel/Redferns (4) Jorgen Angel/Redferns (5) © William Greenblatt Photography (6) Jorgen Angel/Redferns 41 (2) Michael Ochs Archives/Getty Images (3) Courtesy of AIM Inc. 42 (1) Michael Putland/Getty Images (2) Fin Costello/Redferns (3) Fin Costello/Redferns (5) Fin Costello/Redferns (5) Katy Winn/Corbis (6) Roger Ressmeyer/CORBIS (7) Pat Cooley 43 (1) Paul Cullen (2) J. Shearer/WireImage (4) Ron Galella/WireImage (5) John Atashian/CORBIS (6) © 2004 allrightnow.com (7) © Lynn Sorensen (8) Neil Lupin/Redferns 44 (1) Michael Ochs Archives/Getty Images (2) Jan Persson/Redferns (3) Frank Driggs Collection/Getty Images (4) Frank Driggs Collection/Getty Images (5) Gijsbert Hanekroot/Redferns (6) Brigitte Engl/Redferns 45 (1) Jerritt Clark/WireImage (4) © Chris Vitarello 46 (1) Fin Costello/Redferns (2) Fin Costello/Redferns (3) Fin Costello/Redferns (4) Fin Costello/Redferns 48 (1) Hulton Archive/Getty Images (2) Hulton Archive/Getty Images (3) Hulton Archive/Getty Images (4) Hulton Archive/Getty Images (5) Hulton Archive/Getty Images 49 (1) Michael Ochs Archives/Getty Images (2) Central Press/Getty Images (3) RB/Redferns (4) Michael Ochs Archives/Getty Images (5) Michael Ochs Archives/Getty Images 50 tl Michael Ochs Archives/Getty Images tr Michael Ochs Archives/Getty Images c Michael Ochs Archives/Redferns b Michael Ochs Archives/Getty Images 51 tl Gijsbert Hanekroot/Redferns tc Michael Ochs Archives/Getty Images tr RB/Redferns ct Terry Lott/Sony Music Archive/Getty Images cb ABC Photo Archives/ABC via Getty Images b Lionel Flusin/Gamma-Rapho via Getty Images 52 (1) David Farrell/Redferns (2) Fiona Adams/Redferns (3) Michael Ochs Archives/Getty Images (4) Keystone/Getty Images (5) Mark and Colleen Hayward/Redferns (6) Juergen Vollmer/Redferns 54 tl Michael Webb/Getty Images tr Max Scheler - K & K/Redferns cl Bob Thomas/Bob Thomas/Getty Images cr Terry O'Neill/Getty Images bl Hulton Archive/Getty Images br Express/Getty Images 55 tl Robert Whitaker/Getty Images tr BIPS/Getty Images c Hulton Archive/Getty Images b Tom Hanley/Redferns 56 (1) Victor Malafronte/Getty Images (2) © Bureau L.A. Collection/Sygma/Corbis (3) © Mr Bonzai (4) © Mr Bonzai (5) Steven Dewall/Redferns (6) Lester Cohen/WireImage 58 (1) Ian Tyas/Getty Images (2) Michael Putland/Getty Images (3) Keystone/Getty Images (4) Keystone/Getty Images (5) GAB Archive/Redferns 60 t GAB Archive/Redferns cl K & K Ulf Kruger OHG/Redferns cr Waring Abbott/Getty Images bl Waring Abbott/Getty Images br Bobby Bank/WireImage 61 t Michael Putland/Getty Images cl Michael Putland/Getty Images cr Dave Hogan/Getty Images bl © Trinity Mirror/Mirrorpix/Alamy br Chris Walter/WireImage 62 (1) David Redfern/Redferns (2) Ebet Roberts/Redferns (3) Paul Natkin/WireImage (4) © Courtesy Illinois Slim (5) Jan Persson/Redferns (6) David Redfern/Redferns 64 (1) Clayton Call/Redferns (2) Clayton Call/Redferns (3) Clayton Call/Redferns (4) Clayton Call/Redferns (5) Clayton Call/Redferns (6) © Howling Diablo (8) Ray Tamarra/Getty Images 65 (1) Harmony Gerber/Shutterstock.com (2) Ebet Roberts/Redferns (3) Erika Goldring/Getty Images (4) © Greg Rzab (5) © Scott D. Smith/Retna/Retna Ltd./Corbis (6) © Julia Allison (7) © Paul Stacey (8) Ethan Miller/Getty Images 66 (1) Alastair Indge/Photoshot/Getty Images (2) © Alison S. Braun/CORBIS (3) L. Cohen/WireImage (5) Alastair Indge/Photoshot/Getty Images (7) Frank Mullen/WireImage (8) © Copyright 2008 The Autograph Guys, LLC 67 (1) © bbs.sina.com.cn (3) © 12baobao.cn (4) © 12baobao.cn (5) © Yule.sohu.com (6) Xinhua/Guo Cheng 68 (1) Harry Goodwin/Rex Features (2) Harry Goodwin/Rex Features (3) Harry Goodwin/Rex Features (4) Harry Goodwin/Rex Features (5) Chris Walter/WireImage (6) Chris Walter/WireImage 69 (1) Robert Knight Archive/Redferns (2) Jorgen Angel/Redferns (4) © 2002-2012 Encyclopaedia Metallum (6) Fin Costello/Redferns 70 tl Ellen Poppinga - K & K/Redferns tr Chris Walter/WireImage cl Gijsbert Hanekroot/Redferns cr Colin Fuller/Redferns b Jorgen Angel/Redferns 71 tl Denis O'Regan/Getty Images tr Peter Still/Redferns ct Chris Walter/WireImage cb Mick Hutson/Redferns bl Ebet Roberts/Redferns br DMI/Time Life Pictures/Getty Images 72 (1) Jim Steinfeldt/Getty Images (2) Jim Steinfeldt/Getty Images (3) Kristian Dowling/Getty Images (4) Jim Steinfeldt/Getty Images 73 (1) Brian Cooke/Redferns (2) Roberta Bayley/Redferns (3) Maureen Donaldson/Getty Images (4) Maureen Donaldson/Getty Images (5) Michael Ochs Archives/Getty Images (6) Chris Gabrin/Redferns 74 (1) Gems/Redferns (2) Michael Ochs Archives/Getty Images (3) Michael Ochs Archives/Getty Images (4) Michael Ochs Archives/Getty Images (5) Michael Ochs Archives/Getty Images (6) Michael Ochs Archives/Getty Images (7) Michael Ochs Archives/Getty Images (8) Michael Ochs Archives/Getty Images 75 (1) Jorgen Angel/Redferns (2) Jorgen Angel/Redferns (3) Tom Sheehan/Sony Music Archive/Getty Images (4) © LesVegas.com (5) Pete Cronin/Redferns (6) Jorgen Angel/Redferns (7) Pete Cronin/Redferns 76 (1) CARL DE SOUZA/AFP/Getty Images (2) Tony Buckingham/Redferns (3) Alastair Indge/Photoshot/Getty Images (4) Chris Jackson/Getty Images 78 (1) Ebet Roberts/Redferns (2) © Steve Jennings/CORBIS (3) Paul Natkin/Getty Images (4) © Neal Preston/CORBIS (5) Paul Natkin/Getty Images (6) Steve Snowden/Getty Images 79 (1) Mick Hutson/Redferns 80 t Ebet Roberts/Redferns cl Chris Walter/WireImage bl Rob Verhorst/Redferns br Rob Verhorst/Redferns 81 tl Clayton Call/Redferns tr © Jurgen Frank/Corbis ct Ke.Mazur/WireImage cb TORSTEN SILZ/AFP/Getty Images bl JEFF KOWALSKY/AFP/Getty Images br © JEFFREY ARGUEDAS/epa/Corbis 82 (1) Tim Mosenfelder/Getty Images

(2) Ed Peristein/Redferns (3) Richard E. Aaron/Redferns (4) Ed Peristein/Redferns (5) Michael Putland/Getty Images (6) Boston Globe/Boston Globe via Getty Images (7) © David Sikes 83 (1) Tim Mosenfelder/Getty Images (2) © Curly Smith (3) © Troy K Bartlett (4) Mary Schwalm/Getty Images (5) Tim Mosenfelder/Getty Images (6) Jeffrey Mayer/Getty Images (7) © Sayre Berman/Corbis (8) © Sayre Berman/Corbis 84 (1) Michael Putland/Getty Images (2) Terry O'Neill/Getty Images (4) Fin Costello/Redferns (5) Ipo Musto/Rex Features (6) John M. Heller/Getty Images 85 (1) Michael Putland/Getty Images (2) Brian Cooke/Redferns (3) Clayton Call/Redferns (4) © John Soares, courtesy of Reeves Gabrels (5) Ilpo Musto/Rex Features 86 tl Popperfoto/Getty Images tr Michael Ochs Archives/Getty Images c Michael Ochs Archives/Getty Images b Justin de Villeneuve/Getty Images 87 tl Gijsbert Hanekroot/Redferns tr Tim Boxer/Getty Images cl Ron Galella/WireImage cr Simon Ritter/Redferns bl Phil Dent/Redferns br Jeffrey Mayer/WireImage 88 (1) Michael Ochs Archives/Getty Images (2) Michael Ochs Archives/Redferns (3) Michael Ochs Archives/Getty Images (4) Michael Ochs Archives/Getty Images (5) Michael Ochs Archives/Getty Images (6) GAB Archive/Redferns 89 (1) Mick Hutson/Redferns (2) Mick Hutson/Redferns (3) Mick Hutson/Redferns (4) Mick Hutson/Redferns (5) Ethan Miller/Getty Images (6) Kevin Winter/NBCUniversal/Getty Images 90 (1) Fin Costello/Redferns (2) Chris Gabrin/Redferns (3) Peter Noble/Redferns (4) Chris Gabrin/Redferns (5) Chris Gabrin/Redferns (6) Rex Features 91 (2) Simon Horswell/FilmMagic (3) Graham Jepson/WireImage (4) Jo Hale/Getty Images (5) © Gifferette Gonad 92 (1) Ebet Roberts/Redferns (2) Jorgen Angel/Redferns (3) Michael Ochs Archives/Getty Images (4) Michael Putland/Getty Images (5) Gems/Redferns (6) GAB Archive/Redferns 93 (1) Ginny Win/Getty Images (2) Gems/Redferns (3) © 2012 Sarah Morrison Photography (4) Gems/Redferns (5) Gijsbert Hanekroot/Redferns 94 (1) /Michael Putland/Getty Images (4) Leon Morris/Redferns (5) © James Tworow (6) Chris Mills/Redferns (7) Richard E. Aaron/Redferns (8) Brian Cooke/Redferns 95 (1) Petra Niemeier - K & K/Redferns (2) Petra Niemeier - K & K/Redferns (4) Petra Niemeier - K & K/Redferns (5) Petra Niemeier - K & K/Redferns (6) Steve Snowden/Getty Images (7) Steve Snowden/Getty Images (8) Bobby Bank/Getty Images 96 (1) Doug McKenzie/Getty Images (2) Michael Putland/Getty Images (3) Michael Ochs Archives/Getty Images (4) Gems/Redferns (5) Gems/Redferns (6) Michael Ochs Archives/Getty Images 97 (1) Gijsbert Hanekroot/Redferns (3) Michael Ochs Archives/Getty Images (4) Fin Costello/Redferns (6) Petra Niemeier - K & K/Redferns 98 (1) Ebet Roberts/Redferns (2) Ebet Roberts/Redferns (3) Ebet Roberts/Redferns (4) Ebet Roberts/Redferns (5) Ebet Roberts/Redferns 100 (1) Martin Philbey/Redferns (2) Gary Clark/FilmMagic (3) Michael Putland/Getty Images (4) James Emmett/Redferns (7) © Robert Carrithers (8) Jordi Vidal/Redferns 101 (1) © Roland Wolf (2) Jim Dyson/Getty Images (3) Michael Burnell/Redferns (4) Dave Hogan/Getty Images (5) Gary Wolstenholme /Redferns (6) Jim Donnelly/Getty Images (7) Mark Metcalfe/Getty Images (8) GAB Archive/Redferns 102 t Frans Schellekens/Redferns cl Frans Schellekens/Redferns cr Steven Richards/© Photoshot/Retna bl © Gavin Evans/Corbis br Ebet Roberts/Redferns 103 tl Patrick Ford/Redferns tr © Trevor O'Shana/Corbis cl Patrick Ford/Redferns cr Paul Bergen/Redferns b Meghan Sinclair/NBC/NBCU Photo Bank via Getty Images 104 (1) Michael Putland/Getty Images (2) Michael Putland/Getty Images (3) Michael Putland/Getty Images (4) Michael Putland/Getty Images (5) © Neal Preston/CORBIS (6) Chris Walter/WireImage 105 (1) Scott Kirkland/FilmMagic (2) Richard E. Aaron/Redferns (3) David Redfern/Redferns (4) G. Gershoff/WireImage (5) Chris Walter/WireImage (6) Scott Kirkland/FilmMagic (7) Julian Wasser/Time & Life Pictures/Getty Images (8) Larry Marano/Getty Images 106 (1) Ebet Roberts/Redferns (2) Ebet Roberts/Redferns (3) Michael Putland/Getty Images (4) Ebet Roberts/Redferns (5) Peter Noble/Redferns (6) Ray Stevenson/Rex Features 107 (1) Michael Putland/Getty Images (2) Gerry Images/Getty Images (3) Peter Still/Redferns (4) Peter Still/Redferns 108 t David Montgomery/Getty Images c Kevin Cummins/Getty Images bl Ebet Roberts/Redferns br Virginia Turbett/Redferns 109 t /Fraser Gray/Rex Features c Larry Hulst/Getty Images bl Ebet Roberts/Redferns br © Mike Laye/CORBIS 110 (1) Jack Robinson/Getty Images (3) Rob Verhorst/Redferns (4) Michael Putland/Getty Images (5) Jorgen Angel/Redferns (6) Estate Of Keith Morris/Redferns (7) Gems/Redferns 111 (1) Patrick Riviere/Getty Images (2) © Bob King/Corbis (3) Paul McConnell/Getty Images (4) © Bob King/Corbis (7) © Bob King/Corbis 112 (1) Dave Hogan/Getty Images (2) Dave Hogan/Getty Images (3) Dave Hogan/Getty Images (4) Dave Hogan/Getty Images 114 t Mick Hutson/Redferns c Jeff Kravitz/FilmMagic b Nigel Crane/Redferns 115 t Business Wire/Getty Images bl Mick Hutson/Redferns br Peter Wafzig/Getty Images 116 (1) Michael Putland/Getty Images (2) Michael Putland/Getty Images (3) Michael Putland/Getty Images (4) Bobby Bank/WireImage (5) Michael Putland/Getty Images (6) Jorgen Angel/Redferns (7) Jordi Vidal/Redferns (8) Jeff Kravitz/FilmMagic 117 (2) Gary Wolstenholme /Redferns (4) Ebet Roberts/Redferns (4) Bob King/Redferns (5) Tim Mosenfelder/Getty Images (6) Ethan Miller/Getty Images (7) Tabatha Fireman/Redferns (8) Jemal Countess/Getty Images 118 tl Jorgen Angel/Redferns tr Jorgen Angel/Redferns c Terry O'Neill/Getty Images bl Bettmann/CORBIS br © Trinity Mirror/Mirrorpix/Alamy 119 t Fin Costello/Redferns cl © Lynn Goldsmith/Corbis cr Stefan M. Prager/Redferns bl Michel Linssen/Redferns br Chris McKay/WireImage 120 (1) Fin Costello/Redferns (2) © 2011 The Wild Swans (3) © Mick Finkler (4) Harry Goodwin/Rex Features (5) Harry Goodwin/Rex Features (7) Harry Goodwin/Rex Features 121 (1) Ebet Roberts/Redferns (2) © David Fowler/123rf (3) © 2008 Ted Emmett (4) Ebet Roberts/Redferns (5) © Nick Barber/Getty Images 122 (1) Randy Miramontez/Shutterstock.com (2) Randy Miramontez/Shutterstock.com (3) Estate Of Keith Morris/Redferns (4) Randy Miramontez/Shutterstock.com (5) Randy Miramontez/Shutterstock.com 124 tl Kevin Cummins/Getty Images tr Ebet Roberts/Redferns c Roberto Bayley/Redferns bl Michael Grecco/Getty Images 125 br Michael Putland/Getty Images t Rob Verhorst/Redferns cl Estate Of Keith Morris/Redferns cr David Redfern/Redferns bl Michael Caulfield Archive/WireImage br Kevin Mazur/WireImage 126 (1) Jemal Countess/Getty Images (2) David Tonge/Getty Images (3) David Tonge/Getty Images (5) David Tonge/Getty Images (6) © Pam Bogert 127 (1) David Tonge/Getty Images (2) C Flanigan/FilmMagic (3) Joe Scarnici/FilmMagic (4) © Contographer/Corbis 128 (1) David Redfern/Redferns (2) Jan Persson/Redferns (3) Petra Niemeier - K & K/Redferns (4) Sylvia Pitcher/Redferns (5) David Redfern/Redferns (6) Steve Thorne/Redferns 129 (1) Mick Hutson/Redferns (2) Steve Thorne/Redferns 130 tl Paul Popper/Popperfoto/Popperfoto/Getty Images tr Chris Walter/WireImage cl Michael Ochs Archives/Getty Images cr The Estate of David Gahr/Getty Images bl Michael Ochs Archives/Getty Images br Terry O'Neill/Getty Images 131 t Time & Life Pictures/Getty Images c Peter Still/Redferns bl NBC/ NBC via Getty Images br © Gustau Nacarino/Reuters/Corbis 132 (1) Michael Putland/Getty Images (2) Michael Putland/Getty Images (3) Michael Putland/Getty Images (4) Michael Putland/Getty Images 134 (1) Ebet Roberts/Redferns (2) Ebet Roberts/Redferns (3) Ebet Roberts/Redferns (4) Michael Ochs Archives/Getty Images (5) Jack Robinson/Getty Images (6) Jack Robinson/Getty Images (7) Michael Putland/Getty Images (8) Michael Putland/Getty Images 135 (1) Keith Baugh/Redferns (3) © Joseph Lala (5) Clayton Call/Redferns (6) Neville Elder/Redferns (7) Jeff Kravitz/FilmMagic 136 tl © Henry Diltz/CORBIS tr Julian Wasser/Time & Life Pictures/Getty Images c © Henry Diltz/CORBIS bl Terry O'Neill/Getty Images br Jon Sievert/Getty Images 137 tl © Henry Diltz/CORBIS tr © Neal Preston/CORBIS c © Neal Preston/CORBIS bl Steve Eichner/WireImage br Getty Images/Getty Images 138 (1) Tim Mosenfelder/Getty Images (2) Gareth Cattermole/Getty Images (3) Bob King/Redferns (4) Patti Ouderkirk/WireImage (5) Tabatha Fireman/Redferns (6) Kevin Mazur/WireImage 139 (1) Christie Goodwin/Time & Life Pictures/Getty Images (2) © Nen.com.cn 141 (1) Erica Echenberg/Redferns (2) Erica Echenberg/Redferns (3) Erica Echenberg/Redferns (5) Erica Echenberg/Redferns (6) Linda Matlow/Rex Features (7) Jim Steinfeldt/Getty Images 142 (1) Michael Putland/Getty Images (2) Michael Putland/Getty Images (3) Michael Putland/Getty Images (4) Gabor Scott/Redferns (5) Michael Putland/Getty Images 143 (1) Fin Costello/Redferns (2) Fin Costello/Redferns (3) Michael Putland/Getty Images (5) Bob King/Redferns (6) Gustavo Caballero/Getty Images 144 tl Kevin Cummins/Getty Images tr Ebet Roberts/Redferns ct Ebet Roberts/Redferns cb Paul Natkin/WireImage b Rob Verhorst/Redferns 145 tl Michael Putland/Getty Images tr Paul Harris/Getty Images cl Paul Natkin/WireImage cr Liam Nicholls/Getty Images b Jo Hale/Getty Images 146 (1) Estate Of Keith Morris/Redferns (2) Estate Of Keith Morris/Redferns (3) Ian Dickson/Redferns (4) Estate Of Keith Morris/Redferns (5) Paul Natkin/WireImage (6) Marc Marnie/Redferns (7) C Brandon/Redferns (4) Steve Thorne/Redferns 147 (1) Peter Noble/Redferns (2) Peter Noble/Redferns (3) Peter Noble/Redferns (4) Peter Noble/Redferns 148 (1) Fin Costello/Redferns (2) Fin Costello/Redferns (3) Fin Costello/Redferns (4) Jorgen Angel/Redferns (5) Jorgen Angel/Redferns (6) Jorgen Angel/Redferns (7) Jorgen Angel/Redferns (8) Fin Costello/Redferns 149 (1) Fin Costello/Redferns (2) Michael Ochs Archives/Getty Images (3) Ian Dickson/Redferns (4) Ebet Roberts/Redferns (5) Michael Uhll/Redferns (6) David Redfern/Redferns 150 tl John Minihan/Getty Images tr Michael Ochs Archives/Getty Images cl Michael Putland/Getty Images cr Jan Persson/Redferns b Fin Costello/Redferns 151 tl Fin Costello/Redferns tr Peter Still/Redferns c Fin Costello/Redferns bl Mick Hutson/Redferns br Martin Philbey/Redferns 152 (1) Robert Knight Archive/Redferns (2) Robert Knight Archive/Redferns (3) Chris Walter/WireImage (4) Chris Walter/WireImage (5) Robert Knight Archive/Redferns (6) Robert Knight Archive/Redferns 153 (1) Robert Knight Archive/Redferns 154 tl Andre Csillag/Rex Features tr Chris Walter/WireImage c Michael Ochs Archives/Getty Images bl Dave Hogan/Getty Images br Michael Putland/Getty Images 155 tl Andre Csillag/Rex Features tr Harry Herd/Redferns c SGranitz/WireImage bl Jeff Kravitz/FilmMagic br Neil Lupin/Redferns 156 (1) Ebet Roberts/Redferns (2) Randall Michelson Archive/WireImage (3) © Dania Heller (4) © Walter Dietrich (5) © George Berz 157 (1) Gijsbert Hanekroot/Redferns (2) Gijsbert Hanekroot/Redferns (3) Rob Verhorst/Redferns (4) Gijsbert Hanekroot/Redferns (5) Rob Verhorst/Redferns (6) Mark Westwood/Redferns (7) Michael Putland/

Getty Images **(8)** Rob Verhorst/Redferns **158 (1)** RB/Redferns **(2)** RB/Redferns **(3)** Michael Ochs Archives/Getty Images **(4)** RB/Redferns **(5)** RB/Redferns **(6)** Jim Steinfeldt/Getty Images **(7)** RB/Redferns **(8)** Michael Ochs Archives/Getty Images **159 (1)** RB/Redferns **(2)** RB/Redferns **(3)** Clayton Call/Redferns **(4)** Michael Putland/Getty Images **(6)** Clayton Call/Redferns **160 (1)** Michael Ochs Archives/Getty Images **(2)** Chris Walter/WireImage **(3)** Michael Ochs Archives/Getty Images **(4)** Chris Walter/WireImage **162 (1)** Val Wilmer/Redferns **(2)** Michael Ochs Archives/Getty Images **(3)** Gems/Redferns **(4)** © Davis Deluxe **(5)** Michael Ochs Archives/Getty Images **(6)** Richard E. Aaron/Redferns **(7)** Gijsbert Hanekroot/Redferns **(8)** Gijsbert Hanekroot/Redferns **163 (1)** Michael Ochs Archives/Getty Images **(2)** Richard E. Aaron/Redferns **(4)** © Frank Beacham (frankbeacham.com) **(5)** © Stu Kimball **(6)** Fred Hayes/WireImage **(7)** © Frank Beacham (frankbeacham.com) **164 tl** Michael Ochs Archives/Getty Images **tr** Douglas R. Gilbert/Redferns **cl** Fiona Adams/Redferns **cr** Hulton Archive/Getty Images **b** Michael Ochs Archives/Getty Images **165 tl** Alvan Meyerowitz/Getty Images **tr** Jordi Vidal/Redferns **c** The Estate of David Gahr/Getty Images **bl** © John Atashian/CORBIS **br** Sipa Press/Rex Features **166 (1)** Gijsbert Hanekroot/Redferns **(2)** Gijsbert Hanekroot/Redferns **(3)** Gijsbert Hanekroot/Redferns **(4)** Gijsbert Hanekroot/Redferns **(5)** Ed Perlstein/Redferns **(6)** Chris Walter/WireImage **167 (1)** Gijsbert Hanekroot/Redferns **168 t** GAB Archive/Redferns **cl** Gijsbert Hanekroot/Redferns **cr** © Henry Diltz/CORBIS **bl** © Neal Preston/CORBIS **br** © Neal Preston/CORBIS **169 tl** RB/Redferns **tr** Michael Putland/Getty Images **cl** Brad Elterman/FilmMagic **cr** Rob Verhorst/Redferns **b** Brian Rasic/Rex Features **170 (1)** Paul Bergen/Redferns **(2)** Jordi Vidal/Redferns **(3)** © Einsturzende Neubauten **(5)** © VUT **(6)** © 2008-2012 White Trash Fast Food GmbH **171 (1)** © Mote Sinabel Aoki **172 (1)** Michael Putland/Getty Images **(2)** Michael Putland/Getty Images **(3)** Fin Costello/Redferns **(4)** Fin Costello/Redferns **(5)** Fin Costello/Redferns **(6)** Fin Costello/Redferns **173 (1)** Fin Costello/Redferns **(2)** Michael Ochs Archives/Getty Images **(3)** Fin Costello/Redferns **(4)** Fin Costello/Redferns **(5)** © The Orchestra **(6)** Fin Costello/Redferns **174 (1)** Jorgen Angel/Redferns **(2)** Michael Putland/Getty Images **(3)** Jorgen Angel/Redferns **(4)** Gijsbert Hanekroot/Redferns **(5)** © Retroblog.net **176 (1)** Gered Mankowitz/Redferns **(2)** Gered Mankowitz/Redferns **178 (1)** Jodi Hilton/Getty Images **(2)** Matthew J. Lee/Boston Globe via Getty Images **(3)** Matthew J. Lee/Boston Globe via Getty Images **(4)** Matthew J. Lee/Boston Globe via Getty Images **(5)** Andre Csillag/Rex Features **(6)** Andrew Lepley/Redferns **179 (1)** Russian 'Extreme Camp' © 2010-2012 **(2)** Russian 'Extreme Camp' © 2010-2012 **(3)** Russian 'Extreme Camp' © 2010-2012 **180 (1)** Dave Peabody/Redferns **(2)** Jim McCrary/Redferns **(3)** Gems/Redferns **(4)** Ray Stevenson/Rex Features **(5)** Gijsbert Hanekroot/Redferns **(6)** Gems/Redferns **(7)** Dave Peabody/Redferns **(8)** Steve Wood/Evening Standard/Getty Images **181 (1)** Brian Cooke/Redferns **(2)** Jim McCrary/Redferns **(3)** Michael Putland/Getty Images **(4)** Jorgen Angel/Redferns **(5)** Dave Peabody/Redferns **(6)** Christie Goodwin/Redferns **(7)** Jordi Vidal/Redferns **(8)** Jordi Vidal/Redferns **182 (1)** Mick Hutson/Redferns **(2)** Mick Hutson/Redferns **(3)** Mick Hutson/Redferns **(4)** Gary Wolstenholme/Redferns **(5)** © Paul R. Giunta/Corbis **183 (1)** Mick Hutson/Redferns **(2)** © 2002-2012 Encyclopaedia Metallum **(4)** L. Cohen/WireImage **(5)** © Jo Fenn **184 (1)** Gabor Scott/Redferns **(2)** Kevin Cummins/Getty Images **(3)** Kevin Cummins/Getty Images **(4)** Kevin Cummins/Getty Images **(5)** Kevin Cummins/Getty Images **(6)** Kevin Cummins/Getty Images **(7)** © Michael Dawkins **(8)** © Michael Dawkins **185 (1)** © Paul Hanley **(2)** Kerstin Rodgers/Redferns **(4)** © Ding **(5)** Gary Wolstenholme/Redferns **(6)** © Nick Wilkinson **(7)** Astrid Stawiarz/Getty Images **186 (1)** Stephen Lovekin/WireImage **(2)** Stephen Lovekin/WireImage **(3)** Stephen Lovekin/WireImage **(4)** © Html.ucoz.net **(5)** Stephen Lovekin/WireImage **187 (1)** © NDR **(2)** © Michael S. Eisenberg **(3)** © Manuel Wagner **(4)** Mudra László **(5)** © Sigrid Rothe **(6)** © Sigrid Rothe **188 (1)** Giulio Marcocchi/Getty Images **(2)** Lyle A. Waisman/Getty Images **(5)** Dimitri Hakke/Redferns **189 (1)** Scott Legato/Getty Images **(2)** Peter Kramer/Getty Images **190 (1)** Michael Ochs Archives/Getty Images **(2)** Jan Persson/Redferns **(3)** Chris Walter/WireImage **(4)** © Bob Brunning **(5)** Michael Ochs Archives/Getty Images **(6)** RB/Redferns **(7)** Michael Ochs Archives/Getty Images **(8)** GAB Archive/Redferns **191 (1)** Ian Dickson/Redferns **(2)** Michael Putland/Getty Images **(3)** Ebet Roberts/Redferns **(4)** Chris Walter/WireImage **(5)** Time Life Pictures/DMI/Time Life Pictures/Getty Images **(6)** Richard E. Aaron/Redferns **(7)** Donna Santisi/Redferns **(8)** Ron Galella/WireImage **192 tl** Jan Persson/Redferns **tr** Chris Walter/WireImage **cl** Fin Costello/Redferns **cr** Gems/Redferns **b** Fin Costello/Redferns **193 tl** Richard E. Aaron/Redferns **tr** Richard E. Aaron/Redferns **c** © Neal Preston/CORBIS **bl** Time Life Pictures/DMI/Time Life Pictures/Getty Images **br** Kevin Winter/Getty Images **194 (1)** Jim McCrary/Redferns **(2)** Jim McCrary/Redferns **(3)** Jim McCrary/Redferns **(4)** Jim McCrary/Redferns **(5)** Jim McCrary/Michael Ochs Archives/Getty Images **(6)** Jim McCrary/Redferns **(7)** © John Beland **(8)** Gijsbert Hanekroot/Redferns **195 (1)** Gijsbert Hanekroot/Redferns **(2)** Gijsbert Hanekroot/Redferns **(4)** Gijsbert Hanekroot/Redferns **(6)** Gijsbert Hanekroot/Redferns **(7)** Gems/Redferns **196 (1)** Steven Dewall/Redferns **(2)** Scott Gries/Getty Images **(3)** Theo Wargo/WireImage **(4)** Karl Walter/Getty Images **(5)** Mick Hutson/Redferns **(6)** Ian Gavan - MTV/Getty Images **197 (1)** Chris Shiflett/Getty Images **198 (1)** Ebet Roberts/Redferns **(2)** Michael Putland/Getty Images **(3)** © The King Crimson Collectors Club **(4)** © Courtesy Bruce Pilato Archives **(5)** © Courtesy Bruce Pilato Archives **(6)** Ebet Roberts/Redferns **(7)** Gems/Redferns **(8)** Richard Young/Rex Features **199 (1)** © Peterframpton.com **(3)** Lisa Maree Williams/Getty Images **(4)** Christie Goodwin/Redferns **(5)** © Sayre Berman/Corbis **(6)** Christie Goodwin/Redferns **(7)** Christie Goodwin/Redferns **(8)** Tom Pennington/Getty Images **200 (1)** Michael Putland/Getty Images **(2)** Richard E. Aaron/Redferns **(3)** Michael Putland/Getty Images **(4)** Michael Putland/Getty Images **(5)** © John Rabbit Bundrick **(6)** Ian Dickson/Redferns **(7)** Fin Costello/Redferns **201 (1)** Jorgen Angel/Redferns **(2)** Jorgen Angel/Redferns **(3)** Jorgen Angel/Redferns **(4)** Chris Walter/WireImage **(5)** Jorgen Angel/Redferns **(6)** Jorgen Angel/Redferns **202 (1)** Jorgen Angel/Redferns **(2)** Michael Putland/Getty Images **(3)** Graham Tucker/Redferns **(4)** © Pictorial Press Ltd/Alamy **(5)** Phil Dent/Redferns **(6)** © Genesis enthusiast at the English language Wikipedia **(8)** Michael Putland/Getty Images **203 (1)** Denis O'Regan/Getty Images **(2)** Michael Putland/Getty Images **(3)** Ilpo Musto/Rex Features **(4)** Gems/Redferns **(5)** Stefan M. Prager/Redferns **204 tl** Michael Putland/Getty Images **tr** Michael Ochs Archives/Getty Images **cl** © Pictorial Press Ltd/Alamy **cr** Ian Dickson/Redferns **b** Michael Putland/Getty Images **205 tl** Rob Verhorst/Redferns **tr** Jeff Kravitz/FilmMagic **c** Peter Still/Redferns **bl** Denis O'Regan/Getty Images **br** Mick Hutson/Redferns **206 (1)** Michael Ochs Archives/Getty Images **(2)** Time Life Pictures/Getty Images **(3)** Lionel FLUSIN/Gamma-Rapho via Getty Images **(4)** Bertrand LAFORET/Gamma-Rapho via Getty Images **(5)** Lionel FLUSIN/Gamma-Rapho via Getty Images **208 (1)** Richard E. Aaron/Redferns **(2)** Richard E. Aaron/Redferns **(3)** Clayton Call/Redferns **(4)** Gijsbert Hanekroot/Redferns **(5)** Jan Persson/Redferns **(6)** Time & Life Pictures/Getty Images **209 (1)** Jeffrey Ufberg/WireImage **(2)** © 2012 lastsleep.com **(3)** Jan Persson/Redferns **(4)** Tim Mosenfelder/Getty Images **(5)** Steve Eichner/WireImage **(6)** Michael Putland/Getty Images **210 (1)** Scott Gries/Getty Images **(2)** MikeDirnt/Getty Images **(4)** Stephen Lovekin/FilmMagic **212 tl** © Murray Bowles **tr** Robert Knight Archive/Redferns **cl** Tim Mosenfelder/Getty Images **cr** Paul Bergen/Redferns **b** Jeff Kravitz/FilmMagic **213 tl** Graham Knowles/Redferns **tr** Naki/Redferns **cl** KMazur/WireImage **cr** Naki/Redferns **b** C. Taylor Crothers/FilmMagic **214 (1)** Anthony Pidgeon/Redferns **(2)** Kevin Statham/Redferns **(3)** Kevin Statham/Redferns **216 (1)** Ke.Mazur/WireImage **(2)** Ke.Mazur/WireImage **(3)** Mark and Colleen Hayward/Getty Images **(4)** Will Ireland/Classic Rock Magazine via Getty Images **(5)** Bob Krasner/Redferns **(6)** Ethan Miller/Getty Images **(7)** Frank Mullen/WireImage **(8)** Gregg DeGuire/WireImage **217 (1)** Christina Radish/Redferns **(2)** Ethan Miller/Getty Images **(3)** Neil Lupin/Redferns **(4)** Dario Cantatore/Getty Images **(5)** Daniel LeClair/Getty Images via Universal Orlando **(6)** Trish Tokar/Getty Images **(7)** C Flanigan/WireImage **(8)** © W. Axl Rose **218 tl** Larry Busacca/WireImage **tr** Jeffrey Mayer/WireImage **c** Paul Natkin/WireImage **b** Ke.Mazur/WireImage **219 tl** Peter Still/Redferns **tr** Fotos International/Rex Features **cl** Peter Still/Redferns **cr** Peter Still/Redferns **bl** Jerome DOMINE/Gamma-Rapho via Getty Images **br** Sipa Press/Rex Features **220 (1)** David Redfern/Redferns **(2)** Robert Knight Archive/Redferns **(3)** Michael Putland/Getty Images **(4)** Peter Noble/Redferns **(5)** Gareth Davies/Getty Images **222 (1)** Fin Costello/Redferns **(2)** Michael Ochs Archives/Getty Images **(3)** Jorgen Angel/Redferns **(5)** Denis O'Regan/Getty Images **(6)** Michael Ochs Archives/Getty Images **(8)** Michael Ochs Archives/Getty Images **223 (1)** Michael Ochs Archives/Getty Images **(2)** Denis O'Regan/Getty Images **(3)** RB/Redferns **(4)** Jo Astbury/WireImage **(6)** Jo Hale/Getty Images **(7)** © John Chase **(8)** Michael Ochs Archives/Getty Images **224 (1)** Ivan Keeman/Redferns **(2)** Ivan Keeman/Redferns **(3)** Ivan Keeman/Redferns **(4)** Gems/Redferns **(5)** Chris Walter/WireImage **225 (1)** © Juma Sultan **(2)** Barry Z Levine/Getty Images **226 tl** K & K Ulf Kruger OHG/Redferns **tr** K & K Ulf Kruger OHG/Redferns **cl** Terence Donovan Archive/Getty Images **cr** K & K Ulf Kruger OHG/Redferns **b** MARC SHARRATT/Rex Features **227 tl** © Henry Diltz/CORBIS **tr** David Redfern/Redferns **c** Michael Ochs Archives/Getty Images **b** JOEL ELKINS/Rex Features **228 (1)** Darcio Tutak/LatinContent/Getty Images **(2)** Alli Harvey/Getty Images **(3)** © Bruno Medina **(4)** Thiago Piccoli/Getty Images **(5)** © 2012 Na Mira do Groove **229 (1)** Carlos de Andres/Cover/Getty Images **(3)** © Desmotivaciones.es **(4)** © Desmotivaciones.es **(6)** © Alberto P. Veiga/Getty Images **230 (1)** Time & Life Pictures/Getty Images **(2)** A. Nevader/WireImage **(5)** Barry King/WireImage **(6)** CHARLES SYKES/Rex Features **231 (1)** A. Nevader/WireImage **(2)** A. Nevader/WireImage **(3)** Daniel Boczarski/Redferns **(4)** © Stuart Fisher **(5)** Noel Vasquez/Getty Images **232 (1)** RB/Redferns **(2)** Michael Ochs Archives/Getty Images **(3)** RB/Redferns **(4)** RB/Redferns **(5)** Charlie Gillett/Redferns **233 (1)** Dana Frank/Ovoworks/Time Life Pictures/Getty Images **(2)** Dana Frank/Ovoworks/Time Life Pictures/Getty Images **(3)** Dana Frank/Ovoworks/Time Life Pictures/Getty Images **(4)** Dana Frank/Ovoworks/Time Life Pictures/Getty Images **234 (1)** Michael Putland/Getty Images **(2)** Michael Putland/Getty Images **(3)** Michael Putland/Getty Images **(4)** ARALDO DI CROLLALANZA/Rex Features **(5)** Michael Ochs Archives/Getty Images **(7)** Gems/Redferns **235 (1)** Paul Natkin/WireImage **(2)** Paul Natkin/WireImage **(3)** Paul Natkin/WireImage **236 (1)** Mick Hutson/Redferns **(2)** Paul McConnell/Getty Images **(3)** Todd Williamson/FilmMagic **(4)** Katy Winn/Getty Images **(5)** Peter Still/Redferns **(6)** Todd Williamson/FilmMagic **237 (1)** Gaye Gerard/Getty Images **(2)** Todd Williamson/FilmMagic **(3)** Mark Dadswell/Getty Images **238 (1)** Michael Ochs Archives/Getty Images **(2)** © Danny Weis **(3)** Michael Ochs Archives/Getty Images **(4)** Michael Ochs Archives/Getty Images **(5)** GAB Archive/Redferns **(6)** © Larry Reinhardt **(7)** Joey Foley/FilmMagic **239 (1)** GAB Archive/Redferns **(2)** Michael Ochs Archives/Getty Images **(3)** The Elton John Archive **(5)** © DJ Concert Productions **240 (1)** Richard E. Aaron/Redferns **(2)** Michael Ochs Archives/Getty Images **(3)** Annamaria DiSanto/WireImage **(4)** Mick Hutson/Redferns **(5)** Steve Thorne/Redferns **(6)** Odile Noel/Redferns **241 (1)** © Michele Taylor Williams **(5)** Gered Mankowitz/Redferns **(6)** Virginia Turbett/Redferns **(7)** Virginia Turbett/Redferns **(8)** Mick Hutson/Redferns **242 tl** Virginia Turbett/Redferns **tr** Michael Putland/Getty Images **cl** Ebet Roberts/Redferns **cr** Krasner/Trebitz/Redferns **bl** Dave Hogan/Hulton Archive/Getty Images **br** Annamaria DiSanto/WireImage **243 tl** Ebet Roberts/Redferns tr Stuart Mostyn/Redferns c Brigitte Engl/Redferns b /Kevin Nixon/Classic Rock Magazine via Getty Images 244 (1) Peter Noble/Redferns (2) Peter Noble/Redferns (3) Peter Noble/Redferns 246 tl Ian Dickson/Redferns tr © Neal Preston/CORBIS c Steve Morley/Redferns b Ebet Roberts/Redferns 247 t Ebet Roberts/Redferns c Victor Watts/Rex Features bl Gus Stewart/Redferns br ITV/Rex Features 248 (1) Gregg DeGuire/WireImage (2) Nigel Crane/Redferns (3) Valerie Macon/Getty Images (4) Carley Margolis/FilmMagic (5) Barry King/WireImage (6) Jean Baptiste Lacroix/WireImage 249 (1) Jeff Kravitz/FilmMagic (2) © Katy Winn/Corbis 250 (1) Anthony Barboza/Getty Images (2) © Roger Ressmeyer/CORBIS (3) Ed Perlstein/Redferns (4) © Lynn Goldsmith/Corbis (5) © Morton Beebe/CORBIS (6) Blank Archives/Getty Images (7) Clayton Call/Redferns (8) Central Press/Getty Images 251 (1) Michael Ochs Archives/Getty Images (2) Michael Putland/Getty Images (3) Mike FANOUS/Gamma-Rapho via Getty Images (4) Michael Ochs Archives/Getty Images (5) Michael Putland/Getty Images (6) Michael Putland/Getty Images (7) Michael Putland/Getty Images (8) © Lynn Goldsmith/Corbis 252 (1) Jorgen Angel/Redferns (2) Jan Persson/Redferns (3) Harry Goodwin/Rex Features (4) Harry Goodwin/Rex Features (5) Michael Putland/Getty Images (6) Michael Putland/Getty Images (7) Michael Putland/Getty Images (8) Michael Putland/Getty Images 253 (1) Gems Redferns (2) Richard E. Aaron/Redferns (3) Ken Towner/Evening Standard /Rex Features (4) Jordi Vidal/Redferns (5) Pete Cronin/Redferns (6) © M Schurmann (7) Dana Nalbandian/WireImage (8) © Julian Hayr 254 (1) Dave M. Benett/Getty Images (2) GAB Archive/Redferns (4) Harry Goodwin/Rex Features (5) Terry O'Neill/Hulton Archive/Getty Images (6) Michael Putland/Getty Images (7) Robert Knight Archive/Redferns (8) Amanda Edwards/Getty Images 255 (2) The Elton John Archive (3) Jeff Fusco/Getty Images (4) Roberta Parkin/Redferns (5) © John Mahon (6) The Elton John Archive 256 tl Jack Robinson/Hulton Archive/Getty Images tr Michael Putland/Getty Images c David Redfern/Redferns bl Richard Young/Rex Features br Richard E. Aaron/Redferns 257 tl © David Lefranc/Kipa/Corbis tr Tim Mosenfelder/Getty Images c Anwar Hussein/WireImage bl Ida Mae Astute/ABC via Getty Images br KMazur/WireImage 258 (1) Michael Putland/Getty Images (2) Michael Putland/Getty Images (3) Michael Putland/Getty Images (4) Scott Kirkland/FilmMagic (5) © Sayre Berman/Corbis (6) Michael Putland/Getty Images (7) Michael Putland/Getty Images (8) Jeffrey Mayer/WireImage 259 (1) Michael Putland/Getty Images (2) Bobby Bank/WireImage (3) Tim Mosenfelder/Getty Images (4) David Pomponio/FilmMagic (5) Bobby Bank/WireImage (6) Jeffrey Mayer/WireImage 260 (1) Rob Verhorst/Redferns (2) Lisa Haun/Getty Images (3) Lisa Haun/Getty Images (4) Lisa Haun/Getty Images (5) Lisa Haun/Getty Images (6) Jo Hale/Getty Images 261 (1) Tony Woolliscroft/WireImage 262 tl Martin O'Neill/Redferns tr Chris Mills/Redferns clt ITV/Rex Features clb Sheila Rock/Rex Features cr Kerstin Rodgers/Redferns b ITV/Rex Features 263 tl Bob Berg/Getty Images tr Rex Features c Mark Allan/WireImage bl Jon Super/Redferns br Stuart Mostyn/Redferns 264 (2) Paul Natkin/WireImage (3) Paul Natkin/WireImage (4) Chris Mills/WireImage (5) Chris Mills/WireImage (6) Neil Lupin/Redferns (7) Chelsea Lauren/WireImage (8) Chris Walter/WireImage 265 (1) Fin Costello/Redferns (4) © Singerpictures.com (5) Fin Costello/Redferns (6) Naki/Redferns 266 (1) George Pimentel/WireImage (2) Bryan Bedder/Getty Images (6) Lester Cohen/WireImage (7) Bryan Bedder/Getty Images 267 (1) Paul Natkin/WireImage (2) Peter Sanders/Rex Features (3) Peter Sanders/Rex Features (4) Gems/Redferns (5) Michael Ochs Archives/Getty Images (6) Paul Natkin/WireImage (7) Paul Natkin/WireImage (8) Paul Natkin/WireImage 268 (1) Frederick M. Brown/Getty Images (2) Dave Hogan/Getty Images (3) Jerod Harris/WireImage (4) Dave Hogan/Getty Images 270 (1) Gijsbert Hanekroot/Redferns (2) Petra Niemeier - K & K/Redferns (3) DAVID MAGNUS/Rex Features (4) MARK SHARRATT/Rex Features (5) Harry Goodwin/Rex Features (6) Jorgen Angel/Redferns 271 (1) Gijsbert Hanekroot/Redferns (2) Estate Of Keith Morris/Redferns (3) Harry Goodwin/Rex Features 272 (1) © Lynn Goldsmith/Corbis (2) © Lynn Goldsmith/Corbis (3) © Lynn Goldsmith/Corbis (4) © Lynn Goldsmith/Corbis (5) Robert Knight Archive/Redferns 273 (1) © Lynn Goldsmith/Corbis (2) Ebet Roberts/Redferns (4) © Neal Preston/CORBIS (5) Mike Coppola/FilmMagic (6) © Jay Blakesberg/Retna Ltd./Corbis 274 tl Tom Hill/WireImage tr Chris Walter/WireImage ct Michael Putland/Getty Images cb Paul Natkin/Getty Images b Fin Costello/Redferns 275 tl Michael Ochs Archives/Getty Images tr Paul Natkin/Getty Images cl Mick Hutson/Redferns cr KMazur/WireImage b Will Ireland/Class Rock Magazine via Getty Images 276 (1) Paul Hawthorne/Getty Images (2) Annamaria DiSanto/WireImage (3) Bob Berg/Getty Images (4) Christina Radish/Redferns (5) SGranitz/WireImage (6) Jason Merritt/Getty Images 278 (1) Ebet Roberts/Redferns (2) Ebet Roberts/Redferns (3) Michael Ochs Archives/Getty Images (4) Michael Ochs Archives/Getty Images (5) Bob King/Redferns (6) Bob King/Redferns 279 (1) Bob King/Redferns (3) Marc Marnie/Redferns 280 (1) Dave Etheridge-Barnes/Getty Images (2) Kevin Nixon/Classic Rock Magazine via Getty Images (4) © Claudio Leo (6) Steve Brown/Photoshot/Getty Images 281 (1) Kevin Nixon/Classic Rock Magazine via Getty Images (2) Kevin Nixon/Classic Rock Magazine via Getty Images (3) Steve Thorne/Redferns 282 (1) Dick Barnatt/Redferns (2) Chris Walter/WireImage (3) Chris Walter/WireImage (4) Jorgen Angel/Redferns 284 t Jorgen Angel/Redferns cl Charles Bonnay/Time & Life Pictures/Getty Images cr Michael Stroud/Getty Images b Michael Ochs Archives/Getty Images 285 tl David Redfern/Redferns tr Richard E. Aaron/Redferns c Mick Gold/Redferns b Rob Verhorst/Redferns 286 (1) © Ricardo Siqueira (2) Buda Mendes/LatinContent/Getty Images (3) Buda Mendes/LatinContent/Getty Images 288 (1) Susan Wood/Getty Images (2) Susan Wood/Getty Images (3) K & K Ulf Kruger OHG/Redferns (4) Richard Upper/Redferns (5) Ebet Roberts/Redferns (6) Estate Of Keith Morris/Redferns 290 tl John Reader/Time & Life Pictures/Getty Images tr Central Press/Getty Images clt Susan Wood/Getty Images clb Evening Standard/Getty Images cr Terry Disney/Getty Images b Tom Hanley/Redferns 291 tl ABC Photo Archives/ABC via Getty Images tr Michael Ochs Archives/Getty Images cl Steve Morley/Redferns cr Michael Ochs Archives/Getty Images b Michael Ochs Archives/Getty Images 292 (1) Mick Hutson/Redferns (2) Andy Sheppard/Redferns (3) © Markus Cuff/Corbis (4) Mick Hutson/Redferns (5) © Markus Cuff/Corbis (6) Evan Agostini/Getty Images 293 (1) Amy Graves/WireImage (2) Victor Decolongon/Getty Images (3) Victor Decolongon/Getty Images (4) Jon Kopaloff/FilmMagic (5) Brian Ach/WireImage (6) Jim Smeal/WireImage 294 (1) Michael Putland/Getty Images (2) Jim Shea/Getty Images (3) Michael Ochs Archives/Getty Images (4) Petra Niemeier - K & K/Redferns (5) Michael Ochs Archives/Getty Images (6) Michael Ochs Archives/Getty Images 295 (1) Michael Ochs Archives/Getty Images (2) Michael Ochs Archives/Getty Images (3) Michael Ochs Archives/Getty Images (4) Tim Mosenfelder/Redferns (5) Anthony Pidgeon/Redferns 296 (1) © Reuters/CORBIS (2) Ebet Roberts/Redferns (3) © Nelson Onofre (4) © 2002-2012 Encyclopaedia Metallum 297 (1) Jan Persson/Redferns (2) Michael Ochs Archives/Getty Images (3) Michael Ochs Archives/Getty Images (4) Michael Ochs Archives/Getty Images (5) Gilles Petard/Redferns (6) Michael Ochs Archives/Getty Images 298 (1) Tom Hill/WireImage (2) Richard E. Aaron/Redferns (3) Michael Ochs Archives/Getty Images (4) Gems/Redferns (5) Douglas Mason/Getty Images (6) Tim Mosenfelder/Getty Images (7) Michael Ochs Archives/Getty Images (8) Michael Ochs Archives/Getty Images 299 (1) Tom Hill/WireImage (2) Getty Images (3) Michael Ochs Archives/Getty Images (4) Amy Graves/WireImage (5) Derek Storm/FilmMagic (6) Steve Thorne/Redferns (7) Tim Mosenfelder/Getty Images (8) © Jeff Moore/ZUMA/Corbis 300 (1) MARTIN BUREAU/AFP/Getty Images (2) Michael Ochs Archives/Getty Images (4) Michael Ochs Archives/Getty Images (6) Michael Ochs Archives/Getty Images 301 (2) Pascal Le Segretain/Getty Images 302 (1) Chris Walter/WireImage (2) Chris Walter/WireImage (3) Fin Costello/Redferns (4) Ethan Miller/Getty Images (5) Catherine McGann/Getty Images (6) Michael Putland/Getty Images (8) Neil Lupin/Redferns 303 (1) Fotex/Rex Features (2) © Göran Edman (5) © Patrik Hellström (6) Andre Csillag/Rex Features (7) Jordi Vidal/Redferns (8) Naki/Redferns 304 (1) Denis O'Regan/Getty Images (2) Insight-Visual UK/Rex Features (3) Andre Csillag/Rex Features (4) Mick Hutson/Redferns 306 (1) © Kim Kulish/Corbis (2) Foc Kan/WireImage (3) © Jacob Khrist 307 (1) © Wilfried Rebré (3) Lyle A. Waisman/Getty Images (4) Lyle A. Waisman/Getty Images (5) Araya Diaz/WireImage 308 (1) Joby Sessions/Classic Rock Magazine via Getty Images (2) © Mick Pointer (4) Barry Clack/FilmMagic (6) Joby Sessions/Classic Rock Magazine via Getty Images (7) Gary Clark/FilmMagic 309 (1) Fin Costello/Redferns (2) © Jonathan Mover (3) Joby Sessions/Classic Rock Magazine via Getty Images (4) Gary Clark/FilmMagic 310 (1) Stephen Shugerman/Getty Images (2) Kevin Winter/Getty Images (3) Arnold Turner/WireImage (4) John M. Heller/Getty Images (5) Michael Buckner/Getty Images 311 (1) Tim Mosenfelder/Getty Images (2) Tim Mosenfelder/Getty Images (3) Jason Squires/WireImage (4) John Shearer/WireImage (6) Jeff Kravitz/FilmMagic (7) Tim Mosenfelder/Getty Images 312 (1) Ivan Keeman/Redferns (2) Jeffrey Mayer/WireImage (3) Ivan Keeman/Redferns (4) Harry Goodwin/Rex Features (5) Michael Putland/Getty Images (6) Harry Goodwin/Rex Features (7) Bentley Archive/Popperfoto/Getty Images (8) © Roger Ressmeyer/CORBIS 313 (1) Leni Sinclair/Getty Images (2) Leni Sinclair/Getty Images (3) Leni Sinclair/Getty Images (4) Leni Sinclair/Getty Images (5) Leni Sinclair/Getty Images 314 (1) Michael Putland/Getty Images (2) Michael Putland/Getty Images (3) Estate Of Keith Morris/Redferns (4) Estate Of Keith Morris/Redferns (5) Gijsbert Hanekroot/Redferns (6) Richard Blanshard/Getty Images 315 (1) Steve Catlin/Redferns (2) Jim Smeal/BEI/Rex Features (3) Araya Diaz/WireImage (4) Tiffany Rose/WireImage (5) Nick Harvey/WireImage 316 tl Hulton Archive/Getty Images tr Anwar Hussein/Getty Images cl Evening Standard/Getty Images cr Alan Davidson/WireImage bl Keystone-France/Gamma-Keystone via Getty Images br Dave Hogan/Getty Images 317 tl Time & Life Pictures/Getty Images tr Tom Hanley/Redferns c Denis O'Regan/Getty Images b Dave Hogan/Getty Images 318 (1) Michael Ochs Archives/Getty Images (2) Michael Ochs Archives/Getty Images (4) Ron Galella/WireImage (5) Santi Visalli Inc./Getty Images 319 (2) Jesse Grant/WireImage (3) Mark Weiss/WireImage (4) © 2005-2009 Meatloaf Tribute.net (5) Olivia Hemingway/Redferns 320 (1) Chris Walter/WireImage (2) Mark Weiss/Getty Images (3) Kevin Winter/Getty Images (4) Jesse Wild/Rhythm Magazine via Getty Images (5) Mark Weiss/Getty Images (6) Mark Weiss/Getty Images (7) Chris Walter/WireImage (8) Mick Hutson/Redferns 321 (1) Time & Life Pictures/Getty Images (2) Time & Life Pictures/Getty Images (3) Time & Life Pictures/Getty Images (4) Time & Life Pictures/Getty Images (5) Time & Life Pictures/Getty Images 322 (1) Dave Allocca/Time & Life Pictures/Getty Images (2) Hulton Archive/Getty Images (3) Ron Galella Ltd./WireImage (4) Mick Hutson/Redferns (5) Krasner/Trebitz/Redferns 323 (1) Krasner/Trebitz/Redferns (2) Patti Ouderkirk/WireImage 324 tl Larry Hulst/Getty Images tr Fin Costello/Redferns cl Krasner/Trebitz/Redferns cr Ebet Roberts/Redferns b Mick Hutson/Redferns 325 t Tim Mosenfelder/Getty Images cl George De Sota/Redferns cr Paul Bergen/Redferns bl Peter Pakvis/Redferns br Kevin Mazur/WireImage 326 (1) Gaye Gerard/Getty Images (3) Serge Thomann/WireImage (4) Patrick Riviere/Getty Images (5) Gaye Gerard/Getty Images (6) © Tony Mott (7) Frazer Harrison/Getty Images 327 (1) Gijsbert Hanekroot/Redferns (4) Jim Steinfeldt/Getty Images (5) © Ken Cooper (7) Ebet Roberts/Redferns 328 (1) Gems/Redferns (2) Clayton Call/Redferns (3) Clayton

Call/Redferns **(4)** Richard McCaffrey/Getty Images **(5)** Michael Ochs Archives/Getty Images **330 (1)** RB/Redferns **(2)** Gered Mankowitz/Redferns **(3)** Gered Mankowitz/Redferns **(4)** RB/Redferns **(5)** RB/Redferns **(6)** Gered Mankowitz/Redferns **331 (1)** Michael Putland/Getty Images **(2)** Michael Ochs Archives/Getty Images **332 (1)** Gijsbert Hanekroot/Redferns **(2)** Michael Putland/Getty Images **(6)** © Sanford Gossman Photography **(7)** Ebet Roberts/Redferns **333 (1)** Samuel Dietz/Redferns **(2)** © John Allair/John Korty **(3)** Peter Noble/Redferns **(4)** © Ace Conference **(7)** Ollie Millington/Redferns **334 (1)** Ron Galella, Ltd./WireImage **(2)** Ebet Roberts/Redferns **(3)** Robert Knight Archive/Redferns **(4)** Ebet Roberts/Redferns **(5)** Mick Hutson/Redferns **(6)** Paul Natkin/Getty Images **335(1)** A. Nevader/WireImage **336 tl** Chris Walter/WireImage **tr** Peter Still/Redferns **clt** Ron Galella/WireImage **clb** Ebet Roberts/Redferns **cr** Ebet Roberts/Redferns **bl** Ron Galella, Ltd./WireImage **br** © Robb D. Cohen/Retna Ltd./Corbis **337 t** Ron Galella/WireImage **b** Joey Foley/FilmMagic **338 (1)** Fin Costello/Redferns **(2)** Fin Costello/Redferns **(3)** ANAKA/Rex Features **(4)** Estate Of Keith Morris/Redferns **(5)** Ian Dickson/Rex Features **(6)** Fin Costello/Redferns **339 (1)** Estate Of Keith Morris/Redferns **(2)** Fin Costello/Redferns **(3)** Gus Stewart/Redferns **(4)** Fin Costello/Redferns **340 (1)** Gems/Redferns **(2)** Jacques Bernard/Rex Features **(3)** Brian Cooke/Redferns **(4)** Brian Cooke/Redferns **(5)** Ian Tyas/Getty Images **(6)** Gems/Redferns **341 (1)** © Mick Bolton **(2)** Michael Putland/Getty Images **(3)** Michael Putland/Getty Images **(4)** Ivan Keeman/Redferns **(5)** Fin Costello/Redferns **342 (1)** Charles J. Peterson/Time & Life Pictures/Getty Images **(2)** Charles J. Peterson/Time & Life Pictures/Getty Images **(3)** Charles J. Peterson/Time & Life Pictures/Getty Images **(4)** Charles J. Peterson/Time & Life Pictures/Getty Images **(5)** Steven Dewall/Redferns **343 (1)** Benedict Johnson/Redferns **(2)** Mick Hutson/Redferns **(3)** Mick Hutson/Redferns **344 (1)** Mauro Pimentel/LatinContent/Getty Images **(2)** Rui M. Leal/Getty Images **(3)** © Lebrecht Music and Arts Photo Library/Alamy **(4)** © Mario Luiz Thompson/Arquivo **345 (1)** Alastair Indge/Photoshot/Getty Images **(2)** Alastair Indge/Photoshot/Getty Images **(3)** Suzie Gibbons/Redferns **(4)** Photoshot/Getty Images **(5)** Photoshot/Getty Images **346 (4)** © Bryan Spencer **347 (1)** Peter Noble/Redferns **(3)** Erica Echenberg/Redferns **(4)** Michael Ochs Archives/Getty Images **(5)** Ron Galella/WireImage **(6)** Michael Ochs Archives/Getty Images **348 (1)** Peter Pakvis/Redferns **(2)** SGranitz/WireImage **(3)** Kevin Kane/WireImage **(4)** © My Eye & My Lens = My World Photography **(5)** SGranitz/WireImage **(6)** Rob Scott/Rhythm Magazine via Getty Images **350 (1)** Kevin Mazur/WireImage **(2)** Dale Wilcox/WireImage **(3)** Jeffrey Mayer/WireImage **(4)** © Steve Jennings/CORBIS **(6)** Christina Radish/Redferns **(7)** Gary Miller/FilmMagic **(8)** Vince Bucci/Getty Images **351 (3)** © Greg **(4)** Jesse Grant/WireImage **(5)** Annamaria DiSanto/WireImage **(6)** David Livingston/Getty Images **(7)** Astrid Stawiarz/Getty Images **352 (1)** Jeff Kravitz/FilmMagic **(2)** KMazur/WireImage **(3)** Jeff Kravitz/FilmMagic **(4)** © Gillian G. Gaar, 2012 **(5)** David Corio/Redferns **353 (1)** J J Gonson/Redferns **(2)** J J Gonson/Redferns **(3)** Charles J. Peterson/Time & Life Pictures/Getty Images **(4)** Jeff Kravitz/FilmMagic **(5)** Gary Wolstenholme/Redferns **354 tl** J J Gonson/Redferns **tr** Michel Linssen/Redferns **c** J J Gonson/Redferns **bl** Michel Linssen/Redferns **br** Steve Pyke/Getty Images **355 t** Jeff Kravitz/FilmMagic **c** Jeff Kravitz/FilmMagic **b** Frank Micelotta/Getty Images **356 (1)** Dave Hogan/Getty Images **(2)** Dave Hogan/Getty Images **(3)** Jeff Kravitz/FilmMagic **(4)** Mick Hutson/Redferns **(5)** Rex Features **(6)** Mick Hutson/Redferns **357 (1)** Yuji Ohsugi/WireImage **(2)** Tim Mosenfelder/Getty Images **(3)** Dave Hogan/Getty Images **(4)** Lyle A. Waisman/Getty Images **358 (1)** Ian Dickson/Redferns **(2)** Peter Still/Redferns **(3)** Simon Ritter/Redferns **(4)** Dave Hogan/Getty Images **359 (1)** Chris Pizzello/WireImage **(2)** Martin Philbey/Redferns **(3)** JOERG KOCH/AFP/Getty Images **360 (1)** Mark Venema/Getty Images **(2)** Ralph Notaro/Getty Images **(4)** J. Shearer/WireImage **(5)** Ralph Notaro/Getty Images **(6)** John Sciulli/WireImage **361 (1)** © Sayre Berman/Corbis **362 (1)** Fred Duval/FilmMagic **(2)** Robert Knight Archive/Redferns **(3)** Annamaria DiSanto/WireImage **(5)** Ron Galella, Ltd./Getty Images **(6)** © Boss Tweed **363 (1)** James Emmett/Redferns **(2)** Jill Douglas/Redferns **(4)** Tim Mosenfelder/Getty Images **(5)** Gary Wolstenholme/Redferns **(6)** Tim Mosenfelder/Getty Images **364 (1)** Jeff Kravitz/FilmMagic **(2)** Peter Still/Redferns **(3)** Barry Brecheisen/WireImage **(4)** KMazur/WireImage **(5)** Allen Berezovsky/Getty Images **(6)** © 1997 - 2012 Drummerworld.com **365 (1)** Jeff Kravitz/FilmMagic **(2)** Jeff Kravitz/FilmMagic **(3)** Barry Brecheisen/WireImage **(4)** Kevin Mazur/WireImage **366 (1)** C Flanigan/Getty Images **(2)** C Flanigan/Getty Images **(3)** Michael Schwartz/WireImage **(4)** C Flanigan/Getty Images **(5)** Jim Spellman/WireImage **(6)** Jim Spellman/WireImage **367 (1)** Matt Stroshane/Getty Images **(2)** Isaac Brekken/WireImage **(3)** Jeff Kravitz/FilmMagic **368 (1)** HARRY GOODWIN/Rex Features **(2)** Harry Goodwin/Rex Features **(3)** CROLLALANZA/Rex Features **(4)** Harry Goodwin/Rex Features **(6)** Chris Walter/WireImage **370 t** Andrew Whittuck/Redferns **cl** Michael Ochs Archives/Getty Images **cr** Gijsbert Hanekroot/Redferns **bl** David Redfern/Redferns **br** Richard E. Aaron/Redferns **371 t** Ian Dickson/Redferns **cl** Peter Still/Redferns **crt** Moviestore Collection/Rex Features **crb** Rob Verhorst/Redferns **b** Denis O'Regan/Getty Images **372 (1)** Matt Carmichael/Getty Images **(2)** Erik S. Lesser/Getty Images **(3)** J. Shearer/WireImage **(4)** Louise Wilson/Getty Images **373 (1)** Matt Kent/Redferns **(2)** Mike Coppola/Getty Images **(3)** Neil Lupin/Redferns **(4)** D Dipasupil/FilmMagic **(5)** Philip Massey/FilmMagic **(6)** D Dipasupil/FilmMagic **(7)** Gary Wolstenholme/Redferns **(8)** D Dipasupil/FilmMagic **374 (1)** Keystone/Getty Images **(2)** Fin Costello/Redferns **(3)** Ebet Roberts/Redferns **(4)** Ian Dickson/Redferns **376 tl** Janette Beckman/Getty Images **tr** Richard McCaffrey/Getty Images **b** Evening Standard/Getty Images **377 tl** Denis O'Regan/Getty Images **tr** Janette Beckman/Getty Images **cl** © Lynn Goldsmith/Corbis **cr** © Catherine Bauknight/ZUMA/Corbis **b** © Ross Marino/Sygma/Co **378 (1)** Leee Black Childers/Redferns **(2)** Leni Sinclair/Getty Images **(3)** Michael Ochs Archives/Getty Images **(4)** Michael Ochs Archives/Getty Images **(5)** Michael Ochs Archives/Getty Images **(6)** Michael Ochs Archives/Getty Images **(7)** © Scott Weiner/Retna/Retna Ltd./Corbis **(8)** Ebet Roberts/Redferns **379 (1)** Ebet Roberts/Redferns **(2)** Ebet Roberts/Redferns **(3)** Phil Dent/Redferns **(4)** Denis O'Regan/Getty Images **(5)** Greg Williams/Rex Features **(6)** Kevin Winter/DMI/Time Life Pictures/Getty Images **(7)** Tim Mosenfelder/Getty Images **(8)** Samuel Dietz/WireImage **380 tl** Leni Sinclair/Getty Images **tr** Tom Copi/Getty Images **ct** Michael Ochs Archives/Getty Images **cb** Evening Standard/Getty Images **bl** Richard McCaffrey/Getty Images **br** L. Busacca/WireImage **381 t** Time & Life Pictures/Getty Images **c** KMazur/WireImage **bl** Theo Wargo/WireImage **br** Frederic SOULOY/Gamma-Rapho via Getty Images **382 (1)** GAB Archive/Redferns **(3)** Rose Hartman/WireImage **(4)** © Steffen Metzner **(5)** © Conny Veit **(6)** GAB Archive/Redferns **(8)** © Klaus Wiese **383 (4)** © Peter Eising **(5)** © Bernd Wippich **384 (1)** RB/Redferns **(2)** GAB Archive/Redferns **(3)** GAB Archive/Redferns **(5)** Michael Ochs Archives/Getty Images **386 tl** Michael Ochs Archives/Getty Images **tr** Michael Ochs Archives/Getty Images **cl** ABC Photo Archives/ABC via Getty Images **cr** /Paramount Pictures/Courtesy of Getty Images **b** Michael Ochs Archives/Getty Images **387 tl** Michael Ochs Archives/Getty Images **tr** Tom Wargacki/WireImage **c** Michael Ochs Archives/Getty Images **bl** Ron Galella/WireImage **br** Charlyn Zlotnik/Michael Ochs Archives/Getty Images **388 (1)** Fin Costello/Redferns **(2)** © Lynn Goldsmith/Corbis **(3)** L. J. van Houten/Rex Features **(4)** © Lynn Goldsmith/Corbis **(5)** © Michael Ochs Archives/Corbis **(6)** © Michael Ochs Archives/Corbis **(7)** Sarah Kerver/WireImage **(8)** © Tim Mosenfelder/Corbis **390 (1)** Al Pereira/Michael Ochs Archives/Getty Images **(2)** Ebet Roberts/Redferns **(4)** Linda Matlow/Rex Features **(5)** Michael Ochs Archives/Getty Images **(7)** Ebet Roberts/Redferns **391 (1)** Buckmaster © courtesy Eric Leeds **(2)** © Michael Porter **(4)** © 1997 - 2012 Drummerworld.com **(5)** CROLLALANZA/Rex Features **(6)** Steve Eichner/Getty Images **(7)** Michael Ochs Archives/Getty Images **(8)** Michel Linssen/Redferns **392 tl** Waring Abbott/Getty Images **tr** Nancy Heyman/Getty Images **c** Michael Ochs Archives/Getty Images **bl** Frank Micelotta/Getty Images **br** Michael Putland/Getty Images **393 tl** Ilpo Musto/Rex Features **tr** Andre Csillag/Rex Features **cl** Peter Still/Redferns **cr** L. Cohen/WireImage **b** Kristoffer Juel Poulsen/AFP/Getty Images **394 (1)** Michael Tullberg/Getty Images **(2)** Michael Tullberg/Getty Images **(3)** Dave M. Benett/Getty Images **(4)** Tim Roney/Getty Images **396 tl** © Photoshot/Retna **tr** Mick Hutson/Redferns **c** Mick Hutson/Redferns **bl** Mick Hutson/Redferns **br** Neil Lupin/Redferns **397 t** Pat Pope/Rex Features **b** Denis O'Regan/Getty Images **398 (1)** Ollie Millington/Getty Images **(2)** Anthony Pidgeon/Redferns **(3)** Rex Features **(4)** Steve Thorne/Redferns **(5)** Peter Noble/Redferns **(6)** Patrick Ford/Redferns **399 (1)** © Maureen Baker **(3)** © William Sibick **(5)** Stefan M. Prager/Redferns **(6)** Ray Stevenson/Rex Features **400 (1)** Michael Putland/Getty Images **(2)** Michael Putland/Getty Images **(3)** Michael Putland/Getty Images **(4)** Michael Putland/Getty Images **(5)** Dave Hogan/Getty Images **402 tl** Andre Csillag/Rex Features **tr** Keystone Features/Getty Images **ct** David Redfern/Redferns **cb** Ian Dickson/Redferns **bl** Gus Stewart/Redferns **br** Ian Dickson/Redferns **403 tl** Phil Dent/Redferns **tr** Michael Ochs Archives/Getty Images **ct** Popperfoto/Getty Images **cb** Denis O'Regan/Getty Images **bl** Michael Putland/Getty Images **br** Dave Hogan/Getty Images **404 (1)** Neil Lupin/Redferns **(2)** Debbie Smyth/WireImage **(3)** Will Ireland/Classic Rock Magazine via Getty Images **(4)** Lyle A. Waisman/Getty Images **(5)** Jeff Kravitz/FilmMagic **(6)** Iris/WireImage **(7)** Theo Wargo/WireImage **(8)** Nigel Crane/Redferns **405 (1)** Larry Marano/Getty Images **(2)** Larry Marano/Getty Images **(3)** Larry Marano/Getty Images **(4)** Larry Marano/Getty Images **(5)** © Karen Mason Blair/CORBIS **(6)** Annamaria DiSanto/WireImage **(7)** David "Bagel" Ungar/FilmMagic **(8)** Larry Marano/Getty Images **406 (1)** Peter Pakvis/Redferns **(2)** Peter Pakvis/Redferns **(3)** Nick Pickles/WireImage **(4)** Christina Radish/Redferns **(5)** Christina Radish/Redferns **408 tl** Bob Berg/Getty Images **tr** Kevin Cummins/Getty Images **cl** Mick Hutson/Redferns **cr** Paul Bergen/Redferns **b** Larry Marano/Getty Images **409 t** Kevin Westenberg/Contour by Getty Images **c** Mick Hutson/Redferns **b** Kevin Mazur/WireImage **410 (1)** J. Quinton/WireImage **(2)** Brian Rasic/Rex Features **(3)** Startraks Photo/Rex Features **(4)** Gary Miller/FilmMagic **411 (1)** Fin Costello/Redferns **(2)** Fin Costello/Redferns **(3)** Fin Costello/Redferns **(4)** Fin Costello/Redferns **(5)** Gems/Redferns **(6)** IBL/Rex Features **(7)** © Sayre Berman/Corbis **(8)** © 2002-2012 Encyclopaedia Metallum **412 (1)** Mick Hutson/Redferns **(2)** Mick Hutson/Redferns **(3)** Mick Hutson/Redferns **(4)** Mick Hutson/Redferns **(5)** Mick Hutson/Redferns **(6)** Mick Hutson/Redferns **414 (1)** Michael Ochs Archives/Getty Images **(2)** Michael Ochs Archives/Getty Images **(3)** Michael Ochs Archives/Getty Images **(4)** Michael Ochs Archives/Getty Images **(5)** Peter Noble/Redferns**(6)** Henry S. Dziekan III/Getty Images **(7)** Ebet Roberts/Redferns **416 (1)** Dale Woltman/FilmMagic **(2)** Paul Bergen/Redferns **(3)** Michael Zito/WireImage **(4)** SGranitz/WireImage **(5)** Rolf Wolfson/WireImage **(6)** Ebet Roberts Redferns **(8)** Frank Micelotta/Getty Images **417 (1)** Ebet Roberts/Redferns **(2)** Jim Steinfeldt/Getty Images **(3)** Paul Natkin/WireImage **(4)** © ToshiroKitty/Getty Images **(6)** © 4alanis.com **418 t** L. Cohen/WireImage **c** Ebet Roberts/Redferns **bl** Michael Ochs Archives/Getty Images **br** Michel Linssen/Redferns **419 tl** Steve Eichner/WireImage **tr** Tim Mosenfelder/Getty Images **cl** Ebet Roberts/Redferns **crt** Anthony Pidgeon/Redferns **crb** Peter Pakvis/Redferns **bl** Rick Diamond/WireImage **br** Larry Marano/Getty Images **420 (1)** SGranitz/WireImage **(2)** Jeff Kravitz/FilmMagic **(3)** Jeff Kravitz/FilmMagic **(4)** Rick Diamond/WireImage **422 tl** Ebet Roberts/Redferns **tr** Paul Bergen/Redferns **c** Ebet Roberts/Redferns **bl** Michel Linssen/Redferns **br** Theo Wargo/WireImage **423 tl** Dave Benett/Getty

Images tr Jeff Kravitz/FilmMagic ct Frank Micelotta/ImageDirect/Getty Images cb KMazur/WireImage b Scott Gries/Getty Images 424 (1) Richard Wolowicz/ Getty Images (2) Michael Ochs Archives/Getty Images (3) Michael Ochs Archives/Getty Images (4) Popperfoto/Getty Images (5) Terry O'Neill/Getty Images (6) © Ian Stewart @ The Musics Over (8) Alan Messer/Rex Features 425 (1) Michael Ochs Archives/Getty Images (2) Chris Walter/WireImage (3) © Baron Wolman (4) R. Diamond/WireImage (5) Paul Natkin/Getty Images 426 tl David Redfern/Redferns tr Keystone Features/Getty Images ct Jan Olofsson/Redferns cb Keystone-France/Gamma-Keystone via Getty Images bl David Montgomery/Getty Images br Denis O'Regan/Getty Images 427 tl James Garrett/NY Daily News via Getty Images tr Michael Putland/Getty Images cl Denis O'Regan/Getty Images cr Dove Shore/Getty Images b John W. McDonough/Sports Illustrated/Getty Images 428 (1) Brian Cooke/Redferns (2) Brian Cooke/Redferns (3) Brian Cooke/Redferns (5) Brian Cooke/Redferns (6) Brian Cooke/Redferns 429 (1) Time & Life Pictures/Time & Life Pictures/Getty Images (2) © Moody Klingman (5) Clayton Call/Redferns (6) Larry Hulst/Getty Images (7) Clayton Call/ Redferns 430 (1) Fin Costello/Redferns (2) © 2002-2012 Anthem Entertainment (3) Fin Costello/Redferns (4) Fin Costello/Redferns 432 (1) Paul McConnell/Getty Images (2) Mark Metcalfe/Getty Images (3) GAB Archive/Redferns (4) GAB Archive/Redferns (5) Denis O'Regan/Getty Images 434 (1) Robert Altman/Getty Images (2) Richard E. Aaron/Redferns (3) Larry Busacca/Getty Images (4) Michael Ochs Archives/Getty Images (5) Michael Ochs Archives/Getty Images (6) Michael Ochs Archives/Getty Images (7) Michael Ochs Archives/Getty Images (8) Michael Ochs Archives/Getty Images 435 (1) Michael Ochs Archives/ Getty Images (2) Alexander Sibaja/Getty Images (3) Larry Hulst/Getty Images (4) Michael Ochs Archives/Getty Images (5) Michael Caulfield Archive/ WireImage 436 (1) Frazer Harrison/Getty Images (2) Mark Mainz/Getty Images (3) Alexandra Beier/Getty Images (4) Jo Hale/Getty Images (5) Ethan Miller/ Getty Images (6) Krasner/Trebitz/Redferns (7) Krasner/Trebitz/Redferns (8) Steve Thorne/Redferns 437 (2) Jens Hartmann/Rex Features (3) © 2002-2012 Encyclopaedia Metallum (4) Neil Lupin/Redferns (6) © Achim Kirschning (8) Allen Berezovsky/Getty Images 438 t Michael Ochs Archives/Getty Images cl Gus Stewart/Redferns cr Larry Hulst/Getty Images b Michael Ochs Archives/Getty Images 439 tl Michael Ochs Archives/Getty Images tr Georges MERILLON/ Gamma-Rapho via Getty Images cl J. Shearer/WireImage crt Alain BENAINOUS/Gamma-Rapho via Getty Images crb Sipa Press/Rex Features bl Neil Lupin/ Redferns br David Wolff - Patrick/Getty Images 440 (1) Tim Mosenfelder/Getty Images (2) © Tim Mosenfelder/Corbis (3) Malcolm Clarke/Getty Images (4) © Segernet.com (5) Tom Hill/WireImage 441 (2) RB/Redferns (3) © John Atashian/CORBIS 442 (1) Mick Hutson/Redferns (2) Flavia Bechara/Getty Images (3) Mick Hutson/Redferns (4) SGranitz/WireImage (6) Naki/Redferns 443 (1) G. Gershoff/WireImage (2) © Sayre Berman/Corbis (3) © 2002-2012 Encyclopaedia Metallum 444 (1) Express/Getty Images (2) Popperfoto/Getty Images (3) Express/Getty Images (4) Express/Getty Images (5) Express/Getty Images 446 (1) Virginia Turbett/Redferns (2) Virginia Turbett/Redferns (3) Virginia Turbett/Redferns (4) Virginia Turbett/Redferns (5) Virginia Turbett/Redferns (6) Michael Putland/Getty Images (8) Fin Costello/Redferns 447 (1) Peter Still/Redferns (2) Martin McNeil/WireImage (3) Chiaki Nozu/Getty Images (4) Chiaki Nozu/Getty Images (5) Ebet Roberts/Redferns (6) Pete Cronin/Redferns (7) © Mike Peters Organisation/Getty Images 448 (1) CLIVE DIXON/Rex Features (2) Virginia Turbett/ Redferns (3) Fin Costello/Redferns (4) Ray Stevenson/Rex Features (5) Ray Stevenson/Rex Features (6) Gareth Davies/Getty Images 449 (1) Gabor Scott/ Redferns (2) Fin Costello/Redferns (4) Tim Mosenfelder/Getty Images (5) Mick Hutson/Redferns (6) © The Cliks 450 (1) Brian Rasic/Rex Features (2) © Tony Hobdern (3) © Ad v. Mierlo (5) Graham Tucker/Redferns (6) Brian Rasic/Rex Features (8) © Fabio Nosotti/CORBIS 451 (1) Steve Snowden/Getty Images (2) Steve Snowden/Getty Images (4) Annamaria DiSanto/WireImage (5) Astrid Stawiarz/Getty Images (6) Jeff Kravitz/FilmMagic (7) Steve Snowden/Getty Images 452 (1) Michael Putland/Getty Images (2) Michael Ochs Archives/Getty Images (3) Michael Putland/Getty Images (4) Michael Putland/Getty Images 453 (1) Mick Hutson/Redferns (2) Mick Hutson/Redferns (3) Mick Hutson/Redferns (4) Mick Hutson/Redferns (5) Mick Hutson/Redferns 454 (1) © Ravenscape.com (2) © 2002-2012 Encyclopaedia Metallum (3) Paul Archuleta/FilmMagic (4) Eddie Malluk/WireImage (5) Rex Features (6) © Dinho101 at en.wikipedia 455 (1) © Maggotland.net (3) Mick Hutson/Redferns (4) Steve Pope/Getty Images (5) Alexander Sibaja/Getty Images (6) Steve Pope/Getty Images 456 tl © MFKR1.com tr © Ashley Maile/Retna Pictures c © Gene Ambo/Retna Ltd./Corbis b Tim Mosenfelder/Getty Images 457 tl Tim Mosenfelder/Getty Images tr Mick Hutson/Redferns cl Rob Verhorst/Redferns cr Christie Goodwin/Redferns b Gary Miller/FilmMagic 458 (1) CA/Redferns (2) CA/Redferns (3) CA/Redferns (4) CA/Redferns (5) CA/Redferns (6) Courtesy Everett Collection/Rex Features 459 (1) Michael Putland/Getty Images (2) David Reed/Redferns (3) David Reed/ Redferns (4) Andreas Rentz/Getty Images (5) Mike Prior/Redferns 460 tl Jan Persson/Redferns tr Gilles Petard/Redferns c GAB Archive/Redferns bl Jorgen Angel/Redferns br Garry Clarke/Redferns 461 tl Michael Putland/Getty Images tr John Rodgers/Redferns c Michael Putland/Getty Images b Gems/Redferns 462 (1) Paul Redmond/WireImage (2) Mark Renders/Getty Images (3) Patrick Ford/Redferns (4) Valerie Macon/Getty Images (5) Tyrone Kerr/FilmMagic (6) Michael Loccisano/Getty Images 463 (1) Paul Bergen/Redferns (2) Vivien Killilea/WireImage (3) Amanda Edwards/Getty Images (4) Michael Loccisano/ Getty Images 464 (1) Richard E. Aaron/Redferns (2) Kevin Cummins/Getty Images (3) Jorgen Angel/Redferns (4) Michael Ochs Archives/Getty Images (5) Jorgen Angel/Redferns (6) Charlie Gillett Collection/Redferns 465 (1) Leni Sinclair/Getty Images (2) Astrid Stawiarz/Getty Images (3) © Bureau L.A. Collection/CORBIS (4) Sipa Press/Rex Features 466 (1) Kerstin Rodgers/Redferns (2) Ebet Roberts/Redferns (3) Andre Csillag/Rex Features (4) Andre Csillag/Rex Features (5) Andy Kropa/WireImage 468 (1) Michael Caulfield Archive/WireImage (2) Alexander Tamargo/Getty Images (3) JUAN MABROMATA/AFP/Getty Images 470 (1) Jan Persson/Redferns (2) Gijsbert Hanekroot/Redferns (3) Michael Putland/Getty Images (4) Steve Eichner/WireImage (5) Michael Ochs Archives/Getty Images (6) Michael Putland/Getty Images (8) Jeremy Fletcher/Redferns 471 (1) Tony Russell/Redferns (2) Gijsbert Hanekroot/Redferns (3) Tony Russell/Redferns (4) Paul Natkin/WireImage (5) © Howard Denner/Retna/Photoshot (6) Dave Peabody/Redferns (7) Andre Csillag/Rex Features 472 (1) Paul Hawthorne/WireImage (2) Lawrence Lucier/Getty Images (3) Tim Mosenfelder/Getty Images (4) J. Vespa/WireImage (6) Photoshot/Getty Images 473 (1) © Bob Bert (2) Stefan M. Prager/Redferns (3) Marc Andrew Deley/FilmMagic (4) Tim Mosenfelder/Getty Images 474 (1) Nigel Crane/Redferns (3) Mick Hutson/Redferns (4) Mick Hutson/Redferns (5) Alfredo Rocha/WireImage (6) Michael Burnell/Redferns (7) Raymond Boyd/Getty Images 475 (1) David "Bagel" Ungar/FilmMagic (2) Steve Eichner/WireImage (3) © Don Wallen (5) Ron Galella, Ltd./Getty Images (6) JJ Gonson/Redferns (7) Ron Galella, Ltd./Getty Images 476 (1) Theo Wargo/WireImage (2) Debra L Rothenberg/FilmMagic (3) Ed Peristein/Redferns (4) Debra L Rothenberg/FilmMagic (5) Debra L Rothenberg/Getty Images (6) Jeff Kravitz/FilmMagic (7) Scott Halleran/Getty Images 477 (1) ML Layton/Getty Images (2) Terry O'Neill/Getty Images (3) Michael Putland/Getty Images (4) Debra L Rothenberg/FilmMagic (5) Derek Storm/FilmMagic (6) Herry Scott/Redferns 478 tl David Gahr/Getty Images tr Richard E. Aaron/Redferns cl Larry Hulst/Getty Images cr Paul Natkin/WireImage b Mark Weiss/WireImage 479 tl Ron Galella/Getty Images tr DAN GROSHONG/AFP/Getty Images cl Rob Verhorst/Redferns cr Jeff Kravitz/FilmMagic b Kevin Mazur/WireImage 480 (1) Michael Putland/Getty Images (2) Fin Costello/Redferns (3) Terry O'Neill/Getty Images (4) Terry O'Neill/Getty Images (5) Chris Walter/WireImage (6) Gered Mankowitz/Redferns 481 (1) Mark Large/Daily Mail /Rex Features (2) Christie Goodwin/Redferns (3) Christie Goodwin/Redferns (4) Christie Goodwin/Redferns 482 (1) SGranitz/WireImage (2) SGranitz/WireImage (3) David Warner Ellis/ Redferns (4) Michael Ochs Archives/Getty Images (5) David Warner Ellis/Redferns (6) Michael Ochs Archives/Getty Images 483 (1) Jim McCrary/Redferns (2) Michael Ochs Archives/Getty Images 484 (1) Larry Marano/Getty Images (2) © Henry Diltz/CORBIS (3) Michael Ochs Archives/Getty Images (4) © Henry Diltz/CORBIS (5) © Henry Diltz/CORBIS (6) © Henry Diltz/CORBIS (7) Robin Little/Redferns 485 (1) Will Ireland/Classic Rock Magazine via Getty Images (2) Harry Herd/Redferns (3) Shirlaine Forrest/WireImage (4) Shirlaine Forrest/WireImage (5) Dan Kitwood/Getty Images 486 (1) Dave J Hogan/Getty Images (2) Dave J Hogan/Getty Images (4) © Invisible girl music limited 2006 (5) Dave J Hogan/Getty Images (6) Dave J Hogan/Getty Images 487 (1) Jeffrey Mayer/WireImage (2) Joey Foley/FilmMagic (3) Joey Foley/FilmMagic (4) Neil Lupin/Redferns 488 (1) Mike Prior/Redferns (2) Mike Prior/Redferns (3) Mike Prior/Redferns (4) Ollie Millington/Redferns (5) Mike Prior/Redferns 489 (1) Regis Martin/Getty Images (2) © John Ellis 490 (3) Al Pereira/WireImage (4) Ross Gilmore/Redferns (5) Stephen Lovekin/WireImage (6) Evan Agostini/Getty Images (7) Evan Agostini/Getty Images 491 (1) Paul Warner/WireImage (2) Richard E. Aaron/Redferns (3) Rob Verhorst/Redferns (4) Michael Ochs Archives/Getty Images (5) Jeffrey Mayer/WireImage (6) David Livingston/Getty Images (7) Michael Schwartz/WireImage 492 (1) Rob Verhorst/Redferns (2) Hayley Madden/Redferns (3) Michael Putland/Getty Images (4) Michael Putland/Getty Images (5) Michael Putland/Getty Images (6) © Supertramp 493 (1) Gems/Redferns (2) The Image Gate/Getty Images (3) Hulton Archive/Getty Images (4) © Scott Hallock (5) Robert Marquardt/ Getty Images (6) © 21st Century Greenstuff 494 (1) Michael Bezjian/WireImage (2) SGranitz/WireImage (3) Jean-Paul Aussenard/WireImage (5) Marsaili Mcgrath/Getty Images 496 (1) David Mcgough/DMI/Time Life Pictures/Getty Images (2) David Mcgough/DMI/Time Life Pictures/Getty Images (3) David Mcgough/DMI/Time Life Pictures/Getty Images (4) Larry Hulst/Getty Images 498 (1) Michael Putland/Getty Images (2) © Tamara Rafkin/Retna Ltd./Corbis (4) Michael Ochs Archives/Getty Images (5) Michael Putland/Getty Images 499 (1) Frederick M. Brown/Getty Images (4) Marc Broussely/Redferns (5) Brian Rasic/Rex Features 500 (1) Peter Noble/Redferns (2) Peter Noble/Redferns (3) Peter Noble/Redferns (4) Peter Noble/Redferns 501 (1) Kerstin Rodgers/Redferns (2) Stephanie Chernikowski/Michael Ochs Archives/Getty Images (3) Roberta Bayley/Redferns (4) Roberta Bayley/Redferns (5) Roberta Bayley/Redferns (6) © Jimmy Rip 502 (1) Fin Costello/Redferns (2) Michael Putland/Getty Images (3) Jorgen Angel/Redferns (4) Michael Putland/Getty Images (5) Fin Costello/ Redferns (6) Fin Costello/Redferns (7) Jorgen Angel/Redferns (8) Peter Still/Redferns 503 (1) Daniel Boczarski/Redferns (2) Dimitrios Kambouris/Getty Images (3) Christie Goodwin/Getty Images (4) Stephen J. Cohen/Getty Images (5) Jadranka Krsteska/Redferns 504 (1) Sylvia Pitcher/Redferns (2) GAB Archive/ Redferns (3) Michael Putland/Getty Images (4) Michael Putland/Getty Images (5) Richard Upper/Redferns (6) Michael Ochs Archives/Getty Images (7) Brian Cooke/Redferns 505 (1) David Redfern/Redferns (3) Richard E. Aaron/Redferns (4) Rick Diamond/Getty Images (5) © Marc Marot 506 (1) Time & Life Pictures/ Getty Images (2) Bernd Mueller/Redferns (3) SGranitz/WireImage (4) Time & Life Pictures/Getty Images (5) Ebet Roberts/Redferns (6) Robert Knight Archive/ Redferns 508 (1) Gijsbert Hanekroot/Redferns (2) Ebet Roberts/Redferns (3) Estate of Keith Morris/Redferns (4) Estate of Keith Morris/Redferns (6) Estate of Keith

Morris/Redferns **509** (1) Michel Linssen/Redferns (2) © Thetriffids.com (4) Michel Linssen/Redferns (5) Michel Linssen/Redferns (7) Michel Linssen/Redferns (8) Michel Linssen/Redferns **510** (1) Peter Noble/Redferns (2) Peter Noble/Redferns (3) Peter Noble/Redferns (4) Peter Noble/Redferns **512 tl** Virginia Turbett/Redferns **tr** Erica Echenberg/Redferns **ct** Larry Ellis/Getty Images **cb** George Rose/Getty Images **b** © Roger Hutchings/In Pictures/Corbis **513 t** Mick Hutson/Redferns **cl** Paul Bergen/Redferns **cr** KMazur/WireImage **cb** Peter Pakvis/Redferns **bl** © Jason DeCrow/epa/Corbis **br** Mike Coppola/Getty Images **514** (1) © Marie-Emmanuelle Brétel (2) © Univers-zero.com (3) © Marie-Emmanuelle Brétel (4) © Univers-zero.com (5) © Marie-Emmanuelle Brétel (6) © Marie-Emmanuelle Brétel (8) © Marie-Emmanuelle Brétel **515** (1) Fin Costello/Redferns (2) Fin Costello/Redferns (3) Fin Costello/Redferns (6) Jorgen Angel/Getty Images (7) Fin Costello/Redferns (8) Fin Costello/Redferns **516** (1) Richard E. Aaron/Redferns (2) Fin Costello/Redferns (3) © Tina Fultz/ZUMA Press/Corbis (4) Richard E. Aaron/Redferns (5) Chris Walter/WireImage (6) Fin Costello/Redferns **517** (1) Tim Mosenfelder/Getty Images **518 tl** Fin Costello/Redferns **tr** © Scott Weiner/Retna/Retna Ltd./Corbis **cl** Richard E. Aaron/Redferns **cr** Michael Ochs Archives/Getty Images **bl** Rob Verhorst/Redferns **br** Ron Galella/Getty Images **519 tl** Ann Summa/Getty Images **tr** Tim Mosenfelder/Getty Images **c** Kevin Winter/Getty Images **b** Tim Mosenfelder/Getty Images **520** (1) Michael Putland/Getty Images (2) Estate of Keith Morris/Redferns (3) Michael Ochs Archives/Getty Images (5) Michael Ochs Archives/Getty Images (6) Michael Ochs Archives/Getty Images **521** (1) Michael Ochs Archives/Getty Images **522** (1) Bob Berg/Getty Images (2) Bob Berg/Getty Images (3) Bob Berg/Getty Images (4) Bob Berg/Getty Images (5) Peter Pakvis/Redferns **524** (1) CityFlies/WireImage (2) Annamaria DiSanto/WireImage (3) Joey Foley/FilmMagic (4) Fin Costello/Redferns (5) Michael Putland/Getty Images (6) Fin Costello/Redferns (7) Fin Costello/Redferns (8) Fin Costello/Redferns **525** (1) Fin Costello/Redferns (3) Fin Costello/Redferns (4) Richard E. Aaron/Redferns (5) Mick Hutson/Redferns (6) George De Sota/Redferns (7) © Photoshot (8) Frans Schellekens/Redferns **526 tl** Fin Costello/Redferns **tr** Fin Costello/Redferns **cl** Peter Still/Redferns **cr** Fin Costello/Redferns **bl** Dave Hogan/Getty Images **br** George Rose/Getty Images **527 t** Jim Steinfeldt/Getty Images **cl** © Starstock/Photoshot **cr** Harry Herd/WireImage **b** Bob King/Redferns **528** (1) Jan Persson/Redferns (2) Michael Putland/Getty Images (3) Jan Persson/Redferns (5) Chris Morphet/Redferns (6) John Rodgers/Redferns **529** (1) Jon Furniss/WireImage (2) Dave Hogan/Getty Images (3) J. Vespa/WireImage (4) SGranitz/WireImage (5) Paul Bergen/Redferns **530 tl** Jan Persson/Redferns **tr** Richard Young/Rex Features **c** David Montgomery/Getty Images **bl** Graham Lowe/Redferns **br** Eamonn McCabe/Redferns **531 tl** Gijsbert Hanekroot/Redferns **tr** John Rodgers/Redferns **c** Michael Ochs Archives/Getty Images **bl** Graham Wiltshire/Rex Features **br** Tim Mosenfelder/Getty Images **532** (1) David Wolff - Patrick/Getty Images (2) David Wolff - Patrick/Getty Images (4) Gary Miller/Getty Images (6) Gary Miller/Getty Images (7) Jun Sato/WireImage **533** (1) Michael Ochs Archives/Getty Images (2) Michael Ochs Archives/Getty Images (3) Hulton Archive/Getty Images (4) Hulton Archive/Getty Images (6) Michael Ochs Archives/Getty Images (7) Hulton Archive/Getty Images (8) Michael Ochs Archives/Getty Images **534** (1) Michael Putland/Getty Images (2) Ebet Roberts/Redferns (3) Gilles Petard/Redferns (4) Ebet Roberts/Redferns (5) Michael Putland/Getty Images (6) Michael Putland/Getty Images (7) Ian Dickson/Redferns (8) Michael Putland/Getty Images **535** (1) Michael Putland/Getty Images (2) C Brandon/Redferns (3) Ebet Roberts/Redferns (5) Bob Berg/Getty Images (6) Morena Brengola/Getty Images (7) Startraks Photo/Rex Features (8) Ebet Roberts/Redferns **536 tl** Gilles Petard/Redferns **tr** Michael Putland/Getty Images **ct** Michael Putland/Getty Images **cb** Rob Verhorst/Redferns **bl** Michael Putland/Getty Images **br** Michael Putland/Getty Images **537 t** Rob Verhorst/Redferns **c** Rob Verhorst/Redferns **bl** Diana Scrimgeour/Redferns **br** David Livingston/Getty Images **538** (1) Hulton Archive/Getty Images (2) Ebet Roberts/Redferns (3) Ebet Roberts/Redferns (4) Michael Ochs Archives/Getty Images (6) Chris Walter/WireImage (7) Keith Baugh/Redferns (8) © Davis Deluxe **539** (1) Ebet Roberts/Redferns (2) Michael Putland/Getty Images (3) Jorgen Angel/Redferns (4) Fred Duval/FilmMagic (5) Vince Bucci/Getty Images **540 tl** Robert Altman/Getty Images **tr** © Henry Diltz/CORBIS **c** Richard McCaffrey/Getty Images **bl** Michael Ochs Archives/Getty Images **br** Rob Verhorst/Redferns **541 tl** Paul Natkin/WireImage **tr** KMazur/WireImage **cl** Jeff Kravitz/FilmMagic **cr** Tim Mosenfelder/Getty Images **b** Steve Granitz/WireImage **542** (1) Michael Putland/Getty Images (2) © © PA/PA Archive/Press Association Images (3) Petra Niemeier - K & K/Redferns (4) Petra Niemeier - K & K/Redferns (5) Petra Niemeier - K & K/Redferns (6) Jan Persson/Redferns (7) Gijsbert Hanekroot/Redferns (8) Gijsbert Hanekroot/Redferns **543** (2) © Mark R Friedman 2010 (3) Bob Rose/FilmMagic (4) Chris McKay/WireImage (5) Ian Dickson/Rex Features (6) Bob Willoughby/Redferns (7) Jeff Kravitz/FilmMagic (8) Mick Hutson/Redferns **544 tl** Jan Persson/Redferns **tr** David Redfern/Redferns **c** Archive Photos/Getty Images **b** K & K Ulf Kruger OHG/Redferns **545 tl** Gijsbert Hanekroot/Redferns **tr** NBC/NBCU Photo Bank via Getty Images **cl** Michael Ochs Archives/Getty Images **cr** David McGough/Time & Life Pictures/Getty Images **bl** Ebet Roberts/Redferns **br** Frans Schellekens/Redferns **546** (1) Gems/Redferns (2) Gems/Redferns (3) Gems/Redferns

acknowledgments

Quintessence Editions Ltd would like to thank:

Todd Hughes, producer of *Hit So Hard: The Life and Near-Death Story of Drummer Patty Schemel*

Mark Schaffer for his generous and invaluable Tangerine Dream rescue services

Andrew Greenaway, author of *Zappa the Hard Way,* for his much-appreciated assistance with the Frank Zappa and Captain Beefheart sections

Diane Chidrawi at www.totalexposure.co.za for her help with the Prime Circle section

Vinita at www.rocketgirl.co.uk for her help with the My Bloody Valentine section

Hartmut Fischer at www.neubaten.org

Andres Martinez at www.GreenDayAuthority.com

www.nickelbackgeeks.150m.com/index.html

Tristan de Lancey

The general editor would like to thank:

Martin Downham

Colin Hughes

Dave Whitaker

GRAMMY® and the gramophone statuette and logos are registered trademarks of The Recording Academy® and are used under license.

The authors and publisher of this book are responsible for the accuracy of **GRAMMY®** Awards information contained herein.